The Handbook of Practice and Research in Study Abroad

If we are all becoming global citizens, what then are our civic responsibilities? Colleges and universities across the United States have responded to this question by making the development of global citizens part of their core mission. A key strategy for realizing this goal is study abroad. After all, there may be no better way for students to acquire the knowledge, skills, and attitudes required to become effective change-agents in international contexts.

The Handbook of Practice and Research in Study Abroad is a comprehensive survey of the field. Each chapter eloquently conveys an enthusiasm for study abroad alongside a critical assessment of the most up-to-date research, theory, and practice. This contributed volume brings together expert academics, senior administrators, practitioners of study abroad, and policy makers from across the United States, Canada and other part of the world, who meticulously address the following questions:

What do we mean by global citizenship and global competence?

What are the philosophical, pedagogical, and practical challenges facing institutions as they endeavor to create global citizens?

How is study abroad and global citizenship compatible with the role of the academy?

What are the institutional challenges to study abroad, including those related to ethics, infrastructure, finances, accessibility, and quality control?

Which study abroad programs can be called successful?

The Handbook of Practice and Research in Study Abroad is an indispensable reference volume for scholars, higher education faculty, college and university administrators, study abroad professionals, policy makers, and the academic libraries that serve these audiences. It is also appropriate for a wide range of courses in Higher Education Master's and Ph.D. Programs.

Ross Lewin is the Director of Study Abroad at the University of Connecticut. He received his Ph.D. in German Studies from Stanford University.

The Handbook of Practice and Research in Study Abroad

Higher Education and the Quest for Global Citizenship

Ross Lewin

Editor

Association of American Colleges and Universities

NEW YORK AND LONDON

First published 2009
by Routledge
711 Third Ave, New York, NY 10017

Simultaneously published in the UK
by Routledge
2 Park Square, Milton Park, Abingdon, Oxon OX14 4RN

Routledge is an imprint of the Taylor & Francis Group, an informa business

Typeset in Perpetua and Bell Gothic by EvS Communication Networx, Inc.

Library of Congress Cataloging in Publication Data
Handbook of practice and research in study abroad : higher education and the quest for global citizenship / Ross Lewin, editor.
p. cm.
Includes bibliographical references and index.
1. Foreign study—Handbooks, manuals, etc. 2. Education and globalization. 3. World citizenship.
I. Lewin, Ross.
LB2375.H36 2009
378'.016—dc22
2008052463

ISBN 10: 0-415-99160-9 (hbk)
ISBN 10: 0-415-99161-7 (pbk)
ISBN 10: 0-203-87664-4 (ebk)

ISBN 13: 978-0-415-99160-5 (hbk)
ISBN 13: 978-0-415-99161-2 (pbk)
ISBN 13: 978-0-203-87664-0 (ebk)

Contents

CONTENTS

Foreword

Allan Goodman
Institute of International Education

A record number of U.S. students are studying abroad today. According to the most recent *Open Doors 2008* report published by the Institute of International Education and with the support of the U.S. Department of State's Bureau of Educational and Cultural Affairs, over 241,000 Americans received academic credit for courses and research abroad in the 2006–2007 academic year.

This latest number marks a decade of unprecedented growth in this aspect of international education. Ten years ago, the number of Americans studying abroad was less than 100,000 and most were headed to Western Europe. Today, Americans are more frequently choosing nontraditional study abroad destinations. China, Argentina, South Africa, Ecuador, and India each had 20% increases in the 2007–2008 academic year. The discovery that the world is becoming flatter has been hastened by new program opportunities, a growing number of partnerships between higher education institutions, and a greater range of fields, program durations, and types of programs to accommodate the needs of an increasingly diverse U.S. study abroad population. Many more students are expected to study abroad in the decade ahead, and this will open up even more destinations and encourage new program development to accommodate the demand. As this happens, we need to keep updating what we think and do about study abroad. This Handbook is an essential part of the process.

Americans have not always been so globally minded. Thomas Jefferson founded the University of Virginia so that young Americans could avoid altogether the influence and side-effects of foreign travel. Jefferson—who was so international and cosmopolitan in his tastes and quest for knowledge—feared that study abroad would rekindle an interest in monarchy and promote a fondness for wine. The legendary president of Harvard, Charles W. Elliot, believed, as did many of his time, that "in a strong nation, the education of the young is indigenous and national. It is a sign of immaturity or decrepitude when a nation has to import its teachers, or send its scholars abroad." Attitudes like these did not really change until after World War II and with the establishment of the Fulbright Program by act of Congress.

Those of us who are so deeply involved in international education tend to forget how most Americans are disconnected from and ill-informed about the world. Two thirds of college-age Americans do not have a passport. About the same number cannot find Iraq on a map—or Indonesia, Iran, or Israel. Seventy percent cannot name the president of Russia or the Secretary General of the United Nations.

The growing numbers of Americans who do study abroad represent just a fraction of all our citizens in higher education. Educators are now grappling with the issues of how to facilitate the experience so that substantially more will have the chance and will have many more programs and courses to attend.

As the authors of this Handbook make clear, a great deal of work remains in order to integrate study abroad into the mainstream of American higher education. Even if we were to achieve a kind of parity between the numbers of Americans abroad and international students coming here, this would take at least another decade at the present rates of growth. In the process, as the Handbook also makes clear, educational leaders have to change the way not only students but also faculty think about the study abroad experience. What we all have in common is a quest to prepare the next generation to be global citizens.

This is especially important for Americans. At a recent meeting of the World Economic Forum, I sat next to the CEO of a large multinational corporation headquartered in France. He noted that they employed a lot of Americans. I asked how they did. "Not so good," was the answer. "They come to us with very fine degrees and from all the best schools. But they do not really know how to work well with people from other countries. And we cannot afford to keep them long enough to teach them what they should have already learned." The focus of this Handbook is how we can start doing a better job.

In the last era when scholars agreed that the world was flat, St. Thomas Aquinas observed that to become educated without travel "is like trying to read a book without ever turning a page." However each of us critiques and resolves the complex of issues posed in this Handbook, we would do well to remember this counsel.

Acknowledgments

It takes a village to create a volume of this length, and I want to express my deep appreciation to everyone who helped me bring this project to fruition. First and foremost, my profound gratitude goes to all of the contributors to this volume. Their work, both theoretical and practical, continues to inspire me. This is their book as much as mine. I owe my colleague David Moss an enormous thank you. Without him, I never would have conceived of the idea for this volume. I thank Sarah Burrows at Routledge for taking a chance on this project and never getting tired of my phone calls and e-mails. Thanks also to her assistant Alexandra Sharp, who has shown enormous patience in putting all of the pieces together and making last minute changes. Lynn Goeller and her staff at EvS Communications deserve special mention for doing such a careful job copy editing the extremely long manuscript in record time.

My appreciation for the support from my staff, past and present, in the Study Abroad Office at the University of Connecticut runs deep. Aldo Tedjomoeljono helped me prepare parts of the manuscript. Cheryl Blain, Denise Ferreri, Dora Hast, Helen Marx, Lisa McAdam Donegan, Summer Spaderna, Jessica Williamson, and Gretchen Young listened to me rehearse the ideas or read my parts of this volume more times than I can count. They have also all put up with the stress that inevitably accompanies the final days of preparing an edited volume. Andreina Bianchini, Jill Fenton, Peter Fischer, Marita McComiskey, Vernon Rose, and Greg Van Kirk have helped me realize global citizenship study abroad in the field and, as a result, better understand its challenges. Associate Vice Provost Lynne Goodstein, Vice Provost Veronica Makowsky, and Provost Peter Nicholls have provided me with one of the best work environments possible. They have supported my entrepreneurial spirit, encouraging me to take risks in realizing my ideas about global citizenship and study abroad at UConn. I thank Rebecca Hovey and Ben Robinson, who gave me invaluable commentary in the eleventh hour on the Introduction. My colleagues Margaret Lamb and Chris Clark have aided me generously in thinking through study abroad and global citizenship on an institutional level. There are two professors who have lived in my head and heart ever since I studied with them. John Schaar, my undergraduate mentor at the University of California, Santa Cruz, taught me about the value of community, political theory, and to make sure that I understood the arguments of my critics on their own terms before launching into criticism of them. Russell Berman, my graduate mentor at Stanford University, taught me everything I know and much more about the Frankfurt School, Walter Benjamin, and how to think dialectically. My "furst" born Spencer, a Corgi, was my loyal companion on long walks each morning and evening in the Connecticut woods, no matter the weather. He kept it real. To express the depth of my gratitude to Amanda Bailey is impossible. She "gets me" like no one, puts up with my mercurial moments more than she ought, and is the best interlocutor and editor one could ask for. To Amanda, I dedicate this volume.

Introduction

The Quest for Global Citizenship through Study Abroad

Ross Lewin

University of Connecticut

Study abroad is undergoing a revolution in the United States. For over a century, it has been an experience largely reserved for only a handful of students from a small number of institutions and a few academic disciplines. While the percentage of U.S. students pursuing an academic experience in a different country still remains appallingly low, the actual number of American students who engage in an international experience for academic credit has increased dramatically since the late 1990s. Only a fraction of U.S. colleges and universities send students abroad, but their numbers have also grown significantly. It is no longer just humanities students going abroad. Now study abroad programs are populated as much by social science students, and there are increasing numbers of students from the sciences, business, agriculture, engineering, education, nursing, and pharmacy. Study abroad is expensive, which means that it is still predominantly the province of a minority of students. Yet the economic backgrounds of students going to a different country has widened, which has generated a debate as to whether study abroad should be a privilege or a right for every undergraduate in America.

Support for the revolution in study abroad is comprehensive in scope. More than half of all high school seniors express a strong desire to study abroad in college, and this enthusiasm continues well into their first year, even if curricular or financial challenges eventually preclude many students from realizing their dreams. Several university student bodies have voted to collect fees from their members to widen access to study abroad among their peers. There is no generational conflict: parents are as excited as their children about study abroad. Those at the top of the higher education ladder are encouraging students to study abroad as never before, with many central administrations even setting ambitious percentage goals in the name of the "internationalization of higher education." A few colleges have gone so far as to make study abroad a mandatory experience for graduation. Trustees are backing provosts and presidents' prioritization of study abroad, even at public universities where it often comes at the cost of generating tuition revenue. The business community is increasingly funding university study abroad initiatives. Even the U.S. Congress has stated its unequivocal, bipartisan desire for one million American students to study abroad annually by 2017. This is the strongest interest to date in study abroad.

Why is this radical transformation taking place? Answers to this question will vary widely, but there is one response that everyone seems to agree on: globalization. "The world is flat," as Thomas Friedman (2006) has so famously stated. Boundaries between nations are blurring; the production, marketing, and delivery of goods and services have become borderless; the nation-state is fading as the principal site of identity construction. If we are now all competing against each other on a global playing field, it is also the case that global cooperation is essential if political, economic, social, and environmental problems are to be addressed. The revolution in communications technology, particularly the ubiquity of the Internet, has rendered access to information about and contact with other countries virtually instantaneous. Within this new global order, the need for students to obtain extensive exposure to the perspectives and practices of other cultures has been deemed essential for purposes of peace and prosperity, however one defines those terms.

The revolution in study abroad is thus not only numerical, but indeed philosophical. Historically, study abroad has been caught up in the pursuit of high culture. Throughout the late 19th century and during the 20th century, it was primarily an outgrowth of the Grand Tour, which began in 17th-century England, where aristocratic young men were sent to European capitals to complete their classical education. With letters of credit and introduction in hand, these young men, usually accompanied by guardians or tutors, visited private collections of art and the public monuments of antiquity. In the 18th and 19th centuries, the Grand Tour spread across Europe, with aristocratic and bourgeois young adults from Germany, France, and Russia embarking on similar sojourns. By the late 19th century, the practice of the Grand Tour hit the United States, when wealthy Americans began sending their own children to the Continent to absorb and assimilate into high European culture. Throughout the 20th century, and even today, the Grand Tour has informed study abroad in the United States. The vast majority of undergraduates continue to study abroad in European cultural capitals in order to study their art and literature, to acquire their habits, and to gain greater mastery, when appropriate, in their languages. And yet, with the demand for greater participation in study abroad changes in learning outcomes have come about. Much more attention is now paid to developing knowledge, skills, attitudes, and experiences necessary either to compete successfully in the global marketplace or to work toward finding and implementing solutions to problems of global significance.

The democratization of study abroad may be coming at a price, however. Where there are numbers, there is also money. As a result, organizations developing and selling study abroad opportunities have proliferated across the nation and the world, making a strong pitch to American universities and students alike. The business of study abroad is not necessarily a bad thing because much of this entrepreneurial activity has generated new and innovative programming. But growth has commercialized study abroad. As Adrian Shubert (2008) remarks, the commercialism of study abroad is abidingly apparent the moment one walks onto the floor of a NAFSA convention. There are literally hundreds of booths, selling everything from cell phones to security services to study abroad programs. Countries around the globe spend enormous amounts of money erecting elaborate pavilions to advertise their universities as study abroad destinations. American students have become desirable sources of revenue. In addition, most study abroad offices at colleges and universities across the nation are self-supporting, entirely dependent upon generating sufficient revenue in order to keep their staff paid and their doors open. The pressure from upper administration to grow their numbers is phenomenal, and where this pressure exists, the business of study abroad often comes at the expense of academic integrity.

The business of study abroad has, in fact, generated widespread criticism. Some wax nostalgic about the days when only the elite could study abroad. They complain, for example, that the obsession with numbers has resulted in the replacement of academic-year programs in non-English speaking countries with ever shorter programs in either English-speaking countries or non-English-speaking countries where all classes are taught in English. For them, this democratization of study abroad has led to its dumbing down, leaving little opportunity for students to engage in the serious work of cultural acquisition. Others complain that study abroad destinations have become no more than consumer products. They point especially to the growing number of "blockbuster" island programs, in which students never break out of their isolation and mix with the local residents, thus treating the host terrain as nothing more than a playground to chalk up "fun" experiences and a shopping mall to fill their suitcases with "exotic" products. Those who never thought studying abroad was more than just a fanciful semester off, in which students drink their way through Europe and hardly crack a book, now feel completely vindicated. They now seem to have a preponderance of evidence proving that study abroad is nothing more than commercial travel masquerading as academic experience. There are others who express deep skepticism about the shift in goals from cultural acquisition to global citizenship. They are particularly suspicious of the growing number of students serving in developing countries, contending that this is nothing more than a colonialist project of visiting the "natives," a kind of poverty tourism that reinforces stereotypes of themselves and others.

The criticism of study abroad might lead us to wonder whether, in fact, we face an either—or situation: either we endeavor to return to an elitist era of study abroad or we surrender to turning all of our students into global consumers. *The Handbook of Practice and Research in Study Abroad: Higher Education and the Quest for Global Citizenship* will suggest that the pursuit of global citizenship is valuable and possible. The essays contained herein show, each in its own way, that we can democratize study abroad and orient it toward developing critical individuals who are capable of analyzing power structures, building global community, or tangibly helping to improve the lives of people around the world. It does not have to come at the cost of increasing consumerism or colonialism.

In order to understand how we can get there, I suggest we go back to the debate between the critical theorists Max Horkheimer and Theodor Adorno on the one hand and Walter Benjamin on the other over the conflict between the goals of liberalism and the exigencies of capitalism as they relate to the democratization of culture. In a different era and context, Horkheimer and Adorno reflect the concerns of the critics of study abroad, and Walter Benjamin provides us with a theoretical justification for getting beyond them.

In the *Dialectic of Enlightenment*, first published in 1944, Horkheimer and Adorno offered a sustained critique of what they called "The Culture Industry." In exile from Germany and living in Santa Monica, they voiced concern about the decline of high culture and the rise of mass culture, as represented at the time in American film, radio, and magazines. For Horkheimer and Adorno, the mass production of culture certainly gives more people access to its products. Yet in contrast to high culture, mass culture for them is determined by the logic of capitalism, which is invested in the individual spectator not engaging in critical thought. Mass culture instead distracts the observer through the pleasure of escape. Outcomes are prescribed that ensure that nobody questions the system that generates it. The *telos* behind Horkheimer and Adorno's argument would seem to support much of the criticism of study abroad. Study abroad's historical interest in high culture is itself threatened by its mass production. As a result, students decreasingly study high art, which demands critical rigor, and increasingly participate in profit-driven programs that have a stake in ensuring that their experience has a Hollywood ending. The more that study abroad is fueled by the bottom line, the more it will be invested in maintaining compliance to the ideology of the state. Students cannot be expected to think critically about the world, let alone find solutions to the problems confronting it. Instead of becoming global citizens, they become global consumers.

Horkheimer and Adorno's negative outlook on culture and critical thought seems to lend credence to the critics of study abroad. But if we stop with Horkheimer and Adorno, study abroad offices across the United States might as well roll up their carpets and close their doors. Fortunately, at least in my view, there are critical views of Horkheimer and Adorno that can inject hope into the study abroad endeavor. One such voice is Walter Benjamin. In 1936, on the eve of the 20th-century's darkest hour, Benjamin wrote his seminal piece "The Work of Art in the Age of Mechanical Reproduction," which offered a guardedly more optimistic perspective on the implications of mass culture. Benjamin's starting point is a very different one from that of Horkheimer and Adorno. Rather than bemoaning the loss of high culture, Benjamin casts a more critical eye on it. He argues that before the mass production of culture, high culture could not be separated from its unique space, a space defined by a sense of awe, reverence, and magic, which he referred to as its "aura." The aura was not determined by its autonomy so much as it was by the elitist and privileged conditions defining its reception. In contrast to his fellow critical theorists, Benjamin did not believe that one critically engaged with a work of art in this space; one was rather "absorbed" by it. According to Benjamin, the technological dawning of the mass production of art, however, led to the loss of the aura. The work of art was loosened from its space of awe, deracinated from its unique origin. According to Benjamin, the loss of the aura led to a radically different relationship between the artwork and the observer. Rather than being "absorbed" by the work of art, the viewer was now "distracted" by it. Yet for Benjamin, in contrast to Horkheimer and Adorno, distraction was not ipso facto dire. To be sure, the business of mass culture aims to distract the public and transform its members into obedient citizens and mindless consumers. Yet for Benjamin, by preventing the individual from being absorbed by the cultural object, mass produced art could open a space between it and the observer, enabling that observer to engage in criticism. Indeed, mass produced art could, in spite of itself, enable the individual to disclose the ideologies behind the work of art and its production, as well as to generate alternative and productive responses that are unencumbered by those ideologies. The masses of blind consumers now become a democracy of critics and citizens.

The components of Benjamin's argument are, like those in Horkheimer and Adorno's work, also applicable to study abroad. Benjamin's discussion of the aura calls attention to the Grand Tour. Recall that the expressed goal of these tours was to complete a student's classical education through the absorption of masterpieces of art in their privileged spaces. The Grand Tour was thus one of the principal means through which this auratic mode of perception took place. And this auratic mode of experience has seemingly framed the majority of U.S. study abroad programming. Colleges and universities still send an overwhelming number of students to European capitals to discover their magic and treasures. Their main learning activities use "cultural immersion" as their guiding principle in support of the main goal of cultural assimilation. The purpose of assimilation is less to develop students as critics and more to enable them to move seamlessly between North American and European bourgeois culture. This form of study abroad conjures images of First Lady Jacqueline Kennedy speaking flawless French and talking in hushed tones with Charles de Gaulle about who knows what in the State Versailles Room. Jacqueline Kennedy was the paragon of a successful study abroad student. She could move gracefully between cultures. As study abroad undergoes democratization in the United States, this auratic space has been seemingly lost. The more students study abroad, the less study abroad and its relationship to culture preserves that magic. And yet it does not necessarily have to leave colleges and universities transforming their students into global consumers. And it does not have to lead us to wax nostalgic for the good old days when study abroad was not compromised by hoi polloi. Following

Benjamin's logic, we might recognize the space globalization has opened up between students and the cultures they are studying and working in as an opportunity for fostering a new and constructive criticism. That is, the democratization of study abroad may allow us finally to carry out the work of the enlightened university and replace magic with reason, absorption with critical distance, and consumerism with citizenship.

The work before us will not be easy, and some of the signs are not particularly hopeful. It is no surprise that one of the responses in this age of mass produced study abroad has been not to embrace the possibilities but to keep the myth of the aura alive. I particularly see this phenomenon taking place in study abroad's obsession with the "authentic." Study abroad's search for "authentic culture" has tried to deny globalization—read: mass production—either by isolating students in a mythical historical bubble in larger cities or by taking them to ever more remote locations, from smaller towns to rural settings in Europe to more "exotic" lands. In big cities, small towns, and less familiar locations we create the conditions for our students to live in the magical past. Culture becomes the end in and of itself rather than a means for understanding its relationship to the global forces surrounding it. Writing in 1936, when fascism was the ruling ideology in Germany and Italy, Walter Benjamin defined culture as the "aestheticization of politics," whereby ritual replaces critical citizenship, and one wonders whether our search for "authentic culture" and our efforts to create for our students high aesthetic experiences constitute an "aestheticization of academics" that flies in the face of academic goals. Rather than making the authentic its goal, perhaps we need to understand how selling authentic culture is part of the process of globalization. Any walk through London or Florence, for instance, shows that these cities are as littered with chain stores as any American city. The stores may have the look and feel of a small "shoppe"; the bars may have the look and feel of local ownership; retail outfits may be ensconced in Renaissance architecture. Yet multinational corporations they remain, often not even based in the country they are representing. Moreover, it is not as if the "locals" are any less interested in Hip-Hop, Facebook, and the Gap than American students. Small towns, rural villages, and developing countries have not missed the boat on global culture, and what may remain "authentic" is simply sold as souvenirs. Perhaps we need to jump full force into this mass culture and open up a space for students to think about how it functions.

If the democratization of study abroad contains the hope for developing students as critics, it also holds out the possibility for them to engage in more active citizenship, the other antidote to commercialization. Effective citizenship, whether we define that term primarily with respect to rights and responsibilities, participation in civil society, or work toward the common good, requires critical reasoning, empathy toward others, and individual action that goes beyond consumption. Citizenship is not at odds with U.S. higher education; it is embedded in Thomas Jefferson's founding vision of U.S. higher education, which emphasizes the development of democratic citizens and the achievement of "public happiness." Citizenship has also been realized to some extent in the traditions of the liberal arts and land-grant institutions. But citizenship went into retreat in higher education following World War II in favor of a much more exclusive focus on the development of the intellect. Where civic engagement did make a rise in the 1980s and 1990s, it was primarily relegated to domestic internships and service learning. Since the late 1990s, however, civic engagement has gone global. The Association of American Colleges and Universities has spearheaded this movement in a series of recent publications, going so far as to argue that colleges and universities need to provide students with international civic experiences as a means of training them to think liberally and practically about global problems and their resolutions. Even those who are primarily interested in assessment now contend that experiential education is one of the best means for achieving student success, and both civic engagement and study abroad rank high on their list. Against this backdrop, the development of global citizens through study abroad has become a high priority for institutions of higher education across the United States. *The Handbook of Practice and Research in Study Abroad: Higher Education and the Quest for Global Citizenship* will help to provide a roadmap to get there.

As a handbook, this volume is designed to offer readers a sense of the state of the field, a means for becoming more versed in the literature, and a set of examples that they may wish to adapt to their own institutional settings. With its focus on "practice and research," this book is not only an attempt to be comprehensive, but, following in the path of the critical theorists, recognizes that study abroad's turn toward global citizenship is most productive through a dialectic between theory and practice, whereby the latter troubles the former, and the former extends the boundaries of the latter.

If any word stands out in the title it is the word *Quest*. Although colleges and universities are intent on "making" students global citizens, we are at a stage where we are still defining terms, justifying positions, and overcoming barriers—an era of experimentation. Like any quest, this one will probably never be perfected. Like democracy itself, global citizenship is an ongoing voyage, as much a process as a goal.

Finally, I need to say a word about the choice of the term *study abroad*. Over the past decade, professionals in the field have questioned the term *study abroad* as the most felicitous description. Many have opted to replace it with *education abroad* on grounds that the latter term better captures the holistic nature of the experience that undergraduates undergo. Some prefer *international education*, and today we hear more frequent references to *global studies* and *global education*. No doubt, each of these terms has its strengths, and we could spend hours going back and forth as to which is best. I have elected to stick with the term *study abroad*, not because it connotes precisely what takes place, but rather because it is still the term most identifiable by the largest number of constituencies. The argument of this book is that study abroad is changing, and I believe it is important for us to understand that its current redactions are part of a much longer history.

This volume is divided into four sections: "Defining Global Citizenship in Study Abroad," "Aligning Global Citizenship and Study Abroad with the Mission of the Academy," "Institutional Challenges and Strategies to Fostering Global Citizenship Study Abroad," and "Innovative Global Citizenship Study Abroad Models."

The first section recognizes that one of our shortcomings has been our failure to adequately define our terms. If we are going to make an impact on the lives of students or host communities we must make certain that we endeavor to fill these empty ciphers before marketing firms beat us to it. Currently, the concept of global citizenship is heard throughout the administrative and faculty halls of colleges and universities in America. The phrase appears in mission statements; task forces have been created on how to implement it. And yet, everyone seems to be in such a rush to create global citizens out of their students that we seem to have forgotten even to determine what we are even trying to create. Perhaps we avoid definitions not because of our rush to action but out of fear of what we may find. *Global citizenship* is a controversial term, with many people insisting that it cannot exist because it is intimately connected to the nation-state, and others contending that the deployment of global citizenship undermines newer states' long and hard-fought road to achieving citizenship for its own citizens. For these critics, global citizenship is an act of colonialism. Still others assert that while people who engage beyond their borders may be doing something, to call that something global citizenship is erroneous.

While controversy surrounds the term *global citizenship*, as Yonsei University political theorist

Hans Schattle, whose chapter leads off this volume has noted, it is being filled with all sorts of meaning by people who believe they are practicing it. Schattle's contribution sets the stage for other chapters in this section by showing that it is not essential to arrive at a monolithic definition of global citizenship, but that, like democracy and citizenship themselves, there are multiple definitions, and the process and ongoing discussion of the term is as important as any conclusion that we arrive at. For Schattle, global citizenship has its roots in the cosmopolitan tradition, even if it is altering our current notions of citizenship. The next three essays in this section by James Skelly, Rebecca Hovey and Adam Weinberg, and Charles Kolb offer various definitions of global citizenship and how study abroad can be used as a vehicle to achieving them. Skelly, currently at the University of Ulster, argues that study abroad should not be promoted for the purposes of national security or economic competitiveness but rather to foster peace and social justice by getting students more engaged in "global civil society," a sector of world society that stands up to the administrative power of the state. Hovey and Weinberg (World Learning and SIT) contend that we need to create study abroad programs that model democratic values as part of their goals and that transform our students into citizen diplomats capable of creating a global community of learning. Charles Kolb, president of the Committee for Economic Development, the roots of which can be traced back to the development of the Marshall Plan, argues that learning foreign languages and becoming culturally aware of others is the only means for the United States, the only global superpower, to remain economically competitive and nationally secure, which is necessary for the prosperity and peace of the rest of the globe. Ian Davies, University of York, and Graham Pike, Vancouver Island University, writing from a British and Canadian perspective, respectively, frame this section by helping us break down definitions and debates over the meaning of globalization, global education, and global citizenship, in order to posit a new definition of global citizenship defined by a deep understanding of other cultures.

In the second section of *The Handbook*, we shift our focus to aligning the turn in study abroad to global citizenship with the mission of the academy. We recognize in this second section that there are many types of institutions in the United States and beyond, and this section by no means covers them all. We begin with Dieter Wanner at Ohio State University. Worried by the "mass production" of study abroad, Wanner struggles to determine the role of the university in general, and study abroad in particular, to answer the problems of globalization. As a solution, he proposes a maximal model of study abroad as an ideal, which emphasizes long stays, rigorous language learning, and extensive immersion in the host communities. Clemson University professors Megan Che, Mindy Spearman, and Agida Manizade address another aim of higher education, cognitive and emotional development. Calling on the work of Piaget, they contend that both forms of maturation take place best by studying abroad in "less familiar destinations" where students are most apt to encounter "constructive disequilibrium." Kalamazoo College's Joseph Brockington and Margaret Wiedenhoeft examine the mission of the liberal arts college. They draw principally on the work of Martha Nussbaum in contending that global citizenship is most effectively served through an encounter with others' cultures in environments that encourage students to reflect critically on their own experiences and get them to step inside someone else's shoes through intensive immersion experiences.

Connie Currier, James Lucas, and Denise Saint Arnault at Michigan State examine the relationship between study abroad and schools of nursing. They argue that schools of nursing should shift their learning goals from intercultural competences useful in U.S. multicultural medical environments to global competences required to serve in a global environment marked by an ever widening margin between rich and poor. For his part, Kenneth Cushner (Kent State University) is interested in developing students into global citizens eventually capable of addressing problems on a global stage, and to this end, he argues for the necessity of providing student teachers in schools of education with substantive international experiences so that they can most effectively pass on the knowledge, skills, and attitudes in their classrooms. Robert Frost (Oregon State University) and Rosalind Latiner Raby (California State University, Northridge) take on community colleges and global citizenship study abroad. For them, community colleges originated in the principles of universal access and community outreach, and in this new global environment where community extends beyond physical borders, it is essential for community colleges to overcome their institutional challenges and form vibrant study abroad programming.

The second section of this volume ends with three perspectives from outside the United States, one from Canada, a second from Europe, and a third from Singapore. Although the volume calls for more voices from around the world, these three chapters show that global citizenship is culturally and politically determined, as much by the role of higher education and foreign policy as it is by any political theory. Roopa Desai Trilokekar and Adrian Shubert from York University show that, in contrast to the United States, the concept of global citizenship lies at the heart of Canadian national identity, but on account of foreign policy and higher education institutional structures, noncredit bearing international volunteer and cooperative experiences are the main vehicle for its realization among students. Just as it is in Canada, global citizenship is much more organically a part of European identity than it is for Americans. The absence of national policy and a decentralized higher education system in Canada has shaped the parameters of global citizenship. In Europe, however, global citizenship and study abroad are much more connected to the centralized policies and practices of the European Union such as the Bologna Process and the Lisbon Strategy, as described by Hans de Wit, editor of *Journal of Studies in International Education*. Finally, Peter Pang of the National University of Singapore notes that "going global" is a matter of survival in Singapore, and has thus suffused almost every aspect of Singaporean society, including its universities. By examining a few specific study abroad programs, Pang argues that while study abroad has been a national priority for largely economic reasons, it has led to deep partnerships with universities across the world that are collaborating on issues of global import.

We turn in the third section of *The Handbook* to institutional challenges and strategies for realizing global citizenship through study abroad. These are many and varied, given the entrenched histories of study abroad on college campuses across the United States. William Brustein (University of Illinois-Champagne-Urbana) starts this section with a cogent argument that we cannot achieve any isolated goal, including the growth of study abroad, without internationalizing each aspect of the university, and he provides an even more lucid and useful blueprint on how to get there. Riall Nolan from Purdue University casts a wide net, questioning why students are not studying abroad in greater numbers at a time when it has never been more important. For Nolan, it comes down to a lack of university interest in international studies, a healthy dose of faculty skepticism, and little incentive to change. Nolan follows by offering a myriad of practical suggestions to address each of these issues. Joan Gore from the University of Virginia attributes the relative failure of study abroad growth also to faculty antipathy. But rather than talking in the discourse of the institution, she draws on Foucault to analyze the narratives of study abroad which reify a lack of seriousness in its own presentation as a field. Gore counters this reification by telling a new story of study abroad that challenges the old.

In her chapter, Yale graduate student Talya Zemach-Bersin lambastes the marketing of global citizenship and study abroad for turning both into a commodity that promotes consumerist behavior across the world. Zemach-Bersin argues that a key solution is not in the programming itself as much as it is in predeparture training that demands that U.S. students analyze their own cultural assumptions about inequality, race, and power. Earl Picard, Farrah Bernardino, and Kike Ehigiator from Georgia State University examine the seemingly impenetrable problem of increasing the number of minority students in study abroad. Our failure to do so would just widen the achievement gap that so many have fought tirelessly to narrow, and these three authors offer several worthwhile suggestions. If we are determined to make global citizens out of our students using study abroad as a means, then, as Darla Deardorff, Duke University, points out in her chapter, study abroad professionals must become conversant with the myriad theories and tools of assessment in order to learn how to apply them. Short-term programs are here to stay and will be a major strategy for achieving the ambitious participation goals for study abroad. Based on their experience at the University of Delaware, Lisa Chieffo and Lesa Griffiths maintain that short-term programs do not have to be perceived as the poor relation to long-term programs. Not only do they widen access to study abroad, lead to repeat study abroad participation, but also, through carefully planning, can successfully meet many of our learning goals. Another group of students that has been traditionally hard to reach, and yet one that needs global exposure perhaps more than any other group, are science students. Philip Wainwright, Preetha Ram, Daniel Teodorescu, and Dana Tottenham discuss how Emory University was able to overcome institutional and programmatic barriers to attain an extraordinarily high degree of participation. This section closes with Bernhard Streitwieser from Northwestern University tackling the difficult issue of how to engage students in undergraduate research while abroad in a way that fosters global citizenship.

The final section of this volume moves the readers even closer to the ground by offering actual innovative curricular models on how to achieve global citizenship. This part begins with Howard Rollins, who together with colleagues designed Georgia Tech University's award winning International Plan. The International Plan is geared toward making students from all backgrounds, but especially in technological areas, sufficiently globally competent in order to address the challenges of the 21st century. Joan Gillespie and Mary Dwyer of IES Abroad, and Larry Braskamp of Loyola University of Chicago, made their names in part on the basis of the IES-MAP, which served as the basis for The Forum on Education *Standards of Good Practice for Education Abroad*. Here they propose an innovative holistic curricular model that integrates learning in the classroom with engagement in the host communities. The Association of American Colleges and Universities' work *Shared Futures: General Education for Global Learning* project underlies the next chapter. Kevin Hovland, Caryn McTighe Musil, and Amy Jamison, all affiliated with AAC&U, and Ellen Skilton-Sylvester of Arcadia University, present us with a study abroad model that joins global learning abroad with community service at home within the larger theoretical context of using global learning to enhance general education. The leader in service learning in the United States has long been Indiana University-Purdue University Indianapolis (IUPUI). IUPUI's William Plater, Steven Jones (now at the University of Scranton), and Robert Bringle, as well as North Carolina State's Patti Clayton blaze the trail for us in their chapter on how to develop and assess this type of programming in an international setting. In her chapter, Susan Gillespie gathers together voices from her colleagues at Bard and her partners at St. Petersburg State University and the University of Witwatersrand (Wits) to discuss in a very personal way the impact of developing "deep partnerships," guided by the principles of mutuality and equality, that go beyond student mobility to include the college acting as a "global citizen." Jonathan Becker, Bryan Billings, Sergey Bogdanov, Christina Davis, Fazela Haniff, Ayesha Kajee, Thomas Keenan, Nikolay Koposov, Tawana Kupe and Valery Monakhov have played major roles in developing and sustaining either Smolny College, the first liberal arts college in Russia, or the International Human Rights Exchange at Wits in South Africa, and they describe in an unabashedly subjective way the impacts and challenges of these partnerships with Bard College.

We close this final section with two chapters on study abroad initiatives by the University of Connecticut. Maria Martinez, Bidya Ranjeet, and Helen Marx write about the specific challenges of developing study abroad programs for first-generation college students and offer a successful model that they have implemented several times in Liverpool. Greg Van Kirk (CEO of Social Entrepreneur Corps) and I argue in the last chapter for developing study abroad programs that prioritize community development over student development as the best means to achieve both, and we examine the results of this theory through a case study of UConn Social Entrepreneur Corps in Guatemala.

The Handbook of Practice and Research in Study Abroad: Higher Education and the Quest for Global Citizenship is itself a work in progress. As you read through the chapters, you will find strengths and weaknesses. While we attempt to provide as thorough a look at study abroad as possible, we have certainly not covered everything. We hope at least that what lies within these pages can be applied to many of the issues you and your institution are confronting. Most chapters in this volume address, for example, institutional challenges and provide program examples. And many of the chapters beyond the first section offer definitions of global citizenship. The one thing that ties these chapters all together is their quest to transform study abroad into a substantive educational activity that will help students address the most pressing problems of our time.

REFERENCES

Association of American Colleges and Universities. (n.d.). *Shared Futures: Global Learning and Social Responsibility*. Retrieved January 19, 2009, from http:www.aacu.org/SharedFutures/index.cfm

Benjamin, W. (1969). The work of art in the age of mechanical reproduction. In W. Benjamin & H. Arendt (Ed.), *Illuminations* (H. Zohn, Trans., pp. 217–251). New York: Schocken Books. (Original work published 1936)

Friedman, T. L. (2006). *The world is flat: A brief history of the twenty-first century.* New York: Farrar, Straus & Giroux.

Horkheimer, M., & Adorno, T. W. (1972). *Dialectic of enlightenment* (J. Cumming, Trans.). New York: Continuum. (Original work published 1944 under the title *Philosophische Fragmente*)

Shubert, A. (2008, Winter). The pursuit of exotica: A comment. *Frontiers: The Interdisciplinary Journal of Study Abroad 15,* 197–201.

The Forum on Education Abroad. (2008). *Standards of Good Practice for Educations Abroad.* Retrieved January 19, 2009, from http://www.forumea.org/documents/ForumEAStandardsGoodPrctMarch2008.pdf

Part One

Defining Global Citizenship in Study Abroad

Chapter 1

Global Citizenship in Theory and Practice

Hans Schattle

Yonsei University

Perhaps more than any other concept, the idea of global citizenship has emerged since the late 1990s as a key strategic principle in higher education. At scores of colleges and universities in the United States and abroad, the current era of globalization has been accompanied by renewed scholarly interest in an international dimension of citizenship as well as numerous initiatives with the specific aim of inspiring young people to think and live as global citizens. What insights do the historical evolution of cosmopolitan ideals and the recent expansion of the term *global citizenship* in public discourse offer to scholars, teachers, and administrators?

This chapter begins by tracing the origins and development of the cosmopolitan tradition, illustrating how today's multifaceted idea of global citizenship echoes numerous strains within cosmopolitan political thinking that have endured through the ages. Then, the chapter chronicles the recent ascendance of the term *global citizenship*, reviews some of the ongoing scholarly debates surrounding this idea, and explores how contemporary understandings of global citizenship encompass multiple concepts, such as awareness, responsibility, participation, cross-cultural empathy, international mobility, and personal achievement.

THE COSMOPOLITAN TRADITION THROUGHOUT HISTORY

The term *cosmopolitan* is a composite of the Greek words for *order, universe*, and *citizen*. At its heart, the cosmopolitan ideal holds that the inherent dignity and well-being of each human person warrants equal respect and concern,[1] and advocates of the cosmopolitan ideal tend to emphasize universal standards of responsibility that require citizens to "transcend the morally parochial world of the sovereign state" (Linklater, 1999, p. 39). Joshua Cohen (1996) has summarized the essence of cosmopolitanism: "Our highest allegiance must be to the community of humankind, and the first principles of our practical thought must respect the equal worth of all members of that community" (p. vii.).

The earliest political strains of cosmopolitan thinking date back to ancient Greece, where Socrates and Diogenes both identified themselves as citizens of the world.[2] They did so to challenge the bounded civic ideal of the *polis*, which championed locally exclusive ties to one's immediate political community. As Michel de Montaigne wrote of Socrates:

> When someone asked of Socrates of what country he was, he did not reply, "Of Athens," but "of the world." His was a fuller and wider imagination; he embraced the whole world as his city, and extended his acquaintance, his society, and his affections to all mankind. (Montaigne, 1575/1958, p. 63)

As noted by Derek Heater (1996), who has led the way in contemporary historical scholarship of world citizenship, Socrates held a nonpolitical view of world citizenship that envisioned a sense of affinity with all humanity and the universe, as well. Socrates did not renounce his citizenship of Athens; on the contrary, he willingly submitted to a dubious death sentence. In contrast, the Cynics conceived of world citizenship as a direct rebellion against citizenship of the *polis*. Diogenes of Sinope famously made clear his disdain for what he considered the hypocrisy and dishonesty of his fellow citizens and set himself apart by proclaiming himself a citizen of the world.

The notion of world citizenship took a decidedly legalistic turn in ancient Rome, with the ideals of universal law and civic virtue closely intertwined in the writings of Roman Stoic thinkers, such as Cicero, Marcus Aurelius, and Seneca. In the context of an empire of overlapping jurisdictions, Roman political philosophers introduced the idea of multiple citizenships and allegiances radiating from state-based political ties into the international arena. As Seneca emphasized:

> Let us grasp the idea that there are two commonwealths—the one, a vast and truly common state, which embraces alike gods and men, in which we look neither to this corner of earth nor to that, but measure the bounds of our citizenship by the path of the sun; the other to which we have been assigned by the accident of our birth.[3]

By acknowledging citizenship ties based on "the accident of our birth," but awarding higher standing to an envisioned universal political community, the Stoics championed the human capacity to lead a dual civic life—fulfilling obligations to the state while also serving the *cosmopolis* as a virtuous human person. Such ethical perspectives on world citizenship carried into medieval Christian thinking, with Stoic principles related to moral universalism essentially carried forth into the formation of particular Christian teachings and literature, such as *City of God* by St. Augustine.

The single most powerful cosmopolitan thinker from the Age of Enlightenment and early modern period was Immanuel Kant, who advanced the ideal of "cosmopolitan right" secured through an international "pacific federation" among free and independent states. As Kant speculated in his essay, "Perpetual Peace: A Philosophical Sketch," written in 1795: "The peoples of the earth have thus entered in varying degrees into a universal community, and it has developed to the point where a violation of rights in one part of the world is felt everywhere" (Kant, 1991, p. 108). Of course, Kant's linkage of world citizenship to universal human rights echoed the revolutionary declarations of rights written during this period in the emerging American and French *national* republics. Strikingly, at the same time as the U.S. constitutional framers were convening in Philadelphia in 1787, Benjamin Franklin foresaw the eventual prospect of European federation.

During the 20th century, the atrocities and casualties of the two world wars, culminating in the nuclear attacks upon Hiroshima and Nagasaki, reinvigorated campaigns for a cosmopolitan model linked to more cohesive global governing institutions. Immediately following the Second World War, public discourse regarding "world citizenship" revolved heavily around the founding of the United Nations and the hope that this new global institution would foster world peace and nuclear disarmament. Albert Einstein served as one of the most visible advocates of world government, which he believed was necessary to ward off nuclear holocaust. Einstein stated in an interview in the 1940s: "Do I fear the tyranny of a world government? Of course I do. But I fear still more the coming of another war" (quoted in Nathan &Norden, 1968, p. 376).

The founding documents of the United Nations, filled with sweeping affirmations of human rights for all, represented a giant step forward regarding aspirations for a rights-based model of world citizenship. At the same time, the stalemate of the Cold War and the chronic deadlocks between the West and the Soviet bloc—particularly within the United Nations Security Council—underscored the inherent limitations of the United Nations so far as its ability to transcend national sovereignty and power politics. In addition, groups in opposition to the United Nations often invoked "world citizenship" with scorn during the Cold War years. The idea of world citizenship became vulnerable to attack as signaling a remote and tyrannical world government. Some political organizations on the far right, such as the John Birch Society in the United States, even began to equate "world citizenship" with communism, overlooking the fact that Marxist and Leninist aspirations of an international workers utopia amounted to just one of many competing strains of cosmopolitanism as the concept evolved through the ages.

During the 1980s, in what turned out to be the waning years of Soviet communism, the idea of world citizenship had receded to the margins of political discourse. Even within the field of international relations, the term *globalization* was barely on the radar screen. However, this same period brought the early ascendancy of a new model of "global citizenship" that hearkened back to ancient cosmopolitan ideals of a universal human community and the goal of mediating ties and allegiances to overlapping, interdependent political and moral communities. Especially within the educational arenas in the United States and the United Kingdom, professional associations, allied organizations, and educational studies specialists began to show greater interest in designing programs seeking to inspire young people to become global citizens.

As early as 1979, the curriculum guidelines of the National Council for the Social Studies (in the United States) stated that the purpose of social studies education is "to prepare students to be rational, humane, participating citizens in a world that is increasingly interdependent." In 1984, the council's president, Carole Hahn, placed "global citizenship" directly on the agenda of the professional organization with an impassioned argument that can be viewed as a forerunner to the sorts of philosophical arguments in favor of global citizenship that would emerge with much greater force during the 1990s. As Hahn stated in her 1984 presidential address:

> Just as the spread of nationalism since the eighteenth century caused people to rethink the meaning of "citizen," so now it is once again time to rethink that concept in light of our global interdependence. Like it or not, each of us riding on this planet is affected by one another's decisions and actions. We share a common destiny and, to an increasing extent, we share a common culture. Although most of us do not realize it, we are participants in a global society. (Hahn, 1984, p. 297)

The promises of an emerging global society became far more evident in the early 1990s with the political and economic opening of the former Soviet Union and its satellites, the ongoing democratic transformations in formerly authoritarian states such as South Africa and South Korea, and stunning advances in digital technology and telecommunications that made the world seem more interconnected and, indeed, smaller than before.

CONTEMPORARY UNDERSTANDINGS OF GLOBAL CITIZENSHIP

As *globalization* became one of the buzzwords of the approaching new century, the idea of global citizenship became more conspicuous not only within scholarly debates but also as a salient and relevant idea for the general public. International relations theorist Richard Falk (1994) and sociologist John Urry (2000) both captured the new incarnation of global citizenship in separate articles that identified key segments of the population that seemed to fit into categories of prospective global citizens. Their images of global citizens can be consolidated into the following five categories, which overlap with each other:

1 "Global cosmopolitans," as in individuals who develop, often through extensive international travel, "an ideology of openness towards certain 'other' cultures, peoples and environments" (Urry, 2000, p. 73).
2 "Global activists," as in campaigners who take up causes such as human rights, poverty eradication, environmental protection, or who seek to hold accountable international economic institutions. True to the adage "think globally, act locally," these individuals also are often active in their local communities and national political arenas.
3 "Global reformers," who out of concern for all humanity advocate more cohesive and democratically accountable global governing institutions, if not a centralized system of world government, "as indispensable to overcome the chaotic dangers of the degree of political fragmentation and economic disparity that currently exists in the world today" (Falk, 1994, p. 132).
4 "Global managers," as in individuals who work, often in collaboration with the United Nations and other international governing institutions, to resolve borderless problems ranging from climate change to the threat of nuclear weapons.
5 "Global capitalists," as in multinational corporate executives who travel the world and form a "denationalized global elite that at the same time lacks any global civic sense of responsibility" (Falk, 1994, p. 135). Some global capitalists also are seen as willing to assume heavy financial risks in their respective quests to "unify the world around global corporate interests" (Urry, 2000, p. 172).

One category of global citizen that Falk and Urry did not single out—but could have done—is global educators. Classroom teachers and school principals; scholars with international credentials, contacts, and research agendas; leaders of international exchange programs; and educational outreach coordinators for advocacy groups (such as Oxfam International) together comprise a visible and dynamic group of global citizens today. Global educators strive to render their students competitive in the international economy, while also instilling awareness and empathy of other countries, cultures, and issues of common concern across the planet. Although many internationally engaged educators would not necessarily regard themselves as global citizens, they often aspire for the young people whose lives they touch to fit this description.

Recent academic debates surrounding prospects for some sort of international dimension of citizenship can be divided into two major categories. A normative debate on the desirability and feasibility of global citizenship has carried forth among political philosophers and social theorists. Sociologists and international relations scholars focused on developments especially related to international migration and transnational activism have contributed to empirical debates as to whether we are now undergoing a transition away from citizenship as exclusive and bounded within nation-states and domestic politics and toward an expansion of citizenship into an emerging global sphere.

These two categories of academic debates contain many internal divisions. Within recent normative debates on global citizenship, different approaches to global citizenship can be identified, especially when comparing how various scholars on both sides of the Atlantic have approached and framed the concept. In many cases, scholars based in North America have typically framed global citizenship primarily in moral and ethical terms—as a phenomenon dependent primarily on the habits and choices of individuals, irrespective of the state of affairs within any set of governing institutions.

Moral philosopher Martha Nussbaum, for example, is well known for framing global citizenship in a manner that echoes the ancient rationale of Stoic cosmopolitanism: that the well-being of distant strangers should concern everyday people as much as the well-being of their closest neighbors. Nussbaum (1996) advocates world citizenship rather than state or national citizenship, as the appropriate central focus in civic education, on the grounds that education for world citizenship helps promote individual and collective self-awareness, helps promote a spirit of cooperation in solving global problems, and helps acknowledge moral obligations from wealthier and privileged nations to the rest of the world. While Nussbaum focuses not so much on institutional design but on fostering moral sentiments, especially with regard to international distributive justice, her argument takes on political relevance just the same. Nussbaum has argued for an ethic of world citizenship, especially within the United States: "If we really do believe that all human beings are created equal and endowed with certain inalienable rights, we are morally required to think about what that conception requires us to do with and for the rest of the world" (p. 14). In this respect, cosmopolitanism in the present day often emerges as a global extrapolation of classical liberal principles such as liberty, equality, and justice.

In Europe, where a legally binding model of European Union citizenship now complements the institution of national citizenship, scholars often more readily incorporate specific proposals for global governing institutions into arguments advocating global citizenship. The work of international relations theorists David Held (1995, 1999) and Andrew Linklater (1999) provides a good representation of models of global citizenship aligned more closely with institutional cosmopolitanism. David Held, for instance, has linked his understanding of global citizenship to a proposed model of cosmopolitan democracy (1995) that would include an elected worldwide assembly, an international judiciary, military force, and economic policy institutions, as well as transnational referenda and public scrutiny of international nongovernmental organizations (pp. 270–283).

Held argues that states should no longer be regarded as the exclusive power centers within their borders but should be "relocated" within an umbrella of cosmopolitan democratic law, with the sovereign authority of states situated within an overarching global legal framework. In this regard, Held's vision of cosmopolitan citizenship contains world federalist affinities, though Held carefully avoids arguing for any kind of jurisdiction over citizenship to be transferred to a global authority. Rather, he advocates a conceptual enlargement of citizenship in order to account for multiple ties to many different spheres, sustained not only through access to global governing institutions but also through informal networks within transnational civil society. As noted by Held (1999):

> In this system of cosmopolitan governance, people would come to enjoy multiple citizenships—political membership in the diverse political communities which significantly affect them. They would be citizens of their immediate political communities, and of the wider regional and global networks which impacted upon their lives. (p. 107)

7

Likewise, Linklater (1999) has proposed a "dialogic conception" of global citizenship that would emphasize processes of public deliberation in seeking appropriate solutions to common global problems. In Linklater's view:

> World citizens would remain members of bounded communities, each in possession of its rightful sovereign status and free from external intervention. But the act of imagining themselves as participants in a universal society of co-legislators in which all human beings are respected as ends-in-themselves would place moral and psychological constraints on the wrongful exercise of state power. (p. 41)

Such advocates of global citizenship from the academy often share the perspective of placing civic attachments in a series of concentric circles—radiating from one's immediate political communities and then outward to the nation-state and beyond.

Meanwhile, the academic literature on international migration and transnational advocacy networks serves to illustrate how much scholarly disagreement persists as to the extent that various developments and trends associated with globalization actually carry implications for the meaning of citizenship. With regard to international migration, scholars have debated as to whether a possible model of "postnational membership" is displacing national citizenship or whether national citizenship remains resilient, with nation-states still firmly in control of citizenship laws and policies. The central point of contention: Whether international migrants in any given country receive partial membership rights (based on residency) mainly because of the moral force of international human rights or because of national governments acting on their own initiative and following their core principles. Essentially this debate hinges upon whether legal protection granted to migrants traces back to international norms or internal characteristics of domestic political systems.

If an increase in membership rights for noncitizens traces back to international norms, as scholars such as David Jacobson (1996), Yasemin Soysal (1994), and Saskia Sassen (1999) have argued, then national citizenship is regarded as undergoing "devaluation" (Jacobson, 1996, p. 9) or as headed toward obsolescence. Soysal has maintained, based upon the experiences of guestworkers in European countries that: "The recent guestworker experience reflects a time when national citizenship is losing ground to a more universal model of membership, anchored in deterritorialized notions of persons' rights" (p. 3). Likewise, Jacobson has argued that "the polity is in the process of being transposed to a transnational level as an entity based on human rights codes (namely the Euro-Atlantic community) and the state as the institutional forum—the territorial locus—of that legal-political order" (p. 133).

On the other hand, if state recognition of membership rights for migrants stems primarily from attributes and policies within individual host countries—particularly countries subscribing to liberal constitutions—then national citizenship remains resilient. As Randall Hansen (1999) has noted, also arguing that the causal flow is primarily domestic: "The liberal and expansive nature of permanent residents' rights is rooted foremost in the liberal and democratic political process and liberal democratic institutions, above all the judiciary" (p. 436). Similarly, as Christian Joppke (1998) has argued: "If the pressure of human rights meets nation-states from the outside, postnational membership analysts face the problem that this pressure is more urgently felt in the West than elsewhere"[4] (p. 27). At this juncture, the evidence is far from conclusive that membership rights within individual countries, for citizens as well as migrants, have shifted decisively from sources within nation-states to sources beyond them. In keeping humanity subdivided rather than united, the institution of national citizenship still fits Rogers Brubaker's description (1992) as an "international filing system, a mechanism for allocating persons to states" (p. 31). For the vast majority of the world's population, citizenship status is not a matter of choice but an accident of birth.

For transnational activists, in contrast, global civic engagement is indeed a matter of choice. Once again, though, scholars disagree as to whether campaigning on global issues actually amounts to a model of global citizenship. Although "global activists" taken together provide us with a major classification of prospective global citizens, as outlined above, rarely do international relations scholars claim that the proliferation of international nongovernmental organizations lends decisive evidence of an emerging global citizenry. In one the most widely read studies tracing the evolution of transnational civil society, Margaret Keck and Kathryn Sikkink (1998) documented a "boomerang effect" in which domestic grassroots organizations form alliances with international organizations in order to mount both internal and external pressure on state and national governments, especially repressive political authorities in violation of international human rights standards. However, although Keck and Sikkink believe that such nonstate actors in the international arena carry implications for state sovereignty, they do not claim that these transnational networks amount to any sort of cosmopolitan citizenship or global citizenry. This point of view is commonplace in recent scholarship on transnational activism. One prominent exception is the volume *Global Citizen Action*, edited by Michael Edwards and John Gaventa (2001), which specifically links advocacy work on an international scale with the idea of global citizenship. As Gaventa has written:

> Global citizenship is the exercise of the right to participate in decision making in social, economic, cultural and political life, within and across the local, national and global arenas. This is true especially at the global level: Where the institutions and authority of global governance are not so clear, the rights of citizenship are made real not only through legal instruments but through the process of citizen action. (p. 278)[5]

Interestingly, sociologists studying the same phenomenon generally seem less reticent than their political science colleagues when it comes to discussing possible implications of transnational political and social activism for citizenship. In advocating for the development of transnational political parties as a check upon multinational corporations, Ulrich Beck (1999) has noted: "The rank and file of global parties, the 'global citizenry' in its various national colors, composed of multiple branches, should not be confused with a global managerial class. We will have to distinguish between global capitalists and global citizens." Likewise, sociologists Boli and Thomas (1997, 1999) have argued that international nongovernmental organizations carry out the mandate of world citizenship and "translate the diffuse global identity and authority of world citizenship into specific rights, claims, and prescriptions for state behavior" (Boli & Thomas, 1997, p. 182).

CONCEPTS OF GLOBAL CITIZENSHIP IN PUBLIC DISCOURSE

Alongside these empirical debates regarding the feasibility of global citizenship, I have introduced yet another line of inquiry and analysis: how the specific idea of global citizenship is actually being interpreted and communicated in the present day.

Rather than imposing the label of global citizen on particular segments of the population, or arguing whether or not certain trends and patterns of transnational activism or international migration provide us with examples of global citizenship, I have examined how individuals who consider themselves as global citizens have reflected upon global citizenship and applied the idea in their lives. Likewise, I have also examined how numerous organizations and institutions that have adopted the term *global citizenship* into mission statements, programs, and strategies have framed this concept in relation to their endeavors.

By exploring the many pathways followed by self-described global citizens, as well as specific global citizenship agendas taken on by organizations, the key concepts underlying global citizenship in contemporary public discourse come into clearer focus. Awareness, responsibility, and participation are what I consider to be the primary concepts of global citizenship, while cross-cultural empathy, personal achievement, and international mobility are important secondary concepts. In this section of the chapter, I want to cast light upon each of these concepts by conveying insights shared with me during interviews with more than 150 self-identifying global citizens and advocates of global citizenship. These research findings are provided in further detail in my book, *The Practices of Global Citizenship* (2008).

First and foremost, for many individuals global citizenship entails self-awareness as well as outward awareness of one's surroundings and the world. Rather than viewing the idea of global citizenship as implying an absence of place, many self-described global citizens believe the personal relevance of the idea depends on strong and well-defined roots, not only within a particular community but also with respect to one's own individuality. For example, a novelist who lives in New Mexico, along the border separating the United States and Mexico, eloquently defined her idea of a global citizen to me as "somebody that can move between different worlds, what one perceives as these invisible membranes that separate culture and landscape and environment and people from different backgrounds." This person also noted that the individuals she has known with this sense of fluidity share an essential personal quality: "No matter where they were, they were at home; they were comfortable in the universe of their own skin, and consequently that made them available and fresh whenever they met other people in any sort of situation."

Self-awareness, then, can be considered an initial step of global citizenship, providing a lens through which further experiences and insights are perceived. As noted to me by a French-language teacher who has led her students on immersion experiences in Africa: "The thing that I say to my students is becoming a global citizen is not something that happens overnight; it's a process of self-awareness and as you become self-aware, you become more aware of others." Self-awareness also extends into questions of national identity, as some interview respondents who thought of themselves as global citizens flatly rejected the notion that one's sources of national identity should be seen as restricted. As one woman emphasized to me:

> I was born in Korea, and I'm a U.S. citizen. That's a pretty finite state, right? But there's so many more interesting ways of life—and living and being—that's outside of just that finite state of being an immigrant Korean who's now a U.S. citizen. So why not be open to it?

Self-awareness as related to global citizenship, then, means that one avoids clipping one's wings as well as remaining at ease in one's own skin.

Global citizenship as outward awareness entails such personal qualities as understanding complex issues from multiple vantage points, recognizing sources of global interdependence and a "shared fate" that implicates humanity and all life on the planet, and looking beyond distinctions, at least in one's mind, between insiders and outsiders in order to view the human experience in more universal terms. For some individuals, global citizenship involves awakening to new insights about one's native country or continent while gaining perspectives from other lands. One young woman from Ohio, who spent a year in the Netherlands on an exchange through the American Field Service (AFS)—an organization that itself includes "global citizenship" in its mission—said she began to change her position on the gun control debate in the United States after listening to the thoughts of her Dutch classmates following the 1999 massacre at Columbine High School in Littleton, Colorado. An administrator for UNICEF Canada told me that in her view, the essence of global citizenship is found in awareness, not actions such as making ethical purchases: "The action of consuming doesn't make the difference. The shift in attitude or the shift in awareness is what is required. That's the fundamental change." Likewise, a university professor born and raised in Nigeria and now living in Missouri noted that global citizenship, in her mind, has nothing to do with acquiring or giving up national citizenship but is "a mind-set that makes you aware of you as part of the human family, and going beyond your interests to recognize the needs and challenges in resolving some of the problems that the world is faced with."

Many self-described global citizens think about the concept in terms of looking beyond potential barriers that can separate human persons—such as nation, religion, and ethnicity—and then reflecting upon universal commonalities of the human experience, regardless of whatever cultural differences seem to persist. A young medical student from Oregon—who came to regard herself as a global citizen after exploring Europe for six months—said the trip taught her that "young people are really a lot the same, no matter what country they come from. We all kind of have similar ideas and similar kinds of passions about life." Similarly, a community volunteer from Oklahoma expressed how she had grown as a person, first by hosting dozens of visitors from overseas in her home and later through political activism and volunteer work in Mexico, Russia, and Croatia:

> I have learned that people, for the most part, are really wonderful, and that most people, global citizens, want peace in the world; they want better things for their children; they want better health care, better living conditions, and it's shaped me…it has shaped everything about my life.

In short, awareness of the wider world provides the motivation for many self-described global citizens to embark on sustained involvement in society or politics and to begin to take responsibility for a global common good.

The terms *global citizenship* and *global responsibility* often seem interchangeable for people who describe themselves as global citizens or advocate global citizenship. This comes as no surprise, as the aspiration of shared moral obligations across humanity has endured through the ages as a core principle of cosmopolitanism. In the eloquent words of Kwame Anthony Appiah (2006): "The one thought that cosmopolitans share is that no local loyalty can ever justify forgetting that each human being has responsibilities to each other" (p. xvi). Similar to the way that the notion of citizenship is often conceived, global citizenship is interpreted by some as a two-sided coin of universal human rights and corresponding global responsibilities. Consider this perspective from an official associated with the United Nations Global Compact, a collaborative of multinational corporations and civil society organizations:

The beauty of the term [global citizenship] is it brings in the notion of rights that should be balanced with responsibilities…and maybe it is counterproductive, in political terms, to overuse the term because it would provoke all sorts of resistance arguing that there is no such territory beyond the nation-state. But then it offers all the strength of trying to come to grips with a broad definition of our rights and responsibilities in a space that is not yet defined.

The Universal Declaration of Human Rights, signed in 1948 at the founding of the United Nations, is not binding in the same manner as national or state constitutions, but it nevertheless issues key imperatives for national governments, such as the duty to protect refugees and internally displaced persons, as well as any individuals abused or mistreated within their countries of residence. In an interview for my research, a senior United Nations human rights official framed the idea of global citizenship in terms of safeguarding the human rights of those no longer protected by their governments:

In terms of crimes against humanity, and the personal criminal liability of leaders, I think the challenge that we're looking at is how to protect fundamental human rights of those [persons] whose kind of protector, the state, has completely failed…. To the extent that there's been a complete inability or unwillingness of their government to protect their most basic fundamental universal human rights, I think they have a legitimate claim, for that purpose, to turn to the international community. So in that sense, they are the original global citizens. They have no other citizenship, in a sense, than their humanity.

On the other hand, for all the power of rights-based interpretations of global citizenship, self-described global citizens seem to link the idea of global citizenship more commonly with awareness. What responsible global citizenship requires, in the minds of people thinking and talking about the concept, seems to boil down to two key themes: principled decision making and solidarity across humanity. Global citizenship as principled decision making applies every bit as much within local communities as in the international arena. Environmental issues were cited especially often as an area in which responsible and aware global citizens are concerned about the effects of government policies as well as their personal daily choices. For example, an information technology consultant from San Francisco, who defined a global citizen as "someone who makes decisions based on an awareness of the impact of those decisions on the planet," added in the next sentence that she never would buy a sport-utility vehicle. An environmental campaigner based in Washington, DC, framed global citizenship as responsibility to the planet and to future generations:

We have to recognize that given the advances in technology, given the growth in the global economy and the capacity we now have in this country [the United States]—for example, we can unilaterally change the world's climate—in fact, we're almost doing that—and so I think we have to recognize that we have a responsibility now that goes far beyond our boundaries…. Recognizing that the earth is an ecosystem almost automatically defines us as global citizens.

Global citizenship, for many individuals, entails being aware of responsibilities beyond one's immediate communities and making decisions to change habits and behavior patterns accordingly.

The original French usage of *solidarité* signifies collective responsibility (Hayward, 1959), and the self-described global citizens interviewed for my study frequently joined together ideas of global solidarity and global responsibility. This was especially true among individuals who were preoccupied with resolving global problems such as endemic poverty. One respondent, associated with a Catholic international-development organization based in Canada, justified the usage of *global citizenship* rather than alternative terms because, in his words, global citizenship is synonymous with "global equality" and "the notion of solidarity with the poor, the preferential option of the poor.... It's not a question of just promoting love and friendship throughout the world; it's a question of redressing the enormous imbalances that exist."

The most basic examples of global citizenship as participation involve contributing to the political or social life of a community, even if one is not legally a citizen of the country in question. Several self-described global citizens who had lived abroad emphasized that participating in a local community away from home translated, at least in their minds, into global citizenship. One individual who spent several years living overseas made it clear that he regarded himself a global citizen even while lacking the right to vote in his country of residence. When asked, in an interview, if the lack of voting rights impaired his sense of belonging to the various communities in which he lived, he responded that he felt very much a part of political life nevertheless:

> While I was disenfranchised, I still was able to get actively involved in debate, in getting information about the political situation in each country. The very fact that I was involved in university and educational projects meant that invariably I came across quite a bit of political debate—people interested in politics, people moving in and out of politics. I certainly didn't feel a great sense of loss not being able to vote, because I was still able to engage in debate and conversation with people who were voting and was able to get my ideas across anyway.

For this individual, being deprived of voting rights in his adopted country did not leave him feeling deprived of a public voice in his community.

Politically active global citizens focus on directly influencing the practices and decisions of governing institutions—demanding responsible policies from domestic political institutions and subjecting international institutions to public scrutiny. One transnational human rights campaigner interviewed for this book said that global citizenship has to do with "the idea of where should we have, over what institution should we have democratic control, and what are the institutions that really decide over people's lives and against whom we should organize some form of counterpower." For this individual, legally a citizen of France, organizing a teach-in outside the September 2000 meeting in Prague of the International Monetary Fund and World Bank amounted to global citizenship by virtue of trying to hold these powerful institutions accountable. Similarly, with regard to challenging power, the former leader of a transnational advocacy group promoting a human right to food emphasized that the internationalization of corporate power "means the counterbalancing power on the citizen side has to be transnational movements, based on national and regional movements that link globally."

Although political participation in this regard is aimed at promoting responsible decisions by governing institutions, many activists also believe that participation in itself fulfills the moral responsibilities of global citizenship. As an environmental campaigner for the World Council of Churches put it, American church leaders who in early 2001 opposed the United States government's withdrawal from the Kyoto Protocol on climate change were "exercising their responsibility as global citizens within their country to try and change those decisions."

Global citizen activists seeking reforms within governing institutions are motivated by the goal of democratic empowerment as well as idealistic aspirations for human flourishing. Many transnational activists do seem to burn with desire to change the world for the benefit of the least advantaged. For example, a leader of the advocacy group Global Exchange recalled how his experiences traveling in impoverished countries and encountering children facing death left him determined to "get at the causal roots, the institutional causality" of poverty by challenging government and corporate power. Reformers, then, do not merely seek to secure greater democratic control over the institutions they hold under scrutiny; they raise the stakes and strive for change.

Likewise, a prominent Canadian activist who has participated in numerous demonstrations outside meetings of international economic institutions said that in her view, the goal of the "global citizens movement," as she called it, is twofold: first, to amplify the role of politics in the global economy and reclaim political space that has been lost to remote and unaccountable processes of decision making; second, to change the rules in the global economy, particularly with regard to international trade regulations that critics believe are stacked in favor of corporate interests: "I don't believe in a global economy with footloose transnational corporations and transnational capital that is not governed in any way by laws at any level. I [also] don't believe it's enough anymore to do it at the nation-state level. We have to bring the rule of law to global institutions."

By no means must reform-seeking global citizens be transnational activists. In many instances, self-described global citizens carry out quests for reform in their neighborhoods and homes. The organizer of an environmentally innovative cohousing initiative in Cambridge, Massachusetts, noted that many of the participating residents—global citizens, in her mind—could have afforded larger, more expensive houses, but that the community is:

> ...the embodiment of a philosophy that there's a higher standard of living, both socially and spiritually, that can be achieved if we are willing to pull together and invest some time and effort into what the community needs and how we live. And I think that has global ramifications, because if we demonstrate that, then it's there for other people to notice. That's a statement of faith.

Making such a statement of faith, while planted literally in one's own backyard, serves as an interesting counterweight to more overtly political and transnational versions of global citizenship as participation. Global citizenship often signifies forms of civic engagement that are mainly domestic and cross-cultural rather than international and political. Not only does global citizenship involve reclaiming transnational space for the public, but global citizenship also thrives within local public space.

Cross-cultural aspects of global citizenship spring to life in human relationships across many sources of difference, such as ethnicity, language, religion, and social class. For individuals who consider themselves global citizens by virtue of cross-cultural empathy, global citizenship has little, if anything, to do with where a person votes, or from which country one holds a passport, and everything to do with how an individual interacts with others and fits in wherever one should happen to be planted at any moment in time, even if only temporarily. Global citizenship, in this context, implies a readiness to cross intangible borders that others might consider all too formidable. Whether one is an outsider in unfamiliar surroundings or fully entrenched in one's place of birth, global citizenship as cross-cultural empathy depends heavily on a willingness to build personal relationships with those from other backgrounds.

Although an easy acceptance of people from different ethnic and cultural backgrounds might seem largely beyond the sphere of politics, cross-cultural empathy in many circumstances also takes on political significance. An Australian journalist who defined citizenship in terms of rights and responsibilities said that global citizenship, in his view, means not fearing other cultures—both in terms of traveling overseas and welcoming immigrants into Australia. Just one day before this person was interviewed, he participated (as a citizen, not as a reporter) in a mass demonstration in Melbourne in which an estimated 300,000 people called for reconciliation with Australia's aboriginal population:

> We are a migrant culture, and there are enormous numbers of people with different faces and different colored skins and different accents. I don't feel that they're a threat. That's my concept if you talk about a global citizen: it's someone who doesn't feel threatened by other cultures and who sort of feels his own culture is robust enough to stand up amongst them, that that culture itself is a product of diversity.

In keeping with this view of diversity as enriching, a parent from California put her moral vision of global citizenship into practice by enrolling her daughter in a bilingual school that conducts classes in Spanish as well as in English and enrolls a cross-section of youngsters from Anglo and Latino backgrounds. This dual-language experience, in the parent's eyes, lends itself to more than language learning:

> She can share with them (the classmates) what she's learning about being Jewish. They can share with her what they know about their parents and grandparents perhaps being raised in Argentina or Mexico. That's where global citizenship starts. It's how you think of your community.... To be a global citizen, all you have to do is think about somebody else.

Global citizenship, then, not only involves thinking about someone else and absorbing the cultural traditions of others but also involves sharing one's heritage. Being the outsider in another culture entails crossing cultural boundaries with grace and verve; it requires the willingness to nurture a sense of belonging in an unfamiliar setting. Engagement across cultures, meanwhile, requires levels of interest and sensitivity, as well as the willingness to absorb and contribute to communal life and include people who might otherwise feel left at the margins.

Media references to global citizenship occasionally read like a who's who list of celebrities. Journalists around the world have discovered that global citizen works as a convenient catchphrase to describe illustrious individuals—especially those who are world renowned, maintain residences in more than one country, and are also active in various global humanitarian causes. Scores of famous actors, athletes, entrepreneurs, musicians, scientists, spiritual leaders, and writers have been extolled as global citizens in glowing press accounts: Muhammad Ali, Bill Gates, Jane Goodall, Emmylou Harris, Angelina Jolie, the Dalai Lama, Rupert Murdoch, V. S. Naipaul, Yoko Ono, Mary Robinson, Ted Turner, Dionne Warwick, and the late Isaac Stern and Sir Peter Ustinov.

Not everyone labeled a global citizen by virtue of their achievement agrees with the label, however. Several distinguished people declared global citizens by dignitaries, journalists, or awards committees were quite modest during interviews for this study, and, at times, were reluctant to classify themselves as global citizens. On the other hand, global citizenship as a measure of personal achievement is taken more seriously within many schools, colleges, and universities, as many educators aspire to develop a new generation of competent and competitive global citizens. The articulation of global citizenship as achievement was particularly apparent in secondary education, as secondary-school principals espousing global citizenship seemed acutely concerned that their students would advance to universities and reach sufficient academic and technological proficiency to compete in the global marketplace.

For example, a retired secondary school principal from New Zealand said that the term *global citizenship* entered her vocabulary around 1997, as her school began successfully recruiting Asian students from overseas, leading to a much more internationally mobile and culturally diverse student body. Alongside the cultural transformation of her school, which is located in a fairly remote area, the principal associated global citizenship mainly with notions of competence and competitiveness. Upon returning from an international conference for secondary-school principals held in 1998 in Helsinki, Finland, the principal told a local news reporter: "The message that is coming through very clearly is that technology, literacy and numeracy are the keys to global citizenship. We might be relatively isolated in New Zealand, but, through communication, through learning languages and through having an international outlook, we can keep pace with developments in places like Europe" (quoted in Baird, 1999)

To help translate this international outlook into daily life, the school invested NZ$300,000 in a computer network and placed computer terminals in open public spaces rather than in enclosed classrooms. The school provided each student with unlimited Internet access and an e-mail account—an amenity more common at universities than secondary schools and a move that at the time placed the school technologically ahead of every other secondary school in the surrounding region. The principal also placed an emphasis on four extracurricular "quadrants"—sports, cultural activities, leadership, and service. The strategy focused on civic competence and professional competitiveness is working: More than 90% of the school's graduates go on to university education, and half of them become the first university graduates in their families.

Global citizenship as international mobility often tends to be more about professional opportunities and lifestyle options than about political or social responsibility and engagement. Typically, self-described global citizens who approach the concept mainly through their travels have not relocated abroad as immigrants but have moved to pursue career or educational opportunities. For the most part, these mobile individuals seemed to take their national citizenship as given, even as they immersed themselves, albeit partially and temporarily, in unfamiliar territory. In this regard, internationally mobile global citizens engaged in communal life abroad often spoke of being good neighbors while away from home. This did *not* entail, for these individuals, regarding everyone in the world as a "global neighbor." Rather, it meant settling into a new community and becoming part of that community, at least in some modest way.

The sorts of mobile individuals willing to nurture civic ties away from home usually also were the types of people who would simultaneously maintain strong senses of attachment within their countries of origin—and resettle at home eventually. For these sorts of individuals, the sense of belonging that accompanies domestic forms of citizenship is not necessarily diminished by international experiences. Instead, the sense of belonging is transplanted into communities that the expatriates call home for a temporary period of time. For example, a New Zealand television executive said that his family went about "nesting" in various local communities overseas while he held management positions for several years in the United Kingdom and in Australia:

> When we live and work in the UK, particularly in London, which I prefer, we feel like we're part of the UK. We pay our taxes; our kids go to school; we make friends; we have family

there that we can visit on a weekend. When I'm there, I feel like I'm part of the place, so I guess once again, it's an attitude of mind: that when you are in a location other than where you were originally born and brought up, if you feel like a citizen, then consider yourself a citizen.

For other self-described global citizens, international mobility was strongly associated with a sense of distance from one's country of origin. It is difficult to make any cause-and-effect claim in this regard: it is not entirely clear whether a lack of belonging usually prompts international migration or whether international migration erodes one's sense of belonging. Perhaps the relationship between migration and detachment, for some individuals, is mutually reinforcing. In any case, several respondents who think of themselves as global citizens articulated how they came to perceive themselves as being removed from their respective home countries during experiences overseas.

A London advertising executive, for instance, began to feel disengaged from the United Kingdom, first after spending a year in the United States on a management education program, and even more so after his corporate role expanded to include jurisdiction for continental Europe and, eventually, Asia. Although this person had always been based, at least officially, in London, he explained how he quite literally did not have a strong sense of place. He noted that when he traveled on business (60–70% of the time), "frequently I'll wake up somewhere, and it takes me five minutes to work out...remember where I am, and I don't find that at all odd." This person added, talking about flying into Heathrow Airport: "I don't regard it as flying home. I regard it as flying into London."

In other cases, self-described global citizens seem to think about global citizenship simply as an expression that conveys enthusiasm for international travel and a feeling, in some cases, that they could live anywhere, provided that they are able to maintain high living standards. These individuals did not necessarily show an interest in transnational political activism or feel a sense of kinship with humankind; nor were they looking to change their country of citizenship. On the contrary, most of these individuals seemed to recognize the privileges associated with holding passports from the world's wealthier constitutional democracies. This particular strain of global citizenship has little, if anything, to do with political or social engagement and just about everything to do with lifestyle: the term describes an affluent subset of individuals with the means and the will to live on just about any continent, especially if they have reached a point in their lives where residency need not be dictated by employment or other professional considerations.

CONCLUSION

The strains of thinking within contemporary global citizenship discourse that fit together most readily are the ideas of awareness, responsibility, and participation. The ways in which many of today's self-described global citizens often interpret the meaning of "global citizenship" in relation to their lives and endeavors hearken to moral visions of citizenship and cosmopolitanism as these political and social ideals have evolved through the ages. At the same time, other aspects of global citizenship discourse simultaneously challenge conventional assumptions about what counts as citizenship in the present day and prompt questions as to whether notions of global citizenship have become too wide-ranging to provide an coherent picture of a genuinely reconfigured and robust model of citizenship for the 21st century.

As the viability of the current era of globalization itself is increasingly called into question—with growing concern among many international relations scholars that aspirations toward further developments in global governance and collaboration in solving shared global problems are giving way instead to renewed rivalries among multiple national and regional powers—it is not certain that the idea of global citizenship will continue to gain traction in the next decade as much as the past two decades. In a world in which nationalism remains the single most powerful source of political belonging, it is even less certain as to whether global citizenship will begin to move toward the center of the political mainstream across the English-speaking world, let alone take root in public debate elsewhere, particularly in non-Western settings.

Public opinion surveys, though, have shown consistently in recent years that younger generations, at least in the world's more open and affluent constitutional democracies, are more receptive than their elders to the general idea of being an actively engaged participant and a morally responsible member—if not an outright citizen—of communities that reach beyond the boundaries of any given country. Of course, this attitudinal shift owes itself considerably to developments such as the rise of the Internet and other global media platforms, the increased accessibility of international travel, and ongoing social changes that point toward multicultural societies. As illustrated in other chapters in this volume, such developments are inextricably linked with many educational programs that now engage with the specific idea of global citizenship. If global citizenship is to continue gaining traction in the coming years, it will be in no small measure due to the efforts of countless educators, from elementary school teachers to university administrators, who have sought to highlight and advance understandings of global citizenship in curriculum content and extracurricular programs.

As colleges and universities continue building upon strategies with the aims of advancing public understanding of global citizenship and inspiring young people to think and live as global citizens, the insights from past and present renderings of global citizenship leave us with some challenging questions for consideration, which include: Are today's educational initiatives invoking the specific term *global citizenship* really new and distinctive in comparison with other past and present initiatives related to global education or international education? Especially if the specific term *global citizenship* is only hazily defined on campus (or not unpacked at all), to what extent does *global citizenship* bring intellectual substance to the table? How can educators balance the imperatives of fostering a climate on campus in which a plurality of global citizenship understandings coexist while also preventing the idea from lapsing into incoherence and irrelevance? How literally should we take the idea of global citizenship in higher education? Do some self-professed global citizens, especially those who begin to think about global citizenship as a result of short and limited experiences abroad, gravitate to a relatively shallow view of the concept that fails to reckon with persistent cultural differences? And how can we reliably measure and determine, over time, the extent that educational programs for global citizenship actually are making a difference in levels of awareness, responsibility and participation in coming generations of citizens? These sorts of questions will become critically important as university communities work to advance the idea of global citizenship, build upon mission statements and strategic agendas, and design and implement specific programs and activities that will demonstrate how global citizenship imperatives can spring to life.

NOTES

1. As Charles Jones (1999) has defined cosmopolitanism: "The fundamental idea is that each person affected by an institutional arrangement should be given equal consideration. Individuals are the basic units of moral concern, and the interests of individuals should be taken into account by the adoption of an impartial standpoint for evaluation" (p. 15).
2. Historical accounts differ as to whether Socrates and Diogenes each used the term citizen of the world or citizen of the universe. For the sake of consistency, I will use the term citizen of the world.
3. Cited in Heater (1996, p. 221)
4. Joppke's case against "postnational membership" also takes on a normative aspect; he finds it "concretely baffling" that the status of guestworkers in Europe as second-class members, not on track toward full citizenship, is held up as a model by postnationalists: "Independent of the academic stance taken, the actual immigrant-receiving societies have treated post-national membership as an intolerable anomaly.... Denizenship is not celebrated; it is detested" (p. 28). Beyond questions of guestworker status, Peter Schuck (1998) has noted that recent genocides in Bosnia, Somalia, Rwanda, and Cambodia "should remind us that the ostensible goals of post-national citizenship—human rights, cultural autonomy, and full participation in a rich civil society—are tragically elusive" (p. 203).
5. See also Muetzelfeldt and Smith (2002) for an argument that a conception of global citizenship can be linked with the emergence of global civil society and global governing institutions.

REFERENCES

Appiah, K. A. (2006). *Cosmopolitanism: Ethics in a world of strangers*. New York: Norton.

Baird, N. (1999, July 28). Principal urges international outlook. *The Southland Times*.

Beck, U. (1999). *What is globalization?* Cambridge, UK: Polity Press.

Boli, J., & Thomas, G. M. (1997). World culture in the world polity: A century of international non-governmental organization. *American Sociological Review, 62,* 171–190.

Boli, J., & Thomas, G. M. (Eds.). (1999). *Constructing world culture: International non-governmental organizations since 1875*. Stanford, CA: Stanford University Press.

Brubaker, R. (1992). *Citizenship and nationhood in France and Germany*. Cambridge, MA: Harvard University Press.

Cohen, J. (Ed.). (1996). *For love of country? Debating the limits of patriotism*. Boston: Beacon Press.

Edwards, M., & Gaventa, J. (Eds.). (2001). *Global citizen action*. Boulder, CO: Lynne Rienner.

Falk, R. (1994). The making of global citizenship. In B. van Steenbergen (Ed.), *The condition of citizenship* (pp. 127–139). London: Sage.

Gaventa, J. (2001). Global citizen action: Lessons and challenges. In M. Edwards & J. Gaventa (Eds.), *Global citizen action* (pp. 275–287). Boulder, CO: Lynne Rienner.

Hahn, C. L. (1984). Promise and paradox: Challenges to global citizenship. *Social Education, 48,* 240–243, 297–299.

Hansen, R. (1999). Migration, citizenship and race in Europe: Between incorporation and exclusion. *European Journal of Political Research, 35,* 415–444.

Hayward, J. E. S. (1959). Solidarity: The social history of an idea in 19th century France. *International Review of Social History, 4,* 270–271.

Heater, D. (1996). *World citizenship and government: Cosmopolitan ideas in the history of western political thought*. New York: St. Martin's Press.

Heater, D. (2002). *World citizenship: Cosmopolitan thinking and its opponents*. London: Continuum.

Held, D. (1995). *Democracy and the global order*. Cambridge, UK: Polity Press.

Held, D. (1999). The transformation of political community: Rethinking democracy in the context of globalization. In I. Shapiro & C. Hacker-Cordón (Eds.), *Democracy's edges* (pp. 84–111). Cambridge, UK: Cambridge University Press.

Hutchings, K., & Dannreuther. R. (Eds.). (1999). *Cosmopolitan citizenship*. London: Macmillan.

Jacobson, D. (1996). *Rights across borders: Immigration and the decline of citizenship*. Baltimore: Johns Hopkins University Press.

Jones, C. (1999). *Global justice: Defending cosmopolitanism*. Oxford: Oxford University Press.

Joppke, C. (1998). Immigration challenges the nation-state. In C. Joppke (Ed.), *Challenge to the nation-state: Immigration in Western Europe and the United States* (pp. 5–48). Oxford: Oxford University Press.

Kant, I. (1991). Perpetual peace: A philosophical sketch (H. B. Nisbet, Trans.). In H. Reiss (Ed.), *Kant: Political writings* (pp. 93–130). Cambridge, UK: Cambridge University Press. (Original work published 1795)

Keck, M. E., & Sikkink, K. (1998). *Activists beyond borders: Advocacy networks in international politics.* Ithaca, NY: Cornell University Press.

Linklater, A. (1999). Cosmopolitan citizenship. In K. Hutchings & R. Dannreuther (Eds.), *Cosmopolitan citizenship* (pp. 35–59). London: Macmillan.

Montaigne, M. E. (1958). *Essays* (J. M. Cohen, Trans.). Harmondsworth, UK: Penguin. (Original work 1575)

Muetzelfeldt, M., & Smith, G. (2002). Civil society and global governance: The possibilities for global citizenship. *Citizenship Studies, 6,* 55–75.

Nathan, O., & Norden, H. (Eds.). (1968). *Einstein on peace.* New York: Schocken Books.

Nussbaum, M. C. (1996). Patriotism and cosmopolitanism. In J. Cohen (Ed.), *For love of country? Debating the limits of patriotism* (pp. 3–17). Boston: Beacon Press.

Sassen, S. (1999). *Guests and aliens.* New York: New Press.

Schattle, H. (2008). *The practices of global citizenship.* Lanham, MD: Rowman & Littlefield.

Schuck, P. H. (1998). *Citizens, strangers and in-betweens: Essays on immigration and citizenship.* Boulder, CO: Westview Press.

Soysal, Y. N. (1994). *The limits of citizenship.* Chicago: University of Chicago Press.

Urry, J. (2000). *Sociology beyond societies.* London: Routledge.

Chapter 2

Fostering Engagement

The Role of International Education in the Development of Global Civil Society

James M. Skelly
University of Ulster

The future, as we know, looks increasingly problematic. Soil has been rapidly eroding one agriculturally productive land, water is becoming an ever more scarce resource, and biodiversity is in such serious decline that there is an unprecedented mass extinction of species underway (Harper, 2008, pp. 47–57). In tropical forests where 50% of all land species live, estimates suggest that between 4,000 and 6,000 species have been disappearing every year (p. 57). India once produced 30,000 separate varieties of rice, but today most rice production is centered on 10 species. In other words, "the world's available gene pool" (Harper, 2008, p. 62), has shrunk inexorably! And this is to say nothing of climate change, pervasive hunger among many of the world's peoples, or the unsustainable dependence of almost all societies on fossil fuels. James Lovelock, who articulated the Gaia thesis that the earth is a living organism, estimates that by the end of this century there will be nearly 5 billion less people on the planet than there are currently (cited in Aitkenhead, 2008).

In his book *Our Final Century,* Martin Rees (2003), the noted Cambridge scientist, takes an even more grim perspective and estimates that humans have only a 50/50 chance of surviving the current century unless we radically change our approach to our existence on the planet. The question for international educators that arises is, "Are we doing enough to truly meet the challenges of living on this planet that we are sure to face in the coming decades?", as Rees also wonders, or are we blithely proceeding with our professional and personal routines, even though our intuition tells us that the students we are purportedly engaged in educating will face the most profound challenges humanity has ever confronted.

The mission statements of study abroad providers, as well as colleges and universities in the United States and elsewhere, increasingly make a nod to these challenges by often suggesting that they want to educate students to become "sensitive participants in the larger world," or that they are helping to foster "international citizenship," or to create "global citizens." There seems, however, to be a lack of connection between the words in mission statements and the kind of education students are receiving in concrete terms. We know what the challenges are, and that they are global in nature: climate change; poverty; environmental degradation; militarism; and increasing hunger, among myriad others—37 countries were hit by food riots in the first five months of 2008, including Cameroon, Niger, Egypt, and Haiti. Unfortunately, despite the fine sounding words, very few international education programs fundamentally address the problems our students, and humanity more broadly, will face in the decades to come.

Many U.S. supporters of study abroad have felt, however vaguely, that *any* experience abroad for American students would contribute to the general global need for educated citizens and help to foster greater understanding between peoples of different cultures. In this way, study abroad might make a modest contribution to creating a more peaceful and coherent global order. Perhaps this is correct, but the challenges we face are of such magnitude that we must bring much greater intentionality to our programs in the United States and abroad.

This lack of intentionality has been compounded by the fact that many international educators, and the institutions that support them such as NAFSA, have often articulated a truncated view of their work. Thus, international education is often characterized as contributing to "global economic competitiveness," the national security of the United States, or preparing students for a global labor market. From a limited national context there may be nothing wrong with such sentiments, but many of those who work in the field sense that these foci are morally, politically, and intellectually inadequate in facing the global challenges of the future. One reason for this may be that international educators have yet to embed their sentiments in a discourse with solid theoretical foundations that provides an alternative vision that is more in accord with both their own sentiments and the nature of the challenges faced by the people of the planet.

This chapter is an effort to describe the foundational problems in international education and study abroad that constrain our efforts, as well as an attempt to sketch out what we need to do to foster engagement with the monumental problems that humanity faces. In addition, the chapter also endeavors to suggest that international educators embed their work in a broad and compelling discourse that might provide a vision that is not exclusively focused on the state or the market, but is instead global and human centric in its orientation. It should be a requirement at higher education institutions that all students engage in a significant period of study abroad in order to help them see the globe as the context, and fundamental referent, for their lives. This should be the primary task of study abroad programs.

FOUNDATIONAL PROBLEMS

Although the discourse of international education has begun to shift modestly in recent years to one focused on peace, justice, and public diplomacy through the efforts of individuals like recent NAFSA presidents Ron Moffatt and Everett Egginton, the perspective that has been predominant in the United States has tended to distort the inherently global perspective that international education should naturally foster throughout the world. Study abroad, and the hosting of international students, has been seen through the lens of national interest and, as such, tends to put the United States and its individual citizens first. The distorting effects of such a state-centric perspective has also been clearly evident in other areas, such as environmental policy, foreign affairs, and the use of unilateral military force, but the tragedy is that international education should by its very nature transcend such parochialism. The literary critic and public intellectual, Edward Said (1993), argued that we can only overcome this parochialism "by acknowledging that the map of the world has no divinely or dogmatically sanctioned spaces, essences, or privileges" (p. 199).

But the problem is deeply rooted and pervasive. As one of the characters in the Irish playwright Brian Friel's (1981) play *Translations* opines regarding an imperial power that Ireland suffered for too many years, "It can happen that a civilization can be imprisoned in a linguistic contour which no longer matches the landscape of fact" (p. 43). To the extent that study abroad providers focus primarily on issues like "cross-cultural understanding," rather than the deeper structural conditions that create linguistic contours that confine our work, their programs militate against the development of a more generalized sense of global citizenship focused on the concrete problems of humanity. Paulo Freire (1985), the Brazilian educator, has argued instead that we must transcend illusions about a "humanistic education for mankind without the necessary transformation of an oppressed and unjust world." "Such a dream," Freire says, "actually serves the interests of the advantaged..." (p. 113); in other words, most of "us."

The cultural roots of these problems reside not only in the well documented exceptionalism that has defined U.S. political and cultural life, but also in the socialization of a vast number of individual Americans. The sense of being special and feeling entitled is tied to what Christopher Lasch labeled "the culture of narcissism" (1979). Lasch (1984) makes the point that it is not Narcissus' self-love that is problematic, but rather that "he fails to recognize his own reflection" and thus, "lacks any conception of the difference between himself and his surroundings" (p. 184).

This sensibility certainly manifests in the realm of international education, and the consequence is that in spite of our best efforts, many of our students come to think that the world is somehow really about them. A 1995 report by the American Council on Education noted that the fundamental problem in expanding international education was that American "domestic culture is insular, provincial, and parochial," and that too "many Americans, including undergraduates, cling to their own Splendid Isolation" (p. 3). The problem is also captured by the question University of Chicago philosopher Martha Nussbaum asks in her book, *Cultivating Humanity* (1997), "Why should one care about India, if one defines oneself as above all an American?" (p. 67). She answers by arguing that "education for world citizenship requires transcending the inclination of both students and educators to define themselves primarily in terms of local group loyalties and identities" (1997, p. 67).

In addition, and tied to the cultural sensibility discussed above, is the increasingly market-centric perspective that informs international education. This is manifest in the problem of commodification that international education, and education more broadly, faces. Chris Whittle's Channel One, for example, makes the process explicit and sells the attention of students to advertisers by embedding advertisements in "free" news programs and related equipment distributed to schools. Although such practices are well advanced in the United States, seeing higher education as a commodity, and students as consumers, is also becoming predominant in many parts of the world as is evident in the exhibits that tend to dominate the conventions of NAFSA and other educational organizations.

Education as a "service" for which one pays is being resisted by a wide variety of actors in spite of, and because of, its inclusion in the General Agreement on Trade in Services (GATS). Although UNESCO (2004) has suggested that, "The inclusion of trade in higher education services within the framework of GATS is a reality and will not change" (p. 9), the commodification of higher education is being challenged by the European Students' Union, the International Association of Universities, education unions, and various higher education institutions. The Association of Universities and Colleges of Canada, the American Council on Education, the European University Association, and the Council for Higher Education Accreditation issued a Joint Declaration a few years ago in which the first principle states that "Higher education exists to serve the public interest and is not a 'commodity'" (Association of Universities and Colleges of Canada, n.d.). Similarly, the European Students' Union challenged the inclusion of higher education in GATS and rejected "the notion of students as consumers," and instead stated that students "should be seen as partners by the Higher Education Institutions (HEIs) rather than paying customers" (European Students Union, n.d.).

Commodification in study abroad is, however, well advanced, and most providers, as reflected in their marketing, see students as narcissistic consumers. Michael Woolf (2006), of the Foundation for International Education, for example, has argued forcefully that, "The call for programme growth in non-traditional locations is not based on solid academic grounds but on a shallow pursuit of the new" (p. 140). Woolf goes on to suggest that many such marketing efforts use the language of tourism advertisements designed to get the attention of self-centered student consumers; for example, "When you tire of techno, have a quiet drink with Taoist monks," as it says in one advertisement he quotes (2006, p. 137). As the psychoanalyst, Joel Kovel (1981) has noted, the character of contemporary narcissism can be understood as "a neurosis of consumption" (p. 106). The consequence in study abroad marketing according to Woolf, is that "there is rarely a sense of serious exploration beyond the self" (2006, p. 137) and thus, the problem remains of thinking that the world is really about oneself. As the Stoic philosopher Seneca, quoting Socrates, remarked, "Why do you wonder that globe-trotting does not help you, seeing that you always take yourself with you?"

GLOBAL CITIZENSHIP?

The seemingly progressive response to such commodification has been to offer an expanded idea of citizenship, but such notions tend to be rife with confusion. Nussbaum emphasizes "world citizenship," and many other organizations speak of "global citizenship." Even Woolf's foundation reverts to the very kind of advertising that he criticizes when it says that it tries to prepare students for "international citizenship." All of these terms are problematic if seen through the lens of traditional state informed citizenship. However, state-centric notions of citizenship are in decline because of the deep structural crises that have developed in our politics due to globalization and the end of a single dominant conception of history.

Francis Fukuyama (1993) was correct when he suggested that we were at "the end of history" because he assumed a single conception of history had triumphed. What Fukuyama failed to see, however, was that we were at the beginning of a plurality of histories that have engendered a plurality of narratives and spaces. It is within these narratives and spaces, as Paul Barry Clarke argues in *Deep Citizenship* (1996), that we are able to imagine an enhanced politics in which citizenship is revived "while avoiding an extension of the boundaries of the state" (pp. 5–6). The multitude of histories, and the multitude of voices such histories empower, do not therefore look nostalgically at the political citizen of the past, but open up possibilities for a politics and citizenship of the future. Such a citizenship does not deny being a citizen of a state, but radically expands our conception of citizenship to attend to those concerns which states are no longer capable of addressing—in other words, a global citizenship that addresses the global political order and the challenges we face within that order.

The shallowness of traditional notions of citizenship, as well as the fragmentation of societies and the multiple perspectives that have come to the fore, have generated "the possibility of new political spaces and the development of political as well as civil society" at a global level (Clarke, 1996, p. 105). Rather than individuals centered by the master narratives of the past, the consequences of increasing numbers of decentered individuals may actually provide the capacity "to critically take the perspectives of others and engage in an enlargement of the mind" (Clarke,

1996, p. 107). Such a capacity is an absolute necessity "in order to be able to act towards the universal," and without which it is impossible to reach "beyond selfishness, sectionalism, and sectarianism" (Clarke, 1996, p. 107)—or, in the context of this chapter, to become "global citizens" within a global civil society.

GLOBAL CIVIL SOCIETY

Although it has enjoyed much wider currency in academic and intellectual circles in Europe and other parts of the world, the theoretical developments surrounding the idea of "global civil society" may provide the conceptual foundations to further support the development and status of work in international education, as well as providing a discourse that embodies the sometimes inchoate vision that most international educators hold. *Global Civil Society 2002* (Glasius, Kaldor, & Anheier, 2002), the yearbook produced annually by researchers associated with the Centre for the Study of Global Governance at the London School of Economics, mapped the global flows of students studying abroad and argued that, "A growing practice of studying abroad may therefore be one catalyst of the emergence and spread of global civil society" because "students are major transmitters of knowledge and ideas, and interlocutors across cultures" (p. 264).

The idea of "civil society" has a long and distinguished history and can be traced back to Cicero and Aristotle and in recent centuries from Adam Ferguson, through Locke, Adam Smith, Hegel, and, most notably from the perspective of this essay, Jeremy Bentham. In the Greek and Roman conception, which was dominant in European political thought until 1800 or so, civil society was coterminus with the state. In the early 19th century, however, civil society and the state begin to be seen as separate entities, especially in the work of Bentham, who saw them as oppositional.

Although its meaning has changed over the years, the idea of "civil society" was utilized in contemporary times by activists challenging the state in the countries of Central and Eastern Europe under communist rule. It was this distinction between civil society and the state that was seized upon by dissidents who suffered the lack of freedom in the former regimes east of the Iron Curtain. Perhaps the most significant in this regard were Adam Michnik in Poland, György Konrad in Hungary, and Vaclav Havel in the then Czechoslovakia. Michnik's (1987) essay, "The New Evolutionism," Konrad's *Antipolitics* (1984), and Havel's *Living in Truth* (1990), among other works, became required reading for political dissidents in the communist countries. In their writings they focused on people's right to free association—a civil society, in other words rather than a state-centric one within the communist states. The shorthand for this was the idea that "civil society" was in opposition to the pervasive attempts of the state to organize, and therefore control and legitimate, all forms of associational activity on the part of individuals in society. As Mary Kaldor (2003) has noted, "the emphasis was on self-organization and civic autonomy in reaction to the vast increase in the reach of the modern state" (p. 21).

When I went to Hungary for the first time in the summer of 1986, what I encountered then and in subsequent visits during the next several years was the blossoming of associational activity uncontrolled by the state. Those involved understood it as the flowering of "civil society"—and the historic discourse of civil society provided the dissidents involved with a meaningful narrative about their activities, as well as a sense that they were on the "right side of history." To me, *the* exemplar of this flowering was the organization founded by students—the League of Young Democrats, or FIDESZ, as it was known in Hungary. Under communism, the only legitimate organization for young people interested in a political or governmental career was the Young

Communist League, which was approved by the government and the Communist Party. In contrast, FIDESZ was a group of freely associating young people who understood themselves as one of the manifestations of a long suppressed civil society.

Kaldor discusses this particular epoch in Central and Eastern Europe in *Global Civil Society* (2003). In it, she notes how what she calls "The Ideas of 1989," which led to the collapse of the communist states of the Soviet bloc, provided the foundation for the emergence of discussions about a "global civil society" (pp. 50–73). Michael Edwards (2004), director of the Ford Foundation's program on governance and civil society, discusses in more abstract form how those events and perspectives provided the soil within which the global civil society discussions of the 1990s became rooted. He also demonstrates how the larger structural transformations in the global economy during this period created a greater sense of insecurity in many of the world's peoples—thus, what are called "precarity movements," because of the precariousness of contemporary life in ever increasing parts of the world. In other words, as Edwards's asserts, such responses may mean that a global civil society is a manifestation of "people power writ large" (p.15).

In sketching out the basics of three contrasting schools of thought regarding civil society, Edwards suggests that Americans may well resonate most with what he calls the "neo-Tocquevillian" perspective, which focuses on the idea of creating the "good society" (2004, p. 8). While dissidents in Central and Eastern Europe were deploying the discourse of civil society as free associational life to challenge the state, a parallel discourse was developing in the United States that focused on the "good society" in which justice and social equality were valorized. This discourse implicitly challenged the tendencies of large corporations as well as the state, and had its roots in Alexis de Tocqueville's insights into the vitality of American social and political life during his tour of the United States in the 1830s. What Tocqueville noted then were the "habits of the heart" of the Americans that derived from the dominant political discourse that they were historically embedded in—republicanism, and its emphasis on civic virtue both on the part of individual citizens and the Republic itself. These "habits of the heart" were the norms that implicitly contributed to the vitality of American civil society by legitimating a broad spectrum of civically virtuous associational activity on the part of citizens, as Robert Bellah and his colleagues have noted in a book by that name (Bellah, Madsen, Sullivan, Swidler, & Tipton, 2007).

The Good Society (Bellah, Madsen, Sullivan, Swidler, & Tipton, 1992) was more proscriptive and argued for the recovery of the civil society tradition in the United States, which many scholars suggested was under increasing threat. Most notable in this regard was Robert Putnam's *Bowling Alone* (2001), which suggested that Americans were increasingly atomized and isolated. Recent polls have suggested that lack of social engagement has increased even more in the United States since Putnam published *Bowling Alone*, and thus the debate that has developed is about "the value of voluntary associations in curbing the power of centralizing institutions, protecting pluralism, and nurturing constructive social norms especially 'generalized trust and cooperation'" (cited in Edwards, 2004, p. 7).

Edwards, however, argues that there is a third definition of civil society as the "public sphere," which "is the basis for the current and widespread revival of interest in direct, deliberative, or participatory democracy," and which, he argues, is "an essential complement to the representative components of political systems" (2004, p. 59). This kind of "dialogic politics," he argues, may be the only route "to reach a normative consensus around a plurality of interests and positions" (2004, p. 59). However, Edwards makes the important point that the three perspectives on civil society "are not mutually exclusive, since the goals of the good society are most likely to be achieved when an enabling environment for all associational life is combined with support for specific associational forms" (p. 86). This "civil society ecosystem," as Edwards calls it, has one essential component: These are the associations that combine action at both the individual and structural level since they build the dispositions "to care for the common good and to address the barriers that stand in its way" (2004, p. 87). The contemporary German social philosopher Jürgen Habermas articulated similar sentiments when he described the character of contemporary civil society as "composed of those more or less spontaneously emergent associations, organizations, and movements that, attuned to how societal problems resonate in private life spheres, distil and transmit such reactions to the public sphere" (cited in Kaldor, 2003, p. 21). And like Edwards, Habermas emphasizes that, "The core of civil society comprises a network of associations that institutionalizes problem solving discourses of general interest inside the framework of organized public spheres" (cited in Kaldor, 2003, p. 21).

Although the term *global civil society* came to be used in the early 1990s as a counter to what many saw as the increasing power of global corporations, as well as the contemporary state, Edwards argues that the creation of a viable global civil society requires a synthesis of associational life, the good society, and the public sphere. At the global level therefore, states "will remain the duty bearers of international treaties," transnational networks will be "essential to enforce public compliance," and a global public sphere will be "required to foster debates about international norms" (2004, pp. 91–92)

This, of course, is where international education can be truly significant. Broadly speaking our efforts are focused on helping individuals to transcend narrow national cultures and identities through the free association of students within a global context. At the same time we can go several steps further by providing a critical perspective on the imperatives of global corporations and the institutions of states by helping to create a global public sphere where students and faculty, acting as global citizens, can foster much needed debates about international norms on a variety of issues. Unfortunately, this broad context has for the most part not been attended to by international educators, and instead for lack of an alternative vision, the field has tended to focus on the more limited concerns of states and corporations. It is now necessary to begin to broaden that discussion and to lay some modest intellectual foundation for the further development of our understanding of the importance of international education to creation of citizenship within the new global civil society.

WHAT IS TO BE DONE?

There are several levels at which our efforts should be focused in order to concretely achieve such a vision. In general, international educators can help to overcome the distortions that inform parochial educational perspectives by making the principal focus of their efforts be *the globe and its people*. Without question, we must also work to revive civil society in the United States by challenging those who would try to further centralize power through the institutions of the state or through corporate structures. This means that wherever we are engaged, we should help our American colleagues to recover those habits of their hearts that are republican, rather than imperial, in nature. Reviving that individual and collective sense of civic virtue, and the modesty inherent in it, would help to strike a chord with many in the United States and abroad who know, to paraphrase Said (1993, p. 377), that the map of the world does not include any divinely sanctioned spaces and privileges.

As a corollary to the above, we should also move beyond any direct concern with international education as contributing to the national security of the United States. Although the work of international education may in fact contribute to security in the United States, we should follow the lead of the United Nations and think of how our work might contribute to "human security." Human security is informed by the "dual notions of protection and empowerment of people" (UN Commission on Human Security, 2003, p. 121), and the sense that "knowledge, education and democratic engagement are inseparable—and essential" in this task, according to the report issued by the UN Commission on Human Security (2003, p. 120). As educators, we must therefore aim to "raise awareness of the social environment and provide the tools to address problems" by teaching "students to reason, to consider ethical claims, and to understand and work with such fundamental ideas as human rights, human diversity and interdependence" and therefore "instil in the content" of our educational efforts "a new emphasis on ethical values—and on public debate and democracy" (2003, p. 121).

Our most difficult challenge is to resist the consumerist sensibilities that have begun to pervade education both at home and abroad. If we are really to foster global civil society and citizenship, we must not only get students, and their teachers, out of their societies of origin for a significant part of their education, but we also must work to get consumer culture out of students and their teachers. In other words, faculty and higher education administrators should be working against the "relentless commodification" (Said, 1993, p.387) of education in order to help students understand the manner in which the consumerist sensibilities to which they have been socialized distort their understanding of other cultures and peoples, as well as the global problems we face as humans upon the planet.

At a very basic level, students choose to study because they want new understandings and new experiences; this is especially true for students who choose to study in a society and culture other than the one where they underwent primary socialization. However, they face two fundamental challenges: one is that their base realities are often those of television and popular cinema rather than more visceral experiences. Thus, I will often hear American students studying in Ireland, who, when they come upon an old estate, exclaim, "That's just like in Harry Potter," or something similar. Second, their experiences in a new society, and thus their consequent understanding of life's nuances, are increasingly packaged for them even in the realm of study abroad. They may have hoped to encounter the serendipitous while abroad and have experiences unmediated by various interested institutions, but this too is increasingly denied them as international education organizations engage in ever more elaborate projects to assess what students have learned, and thus refine the packaging of student experience. One consequence, as Walter Benjamin (1992, p. 83) has noted, is that "experience has fallen in value" and thus people are unable to tell stories in which the wisdom of personal experience is embedded.

In his essay "The Message in the Bottle," the novelist Walker Percy (1989), captured the desire of people to have bona fide experiences, however seemingly perverse. He posed a series of rhetorical questions at the very beginning of the essay such as, "Why do people often feel so bad in good environments and good in bad environments?" for example. Or, "Why is it harder to study a dogfish on a dissecting board in a zoological laboratory in college where one has proper instruments and a proper light than it would be if one were marooned on an island and, having come upon a dogfish on the beach and having no better instrument than a pocket knife or hair pin, one began to explore the dogfish?" And, "Why was it that when Franz Kafka would read aloud to his friends about the sadness and alienation of life in the twentieth century everyone would laugh until tears came?" (1989, pp. 4—5). Percy goes on to suggest that the answer to these questions is to be found by understanding the manner in which our language, deeply embedded and previously organized into culturally defined packages of knowledge, destroys and constrains our experience of life (1989, p. 6). It is these culturally defined packages that we, and our students, need to transcend.

Without question, NAFSA, other international education associations, and study abroad providers should join with those organizations that resist defining education as a commodity that is a tradable service within the context of GATS. We should affirm that international education exists to serve the global public interest and that it must not be dealt with as a commodity, nor should students be considered consumers. It might also be useful to set standards regarding the "selling" of study abroad programs. In a somewhat light-hearted vein, we could perhaps also join together to provide annual "awards" to those organizations that have engaged in the kind of egregious advertising of study abroad programs that Mike Woolf has highlighted. A bit of derision might go a long way for those who suggest that "when you tire of techno, have a quiet drink with Taoist monks."

The above challenges of a structural and cultural nature also cry out for a more positive strategy with which to inform the programs we create for students. The decision to study abroad suggests that to a greater or lesser extent those students who make that decision are open to experiencing realities that may allow them to situate their home reality as simply one among many—not intrinsically better, nor intrinsically worse, just different. As Clarke notes, such an "expanded consciousness is found in the ability to take one's own private and/or sectional interests and measure them against other perspectives." In other words, "the responsibility of such individuals is that they make reflective judgements" (1996, p. 104).

This perspective should be central to our work as international educators. Regardless of the type of program, we should be building in reflexivity—about the culturally constructed nature of one's self, one's home society, and our understanding of the larger world. This requires that we in particular support a reflexive perspective about how the dominant economic and political structures in the world are constructed and institutionalized so that students recognize that war, injustice, and poverty are institutionalized in the global order. Only by engaging in dialogue with our students and asking, "Why? Does it have to be this way?" as Paulo Freire suggests (1985, p. 113), will we prepare students for the extraordinary challenges they will have to face in the 21st century.

A CAUTIONARY NOTE

Many of us who work in international education are trying to encourage a new mode of thinking—as I am implicitly suggesting above—that may lead to action that helps to create a more peaceful, just, and egalitarian global order. However, we must be wary of the tendency to be utopian.

Writing in the mid-1980s, Vaclav Havel noted that "the word 'peace' has been drained of all content" (1990, p. 166). The problem was, and still is, that "peace," as with other utopian ideas, "ceases to express the transcendent dimension of being human and degenerates into a substitute for it" (Havel, 1990, p. 175). Thus, Havel argued, "the project for a better world, ceases to be an expression of man's responsible identity and begins, on the contrary, to expropriate his responsibility and identity" because "the abstraction ceases to belong to him and he instead begins to belong to it" (1990, p. 175). Havel argued that the genesis of the problem with "peace" is rooted in the anomic individual's desire for mastery and control, in a manner that is not dissimilar in my opinion from that of the nuclear strategists I studied during that period: "They are the people tragically oppressed by the terror of nothingness and fear of their own being, who need to gain inner peace by imposing order ('peace') upon a restless world, placing in a sense their whole unstable existence into that order, ridding themselves of their obsessions once and for all" (1990, p. 173). As with the nuclear strategists, their angst drives them "to construct and impose various projects directed toward a rationally ordered common good" and "their purpose is to make sure that, at long last, things will be clear and comprehensible, that the world will stride onward toward a goal, finally putting an end to all the infuriating contingency of history" (1990, p. 173).

In terms of matters discussed in this essay, what Havel is warning against is an attempt to turn "peace and justice," or "global civil society," for example, into a meta-narrative. Rather than a unitary vision, what international educators may want to do is to help students reflect on the many manifestations of peace and justice, and to celebrate the "infuriating contingency of history." In a similar way, a global civil society is likely to be an untidy phenomenon that resembles a work in progress, rather than a finished totality. This also implies that a different ethical perspective should inform our work.

The contemporary Irish philosopher Richard Kearney has provided some proposals which might make the task more concrete without resorting to a grand meta-narrative of morality and ethics. In *The Wake of Imagination* (1988), Kearney argues that although deconstructive and other forms of postmodern expression have helped to destroy the traditional bases for ethics, an ethical imagination can, and must, be based on the concrete others with whom we are confronted. The only possible response left, Kearney says, is to "the face of the other" (1988, p. 361). This is similar to Martha Nussbaum's insight that, "Citizens who cultivate their humanity need, further, an ability to see themselves…above all, as human beings bound to all other human beings by ties of recognition and concern" (1997, p. 10).

Kearney also notes that it is the face of the other which "resists assimilation to the dehumanising processes of commodity fetishism" (1988, p. 361). The dehumanizing of others in "nontraditional" study abroad locations where the poor, for example, become commodities, is exactly what Mike Woolf is criticizing in his article, "Come and See the Poor People: The Pursuit of Exotica" (2006).

This isn't to suggest that there can't be a universal ethics, but as international educators we should know that the universal must proceed from the particular and not the other way around. In order that such an ethics should not "degenerate into censorious puritanism or nostalgic lamentation," however, Kearney also argues that ethics "must also give full expression to its *poetical* potential" (1988, p. 366). Historically, he claims, the ethical or poetical aspect of the imagination has been dominant, but instead of continuing this separation, he urges a synthesis of the two because the logic of the unconscious imagination "is one of *both/and* rather than *either/or*" (1988, p.368). It is therefore "inclusive and, by extension, tolerant; it allows opposites to stand, irreconcilables to co-exist, refusing to deny the claim of one for the sake of its contrary, to sacrifice the strange on the altar of self-identity" (1988, p. 368). Thus, Kearney wants us to understand poetry as "a creative letting go of the drive for possession, of the calculus of means and ends" (1988, p. 386). Taken together, the poetical and ethical imagination "signals a call to abandon the priority of egological existence," for "without the poetical openness to the pluri-dimensionality of meaning, the ethical imagination might well shrink back into a cheerless moralizing, an authoritarian and fearful censorship" (1988, p. 386).

Aren't these the perspectives that we hope our students will develop when they study abroad?

In my opinion, these are precisely the sentiments necessary to have a viable cosmopolitan civil society at either the local or the global level, and it is this sensibility that should color our work in international education. One person who knew the importance of conjoining such a poetical and ethical imagination, was my friend the late Ron Moffatt, NAFSA's President in 2007. He wrote the following that year:

> As international educators shaping our global future, we share a compelling responsibility and a unique power to envision possibilities commensurate with the challenges we face. We must act now to foster and connect learning communities that will create a more just, compassionate and sustainable world for all. We must prepare tomorrow's leaders to create a global civil society wherein perspectives are exchanged in pursuit of understanding, aspirations are transformed into deeds that enrich the human spirit, borders become invisible, nations become people, common ground is nurtured, partnerships flourish and goodwill prevails.

What I hope is that international educators will individually and through the organizations to which they belong like NAFSA, begin to insure that the educational programs they support truly address the serious systemic problems that we face as humans living on this planet. This cannot be done by simply going about our ordinary routines with our limited personal and national assumptions. International educators, more than other professionals, should see that they are part of a worldwide movement to create a viable, tolerant, and open global civil society that will help to address those problems. NAFSA itself is one of the largest global civil society organizations on the planet, even though its members may for the most part be unconscious of this. The practice of study abroad itself as the yearbook, *Global Civil Society 2002*, pointed out, is a strong indicator of an emerging global civil society, and the express intent of most study abroad programs is to foster the sensibility—cross-cultural learning, immersion, and so on—that is necessary to help create the kinds of citizens that a global civil society requires. Only through such a reconceptualized and engaged citizenship can we hope that our children's children will live on a planet of the sort that Ron Moffatt envisaged.

REFERENCES

Aitkenhead, D. (2008 March 1). *Enjoy life while you can* [Electronic version]. The Guardian, Retrieved from http://www.guardian.co/uk/the guardian/2008/mar/01/scienceofclimatechange.climatechange

American Council on Education. (1995). *Educating Americans for a world in flux: Ten ground rules for internationalizing higher education.* Washington, DC: ACE.

Association of Universities and Colleges of Canada. (n.d.). Retrieved from http://www.aucc.ca/_pdf/english/state-menrs/2001/gats_10_25_e.pdf

Bellah, R., Madsen, R., Sullivan, W. M., Swidler, A., & Tipton, S. (1992). *The good society.* New York: Vintage.

Bellah, R., Madsen, R., Sullivan, W.M., Swidler, A., & Tipton, S. (2007). *Habits of the heart: Individualism and commitment in American life.* Berkeley: University of California Press.

Benjamin, W. (1992). The storyteller. In H. Arendt (Ed.), *Illuminations* (pp. 83–107). London: Fontana Press.

Clarke, P. B. (1996). *Deep citizenship.* London: Pluto Press.

Edwards, M. (2004). *Civil society.* Cambridge, UK: Polity Press.

European Students Union. (n.d.). Reteieved from http://www.esib.org/index.php/issues/Commodification/88-gats-and-education

Freire, P. (1985). *The politics of education: Culture, power, and liberation.* South Hadley, MA: Bergin & Garvey Press.

Friel, B. (1981). *Translations*. London: Faber & Faber.

Fukuyama, F. (1993). *The end of history and the last man*. New York: Harper Perennial.

Glasius, M., Kaldor, M., & Anheier, H. (Eds.). (2002). *Global civil society 2002*. Oxford, UK: Oxford University Press.

Harper, C. (2008). *Environment and society*. Upper Saddle River, NJ: Prentice-Hall.

Havel, V. (1990). *Living in truth*. London: Faber & Faber.

Kaldor, M. (2003). *Global civil society: An answer to war*. Cambridge, UK: Polity Press.

Kearney, R. (1988). *The wake of imagination*. London: Hutchison.

Konrad, G. (1984). *Antipolitics: An essay*. San Diego, CA: Harcourt Brace Jovanovich.

Kovel, J. (1981). *The age of desire*. New York: Pantheon Books.

Lasch, C. (1979). *The culture of narcissism*. New York: Norton.

Lasch, C. (1984). *The minimal self*. New York: Norton.

Michnik, A. (1987). *Letters from prison and other essays*. Berkeley: University of California Press.

Moffatt, R. (2007). *The path ahead: addressing the moral imperatives of our times*. Retrieved October 28, 2008, from http://www.isc.sdsu.edu/current/isc_moffattpublications.htm

Nussbaum, M. (1997). *Cultivating humanity: A classical defense of reform in liberal education*. Cambridge, MA: Harvard University Press.

Percy, W. (1989). *The message in the bottle*. New York: Farrar, Straus, & Giroux.

Putnam, R. (2001). *Bowling alone: The collapse and revival of American community*. New York: Simon & Schuster.

Rees, M. (2003). *Our final century*. London: Random House.

Said, E. (1993). *Culture and imperialism*. London: Chatto & Windus.

UNESCO. (2004). *Higher education in a globalized society*. Paris: UNESCO.

United Nations Commission on Human Security. (2003). *Human security now*. New York: United Nations Commission on Human Security.

Woolf, M. (2006). Come and see the poor people: The pursuit of exotica. *Frontiers: The Interdisciplinary Journal of Study Abroad, 13*, 135–146.

Chapter 3

Global Learning and the Making of Citizen Diplomats

Rebecca Hovey and Adam Weinberg
World Learning/SIT

INTRODUCTION

We begin with two paradoxical observations about American higher education. First, American higher education has deep civic roots, although the full promise of these roots remains unrealized. From the early congregational colleges to Thomas Jefferson's founding of the University of Virginia, American higher education was based on an expressed public purpose (Snyder, 2008; Sullivan, 2000). For 200 years there have been debates over what this means and should mean for undergraduate education, faculty research, and community–campus partnerships. Most recently, this conversation has resurfaced around movements to create "engaged campuses." This work has called for everything from much more fluidity between the college campuses and surrounding communities to a refocus of faculty research and teaching around community-based research and service-learning (Ehrlich, 2000; Mathews, 2008). At the forefront of these efforts has been a more purposeful and intentional movement among educators and administrators for campus-wide civic education efforts.

Second, American higher education is clearly internationalizing, but we do not really know what that means. Open many Web sites or strategic plans, and you will find text on how that university is trying to internationalize. Yet, talk to most presidents and provosts and they will admit that they are not really sure what that means or how to actually do it. There is a lot of work going on. Most of it is very well intentioned. But too much of it feels like the proverbial spinning of the wheels.

We seek to connect the growing body of literature on civic education to this process of internationalization, particularly in the growth of study abroad. The fundamental starting place for our analysis is that study abroad shares many aspects with civic education as both are often incorporated as part of a campus community engagement agenda, service learning initiative, or set of courses designed to instill democratic education. Both frequently involve practical, problem-solving action with disenfranchised communities or grassroots organizations. These two fields, study abroad and civic education, emphasize learning beyond the confines of the classroom to include the knowledge gained by working directly with local communities.

As importantly, civic education and study abroad need each other if both are to flourish in the next decade. Despite the tremendous amount of civic education work on college campuses, it is not clear that most thinking about civic education will actually produce the types of citizens we need in the 21st century. Too much civic education focuses narrowly on traditional approaches where students are presented with information about American history and democratic theory. Educational, psychological, and sociological research suggests that there is little correlation between knowledge about democracy and active civic engagement (Colby, Erlich, Beaumont, & Stephens, 2003; Gibson, 2001; Spiezio, 2002). Knowledge is a necessary, but not sufficient, condition for active citizenship.

Likewise, study abroad needs civic education. While the growth of study abroad is impressive, it is not clear that, as currently practiced, it will sufficiently benefit either students or communities. Study abroad in the United States can either be an extractive enterprise that takes advantage of international partners for our benefit, or it can be a reciprocal enterprise that benefits local communities as well as our students and institutions. It all depends on the models we use, the goals we make explicit, and the learning outcomes that are achieved. The civic education literature can help guide and shape our thinking about appropriate concepts, models, and aspirations.

In the rest of this chapter, we take up the following two questions: What does it mean to prepare students to be citizens in the 21st century? And what role should study abroad play in this process? We build our analysis by exploring and then weaving together three concepts: civic education in study abroad, responsible citizen diplomacy, and what we call a global ecology of learning.

EXPLORING CIVIC EDUCATION: PREPARING STUDENTS FOR CIVIC AGENCY AND PUBLIC WORK

Any definition of civic education must start with a notion of what it is we are hoping to instill within our students and for what purposes we hope to instill it. We want to propose that civic education is fundamentally about preparing students with the capacities and commitments to do public work. Embedded in this statement are some simple assumptions. First, education should prepare people to do the ongoing work of creating and re-creating the places where they live and the communities that anchor their lives. A healthy society is fundamentally dependent upon a citizenry that possesses the capacity and interest to work together as problem solvers and coproducers of public goods (Boyte & Kari, 2000). Second, civic education is a call for an educational system that generates and sustains the capacity for people and institutions to work with others to produce the public goods of our shared community and everyday lives.

At the core of this conception is what Harry Boyte and others have called public work (Boyte, 2008, 2004; Boyte & Kari, 2000; Weinberg, 2005). This conception emphasizes the need for ordinary citizens to come together to produce things or create processes with lasting civic value. Public work is what occurs when ordinary citizens come together, often across differences, to take the actions required to build and sustain our basic public goods and resources. They solve common problems and create common things with lasting value (Boyte, 2004). This work may be paid or voluntary. It may be as part of one's job or as part of one's neighborhood involvements. In perhaps the clearest statement, Colby et al. (2003) state, civic education is about developing a young person's ability to

...recognize himself or herself as a member of a larger social fabric and therefore consider social problems to be at least partially his or her own; such an individual is willing to see the moral and civic dimensions of issues, to make and justify informed moral and civic judgments, and to take action where appropriate. (p. 17)

This framing shifts the question of civic education in two ways that are particularly relevant to study abroad. The first is a shift from civic education as merely a sound understanding of American history and the constitution, or even democratic theory. It reframes the question of civic education as: how do we create situations through education for students to acquire the skills, values, knowledge base, and interest to do public work that can anchor healthy democratic communities in the 21st century? The second is a shift in theories of social change. Too much theorizing, and hence teaching, is embedded with guilt, nihilism, and critique without solutions. Students are presented with case studies and theories about social problems and all the failed attempts to solve them. Or they learn of the historic dimensions of social issues such as racism or colonialism, and the need to "own" these problems, without fully understanding the subjective realities of these issues as lived by diverse communities. Likewise, they are immersed in their own campus communities where they are surrounded by professionals who solve problems for students who are the passive recipients of this help. Unwittingly, we send the message to students that there is not much they can do to make the world a better place, because the problems are too large and their skill sets are much too weak. We are then confounded when students appear disengaged.

Much of the recent theorizing around civic education has used concepts of civic agency to articulate a different way of thinking about education for civic engagement. Civic education instead creates enabling learning environments where students develop hope that they can work with others across differences to solve problems. Citizens replace professionals as the drivers of change, and hope replaces nihilism as the prevailing view about the prospects for change. In a recent article, Boyte (2008) captures this as follows:

> Civic learning enables people to practice civic politics, or self-directed public action. I use the term "politics" here…not as partisan warfare but as something close to the opposite, a method that humans have developed to negotiate different, sometimes conflicting interests and views in order to get things done. The aim is not to do away with conflict—politics sometimes surfaces submerged clashes of interes—but rather to avoid violence and contain conflicts, to generate common work on public questions, and to achieve beneficial public outcomes. (p. 11)

One implication of connecting civic education to study abroad is a powerful proposition for the future of higher education: that learning intercultural awareness and understanding of the global community is critical for the mission of higher education to prepare capable and engaged citizens.

Study abroad proponents argue that international learning can be a cornerstone for an undergraduate education that prepares students to be engaged and informed citizens in an increasingly globalized world. This is part of how we have justified the expense of programs on our campuses. In our view, study abroad is the ideal place to develop the type of agency-driven civic education we have described. We have an enormous opportunity today to build a strong network of supporters: the numbers of students going abroad has increased by almost 10% a year for several years as student seek to gain the skills needed to be successful in today's world. A recent poll of college-bound students found that interest in international learning experiences is strong and more than 55% expect to study abroad as part of their college experience (American Council on Education, 2008).

As study abroad becomes increasingly integrated into U.S. undergraduate curricula, we have a moment to broaden the base of supporters on campuses, while also ensuring that study abroad, when combined with the goals of civic education, can lead the revitalization of higher education in a manner consistent with its original mission. We propose that successful efforts to seize this moment will require us to find the high road of study abroad by identifying the best practices, ethical norms, and quality learning experiences that support this effort.

EXPLORING STUDY ABROAD: FINDING THE HIGH ROAD

A growing body of empirical research suggests that students who have traveled and studied overseas in carefully developed international education programs have greater capacity to develop communicative capacities in languages, interact appropriately in other cultures, and acquire problem-solving strategies for international living (Engle & Engle, 2004; Segalowitz et al., 2004). Many of the capacities needed to compete in what Thomas Friedman (2005) describes as today's "flat" world are acquired through international experiences. We would do well to remember that the desirable outcomes associated with studying abroad are neither automatic nor guaranteed under current conditions, nor can we measure success only by the number of students sent abroad. We need to be intentional and purposeful.

We can think about the practices, norms, experiences, and outcomes of study abroad by distinguishing between what we call low road and high road programs. This distinction of high and low road models is more commonly used to define community economic development initiatives. Low road often refers to efforts by communities and firms to generate more economic activity by enhancing efficiencies, often by squeezing costs while making as few investments in people or production techniques as possible. High road refers to efforts to generate more activity by utilizing the best workers and latest technology to produce products with a high value (Harrison, 1997, 2004). High road organizations emphasize quality control and product innovations over efficiencies. They also rely on high quality labor that can identify, analyze, and solve problems around product design, production, distribution, marketing, and finance. Most often, high road efforts are based on participatory, sustainable, and community-focused principles (Swinney, 1998).

In many ways the high road/low road distinction could be used as a concept to explore larger changes in higher education, although that is well beyond the scope of this paper. Here, we want to use the distinction to tease out what we believe are fundamentally different principles for different types of study abroad programs.

Under low road models, universities and programs send college students into the world, with little preparation, for culturally thin experiences. Students make minimal effort to learn local languages or customs, travel in large groups, and are taught in American-only classrooms. They live and go to bars with other Americans, often drinking too much and getting into trouble. They see local sights through the windows of traveling buses. Far from experiencing another culture deeply and on its own terms, these students (at best) simply get the American college experience in a different time zone. It is worth noting as well that many of the study abroad destinations known as "fun" don't even require language study and offer relatively minimal challenges to students' sense of place and culture. These also happen to be the places with the highest percentage of students.

High road study abroad programs are developed to ensure deep cultural and linguistic immersion. Students are oriented to understand and respect local customs and encouraged to take responsibility for projecting a positive image of Americans. High road programs ensure that students become part of the culture by staying with local families and giving back to local communities. These types of programs are working to create programs where students attend classes and participate in activities with local students and are taught by local staff who are paid fair wages and offer an inside view of the culture. Students learn that they return to the United States with an obligation to stay active, help others learn from their experiences, and push for better understanding from their academic institutions, future workplaces, and political representatives with regard to the world beyond our borders. These students become young intercultural emissaries, global citizens able to adapt and contribute to a complex world.

Without claiming that SIT programs accomplish the above model perfectly, we can offer an example of what a high road program looks like:

Naana Opoku-Agyemang, an African scholar and current Vice-Chancellor of the University of Cape Coast, led multiple groups of 10 to 18 American students who were studying in Ghana for a semester through World Learning's SIT Study Abroad program. The students start the semester with an intense language seminar in Fanti, the local language. Students then attended a series of classes and seminars on the African Diaspora taught by African scholars. During this period, students took a number of excursions, where they spend time immersed in cultural dialogues with Ghanaians—elders, chiefs, healers, scholars, students, families, and townspeople—in settings ranging from classrooms to remote villages. Throughout their visit, they lived with Ghanaian families and worked on community problems. They spent the last 4 weeks of their semester abroad doing an independent research project—a deep, field-based exploration of one aspect of their experience.

"The program is designed with the hope that students will remember that a story is never complete until all sides have been told and heard," says Opoku-Agyemang. Students should leave Ghana understanding how people are shaped by their historical and current realities, and how to bridge those differences in daily life. A student who went on the program a few years ago wrote, "At the end of the program, I finally began to view myself as a citizen of the world. I learned how to adapt to another culture without making it change for me" (personal communication, August 17, 2007).

The distinction between high road and low road is not about length of the program, where the program takes place, or to some extent cost. For example, we both can name semester long and one-week programs that fall into both categories. Rather, the distinction rests on the fundamental principles that guide a program. We want to claim that a high road approach to study abroad starts with a focus on deep cultural and linguistic immersion and should be mindful of four principles:

1. Commitment to scale and access. Study abroad programs face the challenge of being large enough to accommodate student demand, small enough not to overwhelm the host community, diverse enough to represent U.S. demographics, and flexible enough in funding and curricula to provide access to underrepresented populations. Currently, less than 8% of full-time enrolled American college students study abroad, despite polling data that suggest most have an interest in doing so. Of that small percentage, less than 9% are black or Hispanic, even though these students constitute 25% of all college students. Stated differently, about 50% of the students who study abroad come from just one hundred universities and colleges.

We need to do better. As we seek to enroll an even larger share of U.S. university students, we need to design programs and financial opportunities that ensure wide diversity in manageably sized programs.

2. Emphasis on exposing students to less-traveled, less-understood destinations and themes. Two thirds of students who study abroad go to Europe. Only 15% go to Latin America, 7% to Asia, 3% to Africa, and only 0.50% to the Middle East. As geopolitical and economic power shifts, study abroad needs to keep up by including emerging regions of importance. It is critical that students understand how the majority of the world's population is sustained. Of 6.5 billion inhabitants, approximately 1.4 billion, or about 20% of the world's population, live on less than US$1.25 per day. In developing regions such as Sub-Saharan Africa, this percentage often reaches levels of 50% or higher (World Bank, 2008). How our world will address the resource needs, geopolitical conflicts, health and welfare dilemmas of our growing global population needs to be part of every college curriculum. Of course students should still study in Europe, but they should go on programs where they are challenged by important themes in contemporary European society, and learn the necessary linguistic and cultural skills to comprehend these issues from local perspectives.

3. Plans for student "reentry" and opportunities for lifelong engagement. Students return from abroad filled with energy and excitement, often transformed by their experiences, but struggle to find opportunities and outlets for channeling their newfound energies. We need to harness and direct this energy toward lifelong learning, growth, and engagement in communities back home. There has been a tremendous amount of chatter within higher education around civic engagement and undergraduate education. Harnessed correctly, study abroad may be as close to a solution as we will find. In a subsequent section, we will describe how learning global citizenship values is best practiced by example within one's own home community.

4. Commitment to reciprocity. In this context, reciprocity might be defined as operating our programs in ways that strengthen the partners (e.g., community groups, individuals, and communities) we depend upon for the vitality of our programs. International education can either be perceived as an enterprise with little benefit to the rest of the world, or a reciprocal exchange that has economic and social benefits for host countries and communities. High road providers work in partnership with host communities. They contribute needed revenues, networks, and other resources to these communities, while also maintaining a small and respectful footprint.

Some study abroad providers address these principles by paying attention to how they run their operations. They purposefully use local companies, keep the footprint small, and compensate local staff with good wages, benefits, and professional development opportunities. Other providers are using community-based research and service-learning projects to connect students to local development efforts. But reciprocity can and should mean much more. For example, we (SIT) recently signed an agreement with the Royal University of Bhutan (RUB). RUB is hosting SIT Study Abroad undergraduate students for one month in Bhutan. In return, we are offering our network of over 250 colleges and university to serve as a portal for RUB into American higher education. We arranged a tour for RUB administrators to visit their counterparts at a range of public and private universities. In this form, reciprocity connects partners in loops that benefit American universities, study abroad providers, and community partners with clear intentionality and purpose.

EXPLORING THE ECOLOGY OF LEARNING: BUILDING A GLOBAL COMMUNITY OF EDUCATION

Thus far, we have described practices of the high road approach to study abroad which involve immersion in another culture in order to bridge perspectives through language learning, lived experiences, and participation in collaborative work—all based on principles of reciprocity and respect. We have tried to situate these practices within efforts to reinvigorate the U.S. academy with its historical vision of civic engagement and education of citizens for an informed and responsible democracy. In this section, we argue that these educational principles can serve as a foundation for international education as the "campus" of academe extends beyond the national and political borders of a country, requiring new conceptualizations of citizenship and community.

Dewey's early work on experiential education and democracy has been a seminal influence for educators seeking to demonstrate how knowledge gained through civic engagement and community action enhances the more traditional academic learning of the classroom (Dewey, 1899/1990, 1938). Within this education for democracy literature, Cremin (1976) proposed a model of open, community- or field-based learning referred to as the "ecology of learning." Longo (2007) recently reintroduced this concept of an ecology of education in his assessment of how community leaders, neighborhoods, and organizations focused on social change are essential for the revitalization of the public, democratic mission of the university.

Longo describes this ecology of education as the interconnected communities and dimensions of everyday life in which social learning and knowledge creation take place. He explores (2007) a set of case studies as examples of how knowledge and learning from outside the academy can be integral to the educational mission of higher education:

> Education in the community represents a particular way of connecting the many places in which people learn and act collectively; it signifies a way of educating that calls on democratic community building practices, and it utilizes nonprofessional expertise.... [It] can also help leverage the diverse ways citizens act for positive change in communities. In short education in the community can serve as a foundation not only for meaningful learning, but also for a vibrant democracy. (pp. 10–11)

The ecology of education can be used as a guiding concept to develop sound models for educational activities beyond the borders of our local communities and nation, through study abroad, internships, direct enrollment, or employment in another country. Study abroad, as a component of the undergraduate curriculum that takes place outside the formal classroom domain of a student's home campus shares much in common with other extracurricular learning activities such as service learning, civic life, public leadership, and community learning. It expands the borders and space of learning in higher education.

As we described earlier, while there is a call for the internationalization of higher education on most college campuses, the civic engagement literature is still almost entirely focused on the domestic U.S. communities of students or the university neighborhood. Study abroad is rarely associated with this literature on campus civic engagement. Connections with international learning are increasingly found in the offices of service learning and internships, yet these are too often viewed as marginal or secondary to the mission of the university and its faculty. Yet, the study abroad experiences of high-quality, culturally embedded programs are similar to the civic education experiences described by Longo. As described in the example of SIT Study

Abroad, students are open to learning from community practitioners, are able to connect lived experiences with more formal academic knowledge, and learn to build the human connections of trust and collaboration critical to innovative civic action.

Several models exist of how community-based ecologies of learning can provide the structure of educational programs both within the U.S. and in international communities. One of these, the Higher Education Consortium for Urban Affairs (HECUA), grew from an attempt by students and faculty of Augsburg College in 1968 to understand and address issues of U.S. urban unrest and inequality by creating a learning community, entitled the Crisis Colony, based in the inner-city neighborhoods of Minneapolis (HECUA, 2008). Students were taught by community leaders and activists, and lived in the neighborhoods to learn directly from the community, with the goal of working toward social change. This is the kind of U.S.-based community learning model described by Longo in which experiential learning leads to civic engagement. The HECUA Web site describes this as: "HECUA learning is transformational. Our teaching philosophy takes students and faculty into the community to learn from practitioners of social change. The result is informed and engaged student citizens" (HECUA, 2008).

HECUA has taken this model and transferred it to international settings in ways that demonstrate how an ecology of learning approach can be extended to international education and learning. Like SIT Study Abroad, the students learn from a diverse range of local communities and leaders. They have opportunities to volunteer or undertake internships that aim to instill a greater understanding of the challenges of global inequities and cultural change. These programs are also based on carefully chosen partnerships in which a commitment to respect the learning that takes place in a local community is an important part of the pedagogical model. HECUA programs formalize this process through the international inclusion of experiential learning outcomes in which reflection on local practice is a core element of the program. While each of the four semester-long programs offered during 2007 and 2008 varies slightly in structure, they share a similarity in which reflection on individual learning is placed in the context of how one learns to interact in an ethical manner within the local community. For example, as expressed in the curriculum of the HECUA Scandinavian Urban Studies Program, "…you are not simply encouraged to view issues from the neck up, but are encouraged to view yourself as an actor within society with values, decisions and choices which affect our communities, systems, processes and society" (HECUA, 2008).

The HECUA model helps us understand how a community-based ecology of learning can be created outside as easily as within a U.S.-based community. It is delivered in a way that places greater emphasis on the student learning and reflection from the experience. Other programs, many of which are short-term or informal faculty-led programs, emphasize a greater focus on actively contributing to community change through participant action. The student-based group Engineers Without Borders—USA (2008), for example, identifies communities which seek technical advice and support around sustainable engineering and appropriate technology needs, which student groups then organize around and support during short-term field visits overseen by faculty and local technical advisors.

Another example is an informal faculty-led effort by Professor Dan Baker (2007), of the Community Development and Applied Economics Program at the University of Vermont (UVM). Professor Baker's research in Honduras led him to identify rubber tire-burning techniques in sugar cane production as having a serious detrimental impact on the local community. He sought to share innovations in Vermont's own maple sugar burning techniques with the rural Honduran sugar-cane farmers over the course of personal visits, short-term research stints, and the inclusion of a few student internships (Wakefield, 2004). The connection of UVM students eager to learn from the Honduran farmers, and the Honduran farmers' own persistence in seeking ongoing support from Baker and his team, led to a powerful mutual educational learning laboratory with real-life outcomes for the local community in terms of environmental sustainability and improved livelihoods. This project was sustained over several years through the passion, enthusiasm, and commitment to shared goals that marks the best examples of education for civic engagement (Baker, 2007).

The organization Living Routes provides still another model of an ecology of learning through programs that instill values of sustainable development through inclusion of students in intentional communities referred to as "eco-villages." These communities range from the long-standing Findhorn community of northern Scotland, which has practiced a spiritually informed environmental activism since the early 20th century, to indigenous villages welcoming of international student groups, to the educational community of Ecoversidade in Brazil committed to the dissemination and promotion of sustainable living practices in association with local universities, research institutes, and local communities. The commitment of Living Routes to education for sustainability is through the recognition of the need for community itself as a precondition for social change.

> Ever more profound and rapid technological advances are outpacing our collective wisdom and maturity. In other words, we currently know more about computers than about compassion—or community. Of course we need to train scientists. But also, and perhaps more importantly, we need to train community builders—social scientists—with the knowledge, skills, and commitment to create sustainable models of living and working together in peaceful and productive ways. (Living Routes, 2008)

The most significant pedagogical contribution of the civic engagement literature is the notion that education cannot be limited to the formal institutions of schools in isolation from society. This is particularly so with democratic education, in which individuals learn to engage with diverse communities, to participate in discursive and deliberative democratic processes, and to assume the moral responsibility of making decisions for the common good and not just their own individual well-being. If international education and study abroad share one thing in common with the work in U.S. universities around civic engagement, it is this expansion of the learning community beyond the borders and classrooms of the host institution.

The principles connecting this ecology of learning to aspirations of democracy and civic engagement provide a pedagogical framework for study abroad. However, the engagement with communities, political systems, cultures, and notions of democracy beyond our borders calls for a critical rethinking of the notions of citizenship and, in particular, what we mean by the notion of responsible global citizens in the interconnected yet intensely local world of the 21st century. This also requires critical reflection on what we mean by global citizenship.

LINKING THE IDEALS OF GLOBAL CITIZENSHIP WITH EDUCATION FOR RESPONSIBLE CITIZEN DIPLOMACY

A returned SIT Study Abroad student recently published an essay in the Chronicle of Higher Education entitled "American Students Abroad Can't Be 'Global Citizens'" (Zemach-Bersin, 2008).

Zemach-Bersin describes her experience of living with a local exile Tibetan family in cramped quarters with limited food and resources, yet being treated as an honored guest. She realizes when offering them the cash envelope in exchange for their hospitality that this represents the privilege of Western visitors to consume commodified culture. And, she rightfully asks, if study abroad is promoted as education for global citizenship,

> ...such an education may inadvertently be a recipe for the perpetuation of global ignorance, misunderstanding, and prejudice.... [T]here is a vast discrepancy between the rhetoric of international education and the reality of what many students like myself experience while abroad. (Zemach-Bersin, 2008)

This student's critique is an important warning to those of us in study abroad who promote abstract ideals of global citizenship without either a clear understanding of what we mean by the term, or what the expectations of education for global citizenship imply. Examining the power dynamics underlying global citizenship, as Zemach-Bersin implores, compels us to consider how we can create mutually beneficial, reciprocal, and respectful relationships with local communities. We cannot begin to educate within a wider global ecology of education without such relationships because they are central to the ideals of democratic civic engagement.

We attempt to answer some of the questions posed by this critique: What do we mean by global citizenship? Is it limited to those who can study abroad? What about students who do not have the resources, time, or preparation to study abroad? What about members of the local community? How do we achieve goals of citizenship through the public work of building global learning communities?

Hans Schattle (2008) begins to answer some of these questions with his exploration of the practices of global citizenship as expressed by individuals and institutions who identify with this ideal. Schattle's examples include numerous case studies of individuals influenced directly by study abroad or citizen exchange experiences. As we look at how high road study abroad programming can address both the critiques and positive elements expressed in global citizenship, we can learn from his examples of educators and students reflecting on how international exchange sharpens one's own sense of identity and belonging through an awareness of global responsibilities.

Schattle approaches the subject of global citizenship as everyday lived practices articulated and espoused by a range of social, corporate, and institutional actors. He describes it as an emergent "way of living and thinking" with roots in classical ideals of cosmopolitanism that preceded national identities. His examples treat the concept of global citizenship almost as a verb, involving an ongoing commitment to and progression toward a vision of global citizenship. Along the way, the process includes resistance and reflective critique of the notion of global citizens as well. Through interviews, discourse analysis, and empirical observations of a range of practices, he identifies three primary characteristics of global citizenship as a practice: (1) awareness that is both self-awareness and external awareness; (2) responsibility expressed as "principled decision-making" and "solidarity across humanity"; and (3) participation in public affairs focused on accountability and social change (Schattle, 2008, pp. 25–46).

Study abroad, at its best, is our strongest vehicle for creating an enabling environment for students to develop these characteristics. Schattle quotes two women whose study abroad in Africa was influential, but they were reluctant to call themselves "global citizens"; if anything the powerful awareness of other cultures and values gained in Kenya and Senegal led them to emphasize "...how their respective African immersion experiences reinforced their American citizen identities" (Schattle, 2008, p.15). SIT Study Abroad, HECUA, and other like-minded providers often claim that study abroad can help students first and foremost understand themselves, the world around them, and their place in that world. As we hope for our students, these two women returned home to the United States to reengage in their communities in new ways, informed by a broader moral responsibility that would continue to influence their personal and professional lives throughout a range of communities in which they were active.

Several of Schattle's examples highlight the role of educational exchange experiences that provide clarity around an individual's own national or civic identity. In many cases, for students or professionals working abroad, living with a family or host community can frequently provide contrasting moments in intercultural encounters when one is made even more acutely aware of one's own identities and civic origins. These cannot be avoided or forgotten in cross-cultural interactions, especially when they represent relations of political or social power to the members of the other culture.

As students engage with communities abroad, notions of global citizenship provide powerful transformative opportunities to explore one's own identity, lifelong commitments and allegiances. Schattle's research confirms the views of many education abroad professionals—that as students from the United States leave the immediate communities of their home towns and college campuses, they build new allegiances that form part of their identity as global citizens. These observations are consistent with much of the current political theory of global citizenship which finds that through a host of global phenomena, such as transnational social movements, migration, Internet social networking, and ethnic identity formations, the very notion of citizenship is being redefined (Benhabib, Shapiro, & Petranović, 2007; Kabeer, 2005).

The literature on global citizenship speaks directly to this issue of whether citizenship is understood in terms of membership in a formal community. Traditionally, citizenship has been associated with full membership of and rights within a nation. Yet, even within this definition, political scientists have found fault with the effectiveness of such citizenship when practices of discrimination, marginalization, and cultural difference have acted to limit full access to citizenship (Kabeer, 2005). The research and literature in citizenship studies associated with globalization finds that as global networks of technology, corporate structures, social movements, and multilateral cooperative agreements increase, the role and reach of the nation-state is also changing. The impact of these changes, along with historical shifts in postcolonial identities, migration, and the role of communication technology in uniting Diaspora communities, is among many of the influences leading to emergent understandings of citizenship delinked from that of national identity. In some national territories, such as Canada, the view that individuals and communities can have multiple cultural and civic identities is gaining social and political acceptance (Kymlicka, 2007).

Where does this leave us? For the practices of study abroad, the learning of intercultural awareness and respect can and should lead to this reciprocity and commitment to action in reentry that form a foundation for the high road programming discussed in the previous sections. Much of the gain as global citizens may actually take place through the reentry process. At SIT Study Abroad, our students often return with a powerful affective identification with global citizenship as well as the resistance and discomfort with privilege associated with it in some instances. Together, this tension can be the basis for education in global civic responsibility and engagement as students grapple with belonging across multiple communities. The global ecology of learning extends the learning environment to include community partners, but this is not the same as the construction of a new formal community.

In a sense, students come to see citizenship as the emergent meanings of participation in and belonging across communities. They are able to identify with the possibility of multiple and overlapping citizenships (Carens, 2000; Kymlicka, 1995; Taylor, 1992). Williams (2007) describes these as the "citizenships of globalization," a term that provides a way to examine citizenship through differing theorizations of its transnational, cosmopolitan, flexible, Diasporic or postnational meanings. Benhabib et al. (2007) assess this work with questions relevant to international education and the quest for the meaning of global citizenship. They seek to understand: "…why people identify and affiliate themselves with the political projects that they do, how and why they do, and why these allegiances change, and how and why they should change" (Benhabib et al., 2007, p. 1).

The student organization ENGAGE exemplifies this search on the part of returned study abroad students to maintain connections, multiple allegiances, and reciprocal work across communities from a base on their home campuses or in their hometowns. Formed in collaboration with teacher-activists still living at their international program sites, former students convert their initial learning experiences into formal transnational change efforts, such as the Fair Trade Rice or Democracy in Burma initiatives. As expressed on their Web site, this organization models the kind of citizen action linking home communities to the communities abroad that are their global ecologies of learning:

> A growing number of US-based study abroad programs are offering students the opportunity to learn about issues of social justice, human rights, and environmental sustainability in a global context. Further, these programs are directly exposing their students to communities and social movements who are working to create another world. ENGAGE emerged from the energy of these study abroad students when they returned home, as they struggled to answer challenging questions: As students, how do we work in our home communities towards social justice and sustainability? How do we remain connected to, and work alongside, the communities and social movements that inspired us while abroad? How do we turn our education into action? (ENGAGE, 2008).

It is these allegiances and affiliations that are at the heart of new understandings of citizenship and identity. At the same time, while shaped and informed by global phenomena, these allegiances have powerful connections to place—to locally grounded communities and locales— that respect both difference and mutual obligations (Maier, 2007; Sassen, 2006; Stoddard & Cornwell, 2003). This theoretical work informs and supports Schattle's empirical accounts of the discursive practices and concepts articulated by individuals and institutions in the language of global citizenship.

We believe this approach to global citizenship, based in an awareness of one's own community or site of affiliation, is critical for any pedagogical approach to global citizenship. We have started to think about this preparation of students for citizenship as citizen diplomacy. Students in this approach learn to value intercultural experiences, dialogue, and understanding of the other, then they are inspired by their interactions and educational experiences to share and communicate this knowledge of other cultures and human issues to those in their home community. Through educational leadership in the "reentry" phase, this knowledge can lead to new forms of civic engagement around global issues. It is this engagement that is often referred to as "global citizenship." It is not a membership claim or "belonging" to a nonterritorial polity, but a statement of committed action.

We find that the discussion around education for global citizenship leads to the idea of education for responsible citizen diplomacy as we explore this meaning of citizen action across and with multiple communities. As with citizenship, within international relations or foreign policy analysis, citizen diplomacy traditionally associates as the citizen identity with the nation. Citizen or public diplomacy, in this orientation, is frequently couched as part of a formal "soft" form of foreign policy, such as the promotion of Track II citizen diplomacy to Cuba or North Korea (Davies & Kaufman, 2003; Nan & Strimling, 2004). The rethinking of global citizenship allows us to rethink the notion of citizen diplomats in a similar manner. As individuals expand their allegiances to wider, multiple, and overlapping transnational communities, while retaining and "owning" the responsibility of their own primary citizenship identity, they may also be considered to enact roles of "citizen diplomats" as they cross borders, attempt to understand the viewpoints of other communities, and return to their own home community to represent these differences as they engage in new pursuits with a widened worldview.

Many of the proponents of global or transnational activism reflect this view and Web sites such as idealist.org (2008) promote and support active involvement of citizens in resolving crucial human dilemmas. Schattle (2008) also documents the commitment of global activists to working toward common solutions, based on mutual understanding and commitment to peaceful resolution of problems that can be realized by the notion of citizen diplomacy. In an address at Georgetown University, Mary Robinson, former president of Ireland and former UN High Commissioner for Human Rights spoke to the power of an alternative conception of citizen diplomacy (Robinson, 2008a). At the highest level of former leaders-turned-citizens, she participates in such groups as the Club of Madrid and The Elders to engage in citizen peace-building interventions.

Fulbright and Eisenhower saw the potential of citizen diplomacy through education, which they expressed through their belief in people-to-people exchanges. Stated differently, within this potential is a belief that magical things happen when people come together across national boundaries to do things together that are of common interest. People learn that their similarities far outweigh their differences, and that their differences are exciting and fun, not scary. In the course of doing things together, people come to understand each other. They create friendships. They change and they get things done. In the process, the world becomes a better place. There is a belief in the concept that individuals have the right to help shape foreign relations. Echoing the words of Boyte, who we quoted earlier in this paper, the Coalition for Citizen Diplomacy (2008) defines it as the work people do to connect across national differences. It can be paid or voluntary, but it is directed at building the kinds of understandings, relationships, and actions needed to build a more peaceful and prosperous world.

Through Robinson's own organization, Realizing Rights, she emphasizes the value of the UN Declaration of Human Rights, drafted in 1948 and still far from realization, and the need for a wide and diverse range of advocates in a global civil society. This advocacy, while engaged in global efforts, needs to also be built on the responsibility of citizens to act on their global knowledge in their own communities and nations. She quotes from Eleanor Roosevelt, an important supporter of the Declaration: "Without concerted citizen action to uphold human rights close to home, we shall look in vain for progress in the larger world" (Roosevelt cited by Robinson, 2008b).

One action that reflects this dual commitment to global human rights and responsibility for local community action is the initiative to develop a Global Health Worker Migration protocol, aimed at aggressive recruitment by advanced industrial societies of health care workers away from their communities in developing countries. Health care needs in high income countries are resulting in practices that recruit health care workers from lower income countries that already have dire shortages of heath care services and personnel. An awareness of the global needs and supply of health care around the world, and the power of wages and benefits to worsen existing inequities in health care provision, is a place to start in this kind of global citizen action and diplomacy (Realizing Rights, 2007).

This is precisely the kind of global civic action high road study abroad programs aim to inspire. Students come back with the commitments and capacities to engage in public work across national and cultural differences in order to create a better world. They do so with an awareness and responsibility based on their own civic identity, while understanding the need to develop mutual understanding and reciprocal exchange and solidarity with other communities.

CONCLUSION

Global citizenship entails developing the awareness and knowledge to be a globally aware and responsible citizen within overlapping and interconnected communities. To do this involves learning to assume responsibility for one's own citizen commitments while appreciating and developing the ability to respectfully represent differences of other nations, communities and worldviews. We do not want to reproduce a world of privilege in which a passport and a study abroad semester on a CV are a sufficient claim to global citizenship. We want to build quality study abroad programs around the principles outlined in our high road approach—accessibility, understanding of less traditional societies, preparation for reentry to one's country with a renewed commitment to globally informed civic engagement, and an appreciation of the importance of reciprocity and respect for the host communities that are partners in the educational process.

In reconceptualizing principles of education for global citizenship within U.S. higher education, it is important to provide a theoretical framework that is fluid and inclusive enough to allow for intercultural collaboration with a range of communities, institutional partners, and organizations that make up the global ecology of learning for education abroad. As we examine ways in which the principles of quality study abroad meet the core mission and purpose of higher education as it emerges in the 21st century, we seek to ensure that they address existing commitments to civic engagement, moral judgment, and the open pursuit of knowledge needed to perceive and resolve real problems faced by society. Principled and high quality study abroad developed with an intentionality to educate global citizen diplomats will advance the highest ideals of knowledge that serve humanity and an engaged, globally informed democracy.

REFERENCES

American Council on Education. (2008). *College-bound students' interests in study abroad and other international learning activities*. Washington, DC: Author.

Baker, D. (2007, November 30). *Integrating community engagement into study abroad: ensuring academic rigor*. Presentation at the Fostering Global Citizenship in Higher Education Conference, Brattleboro, VT.

Benhabib, S., Shapiro, I., & Petranović, D. (Eds.). (2007). Editors' introduction. In S. Benhabib, I. Shapiro, & D. Petranović (Eds.), *Identities, affiliations, and allegiances* (pp. 1–15). Cambridge, UK: Cambridge University Press.

Boyte, H. (2004). *Everyday politics: Reconnecting citizens and public life*. Philadelphia: University of Pennsylvania Press.

Boyte, H. (2008). Against the current: Developing the civic agency of students. *Change: The Magazine of Higher Learning, 40*(3), 8–15.

Boyte, H. C., & Kari, N. N. (2000). Renewing the democratic spirit in American colleges and universities: Higher education as public work. In T. Erlich (Ed.), *Civic responsibility and higher education* (pp. 37–60) (American Council on Education, Series on Higher Education). Westport, CT: Oryx Press.

Carens, J. H. (2000). *Culture, citizenship, and community.* Oxford, UK: Oxford University Press.

Coalition for Citizen Diplomats. (2008). Retrieved March 21, 2008, from http://www.citizen-diplomacy.org/

Colby, A., Erlich, A., Beaumont, E., & Stephens, J. (2003). *Educating citizens: Preparing America's undergraduates for lives of moral and civic responsibility.* San Francisco: Jossey-Bass.

Collier, P. (2007). *The bottom billion: Why the poorest countries are failing and what can be done about it.* New York: Oxford University Press.

Cremin, L. (1976). *Public education.* New York: Basic Books.

Davies, J., & Kaufman, E. (2003). *Second track/citizens' diplomacy: Concepts and techniques for conflict transformation.* Lanham, MD: Rowman & Littlefield.

Dewey, J. (1938). *Experience and education.* New York: Touchstone.

Dewey, J. (1990). *The school and society.* Chicago: University of Chicago Press. (Original work published 1899)

ENGAGE. (2008). About Engage. Retrieved March 21, 2008, from http://www.engagetheworld.org/aboutENGAGE.html

Engle, L., & Engle, J. (2004). Assessing language acquisition and intercultural sensitivity development in relation to study abroad program design. *Frontiers: The Interdisciplinary Journal of Study Abroad, 10,* 219–236.

Engineers Without Borders–USA. (2008). Retrieved March 21, 2008, from http://www.ewb-usa.org/

Ehrlich, T. (Ed.). (2000). *Civic responsibility and higher education* (American Council on Education, Series on Higher Education). Westport, CT: Oryx Press.

Friedman, T. (2005). *The world is flat: A brief history of the twenty-first century.* New York: Farrar, Straus & Giroux.

Gibson, C. (2001). *From inspiration to participation: A review of perspectives on youth civic engagement.* The Grantmaker Forum on Community and National Service. Retrieved January 22, 2009, from http://www.pace-funders.org/publications/pubs/Moving%20Youth%20report%20REV3.pdf

Harrison, B. (1997). *Lean and mean: Why large corporations will continue to dominate the global economy.* New York: Guilford Press.

Harrison, B. (2004). *Lean and mean: The changing landscape of corporate power in the age of flexibility.* New York: Basic Books.

HECUA. (2008). Scandinavian urban studies term August 2007. Retrieved January 22, 2009, from http://www.hecua.org/pdfs/SUSTSyllabus2007a.pdf p.3

Idealist.org (2008). About us. Retrieved March 21, 2008, from http://www.idealist.org/en/about/mission.html

Kabeer, N. (Ed.). (2005). *Inclusive citizenship: Meanings and expressions.* London: Zed Books.

Kymlicka, W. (1995). *Multicultural citizenship: A liberal theory of minority rights.* Oxford, UK: Oxford University Press.

Kymlicka. W. (2007). Ethnocultural diversity in a liberal state: making sense of the Canadian model(s). In K. Banting, T. Courchene, & L. Seidle (Eds.), *Belonging? Diversity, recognition and shared citizenship in Canada* (pp. 39–86). Montreal: Institute for Research on Public Policy.

Living Routes. (2008). Retrieved March 13, 2008, from http://www.livingroutes.org/programs/education.htm

Longo, N. V. (2007). *Why community matters: Connecting education with civic life.* Albany, NY: SUNY Press.

Maier. C. S. (2007). "Being there": Place, territory, and identity. In S. Benhabib, I. Shapiro, & D. Petranović (Eds.), *Identities, affiliations, and allegiances* (pp. 67–84). New York: Cambridge University Press.

Mathews, D. (2008). Democracy's mega-challenges revisited. In D. Brown & D. Witte (Eds.), *Agent of democracy: Higher education and the HEX journey* (pp. 207–223). Dayton, Ohio: Kettering Foundation Press.

Nan, S. A., & Strimling, A. (2004, January). Track I–track II cooperation. In G. Burgess & H. Burgess (Eds.), *Beyond intractability.* Conflict Research Consortium, University of Colorado, Boulder. Retrieved January 22, from http://www.beyondintractability.org/essay/track_1_2_cooperation/

Realizing Rights. (2007). New initiative seeks practical solutions to tackle health worker migration. Retrieved May 15, 2007, from http://www.realizingrights.org/?option=content&task=view&id=255

Robinson, M. (2008a, March 14). *Citizen diplomacy in a fast-moving world.* World Learning and Georgetown University Mortara Center Citizen Diplomacy Discussion Series Georgetown University, Washington, DC.

Robinson, M. (2008b, January). Realizing rights: Action update. Retrieved January 22, 2009, from http://www.realizingrights.org/index.php?option=com_content&task=view&id=302&Itemid=1

Sassen, S. (2006). *Territory, authority, rights: From medieval to global assemblages.* Princeton, NJ: Princeton University Press.

Schattle, H. (2008). *The practices of global citizenship.* Lanham, MD: Rowman & Littlefield.

Segalowitz, N., Freed, B., Collentine, J., Lafford, B., Lazar, N., and Díaz-Campos., M. (2004, Fall). A comparison of Spanish second language acquisition in two different learning contexts: Study abroad and the domestic classroom. *Frontiers: The Interdisciplinary Journal of Study Abroad, 10,* 1–18.

Snyder, R. C. (2008). Should higher education have a civic mission? Historical reflections. In D. Brown & D. Witte (Eds.), *Agent of democracy: Higher education and the HEX journey* (pp. 53–79). Dayton, Ohio: Kettering Foundation Press.

Spiezio, K. E. (2002, Fall). Pedagogy and political (dis)engagement. *Liberal Education, 88*(4), 14–19. Retrieved January 22, 2009, from ProQuest Central database. (Document ID: 274350261).

Stoddard, E. W., & Cornwell, G. H. (2003). Peripheral visions: Towards a geo-ethics of citizenship. *Liberal Education, 89*(3), 44–51.

Sullivan, W. (2000). Institutional identity and social responsibility in higher education. In T. Ehrlich (Ed.), *Civic responsibility and higher education* (pp. 19–36). Phoenix, AZ: Oryx Press.

Swinney, D. (1998). *Building the bridge to the high road*. Chicago: Midwest Center for Labor Research.

Taylor, C. (1992). *Multiculturalism and the politics of recognition: An essay* (A. Gutman, Ed.). Princeton, NJ: Princeton University Press.

Wakefield, J. (2004, July 21). Sugar technology goes south. *The View*. University of Vermont. Retrieved January 22, 2009, from http://www.uvm.edu/theview/article.php?id=1296.

Weinberg, A. (2005). Residential education for democracy. *Learning for Democracy, 1*, 29–46.

Williams, M. S. (2007). Nonterritorial boundaries of citizenship. In S. Benhabib, I. Shapiro, & D. Petranović (Eds.), *Identities, affiliations, and allegiances* (pp. 226–256). Cambridge, UK: Cambridge University Press.

World Bank. (2008). World Bank updates poverty estimates for the developing world. Retrieved August 6, 2008, from http://go.worldbank.org/14HEAYYGO0.

Zemach-Bersin, T. (2008, March 7). American students abroad can't be "global citizens." *Chronicle of Higher Education, 54*(26). Retrieved January 22, 2009, from ProQuest Central database. (Document ID: 1483699511).

Chapter 4

International Studies and Foreign Languages

A Critical American Priority

Charles Kolb

Committee for Economic Development

The United States entered the 21st century as the undisputed global superpower. It stands as the dominant economic, military, and cultural nation in the world—often, but not always according to some—for the good. No other nation has even approached this degree of power and responsibility.

Moreover, in our increasingly globalized world, there remains the ironic possibility that many of our citizens may react to these circumstances by looking further inward rather than outward: with English becoming the de facto lingua franca, why should Americans take the time to learn a foreign language or study another country's culture? After all, those "foreigners" can do everything *our* way and in *our* language! While perhaps understandable, this attitude is by no means acceptable any more. This chapter will explain why.

In the early years of the 21st century, technological, economic, political, and social forces have created a new era. Technological advancements and lower trade barriers have paved the way for the globalization of world markets, bringing intense competition to the U.S. economy. Political systems and movements around the world are having a profound impact on our national security, as well as on our human security. The increasing diversity of our workplaces, schools, and communities is changing the face of our society. To confront the 21st century challenges to our economy and national security, our education system must be strengthened to increase the foreign language skills and cultural awareness of our students. America's continued global leadership will depend on our students' abilities to interact with the world community both inside and outside our borders.

As one of the world's most open economies, the United States already faces intense global competition, and the emergence of new competitors. Globalization has enabled companies in less-developed countries to compete directly and on a more level playing field with American businesses. Therefore, if U.S. companies of all sizes are to succeed in overseas markets, they require employees with knowledge of foreign languages and cultures, as well as overseas experience.

In the post-Cold War era, nonstate actors who tend to speak languages that are less commonly taught in the United States (e.g., Arabic, Chinese, Hindi, Japanese, Korean, Persian/Farsi, Russian, and Turkish) are challenging U.S. national security. The FBI and other federal government agencies lack sufficient linguists to translate intelligence information in these critical languages in a timely manner. Furthermore, our diplomatic and intelligence efforts often have been hampered by a stunning lack of cultural awareness. It is increasingly important that Americans become better versed in the languages and cultures of other world regions, particularly the Middle East and Asia, so that we can present our nation more clearly to the world.

Today's America is, and will continue to be, characterized by ethnic and linguistic diversity. In many urban, suburban, and even rural school systems, student populations are becoming more diverse. Workplaces and customers also increasingly reflect our multicultural nation, and cultural knowledge has become critical to American businesses. We must educate all of our students about the world or suffer diminished communications among our citizens and a weaker civic culture.

Because most schools have not responded adequately to the challenges of the 21st century, many American students lack sufficient knowledge of other world regions, languages, and cultures. Only about one third of 7th to 12th grade students—and just 5% of elementary school students—study a foreign language. Few students study the less-commonly taught "critical languages" that are vital to national security. State high school graduation requirements often include only minimal course work in international studies. At the postsecondary level, less than 10% of college students enroll in a foreign language and only 1% of undergraduates study abroad (Committee for Economic Development [CED], 2006). These striking characteristics occur at a remarkably important time in American history—a time when many observers recognize our national strengths but are concerned about whether they can be maintained.

"The Future of American Power: How America Can Survive the Rise of the Rest" is excerpted in *Foreign Affairs* from Zakaria's (2008) new book, *The Post-American World*. Zakaria is, on the whole, positive about America's future, but he does caution that complacency can cost us productivity and jeopardize our current economic edge:

> Being on top for so long has its downsides. The U.S. market has been so large that Americans have assumed that the rest of the world would take the trouble to understand it and them. They have not had to reciprocate by learning foreign languages, cultures, or markets. Now, that could leave the United States at a competitive disadvantage. Take the spread of English worldwide as a metaphor. Americans have delighted in this process because it makes it so much easier for them to travel and do business abroad. But it also gives the locals an understanding of and access to two markets and cultures. They can speak English but also Mandarin or Hindu or Portuguese. They can penetrate the U.S. market but also the internal Chinese, Indian, or Brazilian one. Americans, by contrast, have never developed the ability to move into other people's worlds. (p. 7)

With economics and markets more open than ever before, Americans can no longer afford an isolationist posture. General Motors Chairman and CEO Rick Waggoner explains that when he was stationed in Brazil, he took the time to learn Portuguese—not because he needed to, but because he believed that doing so gave him and GM a competitive edge. No doubt Mr. Waggoner could have insisted on conducting all of GM's business in English, but doing so would have positioned both him and GM altogether differently relative to the culture and the company's competition.

The issue of foreign language acquisition, however, goes far beyond issues of education and the relative strength of the economy. On January 5, 2006, President George W. Bush addressed several hundred American college and university presidents at a summit on international education hosted at the U.S. Department of State in Washington, DC. The President's message was straightforward: learning a foreign language and learning more about foreign countries and cultures is not solely an education matter; its importance now extends to questions of America's economic security, our national security, and the effectiveness of our public diplomacy.

In the wake of the September 11, 2001, terrorist attacks, our law enforcement, homeland security, and counterterrorism efforts have been hampered by critical shortages in translators skilled in certain critical foreign languages. Electronic surveillance intelligence gathered by the National Security Agency and the Federal Bureau of Investigation has too frequently been left untranslated because of this severe shortage in qualified translators.

In his message to the educators at the State Department, President Bush (2006) outlined a series of initiatives that his administration would propose to address the critical language shortages. Among the president's proposals, which together comprised the "National Security Language Initiative," were the following:

Expand the number of Americans mastering critical need languages and start at a younger age by:

- Providing $24 million to create incentives to teach and study critical need languages in K-12 by refocusing the Department of Education's Foreign Language Assistance Program (FLAP) grants.
- Building continuous programs of study of critical need languages from kindergarten to university through a new $27 million program, which will start in 27 schools in the next year through DOD's National Security Education Program (NSEP) and the Department of Education, and will likely expand to additional schools in future years.
- Providing State Department scholarships for summer, academic year/semester study abroad, and short-term opportunities for high school students studying critical need languages to up to 3,000 high school students by summer 2009.
- Expanding the State Department Fulbright Foreign Language Teaching Assistant Program, to allow 300 native speakers of critical need languages to come to the U.S. to teach in U.S. universities and schools in 2006–07.
- Establishing a new component in State's Teacher Exchange Programs to annually assist 100 U.S. teachers of critical need languages to study abroad.
- Establishing DNI language study "feeder" programs, grants, and initiatives with K-16 educational institutions to provide summer student and teacher immersion experiences, academic courses and curricula, and other resources for foreign language education in less commonly taught languages targeting 400 students and 400 teachers in five states in 2007 and up to 3,000 students and 3,000 teachers by 2011 in additional states.

Increase the number of advanced-level speakers of foreign languages, with an emphasis on critical needs languages:

- Expand the National Flagship Language Initiative to a $13.2 million program aiming to produce 2,000 advanced speakers of Arabic, Chinese, Russian, Hindi, and Central Asian languages by 2009.
- Increase to up to 200 by 2008 the annual Gilman scholarships for financially needy undergraduates to study critical need languages abroad.

51

- Create new State Department summer immersion study programs for up to 275 university level students per year in critical need languages.
- Add overseas language study to 150 U.S. Fulbright student scholarships annually.
- Increase support for immersion language study centers abroad.

Increase the number of foreign language teachers and the resources for them:

- Establish a National Language Service Corps for Americans with proficiencies in critical languages to serve the nation by:
  - ☐ Working for the federal government; or
  - ☐ Serving in a Civilian Linguist Reserve Corps (CLRC); or
  - ☐ Joining a newly created Language Teacher Corps to teach languages in our nation's elementary, middle, and high schools. This program will direct $14 million in FY07 with the goal of having 1,000 volunteers in the CLRC and 1,000 teachers in our schools before the end of the decade.
- Establish a new $1 million nation-wide distance-education e-Learning Clearinghouse through the Department of Education to deliver foreign language education resources to teachers and students across the country.
- Expand teacher-to-teacher seminars and training through a $3 million Department of Education effort to reach thousands of foreign language teachers in 2007.

President Bush stressed the importance of having "a language-proficient military—to have people that go into the far reaches of this world and be able to communicate in the villages and towns and rural areas and urban centers, to protect the American people." Likewise, President Bush pointed to the need for intelligence officers who

> when somebody says something in Arabic or Farsi or Urdu knows that they're talking about. That's what we need. We need diplomats—when we send them out to help us convince governments that we've got to join together and fight these terrorists who want to destroy life and promote an ideology that is so backwards it's hard to believe. These diplomats need to speak that language.

And, then, President Bush made a very important point which relates directly to the "soft power" aspects of foreign languages and international studies:

> When somebody comes to me and speaks Texan, I know they appreciate the Texas culture. I mean,…somebody takes time to figure out how to speak Arabic, it means they're interested in somebody else's culture. Learning a language—somebody else's language is a kind gesture. It's a gesture of interest. It really is a fundamental way to reach out to somebody and say, I care about you. I want you to know that I'm interested in not only how you talk but how you live. In order for this country to be able to convince others, people have got to be able to see our true worth in our heart. And when Americans learn to speak a language, learn to speak Arabic, those in the Arabic region will say, gosh, America is interested in us. They care enough to learn how we speak.

The President's announcement was criticized by some as not providing resources commensurate with the scope of the problem. While there is little question that more federal dollars could be used in this area, the President's decision to highlight the need, request the funding, and direct federal departments and agencies nonetheless represented an important development—a critical step in establishing the issue as one of critical national priority. His efforts should not, therefore, be trivialized or discounted but, rather, embraced as a very important first step by an American president intent on changing a culture of "inwardness."

A few weeks after the President announced his initiative, the Committee for Economic Development released a new report entitled, "Education for Global Leadership: The Importance of International Studies and Foreign Language Education for U.S. Economic and National Security." Under development for more than a year, the CED report was the work of a subcommittee of several CED Trustees cochaired by John Brademas (an 11-term former Indiana Congressman, former House Majority Whip, and former president of New York University), Alfred Mockett (Chairman and CEO of Corinthian Capital LLC, and the former CEO of American Management Systems), and Charles Kolb (CED's President).[1] What is the significance of CED and its new report on international studies and foreign languages?

Founded in 1942, CED is an independent, nonpartisan group of senior business leaders and university presidents. As a research and public policy organization, CED's mission is "to propose policies that bring about steady economic growth at high employment and reasonably stable prices, increased productivity and living standards, greater and more equal opportunity for every citizen, and an improved quality of life for all." Shortly after its founding, the Committee for Economic Development's business leaders focused on restructuring the post-World War II economy by moving from wartime production to peacetime activity without experiencing a recession. Through the leadership of CED's first Chairman, Studebaker CEO Paul Hoffman, CED also helped develop the outline or design plan for what ultimately became the Marshall Plan for the rebuilding of Western Europe (Committee for Economic Development, 1948).

Throughout much of its history, CED has been concerned about the quality of American education—particularly K-12 education, and especially from a new work-prepared perspective. CED was one of the first business groups to become engaged seriously in education policy reform through a series of studies and recommendations in the wake of the 1983 publication of *A Nation at Risk*. In recent years, CED has issued education policy statements on the importance of investing in universal pre-K programs, the appropriate ways to approach K-12 measurement and testing (an important study that appeared just on the eve of the 2002 passage of the No Child Left Behind Act), and issues relating to school finances. At the same time, other CED subcommittees had been studying topics relating to globalization, trade, and poverty. These two important strands of CED's longstanding policy interests came together in the "Education for Global Leadership" study.

The CED report opens by noting that the 21st century is experiencing a new era that is the result of the convergence of technological, economic, political, and social forces. Through a combination of technological advancements and reduced trade barriers, markets—in commodities, capital, information, even human capital—have become globalized in ways that now mean much more intense competition for American workers and companies. Internally, as immigration from countries around the globe continues to be a positive development for the United States, our young people will face challenges in adapting to increasingly diverse communities inside our borders. As CED's report says, "America's continued global leadership will depend on our students' abilities to interact with the world community both inside and outside our borders" (p. 1).

The release of CED's report came at an unusual time, especially in terms of the national education debate. The passage of the federal No Child Left Behind Act (NCLB) sparked discussions across the country on questions of accountability and testing: What were our children learning, and how did we, in fact, know if they were learning, and at what level of proficiency? The law focused on math and reading assessments during the K-12 curriculum years. Given the unusually strapped financial circumstances of most state and local school system budgets, the media soon began writing stories about how some school boards had to reduce the funding for what were considered "nonessential" activities such as the arts, athletics, and foreign languages. The rationale for these reductions was that scarce resources had to be focused on core curricula priorities under the NCLB Act such as reading and math; everything else was deemed irrelevant.

Given this context and the nature of the debate (plus the related budgetary implications), CED's recommendations make clear from the outset that NCLB's provisions and international studies did not have to be a zero-sum game: international content could, and should be taught across the curriculum and at all levels of learning in a fashion that could expand American students' knowledge of other countries and cultures. The CED report offered the following recommendations:

- International content should be integrated into each state's K-12 curriculum standards and assessment criteria.
- States should require every high school graduate to demonstrate global literacy. High school graduates should achieve proficiency in at least one foreign language, and demonstrate knowledge of the geography and cultures of major regions of the world as well as an understanding of global issues.
- Congress should enact an "Education for Global Leadership Act" that provides funds to modernize and globalize the curricula of elementary and secondary schools to help states and school districts design and create curricula with innovative approaches to teaching international content.
- Teachers should receive professional development training to ensure that they are prepared to teach an international curriculum.
- Colleges and universities should form partnerships with elementary and secondary schools in order to make available their expertise in international studies.
- Colleges and universities should internationalize their campuses by expanding study abroad opportunities for students and faculty and building institutional commitment to international education.
- Teacher education programs in colleges and universities should include a strong international component.
- Corporations should play a more active role to support education in cross-cultural competencies.

The Committee for Economic Development also called for expanding the training pipeline at every level of education to address the paucity of Americans fluent in foreign languages, especially the critical, less-commonly taught languages:

- Federal language initiatives should encourage states and local school districts to implement language programs in the elementary grades and offer more advanced language classes in middle schools and high schools.
- Expanding foreign language instruction in elementary and secondary schools, particularly in critical languages, will require increased professional development for teachers and employing the resources of our heritage language communities.

- To encourage enrollment in higher education programs that lead to careers as language professionals, the federal government should support advanced critical language learning centers and consider incentives, such as loan forgiveness and scholarships.
- To develop a reservoir of critical language practitioners quickly, the federal government should streamline recruitment and training of critical-language and heritage-language speakers.
- University professional programs, such as schools of business administration, engineering, and medicine, should consider incentives to encourage students to pursue high-level foreign language study.

National leaders—political leaders, as well as the business and philanthropic communities, and the media—should also educate the public about the importance of improving education in foreign languages and international studies:

- The President should host a White House Conference on Education for Global Leadership. The Conference would bring together business, education, and national security leaders to assess how our entire education system—kindergarten through postsecondary—can maintain America's economic and national security.
- Governors should take advantage of opportunities to educate their citizens about the link between international commerce and jobs in their states.
- Each governor should convene a high-level review of his or her state's K-12 curriculum and standards by business and education leaders to determine whether they reflect global content.
- Business leaders should champion the issues of international studies and foreign language education by articulating why Americans need to learn more about the world.
- Private philanthropic foundations should intensify their efforts to support an international perspective in the curricula of our elementary and secondary schools.
- The media should increase coverage of global issues and highlight educational programs that are preparing students to become global citizens.

As noted earlier, the CED report unites two strands of CED's ongoing work: its interest in education and its interest in international/globalization issues. But there is also a third strand which has been present in other aspects of CED's policy work over many years that also helps explain the focus of this business-led public policy organization on this important investment. For a whole host of reasons—and in a variety of contexts—we have immense difficulty as a nation, and as individuals, in making appropriate investment decisions that will affect our future productivity, economic growth, and economic security.

Much of CED's recent work has been focused on addressing America's fundamental difficulty in recent decades when it comes to making investment decisions that affect the country's future.[2] For example, it has become abundantly apparent in the last decade that the United States now faces a "triple deficits" problem: we have a massive and growing federal budget deficit, an unsustainable foreign trade imbalance or "current account" deficit, and years when Americans, as individuals, spent more than they earned. These three deficits are interrelated and unsustainable in the medium or long term.

When compared with other developed nations who are members of the Paris-based Organization for Economic Cooperation and Development, the United States clearly underinvests in early childhood education. Countries such as France and the United Kingdom devote far greater resources to ensuring that their youngest children receive the educational, health, and nutritional requirements that will enable them to arrive at school ready to learn.

We also underinvest in our national public infrastructure: our roads, bridges, tunnels, and rail lines are falling apart; our air traffic control system is seriously out-of-date and is limiting future growth and system capacity, not to mention fostering continued airport congestion which means risks to passengers, unacceptable delays, and therefore, lost productivity.

Conversely, we overinvest when it comes to caloric consumption and now face a staggering obesity epidemic throughout the country, which includes young children as well as older adults. For a variety of reasons, it is abundantly apparent that as a nation, we have enormous difficulty in handling investment-type decisions.

In this context, the issue of international studies and foreign language instruction plays a potential role that has significance well beyond the field of education: it illustrates precisely the importance of changing the "habits of mind" of our young people so that they have a better under-standing of and appreciation for the concept of investment. Most of our young people understand that if they want to excel when it comes to athletics, then they need to practice. Many young peo-ple also appreciate this point when it comes to music: learning to play the piano, violin, guitar, or clarinet requires practice, and practice is nothing more than an investment of time directed toward achieving a particular goal: proficiency or expertise. At times, practice even helps identify those individuals who are also truly gifted.

Our current national fixation on short-term approaches to almost everything is seriously undermining our future prosperity. The longest-serving CED Trustee, former Commerce Secre-tary and Blackstone Group cofounder Peter G. Peterson, has repeatedly warned that our inability to curb our deficit-spending ways and restructure our unsustainable entitlement programs (e.g., Medicare, Medicaid, and Social Security) threatens our future and that of our grandchildren. And that is precisely why a greater emphasis on foreign language instruction is so critical: it helps reinforce among our young people a change of focus, away from the current short-term approach to a longer-term approach to their education and their future.

The reason should be obvious: one cannot learn a foreign language overnight. Students can-not take a pill today and wake up tomorrow fluent in Farsi, French, Mandarin, or Arabic. They have to invest years of time to master the rules of grammar and the nuances of pronunciation. Moreover, our school systems and our colleges and universities have to invest resources in train-ing qualified instructors—or be willing to spend the resources to import them from abroad if necessary.

There are other benefits as well to studying foreign countries and foreign languages: one is the greater likelihood that our young people will become lifelong learners. When a young per-son develops an interest in another country, there are related interests that may well follow: in culture, the arts, history, food, geography, and literature. In many cases, these interests have profound educational and career consequences for the individuals who decide to pursue the instruction in order to achieve a measure of proficiency.

It is unrealistic to expect overnight success in this important educational area. After all, with most investments, the payoff lies in the future, and that is precisely why the voice of a busi-ness group such as the Committee for Economic Development is so important when it comes to providing support for international studies and foreign language instruction. Business leaders typically understand the importance of making sound investments that will pay future dividends for their companies and their shareholders. As a nation, we are unlikely to see a sudden, massive increase in the number of schools offering foreign language instruction. For example, we will not see Mandarin being taught in every school in the nation. At the same time, it is vitally important that, as a nation, we begin to make significant marginal progress wherever possible: changing "habits of mind" are never easy, never immediate, and always require patience and persistence to achieve success. Sustained support from the American business community is vital because it can reinforce nationally, within states, and at the school-board level the importance of making the investments now to turn around our current foreign-language deficit.

To this end, CED has also conducted an important effort within the American business community to launch a nationwide endorsement campaign to identify business leaders who are willing to become active in promoting international studies and foreign language instruction. Many of these business leaders will be willing to speak out in their communities, and nationally, to support making these studies an important national priority.

Part of CED's work has also included highlighting companies that are making a difference in this area. For example, in its policy statement, CED noted the program at Boeing Aircraft Corporation which is focused on transforming Boeing into a multinational corporation marketing its products throughout the world. To accomplish this goal, Boeing created several international training options for its employees and executives. The company created a Global Leadership Program through which executives spend a month abroad to enhance their business problem-solving skills while being immersed in that country's culture, business, and politics. For those employees interested in advancing their professional development and international skills, Boeing offers a course on globalization. Additionally, Boeing highlights the importance of international knowledge by linking it directly to future promotion within the company.

Companies such as Boeing are undertaking more internationally focused efforts in large part because they know that it is important for their future business prospects and, as the CED report noted, they are not finding college graduates with sufficient foreign language skills and exposure to international knowledge. U.S. students often lack the cross-cultural skills of their foreign peers. When the RAND Corporation surveyed respondents from 16 global corporations, many were highly critical of U.S. universities' ability to produce graduates with international skills. The CED report cites a marketing manager who said that, compared to their counterparts from universities in other parts of the world, U.S. students are "strong technically" but "shortchanged" in cross-cultural experience and "linguistically deprived" (CED, 2006, p. 6). Another corporate human resource manager explained: "Universities don't think globally—it is not ingrained in their philosophy and curriculum to create the global worker." One corporate respondent went even further: "If I wanted to recruit people who are both technically skilled and culturally aware, I wouldn't even waste time looking for them on U.S. college campuses" (CED, 2006, p. 6).

> It may come as no surprise then, that a 2002 survey of large U.S. corporations found that nearly 30 percent of the companies believed they had failed to exploit fully their international business opportunities due to insufficient personnel with international skills. The consequences of insufficient culturally competent workers, as identified by the firms, included: missed marketing or business opportunities; failure to recognize important shifts in host country policies toward foreign-owned corporations; failure to anticipate the needs of international customers; and failure to take full advantage of expertise available or technological advances occurring abroad. Almost 80 percent of the business leaders surveyed expected their overall business to increase notably if they had more internationally competent employees on staff. (CED, 2006, p. 6)

The difficulties experienced by American business pale in comparison and significance with the problems which inadequate international knowledge and foreign language skills create for our national security and intelligence-gathering actives. In his best-selling history of the Central Intelligence Agency (CIA), *Legacy of Ashes* (2006), *New York Times* reporter Tim Weiner repeatedly describes how our lack of knowledge of foreign cultures and languages led to disastrous consequences for the CIA. Weiner quotes former CIA Director Richard Helms as saying, "The great sadness…was our ignorance—or innocence, if you like—which led us to mis-assess, not comprehend, and make a lot of wrong decisions" (p. 281).

In one specific instance involving an agent placed inside Iran, Weiner quotes an individual who remarked that

> [t]hese Iranians found it inconceivable that the CIA would ever send to such a critical place as Iran someone who was so ignorant of the local culture and language…. It had been difficult enough for them to accept that the CIA would post an inexperienced officer in their country. But it was beyond insult for that officer not to speak the language or know the customs, culture, and history of their country. (pp. 430–431)

Weiner's remarkable, eye-opening history of the CIA is, in fact, punctuated with numerous references to intelligence failures that can be traced to poor or nonexistent foreign-language capabilities.

As noted earlier, one of the difficulties America faces is that developing expertise in international studies and foreign language instruction does not happen immediately; it requires nurturing and investment over time at every level, from our K-12 education system right through postsecondary education. Success will also require addressing "pipeline" issues such as the pool of well-trained instructors. The Goldman Sachs Foundation has been a leader in this area by sponsoring annual prizes for "Excellence in International Education." In partnership with the Asia Society, the Goldman Sachs Foundation makes awards to elementary and middle schools, high schools, states, and media/technology firms that are undertaking innovative approaches to addressing "young Americans' lack of international knowledge and skills in an increasingly global age." The goal is to highlight successful examples and to stimulate others to follow the lead of these innovative projects.

In the late 1990s, former President Gerald Ford was interviewed on the Larry King Live television program. Near the conclusion of the discussion, Larry King asked President Ford whether there was anything that he worried about each evening before he went to sleep. President Ford said, yes: "I worry about the possibility we might drift back into isolationism."

That possibility remains very much alive in 2009. Immigration and the security of American borders were part of the presidential and congressional campaigns, and there are many people who believe strongly that America should close our borders, withdraw from the world, and neglect our leadership opportunities and responsibilities. At a time when globalization is calling for more, not less, openness, it would be tragic for this country to return to isolationism. We need more engagement with the world, and we need to conduct that engagement in a manner that emphasizes what we have in common with countries, cultures, and individuals all around the globe.

One of the most important strategies we can implement to guard against neo-isolationism is to enhance significantly the ability of our young people to speak other languages and to expose them to the culture and history of other countries. As mentioned earlier, this effort will involve changing longstanding habits of mind that are deeply embedded in our own history and culture.

For most of American history, we have existed as if we were an island: we have large oceans off both coasts, a large bilingual neighbor to the north, and a large Spanish-speaking neighbor to the south. Moreover, we have only been invaded twice since we became independent from the United Kingdom: during the War of 1812 and on September 11, 2001. In Europe, by contrast, you can drive just a few hours in almost any direction and find yourself in another country where a different language is spoken: being multilingual in Europe is not uncommon. As Americans, we are simply unaccustomed to living with the same diverse cultures and languages that one often finds in other parts of the world.

For some, this fact has been a luxury, but for the future, this isolated habit of mind will turn out to be an impediment. As this essay has demonstrated, learning more about the rest of the world is not just a nice thing to do, a pleasant extracurricular endeavor that ensures a well-educated, well-rounded young person. The future success of our economy, national security, and our diplomatic relations will be determined by our success in changing American culture in a manner that is significantly more outward-oriented than it has ever been before.

We also have a remarkable history of rising to important national challenges. I remain optimistic that in this endeavor, as well, we will meet these international opportunities in a way that repositions our great country as a positive force for change in a dynamic, interconnected, and global environment.

NOTES

1. The other members of the CED subcommittee were: Bruce K. MacLaury, President Emeritus, The Brookings Institution; Colette Mahoney, President Emeritus, Marymount Manhattan College; Steffen E. Palko, Retired Vice Chairman and President, XTO Energy, Inc.; Donna E. Shalala, President, University of Miami; and Harold M. Williams, President Emeritus, The J. Paul Getty Trust. The project director was Daniel Schecter, and participating guests included: Michele Anciaux Aoki, Project Director, State Innovations Grant, Washington State Coalition for International Education; Barbara Chow, Vice President, Education and Children's Programs, National Geographic Society; Karen Clancy, President, Board of Education, Belmont-Redwood Shores School District; Betsy Devlin-Foltz, Program Director, Longview Foundation; Kathleen Dietz, Chairperson, Office of the New Jersey State Board of Education; Linda Frey, Senior Fellow, Global Affairs Initiative, The William and Flora Hewlett Foundation; John Grandin, Executive Director, International Engineering Program, University of Rhode Island; Teresa Kennedy, Director, International/U.S. Partnerships and Outreach, The GLOBE Program; Barbara Knaggs, Program Manager, Texas Education Agency; Gary Knell, President and CEO, Sesame Workshop; Michael Lemmon, Former Ambassador to Armenia, Faculty Advisor, National War College; Michael Levine, Executive Director, Education, Asia Society; David Skaggs, Executive Director, Center for Democracy & Citizenship, Council for Excellence in Government; Vivien Stewart, Vice President, Education, Asia Society; Shuhan Wang, Education Associate, World Languages & International Education, Delaware Department of Education; and Jeya Wilson, Director, United Nations Development Programme.
2. CED's Longest Serving Trustee, Peter G. Peterson, cofounder of The Blackstone Group and Commerce Secretary in the Nixon Administration, has written repeatedly, and eloquently, on some of these investment-related policy issues. See Peterson (1989, 1993, 1996, 1999, 2004).

REFERENCES

Bush, G. W. (2006). U.S. Department of State Fact Sheet: Office of the Spokesman. Washington, DC: U.S. Department of State.

Committee for Economic Development. (1948). *An American program of European cooperation*. Washington, DC: Committee for Economic.

Committee for Economic Development. (2006). *Education for global leadership: the importance of international studies and foreign language education for U.S. economic and national security*. Washington, DC: Committee for Economic Development.

Peterson, P. G. (1989). *On borrowed time: How the growth in entitlement spending threatens America's future*. Edison, NJ: Transaction.

Peterson, P. G. (1993).*Facing up: How to rescue the economy from crushing debt and restore the American dream*. New York: Simon & Schuster.

Peterson, P. G. (1996). *Will America grow up before it grows old? How the coming social security crisis threatens you, your family and your country*. New York: Random House.

Peterson, P. G. (1999). *Gray dawn: How the coming age wave will transform America and the world*. New York: Random House.

Peterson, P. G. (2004). *Running on empty: How the Democratic and Republican parties are bankrupting our future and what Americans can do about it?* London: Picador.

Weiner, T. (2006). *Legacy of ashes: The history of the CIA*. New York: Anchor Books.

Zakaria, F. (2008). *The Post-American world*. New York: W. W. Norton.

Chapter 5

Global Citizenship Education

Challenges and Possibilities

Ian Davies
University of York

Graham Pike
Vancouver Island University

GLOBALIZATION, GLOBAL EDUCATION, AND CITIZENSHIP EDUCATION

The significance of global citizenship education is currently widely discussed at least in part due to the impact of globalization. As such, any consideration of the nature of global citizenship needs to be undertaken in the context of an appreciation of the meaning of globalization. This is not easily achieved.

Globalization

The scale of comment about globalization is almost overwhelming. Heater (2002) discusses issues in relation to identity, law, social and environmental matters, and political citizenship. Scholte (2000) suggests four major strands of globalization: production, governance, community, and knowledge. Programs of political action relevant to globalization are presented by government departments and agencies (e.g., Department for International Development [DfID], 2000). Over-arching conceptions of the nature of humanity that relate, for example, to rights (e.g., Ignatieff, 2001) have been explored. Feminist debates are clearly of central relevance (e.g., Arnot & Dill-abough, 2000), as are the implications of emerging hybrid identities and multiple loyalties (Appiah, 2006; Merryfield, 2001). Specific areas of the world are explored in the context of globalization (e.g., Hyslop, 1999) and, in this regard, debates about the nature of localism, regionalism, and the nature of states are relevant. It is also important to be able to consider the extent of the commitment that is held toward globalization. Held, McGrew, Goldblatt, and Perraton (1999) refer to hyperglobalists, skeptics, and transformationalists who argue about the potential for positive improvement or deterioration that can occur through globalization (see also Giddens, 1999).

We should, of course, remember that the challenges that are referred to in the above literature at times go further than "mere" opposition to the "delusions" (Gray, 1998) or "follies" (Rosenberg, 2000) of globalization. Indeed, there are questions raised of a fundamental sort. Green (1997), for example, questions the whole basis of the globalization debate. He refers to the large number of new *national* states. He also argues that "economic globalization is a highly contested phenomenon" (p. 161) by showing that internationalization of trade and investment has a long history and that population movements are possibly slowing down. The degree of uniqueness and innovation that is suggested by the term *globalization* is felt by some to be merely the most recent version of internationalization which may depend heavily upon the actions of governments and individuals operating from the perspective of nation-states. Osler and Vincent's (2002) brief assertion that "the focus is now on the consequences of globalization rather than whether or not it exists" (p. 12) still may not be entirely persuasive to some. The need for further elaboration about the nature and impact of globalization is shown even more clearly when one notes Heater's (2002) point that the use of even basic terminology is uncertain. He explains that the terms *world, global*, and *cosmopolitan* citizenship are not used in ways that are either consistent or entirely logical.

In light of the above it is apparent that although it is relatively straightforward to demonstrate the amount of attention given to globalization it is less easy to suggest its meaning. However, it is possible to set some very broad and loose parameters for discussing global matters. Cogan (1998) has outlined several themes that emerge from the literature of globalization. These themes he asserts are to be seen as interwoven rather than being mutually exclusive. They are:

- The global economy in which nothing is overseas and a mesh of interlocking transnational ties focusing more on services and less on goods supplants more traditional activity.
- Technology and communication in which more people have access principally to computers but also to other systems.
- Population and environment in which pollution, genetic engineering, and disparities between the haves and have-nots become the focal points for discussions about sustainability.

The need to explore overlaps and interactions is also made by Isin and Wood (1999), who argue that globalization is a key feature of contemporary reality as well as perception. Although not all can communicate electronically, the scale of the increase of information flow and the ways in which we perceive the amount and pace of change lead them to suggest that globalization is a significant aspect of society. They suggest that we should look at globalization in three diverse ways:

- It is something distinct (in reality and orientation) from Westernization (this relates to debates associated with relativism and universalism of human rights; see also Callan, 1997; Kymlicka, 1995).
- There is a network of flows as opposed to a core—a periphery model (see also Mouffe, 1992).
- We should avoid a narrow perspective and embrace a number of "globalizations" regarding different spheres (economics, politics, culture) and perspectives (see also Featherstone 1995; King, 1991).

This characterization of globalization leads us to suggest that global citizenship education is necessary, highly significant, but extremely challenging. It is to be expected that the nature of global citizenship and the forms whereby it is developed in student teachers is going to be almost inevitably complex and controversial.

The rationale for global citizenship education is developed largely from the perspectives of two significant initiatives in public education in many countries—global education and citizenship education—each of which is discussed separately below prior to bringing them together in an argument for global citizenship education.

What Is Global Education?

Since the late 1960s, global education has developed as a curriculum reform movement that attempts to respond to the increasing interdependence and rapid change that characterizes the contemporary world. Beginning in the developed world, notably in the United States and the United Kingdom (where the term *world studies* was initially preferred), the ideas and practice of global education, in various formats and guises, have gradually spread around the globe and can be found in at least 38 countries on six continents (Tye, 1999). The roots of global education in Europe can be traced back to the interwar movements of the 1920s that sought to use public education as a vehicle to promote a more sustained peace, and post-1945 flourished under the banner of "education for international understanding" (Fujikane, 2003; Heater, 1980; Richardson, 1996). During the Cold War era, seminal work in the United States by Lee Anderson (1979), James Becker (1979), and Robert Hanvey (1975) sought to expand the Eurocentric social studies curriculum by infusing perspectives from other world regions to promote understanding of global systems (Merryfield, 2001). In the final quarter of the 20th century, the rationale for incorporating a global perspective in the curriculum shifted as the multiple and inexorable impacts of globalization became more starkly apparent (Anderson, 1990). During the same period, students' apparent lack of knowledge about global issues and world geography, and their concomitant lack of preparedness to face the realities of an interdependent global system, began to cause alarm among educators in Western nations, particularly in the United States (Merryfield, 1991; Torney, 1977).

Throughout its short history, global education has been characterized—and, some would argue, troubled—by the search for a single, widely accepted definition that encompasses its diverse content, pedagogy, and philosophical positions. Popkewitz (1980, p. 304) contends that the term *global education* operates more as an educational slogan, a label that creates a "unity of feeling and spirit about the tasks to be confronted in schooling." To add to the confusion, global education is regarded by some as an overarching concept that provides unity and coherence to several related fields, including development education, environmental education, human rights education, and peace education (Greig, Pike, & Selby, 1987; Heater, 1980; Tye, 1999). Some clarity is provided by the various conceptual frameworks that are frequently cited in the literature, including those of Case (1993), Hanvey (1975), Kniep (1986), Merryfield (1997, 2001), and Pike and Selby (1995, 1999). From among these frameworks it is possible to discern some common threads that are likely to be found in the conceptual makeup of most theoretical articulations of global education. These are:

- Global connections and interdependence
- Global systems
- Global issues and problems
- Cross-cultural understanding
- Human beliefs and values
- Awareness of choices for the future

The characterization given above could be regarded as the relatively noncontroversial face of global education, an eminently justifiable infusion of a broad set of ideas that emanates from global educators' beliefs about the world and about educators' responsibilities in preparing students for global realities. Beneath this bland visage, however, lie variations of global education, in both theory and practice, that span a spectrum of ideological positions and which, in some cases, have given rise to considerable controversy (Hicks, 2003; Lamy, 1990; Schukar, 1993). Central to the more contentious manifestations is a critique, at times explicit, of the role of schooling in the promotion of nationalism or in supporting the institutions of, and values ascribed to the nation-state (Pike, 2000; Richardson, 1979; Tye, 1999). Robin Richardson (1979), an early pioneer of world studies in the United Kingdom, threw down the gauntlet in constructing "a map of the field," on which he plotted various curriculum initiatives in the United Kingdom and the United States. His "map" suggests that global educators are rooted in divergent educational and political philosophies. This insightful analysis reveals an ideological schism in global education that remains to this day.

Toh (1993, p. 9) explores the schism in depth in his description of two "paradigms of global literacy" which, he suggests, characterize different practices in global education. The "liberal technocratic paradigm," most likely to be found in schools, promotes relatively superficial understanding of other cultures, an uncritical and self-centered acceptance of the nature of interdependence, and a belief in progress through unbridled economic growth (pp. 10–11). The alternative "transformative paradigm" emphasizes ethical concern for victims of injustice, equitable sharing and sustainability of global resources, social and political activism, and a critical and empowering pedagogy (pp. 12–15). These two paradigms highlight distinct differences in the ideological underpinning and pedagogical practice of global education as it is found in classrooms around the world.

What is Citizenship Education?

Citizenship education is now a globally established phenomenon with national governments promoting it beyond Europe; for example, the Discovering Democracy program in Australia (n.d.); Ontario (Ministry of Education and Training, 1999); NGOs such as Oxfam (n.d.); transnational research projects are proliferating (e.g., Fouts & Lee, 2005; Osler & Starkey, 2005). The Council of Europe has been active over many years in the promotion of citizenship education and related initiatives, the European Union funds several relevant projects and programs, and within individual European countries there is some evidence to suggest that the area is enthusiastically embraced; 2005 was designated as the Year of European Citizenship through Education. There is increasing interest in citizenship education in Asia. In China a citizenship education center has been established at Zhengzhou University, and there is an increasing amount of research and development work with Chinese university students that suggests they need more citizenship education alongside the existing forms of patriotic education and moral education (Cheung & Pan, 2006). In Pakistan (Dean, 2005) attempts are being made to promote democracy through citizenship education. In Japan (Parmenter, 2006) the longstanding acceptance of responsibilities by school students has been developed recently by a more explicit focus on what democracy might mean within and perhaps beyond the nation-state (developments include citizenship education being constructed as a new subject in Shinagawa Ward, Tokyo in 2006).

The nature of what is included in citizenship education programs varies across countries. Davies and Issitt (2005), for example, characterized citizenship education textbooks in Australia, Ontario, and the United Kingdom, respectively, as providing social studies (societal understanding that emerges from the development of critical thinking skills related to existing academic subjects such as history and English), civics (provision of information about formal political institutions), and education for citizenship (a broad based promotion of socially useful qualities). However, despite wide variation, citizenship education programs tend in general to cohere around a number of focal points. It is possible to characterize citizenship in relation to legal and political status. This is connected usually with citizenship of a nation-state, although there are forms of transnational legal status (e.g., in the European Union) that are developing and some formal political status that exists below the level of a state (e.g., in the states of the United States). Citizenship also involves identity (Isin & Wood, 1999). This can relate to an individual as well as to a group. There are at times connections between these identities and legal and political status but often less tangible matters are more obviously significant. Citizenship is often perceived as being closely connected to issues of practical engagement (Marinetto, 2003). These matters are not necessarily without problems. The legal status of citizenship can be used to exclude as well as to guarantee rights; a concentration on identity can be used to divide as well as unite societies; an emphasis on participation can be misused by those who wish to use teachers and others to convince learners of the appropriateness of particular forms of action. The ways in which education programs emerge from these sorts of reflections can be seen in the example from Britain where the three fundamental aspects of the citizenship curriculum are political literacy, community involvement, and social and moral responsibility. Forms of this tripartite framework may be seen in many countries.

SEARCHING FOR A COHERENT APPROACH TO GLOBAL CITIZENSHIP EDUCATION

The above separate characterizations of global education and citizenship education suggest that it will not be straightforward to bring these two fields into one coherent whole. These differences have, however, not prevented a range of commentators from attempting to suggest ways in which coherence can be achieved.

Bringing Together Global Education and Citizenship Education

L. Davies (2006) introduces several interpretations through offering different permutations of global + citizenship + education; I. Davies, Evans, and Reid (2005) point to significant differences between citizenship education and global education (focus and origins; degree to which official acceptance has been achieved; and pedagogical processes) but propose a substantive fusion of the two; Andrzejewski and Alessio (1999) suggest that citizenship education should not only be viewed in a global context but should also develop the knowledge and skills essential for social and environmental justice. Several writers focus on the multiple dimensions of citizenship in their rationale for a global conception. Heater (2004) proposes a "cube of citizenship" that illustrates the interplay of three dimensions: elements of citizenship, geographical levels, and education; Selby (1994) highlights the "plural and parallel" allegiances of the global citizen; Cogan and Derricott (1998) propose four dimensions of "multidimensional citizenship": person, social, spatial, and temporal. Dower (2003) explores the many tensions in the idea of global citizenship from ethical and political viewpoints and Pike (2008) relates these dilemmas to the educational context. We suggest on the basis of our analysis of the literature and our own experience in study abroad programs that directly target the clarification and promotion of global citizenship that there are several key challenges to be overcome. These challenges are highlighted below.

Opposition to Global Citizenship Education

While proponents of global citizenship education are increasing in number and visibility, there are still those who strongly oppose the view that this concept should have a place in public education. The opposition might be regarded as emanating from two main camps: the ideological and the pragmatic. In the ideological camp, the central argument posits that teaching global citizenship undermines the development of patriotism and the importance of ensuring that future generations have a sound understanding of their own nation's history and culture. In societies built largely on immigration, such as Canada and the United States, advocates of this view argue that the curriculum should focus principally on the nation in which immigrants have settled, not on the land from whence they, or their ancestors, came. In the telling words of Diane Ravitch (2006):

> How strange to teach a student born in this country to be proud of his parents' or grandparents' land of birth but not of his or her own. Or to teach a student whose family fled to this country from a tyrannical regime or from dire poverty to identify with that nation rather than the one that gave the family refuge. (p. 579)

The pragmatists' arguments, thankfully, are somewhat less supremacist. Central to these is the point that citizenship, as currently defined, is supported at the national level by a complex and sophisticated set of policies, laws, and institutions. Citizenship is conferred upon citizens by virtue of their birth or status and is accompanied by a package of rights and duties, many of which are legally enforceable. Global citizenship has no such trappings: there is no such thing as a world passport, or legislation that permits a person to live, work, pay taxes, or seek legal recourse anywhere in the world they choose. Indeed, the ideological opponents regard with horror the prospect of a global right of passage or a world court. Global citizenship, then, is virtual: it does not exist in any legal or constitutional sense and, in the view of opponents, is open to a plethora of abuses and misinterpretations.

Linked to this argument is the view that individual identity, a significant component of citizenship, is intimately tied to nationhood and, in a sense, becomes meaningless if it takes on global proportions. We define who we are, to a considerable degree, through being American, or Indian, or Kenyan and that definition substantially distinguishes us from those of other nations. Being a global citizen, the argument goes, makes us all the same, a condition that could seriously undermine the cultural and ethnic diversity that adds so much richness to human existence. And how could we possibly educate global citizens to a sufficient level about world culture and world history and thereby nurture the same sense of identity and belonging that is achieved at the national level? Related to this point is the ethical question of whether we really do have or can have serious obligations to all of humanity: is it possible, or even desirable, in a world approaching 7 billion people, for individuals to have the same feelings of empathy for, and solidarity with, citizens living thousands of kilometers away in unknown continents as we do for those in our own nation? If not, should we draw up a priority list to establish which citizens are next in line to receive our support? And what if we don't approve of their customs and practices: are all forms of global citizenship equally acceptable? Such questions, of course, are extremely complex and difficult to answer.

The Case for Global Citizenship Education

In advocating for global citizenship education, we would like to respond to the opposition points presented above, beginning with the nationalist argument that Ravitch represents. Setting aside, for a moment, the imperialist arrogance of the idea that the United States or any other developed country is wholly altruistic in providing "refuge" for immigrants from "a tyrannical regime or from dire poverty," the arguments about the undermining of national identity demand consideration. The key counterpoint to be made here is that the idea of global citizenship in no way demands that citizens of any country loosen or relinquish their legal, physical, or emotional ties to their nation. Aside from the fact that this would be extremely impractical, a point to which we will return, the national versus global citizenship debate is predicated upon the false premise that you cannot have both; indeed, we would suggest that each of us is a "multiple citizen" (Heater, 2004), a person with "plural and parallel" (Selby, 1994) allegiances and responsibilities to community, city, region, continent, and planet as well as to a nation. Furthermore, in an increasingly interconnected and interdependent world, multiple citizenship is the only kind that makes sense. In order to fully understand any nation, particularly a developed nation with its vast web of global economic, cultural, and political connections, a citizen requires knowledge of her nation's relationships, dependencies, and obligations; major policy decisions in the modern nation are rarely made without some degree of influence from other allied or competing nations, whether for reasons of trade, security, or regional solidarity. "Pride" in one's nation, to use Ravitch's term, is therefore "pride" in the whole nest of relationships in which one's nation is embedded, including the historical connections that have prompted immigration. Multiple citizenship, of course, is not straightforward: there will be inevitable tensions among a citizen's loyalties to the various layers of citizenship. As with many of her fellow citizens, Gloria Ladson-Billings' (2006) patriotism, as an African American, was sorely tested by events in the city of New Orleans and by the way in which the Katrina disaster "stripped away the veneer of equity and justice in which American society regularly cloaks itself" (p. 588). But, as she points out, true patriotism demands the insight, the freedom, and the ability to criticize the nation.

The impracticality of global citizenship, from legal and political standpoints, also deserves a reasoned response. We are not proposing the establishment of institutions that will confer the same legal and political trappings of national citizenship but at the global level. It simply wouldn't work, nor is it necessary. Global citizenship is much more of a state of mind, an awareness of the broader context in which each nation is situated and an understanding of citizens' concomitant rights and responsibilities at multiple levels. This intrinsic "virtual" quality contributes to the elusiveness of the concept of global citizenship and underscores the importance of education in helping to give it clarity and substance. As global citizens' identity will not be authenticated in their passports, nor will their pride be swelled by a flag, symbol, or sports team, education has a key role to play in elucidating the concept, nurturing a sense of allegiance at the planetary level, and preparing young people to play active and constructive roles in an interdependent world.

The multiple citizenship concept embodies the ideal that citizens can maintain concurrent allegiances at several levels. As discussed, there may be tensions and the strength of allegiance may differ from one level to another, as well as change over time. The post 9/11 era has likely forced many global citizens through a tortuous maze of sentiments that have seen their allegiances sway and shift as they weigh up the responses to terrorism of their community, their nation, and of multinational alliances, including the United Nations. This "stretching" of allegiance, however, does not diminish or devalue the importance of local citizenship and local culture. Indeed, because of the virtual nature of global citizenship, active local citizenship becomes even more important. Most of us do not have the opportunity to act at a global level but, in a profoundly interlocking global system, we don't have to. Our decisions and actions at a local level have a global impact, whether it be economically, through what we purchase, politically, through our decision to support or not support policies such as sending troops to the Middle East, or environmentally, through our everyday energy consumption. Thus, global citizenship *depends upon* local thought and action.

But how far can we "stretch" our allegiances? Do human beings have an infinite capacity for caring and empathy? Can we really be expected to feel as morally obligated to the millions dying of malnutrition in sub-Saharan Africa as we do to the hungry and needy in our own cities? We don't have a ready answer to such questions, other than suggesting that we don't know, because we haven't really tried. We sense, too, that younger generations see things rather differently. While opinion polls in North America indicate a declining interest by young people in the traditional mechanics of political systems, such as voting, they also suggest that more youth are getting involved in citizenship activism through community and nongovernmental organizations. Furthermore, their focus of concern is increasingly global (O'Neill, 2004; One World U.S. Special Report, 2002). The moral dichotomy implied in the epigram that "charity begins at home" may be weakening as the electronically connected younger generation begins to redefine the exact scope and location of "home." A greater focus on global citizenship may be, in fact, one of the best antidotes to the decline in youth participation at the national political level. However, polls also show that there is a strong positive correlation between young people's knowledge of global issues and their concern about these issues (War Child Canada, 2006). The importance of global citizenship education is highlighted yet again.

CONCLUSIONS AND RECOMMENDATIONS REGARDING THE DEVELOPMENT OF GLOBAL CITIZENSHIP EDUCATION

In this section we draw attention to what we feel are some of the key challenges to the development of global citizenship education and highlight five recommendations that can help us frame the ideas and shape the practices that will lead to a clarification and implementation of global citizenship education. In order to make these recommendations we refer in part to evidence derived from our own experience of working with beginning and experienced teachers, university tutors, and staff from several NGOs in a project that allowed for study abroad by 75 student teachers and 11 staff. Evidence is also drawn from student evaluations of a program that has placed close to 150 student teachers in schools in 28 countries for their final teaching practice.

The Need to Go Beyond the Nation-State

The difficulties of creating global citizenship education are compounded by the alignment between schooling and the nation-state. Any attempts to create global citizenship education through existing institutionally based initiatives are necessary but are likely to be problematic. Green (1997) referred to modern nationhood, seeing the link with education as crucial: "National education systems were first created as part of the state forming process which established the modern nation state" (p. 131). This rather negative form of cohesion can be seen throughout the 19th and

20th centuries. For example, the term *national education*, as employed in the 19th century, did not mean education for the whole nation, but rather an education organized and directed by the wealthy and powerful for the poor and unimportant (Aldrich, 1996, p. 37).

This focus on the nation is also evident in debates about citizenship. Heater (1999) argues that prior to the 18th century four ideas (cosmopolitanism, citizenship, patriotism, and nation) coexisted in European political thought but that by 1800 citizenship and nationality were virtually synonymous terms. He has strongly asserted that: "For two hundred years citizenship and nationality have been political Siamese twins" (1999, p. 95). This generally accepted position (e.g., Smith, 1991, p. 44) does not, of course, mean that the process, which could be seen to promote freedom, cohesion, and allegiance (Heater, 1999), was straightforward or inclusive. Historically, Held (1999) suggests that nation-states have "rarely—if ever—existed in isolation as bounded geographical totalities" (p. 91) and now, in the face of the current form of globalization, nationalism is no longer a position that can be maintained (e.g., Faulks, 2000).

But we suggest that unless great care is exercised in programs of study abroad it is possible that the power of the nation-state will be paramount. In one transatlantic exchange project (Davies et al., 2005), for example, we felt that perhaps in practice the project was helping to develop a sense of multiculturalism in national contexts. To some extent this was highlighted immediately because different—sometimes exhaustive and exhausting—national regulations for the training and certification of teachers hindered simple movement abroad, not to work or to enjoy leisure but to study. The sense of a particular nationality was evident when some of the Europeans remarked very positively on the multicultural nature of some schools in Toronto. The opportunity to see teachers creating simulations in which immigrants had to be attracted, and helped to adapt, to a country was a welcome change of emphasis for some Europeans. It was a curious experience for some of the students from Toronto to be taken from this multicultural context and placed by project staff, who were keen to develop pluralistic understandings, into an environment where as one student remarked "[name of school] is about as un-multicultural as they come." An interesting twist on experiences with multiculturalism was that of the two New Brunswick students who were placed in [name of school] in London. For them this was a real experience with diversity because they came from a relatively monocultural part of Canada to a school with a 100% Bangladeshi Muslim population. Both students, however, commented on the cultural isolation of the school and the lack of interest of students to learn about other cultures. One wrote, "The students at [name of school] are almost 100% Muslim-Bangladeshi, with many students interacting only in this culture both within and outside of school." Another interesting situation was the English students who noted that their host school, which included a large French immersion program and a stated commitment to teaching French as a second language, gave no indication of that in the public spaces (bulletin boards, entry ways, etc), where everything was in English.

The need to go beyond the nation-state (despite the hurdles of nationality that hinder travel) is obviously necessary: the meaning of "the nation" and how we can properly engage with multinational, multicultural contexts through study abroad is less straightforward.

The Need to Go Beyond the Individualism and National Perspective in Forms of International Education

Global citizenship education is not the same thing as international education. Of course, we accept and respect the wide diversity of meaning and activity that takes place within the international education movement and recognize the overlap between it and global citizenship education (Hayden, Levy, & Thompson, 2007). However, while the word *international* suggests that there will be cooperation between individual countries, a good deal of attention in public education seems to have been devoted to organizing traditional educational functions such as organizations (e.g., the International Bureau of Education), qualifications (principally, the International Baccalaureate), and networks of schools (e.g., the International Schools Association) to meet the demands of those parents who, "through their own global professional activities, wish to have their children educated in programs based on international values and often in contexts other than in their home country" (Hayden et al., 2007, p. 1). This desire to meet professional parents' needs, whilst in many ways admirable, is congruent with the impact of study abroad programs on those individuals who use the international experience to develop their own cultural horizons or career prospects. A review of European action programs (e.g., SOCRATES) by the European Commission in 1998 concluded that:

- the most significant contributions made by the programmes is their promotion of transnational and intercultural cooperation and exchange
- the most common participants are those in mainstream high status contexts
- "in practice it could not be said that the majority of the projects they looked at had a primary, explicit and concrete orientation towards learning for active citizenship." (European Commission, 1998, p. 24)

These findings have been supported by others; for example, Grainger (2003); Osler and Starkey (1999); Teichler and Maiworm (1997), and with the latter suggesting:

> there was a consensus that students appeared to be motivated to participate in the ERASMUS/SOCRATES exchange programmes by such goals as the desire to travel and live abroad, experience other cultures, enhance their foreign language skills and in particular, improve their job prospects. (volume 1, p. 40)

During our work in which we helped student teachers and staff to study abroad we were always aware of the possibilities of "merely" encouraging the development of an interesting personal experience which would enhance individual career prospects. In teacher education, we would argue that the explicit goal should be to influence beginning teachers' professional thinking and practice toward the objectives of global citizenship education, particularly in light of the fact that teacher education programs, with a few notable exceptions, are found to be deficient in this regard in most countries (Tye, 1999).

The Need to Enable Deeper Cultural Understanding

Teachers' lack of knowledge and confidence in dealing with cross-cultural and global issues are frequently cited as reasons why they fail to bring a global perspective into their teaching (Andrzejewski & Allessio, 1999; Holden & Hicks, 2007; Yamashita, 2006). In addition to the shortcomings of teacher education programs, a lack of exposure to or direct experience in other cultures or countries contributes to their sense of inadequacy. However, as a student in one of our study abroad programs stated so succinctly, "travel doesn't necessarily change attitudes." Fennes and Hapgood (1997) remind us that outcomes of cross-cultural experience can be confusion, dissatisfaction, or, at worst, a rekindling of xenophobia. Lee and Krugly-Smolska (1999), in their assessment of a group of Canadian student teachers planning to teach overseas, point out that the teachers' lack of more than a superficial understanding of culture may result in substantive bias in their future relationships with, and assessment of, students from another country. Evidence of the latter, fortunately, is not often apparent in our students' evaluations, but a certain air of smug indifference toward the host culture is detectable in a few statements. In the case of one student teaching in a private school in Rome, she was more taken with the fact that one of her students was a prince, another the son of a film star, and that she was staying in an apartment owned by a famous pianist, than she was by the unparalleled monuments to human civilization evident in the city where she lived. Others seem to be able to break through the superficial trappings of an unfamiliar culture to reach profounder learning:

> St. Petersburg is covered with a layer of dirt after weeks of hot weather. But beyond the dirt are the buildings themselves, the architecture is incredible and the views are amazing. Good metaphor for this dirty, noisy, stinking, poor and dangerous place. The good friends and adventures you make prove what a magical, beautiful, warm hearted and fascinating place Russia is....

Or as another wrote:

> Living in Africa has opened my eyes to Africa and Africans. Africa is not what we see on CNN. It is not the land of starvation, AIDS, poverty and suffering. Sure, these things are here, but they are in Canada too.

Such sentiments may not be sophisticated, but they suggest the beginning of an analytical process that questions the cultural assumptions and biases upon which these students had previously built their views of the world. We believe the importance of this should not be underestimated in the formation of global citizens.

The Need to Promote Knowledge and Skills for Public Life

Following the discussion above about the nature of citizenship education and global education there is a need to ensure a coherent framework for global citizenship education. Many curriculum initiatives founder simply because ideas and activities are presented as if they were somehow mutually exclusive. We suggest that within the context of the themes identified as being relevant to global citizenship education we should go beyond the artificial and unhelpful distinctions that are often made in debates about social studies education. The affective and cognitive; private and public; rights and duties while, of course, having distinct meanings, are not mutually exclusive. Rather, they need to be considered together as the means by which learners are helped to understand and contribute to contemporary global society. Analysis of global issues requires awareness and understanding that emerges from and uses perspectives that include both affective and cognitive matters. A carefully constructed rational position must be informed by a sense of and commitment to what is right that at times lies beyond logical positions. Common feelings for humanity have a vital part to play in what some have described as a "sentimental education" (Rorty, 1998). Similarly the private–public dichotomy if asserted without great care simply prevents useful educational developments. Crick, the prime mover of citizenship education in England, and who has been influential elsewhere, has argued repeatedly that educational programs must highlight public issues and that confusion with personal situations must not allow distraction into matters such as health education (Crick & Porter, 1978). In some ways this is a useful distinction in that it encourages proper appreciation of a conceptually based and issue focused political program. But care is needed. There is potential to define politics more broadly than was the case with old style civics programs, but less dynamically than would be required for an understanding and activity that emerges from perspectives on feminism and ethnicity, and this may not be entirely positive. Indeed there is some evidence to suggest that Crick's position is changing to recognize the political in a wider range of contexts and processes in the light of critiques provided by academics such as Kiwan (2007). Kiwan argues that there are various conceptions of citizenship: the moral, legal, participatory, and identity-based. She suggests that the latter (identity-based) has been relatively neglected and proposes an inclusive model of citizenship which consists of two main components: "institutional" multiculturalism and a greater emphasis on the relationship between citizen and state. Crick's glowingly positive foreword to Kiwan's book suggests that some deficiencies have been recognized in earlier models of citizenship. Finally, the rights–duties dichotomy that has concerned many scholars as they have attempted to demonstrate the incompatibility of liberal and civic republican traditions may easily be resisted. The distinct meaning of rights and duties must be borne in mind if we are to avoid unjust impositions of supposed responsibilities by those least able to make contributions to society. But the overlaps between rights and duties should also be recognized. Civic republicanism, generally, has insisted on the primacy of public life over the private. According to the ideology of civic republicanism individuals should search for ways to serve the community. Liberal citizenship, on the other hand, simply stated, emphasizes the importance of rights over duties. Part of Heater's (1999) answer to this dilemma of seemingly contradictory ideologies is to assert that "by being a virtuous, community conscious participant in civic affairs (a republican requirement), a citizen benefits by enhancing his or her own individual development (a liberal objective). Citizenship does not involve an either/or choice" (p. 117). This sort of accommodation between seemingly opposed ideologies makes it possible for some sort of coherence to be developed for global citizenship education.

The Importance of Process

The "content" of what has been suggested above will be meaningful only if it is tackled in an appropriate manner. Many research projects have confirmed that the ways in which education is developed are vitally important and it is insufficient merely to focus on what is taught and learned. Others have already suggested that the spirit of citizenship is more significant than learning about the formal processes of constitutional arrangements (Sears, Voskresenskaya, Hughes, Ioffe, & Jironkina, 2005). We feel that one of the students in one of our projects involving study abroad summed up this position nicely:

> I have concluded that the essential challenge in providing effective citizenship education is not about curriculum and course work, but rather about making a true commitment to democratic processes and a definition of citizenship on a global scale.

We are not suggesting that content does not matter. We are not suggesting that the ends of an educational program are insignificant when compared with how things are managed. There is a need to avoid simplistic judgments that would suggest that there must be simple dichotomies drawn between ends and means. But we do feel that the ways in which people interact in study abroad can make a real difference to the development of their understandings and skills. There are three aspects to this emphasis on process: recognizing the fundamental importance of procedural understanding; developing structural arrangements for engagement; encouraging a particular climate for individual interaction. The first of these matters has been implicitly referred to earlier in this chapter. We wish to suggest that it is possible to go beyond learning about content and context in favor of a more sophisticated conceptual understanding. Concepts may be considered in relation to two main types: substantive (i.e., those concepts which readily suggest particular sorts of content—such as revolution, monarchy, and so on) and procedural (i.e., those concepts—such as evidence, empathy, toleration—that are at the heart of all learning about and for global citizenship). To make these procedural concepts explicit in a study abroad program is not straightforward, but to encourage conceptual learning of this sort will help students to be global citizens and not "just" learn about global citizenship. A student participant in one of our programs appears to have learned this important distinction between cognitive and affective learning as described in her observation:

> I've probably seen 12 different classes and most of them have been the same. I really feel the students here surpass my students in Canada for educational ability. They can quickly get to work at times, they know how to write an essay, they know how to study, they know how to do some of those organizational things, but they don't really know how to behave.

Some of the practical detail of how these matters may be developed can be seen in a range of publications (e.g., Davies & Hogarth, 2004). Second, staff and students who are involved in study abroad programs need to bring these procedural concepts to life by ensuring that there are appropriate mechanisms for consultation and collaboration. It matters who makes decisions about the program, especially a program that focuses on citizenship. The purpose of the program, and its details including accommodation, travel, fund raising as well as other matters should, ideally, be agreed following discussion and deliberation, with key tasks delegated to and by staff and students. Attempts to organize study abroad as if it were a traditional lesson delivered by experts will not do. There is already some research available about, generally, deliberative democracy and, more precisely, about the ways in which student councils can work. Some of the lessons learned from such work can be very useful as the structure within which collaboration can take place is worked out. Finally, we suggest, partly as a result of the first two factors, that the climate or ethos of a study abroad program should develop in a particular way. There are, unfortunately, too many negative examples that can be referred to which will demonstrate how things should not work. A program that has as its goal the development of the skills of intercultural sensitivity should model this in the way that it is organized and led.

This mismatch between content and process, between the teacher's goals for student learning and how he or she strives to pursue these goals, is evident too in the following comments:

> Yesterday I witnessed something really distressing. If I were the girl I would be crying. They have uniforms. Shoes without platforms. You know these girls they are coming into womanhood. We're going on a field trip to [a Church]. The students were told they had to wear flat shoes. They were told that in a letter. The girl with the shoes...I felt it was taken too far. "You are just a stupid girl for wearing those shoes." That would be completely unacceptable [in Canada]. Another example, students had to draw...some pupils did the whole page so she

yelled at them. "You deserve to get a detention." She was so angry about her lesson being off. She threatened them with a detention. A girl got a detention because she didn't bring her pencil crayons. I saw things like that. It's a little bit of an eye opener.

These negative examples should not blind us to the possibilities of more positive outcomes. We know already a good deal about how discussions may be organized in order to allow for mutual respect and the development of learning (e.g., Hess & Avery, 2008). The nature of discussions that can go beyond sharp unthinking exchanges of opinion and allow for a respectful and tolerant style of argumentation is something that is worth striving for (Andrews, 2007). We are already aware of the distinction that can be made between, broadly valuable, authoritative and, broadly problematic, authoritarian teachers and the significance of appropriate relationships between students and teachers (Kakos 2007; Torney-Purta & Amadeo, 2003). The true value of a study abroad program that has, at its heart, the goal of developing global citizens must lie in students' abilities and willingness to question the very structure and processes that have afforded them the opportunity to participate in the study experience. As this student comments, the medium does not always match the message:

> On a number of occasions in the course of my study of citizenship education I found myself wondering if it could be possible that the people involved truly understood the implications of what they were saying for education and society. As teachers, we must surely be aware that it makes little pedagogical sense to attempt to teach students about participatory democracy from within a system of education that is strongly hierarchical in structure, not particularly inclusive, and regulated with powerful social control mechanisms. I think that Professor Crick is quite right that citizenship education can and should be a profoundly transformative activity.

It is common to recommend congruence between aims and processes. The challenges associated with bringing this to fruition should be recognized. Through the development of discussion and engagement we will need to strive continuously if we are to go beyond rhetoric to reality that will include the development of global citizenship education.

REFERENCES

Aldrich, R. (1996). *Education for the nation.* London: Cassell.

Anderson, L. F. (1979). *Schooling for citizenship in a global age: An exploration of the meaning and significance of global education.* Bloomington, IN: Social Studies Development Center.

Anderson, L. F. (1990). A rationale for global education. In K. A. Tye (Ed.), *Global education. From thought to action* (pp. 13–34). Alexandria, VA: Association for Supervision and Curriculum Development.

Andrews, R. (2007). Argumentation, critical thinking and the postgraduate dissertation. *Educational Review, 59*(1), 1–18

Andrzejewski, J., & Alessio, J. (1999). Education for global citizenship and social responsibility. John Dewey Project of Progressive Education, University of Vermont. Retrieved from http://www.uvm.edu/~dewey/monographs/glomono.html

Appiah, K. A. (2006). *Cosmopolitanism: Ethics in a world of strangers.* New York: Norton.

Arnot, M., & Dillabough, J. (2000). *Challenging democracy: International perspectives on gender, education and citizenship.* London, RoutledgeFalmer.

Becker, J. (1979). *Schooling for a global age.* New York: McGraw-Hill.

Callan, E. (1997). *Creating citizens: Political education and liberal democracy.* Oxford, UK: Clarendon.

Case, R. (1993). Key elements of a global perspective. *Social Education, 57*(6), 318–325.

Cheung, K. W., & Pan, S. (2006). Transition of moral education in China: Towards regulated individualism. *Citizenship Teaching and Learning, 2*(2), 37–50.

Cogan, J. J. (1998). Citizenship education for the 21st century: Setting the context. In J. J. Cogan & R. Derricott (Eds.), *Citizenship for the 21st century* (pp. 1–20). London: Kogan Page.

Crick, B., & Porter, A. (1978). *Political education and political literacy*. London: Longman.

Davies, I. (1999). What has happened in the teaching of politics in schools in England during the last three decades, and why? *Oxford Review of Education, 25*(1&2), 125–140.

Davies, I., Evans, M., & Reid, A. (2005). Globalising citizenship education? A critique of "global education" and "citizenship education." *British Journal of Educational Studies, 53*(1), 66–89.

Davies, I., & Hogarth, S. (2004). Political literacy: Issues for teachers and learners. In J. Demaine (Ed.), *Citizenship and political education today* (pp. 181–199). Basingstoke, UK: Palgrave Macmillan.

Davies, I., & Issitt, J. (2005). Citizenship education textbooks in England, Canada and Australia. *Comparative Education, 41*(4), 389–410.

Davies, L. (2006). Global citizenship: Abstraction or framework for action? *Educational Review, 58*(1), 5–25.

Dean, B. (2005). Citizenship education in Pakistani schools: Problems and possibilities. *Citizenship Teaching and Learning, 1*(2), 35–55. Retrieved February 25, 2008, from http://www.citized.info/ejournal

Department for International Development (DfID). (2000). *Eliminating world poverty: Making globalization work for the poor.* Norwich, UK: HM Stationery Office.

Discovering Democracy. (n.d.). Retrieved August 5, 2005, from http://www.curriculum.edu.au/democracy/

Dower, N. (2003). *An introduction to global citizenship.* Edinburgh, Scotland: Edinburgh University Press.

European Commission. (1998). *Education and active citizenship in the European Union.* Brussels: European Commission.

Faulks, K. (2000). *Citizenship.* London, Routledge.

Featherstone, M. (1995). *Undoing culture: Globalization, postmodernism and identity.* London: Sage.

Fennes, H., & Hapgood, K. (1997). *Intercultural learning in the classroom: Crossing borders.* London: Cassell.

Fouts, J., & Lee, W. O. (Eds.). (2005). *Education for social citizenship: Perceptions of teachers in the USA, Australia, Russia and China.* Hong Kong: Hong Kong University Press.

Fujikane, H. (2003). Approaches to global education in the United States, the United Kingdom and Japan. *International Review of Education, 49*(1–2), 133–152.

Giddens, A. (1999). *Social change in Britain.* The 10th Economic and Social Research Council (ESRC) Annual Lecture.

Grainger, N. (2003). *Perceptions of some key respondents of the ERASMUS/SOCRATES programs and the European dimension in education.* Unpublished doctoral thesis, University of York, UK.

Gray, J. (1998). *False dawn: The delusions of global capitalism.* London: Granta.

Green, A. (1997). *Education, globalization and the nation-state.* Basingstoke, UK: Macmillan.

Greig, S., Pike, G., & Selby, D. (1987). *Earthrights: Education as if the planet really mattered.* Godalming, UK: World Wildlife Fund/Kogan Page.

Hanvey, R. G. (1975). *An attainable global perspective.* New York: Center for War/Peace Studies.

Hayden, M., Levy, J., & Thompson, J. (2007). *The Sage handbook of research in international education.* London: Sage.

Heater, D. (1980). *World studies: Education for international understanding in Britain.* London: Harrap.

Heater, D. (1997). The reality of multiple citizenship. In I. Davies & A. Sobisch (Eds.), *Developing European citizens.* Sheffield, UK: Sheffield Hallam University Press.

Heater, D. (1999). *What is citizenship?* Cambridge, UK: Polity Press.

Heater, D. (2002). *World citizenship: Cosmopolitan thinking and its opponents.* London: Continuum.

Heater, D. (2004). *Citizenship. The civic ideal in world history, politics and education* (3rd ed.). Manchester, UK: Manchester University Press.

Held, D. (1999). The transformation of political community: Rethinking democracy in the context of globalization. In I. Shapiro & C. Hacker-Gordon (Eds.), *Democracy's edges.* Cambridge, UK: Cambridge University Press.

Held, D., McGrew, A., Goldblatt, D., & Perraton, J. (1999). *Global transformations: Politics, economics and culture.* Cambridge, UK: Polity Press.

Hess, D., & Avery, P. G. (2008). The discussion of controversial issues as a form and goal of democratic education. In J. Arthur, I. Davies, & C. Hahn (Eds.), *The Sage international handbook of citizenship education and democracy.* London: Sage.

Hicks, D. (2003). Thirty years of global education: A reminder of key principles and precedents. *Educational Review, 55*(3), 265–275.

Holden, C., & Hicks, D. (2007). Making global connections: The knowledge, understanding and motivation of trainee teachers. *Teaching and Teacher Education, 23*(1), 13–23.

Hyslop, J. (Ed.). (1999). *African democracy in the era of globalization.* Johannesburg, South Africa: Witwatersrand University Press.

Ignatieff, M. (2001). *Human rights as politics and idolatry.* Princeton, NJ: Princeton University Press.

Isin, E. F., & Wood, P. K. (1999). *Citizenship and identity.* London: Sage.

Kakos, M. (2007). *Student and teacher interaction in the context of citizenship education.* Unpublished doctoral thesis, University of York, UK.

King, A. (Ed.). (1991). *Culture, globalization and the world system.* London: Macmillan.

Kiwan, D. (2007). *Education for inclusive citizenship.* London: Routledge.

Kniep, W. M. (1986, October). Defining a global education by its content. *Social Education, 437–446.*

Kymlicka, W. (1995). *Multicultural Citizenship.* Oxford, UK: Clarendon.

Ladson-Billings, G. (2006). Once upon a time when patriotism was what you did. *Phi Delta Kappan, 87*(8), 585–588.

Lamy, S. L. (1990). Global education: A conflict of images. In K. A. Tye (Ed.), *Global education. From thought to action* (pp. 49–63). Alexandria, VA: Association for Supervision and Curriculum Development.

Lee, M., & Krugly-Smolska, E. (1999). Cultural understanding in prospective overseas teachers. *Canadian and International Education, 28*(1), 1–16.

Marinetto, M. (2003). Who wants to be an active citizen? The politics and practice of community involvement. *Sociology, 37*(1), 103–120.

Merryfield, M. M. (1991). Preparing American secondary social studies teachers to teach with a global perspective: A status report. *Journal of Teacher Education, 42*(1), 11–20.

Merryfield, M. M. (1997). A framework for teacher education in global perspectives. In M. M. Merryfield, E. Jarchow, & S. Pickert (Eds.), *Preparing teachers to teach global perspectives. A handbook for teacher educators* (pp. 1–24). Thousand Oaks, CA: Corwin Press.

Merryfield, M. M. (2001). Moving the center of global education: From imperial world views that divide the world to double consciousness, contrapuntal pedagogy, hybridity and cross-cultural competence. In W. B. Stanley (Ed.), *Critical issues in social studies research* (pp. 179–208). Greenwich, CT: Information Age.

Mouffe, C. (1992). *Dimensions of radical democracy: Pluralism, citizenship, community.* London: Verso.

O'Neill, M. (2004). *New horizons: Engaging Canadians as active global citizens.* Ottawa: Canadian Council for International Co-operation.

One World U.S. Special Report. (2002). Youth activism and global engagement. Retrieved from http://www.benton.org/OneWorldUS/Aron/

Ontario Ministry of Education and Training. (1999). *Canadian and world studies: The Ontario curriculum grades 9 and 10.* Ontario: Ministry of Education and Training.

Osler, A., & Starkey, H. (1999). Rights, identities and inclusion: European action programs as political education. *Oxford Review of Education, 25*(1&2), 199–215.

Osler, A., & Starkey, H. (2005). *Changing citizenship: Democracy and inclusion in education.* Maidenhead, UK: Open University Press.

Osler, A., & Vincent, K. (2002). *Citizenship and the challenge of global education.* Stoke on Trent, UK: Trentham.

Oxfam. (n.d.). Accessed August 5, 2005, from http://www.oxfam.org.uk/coolplanet/teachers/globciti/key.htm

Parementer, L. (2006) Asian(?) Citizenship and identity in Japanese education. *Citizenship, Teaching and Learning, 2*(2), 8–20.

Pike, G. (2000). Global education and national identity: In pursuit of meaning. *Theory into Practice, 39*(2), 64–73.

Pike, G. (2008). Reconstructing the legend: Educating for global citizenship. In A. Abdi & L. Schultz (Eds.), *Educating for human rights and global citizenship.* Albany: SUNY Press.

Pike, G., & Selby, D. (1995). *Reconnecting. From national to global curriculum.* Godalming, UK: World Wide Fund for Nature UK.

Pike, G., & Selby, D. (1999). *In the global classroom* (Vol. 1). Toronto: Pippin.

Popkewitz, T. S. (1980). Global education as a slogan system. *Curriculum Inquiry, 10*(3), 303–316.

Ravitch, D. (2006). Should we teach patriotism? *Phi Delta Kappan, 87*(8), 579–581.

Richardson, R. (1979). World studies in the 1970s: A review of progress and unresolved tensions. *World Studies Journal, 1*(1), 5–15.

Richardson, R. (1996). The terrestrial teacher. In M. Steiner (Ed.), *Developing the global teacher: Theory and practice in initial teacher education* (pp. 3–10). Stoke-on-Trent, UK: Trentham.

Rorty, R. (1998). *Truth and moral progress: Philosophical papers.* Cambridge, UK: Cambridge University Press.

Rosenberg, J. (2000). *The follies of globalization theory: Polemical essays.* London: Verso.

Scholte, J. A. (2000). *Globalization: A critical introduction.* London: Palgrave.

Schukar, R. (1993). Controversy in global education: Lessons for teacher educators. *Theory into Practice, 32*(1), 52–57.

Sears, A., Voskresenskaya, N., Hughes, A. S., Ioffe, A., & Jironkina, L. (2005). Nurturing the spirit of democracy in Russia and Canada: A collaboration in civic education. Unpublished paper.

Selby, D. (1994). Kaleidoscopic mindset. New meanings within citizenship education. *Global Education, 2,* 20–31.

Smith, A. D. (1991). *National identity.* London: Penguin.

Teichler, U., & Maiworm, F. (1997). *The ERASMUS experience: Major findings of the ERASMUS evaluation research project.* Luxembourg: Office for Official Publications of the European Communities.

Toh, S.-H. (1993). Bringing the world into the classroom. Global literacy and a question of paradigms. *Global Education, 1*(1), 9–17.

Torney, J. (1977). The international knowledge and awareness of adolescents in nine countries. *International Journal of Political Education, 1,* 3–19.

Torney-Purta, J., & Amadeo, J-A. (2003, April). A cross national analysis of political and civic involvement among adolescents. *PSOnline,* 269–274. Retrieved Jnauary 23, 2009, from http://www.apsanet.org

Tye, K. A. (1999). *Global education: A worldwide movement.* Orange, CA: Interdependence Press.

War Child Canada. (2006). *The War Child Canada Youth Opinion Poll.* Toronto: War Child Canada.

Yamashita, H. (2006). Global citizenship education and war: The needs of teachers and learners. *Educational Review, 58*(1), 27–39. Retrieved September 25, 2007, from http://www.gmjyzx.com/

Part Two

Aligning Global Citizenship and Study Abroad With the Mission of the Academy

Chapter 6

Study Abroad and Language

From Maximal to Realistic Models

Dieter Wanner

Ohio State University

Das muss ein schlechter Müller sein,
Dem niemals fiel das Wandern ein.

(Wilhelm Müller–Franz Schubert, 1824)[1]

CONTEXTUALIZING

Study abroad has been growing since the late 1990s. It is set to expand massively in the coming 10 years, spurred by the Senator Paul Simon Study Abroad Foundation Act (2007). The combined thrust of globally fueled internationalization, economic imperatives of competitiveness, national security concerns, the urgency perceived for global academic outreach, ever growing student curiosity, and now finally a programmatic piece of legislation setting a national agenda, have made a hot topic of study abroad as delivered by America's institutions of higher education. If the protagonists in this quest for substantive and experiential internationalization play their cards right, the outcome may be the key to overcoming the nationalistic stalemate of unilateral domination and adversarial perception of global relations that still plague U.S. policy in the early 21st century (O'Connell & Norwood, 2007, pp. 4–5). In order to weave a stronger web for global relations, study abroad needs to be the outgrowth of strategically wise, calculated, and sustainable choices of the goals to be attained as well as their constant reassessment against relevant external milestones. What will count cannot be less than a measurable contribution to global prosperity and peaceful coexistence through mutual understanding between communities, nations, and supraregional blocks, which can be achieved by transcending boundaries of language, culture, and self-centered aspirations.

Within this context, study abroad is one practical, concrete, and highly attainable contribution to the larger goals. For our purposes, study abroad is an activity offered within higher education (abstracting for this essay from programs at the secondary level) in a myriad of shapes and sizes by the highly diverse group of higher education providers and support organizations that so uniquely enrich the U.S. educational landscape (Engle & Engle, 2003). As a result, study abroad is in the first place *study;* that is, an academically motivated activity incorporated into a curricular plan that expresses the mission of the college or university through which the study abroad program is made available to students (Institute of International Education [IIE], 2007). The institution must therefore possess a policy of defining the objectives, the value, the place, and the mode of delivery for functionalized international learning. These goals will need to be aligned with the institution's strategic plan and its values in teaching and research. In combination, these conscious choices provide a roadmap for institutional internationalization relevant in a globalized environment. Such a plan can meaningfully contribute to the public agenda of prosperity and informed and respectful coexistence (National Association of State Universities and Land-Grant Colleges [NASULGC], 2004). An overarching aim of study abroad is the discovery of the individual's self through the other and better understanding of the conditions surrounding our existence through contrast with other realities. This inquisitive program a fortiori embraces the extension to and the inclusion of the other, in this case the international communities, as an organic part of ourselves, elevating a globalized outlook to the conditio sine qua non of a cognitively and socially responsible existence.

While this imperative of becoming aware may recently have taken on a new form and urgency with the key words of *internationalization* and *globalization*, it represents the age-old tradition and irrepressible urge to learn through contact with models and exemplars existing beyond one's immediate reach (the romantic longing of "Wanderlust"). The many travelogues attesting to such physical outreach show us the enduring appeal of this move to the outside: suffering that is ultimately resolved in the *Odyssey*, prophetic and imperial in the *Aeneid*, naively spiritual in the *Pregerinatio ad loca sancta*, learned in al-Idrisí's geographic account of the Islamic West, anthropologically focused in Marco Polo's *Milione*, with a pained ground-level view in Bernal Díaz del Castillo's and Alvar Núñez Cabeza de Vaca's first-hand experiences in the conquest of Mexico and in the latter-day Southern United States, or idealizing in Goethe's Italian travels, to mention just a few older samples from the Western tradition. The medieval tradition of the traveling scholar who brought his learning to others and inevitably enriched his own knowledge, or the elitist model of the Grand Tour of the great sights of Europe in the 17th, 18th, and 19th centuries, setting in motion many travels across Continental Europe and beyond for specifically educational purposes are even more closely aligned with current issues of study abroad. Add to this list the professionally functional period of the *Lehr- und Wanderjahre* which the initial quote evokes in an idyllic version: know the world to become better at your own trade, as clearly expressed in the text: *das muss ein schlecher Müller sein* "it surely is a bad miller," that is, the miller who does not go abroad is supposedly deficient in his profession! In a significant sense, the current thrust to elevate study abroad to an entitlement for college students continues these traditions and gives them a systematic makeover with modern goals, means, and expectations. Yet they still embody an essential part of the quest for self-improvement through knowledge of the other.

STRATEGIES FOR SUCCESS

Even the best intentions require well thought out strategies in a field of focused goals connected to the fundamental functions of the agent in question. The educational content of study abroad is taken here as an absolute imperative; it gives our institutions of higher education the necessary legitimization for providing study abroad directly rather than outsourcing the enterprise wholesale to potentially more efficient providers. Study abroad begins and ends at the student's home institution and its commitment to learning and research. To reach the noble purpose invoked above, and to take at least one step forward, I wish to argue for a maximal model of study abroad as the most, albeit not the only, effective means of reaching a broad array of verifiable targets and thereby getting closer to the overall goal (Task Force on International Education, 2004). For the sake of realism and inclusiveness, various levels of approximation to the ideal will also be considered as valuable for a diversified practice. Four components from general to specific are key for success:

- Institutional commitment to the internationalization of the entire curriculum.
- Knowledge of at least one other language must become a central educational goal.
- Democratize study abroad through multiple means of delivery, locally adapted options for broader student appeal, and deeper penetration of all areas of our world.
- Make study abroad a priority for the establishment of scholarship funds to provide students with better access to affordable study abroad programs in a meaningful setting guaranteed by the students' intellectual, disciplinary, and language preparation.

The following discussion gives some substance to these programmatic points.

Internationalizing the Curriculum

Study abroad flows from a declared institutional commitment to internationalization. For study abroad in particular this presupposes a concerted push to internationalize the curriculum throughout the institution, requiring the organic inclusion of significant international content in all study tracks. This will involve many courses in all disciplines that a priori may not have anything to do with study abroad, but that can use pertinent international information to complement and strengthen domestic materials and general aspects. Given the universal, that is, global nature of human cognition and the decidedly nonnational nature of knowledge in most fields that are not specifically and regionally grounded, this internationalization of the curriculum may exert more or less effort in its initial formulation, but it does not meet with any intellectual, professional, or feasibility barriers. An internationalized curriculum is the foundation for meaningful study abroad that benefits a maximal number of students regardless of their discipline of study. All students will be internationally empowered, and many will have had the chance to deepen their exposure in the field. For such a curriculum redesign to take place, the institutional policies for faculty promotion and tenure also need to express these values unequivocally.[2] The thorough injection of international dimensions in all aspects of the institution's mission and operations provides the only guarantee for internationalization to be an integral part of the institution's fabric.

From current practice, two major strands stand out among the multiple study abroad variants for enriching the curriculum with a hands-on international component. On the one hand, study abroad is conceived of as a service for and benefit to the American student, for which the institutions of higher education carry responsibility. The American institution thereby assumes the concomitant obligation to minimize the socioecological impact on the international communities receiving the increased flux of visitors as a result of study abroad. On the other hand, the service learning and internship options available for students concern the host countries/institutions as they define the dimensions of students' involvement, activities, and benefits. In this case, the American institution needs to look out for the educational welfare of the participants in addition to providing a real service to the local community. Ideally, the two strands come together in mutual responsibility and reinforced commitment to a true international experience with a global horizon. As in other interactive projects, the two sides are required to take full responsibility for their reciprocal impact. This acquires high urgency in a largely unilateral initiative, such as the recent push toward a massive increase in study abroad participation. The benefit to the American student and U.S. society overall implies the potential for equivalent benefit to the host communities. At a minimum this requires the global communities to express acceptance of their host role, and at best the return privilege of study abroad in the United States.[3]

Language Study

Given the healthy state of thousands of languages spoken by communities around the globe, including a much more restricted number of global trade languages, linguistic empowerment of students is a privileged means of internationalizing the curriculum. This instructional commitment enhances students' readiness for a polyglot world more than any other curricular move. Foreign language study must be a second high-ranking platform for institutional internationalization, thereby instituting, maintaining, or broadening a meaningful foreign language requirement for graduation. To give students the chance of interacting with another community on its own terms and in the native language opens up a true experience and appreciation of the other culture. Only in this constructive and engaged way will students be able to conquer any disconcerting sense of otherness in the international setting, further enhanced by a new and unfamiliar language.

The frequent perception that college language curriculum concentrates too much on literature, narrow (high) cultural aspects, and that it neglects more practical aspects, aims at instructional practices that are about to disappear. I am advocating for a language learning experience that takes advantage of state-of-the-art pedagogical practice, that provides pertinent information on subject matters other than language and its immediate usefulness, and that effectively engages students within their educational goals. Varying instructional approaches will be able to further this agenda, from individualized instruction to more of a communicational focus, community engagement, and beyond. For more advanced language students, entire subject courses can be taught in the target language, so long as the instructor has the necessary competencies in language and subject matter. The current heavy burden of much elementary language teaching in the most commonly taught languages must become lighter at the college level to free energies directed toward strategic and less commonly taught languages for the benefit of the larger national requirements of language and cultural preparedness. Higher education institutions will be most successful when they can bring students to higher levels of proficiency in all languages. Ultimately, success can only be measured by a skill level and performance that enables the speaker to operate independently in another language, and only in this way can language learning contribute to the quality of global economic and policy activities.

The individual investment required for reaching this level of proficiency is high, representing long years of intense study and practice in a naturalistic context before the language learner is deemed by native speakers to be an equal partner. A national strategy of benign neglect of languages that relies on a few accomplished speakers, typically concentrated in academe and not available to government, business, and NGOs, is insufficient for the broad demand of international contacts that require bi- or multilingual negotiations, such as business, diplomacy, humanitarian assistance, and more. This is an area where self-sufficiency in another language becomes an aspect of national security.

Aligning the national urgency of an effective language competency goal with the potential of international programs, permits study abroad to claim its educational and societal justification as a necessity. As such, it needs adequate resources for reaching the larger goal. The goals set by the Lincoln Commission and drafted as legislation in the form of the Senator Paul Simon Study Abroad Foundation Act (National Association of State Universities and Land Grant Colleges, 2007, p. 30) must now also address the price this commitment will entail.

Expanding Study Abroad Options

The challenge presented by the daunting size of the proposed increase in study abroad participation by 2016 has repeatedly been noted—fivefold within 10 years, from 200,000 students a year to one million. This creates an urgent need for finding new avenues for letting American students do significant educational work in international settings. Following the principle of study abroad as *study*, the solution must be connected with higher education capacities already available. The European student and curricular mobility created by the ERASMUS program[4] may be used as a point of comparison. This program is built as an exchange among equal institutions that receive funding for student subsidies from a central agency of the European Union (EU), thereby creating a flow of students across the higher education space of the EU. It enables a growing number of students in Europe (close to 1% in 2006) to have a 3- to 12-month experience studying at a university in another European country. The U.S. study abroad cohort numbered 223,000 for 2007, or about 1.3% of higher-education enrollments, exceeding the European model. But where the ERASMUS program has a minimum duration of 3 months, over one-half of U.S. study abroad activity involves short-term programs of 3 weeks or less. Study abroad experiences of more than a semester represent 5.5% of this total, or about 11,000 students while about 100,000 students spend between 3 weeks and one semester in another country compared to the 150,000 in Europe (see http://www.opendoors.iienetwork.org/). The (relative) success of the ERASMUS program highlights some essential dimensions against which one could measure other such enterprises.[5] The parameters of choice regard the establishment of interinstitutional frame conditions, the adaptation of the educational content to the student's curriculum, and the availability of scholarships to help students defray added costs of international study at another institution. ERASMUS is not discussed here as the ideal model that would necessarily fit American aspirations. Rather, it shows that with significant budgetary support a large-scale enterprise of international proportions can sustain student mobility. The model is not only feasible, but it can have a broad impact. Its nuances need massive adjustment for different contexts, and its design can certainly be improved upon. In essence, however, it encourages the collaboration between comparable institutions as a realistic project. If such institutions dispose of spare capacities, they have the opportunity to open their doors for study abroad programs and provide many more students with an integrated learning experience in a new context based on stable contracts negotiated with sending institutions.

The specific conditions, and especially the range of ERASMUS (i.e., Europe), are not really a close model for the expanded study abroad efforts in the United States. Our model is to be global and more diverse, involving all continents and including destinations off the beaten path. This global aspiration cannot count on a similar infrastructure of comparable higher education systems everywhere as is the case across Europe. On the other hand, the success and inherent growth potential of ERASMUS makes clear that existing capacities already are in place, in addition to broad funding, and are a crucial condition for an affordable and immediately approachable delivery mode for study abroad within higher education.[6] Extrapolating from the visionary numbers projected for U.S. participation and the condition of many systems of higher education around the globe, our large-scale efforts will probably be concentrated in a small area of the world compared to true global diversity. The bulk of the new study abroad experiences will take place amid well-established systems of higher education capable of delivering quality instruction and premier research options. The more diverse and adventurous study abroad destinations engaging less developed higher education systems are instead being accessed by a variety of services, from shorter-term programs to NGOs and private entities. The service providers can offer the advantages of relatively easy, targeted access to regions that might not otherwise provide local study abroad capacity, and they typically combine their service with more strictly supervised in-country contact situations than students would find in more traditional study abroad settings. The more challenging external conditions of the exotic destination can always be mitigated with the purchase of more expensive alternatives affording an adaptation to and insulation from the local community, even though this imported infrastructure may contravene the directness of the students' experience in the international setting. Still, complementary forms of study abroad provide a much broader coverage of areas that might not be immediately accessible to traditional forms of study abroad (Engle & Engle, 2003).

Systematic expansion of study abroad appears to involve of necessity going beyond the limits imposed by the language issue, if this endeavor is to touch a much broader segment of the student body and extend far beyond the traditional liberal arts context. Regardless of how desirable a symbiosis between linguistic and in situ expertise may be, it should be considered that English is an academic lingua franca especially in the sciences, business, and engineering, as well as a frequent high-level means of communication in many societies, and not only in the erstwhile British Commonwealth. Even in other regions, science curricula frequently contain English portions or are delivered entirely in English (India, Japan, Turkey, Germany, Netherlands, etc.) for local students. Attracting U.S. students to such curricula, commensurate with their own study plans, is an interesting way of fulfilling different functions in one well-planned study abroad experience: progress toward the degree; international experience in close contact with local students and communities; exposure to a different educational system; and affordable educational, cultural, and social tourism.

Study abroad must take into primary consideration the specific institutional characteristics, from capacity to location, preparedness, and socioeconomic conditions of the student body. One model will obviously not fit every situation, since a fundamental property of study abroad in this view is its embedding in and adaptation to the institutional mission and other specific characteristics. The entire gamut of known study abroad delivery methods is available to institutions and their units to serve the educational needs of their students. Being prescriptive in this aspect is counterproductive. Ultimately, success will be measured by the imaginative solutions that make it possible to send increasing numbers of students outside the United States on affordable budgets, and thereby further the students' education through first-hand international experience.

Study Abroad Access and Funding

From the perspective of public institutions, the appropriate funding of study abroad requires careful planning with the aim to integrate this educational mode into the fiscal reality that underpins the educational success of the college. If study abroad is regarded as an essential and integrated part of college education, rather than an "extra," its funding requires an approach that is similar to that for other essential programs. The fiscal commitment to this component by the institution must fit into its overall mission, yielding a balanced commitment of funds to all important aspects—including study abroad. With a more substantial budget, most challenges can be made to disappear, but this option is not realistic as an operational model for study abroad in public institutions. For most of these institutions, it would seem farfetched to aim for an automatic inclusion of study abroad in the tuition charges that could result in what is considered now as a service becoming an entitlement. Targeted fundraising efforts should, however, be able to yield important means of providing study abroad scholarships to make this experience more broadly and more equitably affordable. At the same time, the institution can systematically strive to hold costs down, not only in the administration of these programs but also in the features composing the in-country activities. Cost-conscious program construction, economies-of-scale, concentration of more students into fewer programs all have the effect of lowering the actual costs to the individual student. The price barrier for study abroad can be lowered sufficiently to bring the crucial international experience within reach of a broader, even though not yet comprehensive, cohort of U.S. undergraduate students. Such cost reduction moves would include a measured injection of central funding, a well-supported development drive for study abroad scholarships, efficient sharing of study abroad advising between a study abroad office and departmental or college efforts, and a cost-containing delivery of in-country programs. Across the United States and with the combined efforts of all institutions, a much higher incidence of international experience represents the infrastructure from which the eventual global preparedness of the American workforce can flow in a natural way. To attain this goal, the study abroad enterprise of any institution of higher education has the obligation to set up a business plan that makes its chosen programmatic goals possible. From a realistic perspective, the ideal condition of a maximal study abroad model needs to be adapted for concrete challenges. This reduced program will still keep the basic tenets viable by nimble implementation and thereby provide a basis on which a meaningful expansion of study abroad can be founded overall and which will benefit ever larger numbers of participants from all academic and social backgrounds.

ASSESSING EFFORTS, OUTCOMES, AND IMPACT

In order to achieve any substantive expansion in the current level of study abroad a realistic assessment of impact and effectiveness will be required. Simple participatory data will not do, even though the IIE Open Doors statistics are a welcome public testament to the growing presence of study abroad. They give a necessary baseline activity level, eventually measuring how the ambitious numerical goals of the Lincoln Commission's recommendations are being implemented. However, beyond headcount of study abroad participants, length of study (credit hour count) should be added as a primary comparative measure. Better still, outcome-oriented units of attainment rather than purely input-defined amount of instructor contact will upgrade the assessment dimension.[7] Another dimension of relevance for student exposure to international conditions is the number of study abroad participants across the undergraduate population of an institution (total participants per graduating class). For the institution, the number of credits (or courses) with significant international content tells us something about the institution's commitment to an internationalized undergraduate education beyond the traditional fields where international topics flourish for intrinsic reasons. These dimensions are easily gauged and they can yield a moving indicator of internationalization at an institution.

They still cannot measure the desired effect on a student's cognitive gain or effective educational achievement. Such targets remain at this point undefined and so far have escaped meaningful assessment. Relevant gauges here need to look at the eventual outcome of education, especially how it translates into work dimensions of significant international engagement, and how this base of international skills, knowledge, and experience derives at least in part from the study abroad component of the individual's education (Teichler & Maiworm, 1994). Undoubtedly, this core dimension suffers from the difficulty of attributing the desired (vague) effects to a single (precise) cause, such as study abroad. As the best available current substitute for an outcome or even impact perspective, we will need to use self-assessment of study abroad graduates at different points of their professional careers. The self-perception of the effects of study abroad on what the students are doing later on in their professional environment might indicate that the effort put into study abroad at the college level is worth its price in time and money. An impressionistic dimension must at present suffice to guide the current drive of doing ever more study abroad and help channel it into a better and more strictly educational endeavor.

The difficulty is that we do not know whether the international dimension is important to students or whether it is important in the professional field overall. There is no doubt from the perspective of how global communications, business, and research is developing that this dimension is, and will become even more of a central aspect in the working world. But it is a different question if we are to measure what contribution the study abroad experience has made in reaching this goal (NASULGC, 2007, p. 36). In the end, a justification of the practice of study abroad must come from a commonly shared belief, based on concrete evidence, that this is an excellent way to foster the a priori goal of international competency and globalized consciousness, and that it therefore belongs to the foundational ingredients of education in the 21st century. The absence of international competency can then be expected to leave a graduate at the same disadvantage that currently adheres to the lack of a college degree. Since this latter perception is directly predicated on the reality of the current job market (employment opportunities, wage potential, empowerment), the way to see internationalization integrated into the social values of this country rests with the evolution of corporate and government hiring and reward guidelines. These qualifications will inexorably impose themselves as international competition for the global markets increases and participants become better prepared for the global scene.

We are not yet at the point of fully acknowledging this thrust toward internationalization as an operational principle, as the newest survey of efforts and attitudes documents again (American Council on Education, 2008a, *passim*). For an anecdotal vignette, a recent workshop for foreign language education providers and business and government leaders on the demand side showed the still very limited relevance of foreign language knowledge in the job market (Ohio Language Summit, 2007).[8] Foreign language competence may still be a rather exceptional qualification specifically sought after for internationalizing the work force in business. In view of our arguments about the importance of mastering another language for national security and productive development of business on a global scale, there is a considerable way to go before reaching the desired goal.

Ultimately, the incidence of international qualifications, including language skills, as announced in job ads from education, business, industry, and government, yields a crude, but effective impact measure of internationalization. The eventual requirement of such qualifications for job candidates will indicate that a qualified pool of talent is indeed available; that is, job seekers will have had the necessary education to prepare them for their professional careers (NASULOC, 2007, p. 36). Since business and industry approach such questions with a data-driven attitude (i.e., the qualifications need to be concrete, verifiable, and useful), the study abroad component of education and professional formation takes on the role of documented internationalization, even though limited to measuring the input level. Concrete, functionalized, and prolonged contact with international settings will give the employer a staff member who does not have to be brought up to standards on company time.

Challenges

The challenges for meaningful study abroad, especially for the maximal model advocated here, are considerable, but by no means insurmountable. Let's recall the main features of this approach: study, time, language, access, and reciprocity.

- Study abroad is study-connected in forms that are specific to higher education institutions.
- Due to the relatively slow acquisition of complex environmental conditions, especially language and social networks, extended time is an important factor in the value of study abroad venues.
- Doing study abroad *in lingua* is the highest level of accomplishment for reasons of authenticity, directness of communication, and maximal contribution to the internationalization of U.S. business and policy.
- Study abroad must be available as an opportunity for all students in good standing regardless of means and discipline.
- Study abroad providers are self-policing for the socioecological impact of study abroad and, if service oriented, respond to the initiative of the international partner.

The most pressing challenges in this context on the one hand concern language, due to the rather difficult situation it represents as a shared social value (see below on language attitude) and the objective complexity and uniqueness of its nature (see below on misleading expectations of compartmentalizing language learning). On the other hand, institutional challenges concern the delivery of study abroad in an effective way so that it is priced reasonably and affordably in order to expand its clientele. In particular, the questions of quantity vs. quality and the effects of the massive increase in projected study abroad for the host countries demand to be confronted with a sense of urgency in light of the implications of the Lincoln Commission report and its unilateral implementation in the Simon Foundation Act. Both topics are not only in the forefront for higher education institutions, but they also embody challenges for a broad application of the ambitious study abroad model developed here. The recommendations below propose a more varied picture that establishes a balance between the competing trends, arguing for the need to make use of a broad variety of approaches if an increasingly maximal model is to have any chance of being realized in the future for a growing segment of new college cohorts.

Language Attitude and Opportunities

The maximal model confronts various difficulties; two major ones derive from the function of language and current attitudes about this basic human communicational domain. The Anglophone world, in particular the United States, is in general not especially attuned to language as an essential cultural value beyond its communicational domain. Clarity and simplicity of expression trump other considerations; using another language is in this context only a hindrance to effective communication. As a consequence, the emphasis on language in the educational system is subdued and rather utilitarian, risking a failure to instill in students a linguistic pride in English as their shared language. This value, deriving from conscious knowledge of what a language can accomplish and how it functions, translates into the curiosity, capacity, and thus the necessary inducement to learn another language. In the context of the socioethical commitment to converge, for practical and communitarian purposes, toward a single language, the inherent reticence against learning another language as an alternative reality becomes more comprehensible. The effort required to acquire functional skills in another language is not generally seen as worth the time that could be spent on something perceived as more useful or productive. This, in turn, leads to curricular constraints on language learning, especially at the college level. In addition, since so much of international communication converges effectively on English in vital fields of scientific and applied knowledge, it suggests to many more students that learning a foreign language may not be a matter of utility or urgency.

This is the place where a challenging yet flexible approach to study abroad can offer functional solutions. Beyond language-based learning as the ideal case, the delivery of a student's subject matter in English in the international study location offers a way to decouple a specific language from content, as is the general situation in the human quest for knowledge. Yet this study abroad practice will still produce the desired awareness of and empathy with the international culture and its communities through an effective period of focused and functional studies.

Readiness for Foreign Language Learning

Beyond the concerns about language attitude working against a maximal study abroad practice, there exists an additional challenge in the broader implementation of a study abroad model based on language skills. On the one hand, a recent survey of college-bound high school students (American Council on Education, 2008b) shows the interest in learning another language to be prominent in what students express about their desires of learning in college. On the other hand, the readiness to translate this self-perceived desire to go through the process of acquiring skills in a language is significantly curtailed when it comes time to make curricular choices. In this survey, two cross-validating questions reveal an ambiguity between what students want and what they are ready to actually carry out: 71% of those wishing to study abroad in college express their intention to learn a foreign language, either "fluently" or "enough to converse with speakers of the language" (Chart 2, p. 19). Yet only 21% of the same population would welcome a curriculum that required some foreign language study before participating in a study abroad program, and 42% would feel discouraged by this imposition (Chart 13, p. 22). A similar discrepancy between projection and readiness derives from the comparison of Charts 6 (p. 20, "Motivation to study abroad") and 15 (p. 23, "Agreement about benefits of study abroad"). While 92% (strongly) agree that study abroad is the best way to learn or improve a foreign language, only 9% mention learning a foreign language as their primary objective in study abroad. The incongruence between perception of value and engagement to obtain the necessary skills is rather pronounced, but in no way surprising. If a foreign language mainly represents one of the many requirements for graduation, it risks being tainted with an acutely negative flavor. This disincentive to learning a language is supported by the common perception of the purported drudgery of acquiring this skill. The affective energy in language learning is understandably flowing toward the communicative function of being in touch with the people in another culture. Half of those wishing to learn another language would be content with limited skills that let them converse with their acquaintances and friends from the other linguistic culture (Chart 2, p. 19).

The recurring notion of knowing enough to survive in a language, but in no way with an ambitious level of skills, consistently permeates the discussion about language learning from the demand side. It shows up in the request for courses covering the essentials for tourism, for some social interactions among business people, and for casual conversational capabilities. The challenge with this perception is the discrepancy between a functionally limited need by the learner and the unitary nature of language as an instrument with a determined form and modus operandi. In fact, casual conversation is not linguistically simpler in a true sense. It may depend on a more limited, immediately shared, and experiential vocabulary supported by the specific context. The sentences are certainly not of a stylistically elevated level or even literary in their aspirations. Much of such conversation is also situationally (and thus linguistically) anchored to a much greater degree than more ambitious modes of discourse. But the typical conversational style contains structures of very different complexity; if it uses fixed expressions, they occur in free co-occurrence that requires the ability to efficiently process recombinant pieces. The strong contextual anchoring of casual conversation also implies a high degree of ellipsis, allusion, and other intratextual strategies in a different cultural setting that significantly complicate the processing of language for beginning to intermediate speakers. The challenge for limited register speech is not so much in what low-proficiency speakers must have at their active disposal; there are many ways of getting around one's limitations by using perhaps less than elegant, but in the end effective circumlocutions. The native partners, however, will not hold themselves to a range of vocabulary, expressions, constructions, and limited circumstantial knowledge corresponding to the interlocutor. The ensuing communicational difficulty, especially in the foreign-language speakers' comprehension of what is being said to them, reduces the value of this kind of communicative exercise to rather trivial levels of interchange. Except for an empathetic community feeling and the consciousness of having made a good-faith effort, any more significant exchange of ideas and broader aspirations will be abandoned. The consequence may very well be the language learners' frustration and consequent devaluation of language learning as a valued pursuit, since the projected benefits cannot (easily or rapidly) be obtained. Compare this to the situation of many fields of knowledge or expertise which permit different levels of attainment with perfectly cohesive results for everyday purposes: some arithmetic for the proverbial balancing of the checkbook; limited skills dealing with software, but entirely sufficient for everyday computer use; or a modest understanding of complex financial instruments that is nevertheless sufficient for steering one's own investments. As a communicational tool, language does not possess the same graduated complexity, since it depends on the same core grammar representing the structures that permit the expression of the conversationally "simple" exchanges as well as polished rhetorical texts. The known amount of time required to learn to speak a foreign language and the holistic nature of essential language skills deny the viability of a compartmentalized approach (e.g., tourist Russian, just business Chinese, etc.). It will not work for anything approaching a solution of value to the language learner. Language does not permit this kind of a shortcut.

Still, there are ways of using focused methods to accelerate learning. The current trend to steer language learning away from form and linguistic aspects to the content sphere provides language learners with very positive information about the circumstances, values, and practices of the linguistic community they are studying. This content reorientation may seem to be at the expense of acquiring the linguistic competence that will sustain skills acceptable to the foreign language community. While the complexity of the linguistic task remains unchanged, the useful information gained in this approach provides students with motivation and significant content that translates into a real gain. It will be the learner's individual challenge to reach a language competency sufficient for the intended purpose of successful communication. Time and effort are still needed, but the overall activity may thus appear (more) worthwhile and the time required becomes a recoverable investment.

Institutional Challenges

Study abroad will have its best results if it is an integral part of a student's chosen curriculum, flowing without artificial boundaries from the home campus to an international site and back. While this is achievable by building international content into the materials used in courses, the right academic context must be postulated by institutional leadership. This engagement will permit the transformation to extend from programmatic statements by campus leaders to attribution of resources and eventually direct actions by the faculty (Task Force on International Education, 2004). International considerations need to form an important part not only of the curriculum, but also of faculty guidance and incentive structures (appointment, promotion, and salary adjustment dimensions), fully equivalent to the dimensions of institutionally apprised faculty and staff activities in research and teaching. In this way, the senior officer in charge of internationalization has the opportunity to provide the institution with a comprehensive action plan for international engagement in all domains (Heyl, 2007, pp. 20–42).

In spite of the extensive practice of study abroad, the field has not yet reached a state of confident codification that can be adopted by newcomers and more seasoned practitioners as a secure base for consolidating and extending their programs. The reasons are multiple. Chief among them is the question of how study abroad can be made more affordable short of investing in it the large sums some private institutions have at their disposal. The major disconnect comes from the commonly shared flaw that institutional budget systems were built without considering the unique conditions of study abroad; it is unclear whether that is due to an oversight, the late development of study abroad for a college, or the inherent complexity of the field. As argued above, the focus for letting study abroad flourish must be on the delivery methods that guarantee the educational goals and do so by keeping costs low through an economy of scale and a rationalization of the programs. One time-honored and rather successful model operates with a stable international presence for a program or institution (*University X in Country Y*), offering multiple courses of study in a stable environment. Many universities have (mostly) European minicampuses that provide easily accessible international experiences, usually for the duration of a semester or a year. In addition to its clear advantages, the drawbacks of this model derive from the geographic limitation to one site and the academic restriction to a single host institution or even a stand-alone minicampus of the American institution. The single location may not satisfy many disciplines and colleges as the best partnership for research and instructional contacts. The accumulation of a relatively large number of U.S. students in one small expatriate institute might also be seen as problematic, possibly leading to social coagulation of the nonlocals and thereby jeopardizing the central study abroad benefit of meeting the other.

Quantity and Still Quality

The current challenge of reaching much higher greater participation in study abroad across all demographic strata only becomes bigger with the projected number of students that we wish to become involved in quality educational activities. There are two dimensions through which we can approach the issue of quantity versus quality: language and time. Neither of these yields an ideal solution, and neither can be dismissed out of hand; both have appealing features, yet neither is fully attuned to realities or quality requirements. This essay, arguing for the crucial impact of time and advocating long-term exposure cannot coherently deal with a reduced time dimension and do it justice in the available space. Short-term programs have their value, but they serve a purpose that is different from the thrust of a maximal practice of study abroad. They will not be further considered here; for some discussion see chapter 21 of this volume. Increased quantity can be achieved by simplifying the study abroad process and the product, and taking it to the level of mass-produced goods, demanding that we again evaluate the role of language in this context. While a strong language requirement before studying abroad could be imposed on maximal programs, this condition is potentially elitist and definitely unrealistic in the short term. Let's consider this question in greater detail as it relates to more broadly implemented study abroad experiences.

Mass-produced study abroad, with or without language, might at first glance imply a lowering of standards for large-scale participation: it gets you there, it delivers on the essentials, in this case the foreign experience, and if done right can also provide the necessary contact with people in the international setting. With a greater number of students served, the cost per student can be expected to drop to a level that makes broad access much more realistic than is currently the case. However, we need to consider individual needs and expectations, ranging from much simplified predeparture counseling (largely Web-based processes to save on personnel costs), to standardized in-country guides for larger groups, and to fewer options so as to streamline delivery. The practice of study abroad will certainly move in this direction to some degree; but the trend needs to be checked by the benchmarks of educational quality demanded by a given institution, by higher education in general, and, above all, by the students obtaining their international education in this form. The idea of study abroad as *study* prevents the simplification from undermining the academic values that justify the practice in the first place.

The mass-migratory approach cannot do justice to the basic tenet of maximal study abroad which involves language immersion. The difficulty here stems from the sluggish way in which enrollment in language courses can be increased, similar to other experiences in trying to upgrade standards in a complex system such as secondary and tertiary education: they take a lot of time to get underway. The corresponding increase in numbers of successful, that is, proficient, language learners will depend on a generational shift in the education system that must first permeate the relevant institutions of learning. The fiscal and personnel dimensions of this increase in foreign language delivery make any impact on the Simon legislative goal highly unlikely, regardless of the readiness by so many students to take language study seriously as a preparation for study abroad.

The need to mass-produce programs to let the greatest number of students study abroad can only be met by disassociating it in part from the language question, and focusing instead on an approach that offers substantive educational content in English that takes place at a site outside the United States. Building such a network of delivery institutions on a grand scale may not be easy, but it can definitely be undertaken. It depends on the organizational focus of our higher education institutions to define standards and transmit them to potential international providers. For quality purposes these providers will preferably be colleges and universities abroad ready to deliver the instruction and equipped to serve U.S. students in appropriate ways. Each institution may individually determine acceptable content, quality, and level of instruction sought in such a third-party provider program. The current model where each U.S. institution works on its own to find international partners has the advantage of maintaining institutional control to the highest degree, but at the same time it has also proved to be enormously time and labor intensive for identifying and maintaining multiple small-scale ("boutique") programs. The depth and breath of the vision mandated by the Simon legislation requires an enormous increase in the size of study abroad programs, a category that simply cannot be delivered based on the current approach of institution by institution. It is important for our institutions of higher education to cooperate as consortia in order to assure appropriateness and quality control of the services being delivered by third-party providers. Even though issues such as individual attention, broad access, relative affordability, and simplification of internationalization for students all need to be addressed, there is no excuse for U.S. colleges and universities not to be in command of quality control. It is a classical situation of necessary outsourcing. The challenge is to define what the product should be, how it can be strictly controlled for quality, and how it will be assessed on a regular basis. This is the dimension which cannot be abandoned.

A look at the current study abroad statistics and their implications for the Lincoln/Simon expansion also is a clear reminder that one size and one type of study abroad will never be adequate for reaching the numerical targets within the limits of currently projected resources. The participants in this mass mobility have broadly divergent needs and interests that require a more flexible approach. It is prudent not to expect much new federal funding to achieve this goal, which means the new reality must be created out of existing pieces and resources. There is no way around rationalizing all aspects that can thereby increase efficiency while safeguarding the educational purpose and quality. At the same time, these streamlining measures must also be able to correct the known defects of study abroad as it has developed so far. One immediate dimension of intervention concerns the demographic distribution of study abroad participation that does not correspond well with the null hypothesis of proportional representation of all groups. Compared to the pool of college students, and even more so to the proportions in the population at large, White students and women are largely dominant as participants in study abroad. All other groups, African Americans, Hispanics, Asian Americans, and Native Americans, remain somewhat or even very far below a representative level, most dramatically so for African Americans. Extrapolation to the projected overall number of students from the current figures yields differential factors that correct for a demographically validated participation rate. Figure 6.1 provides a comparative view of this calculated increase. Where participation by White students needs to rise by a factor of about 2.7, for African Americans this number is 13.3, and for Hispanics and Native Americans the projected factor is 6.7, given their currently much lower participation rates (see also chapter 19 of this volume). It may not be sufficient to look just at the economics of the student population and subsequently provide funding to bankroll study abroad for underrepresented groups. Thus, assuming the economic conditions self-correct in the foreseeable future, it would still not be the case that the study abroad figures would therefore automatically rise in parallel with economic recovery—that would be quite unrealistic; equally, the foreign language learning framework will not have sufficiently adjusted in the next decade. The numerically challenged study abroad groups evidently require further, stronger, and better reasons for participating in study abroad before their engagement will reach more representative levels. The discrepancy in participation rates makes it crucial to provide these (self?-) marginalized participants with clear perspectives of what they have to gain by opting in. The question for them should not be whether they should be part of the effort, but only which form and theme of study abroad they can choose that best fits their curriculum and career plans. The transition into this proactive approach requires intermediate steps to reach the expected level as a natural extension. The reassuring aspect in this urgent challenge is that the ingenuity required to make study abroad a standard educational tool for many is the best precondition for providing the variety of formats, delivery, and content areas that will permit all demographic strata to find reasons and means to engage in this activity.

The vision for study abroad needs to acquire more structure, different layers, and an adaptive approach for different needs. The maximal model requires an adjustment of its scope given all the considerations of access, participation, integration, and educational preparation. Study abroad

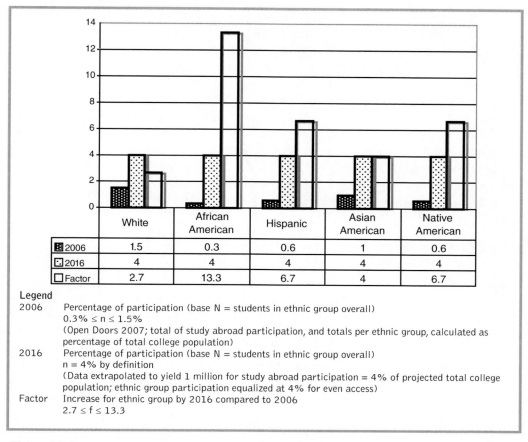

	White	African American	Hispanic	Asian American	Native American
2006	1.5	0.3	0.6	1	0.6
2016	4	4	4	4	4
Factor	2.7	13.3	6.7	4	6.7

Legend

2006   Percentage of participation (base N = students in ethnic group overall)
        $0.3\% \leq n \leq 1.5\%$
        (Open Doors 2007; total of study abroad participation, and totals per ethnic group, calculated as
        percentage of total college population)

2016   Percentage of participation (base N = students in ethnic group overall)
        n = 4% by definition
        (Data extrapolated to yield 1 million for study abroad participation = 4% of projected total college
        population; ethnic group participation equalized at 4% for even access)

Factor Increase for ethnic group by 2016 compared to 2006
        $2.7 \leq f \leq 13.3$

Figure 6.1 *Factors of Increase for Different Ethnic Groups 2006 to 2016*

should offer the option of concentric circles, with expansion between iterations. While many
students will continue to take immediate advantage of the long-term study options, many others
may be initiated through short-term study abroad programs, gain confidence and, one hopes,
recognize the value of setting their sights far beyond national boundaries and the comforting
short-term horizon. The challenging linguistic front will also profit from a layered model with
earlier short-term experience progressing to a more effective quarter or semester length program, because the initial international contact will most easily open the participants' eyes to the
reality of alternative language contexts. If this happens early on in the study career, students have
the time to dedicate their effort among other things to building language studies into their curricular program. In this indirect way, the deeper commitments of maximal study abroad may also
be furthered by the study tours and their limited, special contribution to internationalization.

More Challenges

Study abroad that is provided in a responsible, accessible, affordable, and educationally meaningful way needs to be considered with all urgency in the context of the above and for many more
reasons. The issues related to security and health in the international setting come to mind as
real threats to even the best designed study abroad programs. These challenges remain entirely

outside the realm of active control by U.S. institutions other than in an entirely reactive way. Public perceptions of the appropriateness of what is going on in universities may add considerable headaches; it suffices to remind us of the more or less serious storm clouds recently gathering over the issue of third-party providers and acceptable collaborative arrangements between these companies and accredited colleges outsourcing study abroad experiences (Farrell, 2007; In study abroad, gifts and money for universities, 2007). Other contributions to this volume make abundantly clear how complex is the entire domain of study abroad within the higher education enterprise and how much individual institutions are expected to act as imaginative entrepreneurs. Maximal study abroad options address one central concern of this long list of challenges. Maximal study abroad is a pivotal component for the success of the entire exercise, but it is only one aspect of the daunting challenge of putting enough U.S. students in meaningful contact with international conditions as they exist in diverse regions of the world.

CONCLUSION

Study abroad has much potential for benefiting society in a broad way, affecting the welfare of business, government, and social coexistence. The challenges for productive implementation are considerable, but they are challenges that can be overcome with ingenuity, dedication, and allocation of resources. Study abroad addresses the burning issue of global involvement for society at large; it is one of many avenues open for development. It has a privileged function within higher education where it is a formative experience for the new generation of socially responsible leaders on the local, national, and global stage in the years to come. In arguing for a maximal model of study abroad as an ideal goal, this essay wishes to stress the need for a much wider presence of functional language skills in the population at large. To this end, an extended international experience becomes an obligation and a personal commitment. The fun and experiential enjoyment inherent in study abroad represents an integral force that drives this activity; the educational component then becomes even more important for the delivery of international empowerment as the value-added aspect that the higher education institution can guarantee.

Study abroad is a give-and-take experience. The students give of themselves to perform as closely as possible as regular members of their host community, including language, knowledge about people and their culture, fitting into the study, work, and everyday context as smoothly as they can manage. They take away from it a healthy relativization of their original values that lets them ground their own position as reflected in the two existential modes, one native and one acquired. This comprehensive identity search through the other is the necessary antidote to the trend toward identity politics coming to a grinding halt in parochial self-affirmation. The international horizon will enlarge the narrower frame of reference and enable the graduate of this experience to approach challenges at home and abroad in a much more analytic and reflective way. The language issue looms large and inevitably requires personal engagement, time, and long-term effort to reach a noticeable improvement; however, it is fully within reach if appropriate measures are taken throughout the educational domain.

Concrete institutional policies for higher education were mapped out in eloquent terms in the report by the Task Force on International Education (2004) and a host of parallel game plans by professional associations. The primary ingredient remains the unequivocal centrality of internationalization and global awareness professed by an institution's leadership, coupled with the necessary and balanced realignment of resources to make such policy directions a reality. U.S.

colleges and universities have the knowledge, the organizational capacity, and the inventive ingenuity to make large-scale study abroad happen in a responsible framework and with the clear goal of contributing to the overall welfare of our society by engaging with other societies and cultures on a global scale.

NOTES

1. Translation: "It must be a bad miller who never got the idea of traveling."
2. See Task Force on International Education (2004). The continuing need to advance on this front is again expressed very clearly in the survey by the American Council on Education (2008b).
3. This is the spirit in which the late Senator Paul Simon approached the question: an exchange for mutual benefit through open communication and shared experience.
4. See http://ec.europa.eu/education/programmes/llp/erasmus with a number of regulatory and evaluative reports detailing the conditions applicable for this program; retrieved January 19, 2009.
5. See the early assessment of Teichler and Maiworm (1994) looking into various dimensions of input, output, and impact of the ERAMUS framework and its financial support arm. The concerns over effectiveness and challenges in delivery in the early nineties still correspond to the current challenges in the U.S. practice of study abroad.
6. Not everything is perfect in the delivery or structure of this program, between a high level of bureaucracy, insufficient language preparation of the students to profit from classes taught in the local language, and complications of everyday living frequently encountered and not always successfully solved by the institutions or the participants. See Teichler (2004), and the most recent critical reports on the various study areas available on the ERASMUS Web site, retrieved January 19, 2009, from, http://ec.europa.eu/education/programmes/llp/erasmus/public_en.html.
7. The assessment-oriented credit notion inherent in the European Bologna program represents a next step in this important direction. Given the entrenchment of the credit (faculty contact) hour in the U.S. system, I will not further question its pertinence for this early phase, even though better measures will certainly be developed and eventually accepted in the profession.
8. See http://chineseflagship.osu.edu/ohiolanguagesummit/ for Ohio (retrieved Januaruy 19, 2009). Similar events took place in Texas and Oregon under the auspices of local language Flagship programs. The three Language Summit conferences were sponsored by the U.S. Department of Education.

REFERENCES

American Council on Education. (2008a). *Mapping internationalization on U.S. campuses.* Washington, DC: Author.

American Council on Education. (2008b). *College-bound students' interests in study abroad and other international learning activities.* Washington, DC: Author.

Engle, L., & Engle, J. (2003). Study abroad levels: Toward a classification of program types. *Frontiers: The Interdisciplinary Journal of Study Abroad, 5*(2), 39–59.

Farrell, E. F. (2007, August 15). As interest in studying abroad grows, colleges struggle with cost, quality, and oversight. *Chronicle of Higher Education, 54*(2), A1.

Heyl, J. D. (2007). *The senior international officer (SIO) as change agent.* Durham, NC: Association of International Education Administrators.

Institute of International Education (IIE). (2007). *Meeting America's global education challenge* (IIE study abroad White Paper Series 1). New York: Author.

In study abroad, gifts and money for universities. (2007, August 13). *New York Times,* A1.

Lincoln Commission Report. (n.d.). Retrieved January 20, 2009, from http://www.nafsa.org/public_policy.sec/public_policy_document/study_abroad_1/lincoln_commission_report

National Association of State Universities and Land Grant Colleges (NASULGC). (2007). *Proceedings of the forum on study abroad and economic competitiveness.* Retrieved January 20, 2009, from http://www.aifs.com/media/articles.2007)02)06_study_abroad_lincoln_commisison_gertz.asp

O'Connell, M. E., & Norwood, J. L. (Eds.). (2007). *International education and foreign languages. Keys to securing America's future.* Committee to review the Title VI and Fulbright-Hays International Education programs. Washington, DC: National Academies Press.

Ohio Language Summit. (2007). Retrieved January 20, 2009, from http://www.chineseflafship.osu.edu/ohiolangiagesummit/

Schubert, F. (1824). Das Wandern. From *Die schöne Müllerin. Ein Liedzyklus von Wilhelm Müller* [Score]. In M. Friedlaender (Ed.), *Schubert Album* (Vol. 1, pp. 4–5). Leipzig: Peters.

Study Abroad Foundation Act. (2007). Retrieved January 20, 2009, from http://www.govtrack.us/congress/bill.xpd?bill=h110-1469

Task Force on International Education. (2004). *A call to leadership. The presidential role in internationalizing the university*. Washington, DC: NASULGC.

Teichler, U. (2004). Temporary study abroad: The life of ERASMUS students. *European Journal of Education, 39*(4), 395–408.

Teichler, U., & Maiworm, F. (1994). *Transition to work: The experiences of former ERASMUS students*. (Higher Education Policy Series 28, ERASUMS Monograph 18). London and Bristol, PA: Kingsley.

Chapter 7

Constructive Disequilibrium

Cognitive and Emotional Development through Dissonant Experiences in Less Familiar Destinations

S. Megan Che, Mindy Spearman, and Agida Manizade

Clemson University

This chapter highlights the connections between purposes of higher education institutions and study abroad programs in less familiar destinations, particularly those programs that effectively facilitate participants' transformation and growth. We construct an academic, theoretical justification for increased participation in study abroad programs to less familiar destinations as one largely underutilized but powerful way to meet the purpose of postsecondary education of student development. This chapter opens with a discussion of the aims and purposes of institutions of higher education. Among other areas, mission statements of such institutions support goals of increased awareness and personal growth, the potential for which is inherent to study abroad programs to less familiar destinations. We turn next to cognitive and psychological theories of learning and development for insight as to how the mind, intellect, and personality develop. We focus particularly on the concepts of stress, struggle, and disequilibrium in Vygotsky's and Piaget's theories of learning and development. Understanding processes of learning and maturation is essential to facilitating such development. Then we emphasize relationships between study abroad programs and theories of human development—in this section, we underscore the increased potential, arising from psychological and cognitive unease and dissonance, of study abroad programs to less familiar destinations to further participants' development. In the next section, we empirically outline the popularity of various study abroad destinations by geographic location. This chapter closes with a cautionary articulation of some of the risks of conducting study abroad programs in less familiar destinations, focusing particularly on the risk of perpetuating colonial practices

PURPOSES AND AIMS OF HIGHER EDUCATION INSTITUTIONS

What roles do study abroad programs—especially those to places that are less traveled by U.S. students—play in fulfilling the goals, purposes, and aims of postsecondary education? To discover the extent that institutions of higher education support studying abroad as part of a students' higher education experience, we must briefly investigate the general purposes and aims of American colleges and universities. Importantly, the 21st century has ushered in new factors which have begun to change the discourse about the philosophy of higher education. Barnett has noted several factors that play into contemporary contextualization of university purposes, including: globalization, technology, social equity, and competition (2004). He concludes that these factors have caused the traditional functions of universities—objective knowledge, critical thinking, and institutional autonomy—to be "put in doubt" (p. 72) and that contemporary institutions must be aware of the larger global arena to truly be universal universities. As the 21st century continues, higher education purposes will continue to be restructured with international as opposed to national foci.

Investigation of more specific operational university goals is more complicated. Tuckerman and Chang have referred to a "definitional problem" in the analysis of university purposes because scholars have failed to agree on exactly what a university "purpose" entails (1988, p. 611). This problem is exacerbated in the literature by the use of several different terms to describe university purpose, including *aim, mission, objective,* and *priorities* (p. 612). We follow Tuckerman and Chang in their use of Pratt and Richard's 1983 definition of a university mission that is "a statement of educational philosophy which provides a long-term sense of institutional identity" (cited in Tuckerman & Chang, 1988, p. 612). While institutions of higher education often take inspiration for their goals from multiple sources, the "mission statement" is the most common publicly visible document that articulates the purposes, practices, and future goals of a particular college or university.

The prevalence of mission statements among American institutions of higher learning is so widespread that to not have one "begs the very legitimacy of a college or university" (Morphew & Hartley, 2006, p. 456). These statements are perceived to be formal articulations of a university's culture and academic leadership manuals urge administrators to treat university mission statements as the "foundation on which priorities are established and decisions are made" (Diamond, 2002, p. 18). Many scholars who have researched mission statements complain that they are so rhetorical that they "evoke an all-purpose purpose" (Morphew & Hartley, 2006, p. 458). However, Morphew and Hartley, in an analysis of a random sampling of 300 mission statements from American 4-year colleges and universities, have demonstrated that mission statements are not as meaningless as many scholars have previously assumed (2006). These statements demonstrate political complexities that merit further research.

Scott has revealed university mission statements have existed since the medieval period (2006). He has traced the evolution of six major periods of university mission themes which chronologically change from *teaching* (Middle Ages) to *nationalization* (Early Modern Europe) to *democratization* (19th century America) simultaneous with *research* (European Enlightenment) to *public service* (20th century America) to the contemporary period of *internationalization* (Scott, 2006, pp. 5–6). The internationalization period is particularly interesting for those scholars interested in postsecondary study abroad programs. Does this new global perspective of mission statements reflect any goals that might be met through concerted efforts to expand study abroad experiences amongst American undergraduates?

To better understand the relationships between expanded study abroad endeavors and the missions of higher education institutions in this country, we sought out mission statements from universities listed as "Top National Universities" by *U.S. News & World Report's* 2008 ranking system (2008). To this date, we have located and coded statements from 81 of these universities. The mission statements that we analyzed spoke mainly to three domains: scholarship (construction of and contribution to knowledge), teaching, and outreach. Almost all study abroad programs have an explicit and primary educational goal; study abroad programs generally seek to improve or increase students' understandings about themselves, the world, or their particular area of study. Given this instructional goal, most study abroad programs interact with higher education mission statements in the realm of teaching or education. Further, there are many study abroad programs that incorporate a service-learning aspect—these programs connect to two of the three domains of mission statements: outreach and education. Given this close relationship between the purposes of study abroad programs and the purposes of higher education institutions, it is not surprising that many higher education institutions (particularly smaller liberal arts colleges) actively support study abroad programs. Some of these higher education institutions even require an educational experience abroad as a condition of graduation.

In addition to a focus on teaching, another common theme among these mission statements was an explicit connection to diversity (respecting diversity, attracting a diverse faculty or student body), or an acknowledgment of the increasing importance of international considerations (preparing students for the world, age of a global community, constructing a global perspective). Over half of the mission statements that we investigated acknowledged the increasing importance of international considerations (preparing students for the world, age of a global community, constructing a global perspective), echoing Scott's findings that mission statements from American universities and colleges are now entering a theme of "internationalization" (2006). It is in this recently emerging theme in mission statements that endeavors at expanded study abroad programs are particularly supported.

Mission statements clearly reflect that a large number of colleges and universities are seeking to produce graduates who are, among other things, culturally aware and global-minded. Culturally aware students possess what King and Magolda (2005) call "intercultural maturity"—that is, the ability to respect differences in ethnic, religious, and political perspectives while still maintaining a strong sense of self-identity. These individuals not only appreciate other cultural viewpoints but also come to more critical understandings about their own, personal cultural backgrounds. Students who posses global-minded attitudes are more likely to view events from a world perspective and value solutions to problems that will not only benefit them, but that will also benefit the broader world arena.

In sum, aims of institutions of higher education, articulated through mission statements, emphasize the development of student understanding, including an awareness of themselves and the way they interact within the world. The next question is how such development happens and what can be done to facilitate student development and learning. Having an insight into learning and development clarifies the roles of study abroad programs in fulfilling aims of institutions of higher education.

THEORIES OF LEARNING AND DEVELOPMENT

For the last few decades, many in education—particularly mathematics and science education—have relied on two scholars, Jean Piaget and Lev Vygotsky, for theories of intellectual development (Confrey, 1994). In this section we focus on particular aspects of both Vygotsky's and Piaget's theories—we consider primarily those aspects most closely related to our discussion of study abroad programs' potential for furthering student development. To be clear, we are not presenting a thorough consideration or even a complete overview of Piaget's or Vygotsky's theories. For more comprehensive treatments of these theories, the reader can consult translations of original works of these theorists (Piaget, 1961, 1985; Vygotsky, 1978, among others), or Confrey's synthesis of the two theorists into a revised perspective (Confrey, 1994, 1995a, 1995b).

Vygotsky is well-known for his concept of the Zone of Proximal Development (ZPD), which is "the distance between the actual developmental level as determined by independent problem solving and the level of potential development as determined through problem solving under adult guidance or in collaboration with more capable peers" (Vygotsky, 1978, p. 90). Thus, development is a social process involving interaction (cooperation and collaboration) with others. Vygotsky saw development as a dynamic interplay between prior psychological states or functions, the present environment and experience, and future potential. Such development is a non-linear process in which "a personality struggle with the new demands of a specific environment during a period of crisis" brings about a "neoformation," the formation of a new mental structure or system (Levykh, 2008, p. 86). Two implications of this theory of development are relevant to study abroad programs that challenge participants with experiences that depart from the participants' comfort zone. These implications are that learning (or educational experiences designed to facilitate learning) directed to one's current level of development are inadequate, and that development involves struggle and dissonance (Levykh, 2008).

From Vygotsky's perspective, social interaction and participation in social practice is crucial to learning; by interacting with others whose experience differs from ours, we learn. "When people participate in a social practice that is more advanced than what they can do independently by themselves, a *zone of proximal development* occurs" (Havnes, 2008, p. 199, italics in the original). Though we can take issue with the hierarchical structure implied in this assertion, and contend that the notion of "advanced" is not as viable as the notion of "diverse," the central point is that, by engaging socially with those around us whose knowledge and experience diverge from ours, we construct a zone or space wherein development is facilitated. It follows that experiences consistent with one's current level of development do not have the same (in terms of quantity and quality) potential for growth as do experiences beyond one's current level of development. By the same token, experiences that are on a level too far beyond one's current level also do not have the same potential for growth as experiences closer to but distinct from one's current level (Levykh, 2008). If there is too much space between a learning experience and one's developmental level, it is likely that the learning experience will simply pass one by, or that, in the attempt to engage with the learning experience, one will become frustrated to a degree that is nonconstructive. Learning experiences must dance with (that is, dynamically and nonlinearly engage) the dialectics of closeness and space, familiarity and novelty. We will discuss shortly the potential for study abroad programs, and particularly those programs to less-familiar destinations, to facilitate students' participation in their zone of proximal development. First we consider Vygotsky's view of the role of struggle in development.

Tension and struggle arise when one encounters unfamiliar or challenging experiences. In Vygotsky's theory, growth is a result of external struggle between the individual and her or his environment and an internal struggle *within* mental functions (Levykh, 2008). Though the result may be positive, this struggle is often, if not always, emotionally painful:

> The word "struggle" first and foremost denotes a negative emotional experience because of the negative origin of the word itself. On the one hand, the struggle itself is initiated by the experience of emotional dissonance between opposing forces, and, on the other hand, the struggle results in an emotional outcome…. As a result of the struggle, new culturally developed emotions reflect a wide spectrum of complexity, penetrate the deepest layers of the culturally-developed personality, and emerge in every stage and process of [one's] cultural development. (Levykh, 2008, p. 87)

Aside from the cognitive challenges one may encounter, learning is also not emotionally easy or simple. There is an element of uneasiness and discomfort in the process of development. Though with a less explicit affective focus, Piaget also acknowledged the central role of strife, or disequilibrium, in learning.

For Piaget, the role of perturbation that is consciously felt by the learner is central to the emergence of new cognitive structures, or schemes. Becker (2004, pp. 79–80) quotes Piaget as asserting in his 1975 work *The Equilibration of Cognitive Structures*, "Disequilibria alone force the subject to go beyond his current state and strike out in new directions." This disequilibrium occurs when one becomes aware of contradictions or inconsistencies in one's schemes, and when this awareness results in dissatisfaction or discomfort with one's current state. Piaget insisted that conscious or felt perturbation was vital for development, going so far as to claim that, "The most influential factor in acquiring new knowledge structures is perturbation or conflict" (quoted in Becker, 2004, p. 82). The emergent knowledge structures bring about a reorganization of one's cognitive schemes, the aim of which is to enable one to better interact with one's environment (Becker, 2004). Felt perturbation or disequilibrium is important because it represents a point of no return—once one is aware of inadequacies in one's cognitive structures, one cannot be satisfied with retreating, so the construction of new spaces of meaning that expand and modify existing schema becomes more likely. Study abroad programs to less familiar destinations—because they are distinct but not disjoint from one's prior experiences—abound with opportunities to perturb one's perspective to the point of constructive disequilibrium.

The affective social environment that is conducive for learning and development is our final point in this discussion of learning and development. Though struggle and strife, as we have argued above, are inherent to learning, development is facilitated when this discomfort is experienced within a social setting that provides safety and nurture. When new understandings are constructed this implies reaching a different level of development through the modification of one's prior cognitive structures—which means that one's prior cognitive structures were not adequate for interacting with the experiences that bring about the cognitive reorganization. It is very often an uneasy proposition to recognize, feel, and openly acknowledge the inadequacies in one's cognitive structures, but this step forward is aided by a caring, social environment that rewards cognitive risk taking (Houser, 1996; Levykh, 2008).

When dissonance is experienced in a context that does not provide support and affirmation for the learner as a person, frustration and even fear can arise. These emotions of frustration and fear can result in the premature dismissal of perturbing experiences and ideas. Thus, there is the risk that frustration and fear can inhibit the ability to learn (Houser, 1996). The struggle, discomfort, and disequilibrium inherent to generating new understandings must be supported within a safe, affirming emotional environment (Houser, 1996). A student needs to feel safe enough to express what she does not know, to ask questions, and to take risks, but she also needs cognitive challenges. In such situations, constructive disequilibrium—that dissonance which results in construction of new meanings—is facilitated. The comfort arising from the structure of study abroad programs can provide the safe environment necessary for constructive disequilibrium.

We have established thus far in our essay that an important reason for the existence of institutions of higher education is for the development of the student. We have outlined theories of development and the roles of dissonance or disequilibrium and novel experiences in these theories. We have also stressed the importance of a balance between nurture and challenge to facilitate one's engagement in an environment conducive for learning. We next illustrate the ways in which study abroad programs, and particularly those set in less familiar destinations, can engage students in these learning and development processes. We contend that study abroad programs in less familiar locales offer a unique potential to perturb American students' perspectives to the point of constructive disequilibrium within the context of a relatively safe, structured experience.

LESS FAMILIAR STUDY ABROAD DESTINATIONS

Institutions of higher education have broad purposes of developing students and contributing so the greater social good. Socially just, globally conscious study abroad programs, regardless of destination, can address these purposes; as research has shown, sustained, personal experiences with others play a critical role in cultural understandings (Bennett, 1993; Cushner & Brislin, 1996). Further, because of the possibility of much learning occurring outside of classrooms in direct experience with other cultures, all study abroad programs carry the potential to be experiential (though not all programs fulfill this potential) (Lutterman-Aguilar & Gingerich, 2002). Although most study abroad experiences do feature formal academic settings as an integral part of the program, student participants report learning more from field-experiences, people encountered, living situations and personal explorations than from program or university courses (Steinberg, 2002, p. 215).

However, we propose that study abroad programs targeting less familiar destinations have a potential for student development, social good, and for increasing cultural awareness and global mindedness to a greater degree than those that target more familiar locations. This is because the more rich opportunities to experience struggle and cognitive dissonance while simultaneously interacting with more capable others contributes to a higher likelihood of the construction of an authentic, deep space or zone for development and transformation. Further, the stable, nurturing structure of study abroad programs will ideally provide the emotional safety necessary if the dissonance is to result in constructive disequilibrium and learning.

The importance of novel experiences in learning and development implies that those destinations with which one is less familiar offer a broader domain of opportunities for transformation. This is not to say that one will not learn when seeing Big Ben in person for the first time or when visiting a French café, but the familiarity most Americans have with Western European cultures influences the development potential in both qualitative and quantitative ways. That is, not only does familiarity with the destination's geography and culture influence the amount of development opportunities, but it also influences the type of development likely to occur. Critical self-examination, an aspect of individual development, is not dependent on physical location but is also not wholly unrelated to it. Personal transformation can happen anywhere, but because of the role of novelty in perturbing our perspectives, personal transformation becomes more possible when we encounter and experience that which we have not encountered before. As long as such personal change is supported in an affirming, safe social environment, experiences in less familiar (both physically and culturally) destinations abound with potential for personal growth.

Because the potential for learning exists when one encounters novelty, the fewer experiences (direct and indirect) one has had with the peoples or cultures of a particular place, the more abundant are the opportunities for transformation and growth. For instance, finding oneself lost in a sea of more culturally capable others while simultaneously experiencing the novelty of a continual spotlight because one's skin color is different from those around one is a powerful catalyst for critical self-examination (Che, 2005). Other distinctions such as language, accent, dress, and mannerisms can also contribute to a change in perspective; being the nonnorm in many aspects (appearance, speech, or ethnicity) gives one lenses through which to view oneself and one's culture, as well as other people and other cultures, from vantage points that were previously inaccessible. This potential for transformation does not rest at the level of the individual, however. At a societal level, there is greater potential for deeper and richer understandings of realities of women and minorities as more members of society—particularly those from dominant groups—experience being a cultural and racial minority. One tends to view, for example, the experience of underrepresented groups in one's country from a different perspective when one has repeatedly experienced being the only one looking different in gatherings of tens and hundreds of people; such a transformation of perspective would likely not be as deeply "felt" or internalized if one merely reads or watches about minority experience.

It is important to understand that the term *novelty* as we are using it here does not mean completely alien—in learning and developing, one must be able to form bridges to new information, new ideas, and new meanings from what one's mind and personality was before the transformation began. Development denotes a continual, not a disjointed, process in which the direction and degree of transformation is in relationship with prior personal and cognitive states. That is one reason why two people having the "same" experience will likely not share the same growth or construct the same understandings from the experience. To construct meaning, we relate what is new to what we knew before. Therein lies another potential of study abroad programs to less familiar destinations—though the cultural and geographical realities of the destination will be dissimilar enough to pose fruitful perturbations, there are still spaces of shared human existence. These pockets of familiarity—recognizing what we share because we are human—can aid in understanding the meaning of humanity.

MORE/LESS FAMILIAR DESTINATIONS

We have been using the term *familiarity* to describe the degree of one's closeness with a particular study abroad destination. Obviously, familiarity will vary by student, depending on their background and their prior experiences, but there are some patterns in study abroad destination selection that may point to those locations that could offer increased potential, through decreased familiarity, for development and transformation. To start, let us make the point that the vast majority of students coming from public schools in the United States are already more familiar with cultural practices of Western Europe than those of other regions because of the commonly Eurocentric focus of the social studies curriculum (Merryfield, 2002).

Paralleling this Eurocentric curricular focus, participation in study abroad programs is highly concentrated in a small number of destinations (Institute of International Education [IIE], 2007). *Open Doors 2006*, the annual report on international education published by the Institute of International Education and funded by the U.S. Department of State's Bureau of Educational and Cultural Affairs, presented findings on over 200 host countries worldwide. According to this report (IEE, 2007), 140 countries hosted less than 100 students each, out of the 223,534 U.S. students traveling abroad. Forty-six of these countries hosted no more than 5 students each. Over 180 countries individually hosted less than 1% of the total number of U.S. students traveling abroad. Therefore, fewer than 20 countries provide experiences for a substantial majority of study abroad participants.

Based on the 2006 *Open Doors* report, the top 10 destinations for studying abroad include (in

105

order from highest to lowest participation rate, expressed as a percentage of all study abroad participants) United Kingdom (14% share of study abroad participants), Italy (12%), Spain (10%), France (7%), Australia (5%), Mexico (4%), China (4%), Germany (3%), Costa Rica (2%), and Ireland (2%). Combined, these 10 countries host 64% of the entire population traveling in study abroad programs. More than 75% of American students studying abroad do so in fewer than 20 host countries (the top 10 listed above plus Japan, Greece, Argentina, Czech Republic, Austria, Chile, New Zealand, South Africa, and Brazil). Each of these countries hosts more than 1% of U.S. students traveling abroad. Students in these host countries range in number from 32,109 (United Kingdom) to 2,328 (Brazil).

Figure 7.1 illustrates participation rates by undergraduate and graduate students from the U.S. to study abroad programs by country. Darker shades of red indicate higher participation rates. A country colored white has less than 1% of the total number of students studying abroad. The map in Figure 7.1 clearly shows the concentration of students studying abroad in just a few countries—the United Kingdom, Italy, and Spain alone account for more than a third of those studying abroad. Western Europe in general accounts for much of the population of students studying abroad—a close-up of Europe is provided in Figure 7.2. Much of the globe has a very small share of the students studying abroad, including Northern and Eastern Europe, much of Asia, almost all of Africa, and most of Northern, Central, and South America. Our analysis of the data provided by *Open Doors* (IEE, 2007) is corroborated by the findings in the Lincoln Commission report from a year earlier (Abraham Lincoln Study Abroad, 2005).

Some destinations which are included less often in study abroad programs may be part of a list of countries which U.S. citizens are warned away from. The U.S. Department of State, Bureau of Consular Affairs regularly lists travel warnings for countries that are not deemed safe for travel (2008). In Figure 7.3, we have accounted for these countries by shading them in gray (updated as of February 25, 2008). Many universities do not allow study abroad programs to occur in countries on the travel warning list; however, even with this consideration, there remains a persistent disparity in participation rates in study abroad programs, with a high concentration in Western Europe. Given the primarily Eurocentric curricular focus common to social studies, and given the concentration of participation in study abroad programs in Western Europe, it is likely that study abroad programs that seek to present students with experiences of less familiar cultures will turn to geographic regions outside of Western Europe. As noted earlier, developing a globally minded perspective (an aim supported by many institutions of higher education) includes a critical awareness and understanding of other cultures and ethnic groups—fulfilling this aim can carry one to less familiar destinations.

GLOBAL CITIZENSHIP

Several of the mission statements from institutions of higher education that we analyzed for this chapter included a consideration of global relationships (e.g., "learning relevant to a changing global society," Rodin, 1995) or the need to contribute to students' global perspectives (e.g., "a global perspective on the human condition," Emory University, n.d.). For instance, this longer statement typifies the position of several higher education institutions on the importance of an informed worldview:

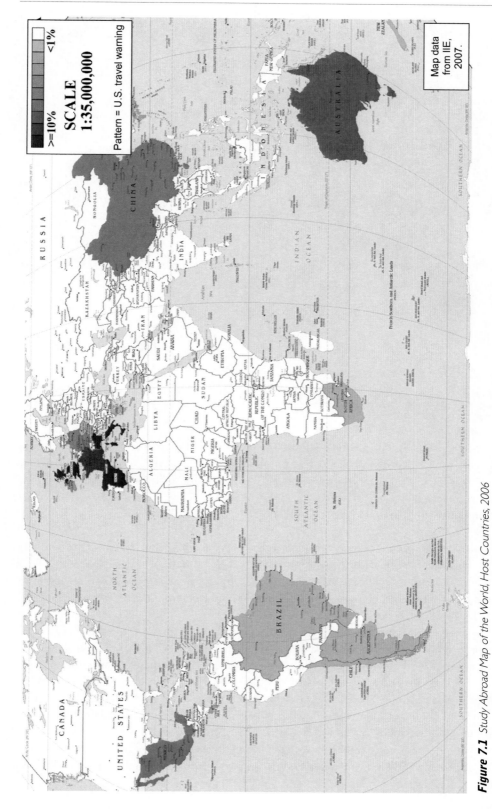

Figure 7.1 *Study Abroad Map of the World, Host Countries, 2006*

Note: The gray-tones indicate the percentage of students traveling to each country out of all undergraduate and graduate U.S. students participating in study abroad programs. The darker the gray-tone represents higher participation rates. Countries in white host less than 1% of the U.S. students studying abroad.

Figure 7.2 *Study Abroad Map of Europe, Host Countries, 2006*

Note: The gray-tones indicate the percentage of students traveling to each country out of all undergraduate and graduate U.S. students participating in study abroad programs. The darker the gray-tone represents higher participation rates. Countries in white host less than 1% of the U.S. students studying abroad.

[to] participate(s) in international efforts to alleviate world hunger and poverty, to prepare students and faculty to be productive and responsible citizens of the world, and to contribute to increased cultural, educational, economic, scientific, and socio-political interchange and understanding between and among [members of our state] and other members of the world community. (Iowa State University, 2007)

Many of these higher education institutions refer to global citizenship, but their mission statements do not elaborate on what it might mean to be a global citizen. In fact, there are several disciplinary constructs of global citizenship, and it is especially important, as we discuss in the next section, for programs in less-familiar destinations to be cognizant of and to articulate their meaning for global citizenship.

Of the several varying perspectives on global citizenship, we focus on the social justice perspective favored by scholars of social studies education. In this view, global citizenship involves working toward world common good while remaining attentive to the responsibilities of a citizen in a pluralistic society (Cogan, Grossman, & Mei-Hui-Lui, 2000; Grelle & Meztger, 1996; Merryfield & Kasai, 2004). Specifically, students should strive to view manifestations of citizenship from "non-dominant, non-western perspectives," understand their own place(s) in a global society, and embrace social action for global welfare (Andrzejewski & Alessio, 1999). Global citizenship implies more action than global education; citizenship brings rights and responsibilities. Understanding nondominant and non-Western perspectives implies that one can recognize dominance, power, and hierarchies, and that one can begin to position oneself with respect to

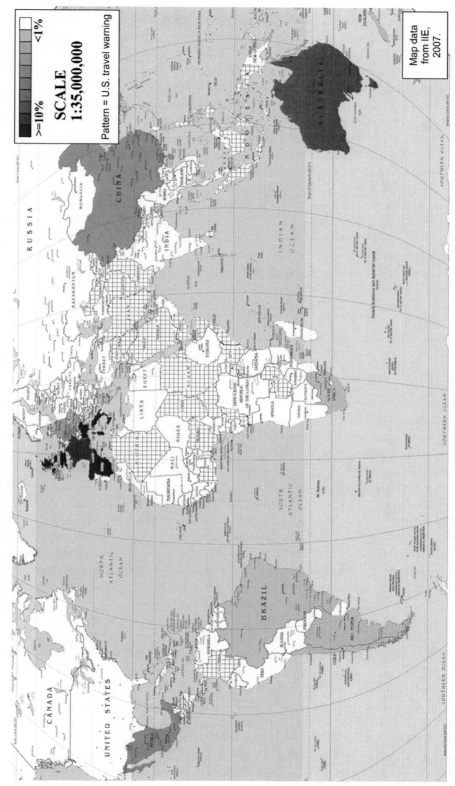

Figure 7.3 *Study Abroad Map of the Travel World, Host Countries with Travel Warnings, 2006*

Note: The gray-tones indicate the percentage of students traveling to each country out of all undergraduate and graduate U.S. students participating in study abroad programs. The darker the gray-tone represents higher participation rates. Countries in white host less than 1% of the U.S. students studying abroad. Travel warnings have been issued for countries shaded in the cross-hatched pattern.

these webs of influence. For students in the United States, this process of becoming more fully aware of one's relationship to hegemony and oppression can be emotionally and intellectually challenging.

For those hoping to cultivate their "intercultural maturity" (King & Magolda, 2005) and thereby become a more global citizen, awareness of power structures and power relations at work internationally and locally, and means by which such structures and relations are maintained and perpetuated become critically important. Both theoretical (from critical theory, antiracist theory, and postcolonial theory) and empirical (from trade agreements, consumption information, and document analysis) explorations of ways we Americans view the world and how others might see the world are helpful in forming an image of historical and current, dynamic yet patterned interactions among and between nations and states.

Thinking about connections between our individuality and our commonality, our uniqueness and our shared experience (as we perceive them) is one way to begin to create a perspective of who and where we are. (Note that the word *are* here is used not in the static sense but as a dynamic, continually shifting being-with and being-in the world [in the Heiddeggerian sense]). In what sense are we connected with the actions of those who came before us? Who and where are we in relation to actions taken by political leaders? What do we have to do with historical and current actions taken in the interest of our community, our state, our nation, or our region? What is citizenship? What does it mean to be an American? What is power? Why and through what means did some nations colonize other nations? How am I connected with that process of colonization?

Postcolonialism

Thoughtful and well-considered study abroad programs to less familiar destinations have the potential to challenge and stretch American students' perspectives and paradigms, thus contributing to a more aware global citizenry. There is a high probability that such study abroad programs will occur in former colonies; by the 1930s, colonies and ex-colonies (of formal European governments) covered 84.6% of the land surface of the globe (Loomba, 2005). Given this colonial context, formal educational endeavors such as study abroad programs conducted in less familiar destinations carry a risk of perpetuating highly inequitable practices and relationships rooted in the earliest West/non-West interactions and continued to this day, despite the nominal independence of former colonies. This risk increases as one's level of understanding about global, international relationships decreases. That is, we are positing that the less one knows and understands about the influences and actions at work when two nations come into contact, and the historical implications behind such contacts, the more one is likely to think and behave in a manner destructive to the people, culture, or environment of the less familiar destination. Students who understand what it can mean to be socially conscious and who are actively becoming more socially conscious can engage in decolonization (San Juan, Jr., 1999). Understanding theories of postcolonialism and privilege can broaden one's understanding of historical and current global interactions and the power structures embedded therein, thereby increasing the possibilities for a more responsible, authentic international exchange.

The term *postcolonialism*, in the context of this chapter, is not intended to denote a rupture from or a discontinuation of colonialism; thus we are using postcolonialism rather than post-colonialism as an indication of our awareness that colonial practices are continued and ongoing. Postcolonialism, though a theory, illuminates and contests inequitable power relations—which means that postcolonialism also involves actions or practice (Quayson, 2000; Urrieta, 2004).

Tied also to constructs of identity (Fanon, 1967; Freire, 1970/2000), nationalism (Bhabha, 1994; Fanon, 1967), and otherness (Said, 1978), postcolonialism is a historied perspective and endeavor that is centuries old. Postcolonial perspectives and endeavors acknowledge that the experiences of colonialism varied widely—it was not the same for everyone and in every place (Loomba, 2005). Understanding shared and distinctive features of the colonial project will be highly important for study abroad programs that aim for a critical global consciousness, an aim that we advocate all study abroad programs share, but particularly those that enable students to visit less familiar (likely once colonial) locales.

One strategy through which students can begin to become more socially conscious—including constructing a more nuanced perspective of culture and the relationships between culture, nationality, and identity—is through the critical pedagogy of problem-posing education introduced by Freire (1970/2000) and linked to postcolonialism through San Juan, Jr. (1999) and others (Margonis, 2003). This pedagogy is an educational process which utilizes dialogue at all phases to address rather than avoid controversial issues and social contradictions. Urrieta (2004) pointed out, though, that strategies that seek to problematize perspectives of culture and nationality must "incorporate more than a festive approach" (p. 453). That is, a festive approach to culture—superficial understandings of the food, language, and celebrations of a culture—is not enough to "purposefully disrupt oppressive paradigms" (p. 453). A critical pedagogy that aims to engage students in postcolonialism must, according to Urrieta (2004), be inclusive of and seek alternative, non-Western epistemologies and perspectives. We would also note here that peoples in less familiar host countries are not the only ones who can benefit from socially conscious, postcolonial visitors; the visitors themselves can transform their perspectives and paradigms through the process of becoming more socially, critically aware. Indeed, Urrieta (2004) is among those who encourage "transnational cultural experiences through structured cultural exchange programs" (p. 452).

Specific resources for socially conscious study abroad leaders abound, and the choice of materials for preparing students for their experience in a less-familiar destination will likely depend on that destination. Artifacts that transcend spatial and temporal boundaries include official colonial documents and contemporary trade agreements. Document analysis of international conferences such as the Berlin Conference of 1884 (Forster, Mommsen, & Robinson, 1988) and numerous colonial orders or decrees that redefined traditional authority figures also facilitate the exploration and examination of colonial practices and postcolonial opposition or resistance. Further, Rodney (1982) explicates several specific methods through which inequitable international relations were established—students and study abroad facilitators can examine current trade agreements, among other documents, to understand to what extent these international relations are continued to the present day.

A few of the questions students and facilitators can contemplate as they are in the process of constructing a more socially and globally aware image of their identity and their positionality (again, let us reiterate that we view neither identity nor positionality as static—we view these notions as more process than object) include: "Are human beings essentially the same or different? How is difference defined?" (Loomba, 2005, p. 90). Who defines or names difference? What is privilege? This last construct, privilege, has particular importance for study abroad programs to former colonies or to "developing" nations. Asymmetries in power relations, maintained and perpetuated through hegemonies, contribute to privilege, an inequitable position generally denoting comparatively more influential material and social capital or access to such capital.

White middle and upper class Americans are generally loath to admit privileges attendant, in this society, to their race and class (Solomon, Porteilli, Daniel, & Campbell, 2005); in the United States, personal compromise and modification of beliefs and actions are commonly expected more often of women and underrepresented groups (Houser, 1996). Presented with the possibility that their cultural and social status, or position, is dependent on advantages stemming from the fact that they happened to be born a particular race or in a particular place, or of a particular economic status, many students at first tend to either negate capital stemming from race, to assert ideals of individual effort and meritocracy, or feel discomfited, resentful, or even angry (Solomon et al., 2005). As we argued above, however, transformation and growth require an element of unease, and developing an understanding of privilege—attempting to locate oneself in the intricate series of power relations that define, to some extent, one's reality—is imperative for socially just, globally conscious study abroad programs. Study abroad participants—especially those from dominant groups—that have not started to problematize their (ethnic, economic, social, or sociopolitical) status or critically examine privilege may not be prepared to constructively engage with experiences in stark contrast to their lived reality, such as encountering apparently impoverished peoples (Barbour, 2006).

There are various ways through which people become conscious of their race or class-based privilege; there are many resources on which to draw. McIntosh's highly influential work (1989) outlines specific instances of White privilege in particular, at least some of which most students will be able to relate to. McIntosh's work may well be a good starting point for the often uncomfortable process of owning inequitable and unjust benefits. Having admitted to privilege, no matter how small, one may then be able to more authentically hear from Baldwin, hooks, W. E. B. DuBois, and others.

To illuminate more tangibly notions of postcolonialism and privilege, one can also, during predeparture educational sessions, engage students in discourse about ethical dilemmas they may face as they travel, and how postcolonial theory on the one hand and continued colonialization on the other might respond to such situations. For example, Barbour (2006) discusses the reactions and emotions of study abroad participants when faced with a young beggar. What is an ethical, just response? How would postcolonialism speak to the question? In what ways might the potential responses perpetuate or contest colonial relationships? Another controversial issue which can highlight meanings of and purposes for postcolonialism is that of Western aid to less "developed" countries. To what extent does such aid perpetuate colonial inequities? Exactly what are less "developed" countries in need of, that we think we can give them? What does it mean to be less "developed" or "third world"? Who defines these terms, and for what purposes? Dialoguing with study abroad participants in contemplation of these issues can lay the groundwork for constructive critical examination of one's lived experience.

One's privilege is starkly illuminated when one witnesses young children scavenging in garbage (Barbour, 2006). Familiarizing—predeparture—those intending to study abroad with the notion of privilege and the exploration of their location, position, and privilege can help prepare facilitators and students for the perturbations of such experiences, so that participants can acknowledge the guilt and shame they may likely feel (Barbour, 2006), but also learn from the experience and ideally move toward globally and socially just action. We agree with Barbour (2006) that, "To wrestle with the moral ambiguity of tourism—and of our educational programs— is vitally important. One outcome of traveling should be to develop an uneasy conscience and a critical self-consciousness about our practices when we go abroad" (p. 24). We would add that this process of feeling uneasy and critically examining oneself, if it is begun in a predeparture domestic setting through discussions about postcolonialism and privilege, could facilitate intellectual and emotional growth once study abroad participants witness and experience dilemmas first-hand. We would also stress that problematizing one's conscience and self-consciousness should not be reserved solely for travel abroad; as long as we are mindful of inequity and privilege, we are not likely to be at our ease even in the comforts of home.

It is important to distinguish between privilege and superiority. Encounters with beggars and scavenging children can often arouse guilt, shame, and sympathy, along with an urge to do some-thing for those "less fortunate." Just because, however, one may have (likely through the acciden-tal, coincidental context of one's birth) accrued, or may have access to more material and social capital—does not mean that one is superior to those with relatively less capital. It does not even mean that all those with less capital are to be pitied for their assumed unenviable state. Many cultures, particularly indigenous cultures, perceive of success, wealth, and well-being in terms of family and community relationships more than in financial terms. Rich cultural traditions and extended familial bonds can more than make up for a state that Americans would likely view as impoverished. Further, there are other cultures and locales in which an average American would likely feel relatively impoverished, so before traveling abroad, it can be helpful to confront the assumption of American superiority (Alles, 2006) and our narrow, confined, and restrictive definitions of wealth. Understanding alternative constructs of wealth is one specific example of including non-Western, alternative perspectives in preparation for study abroad. Such explora-tions of different perspectives contribute to the development of a globally minded citizen, one of the aims of many higher education institutions. Following these explorations with actual, lived experiences with less familiar locations further facilitates, through the perturbations and struggle arising from making sense of novelty in a supportive learning environment, critical self-reflection and development of the student as a whole—another aim of higher education institutions.

Need for Further Research

The arguments in this chapter have been largely theoretical; much empirical research is needed to understand more about actualities of study abroad programs in less familiar destinations. Recent research on college student development has suggested that the immersive nature of study abroad experiences does indeed help students become culturally competent and tolerant (Pascarella & Terenzini, 2005, p. 316). Students that engage in study abroad might improve their critical think-ing skills, reduce their ethnocentrism, and become increasingly concerned with global issues. Interestingly, Pascarella and Terenzini have called attention to the fact that most study abroad experiences seem to promote these benefits, regardless of program focus, length, and location. They have been careful to note, however, that the studies which contributed to this generalization are "small-scale and leave uncontrolled numerous factors" (2005, p. 316).

Pascarella and Terezini have suggested that scholars looking for a more extensive analysis of study abroad experiences might turn towards the Study Abroad Evaluation Project (SEAP, Carlson, Burn, Useem, & Yachimovicz, 1990), which investigated the experiences of American students studying abroad in European host countries during the 1984–1985 school year. SEAP researchers have noted that the analysis of some interrelationships between student development and particular program characteristics were not possible due to data limitations (Carlson et al., 1990). They have suggested that one important future research direction might involve inter-relationships between the degree of learning and the geographic focus of the study abroad pro-gram (Carlson et al., 1990, p. 124). Importantly, SEAP researches have lamented the dearth of study abroad programs in "non-Western and developing countries" and challenged the federal government to provide funding for these sorts of experiences (Carlson et al., 1990, p. 122). Indeed, the Lincoln Commission report has listed diversity of destinations as a major objective for American study abroad experiences (Abraham Lincoln Study Abroad, 2005). Likewise, NAFSA: Association of International Educators has long called for movement away from Eurocentrism and has continued to repeat this plea during the first part of the 21st century. Their 2007 policy has urged Congress to, among other things, "Promote the diversification of the study-abroad experience, including: increased study in locations outside Western Europe, especially in the developing countries" (NAFSA, 2007, p. 4).

Yet not all educators have echoed this recent push. Some have criticized an emphasis on non-traditional destinations as an affront to the cultural value of Europe as a study abroad location (Gore, 2005, p. 145). Woolf has stated that the "seductive images of exotica" negatively impact Western European destinations by implying that students who study there get something that is "less valued, less 'exciting'" (2007, p. 505). Specifically, he has asserted that the push for non-traditional locations "is driven by an unholy trinity of national political interest, the pursuit of the exotic, and a missionary tendency" (2007, p. 507). More research on student and facilitator motivation for destination choice is needed to better understand the current distribution of study abroad programs as well as future directions for study abroad participation.

Others have also advocated for study abroad programs to less familiar destinations, a reason for which includes the possibility for less familiar destinations to encourage increased male student participation in study abroad programs. Women have traditionally outnumbered men in study abroad programs in a 2:1 ratio and this gender gap may be widening (Shirley, 2006). Some think that a greater number of men might be drawn into the study abroad experience through the increase of the number of programs located in non-Western countries. Perhaps this might be based on a stereotype that men might be attracted to extreme situations more often than women. Or, that women are more fearful of traveling to less familiar study abroad locals than men due to security reasons (Thomlison, 1991, p. 32). Clearly, more research is merited in this area.

Another consideration for students wanting to study abroad is how the experience relates to their academic discipline. It could be that some destinations are more educationally fruitful than others, depending on the field of study. For instance, it may be that a microbiology student is likely to study abroad in a different country from a student interested in classics, although more research is needed to understand students' priorities in selecting study abroad programs. Though it seems reasonable that academic discipline could influence the study abroad destination, within a single field of study (such as landscape architecture), participation rates may show patterns similar to the trends discussed in this section (Hewitt & Nassar, 2005).

CONCLUSION

Conducting study abroad programs in less-familiar destinations is not a task to be taken lightly, given the stakes of all those connected with such endeavors. However, carefully considered, thoughtfully prepared facilitators and students who seek to explore difference, who understand the necessity of diversity, and who are genuinely curious about alternative perspectives can be transformed by visiting with and being-in a less familiar locale. Such study abroad programs are supported by mission statements of higher education institutions, by student development theory, and by cognitive perspectives of learning. Participants—both facilitators and students—in study abroad programs in less familiar destinations will likely be traveling to former colonies, and thus need to be thoroughly prepared in terms of historical understandings about international relationships and in terms of understanding what responsible global citizenship entails. While participants in study abroad programs must avoid as much as possible perpetuation of colonial practices, it does not follow that study abroad programs should continue to be highly concentrated in more familiar destinations.

REFERENCES

Abraham Lincoln Study Abroad Fellowship Program, Commission on the (2005). *Global competence and national needs: One million Americans studying abroad*. Washington, DC: Author.

Alles, G. D. (2006). Richer? Superior? Americans abroad. *Chronicle of Higher Education, 53*(13), 17–18.

Andrzejewski, J., & Alessio, J. (1999). Education for global citizenship and social responsibility [Monograph]. *Progressive Perspectives, 1*(2).

Barbour, J. (2006). The moral ambiguity of study abroad. *Chronicle of Higher Education, 53*(7), 59.

Barnett, R. (2004). The purposes of higher education and the changing face of academia. *London Review of Education, 2*(1), 61–73.

Becker, J. (2004). Reconsidering the role of overcoming perturbations in cognitive development: Constructivism and consciousness. *Human Development, 47*, 77–93.

Bennett, M. (1993). Towards ethnorelativism: A developmental model of intercultural sensitivity. In M. Paige (Ed.), *Cross-cultural orientation* (pp. 27–69). Lanham, MD: University Press of America.

Bhabha, H. (1994). *The location of culture*. London: Routledge.

Carlson, J., Burn, B., Useem, J., & Yachimovicz, D. (1990). *Study abroad: The experience of American undergraduates*. Westport, CT: Greenwood Press.

Che, S. M. (2005). *Cameroonian teachers' perceptions of culture, education, and mathematics*. Unpublished doctoral dissertation, University of Oklahoma, Norman, OK.

Cogan, J. J., Grossman, J. D., & Liu, M. (2000). Citizenship: The democratic imagination in a global/local context. *Social Education, 64*, 48–52.

Confrey, J. (1994). A theory of intellectual development, Part I. *For the Learning of Mathematics, 14*(3), 2–8.

Confrey, J. (1995a). A theory of intellectual development, Part II. *For the Learning of Mathematics, 15*(1), 38–48.

Confrey, J. (1995b). A theory of intellectual development, Part III. *For the Learning of Mathematics, 15*(2), 36–45.

Cushner, K., & Brislin, R. (1996). *Intercultural interactions: A practical guide* (2nd ed.). Thousand Oaks, CA: Sage.

Diamond, R. (2002). *Field guide to academic leadership*. San Francisco: Jossey-Bass.

Emory University. (n.d.). *University mission statement*. Retrieved January 7, 2008, from http://www.college.emory.edu/current/standards/pdf/mission.pdf

Fanon, F. (1967). *Black skin, white masks*. New York: Grove Press.

Forster, S., Mommsen, W. J., & Robinson, R. (Eds.). (1988). *Bismarck, Europe, and Africa: The Berlin Africa Conference 1884–1885 and the onset of partition*. New York: Oxford University Press.

Freire, P. (2000). *Pedagogy of the oppressed*. New York: Continuum. (Original work published 1970)

Gore, J. E. (2005). *Dominant beliefs and alternative voices: Discourse, belief and gender in American study abroad*. New York: Routledge.

Grelle, B., & Metzger, D. (1996). Beyond socialization and multiculturalism: Rethinking the task of citizenship education in a pluralistic society. *Social Education, 60*, 147–151.

Havnes, A. (2008). Peer-mediated learning beyond the curriculum. *Studies in Higher Education, 33*(2), 193–204.

Hewitt, R., & Nassar, H. F. (2005). Assessing international education in contemporary landscape architecture. *Landscape Journal, 22*(2), 185–197.

Houser, N. O. (1996). Negotiating dissonance and safety for the common good: Social education in the elementary classroom. *Theory and Research in Social Education, 24*(3), 294–312.

Institute of International Education (IIE). (2007, November). *Open doors 2006*. New York: Author.

Iowa State University. (1997). *The strategic plan for 1995–2000*. Retrieved January 7, 2008, from http://www.president.iastate.edu/plan/2000/plan.html

King, B., & Magolda, M. B. (2005). A developmental model of intercultural maturity. *Journal of College Student Development, 46*(6), 571–592.

Levykh, M. G. (2008). The affective establishment and maintenance of Vygotsky's zone of proximal development. *Educational Theory, 58*(1), 83–101.

Loomba, A. (2005). *Colonialism/postcolonialism* (2nd ed.). New York: Routledge.

Lutterman-Aguilar, A., & Gingerich, O. (2002). Experiential pedagogy for study abroad: Education for global citizenship. *Frontiers, 8,* 41–82.

Margonis, F. (2003). Paulo Freire and post-colonial dilemmas. *Studies in Philosophy and Education, 22,* 145–156.

McIntosh, P. (1989). White privilege: Unpacking the invisible knapsack. *Peace and Freedom,* 10–12.

Merryfield, M. (2002). Rethinking our framework for understanding the world. *Theory and Research in Social Education, 30*(1), 148–151.

Merryfield, M., & Kasai, M. (2004). How are teachers responding to globalization? *Social Education, 68,* 354–359.

Morphew C., & Heartly, M. (2006). Mission statements: A thematic analysis of rhetoric across institutional type. *The Journal of Higher Education, 77*(3), 456–471.

NAFSA: Association of International Educators. (2007, October). *An international education policy for U.S. leadership, competiveness and security.* Retrieved January 5, 2008, from http://www.nafsa.org/_/File/_/neip_rev.pdf

Pascarella, E., & Terenzini, P. (2005). *How college affects students: Vol. 2. A third decade of research.* San Francisco: Jossey-Bass.

Piaget, J. (1961). *Psychology of intelligence.* Totowa, NJ: Littlefield, Adams.

Piaget, J. (1985). *The equilibration of cognitive structures: The central problem of intellectual development.* Chicago: University of Chicago Press.

Quayson, A. (2000). *Postcolonialism, theory, practice or process?* Cambridge, MA: Polity Press.

Rodin, J. (1995). *The agenda for excellence: President's message, 1995 annual report.* Retrieved January 7, 2008, from http://www.upenn.edu/president/Annual_Report_95_96.html

Rodney, W. (1982). *How Europe underdeveloped Africa.* Washington, DC: Howard University Press.

Said, E. (1978). *Orientalism.* New York: Vintage.

San Juan, E., Jr. (1999). *Beyond postcolonial theory.* New York: St. Martin's Press.

Scott, J. (2006). The mission of the university: Medieval to postmodern transformations. *The Journal of Higher Education, 77*(1), 1–39.

Shirley, S. (2006). *The gender gap in post secondary study abroad: Understanding and marketing to male students.* Unpublished doctoral dissertation, University of North Dakota.

Solomon, R. P., Porteilli, J. P., Daniel, B-J., & Campbell, A. (2005). The discourse of denial: How white teacher candidates construct race, racism and "white privilege." *Race Ethnicity and Education, 8*(2), 147–169.

Steinberg, M. (2002). "Involve me and I will understand": Academic quality in experiential programs abroad. *Frontiers: The Interdisciplinary Journal of Study Abroad, 8,* 207–229.

Thomlison, T. (1991). Effects of a study-abroad program on university students: Toward a predictive theory of intercultural contact . (ERIC Document Reproduction Service, No ED 332629)

Tuckerman, H. P., & Chang, C. (1988). Conflict, congruence, and generic university goals. *The Journal of Higher Education, 59*(6), 611–633.

Urrieta, L., Jr. (2004). Dis-connections in "American" citizenship and the post/neo-colonial: People of Mexican descent and whitestream pedagogy and curriculum. *Theory and Research in Social Education, 32*(4), 433–458.

U.S. Department of State, Bureau of Consular Affairs. (2008). *Current travel warnings.* Retrieved February 25, 2008, from http://travel.state.gov/travel/cis_pa_tw/tw/tw_1764.html

U.S. News & World Report. (2008). *America's best colleges 2008: National universities: Top schools.* Retrieved March 15, 2008, from http://www.usnews.com/usnews/edu/college/rankings/brief/t1natudoc_brief.php

Vygotsky, L. (1978). *Mind in society: The development of higher psychological processes.* Cambridge, MA: Harvard University Press.

Wolfe, M. (2007). Impossible things before breakfast: Myths in education abroad. *Journal of Studies in International Education,11,* 496–509.

Chapter 8

The Liberal Arts and Global Citizenship

Fostering Intercultural Engagement Through Integrative Experiences and Structured Reflection

Joseph L. Brockington and Margaret D. Wiedenhoeft
Kalamazoo College

The question of how study abroad fosters global citizenship is ideally posed within the context of American liberal arts colleges. Not only are study abroad participation rates (in terms of the percentage of graduates) higher among liberal arts colleges than for other types of institutions (Bhandari & Chow, 2008), the liberal arts have a long tradition of preparing graduates for citizenship. Increasingly, liberal arts colleges are adding experiential opportunities to their curriculum acknowledging that a whole-person education necessarily takes place within a whole-world context. While not universal among liberal arts colleges, these institutions are increasing their attention to the development of global citizens in their mission statements' regarding expected educational outcomes.

A cursory look at mission statements from some of the top 40 baccalaureate study abroad institutions from the 2007 *Open Doors* (Bhandari & Chow, 2008) report shows that fully three-quarters of them reference some type of citizenship education or civic engagement. Half of the institutions include some reference to a larger world. For example, Rollins College "educates students for global citizenship and responsible leadership…"; Pitzer College "produces engaged, socially responsible citizens of the world through an academically rigorous, interdisciplinary liberal arts education emphasizing social justice, intercultural understanding and environmental sensitivity." Middlebury College strives to engage "students' capacity for rigorous analysis and independent thought within a wide range of disciplines and endeavors, and to cultivate the intellectual, creative, physical, ethical, and social qualities essential for leadership in a rapidly changing global community." In its mission statement, St. Olaf College challenges students to become "responsible and knowledgeable citizens of the world." Earlham College "stresses global education, peaceful resolution of conflict, equality of persons, and high moral standards of personal conduct." The mission of Lewis & Clark College is to enable students to pursue "the aims of all liberal learning: to seek knowledge for its own sake and to prepare for civic leadership." And finally our own institution, Kalamazoo College, seeks "to prepare its graduates to better understand, live successfully within, and provide enlightened leadership to a richly diverse and increasingly complex world." These stand in contrast to what Meacham and Gaff found in their analysis of mission statements from 331 highly ranked colleges and universities (not just liberal arts colleges) where only about one-third included some aspect of values, character, or civic engagement (Hersh & Schneider, 2005, p. 8).

While many modern liberal arts colleges embrace certain religious values in their missions, this does not detract from their overall goal of educating engaged citizens. Liberal education has always been about values since its origins in ancient Greece. It is a peculiar education that "makes the person competent, not merely to know or do, but also, and indeed chiefly, to be" (Van Doren, 1959, p. 67). It is a kind of "whole person" education almost exclusively located in an American environment. In the 21st century, it is vital that this wholly educated person be at home in the world and ready to provide the kind of "enlightened leadership" called for in our colleges' mission statements.

Since its inception in 2002, the "Greater Expectations" project of the Association of American Colleges and Universities (AAC&U, 2002) has sought to provide the type of reform that would reassert the place of the liberal arts in U.S. postsecondary education. It is worth mentioning that the report calls for an "empowered" type of liberal education that is engaged by "intentional" learners (p. xi). Among other things, the intentional learner will be able to communicate in a second language, learn about the products of many cultures and "interrelations within and among global and cross-cultural communities" (p. 23). In addition to these international and intercultural goals, the intentional learner described in the report is also to develop competencies for responsible personal actions and civic values (p. 23).

LIBERAL ARTS: FROM CITIZENSHIP EDUCATION TO GLOBAL CITIZENSHIP

Few would argue with the assertion that one of the most consistent goals of liberal education over the past two millennia has been the production of civically engaged citizens. In her seminal work on the liberal arts and world citizenship, *Cultivating Humanity: A Classical Defense of Reform in Liberal Education* (1997), Martha Nussbaum argues that at the center of education for citizenship in a diverse world should be an ability to negotiate difference:

> The present-day world is inescapably multicultural and multinational. Many of our most pressing problems require for their intelligent, cooperative solution a dialogue that brings together people from many different national and cultural and religious backgrounds. Even those issues that seem closest to home—issues, for example, about the structure of the family, the regulation of sexuality, the future of children—need to be approached with a broad historical and cross-cultural understanding. A graduate of a U.S. university or college ought to be the sort of citizen who can become an intelligent participant in debates involving these differences, whether professionally or simply as a voter, a juror, a friend. (p. 8)

Education for citizenship should be cooperative, multicultural, multinational, broadly historical, infused with cross-cultural understanding, and aware of and sensitive to difference. "The new emphasis on 'diversity' in college and university curricula is above all a way of grappling with the altered requirements of citizenship, an attempt to produce adults who can function as citizens not just of some local region or group but also, and more importantly, as citizens of a complex interlocking world" (p. 6). Nussbaum goes on to note that citizens of the world need not give up the local affiliations that so often enrich their lives. Rather we, like the ancient Stoics, should think of ourselves surrounded by a series of "concentric circles" (self; immediate family; extended family, neighbors or local group, city-dwellers, fellow countrymen, ethnic, religious, linguistic, historical, professional, gender identities, etc.) (p. 60). "Our task as citizens of the world, and as educators who prepare people to be citizens of the world, will be to 'draw the circles somehow towards the center,' making all human beings like our fellow city-dwellers" (p. 60–61).

When it comes to developing curricula that get students to see beyond their localities, not surprisingly Nussbaum notes that, "it is also very important for students to understand what it is like to see the world through the perspective of another language, an experience that quickly shows that human complexity and rationality are not the monopoly of a single linguistic community" (p. 62). This fits with what could be seen as her general goal for the curriculum: "education for world citizenship requires transcending the inclination of both students and educators to define themselves primarily in terms of local group loyalties and identities" (p. 67). Thus for Nussbaum, a liberal education becomes in a very tangible way, the cultivation of the capacity for students to recognize the humanity of the other and, having done so, to respond in a humane manner. By extending the citizenship franchise to include any number of identity groups, she is arguing against parochialism and xenophobia. However, this very broad definition does beg the question of the place of difference in this schema. Are we to make all humans "like our fellow city-dwellers" (p. 61) through accentuating the similarities or by accepting their differences?

In a series of articles in *Liberal Education* and in their AAC&U report *Globalizing Knowledge* (1999), Grant Cornwell and Eve Stoddard have considered how a liberal arts education can foster global citizenship. Drawing on the work of Nussbaum and others, they argue that

> The work of liberal education is, on the one hand, to create citizens who have the ability to move easily among different cultures, who give the benefit of the doubt to diverse ways of thinking, who go beyond applying their own labels and categories to practices which seem strange, and who seek out the common humanity in those whose beliefs and practices are different. It is, on the other hand, to create citizens who will be critical consumers of commodities, media reports, and economic policies, who will ask questions beyond that of individual or national self-interest when they assess the equity of economic and political choices. (pp. 35–36)

They are firmly on Nussbaum's side when it comes to having students learn how to live in multiple communities (Nussbaum's concentric circles) and be able to appreciate others' points of view. They note that this involves an understanding and appreciation of perspectives. "If education for citizenship is indeed a goal of American higher education, students have to learn both how to locate themselves, how to think critically about their own positionalities, and how to engage various other perspectives on the issues they seek to understand and to judge" (Cornwell & Stoddard, 2006, p. 33).

Cornwell and Stoddard see education for and in perspective as involving more than changes to the on-campus curriculum. Students and faculty will need to venture outside their comfort zones and encounter different communities firsthand. Through those encounters they will begin to develop the important skills of a global citizen.

> The curriculum can represent diverse points of view, but that is not enough. Precisely because the world looks different from different vantage points, the students and faculty who comprise a campus need to have different life experiences and different social locations that they can bring to the table in a collaborative or dialogic process of knowledge creation. They

also need to get outside the campus, to gather perspectives from the local communities, the nation, and from other parts of the world, and then to subject those triangulations to interpretation and evaluation. (2006, p. 33)

For the modern curriculum with global citizenship as its goal, of course this means study abroad. However, like all experiential endeavors, one gets better with practice. For some that may mean multiple study abroad sojourns. For others, study abroad may be preceded with a service–learning or internship experience. Three elements are needed in order for these experiences to prepare the student for study abroad: the experience (1) must be intentional; (2) must include some form of structured reflection; and (3) must provide for intensive contact with a group or culture different than the student's own. Like any pedagogical method, the mode of learning experientially can be taught and must be internalized before students will achieve the greatest progress. Particularly if we are to have students and faculty venturing outside their academic and personal "comfort zones," we will need to ensure that they have the proper tools to make sense of their experiences.

FROM THE IDEA OF GLOBAL COMPETENCE TO GLOBAL CITIZENSHIP

In the wide variety of the various liberal arts curricula (and mission statements) we see the specifics of how individual colleges have chosen to address the goal of global citizenship. Some take a more direct approach, while others are more indirect. Some institutions have a long history of educating for world citizenship; others have come to this more recently. In each instance, however, the fundamental question remains the same: How do we get students to become both rooted in and unrooted from their localities? How do we get students to acknowledge their intersections with the larger world and the peoples and persons living within it? To think of themselves as both/and—both a citizen of a local community and also a member of a global one as well?

Over the years, numerous scholars have proposed various curricular goals for education for world citizenship. Among the first in the recent era was Robert Hanvey (1976). Here Hanvey proposes five dimensions of a global perspective.

1. Perspective Consciousness: the recognition or awareness on the part of the individual that he or she has a view of the world that is not universally shared.... (p. 4)
2. State of Planet Awareness: awareness of prevailing world conditions and developments, including emergent conditions and trends.... (p. 6)
3. Cross-cultural Awareness: awareness of the diversity of ideas and practices to be found in human societies around the world, of how such ideas and practices compare, and including some limited recognition of how the ideas and ways of one's own society might be viewed from other vantage points. (p. 9)
4. Knowledge of Global Dynamics: some modes of comprehension of key traits and mechanisms of the world system, with emphasis on theories and concepts that may increase intelligent consciousness of global change. (p. 16)
5. Awareness of Human Choices: some awareness of the problems of choice confronting individuals, nations, and the human species as consciousness and knowledge of the global system expands. (p. 28)

Hanvey's ideas continued to find support through the 1990s in the work of scholars such as McCarthy (1998, p. 68) and Tonkin (1994, p. 179).

Nussbaum's goals of both a local and global point of view as well as Cornwell and Stoddard's argument for citizens who can move among different cultures are similar to each other as well as to Hanvey's goals. Further similarities among global competence goals are seen in Cornwell and Stoddard's four interrelated goals for undergraduate students:

1. Understanding diverse cultures and understanding cultures as diverse;
2. Developing intercultural skills (through second language study; intercultural experiential learning; college campuses as intercultural laboratories; study abroad; service learning);
3. Understanding global processes;
4. Preparing for citizenship, both local and global (1999, p. 21).

The Global Competence project came into its own in 1988 with the publication by the Council on International Educational Exchange (CIEE) of "Educating for Global Competence" followed by *Educational Exchange and Global Competence* in 1994 (Lambert, 1994a). This latter volume was among the first to take on the definition of the term *global competence* and to offer insights into how programs of study, especially study abroad, contribute to the development of a globally competent student. Wilson lists five "attributes" of global competence: substantive knowledge, perceptual understanding, capacity for personal growth, ability to develop international interpersonal relationships, and ability to act as a cultural mediator (1994, pp. 42–44). Lambert sees five different components of global competence: knowledge, empathy, approval (of other peoples and cultures), foreign language competence, and task performance (in a different cultural setting) (1994b, p 12). Byram (1997) expanded the list to include, "Knowledge of others; knowledge of self; skills to interpret and relate; skills to discover and/or to interact; valuing others' values, beliefs, and behaviors; and relativizing one's self. Linguistic competence plays a key role" (p. 34). In her 2006 study, Deardorf noted that intercultural experts found Byram's definition of intercultural competence most acceptable, followed by those of Lambert (Deardorf, 2006, p. 248).

LANGUAGE SKILLS, GLOBAL COMPETENCE, AND GLOBAL CITIZENSHIP

Given the importance that Nussbaum and Cornwell and Stoddard place on perspective, especially understanding the perspective of others, it is easy to see why language learning is prominently featured in their objectives. While the curricular goals of global competence and global citizenship share many of the same attributes, education for global citizenship extends global competence by the addition of instilling in students a respect for and desire to connect with others different from themselves. "A liberal arts college or university that helps young people learn to speak in their own voices and to respect the voices of others will have done a great deal to produce thoughtful and potentially creative world citizens" (Nussbaum, 2004, p. 44). The ability to communicate across cultures and difference will be of fundamental importance to the global citizen—even more important than certain technical skills.

We are told that technical proficiency will one day become the only real passport needed by a citizen of the world. But such a passport will not be enough to flourish in the cultures to which it gives access. Communication skills, the ability to interact with others, histori-cal awareness, analytical abilities, the mastery of several languages, and the cross-cultural knowledge to hear our polyphonic planet are some of the most important tools that we can provide students. And it is equally important, in my view, that we teach them how to think about, and through, this new fluidity. (de Courtivron, p. 2000)

The importance of proficiency in a second or third language for those who aspire to global citi-zenship cannot be overemphasized. When viewed through the lens of their own language, societ-ies and even individuals reveal cultural nuances that are simply lost in translation. One claims citizenship of a locality by virtue of birth or by long-term residence and the gradual acquiring of local knowledge, customs, and language. And while it is impossible for a global citizen to have a command of all of the languages of the world, it is possible to develop an appreciation for the linguistic diversity of the world's peoples and begin to recognize those things that have special linguistic relevance to them.

A CURRICULUM FOR GLOBAL CITIZENSHIP

However, when it comes to the acquisition of these necessary cross-cultural skills and insights and the relevant knowledge, the curricula in question often consist of fragmented courses and experiences. Students are expected to achieve a certain technical skill level in various areas, such as a foreign language, international relations, or history, and perhaps study abroad, whereupon they can be sent off to practice in the world. Even the most carefully crafted set of international learning outcomes or lavishly funded international studies program won't ensure that students will emerge with the knowledge, skills, and attitudes that will make them engaged global citizens. Richard Hersh (1999) has lamented that a liberal arts education in general too often becomes an amalgam of disparate parts, courses, facts, and experiences, with nothing to tie it together; Patti McGill Peterson has similar worries about international education. Study abroad, foreign students, and area studies courses "do not in and of them themselves make for a worldly campus. All too often, they add up to merely a list of disconnected activities, lacking a coherent sense of purpose or a comprehensive vision of what it means to be educated" (2000, p. 3).

Looking at some of the curricula that list world or global citizenship among their outcomes, we see some not unexpected similarities: on-campus coursework in international studies, addi-tional coursework in related disciplines (foreign language, anthropology, political science, art, music, literature, history, etc.), study abroad, and a capstone seminar (e.g., Pitzer, Macalester, Middlebury). On other campuses, study abroad seems to be optional for the global or interna-tional studies major (cf. Rhodes College, Willamette University, or Earlham College which offers both language/study abroad and nonlanguage/nonstudy abroad tracks).

Study abroad, a capstone seminar, an internship, a service–learning course, any of these can provide the unifying vision to a curriculum for global citizenship. However, it is not enough merely to provide students with the opportunity to engage in these experiences. They must also have time to reflect, in writing or through discussion, about what they experienced and thus begin the process of translating the experience into learning (Kolb, 1984). The question may have been stated backwards. Perhaps we should not be considering whether (or how or the extent to which) study abroad fosters global citizenship, but rather the processes through which students learn (by experience and experiment) and test their engagement in various societal levels. This takes off from the old saw of "all politics are local." So is all citizenship—but it is possible to have citizenship acquired, honorary, or assumed in several groups, thus making it possible to belong to many localities.

THE LIBERAL ARTS, STUDY ABROAD, AND GLOBAL CITIZENSHIP

Educational psychologists tell us that learning proceeds from a sense of dislocation; so it is not surprising when Kiely (2005) asserts that "transformational learning" results from "high intensity dissonance" (p. 11). Students experience high intensity dissonance when they encounter a situation or relationship for which their knowledge is insufficient to help them interpret the new experience. Most learning situations provide some measure of dislocation and dissonance. Study abroad can be entirely dislocating. Students are removed from home and hearth and transported to somewhere unfamiliar. They are then left with the task of figuring out how things work in their new surroundings, ideally without offending too many of the local people. In the "figuring out" phase of their sojourns, students ideally accumulate experiences that will become the stuff of their education for global citizenship. They make mistakes. They react badly. They make linguistic and cultural faux pas. They become frustrated. They want to quit and go home. They may retreat from the host culture into a bar-based American student culture where English is king and the Knicks are on TV. Engle and Engle decry the magical thinking of American international educators who believe that their students will make progress interculturally, linguistically, and personally just by being somewhere else (2003, pp. 26–27). But through their mistakes and cultural experiments, American students are learning something while abroad. The question is what?

The study abroad experience is vastly different from what it was 30 or 40 years ago. The prevalence today of the ATM, Golden Arches, the Gap, Citi Bank, and other multinational corporations even in some of the most remote locations can lead students to the conclusion that we're not so different after all. And while there are genuine differences, as Engle and Engle note, "these differences are less visible to the unguided or unprepared, and it has without doubt become considerably easier to skate smoothly above them" (p. 27). Benjamin Barber has dubbed this transformation of modern life that of "McWorld as Theme Park" (1995, p. 128). Both of these issues are not unique to liberal arts colleges. Indeed, as Engle and Engle argue they may be more dependent on program design than anything else (pp. 33–36). If a study abroad program is to foster global citizenship, defined for now using Cornwell and Stoddard's goals (understanding diverse cultures and understanding cultures as diverse; developing intercultural skills; understanding global processes; preparing for citizenship, both local and global), there needs to be a curricular intervention or program structure that will lead students past superficial contact with the host culture into a deeper, more meaningful cultural experience. For Earlham College (Indiana) that is the ethnographic project; for Kalamazoo College (Michigan), it is the Integrative Cultural Research Project (ICRP).

EARLHAM COLLEGE'S ETHNOGRAPHY PROJECT

A small college of some 1,200 students, Earlham has a tradition of study abroad that dates from the late 1950s. The ethnographic project was introduced into certain Earlham faculty-led programs in the late 1970s to enhance learning during study abroad, provide avenues for students to gain insights into the complex societies where they were studying, and strengthen the connection between on- and off-campus learning (Jurasek, Howard, & O'Maley, 1996). Since that time, the field study ethnography has evolved. The ethnographies represent "an intensified experience by which students develop insights through an ongoing reflective and interactive process" (pp. 24–25). The projects are completed in conjunction with a field studies course or internship placement and are a significant component of the overall academic program abroad. Students receive instruction in participant observation techniques, make field notes, and keep a reflective journal of their experiences. During the project, students have regular meetings and feedback with a project supervisor or course instructor during which they can ask questions about their placements, process their field notes, and discuss what they have experienced. The program leaders inoculate the students to the challenging aspects of the project and stress that it is a multilevel process with several key moments of epiphany. During the journey there may be bumps, bruises, emotional highs and lows, but students have to figure out strategies to move forward. The paper and presentation are the culminating moments in the process.

A review of student learning from Earlham study abroad programs with ethnographic projects found that students demonstrated

- An enriched language experience
- Insight into the complexity of cultures and societies
- Involvement and investment in the cultural learning process
- Meaningful interaction with members of other cultures
- Increased flexibility of thought, reflection, and self-reflection. (Jurasek et al., 1996, p. 24)

Field study placements have included sites such as an integrated school and a large reconciliation center in Northern Ireland; a veterinarian or preschool in Cuautla, Mexico; a midwifery clinic or house construction in Tanzania. Here

> students observe, participate, and engage in meaningful conversations in which the complexities and contradictions of individuals and cultures are constantly in play on both sides—which is so critical in cultural interactions. Views and perspectives must constantly be refined for understanding to occur. (p. 29)

Students and faculty report that the projects are: "often the most rewarding and meaningful components of the students' experience abroad, as well as the most difficult and the most challenging" (p. 29).

Over time, the field study and ethnographic projects have taken on different characteristics as they have adapted to the realities of the programs. For example, the goal of the Earlham program in Northern Ireland is to increase students' understanding of the complexities of the conflict and the peace process in Northern Ireland and to use the knowledge gained to analyze and to increase understanding of conflict in their own and other societies. The supervised field study is a significant component of this program. Resident director Mervyn Love states, "each placement is relevant to the idea of promoting either cross-community engagement or some aspect of peace and reconciliation work" (Love, 2007). This can create a very powerful learning experience as a 2007 participant wrote in an evaluation, "the cross-community aspect was the most meaningful for me. To see two divided peoples come together to put their experiences into art in an effort to bridge the gap years of segregation has created was astoundingly moving." The field studies are designed to bring the different components of the program together in new ways. "The placement tied together all the separate aspects of the program into one experience where every part was represented but not overwhelming. It was a wonderful capstone experience" (student evaluation from 2007 program).

In her 2002 article, "Letter from the Editor: The Critical Pedagogy of Ethnography in the Border Studies Program," Joanna Swanger further describes the function and intended outcomes of ethnography in another one of Earlham's off-campus programs. As described in this article, the Border Studies program is located in Ciudad Juárez and El Paso, with students living in homestays and taking classes in both cities. Like the other study abroad programs, Border Studies includes a field study/internship with an ethnographic aspect. The idea is not "to create professional ethnographers, but rather to employ ethnography as a pedagogical tool to help students develop more effective ways of seeing other cultures as well as their own" (p. 1). Among the many topics considered by the program is globalization and its effects on the U.S. and Mexican sides of the border.

> Because it is concerned with understanding the processes referred to in shorthand as "globalization," the Border Studies Program takes as its point of departure the pedagogical desire to link knowledge, social responsibility, and collective action toward greater social justice. The program attempts to transform the worldviews of students by getting them to think critically about where they stand in relation to the world around them. It also attempts to empower them so that they can move beyond the role that society dictates is most appropriate for us: that of passive consumer. (p. 2)

As a high-dissonance learning opportunity, ethnography has the potential to be a powerful and transformative learning experience for students. Through their field notes and reflective journals, students maintain a "dialogue" with subjects of their ethnographies. In writing about their field experiences students are asked to "(1) pay attention to the language used by 'insiders' and respect this language as descriptive of their reality; (2) continue to ask *why* the situation they are analyzing is the way it is and try to determine in detail how they arrived at their conclusions; and (3) continue to be aware of the effects of their presence and try to determine how their presence might be affecting the dynamics of the field-study setting." Given the reflective and self-reflective nature of the ethnographies, it is little wonder that stereotypes are quickly tackled. Students develop an "empathic understanding" of a culture (p. 3).

On the U.S.–Mexico border, students participated in field studies in hospitals, midwifery clinics, law offices and legal aid, women's shelters, homeless shelters, environmental agencies, schools, labor organizations, human rights organizations, youth shelters, all organizations that work directly with issues of the border, and, as one student said, "all inclined to shelter the human family in some capacity." A student from the 2007 Border Studies program gives some insights into her field study within the context of the program as a whole:

> I am only beginning to realize how deeply the Border Studies program affected my life. I left that place, the Border, with all its contradictions and confrontations, and could not imagine how I would metabolize all that I had seen and experienced. I worked in a detention center where I met and worked with scores of kids who had just been deported from the U.S.... What lies on the border is a complicated world filled with questions, some answers, privilege, history and a future that is yet to be determined. What do I understand to be my experience on the Border? Well, it's not over yet. (Leigh, 2008)

KALAMAZOO COLLEGE'S INTEGRATIVE CULTURAL RESEARCH PROJECT (ICRP)

Kalamazoo College is a liberal arts college with 1,340 students and 105 faculty located in southwest Michigan. The College offers an experience-rich curriculum called the K-Plan that combines rigorous coursework in the liberal arts with experiential education components. Every student is required to achieve intermediate proficiency in a foreign language, pass comprehensive examinations in the major, and complete a senior individualized project. Over 80% of Kalamazoo students, including 80% of science majors, participate in an intensive study abroad program. Most students study abroad for 6 months in one of our 45 programs in 25 countries around the world. The majority of Kalamazoo students (about 60%) also participate in service–learning projects in the local community, and an equal number complete at least one career internship or externship.

The Kalamazoo ICRP began in the mid-1990s as an ethnography-type project following the Earlham model. It was introduced for many of the same reasons that were cited at Earlham. We were looking for a way to have our students engage the local culture in a more meaningful fashion and make greater use of their developing language skills, to name just two goals. Students are required to keep a field journal, meet at regular intervals with the project supervisor, and prepare and present a reflective paper at the end of the project. As the ICRPs have developed over the years, they continue to emphasize hands-on interaction with local communities, groups, agencies, and organizations. The final written projects, however, are no longer ethnographic in nature. Instead emphasis is placed on understanding how and where the activity at the project site is located in a larger cultural context. The learning outcomes we strive for in the ICRP include:

- Improved use of the target language
- Increased understanding of the local culture
- Firsthand experience with a facet of everyday life in the host culture
- Meaningful interaction with local people
- Improved analytical and problem-solving skills

Of particular importance in the execution of the ICRP is that students are not to be in charge of activities in which they are involved. They are to be participants, not directors. Students are there to learn how to work with local people on local projects that meet local needs using local resources in a locally responsible manner. During their orientation to the project, students are taught the DIVE observation methodology:

- **D**escribe in value neutral terms.
- **I**nterpret what is happening within the local context.
- **V**erify your interpretation with a local person.
- **E**valuate how well it seems to be working within the local context.

The ICRP deliberately tries to steer students away from comparisons between their local placements and what they know from home. Rather we encourage them to invest their energy into trying to understand what is going on around them in their new culture, while avoiding superficialities and stereotypes.

For their final ICRP reflective paper, students are asked to consider a number of guiding questions:

- What is the main activity of the agency or organization? What is produced?
- What are the goals and mission of the organization?
- Where does this particular organization stand in relation to similar ones in the city? In the region? In the state? In the country?
- Whom does this organization serve?
- How do people view this organization and its mission?
- What problems and tasks are to be accomplished?
- How is this done?
- How successful is the organization?
- What are the basic skills and knowledge needed to work for this organization?
- Describe a typical day or week in the organization?
- What were your responsibilities?
- What contribution did you make to help the organization achieve its goals?

As with the Earlham ethnography project, the focus here is to understand the activity at the project site from the point of view of the local participants. By breaking down stereotypes through the use of the DIVE methodology and by using authentic descriptive language, students gain insight into local perspectives on this small slice of daily local life. The need for students to understand first what is happening at their ICRP placements, and second to look for connections between those placements and the broader host society are further reasons why the ICRP projects do not ask students for comparisons with their home culture.

The ICRP experience, as described by students Hannah and Tania, illustrates both the concentric circles of Nussbaum and the importance of linguistic competence. Hannah and Tania began their college career at Kalamazoo in a first year seminar titled, "Commitments." The professor designed this course to help students understand the importance of local issues and how to make a "commitment" to a local community. For one of their class projects, the students proposed examining the local food movement in Kalamazoo and to study the feasibility of supplying local food to the cafeteria. As a result of their efforts, cafeteria management agreed to use some local suppliers to the extent possible. In their second year, Hannah and Tania became more involved in cocurricular service—learning projects. Hannah worked in a juvenile home as a youth mediator, designing a program to help local youth talk to each other in a meaningful, nonviolent manner. Eventually she gathered additional students to serve as volunteers and began a formal cocurricular project that continues, allowing Kalamazoo students to work with the organization.

Both Hannah and Tania decided to study abroad during their junior year. They intentionally selected a program including social justice and sustainability issues as part of the curriculum. While studying at the International Sustainable Development Studies Institute in Chiang Mai, Thailand, both students worked with Burmese immigrants as part of their ICRP project. In working with the local Burmese groups, the students became very interested in how they could offer sustainable and meaningful support to the organization. How could they demonstrate a "commitment" to this group? The students asked what skills they needed to develop? The reply from the locals was that they needed to become proficient in grant writing to help attract funding. As part of working to achieve this goal upon return to the United States, both students enrolled in an intensive language program to learn Burmese. They completed a joint senior thesis project examining leadership in grass-roots organizations. Before they graduated, they, along with a third student, applied for and received $10,000 from a national foundation to travel to northern Thailand to work with local agencies in providing mosquito nets and malaria-prevention education to internally displaced people along the Thai–Burma border. In describing this journey that started with the first year seminar, both students describe how they adjusted their presumed level of knowledge with each new experience, both at home and in Thailand, moving beyond assumptions by learning the perspective of the other.

Another student, Laura, also describes her on-campus coursework as an important component of her pathway between international and domestic issues particular to migrant communities. Laura knew she wanted to use her Spanish skills and she knew she wanted to work with individuals who were disenfranchised from the local community. After her first year of college, she lived in Florida for a summer as a volunteer in a program that provided support services for seafarers coming into port. This population often needs medical services or translation assistance. Her job was first to listen, then assist. The next summer she traveled to south Texas to volunteer for an organization providing legal assistance to migrant farm workers.

During her junior year, she studied abroad in Quito, Ecuador and worked at a day shelter for "street grandmothers" for her ICRP. She explains her work with migrant and indigent populations as an obligation she feels as an engaged citizen, whether that is working with homeless populations in Kalamazoo or in Quito, Ecuador. As a sociology and anthropology major, she describes her understanding of the relationship between the academic and the experiential in this way: The academic program has given her theoretical knowledge of the issues but it is the experiential opportunities, through service–learning coursework, cocurricular service–learning, and study abroad that has helped her see the "how" or the practical applications of the knowledge. When she is involved in projects or organizations, she is better informed about "what" questions she should be asking, by asking different questions or exploring more of the academic side, this will change "how" she continues to approach the issues. She discusses further how her work continues to focus on recognizing the disparities between individuals and their relationship with the surrounding community.

In explaining their courses and activities, all three of these students emphasized that on-campus coursework and involvement in experiential programs, such as service-learning, helped them to develop both an "ability to fail" and a skill set to navigate unknown environments. Hannah, Tania, and Laura also described how their idea of citizenship, whether global or local, became informed by the idea of involvement and commitment, in a locally appropriate way (as described by the locals) and as indicated by the organizations and individuals involved. Having multiple opportunities to explore unscripted situations including sensitive socioeconomic issues, these students described becoming better at understanding what involvement in the local community truly means. These tools and attitudes served them well when they met the "dissonance" described by Kiely.

The power of these projects in both the Earlham and Kalamazoo study abroad programs lies in the dual function of description and reflection. We know from the experiential learning theory of David Kolb, that "learning, the creation of knowledge and meaning, occurs through the active extension and grounding of ideas *and* experiences in the external world and through internal reflection about the attributes of these experiences and ideas" (Kolb, 1984, p. 52). Description helps the students understand what is going on around them and reflects what is going on within.

> Living, learning, and working alongside people from the host culture in an attempt to understand a setting enhances the willingness to reserve judgment, to test hypotheses, and to reevaluate what one has observed. Most important, this change in the way one perceives a microculture also affects the way students deal with the entire experience abroad. Rather than defensively shying away from meaningful encounters with members of the culture,

this feeling of connectedness to the other, developed during the ethnography, makes study abroad a much deeper experience than simply inhabiting the space of that culture. (Jurasek et al., 1996, p. 43)

Both the Kalamazoo College ICRP and the Earlham ethnography projects lead students to what Hanvey has called "perspective consciousness," a recognition of other worldviews. By having the students focus much of their efforts on describing the activities of their placement sites, the paper becomes what Stoddard and Cornwell (2003) have termed a "peripheral vision," a story told from a different perspective. In their article of the same name, Stoddard and Cornwell advance a concept of global citizens who deliberately seek multiple points of view and perspectives when trying to determine their stance on issues.

The chief epistemological virtue here is the capacity to listen for and across differences. Second in line is a disposition not to meet differences with a desire to win, to have one's own point of view triumph over others, but instead to meet differences as a project, a sign that power and point of view are likely in play. Intercultural communication skills emerge by this analysis not simply as useful in getting by in a diverse world, but as capacities essential to build a complex account of what is the case and what it is important to do. Filling out the meaning of responsible global citizenship is necessarily a collaborative process, and the more points of view that are brought into triangulation, the more confidence one can have about where one is standing. (pp. 50–51)

GLOBAL CITIZENSHIP: AT HOME IN THE WORLD

As we have seen, the project of education for citizenship is closely aligned with that of a liberal arts education. It becomes education for global citizenship when attention is given to internationalizing the outcomes of that liberal education in such a way that graduates will have had significant international and intercultural experiences in and out of the classroom. Study abroad is often seen as the culminating intercultural experience, after which students are able to demonstrate all of the attributes of a global citizen. Unfortunately, that is rarely the case.

In a provocative commentary with the title, "American Students Abroad Can't Be 'Global Citizens'," 2007 Wesleyan University graduate Talya Zemach-Bersin describes her semester abroad in India and Nepal. Throughout her program she wrestled with the discrepancy between program rhetoric and personal perceptions. "Caught between a study-abroad education that demanded that I 'fit in,' and an experiential reality that forced me to think critically about what it means to be an American abroad, I found I had not been prepared with the necessary tools to fully engage with, and learn from my experiences" (2008, p. A34). The tools she is searching for are to be found in Nussbaum's *Cultivating Humanity*, Stoddard and Cornwell's "Peripheral Visions," Hanvey's perspectives, and the field notes and final paper of the Earlham ethnography and Kalamazoo ICRP. Zemach-Bersin reaches a similar conclusion when she acknowledges the need for "critical discussions about the ways in which my classmates and I were interacting with our surroundings…" (p. A34). Absent the opportunity for structured reflection as part of the experience abroad, she returned home "confused and unable to respond to the flood of questions" about her time abroad. And without the opportunity for structured reflection upon her return, she found herself confronted with all of the important questions:

> Why had we not analyzed race, identity, and privilege when those factors were informing every one of our interactions? Why was there never a discussion about commodification when our relationships with host families were built on a commodified relationship? Wasn't a history of colonialism and contemporary imperialism affecting the majority of our experiences and influencing how host nationals viewed us? Was there nothing to be said about the power dynamics of claiming global citizenship? (p. A34)

And there was no forum for discussing responses to these questions.

In a response to Zemach-Bersin, Erin Costello (2008) argues that if the program did not initiate the discussions she sought, then she ought to have done so herself. "Study and travel abroad is like anything else in life: You get out of it what you put into it." For Costello, the special power of her experience abroad came from the relationships she was able to forge through her ability to use the language to access the local culture.

> I was able to easily assimilate into Spanish culture, but the international dialogue between local peoples everywhere and foreign students is ongoing; students simply need to go out of their comfort zones, find it, and join the conversation. I had to work a little harder to really see what it was like to be an everyday Spaniard, instead of an everyday American in Spain. That work paid off and allowed me to have a life-changing, perspective-shattering experience as a student abroad. (p. A55)

Costello's experience is that of a student who has been able to move from one locality to another, to join more than one conversation, and to gain another peripheral vision.

Zemach-Bersin's experience underscores the dangers of assuming a causal relationship between study abroad participation and global citizenship. Moreover, her experiences show the importance of creating intentional learning structures that encourage students to go out of their comfort zones and face cognitive dissonance and that then engaging them in structured reflection so that they can transform dissonant elements into profound learning experiences. At its best, study abroad is an experience of "intense dissonance and dislocation" (Kiely, 2005) that requires participants to construct a new worldview. For traditional age students (i.e., 20-year-olds), that project occurs concomitantly with their own age-related inquiries into identity (Chickering & Reisser, 1993). Thus it is not surprising that Zemach-Bersin should include identity among the questions that arose while she was overseas. The question of identity also underlies the challenge of stereotypes, which when exposed, can lead to fruitful discussions of power, privilege, and race (Swanger, 2002).

Study abroad is not an inoculation that one gets and which immediately confers global citizenship. Nussbaum, Cornwell and Stoddard, and others have noted that citizenship in general and global citizenship in particular are habits of mind and heart that are developed over time. Study abroad offers one, for many U.S. students a first, intensive encounter with another culture and perspective. However, simply showing up on a study abroad program should not be enough. As Zemach-Bersin's example illustrates, simply participating in a program abroad is insufficient for achieving a goal of global citizenship. She was left with too many questions and too many unreflected observations. Without an opportunity for intensive integrative cultural experiences coupled with structured reflection, the "dissonance" of the study abroad situation can overwhelm the participant, causing some to retreat into stereotypes, others into the Westernized (often bar-based) culture present in most larger cities around the world, and a few, like Zemach-Bersin, into frustration and anger. Students who wrestle with dissonance of study abroad in the context of a program that has equipped them with tools of observation and analysis and has provided them with regular opportunities for reflection on what they are experiencing will often find that they move more quickly through the stages of frustration to meaning making and finally to an understanding of their surroundings and their own place in them.

Institutions wishing to train future global citizens must also be willing to create learning experiences that challenge students (both locally and internationally) to learn different perspectives while at the same time gaining a better perspective of themselves as individual cultural beings. Nor should they neglect the basics of an education for global citizenship. There should be a rigorous on-campus program that promotes: understanding diverse cultures and understanding cultures as diverse; developing intercultural skills; understanding global processes; preparing for citizenship, both local and global. A study abroad program that is integrated into an on-campus curriculum and that also seeks to integrate and support students in new intercultural settings will do much to produce global citizens who are at home in the world.

REFERENCES

Association of American Colleges and Universities (AAC&U). (2002). *Greater expectations: A new vision for learning as a nation goes to College*. Washington, DC: Author.

Barber, B. R. (1995). *Jihad vs. McWorld*. New York: Ballantine Books.

Bhandari, R., & Chow, P. (2008). *Open Doors 2007: Report on international educational exchange*. New York: Institute of International Education.

Byram, M. (1997). *Teaching and assessing intercultural communicative competence*. Clevedon, UK: Multilingual Matters.

Chickering, A. W., & Reisser, L. (1993). *Education and identity*. San Francisco: Jossey-Bass.

Cornwell, G. H., & Stoddard, E. W. (1999). *Globalizing knowledge: Connecting international and intercultural studies*. Washington, DC: Association of American Colleges and Universities.

Cornwell, G. H., & Stoddard, E. W. (2006). Freedom, diversity, and global citizenship. *Liberal Education, 92*(2), 26–33.

Costello, E. (2008, April 18). Students' responsibility for education abroad. *Chronicle of Higher Education, 54*(35), A55.

Deardorff, D. K. (2006). Identification and assessment of intercultural competence as a student outcome of internationalization. *Journal of Studies in International Education, 10*, 241–266.

De Courtivron, I. (2000, July 7). Educating the global student, whose identity is always a matter of choice. *Chronicle of Higher Education, 46*(45), B4.

Engle, J., & Engle, L. (2003). Neither international nor educative: Study abroad in the time of globalization. In W. Grünzweig & N. Rinehart (Eds.), *Rockin' in red square* (pp. 25–39). Münster, Germany: LIT Verlag.

Hanvey, R. G. (1976). *An attainable global perspective*. New York: The American Forum for Global Education.

Hersh, R. H. (1999). Generating ideals and transforming lives: A contemporary case for the residential liberal arts college. *Daedalus, 128*(1), 173–194.

Hersh, R. H., & Schneider, C. G. (2005). Fostering personal and social responsibility on college and university campuses. *Liberal Education, 91*(3–4), 6–13.

Jurasek, R., Howard, L., & O'Maley P. (1996). Ethnographic learning while studying abroad. *Frontiers: The Interdisciplinary Journal of Study Abroad, 2*(1), 23–44.

Kiely, R. (2005). A transformative learning model for service-learning: A longitudinal case study. *Michigan Journal of Community Service Learning, 12*(1), 5–22.

Kolb, D. (1984). *Experiential learning*. Englewood Cliffs, NJ: Prentice-Hall.

Lambert, R. D. (Ed.). (1994a). *Educational exchange and global competence*. New York: Council on International Educational Exchange.

Lambert, R. D. (1994b). Parsing the concept of global competence. In R. D. Lambert (Ed.), *Educational exchange and global competence* (pp. 11–23). New York: Council on International Educational Exchange.

Leigh, G. (2008). Participant profiles. Retrieved August 12, 2008 from http://www.earlham.edu/~borders/participants/index.html

Love, M. (2007). *Program materials: Northern Ireland*. Richmond, IN: Earlham College.

McCarthy, J. S. (1998). Continuing and emerging national needs for the internationalization of undergraduate education. In J. N. Hawkins, C. M. Haro, M. A. Kazanjian, G. W. Merkx, & D. Wiley (Eds.), *International education in the new global era: Proceedings of a national policy conference on the higher education act, title VI, and Fulbright-Hays programs* (pp. 65–75). Los Angeles: International Studies and Overseas Programs, University of California Los Angeles..

Nussbaum, M. (1997). *Cultivating humanity: A classical defense of reform in liberal education.* Cambridge, MA: Harvard University Press.

Nussbaum, M. (2004). Liberal education and global community. *Liberal Education, 90* (1), 42–47.

Peterson, P. McG. (2000). The worthy goal of a worldly faculty. *Peer Review, 3*(1), 3–7.

Stoddard, E. W., & Cornwell, G. H. (2003). Peripheral visions: Towards a geoethics of citizenship. *Liberal Education, 89*(3), 44–51.

Swanger, J. (2002). Letter from the editor: The critical pedagogy of ethnography in the border studies program. *International Journal of Qualitative Studies in Education, 16*(1), 1–10.

Tonkin, H. (1994). Higher education and global competence: Diversity, technology, global resources. In R. D. Lambert (Ed.), *Educational exchange and global competence* (pp. 179–185). New York: Council on International Educational Exchange.

Van Doren, M. (1959). *Liberal education.* Boston. Beacon Press.

Wilson, A. (1994). The attributes and tasks of global competence. In R. D. Lambert (Ed.), *Educational exchange and global competence* (pp 37–50). New York: Council on International Educational Exchange.

Zemach-Bersin, T. (2008, March 7). American students abroad can't be global citizens. *Chronicle of Higher Education, 54*(26), A34.

Chapter 9

Study Abroad and Nursing

From Cultural to Global Competence

Connie Currier, James Lucas, and Denise Saint Arnault
Michigan State University

The nursing profession educates its members to be culturally competent so they will be capable of providing high quality, culturally appropriate health care. A number of pedagogical methods are used in nursing to teach cultural competence, including study abroad. While cultural competence is an important indicator of competence in clinical practice, *global competence* is a broader concept that can prepare nurses to work, not only in multicultural settings in the United States, but internationally as well. Nursing and health care are global issues that require an awareness of the complex cultural, social, political, and economic interrelationships within and between nations, and the moral obligations that unite us as a world community. With this knowledge and contextual understanding, a globally competent nurse will have a more holistic perspective of the health beliefs and practices of an individual from another country/culture, and as a result will be better prepared to provide culturally appropriate health care in any setting. Although study abroad is a means to teach cultural competence, and can be a vehicle for teaching global competence as well, we know very little about how, or to what extent study abroad affects the clinical practice of nurses in the field, or to what extent changes in clinical practice affect patient outcomes.

By 2050, it is expected that Hispanics and minority racial groups (including non-Hispanic Blacks, Asians, and American Indians) will account for almost half of the U.S. population (Passel & Cohn, 2008). Currently, immigrants make up approximately 12% of the U.S. population—up from a low of about 5% in 1970 (Swanbrow, 2006). Eighteen percent of American households speak a language other than English (Shin & Bruno, 2003). Racial and ethnic disparities in health persist in the United States and many parts of the health care system, including health insurance plans, patients, and health care providers, contribute to these disparities (Smedley, Stith, & Nelson, 2003).

The nursing workforce is not keeping pace with the demographic changes in the U.S. population, and minorities are underrepresented in the nursing workforce. There are "too few...minority nurses available to serve an increasing minority population" (Brown & Marshall, 2008, p. 21). In a survey of the racial and ethnic distribution of the nursing workforce conducted by the U.S. Department of Health and Human Services (HRSA) in 2000, 86.6% of registered nurses (RNs) were White (non-Hispanic), whereas 69.1% of the general population was White (non-Hispanic); approximately 12% of RNs were minorities, and approximately 29% of the general population was White (non-Hispanic) (HRSA, 2006).

International recruitment of nurses and nurse migration may influence the diversity and training needs of the U.S. nursing workforce. The nursing shortage in the United States has led to recruitment of nurses from less developed countries. Migration is occurring from countries such as India, Korea, and the Philippines, countries with an apparent oversupply of nurses (Rosenko-etter & Nardi, 2007). The number of foreign-trained nurses entering the U.S. workforce nearly doubled between 1990 and 2000, increasing from 8.8% to 15.3% (Polka, Sochalski, Aiken, & Cooper, 2007). This influx of foreign nurses has implications for employers who:

> …must be sensitive to cultural values and practices that could affect the foreign nurse's abil-ity to practice safely as well as [have an] impact on existing staff. Local professional staff and the immigrating nurse must receive diversity training if foreign nurses are to assimilate into a collaborative health care environment. (Rosenkoetter & Nardi, 2007, p. 311)

The concept of global health is now more commonly used in the nursing literature than during previous periods because of events with global implications such as a possible outbreak of pan-demic avian flu, and disasters such as the 2004 Indian Ocean tsunami which killed over 350,000 people. This has been accompanied by a growing recognition in nursing that "international social, political, economic, environmental, and cultural issues affect health and health care around the world" (Carlton, Ryan, Ali, & Kelsey, 2007, p. 124).

Nurses represent the largest group of providers in the health care workforce worldwide, and they are likely to be among the first responders in a global health crisis (WHO, 2006). Under these circumstances, all nurses will need to possess the ability to work across cultures—both domestic and global, and use a systems approach to understanding the broader context within which health problems take place.

To provide the very best health care to an increasingly diverse population, the nursing pro-fession has, until now, focused on developing "culturally competent" nurses (de Leon Sianz & Meleis, 2007; Gonczi, 1994; Liu, Pothiban, Lu, & Khamphonsiri, 2000). Although no univer-sally accepted definition of cultural competence exists, the term generally refers to a profession-al's ability to identify, understand, appreciate, and act upon cultural factors in resolving a human health need (de Leon Sianz & Meleis, 2007; Green, 1989, 1995). While cultural competence is a critical indicator of competence for the nursing profession; it is important that the profession broaden its objectives and educate nurses not only for *cultural competence*, but *global competence* for the purpose of developing *global citizens*.

Within higher education, the events of September 11, 2001 have prompted a greater empha-sis on the development of *global competence* and *global citizenship*. Global competence has been framed in such a way that "global" encompasses a broader perspective than "cultural" competence (Hunter, 2004). As with *cultural competence*, *global competence* has no unifying or singular defini-tion, yet the term is frequently described in terms of the knowledge, attitudes, and skills required by today's professional to live and work in an increasingly "flat" world (Friedman, 2005; Green & Olson, 2003). A globally competent person:

> …demonstrates knowledge of world geography, conditions, and events [and] has an aware-ness of the complexity and interdependency of world issues and events and an understanding of the historical forces that have shaped the current world system. In terms of attitudes, a globally competent person has a sensitivity and respect for personal and cultural differ-ences [and] is capable of empathy and can handle ambiguity and unfamiliarity. Regarding skills, a globally competent person has critical thinking and comparative skills, including the ability to think creatively and integrate knowledge. Also, it is a person who has effective

communications skills including an understanding of intercultural communication concepts. (Green & Olson, 2003)

Some authors also see global competence as a prerequisite for global *citizenship,* which requires that an individual have a sense of responsibility and commitment to global values as a member of the world community (Heilman, 2007).

In response to the need to develop global citizens and educate for global competence, higher education has begun to emphasize campus internationalization (Green & Olson, 2003). This process includes an array of programs and experiences for students, including curricular options such as language and internationally based majors, internships, service learning, and most prominently study abroad. According to the data, study abroad represents a unique and powerful way to promote learning (Carlson, Burn, Useem, & Yachimowicz, 1990; Dwyer & Peters, 2004; Garraty, Kemperer, & Taylor, 1981; Kauffmann, Martin, & Weaver, 1992; Opper, Teichler, & Carlson, 1990). Although other programs, such as interaction with international students or language instruction, can improve global knowledge and understanding, research shows that the disorientation of international travel produces significant personal and cultural learning beyond what can occur domestically (Deardorff, 2006; Erwin & Colman, 1998; Sell, 1983). While the nursing profession has employed a number of strategies to teach students about culture and international topics, study abroad is considered one of the most successful for teaching nursing students cultural competence (Bentley & Ellison, 2007; Boyle, 2007; Caffrey, Neander, Markle, & Stewart, 2005; Currier, Canady, & Saint Arnault, 2007; Fahrenwald, Boysen, Fischer, & Laurer, 2001; Lipson & deSantis, 2007; St. Clair & McKenry, 1999).

This chapter argues that in addition to cultural competence, global competence is an increasingly important area for nursing and that participation in study abroad programming offers a major contribution to the development of global competence for nursing students and enables them to develop knowledge, attitudes, and skills to be better global citizens. For nursing, a shift from cultural to global competence would require that nurses not only develop knowledge, attitudes, and skills about cultural differences, but also about the cultural, social, political, and economic systems that shape individuals' lives on a global scale, the complex interactions among people, the moral and ethical obligations people have to one another, and how these influence health and health care. By developing global competence, nurses can address the health care needs of any person they encounter, regardless of their cultural background. They can do this because they possess the knowledge, critical thinking, creativity, and problem-solving abilities to situate a given individual into the larger field of complex interacting forces that affect both their health and their access to the resources they need to regain their health. At present, there is little data in the assessment literature to demonstrate that the development of cultural competence through study abroad has an impact on nursing practice in the field, or that changes in nursing practice affect patient outcomes. Nevertheless, evidence on the outcomes from study abroad related to cultural competence for nurses, and evidence from other study abroad programming suggest that study abroad could provide the broader contextual learning environment needed to achieve global competence and an awareness of health as a global concept (Currier et al., 2007; Ryan, Twibell, Brigham, & Bennett, 2000).

The chapter begins with a review of the history of cultural competence movements in nursing and a critique that asserts a global view is more effective for interaction with people from a wide variety of cultures. Then study abroad is discussed as a primary mechanism to provide global competence. Finally, the chapter concludes by stating that study abroad programs in nursing with a goal to develop global competence must include, not only content about nursing and health care in a country/culture, but should offer content about the broader historical, economic, political, social, cultural and ethical environment in which that care is provided. In other words, participation on study abroad alone does not produce globally competent persons or citizens, but rather faculty members and educators must purposefully craft the structure and pedagogy of study abroad to produce these outcomes.

CURRENT STATUS OF CULTURAL COMPETENCE IN NURSING

The nursing profession has, until now, focused on educating nurses to be culturally competent and not globally competent. While the nursing profession has a long history of commitment to international health and education dating back to 1899, and the founding of the International Council of Nurses (ICN; 2007), evolution of the importance of cultural competence in nursing originated during the 1960s as the Civil Rights movement gained momentum, and lack of access to health care surfaced as a concern for minority and disadvantaged populations (Branch & Paxton, 1976). In 1978, Leininger's culture care theory established the field of transcultural nursing (TCN), now a specialized area of nursing knowledge and practice. The purpose of Leininger's culture care theory, which is now implemented in nursing programs around the world, is to use research findings to provide "culturally congruent care" defined as:

> Those cognitively based assistive, supportive, facilitative, or enabling acts or decisions that are tailor made to fit with individual, group, or institutional cultural values, beliefs, and lifeways in order to provide or support meaningful, beneficial, and satisfying health care or well-being services. (Leininger, 1991, p. 49)

Since Leininger presented her theory, other theorists have presented models of what is now more commonly called *cultural competence*. The Purnell model for cultural competence (2002), Campinha-Bacote's culturally competent model of care (2003), and the Giger-Davidhizar model of transcultural nursing assessment (Giger & Davidhizar, 2002) are all widely used in nursing education. Each of these models defines cultural competence as a process which can be applied in clinical practice. Purnell's model has been used by professionals from a number of different disciplines in multiple clinical settings in many different countries (Purnell, 2002). It has been used to teach population-based care, and has been used in acute care, long-term care, and home care settings. It states that individuals develop along a continuum from unconsciously incompetent to unconsciously competent (Purnell, 2002). The model, described as an organizational framework, is circular with 12 cultural domains that represent general concepts such as health care practice, nutrition, and spirituality. Within each domain, a list of more specific concepts relates to each domain. For example, the concepts "religious practices," "use of prayer," and "meaning of life" are found under spirituality. Campinha-Bacote's model is also used to teach population-based care (Fahrenwald et al., 2001), and is used in mental health, home health, gerontology, rehabilitation, maternal child nursing, and community services (Campinha-Bacote, 1999, 2002). The model has five constructs depicted as *cultural desire* burning within a volcano which erupts as the motivation to seek *cultural encounters*, which lead to obtaining *cultural awareness, cultural knowledge,* and *cultural skill* (Campinha-Bacote, 2002). Each of these constructs is composed of a number of concepts, for example "cultural knowledge" includes an understanding of health-related beliefs and cultural values, disease incidence and prevalence, and treatment efficacy. Giger and Davidhizar's transcultural assessment model was developed to assist undergraduate students in the process of assessing culturally diverse patients (Giger & Davidhizar, 2002). The model has six cultural phenomena which are categories for assessment: communication, space, social organization, time, environmental control, and biological variations (Giger & Davidhizar, 2002). Each of these models defines cultural competence somewhat differently and uses broad constructs to describe concepts that are difficult to operationalize as measurable variables. As a result, there is little evidence in the nursing literature to support that these models have contributed to our understanding of how cultural competence improves nursing care or patient outcomes.

A review of the general literature on the effectiveness of cultural competency in reducing health disparities has found that researchers focus mostly on the sources of disparities, and very little on the various cultural competency techniques for reducing disparities, such as training health workers and immersion into another culture (Brach & Fraserirector, 2000). Cultural competency techniques are rarely linked with the outcomes that could be expected to follow from them. According to Brach & Fraserirector:

> Unfortunately, at this point there is little by way of rigorous research evaluating the impact of particular cultural competency techniques on any outcomes, including the reduction of racial and ethnic disparities.... Most linkages among cultural competency techniques, the processes of health care service delivery, and patient outcomes have yet to be empirically tested. (p. 203)

Despite the difficulty of linking cultural competence with specific outcomes, all of the cultural competence models mentioned continue to be commonly used in the health literature.

At the same time that Leininger introduced her culture care theory, nursing organizations that accredit nursing academic programs began requiring cultural content in nursing curricula. Specifically, the NLN began requiring cultural content in nursing curricula in 1977 (DeSantis & Lipson, 2007), and in 1983, the NLN developed criteria for inclusion of racial and ethnic diversity content in curricula. In 1996, the American Academy of Colleges of Nursing's *Essentials of Master's Education for Advanced Practice Nursing* included cultural competence as required graduate core curriculum content for all students who pursue a master's degree in nursing, regardless of specialty or functional focus (American Association of Colleges of Nursing [AACN], 1996, p. 11). In 1998, the revised version of the American Academy of Colleges of Nursing *Essentials of Baccalaureate Education for Professional Nursing* included global health care as required core knowledge for the preparation of baccalaureate nurses, defined as "an understanding of the implications of living with transportation and information technology that link all parts of the world" and "information about the effects of the global community on such areas as disease transmission, health policy and health care economics" (AACN, 1998, p. 15).

During that same time period, the American Nurses Association (ANA, 1998), the professional organization representing the nation's nurses, similarly endorsed the inclusion of culture in nursing curricula. In 1986, the ANA identified several methods for integrating *cultural diversity* content into nursing curricula. The Association suggested that curricula include content that (1) integrated the concepts throughout the curriculum; (2) taught culturally relevant aspects of nursing care in specific courses; or (3) offered a required or elective course on cultural diversity. In

1992, the American Academy of Nursing Expert Panel on Culturally Competent Nursing Care published a white paper defining culturally competent care as:

> ...care that is sensitive to issues related to culture, race, gender, and sexual orientation. This care is provided by nurses who use cross-cultural nursing theory, models, and research principles in identifying health care needs and in providing and evaluating the care provided. It is also care that is provided within the cultural context of the clients. (Meleis, 1992, p. 278)

As nursing accreditation and professional organizations were working to incorporate cultural competence into nursing education and practice, a series of documents were published that influenced the medical profession and other health professionals with regard to cultural competence. In 1998, the Pew Health Professions Commission released a report (Pew Health Professions Commission, 1998) that called for the ability to "provide culturally sensitive care to a diverse society." National standards for "culturally and linguistically appropriate services" (CLAS) were released by the U.S. Department of Health and Human Services (DHHS) Office of Minority Health (OMH) in December 2000 (U.S DHHS, 2001). *Unequal Treatment*, published in 2002 by the Institute of Medicine (IOM), assessed the extent of disparities in the types and quality of health services received by U.S. racial and ethnic minorities and nonminorities, and found evidence to suggest that, "bias, prejudice and stereotyping on the part of healthcare providers may contribute to differences in care" (Smedley et al., 2003). One of the key recommendations of the IOM report (recommendation 6-1) was to: "Integrate cross-cultural education into the training of all current and future health care professionals" (Smedley et al., 2003, p. 20). These documents have been highly influential in driving curricular changes to support the development of cultural competence in the education of health professionals (Giger et al., 2007).

Accrediting agencies in nursing and other organizations responsible for establishing standards for the health professions have clearly articulated the importance of cultural competence for clinical practice. Although accrediting agencies in nursing and expert panels have made recommendations that cultural competence content be included in nursing curricula, little direction is given for how this can best be accomplished. As a result, as Lipson and DeSantis point out, there is a "lack of consensus on what should be taught, lack of standards, limited and inconsistent formal evaluation of effectiveness, a decline of curricular specialty courses on culture, and a focus on the microlevel of the nurse-patient encounter" (2007, p. 10S).

STRATEGIES FOR TEACHING CULTURAL COMPETENCE IN NURSING

Therefore, with cultural competence as the goal, nursing has utilized a variety of teaching strategies to integrate cultural content into nursing curricula including program specializations, required courses, teaching of cultural competence models, immersion experiences, and distance learning or simulation (Boyle, 2007; LaVerne & Letzring, 2003; Lipson & DeSantis, 2007; Purnell, 2007). A few nursing schools offer programs that lead to a degree with a specialization in cross-cultural nursing, usually at the master's level. For example the Graduate Program in Cross-Cultural Nursing offered by the University of Washington began in 1974, and is designed to prepare professional nurses for roles in cross-cultural and international systems of health care delivery so that they may function effectively among people of different subcultures within Western and non-Western societies (University of Washington, 2008).

Some schools of nursing adopt one particular model of cultural competence around which it organizes its courses or programs (Lipson & DeSantis, 2007). For example, Excelsior College in New York uses Dr. Purnell's model for cultural competence in its undergraduate distance learning school of nursing, and Ball State University in Indiana uses Giger and Davidhizar's Transcultural Assessment Model throughout their curriculum (Lipson & DeSantis, 2007).

Many schools require courses with cultural competence as the focus at both the undergraduate and graduate levels (LaVerne & Letzring, 2003; Lindquist, 1990; Lipson & DeSantis, 2007). These courses tend to include content on a nursing model or models of cultural competence in a course dedicated to cultural competency. They may also include cultural content from an anthropological perspective, which may focus on health beliefs and practices or explanatory models of people from various cultures, as well as "typical" beliefs and practices that have been described as a "cookbook" approach to culture. Broader content may also be included related to international health organizations and the role of nursing in an international context. Socioeconomic and international comparisons, issues of diversity, and health disparities are often addressed as well. The cookbook approach can be criticized for three major flaws. The first is that it does not address the political, economic, and historical differences between people from *within* any given culture. The second criticism is that students do not necessarily make the cognitive leap between cultural differences and their implications on health care. Finally, these courses tend to be content rather than skill oriented, thereby failing to provide the necessary skill set necessary in cross-cultural situations.

More commonly, however, cultural content is threaded throughout a nursing curriculum. This can occur in a variety of ways; for example, a lecture on global health may be included in a course on community health nursing, or health beliefs and practices of people from different cultures might be addressed in a physical assessment course. This approach is problematic for several reasons. First, it makes it difficult for students and evaluators to track the outcomes of inclusion of cultural content on student learning. Second, the incorporation of cultural content into various courses or dedicating courses to cultural issues is sometimes perceived as competing with clinical and theoretical nursing content, which is seen by some to be relatively more critical to the discipline of nursing in the clinical practice setting. Third, while these methods provide information about culture, they lack the opportunity for students to apply what they have learned in real-life settings.

Some schools are developing innovative strategies for incorporating cultural content into nursing curricula. The University of Arizona uses simulations to extend cultural content into clinical situations using problem-based learning. For example, simulations have been developed related to patient experiences of death and dying, childbearing, and traditional beliefs and practices (Boyle, 2007.) Limitations to this approach include the inability to provide the sociocultural context of the patient situation in the simulation experience (Lipson & DeSantis, 2007).

Many nursing schools offer immersion experiences in another culture, either domestically or internationally. Domestically, experiences are often integrated into senior level courses for undergraduates (Lipson & DeSantis, 2007). Examples include home visits to Southeast Asian and Hispanic clients as part of a clinical experience in a community health course in the Boston area (Williamson, Stecchi, Allen, & Coppens, 1996), conducting a community health assessment as part of a public health nursing course with the Hutterites in South Dakota (Fahrenwald et al., 2001), or a series of assignments as part of a community health program developed to work with a migrant population in Colorado (Brown & Barton, 1992). All of these examples immerse students within a culture other than their own and according to student self-reports, help to develop cultural competence. Although these experiences expose students to cultural differences, students have the opportunity to disengage from the foreign culture and reimmerse in their own culture on a daily basis. That is, they continue to be exposed to U.S. media, cuisine, values, language, culture, and retain access to their cell phone and computer. U.S.-based immersion experiences differ from foreign immersion experiences in that U.S.-based immersions do not provide students with the lived experience of the original social, cultural, economic, or historical context from which these transplanted cultures came. While students can experience what it is like to live in another *culture*, they are unable to experience what it is like to live in another *country*. To increase the level of immersion and opportunities for exposure to diverse cultures as a means of teaching cultural competence to students, nursing has increasingly focused on the importance of international study abroad (Caffrey et al., 2005; Harrison & Malone, 2004; St. Clair & McKenry, 1999).

STUDY ABROAD: FROM CULTURAL TO GLOBAL COMPETENCE

According to the data, study abroad represents a unique and powerful way to promote student learning and contribute to students' cultural competence. The data suggest that study abroad would be a key method for teaching students global competence as well. A summary of this literature indicates that study abroad benefits students' learning in one or more of the following three general domains: academic knowledge and skills, personal growth, and intercultural sensitivity (Carlson et al., 1990; Dwyer & Peters, 2004; Garraty et al., 1981; Kauffmann et al., 1992; Opper et al., 1990). Each of these is addressed below.

First, in terms of knowledge-based skills, Garraty et al. (1981) and Kauffmann et al. (1992) suggest that learning occurs best in a relevant context and that studying abroad increases understanding and retention of language abilities and content-knowledge as related to one's major or career goals (Carlson et al., 1990; Dwyer & Peters, 2004; Ingraham & Peterson, 2004; Opper et al., 1990). Although study abroad traditionally served language learners, Garraty et al. showed that learning abroad can benefit all disciplines by providing an experiential context (Dewey, 1963). For example, students in environmental science could gain a better understanding of water shortages by visiting drought ridden Australia or Africa. Carlson et al. (1990) indicated that students who study abroad demonstrate increased ability to integrate concepts from other disciplines into their thinking, so as an example, architectural and engineering students might gain an appreciation for the cultural factors influencing design, learning to think beyond science alone. Similarly, nursing students abroad could develop a greater appreciation for the influence of culture, socioeconomic status, history, the political environment, and other factors that impact on health beliefs and practices and health care systems in another country.

Although gains in academic ability are significant on study abroad programs, Ingraham and Peterson (2004) also reported a potential for negative academic learning due to the presence of intervening variables such as program structure, student preparation, and the availability of alcohol and drugs. Their study showed that if a program is too short or faculty members do not adequately prepare students for intercultural interactions and learning, students might not need to confront— or could have a negative reaction to—cultural differences and thus reinforce stereotypes (Bennett, 1993). Similarly, if alcohol and drugs are readily available for students, study abroad may facilitate or engender a vacationlike atmosphere, which will decrease academic motivation and learning.

Second, in terms of improvement in personal growth, study abroad programs have been found to increase students' confidence, maturity and self-reliance, ability to work with others, ability to clarify values, and willingness to accept new ideas (Carlson et al., 1990; Erwin & Coleman, 1998; Ingraham & Peterson, 2004; Kauffmann et al., 1992; Opper et al., 1990). Navigating life in a foreign culture necessarily challenges students on a daily basis, requiring them to find new ways of performing typically simple tasks such as asking for directions. If they can successfully live in such an environment, they achieve a greater sense of confidence and self-esteem (Garraty et al., 1981). Dwyer and Peters (2004) reported a 98% increase in students' self-confidence after one year abroad, and suggest that programs longer than 6 weeks result in significantly more growth in this domain than shorter programs.

Finally, the research on intercultural sensitivity shows student improvement in three areas: interest in global issues, ability to interpret ideas from different perspectives, and ability to have empathy and relate to difference (Carlson et al., 1990; Dwyer & Peters, 2004; Erwin & Coleman, 1998; Ingraham & Peterson, 2004; Kauffmann et al., 1992; Medina-López-Portillo, 2004; Opper et al., 1990; Sell, 1983). Researchers believe that through comparison of their home culture to their host culture, students gain a better appreciation of both by expanding their overall understanding of the world in a broader context (Dwyer & Peters, 2004; Kauffmann et al., 1992; Kirkwood, 2001; Sell, 1983). Erwin and Coleman (1998) and Kauffmann et al. (1992) also suggest that students begin to question their native culture as they interact with the new ideas, lifestyles, and standards experienced in the host culture. Ingraham and Peterson's (2004) study showed that of all the outcome domains, intercultural sensitivity increased the most regardless of intervening factors such as program structure or duration. For this reason and those cited above, study abroad provides an important and unique experience for students, and may also serve as the necessary modality to provide nurses with *both* the *cultural* and the *global* competence that is so critically needed. While there is little in the study abroad literature that specifically relates to the development of global competence or evaluation of the translation of these skills on nurses' clinical skills and career choices, the research indicates that the disorientation of international travel produces significant personal and cultural learning that cannot be achieved domestically (Deardorff, 2006; Erwin & Colman, 1998; Sell, 1983). While other campus activities and programs, such as interaction with international students, cross-cultural internships, or language instruction, can improve intercultural knowledge and understanding, we believe that by providing students with an opportunity to examine the social, cultural, political, and economic environment of a place in context, examining health from a systems perspective, and providing an opportunity to learn and appreciate global values, the study abroad experience can make the critical difference in the ability of the health care provider to truly become *globally* competent. As will be shown below, study abroad has been successful in developing these same three general characteristics in nursing students—academic knowledge and skills, personal growth, and intercultural sensitivity, and contributes to the development of cultural and global competence.

STUDY ABROAD AND NURSING

References to early international exchange programs in nursing first appeared in the literature in the 1960s (Karashima, 1969; Phillips, 1966). The current structure of study abroad programs available to nursing students varies from international student exchange (Penman & Ellis, 2004), courses partially or entirely based on community service or service learning opportunities (Evanson & Zust, 2004; Riner & Mecklenburg 2001; Walsh & DeJoseph, 2001), and immersion programs which extend anywhere from 1 to 6 weeks (Caffrey et al., 2005; Frisch, 1990; Haloburdo & Thompson, 1998; Harrison & Malone, 2004; Johanson, 2006; St. Clair & McKenry, 1999; Tabi & Mukherjee, 2003; Talarczyk, Curtis, & McCartney, 1988) to a full semester or longer (Currier, Omar, Talarczyk, & Guerrero, 2000; Haloburdo & Thompson, 1998). Most programs are faculty led (Evanson & Zust, 2004; Frisch, 1990; Harrison & Malone, 2004; Walsh & DeJoseph, 2003; Zorn, Ponick, & Peck, 1995) with nursing faculty accompanying students at all times, with some exceptions (Currier et al., 2000; Haloburdo & Thompson, 1998; Thompson, Boore, & Deeny, 2000). Those programs without faculty on-site at all times may be direct enrollment programs, programs arranged by a contracted agency, or, as was the case with the Michigan State University (MSU) semester program in Mexico (Currier et al., 2000), a faculty member visited students three times over the course of the semester to monitor progress and supervise clinical experiences.

Of those programs in countries where a language other than English is spoken, often language is not required (Frisch, 1990; Harrison & Malone, 2003; Walsh & DeJoseph, 2003) due to the program's short duration or difficulties in requiring language in an already tight curriculum. Students may stay in dormitories (Haloburdo & Thompson, 1998; Zorn et al., 1995), hotels (Frisch, 1990; Haloburdo & Thompson, 1998), or with families (Currier et al., 2000; Harrison & Malone, 2004). Most programs offer hands-on clinical experiences as part of required nursing courses (Caffrey et al., 2005; Evanson & Zust, 2004, 2006; Frisch, 1990; St. Clair & McKenry, 1999; Walsh & DeJoseph, 2003). Some programs offer no hands-on clinical experiences, but are comparative in nature, and examine the local health care system in contrast to that of the United States (DeDee & Stewart, 2003; Harrison & Malone, 2004; Talarczyk et al., 1988). The content of the majority of study abroad programs in nursing focuses solely on nursing and health care in the country under study. A few programs include selected demographic, social, and other characteristics about a country in the content that is offered (Harrison & Malone, 2004), but rarely does a program comprehensively address the historical, political, economic, social, and cultural environment of the country or region to provide an understanding of health and health care in a broader context (Currier et al., 2007). Students travel to both developed (DeDee & Stewart, 2003; St. Clair & McKenry, 1999; Talarczyk et al., 1988; Thompson et al., 2000; Zorn, 1996; Zorn et al., 1995) and developing countries (Caffrey et al., 2005; Currier et al., 2000; Evanson & Zust, 2004, 2006; Frisch, 1990; St. Clair & McKenry, 1999; Thompson et al., 2000; Walsh & DeJoseph, 2003).

The number of nursing programs abroad has steadily increased since the late 1970s. In 1986, Lindquist surveyed 403 U.S. baccalaureate nursing schools to determine ways in which their curricula were internationalized. Of the 319 schools that responded, 43 (14%) offered study abroad programs for students in 104 different countries. Programs ranged in length from one week to one academic year, with the majority being one-month long. Over 50% of programs identified were offered during the summer, between semesters or on breaks. A recent survey of U.S. nursing schools conducted by Thompson and Haloburdo (2006) (437 surveys were returned for a response rate of 65%) reported that approximately 30% of nursing schools provide some type of study abroad opportunity; an additional 30% plan to offer a program in the future. The majority of schools offer short-term study abroad options (2 to 4 weeks) for fewer than 20 students per year. The study found that students studied in 96 different countries, both developed and less developed.

With the increase in the number of study abroad programs for nursing students since the late 1980s, Thompson and Haloburdo concluded that, "[nursing] programs have begun to recognize the value of such experiences for internationalizing the curriculum and for the personal and professional growth of students" (2006). However, the majority of study abroad programs in nursing today—as was true at the time Lindquist first conducted her survey in 1986—continue to be short term or are offered during the summer when students are often free to take courses outside of the required nursing curriculum (Anders, 2001; Bond & Jones, 1994; Colling & Wilson, 1998; Cummings, 1998; Stevens, 1998).

ASSESSMENT OF STUDY ABROAD AND CULTURAL COMPETENCE IN NURSING

Assessment of study abroad program outcomes is an area that has received insufficient attention in nursing education and merits further study, particularly as it relates to the acquisition of cultural competence (Lipson & DeSantis, 2007). Most assessments of study abroad programs in nursing involve small convenience samples, a few employ quantitative methods using survey instruments (Caffrey et al., 2005; DeDee & Stewart, 2003; Frisch, 1990; St. Clair & McKenry, 1999; Thompson et al., 1999; Zorn, 1996; Zorn et al., 1995), and many are qualitative and assess how the international experience influenced students' personal and professional development (Evanson & Zust, 2004; Haloburdo & Thompson, 1998; Harrison & Malone, 2004; Lee, 2004; Ryan et al., 2000; Ryan & Twibell, 2002; Walsh & DeJoseph, 2003). Qualitative examinations of study abroad programs in the nursing literature typically involve analysis of student journals, one-on-one interviews, and focus group discussions with students following the study abroad experience. Similar to the general study abroad literature, outcomes of quantitative and qualitative studies of study abroad programs in nursing include academic knowledge and skills (Frisch, 1990; Thompson et al., 1999; Zorn, 1996; Zorn et al., 1995), personal growth (DeDee & Stewart, 2003; Haloburdo & Thompson, 1998; Lee, 2004; Ryan & Twibell, 2002; Ryan et al., 2000; Walsh & DeJoseph, 2003), and intercultural sensitivity (Caffrey et al., 2005; Ryan & Twibell, 2002; St. Clair & McKenry, 1999; Walsh & DeJoseph, 2003; Zorn, 1996). Additional outcomes reported include professional growth and changing perceptions of the professional nurse role[1] (DeDee & Stewart, 2003; Evanson & Zust, 2004; Lee, 2004; Thompson et al., 1999).

Few studies consider the impact of study abroad on clinical nursing practice. Ryan et al. (2000) conducted a qualitative study of nursing program graduates to describe the process and outcomes of cultural immersion experiences. Students participated in immersion experiences in both domestic and international settings in India, Korea, Honduras, Guyana, and Washington, DC. Outcomes included personal growth, changes in values, increased communication skills, and professional growth that included the development of culturally focused nursing practice:

> Respondents asserted that adaptation to cultural differences in an immersion experience affected them personally and professionally as evidenced by how they practiced nursing, both during the experience and in later professional careers…as a result of the immersion experience, respondents assessed cultural differences, identified personal biases, recognized the need for culturally competent care, and resolved to deliver culturally sensitive care. (pp. 405–406)

However, the authors did not indicate if there were differences in outcomes between domestic and international immersion experiences, nor were specific examples given of changes in clinical practice.

Several studies compare the effect of different study abroad program designs on the development of cultural competence among nursing students. Zorn (1996) found that nursing students who participated in longer study abroad programs (12–16 weeks) reported higher long-term impact (in terms of enhanced international perspective, personal development, intellectual development, and change in view of professional nurse role) than those who participated in shorter study abroad programs, although this impact decreased over time. Comparisons of the outcomes of developed vs. developing country programs differ. Haloburdo and Thompson (1998) found reports of students' personal and professional growth from developed and developing country programs to be similar, whereas Thompson et al. (1999) reported students who had studied in developing countries gained more in terms of international perspectives, personal development, and intellectual development than those who studied in developed countries. They concluded,

> It appears that the very considerable contrast from [the nursing students'] own country in terms of living conditions, culture and values, common health problems, and the quality of healthcare and nursing provided stimulates a re-evaluation of the students' own circumstances and their personal and professional values. (p. 489)

Cultural immersion is consistently reported to be one of the most effective ways of teaching cultural competence in the nursing literature (Caffrey et al., 2005; Currier et al., 2007; Ryan et al., 2000; St. Clair & McKenry, 1999), although there is no consistent definition of "immersion." It may mean students engage in hands-on clinical practice in one study, and in another it may mean students live with local families during the program. Caffrey et al. (2005) compared nursing students who had cultural content integrated into their undergraduate nursing curricula (ICC) to students with cultural content integrated into their undergraduate nursing curricula plus a 5-week clinical immersion in international nursing (ICC plus). International nursing (ICC plus) students gained significantly more than their ICC classmates in perceived cultural competence as a result of the international immersion program. St. Clair and McKenry (1999) observed a similar difference between students who participated in international immersion experiences and U.S.-based experiences:

> …working with culturally diverse patients in community-based practices—where the nurses visit patients in their homes but return to their own homes and communities [in the U.S.] can contribute to the development of cultural awareness, but appears to do little, if anything, in helping students overcome their ethnocentrism. [On the other hand], being culturally immersed [in a foreign country] and living and working with different people on their terms and within their communities made the difference in the students' ability to sustain the transformational process in their practice long after their return from foreign locations…it may be essential to propose that the concept of cultural competence include the phenomena of cultural sensitivity, self-efficacy, perspective transformation, and achievement of ethnorelativism. (p. 233)

From these studies it is apparent that study abroad affects the development of nursing students' cultural competence in terms of personal development, intellectual development, international perspectives and professional growth/changing perceptions of the professional nurse role. However, in addition to these outcomes, defined as "cultural competence" in the nursing literature, many of the outcomes descriptive of global competence were reported by nursing study abroad programs as well including: an understanding of the cultural, social, political, and economic context in which health occurs (Currier et al., 2007); an awareness of the complex and interdependent interactions among people and world events (DeDee & Stewart, 2003); a focus on global values and justice and the moral and ethical obligations people have to one another (Evanson & Zust, 2004); and a global sense of citizenship and community (Haloburdo & Thompson, 1998; Walsh & DeJoseph, 2003; Zorn, 1996).

However, we know little about the long-term effects of study abroad in nursing (Zorn, 1996). Studies that compare study abroad program design are lacking, and while some suggest that longer programs, and programs in developing countries may contribute more to the development of cultural, and potentially global, competence, additional research is needed. Empirical studies are needed to determine if cultural/global competence acquired through international immersion programs or study abroad translates to changes in clinical nursing practice (Caffrey, et al., 2005; Walsh & DeJoseph, 2003), and if improved clinical practice translates to better patient outcomes.

RECOMMENDATIONS

Given the importance of global competence for the nursing profession and the life-changing potential of study abroad programs for nurses, it is recommended that:

- The profession takes its efforts to the next level and begins educating nurses for global competence.
- All nursing programs offer multiple study abroad programs.
- Existing study abroad programs in nursing incorporate content about the historical, political, social, and cultural context of the country/culture under study.
- Further research is needed to address the following questions:
  - □ "With regard to cultural competence, can students have immersion experiences in culturally diverse communities in the U.S. with results similar to those students have internationally?" (St. Clair & McKenry, 1999, p. 234)
  - □ Does cultural (or global) competence in nursing acquired through study abroad translate to clinical practice with clients/patients in the U.S., and if so, how?
  - □ If cultural/global competence in nursing acquired through study abroad *does* translate to clinical practice, does it have an impact on patient outcomes?
  - □ Are there generic cultural/global concepts that form a "cultural template" that can be learned and taught that are relevant for, and can be applied to, all cultures and that would be useful for health care providers in clinical practice?
  - □ Do some types of study abroad programs contribute "more" to the development of global competence than others (short vs. long; developed vs. developing country; immersion vs. nonimmersion; programs/courses with content about the historical, economic, social, and cultural context of a country vs. others that do not provide a context)?

ONGOING CHALLENGES

The literature supports that study abroad is one of the best educational strategies available for teaching cultural and global competence to nursing students. However, a number of challenges remain, both programmatically and for students wishing to participate in programs. It is often very difficult to find nursing faculty with expertise in culture or transcultural nursing to teach global health concepts in the nursing curriculum (Carlton et al., 2007; Leininger, 1995) or to teach study abroad (Thompson & Haloburdo, 2006). Grant support to fund international travel to develop new programs is frequently difficult to obtain (Carlton et al., 2007). Similarly, a study abroad program may last only as long as an individual faculty member with the expertise in a particular country or subject area is available to offer the program or course (LaVerne & Letzring, 2003; Lipson & DeSantis, 2007). Other commitments, including clinical assignments and research obligations, frequently preclude faculty from taking on the responsibilities of a study abroad program (Boyle, 2007; Ekstrom & Sigurdsson, 2002).

Currier et al. (2000) noted several characteristics of nursing education that tend to make nursing curricula less flexible than those of other disciplines. These characteristics may prevent many nursing students from studying abroad for long periods of time unless they extend the time to degree completion. They may also inhibit many nursing programs from initiating efforts to develop longer term study-abroad programs. For example, nursing students must take a number of required courses in a predetermined sequence. This often requires that they spend an entire fall and spring semester taking a sequence of nursing courses. Clinical requirements must comply with State Board of Nursing regulations, and to assure student success, course and clinical content must include material tested by the National Council Licensure Examination (NCLEX). Liability issues often limit the ability to offer direct patient care experiences as part of a study abroad program. These constraints make short-term or summer programs a more feasible option for nursing students who wish to study abroad and increase the likelihood that nursing programs will develop the shorter length programs that include courses as electives rather than courses for required credit (Currier et al., 2000; Ekstrom & Sigurdsson, 2002).

Additional barriers exist for nursing student participation in study abroad programs that would facilitate the development of global competence. Nursing students often consider the cost of study abroad to be prohibitive (Ekstrom & Sigurdsson, 2002; Lipson & DeSantis, 2007; Johanson, 2006; Tabi & Mukherjee, 2003; Thompson & Haloburdo, 2006), and the current U.S. economy is making foreign travel less attractive than in previous years. Often a limited number of students are able to participate in nursing study abroad programs due to the clinical focus of the programs and the need to keep the study/faculty clinical ratio at an appropriate level (Johanson, 2006; Lipson & DeSantis, 2007). Since study abroad courses in nursing are typically offered for elective credit, they compete for space in an already constrained nursing curriculum (Carlton et al., 2007; Johanson, 2006; Lipson & DeSantis, 2007). Nursing students must sometimes decide to take courses over and above what is necessary for graduation to participate in study abroad. Revising existing courses to incorporate content about the historical, political, social, and cultural context of the country under study could pose similar problems. If adding this content was achieved by developing a new course, it is likely the course would be another elective in a potentially oversubscribed curriculum.

CONCLUSION

In an increasingly global world, all students, and especially those in the health service professions, need to have the ability to work, learn, and live across cultural boundaries (Deardorff, 2004; Kirkwood, 2001). Nursing has placed considerable emphasis on the acquisition of cultural competence for members of the profession, and cultural competence has been taught in nursing curricula using a variety of strategies. While cultural competence requires that nurses develop an awareness and understanding of cultural factors and the ability to apply that knowledge in the delivery of health care in different cultural settings, whether domestic or international, developing global competence involves understanding the interactions among the socioeconomic, political, and historical forces that operate within the global economy, and how these forces affect health and well-being. Global competence in health care emphasizes that issues are often complex and transcend national boundaries, such as environmental pollution, human rights, and poverty. A globally competent health care provider embraces the belief that all humans have moral and ethical obligations and responsibilities to all people (Clipsham, n.d.; Gaudelli, 2003; Heilman, 2005; Kirkwood, 2001; Wang, 2005). International immersion experiences have the potential to develop globally competent nurses who can act as global citizens so necessary in an increasingly diverse workplace and a world growing ever "smaller." Learning experiences that are intentionally designed by faculty and provided through international study abroad enable the nurse to develop global competencies such as knowledge, systems thinking, imagination, communication skills, and problem solving, and apply a global understanding of health and disease across cultures and in multiple cultural settings. Combined with a focus on global values and justice, these attributes contribute to the development of nurses as global citizens.

NOTES

1. Questions about the professional nurse role from the International Education Survey (DeDee & Stewart, 2003) were related to the influence of study abroad programs on the nursing student:
   a. Had a long-term impact on your practice as a professional nurse?
   b. Been relevant to your professional career?
   c. Enhanced your effectiveness as a professional nurse?
   d. Improved your efficiency as a professional nurse?
   e. Affected your progress as a professional nurse?

REFERENCES

American Association of Colleges of Nursing. (1996). *The essentials of master's education for advanced practice nursing*. Washington, DC: Author.

American Association of Colleges of Nursing. (1998). *The essentials of baccalaureate education for professional nursing practice*. Washington, DC: Author.

American Nurses Association (ANA). (1986). *Cultural diversity in nursing curriculum: A guide for implementation*. Washington, DC: Author.

American Nurses Association (ANA). (1998). *Standards of clinical nursing practice* (2nd ed.). Washington, DC: Author.

Anders, R. L. (2001). A nursing study abroad opportunity. *Nursing and Health Care Perspectives, 22*(3), 118–121.

Bennett, M. J. (1993). Towards enthnorelativism: A developmental model of intercultural sensitivity. In R. M. Paige (Ed.), *Education for the intercultural experience* (pp. 21–71). Yarmouth, ME: Intercultural Press.

Bentley, R., & Ellison, K. (2007). Increasing cultural competence in nursing through international service-learning experiences. *Nurse Educator, 32*(5), 207–211.

Bond, J. L., & Jones, M. E. (1994). Short-term cultural immersion in Mexico. *Nursing & Health Care, 15*, 248–253.

Boyle, J. (2007). Commentary on "current approaches to integrating elements of cultural competence in nursing education." *Journal of Transcultural Nursing, 18*(1), 21S–22S.

Brach, C., & Fraserirector, I. (2000, November). Can cultural competency reduce racial and ethnic health disparities? A review and conceptual model. *Medical Care Research and Review, 57*(Suppl. 1), 181–217.

Branch, M. F., & Paxton, P. P. (Eds.). (1976). *Providing safe nursing care for ethnic people of color*. London: Appleton-Century-Crofts.

Brown, J., & Marshall, B. L. (2008). A historically Black university's baccalaureate enrollment and success tactics for registered nurses. *Journal of Professional Nursing, 24*(1), 21–29.

Brown, N. J., & Barton, J. A. (1992). A collaborative effort between a state migrant health program and a baccalaureate nursing program. *Journal of Community Health Nursing, 9*(3), 151–159.

Caffrey, R., Neander, W., Markle, D., & Stewart, B. (2005). Improving the cultural competence of nursing students: Results of integrating cultural content in the curriculum and an international immersion experience. *Journal of Nursing Education, 44*(5), 234–240.

Campinha-Bacote, J. (1999). A model and instrument for addressing cultural competence in health care. *Journal of Nursing Education, 8,* 203–207.

Campinha-Bacote, J. (2002). Cultural competence in psychiatric nursing: Have you "ASKED" the right questions? *Journal of the American Psychiatric Nurses Association, 8*(6), 183–187.

Campinha-Bacote, J. (2003). *The process of cultural competence in the delivery of healthcare services* (4th ed.). Cincinnati, OH: Transcultural C.A.R.E. Associates Press.

Carlson, J. S., Burn, B. B., Useem, J., & Yachimowicz, D. (1990). *Study abroad: The experiences of American undergraduates.* Westport, CT: Greenwood Press.

Carlton, K. H., Ryan, M., Ali, N. S., & Kelsey, B. (2007). Integration of global health concepts in nursing curricula: A national study. *Nursing Education Perspectives, 28*(3), 124–129.

Clipsham, D. (n.d.). Guide to infusing global education into the curriculum. Retrieved September 7, 2006, from http://www.global-ed.org/curriculum-guide.doc

Colling, J., & Wilson, T. (1998). Short-term reciprocal international academic exchange program. *Journal of Nursing Education, 37,* 34–36.

Cummings, P. H. (1998). Nursing in Barbados: A fourth-year elective practice experience for nursing students and registered nurses. *Journal of Nursing Education, 37,* 43–44.

Currier, C., Canady, R., & Saint Arnault, D. (2007, Spring). Study abroad in Ghana: A path to cultural competence. *Medical Humanities Report, Michigan State University, 28*(4), 5–6, continued online. Retrieved March 24, 2008, from http://www.bioethics.msu.edu/mhr/contents.html

Currier, C., Omar, M., Talarczyk, G., & Guerrero, R. D. (2000). Development and implementation of a semester program in Mexico for senior nursing students. *Journal of Professional Nursing, 16*(5), 293–299.

Deardorff, D. K. (2004, Spring). Internationalization: In search of international competence. *International Educator, 23,* 13–15.

Deardorff, D. K. (2006). Identification and assessment of intercultural competence as a student outcome of internationalization. *Journal of Studies in International Education, 10*(3), 241–266.

DeDee, L., & Stewart, S. (2003). The effect of student participation in international study. *Journal of Professional Nursing, 19*(4), 237–242.

deLeon Sianz, M. L., & Meleis, A. I. (2007). Integrating cultural competence into nursing education and practice: 21st century action steps. *Journal of Transcultural Nursing, 18*(86), 86S–90S.

DeSantis, L. A., & Lipson, J. G. (2007). Brief history of inclusion of content on culture in nursing education. *Journal of Transcultural Nursing, 18,* 7S–9S.

Dewey, J. (1963). *Experience and education.* New York: Macmillan.

Dwyer, M. M., & Peters, C. K. (2004). The benefits of study abroad: New study confirms significant gains. *Transitions Abroad, 27*(5), 56–59.

Ekstrom, D. N., & Sigurdsson, H. O. (2002). An international collaboration in nursing education viewed through the lens of critical social theory. *Journal of Nursing Education, 41*(7), 289–294.

Erwin, T. D., & Coleman, P. K. (1998). The influence of intercultural experiences and second language proficiency on college students' cross-cultural adaptability. *International Education, 28*(1), 5–25.

Evanson, T. A., & Zust, B. L. (2004). The meaning of participation in an international service experience among baccalaureate nursing students. *International Journal of Nursing Education Scholarship, 1*(1), 1–14.

Evanson, T., & Zust, B. L. (2006). Bittersweet knowledge: The long-term impact of an international service experience. *Journal of Nursing Education, 45*(10), 412–419.

Fahrenwald, F. L., Boysen, R., Fischer, C., & Laurer, R. (2001). Developing cultural competence in the baccalaureate nursing student: A population-based project with the Hutterites. *Journal of Transcultural Nursing, 12*(1), 48–55.

Friedman, T. L. (2005). *The world is flat: A brief history of the twenty-first century.* New York: Farrar, Straus & Giroux.

Frisch, N. (1990). An international nursing student exchange program: An educational experience that enhanced student cognitive development. *Journal of Nursing Education, 29*(1), 10–12.

Garraty, J. A., Kemperer, L., & Taylor, C. J. H. (1981). *The new guide to study abroad.* New York: Harper & Row.

Gaudelli, W. (2003). *World class: Teaching and learning in global times.* Mahwah, NJ: Erlbaum.

Giger, J. N., & Davidhizar, R. E. (2002). The Giger and Davidhizar transcultural assessment model. *Journal of Transcultural Nursing, 13*(3), 185–188.

Giger, J., Davidhizar, R. E., Purnell, L, Harden, J. T., Phillips, J., & Strikland, O. (2007). American Academy of Nursing Expert Panel Report: Developing cultural competence to eliminate health disparities in ethnic minorities and other vulnerable populations. *Journal of Transcultural Nursing, 18*(2), 95–102.

Gonczi, A. (1994). Competency based assessment in the professions in Australia. *Assessment in Education: Principles, Policy & Practice, 1*(1), 27–44.

Green, J. (1989). *Cultural awareness in the human services: A multiethnic approach.* Toronto: Allyn & Bacon.

Green, J. (1995). *Cultural awareness in the human services: A multiethnic approach* (2nd ed.). Toronto: Allyn & Bacon.

Green, M. F., & Olson C. (2003). *Internationalizing the campus: A user's guide.* Washington, DC: American Council on Education.

Haloburdo, E. P., & Thompson, M. A. (1998). A comparison of international learning experiences for baccalaureate nursing students: Developed and developing countries. *Journal of Nursing Education, 37,* 13–21.

Harrison, L., & Malone, K. (2004). A study abroad experience in Guatemala: Learning first-hand about health, education, and social welfare in a low-resource country. *International Journal of Nursing Education Scholarship, 1*(1), 1–15.

Heilman, E. (2005). Critical, liberal, and poststructural challenges for global education. In C. H. Cherryholmes, E. Heilman, & A. Segall (Eds.), *Counterpoints: Studies in the postmodern theory of education: Vol. 272. Social studies—The next generation: Re-searching in the postmodern* (pp. 189–208). New York: Lang.

Heilman, E. (2007). (Dis)locating imaginative and ethical aims of global education. In K. Roth & I. Gur-Ze'ev (Eds.), Philosophy and education: Vol. 16. *Education in the era of globalization* (pp. 83–104). New York: Springer.

Hunter, W. D. (2004). Got global competency? *International Educator, 13*(10), 6–12.

Ingraham, E., & Peterson, D. (2004). Assessing the impact of study abroad on study learning at Michigan State University. *Frontiers: The Interdisciplinary Journal of Study Abroad, 10,* 83–100.

International Council of Nurses. (2007). *The ICN vision.* Retrieved December 20, 2007, from http://www.icn.ch/vision.htm

Johanson, L. (2006). The implementation of a study abroad course for nursing. *Nurse Educator, 31*(3), 129–131.

Karashima, S. (1969). Experience of an exchange student nurse in the U.S. *Nursing Technique, 5,* 133–135.

Kauffmann, N. L., Martin, J. N., & Weaver, H. D. (1992). *Students abroad: Strangers at home.* Yarmouth, ME: Intercultural Press.

Kirkwood, T. F. (2001). Our global age requires global education: Clarifying definitional ambiguities. *The Social Sciences, 92*(1), 10–15.

LaVerne, G., & Letzring, T. (2003). Status of cultural competence in nursing education: A literature review. *Journal of Multicultural Nursing and Health, 9*(2), 6–13.

Lee, N. J. (2004). The impact of international experience on student nurses' personal and professional development. *International Nursing Review, 51,* 113–122.

Leininger, M. M. (1991). *Culture care diversity and universality: A theory of nursing.* New York: National League for Nursing.

Leininger, M. M. (1995). *Transcultural nursing: Concepts, theories, research and practices.* New York: McGraw-Hill.

Lindquist, G. J. (1986). Programs that internationalize nursing curricula in baccalaureate schools of nursing in the United States. *Journal of Professional Nursing, 2,* 143–150.

Lindquist, G. J. (1990). Integration of international and transcultural content in nursing curricula: A process for change. *Journal of Professional Nursing, 6*(5), 272–279.

Lipson J. G., & DeSantis, L. A. (2007). Current approaches to integrating elements of cultural competence in nursing education. *Journal of Transcultural Nursing, 18*(1), 10S–20S.

Liu, J. E., Pothiban, L., Lu, Z., & Khamphonsiri, T. (2000). Computer knowledge, attitudes, and skills of nurses in People's Hospital of Beijing Medical University. *Computer Nurse, 18*(4), 197–206.

Medina-López-Portillo, A. (2004). Intercultural learning assessment: The link between program duration and the development of intercultural sensitivity. *Frontiers: The Interdisciplinary Journal of Study Abroad, 10,* 179–200.

Meleis, A. I. (1992). AAN expert panel report: Culturally competent health care. *Nursing Outlook, 40*(6), 277–283.

Opper, S., Teichler, U., & Carlson, J. (1990). *Impacts of study abroad programmes on students and graduates.* London: Kingsley.

Passel, J., & Cohn, D. (2008). *Immigration to play lead role in future U.S. growth.* Pew Research Center Publications. Retrieved May 26, 2008, from http://pewresearch.org/pubs/729/united-states-population-projections

Penman, J., & Ellis, B. J. (2004). Philippine academic visit: Brief but life changing. *International Journal of Nursing Education Scholarship, 1*(1), 1–12.

Pew Health Professions Commission. (1998). *Recreating health professional practice for a new century.* Retrieved March 1, 2008, from http://www.futurehealth.ucsf.edu/pdf_files/recreate.pdf

Phillips, D. (1966). A report by the 1st exchange nurse to Japan. *Japanese Journal of Nursing, 18*(1), 62–66.

Polsky, D., Sochalski, J., Aiken, L. H., & Cooper, R. A. (2007). Medical migration to the U.S.: Trends and impact. *LDI Issue Brief, Leonard Davis Institute of Health Economics, 12*(6), 1–4.

Purnell, L. (2002). The Purnell model for cultural competence. *Journal of Transcultural Nursing, 13*(3), 193–196.

Purnell, L. (2007). Commentary on "current approaches to integrating elements of cultural competence in nursing education." *Journal of Transcultural Nursing, 18*(1), 23S–24S.

Riner, M. E., & Mecklenberg, A. (2001). Partnering with a sister city organization for an international service–learning experience. *Journal of Transcultural Nursing, 12*(3), 234–240.

Rosenkoetter, M. M., & Nardi, D. A. (2007). American Academy of Nursing experts panel on global nursing and health: White paper on global nursing and health. *Journal of Transcultural Nursing, 18*(4), 305–315.

Ryan, M., & Twibell, R. S. (2002). Outcomes of a transcultural nursing immersion experience: Confirmation of a dimensional matrix. *Journal of Transcultural Nursing, 13*(30), 30–39.

Ryan, M., Twibell, R., Brigham, C., & Bennett, P. (2000). Learning to care for clients in their world, not mine. *Journal of Nursing Education, 39*(9), 401–408.

St. Clair, A., & McKenry, L. (1999). Preparing culturally competent practitioners. *Journal of Nursing Education, 38*(5), 228–234.

Sell, D. K. (1983). Attitude change in foreign study participants. *International Journal of Intercultural Relations, 7,* 131–147.

Shin, H. B., & Bruno, R. (2003, October). *Language use and English speaking ability: 2000* (Census 2000 brief). Washington, DC: U.S. Census Bureau.

Smedley, B. D., Stith, A. Y., & Nelson, A. R. (Eds.). (2003). *Unequal treatment: Confronting racial and ethnic disparities in health care.* Washington, DC: National Academies Press.

Stevens, G. L. (1998). Experience the culture. *Journal of Nursing Education, 37,* 30–33.

Swanbrow, D. (2006). The changing face of U.S. immigration. *ISR Research Update.* Ann Arbor: The University of Michigan. Retrieved September 24, 2008, from http://www.isr.umich.edu/home/news/research-update/2006-04.pdf

Tabi, M. M., & Mukherjee, S. (2003). Nursing in a global community: A study abroad program. *Journal of Transcultural Nursing, 14*(2), 134–138.

Talarczyk, G., Curtis, J., & McCartney, M. (1988). Overseas study in a baccalaureate program. *Journal of Nursing Education, 27*(4), 180–182.

Thompson, K., Boore, J., & Deeny, P. (1999). A comparison of an international experience for nursing students in developed and developing countries. *International Journal of Nursing Studies, 37,* 481–492.

Thompson, M. A., & Haloburdo, E. P. (2006). *Study abroad experiences for nursing students in U.S. undergraduate and graduate programs.* Paper presented at the Sigma Theta Tau International Conference.

Transcultural Nursing Society. (n.d.). Retrieved December 20, 2007, from http://www.tcns.org/

U.S. Department of Health and Human Services. (2001, March). *National standards for culturally and linguistically appropriate services in healthcare.* Retrieved March 10, 2008, from http://www.omhrc.gov/assets/pdf/checked/finalreport.pdf

U.S. Department of Health and Human Services. (2006, August 21). *Changing demographics and the implications for physicians, nurses, and other health workers.* Retrieved April 14, 2008, from http://bhpr.hrsa.gov/healthworkforce/reports/changedemo/composition.htm#3.3.2

University of Washington. (2008). *Advanced practice community health systems nursing.* Retrieved March 5, 2008, from http://www.son.washington.edu/eo/apchs/cognates.asp

Walsh, L. V., & De Joseph, J. (2003). "I saw it in a different light": International learning experiences in baccalaureate nursing education. *Journal of Nursing Education, 42*(6), 266–272.

Wang, L. (Ed.). (2005). *Global perspectives: A statement on global education for Australian schools.* Carlton, Australia: Curriculum.

Williamson, E., Stecchi, J. M, Allen, B. B., & Coppens, N. M. (1996). Multiethnic experiences enhance nursing students' learning. *Journal of Community Health Nursing, 13*(2), 73–81.

World Health Organization. (2006). *The world health report 2006: Working together for health.* Retrieved September 15, 2008, from http://www.who.int/whr/2006/en/index.html

Zorn, C. R. (1996). The long-term impact on nursing students of participation in international education. *Journal of Professional Nursing, 12*(2), 106–110.

Zorn, C. R., Ponick, D. A., & Peck, S. D. (1995). An analysis of the impact of participation in an international study program on the cognitive development of senior baccalaureate nursing students. *Journal of Nursing Education, 34*(2), 67–70.

Chapter 10

The Role of Study Abroad in Preparing Globally Responsible Teachers

Kenneth Cushner

Kent State University

Now I know that the United States is not the center of the universe.

Being in a new and different situation gave me the opportunity to experience what it feels like to be away from one's familiar surroundings and to be the odd person out. It can be very scary and lonely at times, but you do get over it. This is one way I have become more sensitive. This will definitely help me if I ever get a student who is from another country, or even another state, in my classroom. I learned so much, especially about myself—and the world.

Statements such as these, made by students who have just returned from an overseas student teaching experience, illustrate the impact a study abroad experience can have in their preparation as professional educators. Teachers play a critical role in enhancing the ability of the next generation of young people to better understand the world around them and to be able to collaborate with others in the resolution of global problems. The degree to which teachers can do this, however, is dependent on their own knowledge, experience, and ability to transmit this knowledge and skill-set to the students in their charge.

The field of teacher education has been criticized by some for insufficiently preparing teachers to work with diverse populations (e.g., Gay, 2002; Ladson-Billings, 1999), while others have questioned whether education schools adequately address global issues (Jennings, 2006). In a recent issue of *AACTE Briefs*, Jennings pointed out that "Americans, throughout their school years especially…do not study about other people in the world, people whose beliefs, cultures, and status will directly impact their own lives in ways that were not even imagined a generation ago" (p. 2). These admonitions remind us that as schools of education endeavor to help their candidates develop pedagogical competence they must also consider cultural competence as part of their professional preparation. Teachers in the 21st century must be able to assist their students to function effectively and contribute to life in a global society, or as Jennings has suggested, deal with "complicated issues in both local and global communities" (p. 2). This is no easy task given what we know about teacher education students in general, the manner in which people learn to be effective across cultures, and the contextual constraints that are unique to teacher education.

Ausubel (1963) referred to cognitive structures as a person's knowledge of a particular subject matter and how well organized it is at a particular point in time. Existing cognitive structures can be the critical factor in determining whether new material will be meaningful and how the information will be acquired and retained. The stronger the individual's cognitive structures, the more new information will be integrated and retained.

Studies designed to investigate the importance of prior knowledge on new learning report that up to 80% of what is learned in an educational experience can be directly dependent upon what an individual knows even before stepping into the classroom (Bransford, 1979). This is a particularly sober finding for those concerned with the intercultural development of educators who find that teacher education students (and most teachers) have limited prior international knowledge and experience. While most teachers may be competent in the subject matter that they have studied, they may lack the necessary prior knowledge, attitude, and skills essential to teach toward a global or intercultural perspective. The most common approaches to enhancing intercultural knowledge of preservice teachers—the addition of coursework or field experiences in culturally diverse settings (e.g., urban schools), has limited, if any, impact on enhancing their international and intercultural sensitivity (Pajares, 1992; Zeichner & Melnick, 1996).

I will argue in this chapter that the study abroad experience can provide the crucial "prior knowledge" that can facilitate preservice teachers' ability to learn more about the world and become more interculturally effective. This chapter reviews the current state of affairs of teacher and student readiness to address international concerns; presents some of the challenges as well as approaches to integrating international experience into the education of pre-service and in-service teachers; looks at the impact of study abroad as a critical component in the teacher education curriculum; and finally, offers suggestions for integrating more focused attention to international and intercultural aspects in the teacher education curriculum.

THE INTERCULTURAL READINESS OF TEACHERS AND TEACHER EDUCATION STUDENTS

The demographics of the teaching profession in the United States have not changed appreciably nor diversified sufficiently to match the increasing cultural and ethnic diversity of students in most schools (Come back Mr. Chips, 2007; Gay, 1993; Hodgkinson, 2002; Zimpher, 1989). Even with the increased attention to the recruitment of underrepresented groups into the profession, teaching in the United States, as elsewhere around the globe, remains a rather homogeneous profession (Cushner, 1998). In schools across the United States, the majority of those in the teaching profession are European American, with fewer that 15% being teachers or administrators of color. Females continue to dominate the field, representing 75% of teachers in general, and more than 90% in the elementary grades. Most teachers come from middle class backgrounds and live in small- to medium-sized suburban communities. This is in sharp contrast to the increasing percentage of students of color in American public schools, who represent close to 40% of school population nationwide, with an increasing number living in poverty.

Teacher education students continue to reflect these demographics (Glazier, 2003) while at the same time being relatively cross-culturally inexperienced. The majority of today's teacher education students wish to teach where they grew up or in schools very similar to the ones they experienced, with fewer than 10% reporting an eagerness to teach in urban or multicultural environments. The situation appears increasingly grim when we add to this the fact that fewer than 5% of American teachers are fluent and able to teach in any second language and that the majority of teacher education students spend all or most of their time with people of their own ethnic and racial group. Teachers and teachers in training seem to live in vastly different worlds from the students in their charge.

INTERNATIONAL KNOWLEDGE OF TEACHERS AND TEACHER EDUCATION STUDENTS

Adding to the need to address domestic multicultural concerns in schools is the increasing responsibility to provide future teachers with a global and international education. Today's students must be prepared to live and work in the global marketplace and have the skills necessary to solve problems that are increasingly complex and global in nature and scope. Nevertheless, we are continually reminded that most American do not seem to be up to the task. This is not a new concern. President Carter's 1979 Commission on Foreign Language and International Studies warned of dire consequences if our educational system did not more effectively address international studies, geography, and foreign languages (Heyl & McCarthy, 2003).

While we lack current data on the international knowledge of preservice teachers in particular, we do know that the international knowledge of the population in general has not improved much since 1979. Results of the 2002 National Geographic–Roper (NGR) *Survey of Geographic Literacy* ranked U.S. young people next to last from among nine nations, scoring slightly above Mexico (NGR, 2002), with a more recent assessment among 18- to 24-year-olds again documenting their limited knowledge of their world (NGR, 2006). While these are limited to knowledge-level indicators, the NGR 2006 study revealed that only 37% of young Americans could find Iraq on a map—although U.S. troops have been in the country since 2003; 20% of young Americans think that Sudan is in Asia; and 48% believe the majority population of India is Muslim. In the 2002 study, only 15% could locate Israel and 17% could locate Afghanistan on the map; 29% could not identify the Pacific Ocean; 69% could not identify the United Kingdom; only half could find New York; and 11% could not even locate the United States on a map.

These findings suggest that young people in the United States—the most recent graduates of our educational system and the cohort from which teacher education students are drawn—are unprepared, at least on the knowledge level, for an increasingly global future. Smith (2002) reports that the most serious problem facing the internationalization of education is the inadequate knowledge that teachers have about the world, citing the point that many states license teachers even in the social studies or history without requiring coursework in geography or world history. It is far fewer elementary school teachers who have had any such courses.

In spite of all this evidence of a critical knowledge deficit, there remains insufficient attempt to remedy the situation among those studying to be teachers in the United States. A study of nearly 50 colleges and universities undertaken by Lambert in 1989 found that the average teacher education student took fewer than 1.5 internationally focused courses compared with 2.4 courses taken by all majors (pp. 67–69, 122–125). Schneider's (2003) report showed that in an 18-year period, little had changed in the international exposure of preservice teachers. No appreciable gains had been made in forging linkages between area studies programs in colleges of arts and sciences and colleges of education, for instance. Similarly, the three strategies most often cited to internationalize teacher training—encouraging faculty travel abroad, admitting foreign students, and study abroad or overseas internships had not changed; with only 5% favoring curriculum revision to include international content in the preparation of teachers. The same holds true for foreign language study among teacher education students. While the majority of those polled in Schneider's

2003 student survey reportedly support foreign language education for teachers, an analysis of teacher education students at three universities reports that 76% had no college-level foreign language study, with the majority of those who did have such study having completed only one to two semesters (Heyl & McCarthy, 2003).

THE SIGNIFICANCE OF AN INTERNATIONAL EXPERIENCE

Many teacher educators recognize that coursework alone is insufficient when it comes to changing preservice teachers' beliefs about those from other cultures. Zeichner and Melnick (1996), for instance, call for

> an experiential component in teacher education programs that helps prospective teachers examine themselves and their attitudes toward others, and helps them develop greater intercultural competence. The preparation of teachers for cultural diversity involves a fundamental transformation of people's world views and goes far beyond giving information about cultures, curriculum, and instruction.... (p. 178)

This is supported by research in the field of cross-cultural training that continues to demonstrate that the most effective way to enhance the skills required of individuals living and working among cultures other than their own demands significant, long-term, direct personal interaction with people and contexts different from those with which they are most familiar (Cushner, 2007; Cushner & Brislin, 1996; Dwyer, 2004; Landis, Bennett, & Bennett, 2004; Stephan & Vogt, 2004).

At the same time, there is increasing evidence that for maximum impact with preservice teachers, such experiences may need to be outside the home country. Traditional approaches, some argue, even taking preservice teachers to urban settings, still place students within the larger dominant cultural context. Most White preservice teachers have had few significant cross-cultural experiences and have been socialized within the dominant Eurocentric school setting. Upon entering schools in culturally diverse domestic settings, they continue to view the school through the cultural filters and preconceptions with which they have been socialized, thereby seeing the school within the cultural paradigm with which they are comfortable. Although children and families may appear different, schools typically look the same, resulting in a tendency to view the school structure and values from the perspective with which one is familiar, thus reinforcing certain stereotypes. Students, thus, are prevented from fully examining their own beliefs and assumptions. As Marx (2008) has suggested, if cross-cultural placements are to move students' intercultural development forward, they must be designed so that preservice teachers cannot "return to normalcy" to explain what they are experiencing. This is much more difficult to achieve in domestic placements.

OPPORTUNITIES AND OBSTACLES TO INTEGRATING STUDY ABROAD IN TEACHER EDUCATION

Schneider's research report, *Internationalizing Teacher Education: What Can be Done?* (2003) on the undergraduate training of secondary school teachers, revealed that two thirds of in-service teachers feel that study abroad should be part of the undergraduate experience, and that current students in education would like to see more study abroad opportunities available to them. Faculty and administrators in most colleges and universities also recognize the importance of teachers gaining an international perspective and the role that study abroad can play in achieving these ends.

Given that 55% of incoming freshmen state that they intend to study abroad in their college years and another 26% would like to do so (American Council on Education [ACE], 2008), we should not be surprised by the increase we have witnessed in recent years in the number of students who embark on such experiences. However, even with this growing interest and participation, fewer than 5% of students nationwide study abroad—and the number is even less for education students. The Institute of International Education (IIE) reports that in the 2005–2006 academic year, only 4% of all study abroad participants were in the field of education (IIE, 2007); translating to roughly 1% of all teacher education students. This percentage remains consistent over the previous 10 years, with the majority of the study abroad experiences being short-term in duration. Reasons for the low participation rates of education majors in study abroad may be attributed to a variety of institutional and disciplinary constraints, while interest in intercultural affairs may be attributed, at least in part, to the levels of intercultural sensitivity of both teachers and students.

INSTITUTIONAL AND DISCIPLINARY BARRIERS

Gaining international knowledge and experience for teacher education students is hampered by a number of factors at the institutional level. Foreign language education, the discipline where most students first come into sustained contact with international concepts, has never been strongly encouraged or endorsed in American education. Although 95% of college-bound students reportedly have studied a foreign language in high school (ACE, 2008), subsequent participation in university is far lower. Fewer than 40% of universities across the nation have a foreign language requirement, and it is virtually nonexistent in the teacher education curriculum nor required by most state and professional teacher accrediting agencies. Additionally, as many as 50% of education majors may be transfer students from community colleges where there are few, if any, international or foreign language requirements.

Additional institutional obstacles to integrating study abroad into the teacher education experience include the financial cost for both student and institution; time away from campus and home; and evidence that academic advisors for education majors rarely provide students with information on study abroad or other international opportunities (Schneider, 2003).

Teachers may also know little about the world and show relatively little interest in expanding their knowledge and experience because little is asked of them by the profession. State and professional accrediting agencies rarely require or encourage international or foreign language competence for licensure, and few universities require significant international coursework to fulfill general education requirements for teacher education students. Additionally, state-level teacher licensing boards increasingly add requirements to an already overcrowded teacher education curriculum, making it virtually impossible for students to take time away from their studies to pursue education-related courses overseas.

INTERCULTURAL SENSITIVITY OF TEACHERS AND THEIR STUDENTS

Intercultural sensitivity refers to an understanding that there exist multiple ways of viewing and interacting in the world, and that others may have approaches that are significantly different from one's own. The Intercultural Development Inventory (IDI; Hammer & Bennett, 1998), based on the developmental model of intercultural sensitivity (DMIS; Bennett, 1993) is perhaps the most comprehensive assessment tool designed to identify where an individual falls along a continuum of intercultural sensitivity from highly ethnocentric to highly ethnorelative. Three stages lie on the ethnocentric side of the continuum (Denial, Defense, or Minimization), and three stages reflect increasingly ethnorelative perspectives and sensitivities (Acceptance, Adaptability, or Integration). Recent studies employing the IDI support the notion that today's teachers may not have the degree of intercultural sensitivity that is required of them to be effective international educators. This may also explain why it may be difficult to advance toward more advanced stages.

Mahon (2003) studied 155 teachers from the American Midwest and reported that all had IDI scores that placed them at minimization or below—all on the ethnocentric side of the scale. Similar results were found by Grossman and Yuen (2006) in a study that sampled 107 teachers in schools in Hong Kong. They report 55% of teachers in Denial/Defense, and 43% in Minimization, with only 2% in the Acceptance or Adaptation stages. This presents a somewhat worrisome scenario. An individual in Minimization is typically "color-blind," focusing on commonalities and universal values, emphasizing similarities, and holding the belief that all people are fundamentally the same. Although cultural differences may be recognized, these differences are "minimized" and not seen as important as the similarities. As a result, significant and oftentimes deep cultural differences may be trivialized, romanticized, or ignored. Teachers in Minimization tend to report not seeing color or difference, treating all children alike, or not discriminating, which according to Mahon (2006) is exactly the skill teachers need to develop. Complicating the situation is the fact that teachers tend to overestimate their intercultural sensitivity as reported by their Perceived Means. Thus, they believe they are doing well and feel good because of this, making it all the more difficult to advance to a more ethnorelative stage.

In a related study of preservice early childhood teacher education students, Pappamihiel (2004) found that students who had taken one class in multicultural education and another class specific to the needs of English language learners still exhibited a low level of intercultural sensitivity. Basing her study on the DMIS but not utilizing the IDI, Pappamihiel asked respondents to compare how they would express caring behaviors to children in general compared to a group of English as a second language (ESL) students. Very few of the 28 respondents demonstrated any indication that they understood, accepted, and valued cultural differences between these groups of students, or that they would behave any differently in their interactions. Like others in Minimization, they reported that they would ignore any differences by offering "hugs and smiles" as the predominant way to express caring to all, regardless of the cultural-appropriateness of the behavior and the background of their students. Coursework alone did not seem to be sufficient to bring about the desired changes in preservice teachers' understanding of culture and how it manifests itself in the classroom.

There is evidence of a surprising disparity between teachers, teacher education students, and the children they are preparing to teach, with young people demonstrating higher levels of intercultural sensitivity than their teachers. Although not normed on young people, Pederson (1997) administered a modified version of the IDI to 145 seventh-grade students in six social studies classrooms from three schools (one each from urban, rural, and suburban settings). Contrary to the teachers sampled in the studies referenced above, more than 70% of these middle school students were found to be in high Minimization or Acceptance (53 in Minimization and 52 in Acceptance).

A more recent and related study by Straffon (2003) found even greater disparity between students' levels of intercultural sensitivity and that of the teachers reported above. Assessing the levels of intercultural sensitivity of 336 high school students who attended an international school in Southeast Asia, he found only 3% on the ethnocentric side of the IDI. In this study, the longer students were in attendance in the school (mean length of time in this school was 5.7 years), the higher their IDI score, with 71% in Acceptance and 26% in Cognitive Adaptation.

Recent analysis of the international socialization of young people suggests that the middle childhood years, between the ages of 8 and 12, may represent the critical period in the development of an international or intercultural perspective in children (Cushner, 2008), thus making it all the more important that teachers not only have sufficient international knowledge, but the skill and motivation needed to transfer this to the students in their charge. Psychosocial development at this age seems to be characterized by rapid cognitive development, especially related to perspective and role-taking ability; low rejection of groups; high attitude flexibility; development of more differentiated intergroup perceptions; and, is a time when one is able to perceive another's point of view. Additionally, for those concerned with the role of experience in international socialization, this represents an ideal time to begin traveling with young people and having them participate in international and intercultural youth programs and exchange experiences. Children at this age are comfortable being away from home, interact with relative ease nonverbally through games and other activities, and are eager and willing to learn new languages. Educational efforts to develop an international and intercultural perspective should begin during these years.

Opportunities and encouragement to internationalize the field of teacher education can be found in a variety of places, including professional associations and accrediting bodies, as well as through creative course delivery and international internships. Schools of education are responding with some innovative and powerful approaches, of which study abroad can be a key.

PROFESSIONAL ASSOCIATIONS

The National Council for the Accreditation of Teacher Education (NCATE) now requires teacher education programs undergoing accreditation reviews to show evidence of how the curriculum addresses issues related to diversity, and by inference, the global dimension of teaching and learning. Standard Four, Diversity, states, "Regardless of whether they live in areas with great diversity, candidates must develop knowledge of diversity in the United States and the world, dispositions that respect and value differences, and skills for working in diverse settings" (NCATE, 2006). It continues, "One of the goals of this standard is the development of educators who can help all students learn and who can teach from multicultural and global perspectives that draw on the histories, experiences, and representations of students from diverse cultural backgrounds" (p. 31). Additionally, most of the discipline-based organizations and professional association (e.g., National Council for the Social Studies, National Association of the Education of Young Children) now encourage all teachers to address diversity in a more focused and strategic manner; some of them stressing international or global competence.

Perhaps the most effective way to help prospective teachers become more internationally minded, and thus to acquire the foundational skills and motivation required to prepare their young students for global citizenship, is through carefully structured international or intercultural experiences. Teacher education curriculums, driven in large part by a plethora of state licensing and assessment mandates, typically make this difficult to achieve. With such highly prescriptive course requirements, if study abroad is not undertaken early in the general education curriculum, it can be quite difficult to integrate in the professional program. Finding ways to integrate a meaningful international experience in the preservice teacher education curriculum, although difficult due to required course demands, has been approached in a number of innovative ways, from short-term content-specific courses to long-term overseas student teaching internships.

CREATIVE COURSE DELIVERY

One strategy a number of institutions are beginning to employ is to offer special sections of the standard required foundations courses in overseas settings, thus providing an international experience that is specific to the discipline while engaging with the content in a comparative approach. For example, since 2002 my own institution has offered overseas sections of such required courses as educational psychology or school and society. The traditional educational psychology course, in this instance, utilizes a comparative approach in Italy while visiting the community of Reggio Amelia, looking at Montessori education, as well as how education is carried out in American or international schools. The school and society course found in most education programs has taken place in Mexico, enabling students to take a comparative look at Latino/a and bilingual education, and in Ireland, where students have a firsthand opportunity to compare urban and rural educational issues. In all of these instances, coursework begins at the home campus and sets the stage for and is complemented by a 2-week study–travel experience in the host country.

INTERNATIONAL INTERNSHIPS—STUDENT TEACHING ABROAD

One of the best ways to help teachers to understand the challenges associated with teaching children in a global age is through carefully structured, intercultural field experiences where candidates are immersed in another culture. Since student teaching requires candidates to show they can translate theory into practice over an extended period of time, this capstone event is ideally suited for strengthening candidates' intercultural and international understanding.

Study abroad programs can be classified by their structure according to the degree of immersion into the host culture that the experience provides, with the assumption that the more integrated a student is in the host culture, the better the program is at assisting the student to develop intercultural competence (Engle & Engle, 2003). Student teaching in other cultural contexts enables teacher candidates to simultaneously strengthen their practice and personally stretch beyond their traditional zone of comfort—away from support networks provided at home, in school, or by friends, and to develop interpersonal relationships with host nationals. In addition, unlike many study abroad experiences where participants spend most of their time with others from their own country, overseas student teachers are generally on their own where increased self-efficacy becomes possible. And, because the curriculum, instructional material, and approach to teaching that one encounters when placed in a school overseas are all likely to be different from what the student would experience in a local placement, the student has increased opportunities to examine alternative approaches to teaching. Finally, opportunities exist for student teachers to broaden their cultural knowledge, learn about another's view of the world from an insider's perspective, develop a global perspective, and increase their understanding of the value of multicultural education through interaction with children, other professionals, and adults from varying cultural backgrounds.

An increasing number of universities now offer overseas student teaching placements for their students. The Consortium for Overseas Student Teaching (COST), the International Teacher Education Program (ITEP) in the California State University System, and the Cultural Immersion Projects at Indiana University represent three programs that have each provided coordinated and sustained structured intercultural field experiences for student teachers for many years.

Cited as one of the oldest organizations facilitating international student teaching placements (Heyl & McCarthy, 2003), the Consortium for Overseas Student Teaching (COST) was formally established in 1973 through an alliance of faculty from six universities, out of concern that students who attended their institutions had little or no intercultural experiences; many, in fact, having never traveled beyond the region in which they lived. Since its inception, COST has placed thousands of teacher candidates in international settings. The author of this chapter served as director of COST from 1995 to 2000, and still serves on its Executive Board. The Cultural Immersion Project and Overseas Student Teaching Project, both offered at Indiana University, give teacher candidates opportunities to broaden their intercultural horizons with placements in international as well as domestic settings. For the past 30 years, candidates have been afforded opportunities to student teach on Native American reservations in the southwest as well as in various international locations. Using the motto "education unites the world," the overseas project has been recognized for excellence by the American Association of Colleges for Teacher Education, the Goldman Sachs Foundation and the Asia Society. A considerable amount of research data has been collected over the years about the efficacy of these programs (Stachowski, 2007; Stachowski & Chleb, 1998; Stachowski & Visconti, 1997).

The California State University's International Teacher Education Program was established in 1994 to provide bilingual student teaching experiences in neighboring Mexico. It is authorized to credential teacher candidates seeking a multiple-subject credential with a Spanish/English authorization. Today, it is in partnership with Mexico's State Department of Education and is the only international credential program in California that is approved by the California Commission on Teacher Credentialing.

Impact of Study Abroad on Teacher Education Students

Achieving positive impact on intercultural development as a result of study abroad depends on the quality and design of the experience, the degree of immersion into the host culture, opportunities to develop relationships with people from the culture, and program support for guided critical cultural self-reflection. Research related to cross-cultural learning and the development of intercultural competence reports growth in a number of related areas as a result of the study abroad experience (Cushner & Karim, 2004; Kauffman Martin, & Weaver, 1992; and elsewhere in this volume), including the development of intercultural sensitivity (Anderson, Lawton, Rexeisen, & Hubbard, 2006; Marx, 2008; Medina-López-Portillo, 2004; Olson & Kroeger, 2001); intercultural communications competence (Olson & Kroeger, 2001; Williams, 2005); global perspective and world-mindedness (Douglas & Jones-Rikkers, 2001; Hassard & Weisberg, 1999); and increased intercultural and cross-cultural awareness (Hassard & Weisberg, 1999).

In recent years, researchers have begun looking at the nature of the international student teaching experience and its impact on professional and personal development (Mahon & Cushner, 2007; Marx, 2008; Stachowski & Sparks, 2007). Consistent with what the research says about study abroad in general, student teaching overseas impacts preservice teachers profoundly in both personal as well as professional ways. In addition to being exposed to new pedagogical approaches and educational philosophies, overseas student teachers gain a significant amount of self-knowledge, develop personal confidence, professional competence, and a greater understanding of both global and domestic diversity.

Personal Growth and Development

Traveling independently and living abroad, many for the very first time, overseas student teachers often confront a range of personal anxieties and test their own limitations. As a result of the experience, most report an increase in self-awareness, self-confidence, and esteem; increased adaptability, persistence, strength, and risk-taking; enhanced relationships with others; and, stepping outside of one's traditional comfort zone and developing a sense of "being otherwise." Quezada and Alfaro (2007) report that students in their biliteracy program in Mexico recognize that they have the power to be agents of change in their own classrooms. This increased self-efficacy has professional benefits as well, because teachers with high self-efficacy motivate and praise students more, and are better able to guide students in their learning by promoting or offering probing questions (Gibson & Dembo, 1984). Student comments like, "I am more independent and self-sufficient than I had originally thought," "I've learned to take chances in my life—which I really never did before," or, "I've become resourceful in the respect that I am able to deal emotionally in a wide variety of circumstances," reflect this increased sense of self-assurance and a sense of accomplishment.

A recognition of "being otherwise" is an unanticipated outcome of the experience, directly affecting students' interaction with others in the host community by encouraging them to experiment with a different way of being. Students who were more solitary or independent for instance, learn the value of working with others and reaching out to meet new people. For some, suddenly having to rely on others prompts a transition from individuality toward collectivism, recognizing the value that support networks can have on the quality of one's experience. And these support networks can exist in both the new overseas location through host families, teachers, and local community members, or through electronic connections to those remaining back home. The more socially oriented students begin to recognize the value of slowing down, becoming more reflective, or simply gaining comfort while being on their own.

Increase in Cultural Knowledge

Throughout the course of an international teaching experience students begin to challenge their beliefs about the world and its people, develop empathy for and trust in others, learn a significant amount about at least one other culture, and often to their surprise, learn quite a lot about their own culture, developing a greater appreciation of home. Interacting with others and hearing new perspectives on their own nation and culture, students are able to reflect on the country they left, examining it from new and different points of view. Stachowski and Brantmeier (2002) report that student teachers begin to "see the self through the other," and thus experience a perspective shift. Sometimes, students do not necessarily like what they see. As one COST student noted, "I learned that other cultures are not as openly racist as in the United States, and that other cultures are more open to African Americans. I felt more welcome as an African American in Europe that I typically do at home." Another explained, "I have become more knowledgeable about world events and less ethnocentric. I know that the U.S. is not the center of everyone's thoughts and actions." Still another noted, "Americans know so little about Australians and I think that is sad. Australians know so much about what happens in the U.S."

■ **160**

Additionally, students begin to examine the stereotypes they may have held of others, to question aspects of their own culture which had previously gone unexamined, and to develop greater empathy. This ability to place oneself in another's shoes and to shift perspectives is critical to developing effective cross-cultural understanding and maintaining good communication (Bennett, 1993).

Professional Impact

Student teachers grow professionally, too, as a result of their overseas experience. In addition to gaining greater understanding of another educational system and an enhanced ability to work with different colleagues, there is evidence that student teachers become more flexible and are better able to adapt their teaching to individual student differences. One student reported that she now referred to herself as a facilitator rather than a "knowledge-giver" adding, "My time at (host school) taught me to focus on the needs of children that I was teaching. Because of this experience, I will be more thoughtful in my approach to the children that I teach." Another student reported a similar impact, stating,

> I have had to alter the work level to fit each student's needs. Many times I have stopped class and discussed the different strategies people have used to solve problems. Looking at everyone's ideas helps others to see that there isn't just one right or wrong answer. Some of the students from different nationalities have used strategies that other students were unaware of.

Student teachers placed in English-speaking as well as non-English speaking countries report new understandings about language teaching and an increased ability to work with second language learners. One student placed in an international classroom in Switzerland where English was the language of instruction reported how surprised she was that the differences in native languages would affect her classroom. She stated,

> I have learned that I can never take for granted what the students understand. When asked, 95% of the time the student will tell me that he or she understands even when it is clear that he or she does not. It has become paramount that I encourage questions even when it disrupts the immediate lesson. After all, when my students don't understand, what sort of lesson is it anyway? Even if generally speaking we are all using the same language, there are so many subtleties within that language that it has significant implications for how the class learns.

Another student, rather proficient in Spanish and placed in a Mexican public school for her student teaching, attested to the impact it had on her skills as a teacher when she returned to the United States. She reported,

> I now know where many of my students come from. I have many students who come from public schools in Mexico, and because I know the Mexican curriculum, I am able to help students and families with their transitions to the United States. In turn, I help the administration and teaching staff interpret scores and grade levels of students based on their outcome in the Mexican school setting.

One student resonated more with multicultural education after her experience, stating, "The biggest change that happened to me was that I become much more multicultural in my view of the world. I believe that multicultural education happens every day, and that this can become a mindset for the teacher, rather than an occasional effort. I owe this to my overseas teaching experience."

Finally, some draw upon their overseas experience to help them succeed in new jobs in urban environments. One student who took a position in a large Midwestern urban district stated,

> Professionally, I could have never thrived in the situation I am currently in without the experience with COST. Six months after my return I was knee deep in (City name) Public Schools, with a class that spoke English, but somehow it was all a different language. This wasn't much different than being in Mexico, a whole different culture that I knew little about. I was plucked out of my small town in the UP (Michigan's Upper Peninsula) and put into a new world that I had no experience with, everything was new and different. Personally, being alone in a big city again after living in Mexico City was not as much of a shock as it would have been otherwise. I know I would have never made it through the first year of teaching here without my COST experience. COST provided me with a safe and supportive environment to test and retest my knowledge and skills—it has made all the difference.

These observations are consistent with what other global educators have proposed. Merryfield (2001) reports that many educators find parallels between the multiple realties that exist in a community or a given country as well as globally, stating,

> This recognition is what has led many people concerned with domestic diversity and equity to make connections with global diversity and equity and become interested in how global perspectives can inform multicultural education. For others, the recognition of the interconnectedness of local and global intersections of power, discrimination and identity turned their attention to domestic diversity in order to pursue local ramifications of globalization. (p.6)

ONGOING CHALLENGES AND QUESTIONS ABOUT STUDY ABROAD AND TEACHER EDUCATION

In addition to the obstacles to integrating study abroad as well as international content into the teacher education curriculum previously discussed, a variety of other issues are worth considering. Questions arise around one's reluctance to engage in meaningful ways with the host community and thus resist intercultural growth; the degree to which language familiarity facilitates or inhibits intercultural development; length of experience; and the degree to which an international experience can also facilitate greater sensitivity to domestic diversity are all issues of concern and question.

Resistance

Not all students, for instance, become more interculturally sensitive simply by having an international experience, no matter how great the impact may be. Although the IDI has not been used to date to monitor intercultural development as a result of an overseas student teaching assignment, responses from some international student teachers indicate a continuing lack of ability to detect or discriminate cultural nuances, making statements that suggest they continue to minimize cultural differences—a kind of "kids are kids the world over" sentiment. One student, for instance, commented: "Teenagers are teenagers, I found that my kids, all mostly Polynesian, were very loving and forgiving." Another noted at the end of her 12-week experience, "I will use my experience to study other cultures as well as the Australian culture. Also, to help emphasize that people are the same despite some cultural differences."

In some cases, these nuances were related to the students' assessments of the similarities of the United States versus an international teaching context. Having observed a professional development day which highlighted differences between teachers and administrators, one student noted, "This distance (between teachers and administrators) is something I have picked up on in virtually every school I have been a part of in the States. It was fascinating to see the same problem existing in a different country." Another student working in Ecuador noted, "I think my teaching experience was almost equivalent to an experience in the States. What I did learn was how important goals are to the atmosphere and success of a school, which could have been learned anywhere." Another student who traveled to South Africa explained, "Teaching children seems to be the same no matter what continent you are on. Of course there are little differences, but overall, you need to apply the same things to students in Africa as you need to in the U.S. Kids are the same everywhere."

Some initially report experiencing no real differences, even though the remainder of their responses suggest otherwise. For example, when asked about the possible change in one's philosophy after an overseas teaching experience, one student teacher responded, "I don't believe it really has [changed] other than the fact that I want to make my students more culturally aware through education." Or, in detecting differences between themselves and their U.S. counterparts, one student teacher commented, "I don't necessarily believe I am really different except I have more knowledge about Australia. Someone else may know more about Europe though, so I don't see it as a huge deal."

It is possible that it is easier to move from Denial or Defense to Minimization than it is to move out of Minimization. Being in Minimization is a comfortable place to be, and movement from there may require more time or focused reflection—something that will demand greater attention on the part of university faculty.

Similarity of Language

Unique and oftentimes unexpected obstacles can also exist when the host language is the same as the student's. The majority of students in the COST network, for instance, request and are placed in English-speaking countries (76% between Fall 2006 and Summer 2008) versus non-English-speaking countries (24%). Sharing a common language may, on the surface at least, appear to allow U.S. students to communicate with more ease than in countries where students need to struggle with speaking a foreign language. Two possibly negative scenarios, however, may develop. As Marx (2008) suggests, U. S. students in other English-speaking countries may be able to function at a relatively high level, thus creating an illusion of cultural immersion while masking some very substantive cultural differences. This language similarity may also allow people to engage in more substantive conversations with hosts, leading to the possibility that they will delve into deeper and more sensitive interpersonal areas before a strong relationship of trust and mutual understanding has truly developed. When the languages differ between the host and sojourner, in the course of struggling to communicate, they also have a longer period of time with which to develop the level of trust and cultural understanding that is needed before moving into more sensitive areas of discussion.

As a general rule of thumb, short-term study abroad programs that take place within countries where a common language exists between host and sojourner must be especially sensitive to these issues and provide more, rather than less structure, and thus design opportunities that allow students to experience a sufficient degree of cultural disequilibrium that acts as a catalyst for the student to engage in intercultural development. In the case of COST and other international student teaching programs where students might request English-speaking countries, special attempts must be made to encourage students to teach (usually in English-language medium schools) in non-English speaking countries.

Program Length

The question of length of experience on impact, especially when considering the difficulty education students have in finding time and space in their professional program for study abroad is also a consideration. The literature in this regard is not clear. Three studies that focused on language development experiences among students having substantial background in the host language show mixed results. Medina-López-Portillo (2004) report little significant evidence of gain in intercultural sensitivity as a result of either a 7-week or semester-long language program in Mexico. Paige, Cohen, and Shively (2004), however, report that students spending a semester abroad in French- and Spanish-speaking countries made significant gains on intercultural sensitivity. And Engle and Engle (2004) report similar gains among students in semester-long programs, with even larger gains made among students in year-long programs. Dwyer (2004), too, compares year-long, semester, and summer study abroad programs finding that the longer the program, the greater the impact.

There is recent evidence that a short-term study abroad experience can have a positive impact on intercultural sensitivity. This offers promise to teacher education programs, especially given the fact that most study abroad programs are becoming increasingly shorter in duration and led by faculty from the home campus. Anderson et al. (2006) report modest gains on intercultural sensitivity using the IDI as a result of a 4-week, non-language-based study abroad experience in England and Ireland. The quality and attention to such factors as type of housing, degree of cultural immersion, and meaningful interaction with locals, use of host faculty, and pre- and post-orientation on such programs seems critical to assure that the experience moves beyond tourism. Barkhuizen and Feryok (2006) report this as a major drawback to their language experience programs for a cohort of Hong Kong preservice ESL teacher education students spending 6 weeks in New Zealand where students were limited to relatively surface-level interaction with hosts.

Although the jury is still out in terms of the impact on intercultural development, short-term study abroad programs may serve other valuable purposes, especially for preservice teachers. Such programs offer opportunities for comparative educational experiences, and may, in some instances, include visits to schools that parents of immigrant children have attended, thus allowing preservice teachers to learn more about the educational assumptions, perspectives and experiences of some of their students. Or, short-term skill-development programs, such as study trips that focus on whole language literacy programs in New Zealand or short-term foreign language immersion experiences, while not necessarily enhancing intercultural sensitivity, may be the stimulus that leads an individual to consider further education or subsequent study abroad upon her or his return home.

Cushner and Karim (2004) summarized the research related to this issue as follows:

...it appears that although both short- and long-term study-abroad programs have an impact on participants, the longer and the more fully integrated the program, the greater the potential for impact. Short-term programs may not be sufficient to affect psychosocial developmental outcomes or for the impact to remain after a period of time. There also continue to be conflicting results between quantitative and qualitative studies. In many instances, where quantitative analysis may reveal little in the way of impact, qualitative analysis demonstrates impact. (p. 300)

Connecting International Diversity to Domestic Concerns

Advancing educators' sensitivity and ability to work effectively across cultures on the domestic front is of utmost concern among most teacher educators in the United States. Some researchers report that a successful international experience can serve as a stimulus to advance pre-service teachers' intranational knowledge and skills (Baker, 1999; Brown & Kysilka, 2002), while others remain skeptical, concerned that a focus on international diversity and interpersonal change enables students to avoid critical issues of power and privilege that contribute to inequality (Banks, 2001).

Merryfield (2000) addressed this intersection in her study of 80 teacher educators recognized by their peers for their success in preparing teachers in both multicultural and global education. What she discovered is of critical importance to teacher educators concerned with the intercultural development of preservice teachers.

Merryfield found there to be significant differences between the experiences of people of color and European Americans that reflect the importance of impactful, experiential learning. Most American teachers of color have a double consciousness (DuBois, 1903/1989). That is, many have grown up conscious of both their own primary culture as well as having experienced discrimination and the status of being an outsider by encountering a society characterized by White privilege and racism. Middle-class White teacher educators who are effective at teaching for diversity had their most profound and impactful experiences while living outside their own country. These teachers had, thus, encountered discrimination and exclusion by being an outsider within another cultural context, and they had found ways to bring this to their teaching.

As Merryfield's study suggests, those who leave the comfort of their home society for an extended period of time come to understand what it is like to live outside the mainstream and to be perceived as the other. It is the impactful international experience, like that provided by overseas student teaching, that has facilitated many European-American mainstream teachers to become more ethnorelative in their understanding of others, more skilled at crossing cultures, and committed to bringing about change through their work. A significant international experience, thus, leads to new, firsthand understandings of what it means to be marginalized, to be a victim of stereotypes and prejudice, and how this might affect people.

Travel and living abroad also affords people the opportunity to experience what happens to their identity when they are no longer in control, and the contradictions between people's beliefs, expectations, and knowledge and the multiple realities of others (Merryfield, 2000). As one COST student teacher remarked, "I learned what it is like to be an outsider, to not understand what others around me take for granted. This is extremely helpful to me as I think about teaching children from different backgrounds now that I have returned home." When this experience is recognized in a real-life context, it forces people to reflect and question, thus deconstructing previously held assumptions or knowledge about themselves and others. Thus, the international

165

lived experience sets the stage for developing a consciousness of multiple realities and serves as the stimulus that prompts new learning.

RECOMMENDATIONS FOR FUTURE ACTION AND RESEARCH

A strong rationale for integrating an international experience in teacher education can be found in the context of situative theory (Putnam & Borko, 2000). Since so much of learning occurs within the confines of a typical classroom setting, behaviors of both teachers and learners often become routine and automatic. In situative learning, the context in which the individual learns is seen as integral to one's cognition. It is the outside experiences and encounters that facilitate the individual development of alternative perspectives, thus helping preservice teachers to understand more fully the ways of others, and to begin seeing themselves as global citizens with others as potential partners. These outside experiences encountered through study abroad may provide the necessary context for this to occur.

It is clear from the research on study abroad in general, as well as from what we are beginning to learn from the experiences of preservice students, that individuals are impacted on the personal level. Marx's case study of one student teacher in London (2008) documented movement from Minimization to Acceptance/Adaptation on the IDI over the course of a semester-long student teaching experience. A number of qualitative studies reviewed in this chapter also suggest that a carefully structured immersion experience can have a significant impact on teacher education students. We do need to investigate intercultural development that more fully utilizes the IDI (or other valid and reliable assessment tools) on larger numbers of preservice teachers to better understand the process.

What is still not clear is the extent to which either a short- or long-term international experience impacts one's professional teaching practice in the United States. Thomas (2001) provides evidence that extensive international volunteer experience among British teachers enhances their confidence and ability to bring the international dimension into their teaching. We need to know in what ways people teach differently after having had international experiences in teacher education programs. Are those who have student taught overseas more inclined to seek positions in culturally diverse communities when they return? If they do teach in diverse school settings, are they more effective? Do they remain in their positions longer than those who have not had international experience? Do these teachers develop more meaningful and productive relationships with families and others in their community? How do they translate their own personal experience into curricular experiences that they then share with their students or other teachers? Are they more inclined to seek out further international experiences or to pursue subsequent study of internationally-related topics or learn more foreign language upon their return? These are all areas of fruitful inquiry.

The challenges to integrating an international experience into the education of teachers are numerous, especially when considering the many demands that already face the field of education. Yet, given the times and circumstances in which we live, and the relative lack of intercultural competence on the part of most teachers, this represents a component of the education of teachers that cannot be ignored because it shows promise on both the domestic as well as international front.

REFERENCES

American Council on Education. (2008). College bound students' interests in study abroad and other international activities. Retrieved June 23, 2008 from http://www.acenet.edu/AM/Template.cfm?Section=Home&Template=/CM/ContentDisplay.cfm&ContentFileID=3997

Anderson, P., Lawton, L., Rexeisen, R., & Hubbard, A. (2006). Short-term study abroad and intercultural sensitivity: A pilot study. *International Journal of Intercultural Relations, 30*, 457–469.

Ausubel, D. (1963). *The psychology of meaningful verbal learning*. New York: Grune & Stratton.

Baker, F. (1999, Fall). Multicultural versus global education: Why not two sides of the same coin? *Teacher Education, 12,* 97–101.

Banks, C. A. M. (2001). Becoming a cross-cultural teacher. In C. Díaz (Ed.), *Multicultural education for the 21st century* (pp. 171–193). New York: Longman.

Barkhuizen, G., & Feryok, A. (2006). Pre-service teachers' perceptions of a short-term international experience programme. *Asia-Pacific Journal of Teacher Education, 34*(1), 115–134.

Bennett, J. M., & Bennett, M. J. (2004). Developing intercultural sensitivity: An integrative approach to global and domestic diversity In D. Landis, J. M. Bennett, & M. J. Bennett (Eds.), *Handbook of intercultural training* (3rd ed., pp. 147–166). Thousand Oaks, CA: Sage.

Bennett, M. (1993). Towards ethnorelativism: A developmental model of intercultural sensitivity. In M. Paige (Ed), *Cross-cultural orientation* (pp. 27–69). Lanham, MD: University Press of America.

Bransford, J. (1979). *Human cognition: Learning, understanding and remembering*. Belmont, CA: Wadsworth.

Brown, S. C., & Kysilka, M. L. (2002). *Applying multicultural and global concepts in the classroom and beyond*. Boston: Allyn & Bacon.

Come back, Mr. Chips. (2007, September 17). *Newsweek*, 44.

Cushner, K. (1998). *International perspectives on intercultural education*. Mahwah, NJ: Erlbaum.

Cushner, K. (2007). The role of experience in the making of internationally-minded teachers. *Teacher Education Quarterly, 34*(1), 27–40.

Cushner, K. (2008). International socialization of young people: Obstacles and opportunities. *International Journal of Intercultural Relations, 32*(2), 164–173.

Cushner, K., & Brislin, R. (1996). *Intercultural interactions: A practical guide* (2nd ed.). Thousand Oaks, CA: Sage.

Cushner, K., & Karim, A. U. (2004). Study abroad at the university level In D. Landis, J. M. Bennett, & M. J. Bennett (Eds.), *Handbook of intercultural training* (3rd ed., pp. 289–308). Thousand Oaks, CA: Sage.

Douglas, C., & Jones-Rikkers, C. (2001). Study abroad programs and American student world mindedness: An empirical analysis. *Journal of Teaching in International Business, 13*(1), 56–65.

DuBois, W. E. B. (1989). *The souls of Black folks*. New York: Bantam Books. (Original work published 1903)

Dwyer, M. W. (2004, Fall). More is better: The impact of study abroad program duration. *Frontiers: The Interdisciplinary Journal of Study Abroad, 10,* 151–164.

Engle, L., & Engle, J. (2003). Study abroad levels: Toward a classification of program types. *Frontiers: The Interdisciplinary Journal of Study Abroad, 9,* 1–20.

Engle, L., & Engle, J. (2004, Fall). Assessing language acquisition and intercultural sensitivity development in relation to study abroad program design. *Frontiers: The Interdisciplinary Journal of Study Abroad, 10,* 219–236.

Gay, G. (1993). Building cultural bridges: A bold proposal for teacher education. *Education and Urban Society, 25*(3), 284–299.

Gay, G. (2002). Preparing for culturally responsive teaching. *Journal of Teacher Education, 53*(2), 106–116.

Gibson, S., & Dembo, M. H. (1984). Teacher efficacy: A construct validation. *Journal of Educational Psychology, 76*(4), 569–582.

Glazier, J. A. (2003). Moving closer to speaking the unspeakable: White teachers talking about race. *Teacher Education Quarterly, 30,* 73–94.

Grossman, D., & Yuen, C. (2006). Beyond the rhetoric: A study of the intercultural sensitivity of Hong Kong secondary school teachers. *Pacific Asian Education, 18*(1), 70–87.

Hammer. M. R., & Bennett, M. J. (1998). *The intercultural development inventory (IDI) manual*. Portland, OR: Intercultural Communication Institute.

Hassard, J., & Weisberg, J. (1999). The emergence of global thinking among American and Russian youth as a contribution to public understanding. *International Journal of Science Education, 21*(7), 731–743.

Heyl, J. D., & McCarthy, J. (2003, January 24). *International education and teacher preparation in the U.S.* Presentation at the national conference Global Challenges and U. S. Higher Education: National Needs and Policy Implications, Duke University, NC.

Institute of International Education, IIE Network. (2007). *Open doors*. Retrieved June 24, 2008, from http://opendoors.iienetwork.org

Jennings, C. (2006, April 24). *Teacher education: Building a foundation for the global workforce* (AACTE Briefs). Washington, DC: American Association of Colleges for Teacher Education.

Kauffman, N., Martin, J. N., & Weaver, H. (1992). *Students abroad, strangers at home*. Yarmouth, ME: Intercultural Press.

Ladson-Billings, G. (1999). Preparing teachers for diverse student populations. *Review of Research in Education, 24,* 211–248.

Lambert, R. (1989). *International studies and the undergraduate*. Washington, DC: American Council on Education.

Landis, D., Bennett, J., & Bennett, M. (2004). *Handbook of intercultural training* (3rd ed.). Thousand Oaks, CA: Sage.

Mahon, J. (2003). Intercultural sensitivity development among practicing teachers: Life history perspectives. *Dissertation Abstracts International* (UMI No. 3097199).

Mahon, J. (2006). Under the invisibility cloak? Teacher understanding of cultural difference. *Intercultural Education, 17*(4), 391–405.

Mahon, J., & Cushner, K. (2007). The impact of overseas student teaching on personal and professional development. In K. Cushner & S. Brennan (Eds.), *Intercultural student teaching: A bridge to global competence* (pp. 57–87). Lanham, MD: Rowman & Littlefield.

Marx, H. A. (2008). *Please mind the gap: A pre-service teacher's intercultural development during a study abroad program*. Unpublished dissertation, University of Connecticut, Storrs, CT.

Medina-López-Portillo, A. (2004). Intercultural learning assessment: The link between program duration and the development of intercultural sensitivity. *Frontiers: The Interdisciplinary Journal of Study Abroad, 10,* 179–200.

Merryfield. K. M. (2000). Why aren't teachers being prepared to teach for diversity, equity and global interconnectedness? A study of lived experiences in the making of multicultural and global educators. *Teaching and Teacher Education, 16,* 429–443.

Merryfield, M. M. (2001, March 3). *Implications of globalization for teacher education in the United States: Towards a framework for globally competent teacher educators*. Paper presented at the 53rd Annual Meeting, American Association of Colleges for Teacher Education, Dallas, TX.

National Council for Accreditation of Teacher Education (NCATE). (2006). *NCATE: Professional standards for the accreditation of schools, colleges and departments of education*. Washington, DC: Author.

National Geographic–Roper. (2002). *Survey of geographic literacy*. Retrieved from http://news.nationalgeographic.com/news/2002/11/1126_021120_TVGeoRoperSurvey.html

National Geographic–Roper. (2006). *Survey of geographic literacy*. Retrieved from http://www.nationalgeographic.com/roper2006/findings.html

Olson, C. L., & Kroeger, K. R. (2001). Global competency and intercultural sensitivity. *Journal of Studies in International Education, 5*(2), 116–137.

Paige, R. M., Cohen, A. D., & Shively, R. L. (2004). Assessing the impact of a strategies-based curriculum on language and culture learning abroad. *Frontiers: The Interdisciplinary Journal of Study Abroad, 10,* 253–276.

Pajares, M. F. (1992). Teachers' beliefs and educational research: Cleaning up a messy construct. *Review of Educational Research, 62*(3), 307–332.

Pappamihiel, E. (2004). Hugs and smiles: Demonstrating caring in a multicultural early childhood classroom. *Early childhood development and care, 174*(6), 539–548.

Pederson. P. (1997, November 20–23). *Intercultural sensitivity and the early adolescent*. Paper presented at the 77th Conference of the National Council for Social Studies, Cincinnati, OH.

Putnam, R. T., & Borko, H. (2000). What do new views of knowledge and thinking have to say about research on teacher learning? *Educational Researcher, 29*(1), 4–16.

Quezada, R., & Alfaro, C. (2007). Developing biliteracy teachers: Moving toward culture and linguistic global competence in teacher education. In K. Cushner & S. Brennan (Eds.), *Intercultural student teaching: A bridge to global competence* (pp. 57–87). Lanham, MD: Rowman & Littlefield.

Schneider, A. I. (2003). Internationalizing teacher education: What can be done? A research report on the undergraduate training of secondary school teachers. *International Studies Perspectives, 5,* 316–320.

Smith, A. F. (2002). How global is the curriculum? *Educational Leadership, 60*(2), 39–40.

Stachowski, L. (2007). A world of possibilities within the United States: Integrating meaningful domestic intercultural teaching experiences into education. In K. Cushner & S. Brennan (Eds.), *Intercultural student teaching: A bridge to global competence* (pp. 88–122). Lanham, MD: Rowman & Littlefield.

Stachowski, L., & Brantmeier, E. J. (2002). Understanding self through the other: Changes in student teacher perception of home culture from immersion in Navajoland and overseas. *International Education, 32*(1), 5–18.

Stachowski, L., & Chleb, J. (1998). Foreign educators provide feedback for the improvement of international student teaching experiences. *Action in Teacher Education, 19*(4), 119–130.

Stachowski, L., & Sparks, T. (2007). Thirty years and 2,000 student teachers later: An overseas student teaching project that is popular, successful, and replicable. *Teacher Education Quarterly, 34*(1), 115–132.

Stachowski, L., & Visconti, V. (1997). Adaptations for success: U.S. student teachers living and teaching abroad. *International Education, 26,* 5–20.

Stephan, W. G., & Vogt, W. P. (2004). *Education programs for improving intergroup relations.* New York: Teachers College Press.

Straffon, D. A. (2003). Assessing the intercultural sensitivity of high school students attending an international school. *International Journal of Intercultural Relations, 27,* 487–501.

Thomas, G. (2001). *Human traffic: Skills, employers and international volunteering.* London: Demos.

Williams, T. R. (2005). Exploring the impact of study abroad on students' intercultural communication skills: Adaptability and sensitivity. *Journal of Studies in International Education, 9*(4), 356–371.

Zeichner, K. M., & Melnick, S. L. (1996). The role of community field experiences in preparing teachers for cultural diversity. In K. M. Zeichner, S. L. Melnick, & M. L. Gomez (Eds.), *Currents of reform in pre-service teacher education* (pp. 176–198). New York: Teachers College Press.

Zimpher, N. L. (1989). The RATE project: A profile of teacher education students. *Journal of Teacher Education, 40*(6), 27–30.

Chapter 11

Democratizing Study Abroad

Challenges of Open Access, Local Commitments, and Global Competence in Community Colleges

Robert A. Frost
Oregon State University

Rosalind Latiner Raby
California State University, Northridge

INTRODUCTION

Since their phenomenal expansion in the 1960s, community colleges have grown with unique missions that emphasize open access, local commitments, and workforce preparation. We argue that each has always had a foundation in global competency and that education abroad, specifically, helps to secure these skills. However, the key education abroad issues identified by Freeman (1966) are the same issues defined by Hess (1982) in the first book that focused exclusively on community college education abroad. Twenty-six years later, these issues are still being cited by community college leadership (Institute of International Education [IIE], 2007): Thriving education abroad programs must have (1) support from the chief administrative officer; (2) commitment from faculty; and (3) a specific coordinator position with a centrally placed and staffed office. Those distinctive characteristics that define community colleges: a community-first mission, nontraditional students, an institutional culture built on making do with limited funding, stakeholder conflicts, and a sometimes parochial orientation, are the same issues that separate community colleges from their university counterparts, even urban universities with a largely urban commuter student body.

The continued narrow pathway for community college education abroad, staff, office, program development, and student advisement is echoed in best practice reports from individual community colleges.[1] However, scholarly critical data on what education abroad represents to community colleges, how education abroad exists within core educational goals, and how community college programming is distinct from other institutions, remains lacking (Dudderar, 2002; Frost, 2007; Korbel, 1998; Raby, 2007; Raby & Swadago, 2005). Moreover, even though noted best practices exist, they are infrequently applied in community college planning contexts. All of these challenges remain, even as community college enrollments in study abroad programs are expanding faster than any other higher education sector (IIE, 2007).

This chapter examines the need for integrated education abroad in the community college. Access to education abroad by diverse populations, the challenges of local–global relationships, and ensuring responsive workforce preparation are key areas where community colleges contribute to the field but are also most vulnerable. By contextualizing how conflicts and limitations are viewed within community colleges, the chapter opens up a dialogue for change. The conclusion shares a vision for community college education abroad, and links the reimagining of programming with other novel efforts necessary to build curriculum for the emerging generation of global citizens.

PERTINENCE OF GLOBAL CITIZEN TO COMMUNITY COLLEGES

Production of the *global citizen* is at the core of community college education. This chapter defines the global citizen as meaning someone trained to observe, reflect, interpret, and particularly, contribute to improving global society. A global citizen embodies the traits and learning outcomes associated with intercultural, multicultural, and international education, particularly including the desire to learn more about other peoples and possess the skills to live, work, and transact with those from radically different backgrounds within and across borders. Thus, global citizens apply international literacy, which enables them to interpret and utilize value judgment skills that result in positive and sustainable social interaction and social responsibility.

In the early twentieth century, community (or "junior" colleges at the time) colleges were formed to help solve the common problems of society, produce an educated citizenry that would assure social order, and promote a common humanity and culture (Cohen & Brawer, 2003; Eells, 1931; Koos, 1924). For community colleges, the call to produce a global citizenry did not start in 2001 with the World Trade Center, the 1990s with NAFTA, the 1980s with deténte, or even the 1950s with Sputnik. Instead, it started with the 1947 *The President's Commission on Higher Education*, popularly known as the Truman Commission Report which, in part, encouraged all higher educational institutions to produce an international citizenry (Zook, 1947). Since this report, community college international educators have been defining and refining the connection between international literacy and global citizenry (American Council on International Intercultural Education [ACIIE], 1994; Hess, 1982; Raby, 2005). The landmark Truman Report defined community colleges as part of the higher education spectrum as it delineated a shift from a "junior" to "community" college model, and recommended that higher education open its doors to *all* citizens; *all* students to gain international understanding; and education be the solution to social problems and administration of public affairs (Russell, 1949; Zook, 1947). One subheading in this document, "Preparation for World Citizenship," states,

> In speed of transportation and communication and in economic interdependence the nations of the globe already are one world; the task is to secure recognition and acceptance of this oneness in the thinking of the people, so that the concept of one world may be realized psychologically, socially, and in good time politically.... For effective international understanding and cooperation we need to acquire knowledge of, and respect for, other peoples and their cultures—their traditions, their customs, and attitudes, their social institutions, their needs and aspirations for the future. We must learn to admit the possible worth of human values and ways of living we ourselves do not accept. (pp. 14–15)

This document castigated higher education for its elitism through intentional limits to admissions (including race-based) and intensified the mission of educating those left out by universities. Of pertinence to this chapter is that the discussion of the need for a global citizenry began at the same time community colleges took root.

Even as he charged both junior colleges and their university counterparts with achieving these goals, George Zook, Truman Commission Chair, could not have imagined that one day community colleges would educate one-half of all national undergraduates in some, if not all of their higher education (Cohen & Brawer, 2003). Although some lament that barely 20% of those ever finish a bachelor's degree, others view this as a unique characteristic that indicates the diverse goals of community college students (Levinson, 2005). Regardless of intent, be it transfer, life-long learning, or trade/service careers, all community college students benefit from the higher education they receive. In the context of this chapter, however, once it is understood that most community college students *do not* finish a bachelor's degree, it is even more critical to promote global education experiences in the community college context.

Community college international education literature defines four rationales for why community colleges should promote international education: political, economic, academic integrity, and humanistic (Council on Learning, 1981; Raby & Tarrow, 1996; Valeau & Raby, 2007; Scanlon, 1990). The first three rationales discuss how an internationalized curriculum is a pragmatic tool that ensures national security, prepares students for a globalized job market, and helps keep all academic, technical, occupational, and vocational college courses updated and with accurate information. While all three rationales are important, it is the humanistic rationale that links them to the goal referenced from the Truman Commission Report: developing a well-informed and internationalized citizenry with a common humanity.

The humanist rationale promotes international education as a process that is necessary in order to understand other languages and cultures in our now permanently multicultural society, thus contributing directly to building tolerance and peace. Education abroad assists this education by securing cross-cultural communication skills through which students can reconcile conflicting ideologies, perceive multiple perspectives, and respect a relativity of differences. Following the humanist rationale, education abroad graduates gain skills to serve their country in professions of political sensitivity or in professions that support the country's economy, and overall, empower active participants as global citizens in a democratic society. Not only does this literacy provide the foundation for effective citizenship training, but it adheres to the historical mission of the community college to educate to bind society together as it increases students' employability and potential throughout life.

Community colleges may be the final opportunity for many students to study abroad, to learn with international peers, to gain experiential learning for career enhancement, and to test their own intercultural abilities. As such, community colleges are key contributors to the success of our multicultural society; preparing students both for careers and broad participation in the American democratic experience, and in securing the skills needed for *global citizenry*.

Unique Characteristics of Community Colleges

The community college mission prioritizes learning experiences that integrate academic knowledge with cognitive and social skills. This approach is designed to produce citizens who support the local community, hold shared identities, and support successful collective action. In this mission resides yet untapped sources to establish global citizenry skills. Educating the individual, be it student, administrator or trustee, teacher, or staff, is the foundation upon which international competency is built. When entire disciplines are internationalized, even greater numbers of students are affected. In this process, three characteristics help place education abroad within the community college context, but also have the greatest potential to hinder future growth as they are at the foundation of all problems profiled in this chapter: access, a local/global dichotomy, and workforce preparation.

Open access is perhaps the one key term necessary to understand the community college mission because all community colleges embody this philosophy. For many students these colleges represent their last chance for personal and professional growth. Whether for terminal certificates or potential transfer to universities, community colleges remain the first rung up the social ladder. For education abroad, simply by allowing freshmen, sophomores, and nondegree students to study abroad, often with only minimal or no previous college credit earned, and few GPA restrictions, community colleges have transformed the once elitist junior year abroad foundation.

The local–global dichotomy has existed since the formation of district boundaries to serve the needs of the geographic community, and since 1972, community colleges have been located within 25 miles of nearly every potential student (Cohen, 1972). On the surface, this local emphasis seems to bind students to transfer to local 4-year universities or for employment at local businesses. In this light, preparing students for anything external to the direct connection with the local is a luxury. However, Raby and Valeau (2007) suggest that when defined globally, the term *community* expands global networks that demand colleges no longer think in linear relationships across borders, but in educating students as *global citizens*. Such education is then crucial for all students.

Workforce preparation remains a key charge of the community college. Globalization has changed the employment field, and small, large, local, and multinational businesses need employees with international literacy skills: "the United States continues to need informed and tolerant citizens, members of the workforce who can function in multicultural environments, and language and area experts to teach and serve in government" (Green, 2007, p. 15). Little doubt remains that the world will demand increasing economic communications, environmental, technical, and scientific competencies (Dellow, 2007; Milliron, 2007), and that teaching these subjects is no longer a question of if, but how soon they are integrated within all community college disciplines (Levin, 2002). Both the American Association for Community Colleges (AACC) and the Association of Community College Trustees (ACCT) assert that "a rededication to global education is required that will inspire and shape new educational strategies initiated to promote the shared goals of global connectedness and understanding" (AACC, 2006).

The problem remains that when global citizenship is juxtaposed against funding limits, the predominating "local mission" philosophy appears. As community college state and district revenues continue to shrink, the differences are increasingly made up by student tuition, grant and endowment funding, and student fees (Bailey & Morest, 2006). Fees can include charges for program services, orientation activities, application processing, placement in an external program, or transcripting credit earned while abroad. As a result, student funds are strained for any off-campus learning experiences while budgets for academic programs are consolidated to reduce staff or are cut altogether. In education abroad, this means that the people who teach, advise, and provide services to diverse constituencies have to do all of the above in one job.

Hence, this Catch-22 situation promotes the continued lack of a critical mass of students, dedicated staff, and programs themselves. The resulting low numbers maintain international programs on the college periphery and thereby ensure that they are subject to underfunding, inadequate support, and low visibility. In turn, this negative cycle limits access, which is the antithesis of the community college open access policy.

Community College Program and Student Profile

Although community colleges have been offering education abroad since 1967,[2] data indicate less than 15% of all community colleges do so.[3] In 2002, the Institute of International Education's (IEE) *Open Doors* reported the first community college responses as an aggregate sample and since it included both headcounts and college programs, it remains the field's baseline in which 143 community colleges are listed, of which, 94 had programs that sent a total of 4,085 students abroad. The 2007 report included 151 colleges, of which, 114 had programs that served 6,957 students. While the number of programs only grew by 7%, a notable 41% increase of students indicates that the demand is there when the opportunity exists.

Community college students include those who historically have been denied any privileged educational opportunities. Seventy-three percent of community college students are defined as nontraditional, with 50% first-generation college attendees, 40% over the age of 25, and 64% enrolled part-time (Cohen, 2009). This student population is considered "bifurcated" (Levinson, 2005, pp. 18–20) due to the split between traditional transfer-bound students, and others. These student characteristics are key considerations for advising, program logistics, and other education abroad topics addressed below.

While the field overall has a paltry percentage of underrepresented students, this number would be more embarrassing without the contributions of community colleges. Patterns indicate that community colleges send a more diverse student body abroad than 4-year higher educational institutions. Since community colleges more closely mirror the diversity of their local communities, and many of these communities are majority minority and lower income, this student profile should not be surprising. Table 11.1 shows comparative data.

Finally, when social class and cultural markers are analyzed, community college students' motivations and approaches are distinct from those of their university counterparts. When community college students go to nontraditional countries, it is frequently as a heritage student. Moreover, the experiences abroad and those brought home by minority students (who are much more highly represented in community colleges), in any location, remains distinct from their European-American classmates. For example, while all students abroad may experience prejudice as a result of being Americans, students of color and lower-class students experience additional issues of racism and lack of privilege. As a result, the intersection of diversity in age, gender, career interests, and class backgrounds has made the impact on the study abroad field of community college education abroad undeniable.

Table 11.1 *Comparison by Ethnicity between Total Numbers of Community College and University Study Abroad Participants.*

Race	Community College %	University %
White/Caucasian	69.0%	83.0%
Hispanic/Latino	13.1%	5.4%
Multiracial	9.1%	1.2%
African-American	5.0%	3.5%
Asian-American Pacific Islander	3.4%	6.3%
Native American/Alaskan Native	0.5%	0.6%

Source: IIE Open Doors, 2007

Contextualizing Current Problems

This section depicts problem areas that disable education abroad as a critical catalyst for community colleges and their students to advance toward global citizenship: (1) administration and stakeholder considerations; (2) staffing; (3) finance and budgeting; (4) program logistics and choice of program options; (5) curriculum; (6) program quality and assessment; and (7) student access and student funding. The intent is for each section to speak to the representative college leaders and staff who can most impact the future of education abroad in community colleges. Because of the range of colleges that can be profiled in each section, we are including individual examples as endnotes.

Administration and Stakeholder Considerations

Central to this discussion is the creation of an institutional commitment that includes international education in general and education abroad in particular. A lack of communication feeds the lack of commitment. Historically, community colleges did not share information beyond the local level due to local governance issues and an uncertainty about their place in higher education (Cohen & Brawer, 2003; Clark, 1960; Gleazer, 1980). Due to the prevailing local emphasis, education abroad was never fully adopted by community colleges and those who were early advocates felt that if they called attention to their activities, opposition would cause their elimination. Indeed, history shows a pattern of colleges with prolific programs being totally eliminated without warning. As a result, communication was sparse and most colleges grew their abroad programs with a singular programmatic emphasis which ensured survival, but did not garner widespread support among community college stakeholders. Despite recent live and satellite conferences on community college education abroad,[4] the fears of being "shut down" remain.

In order to rectify this situation, we contend that all stakeholders provide the foundational support needed to "believe" a globalized campus is desirable and to build strong campus-wide networks to support program activities. In the understaffed world of community colleges, it takes a great commitment to connect diverse groups like senior administration, trustees, student government, faculty senate, registrar's office, curriculum committees, counseling staff, financial aid staff, and college Web master. For trustees, a shift in priority includes developing expansive educational and economic networks that link education abroad to other service and learning communities. For administrators, open, deep, and directed discussions (Wheatley, 2006) with diverse staff groups about fitting education abroad into the larger college philosophy and curriculum will help recognize how the past limits the present and how the present must reshape the future. For faculty, engagement occurs through their own preparation for the new learning environment, in internationalizing their courses, in program evaluation, and in forming instructional partnerships overseas. In turn, college policy needs to honor faculty and staff with international knowledge and who infuse the wider college curriculum with that knowledge and continue that connection throughout the college in new student orientations, college functions, and student services programs.

Suffice it to say that perhaps the greatest requirement for success is long-term commitment by senior leaders to globalize their college and the insistence of faculty to offer diverse education abroad experiences that support cross-campus and inter-community networks.[5] Such reconsideration of access to global learning can break down silos, integrate learning activities, and even reenergize traditional access points associated with developmental and transfer education.

Staffing

Every community college is distinct in its location (rural or urban), finances (funding formulas and local wealth), and special needs (high developmental, faculty competencies, internal governance and location). Thus, there is no one staffing plan. Some community colleges combine education abroad with other international programs or even service learning with a single staff in one large office.[6] In this setting, there must be a clear understanding about the nature and roles of each program. Other colleges support individual offices for each international educational program.[7] In this setting, communication and collaboration must be stressed. Most community colleges have no special office for education abroad, so it remains a small portion of a faculty's, dean's, senior administrator's, or even executive assistant's assignment (many of whom have no experience in the field), and whose work is conducted in addition to paid hours.

Enhancing community college education (as advocated by Hess, 1982) begins with the college providing a visible location in which a range of study abroad program options are displayed. Unlike Hess, we advocate that it is not enough to have a staffed office. Today, community college education abroad staff should be built around expected outcomes that include not only recruiting, counseling, orientation, reentry, student support, and faculty program development and evaluation, but also the building of cross-college relationships. Thus, success on the job is not only measured in terms of a percentage increase in students or total FTE, but in a complete accounting for how global learning is being woven into the college curriculum. Support staff can address day-to-day inquiries, maintenance of program literature and Web sites, and preparations for internal forums and community outreach. In addition, leadership must link students, faculty, and community with programs and partners *outside the district*, define faculty selection, secure long-range planning, and adhere to related risk management plans. The authority to supervise valid assessment is vital, as is the ability to rein in excessive travel when poor results are measured. Absence of these very activities, or poor oversight of these roles, has been a primary criticism of community college international programs, and a cause of liability suits (students cannot learn of or prepare for risks when faculty act independently of college guidelines). This external role has been commonly underestimated, or not addressed, in budgeting for staff in the past. Perhaps most importantly, students become ambassadors for these new connections when, through consistent college mentors, their learning is specialized and connected to the wider world. Many colleges with multiple dedicated positions gain national attention and awards for their work in the field.[8]

Finance and Budgeting

If the larger goal is to maximize student access by integrating education abroad into the college and community, then staff must have the resources to support vested players and invest in long-term programming. Ninety percent of those who responded to a survey on SECUSS-L and SECUSSCC listservs, indicated that their education abroad office is funded out of general college funds, that most do not even have a directed budget for education abroad, and those who do, typically operate their education abroad on an annual base commitment of under $5,000. We contend that this is not enough money to adequately secure a staff, travel for site visits, evaluations, conference training, conduct new program and faculty professional development, develop faculty projects that link curriculum home and abroad, and offer small scholarship funds to increase student access.

In order to rectify this situation, stakeholders must provide the budgetary support and build education abroad into the larger staffing plan and job descriptions that provide more than minimal release time for faculty and staff. A dramatic irony exists in that community college programs that result in revenue enhancements, such as grant-making activities and international students, show dramatic expansion, while nonincome generating programs, such as education abroad, do not. Few community college education abroad programs are for-profit since profit means that open access is at risk because it favors the wealthy. Hence, it is important to note that a dollar spent for other programs, such as international student support, can also be a dollar for study abroad, if salary lines are under the "international" heading. Some colleges supplement funding by applying all international revenues to college internationalization or grant revenues to support faculty development or leverage cooperative funding with consortia.[9] This distinguishes how strongly the role of funding affects access to education abroad.

Similar to other small, yet labor intensive academic programs, education abroad is a cost effective learning activity when measured against the knowledge and experience gained. Learning outcomes may result from a variety of activities associated with several fee sources (administrative, tuition, on-site excursions, foundation) especially given the above considerations on collegewide integration. A transparent budget model with line items that respond to actual planning, programming, and learning will keep all players focused on outcomes and avoid the need for constant permissions, reconsideration, and problem-based management.

Program Logistics and Choice of Program Options

The vast distinctions between small and rural colleges with under 2,000 students and the large urban districts with over 10,000 students underscore the variation in program logistics.[10] Central to any program design is the ability to fit the needs and lifestyles of students, as well as to understanding why budgeting, staffing, and alternatives to traditional programming are necessary to reach most community college students. The categories below are addressed under vastly different circumstances from one college to the next, but will appeal to distinct populations of this majority of nontraditional students.

Length of Time

Although many community colleges advocate for short-term programs of 17 days to 4 weeks as an optimal fit for older, working, and career students, and in fact, 90% of community college programs are short-term, there is a noted increase in community college semester programs. In the community college student context, any time spent learning abroad is valuable so long as it is connected with future intercultural or career learning activities and goals that then include integration with formal campus, classroom, and community learning (Frost, 2007; Raby, 2007).

Program Design

The unique nature of the relationship between faculty and students at community colleges increases the popularity of campus-based faculty-led programs. Increased understanding of institutional risk reinforces the need for faculty to work in alignment with a designated campus office or committee which then authorizes who teaches, what courses are taught, and who oversees logistics. A key consideration for community college students is to ensure that credits are either

177 ▪

transferable or apply toward degree/certificate attainment. Due to limited qualified counseling staff, and higher costs, few students participate in direct-enrollment third-party programs or in year-long programs. While students will discover (often on campus bulletin boards or via the Web) and bring information of these options to a counselor's attention, staff (if it exists) rarely have time to work with admissions to advocate for transfer credit, or provide proper counsel. Finally, travel arrangements are often contracted out, since some consider this further reduces college liability. Above all, the close connection between costs, institutional risk, and immediate career benefit is obvious to community college staff.

Faculty Selection

Faculty selection varies as some colleges see an advantage to sending the same (reliable) faculty abroad annually to build a following; others discourage such exclusivity as it fails to insure college integration. The same holds true for those who administer programs.[11] Overall, the more areas of the college that are involved, the less peripheral education abroad becomes. Also, program design should include checks and balances between the coordinator, program faculty, and the international education committee/council. This insures that learning outcomes, faculty development, and evaluation and improvement are built into each program and everyone's formal responsibilities.

State or Regional Consortia

State or regional consortia allow colleges to work together to design, offer, and market programs, share costs, and accept the transfer of credits.[12] This joint work helps counter high logistical overhead and provides a critical mass of students. One model designates a "lead college" that designs a program, sends its own faculty to lead the program, and receives all student tuition and state apportionment. Another model changes the "lead" college annually to allow each consortium member a chance to build brand loyalty within the college by sending its own faculty abroad and by receiving tuition. Korbel (2007) profiles successes where a college can send just one student and yet be involved in promoting education abroad without overhead costs as well as challenges which include issues of accreditation, financial aid sharing, and lack of institutionalization when colleges do not "own" their own programs.

Curriculum

Community college education abroad curriculum is as diverse as the colleges themselves. While a clear distinction exists between education abroad (credit) and study tours (noncredit community education), the former is in adherence to the field, and the latter remains attractive to many community college stakeholders. Unlike upper division, or graduate credits, community college transfer courses articulate through a college, a university system, and then state approval process. This takes six months to over a year. While faculty can create "special topics" courses for an abroad experience (for-credit), students shy away from programs that cannot guarantee transfer credit. More commonly, faculty will offer special topics within an existing course, such as a focus on Mayan civilization in a Latin America studies or introduction to humanities course offered in Guatemala. Abroad courses may have distinct features to address the learning context, but they are almost always articulated and approved for transfer credit well before a program is advertised. This ensures that curriculum options are within the state's transfer system. For example, in states where foreign language is not well articulated, less programming based on language acquisition occurs. Given lower division coursework criteria, the following five learning approaches define appeals to certain learners based on their levels of experience, funding, and future interests.

Locations and Disciplines

Locations and disciplines are offered in some countries that are similar to those found in universities, and yet, their academic focus is distinct because they cater to the career or nontransfer student by offering both academic courses for transfer and courses only offered by community colleges, such as those in technical, vocational, and occupational fields. It is therefore, not surprising that community colleges offer more programs in foreign languages, health sciences, fine or applied arts, and education than 4-year universities (IIE, 2007). An often added-value are courses that compare sociopolitical issues or contexts abroad that are also present in the students' home community.[13] Programs remain popular that combine the academic with the experiential and offer service components such as student internships for co-op work credit, work-shadowing, or extended research assignments to connect class learning with intercultural experience.

Singular Departmental or Individual Focus

Singular departmental or individual focus has defined community college programs. It has been detrimental to the programs over time that the individualized construct acculturated people into believing that such programs could be run on a shoestring, independently, and under the radar. Unlike the past, expansive and continual discussion between representatives across the institution will redefine education abroad as no longer being one person's pet project or the ownership of a single department. When education abroad funds go to support one faculty member who leads a summer program to Spain for students interested in that language, there are many other students whose interests are not met in diverse fields such as business, nursing, and Asian studies. If study abroad is limited to modern language students, holistic cross-campus connections are not being met.

Integrating Education Abroad with Wider College-Community Learning Initiatives

Integrating education abroad with wider college–community learning initiatives, while not common, is beneficial to making education abroad a holistic part of the total college environment. Some colleges offer education abroad and then initiate internationalizing curriculum, international business, and international student programs. Other colleges develop international development programs, added internationalizing curricula, and finally link the two with education abroad.[14]

Independent Study

Independent study appeals to students who (1) participate in direct enrollment in international universities;[15] (2) live/work abroad and seek the means to integrate their life experiences with independent study designed with a designated faculty; or (3) live/study abroad and take online courses offered by their home institution. Since community college students already have vast life experience, with an average age of 29, some are willing to take classes in which not all credits transfer, or design their own programs to enhance their intercultural and academic experiences while living/working abroad.[16] Distance education allows different dimensions for independent study. Some students who live abroad can earn academic credit by sharing their abroad experiences with others in the college online learning community. Alternatively, students in group abroad programs can share their abroad experiences in similar online learning communities.[17]

Work, Work/Study, Internships, Service, and Volunteering Abroad

Work, work/study, internships, service, and volunteering abroad meet many needs of nontraditional students, especially because it matches similar internship, laboratory, or experiential learning activities traditionally arranged in the home community. However, lack of specialized staff to coordinate admissions, academics, secure credit, and the high cost of these programs results in limited community college participation. In these programs, advanced activity planning and organization partnerships with overseas institutions ensure that participants are assigned tasks and activities that can result in meaningful learning and service rendered.[18]

Program Quality and Assessment

Unique community college characteristics are visible in key education abroad issues associated with quality including evaluation; predeparture and reentry training; and health, safety, and risk management.

Evaluation

Due to strict accreditation oversight, the open access philosophy, and the limits to transferability, community college education abroad courses are evaluated on terms very similar to those offered on campus, except for particulars special to a given location (dorms or host family) and approaches (experiential) to learning. Basic formal evaluations include a standard Likert-scale end-of-course and instructor evaluations. The field indicates increasing attention to measuring student learning and the need for both ongoing and transparent quality improvement assessment. This is especially important in allowing program leaders to be in close contact with students' thoughts and emotions as they adjust to new living and learning environments and how they relate their overall learning experience to their college community. Successful evaluation tools, such as those promoted by The American Council on Education (ACE), were hardly common until recently, and even today many colleges run programs with only a limited association with wider college assessment processes that promote professionalism and advertise associated learning outcomes to deans, presidents, and trustees and connect those outcomes to college education abroad and strategic plan goals. The Forum on Education Abroad, *Standards of Best Practice* (2007) was the first time widespread standards were piloted by 10 community colleges. No longer must community colleges adapt a university model; this time community colleges were part of the review and approval process.

Predeparture and Reentry Programs

Due to a lack of devoted and professional staff, orientation programs are frequently linked with marketing efforts. Some colleges offer Web-based tutorials, such as *PLATO,* or have third-party providers offer airport-based predeparture programs because sometimes this is the first point where all students, from multiple colleges, are in the same place. Few colleges offer multihour/day predeparture programs that are independent of orientation. Reentry programs range from on-site evaluation to dedicated workshops that take place at the conclusion of the course. Given the short duration of many programs and the expansion of individualized projects abroad, defined and quality reentry programs are crucial. However, without support networks, or follow-on assignments associated with the credit-based course, students are largely left on their own to follow up on their abroad experience. Following the lead of the Gilman International Scholarships, some colleges encourage students to conduct follow-on or outreach projects that help reconcile their learning experiences abroad with their educational and professional goals (IIE, 2009).

Health, Safety, and Legal Issues

Health, safety and legal issues that were addressed in the 1985 California Colleges for International Education (CCIE) "Study Abroad Bylaws"[19] share similarities to the 2001 Community Colleges for International Development (CCID) satellite conference on *Legal Issues in Study Abroad* and echo sentiments in NAFSA's *Guide* (Brockington, Hoffa, & Martin, 2005). Knowledge of these issues depends on the longevity and professionalism of the education abroad director, and the overall college support. Therefore, the right investment of human resources for staff development and collaboration with an in-house legal office ensures a safety and risk management plan that works for that particular community college. New challenges to the field include unique issues, such as allowing concurrent enrollment of high school students on programs, adult liability issues, mobility limitations, compliance in some countries for other-abled students, and inability to secure personal insurance for senior citizen students.

Three distinctive problems remain. The first involves leadership that does not distinguish risk management from local–global mission debates. Administrators who argue against education abroad in the context of "I do not want to see a headline that says 'College students hurt in bus accident'" are not likely to prioritize risk management over pure avoidance. The second is a lack of staff to conduct training, and establish campus-wide relationships to secure a solid risk management plan that meets local campus needs. With limited staff, many community colleges utilize a risk management plan that is offered not by their college but by a third-party provider. Finally, continued periphery status results when education abroad is not fully integrated into the college. This causes nonconventional patterns to emerge, such as programs run for profit or recreation, use of a provider not sanctioned by the college, and renegade faculty who use college name/logo, their staff position, and even hold on-campus orientations and utilize official registration, all without permission of the college. These activities expose the college to severe legal risk, and more than any other issue, speak to the peripheral nature, limited attention, and limited financing in community college education abroad.

Student Access and Student Funding

Community college student access to education abroad is based on both personal and institutional factors. Personal issues include economic barriers, difficulty in reconciling family and work obligations, and lack of cultural capital that stems from being first generation college goers or first generation Americans. Since community colleges represent their local communities and many of those communities are economically challenged, financial cost is a key component. As such, extensive financial aid counseling and knowledge by college staff that it *is* within federal regulations to use financial aid to study abroad, even for short-term programs, must exist. Financial resources are also needed to support students who are unable to obtain financial aid, but who are still struggling economically. There are passionate advocates for creative financing, but that does not mean that priority is given by the college to education abroad. Best practices include scholarships funded by endowments, fund-raising efforts, or using a portion of student fees.[20] Offsetting costs and linking scholarships to a for-profit model is limited since so few programs generate profit.

Program cost, as detailed in Table 11.2 below, is central in the planning and marketing of programs. Faculty-led community college programs include a $785 (one-week volunteer health program between border states, or a two-week marine biology course in Baja, Mexico) as well programs for $ 3,000 to $ 8,400 that last 3 to 16 weeks. A SECUSSA-CC survey lists the most expensive community college semester program (2008–2009) at $8,400.[21] Even discounted as compared to university programs, these are out of the reach for most students. Frequent bidding to third-party providers and utilization of home-stays and dormitories helps assure the highest academic quality at the lowest cost. It is not uncommon for students to complete extensive advance planning in order to go abroad, even 1 to 2 years in advance. When education abroad is designed through attention to all of these programming components, and fits the needs and lifestyles of nontraditional students, they are the most successful (Raby & Sawadogo, 2005).

Access to global learning opportunities continues to be defined by cost, program packaging, and transferability of completed coursework. High value with low cost is a hallmark of the community college; the same is not so easy in an experiential and international setting. Matching real costs with funding efforts remains a key challenge to community college international educators.

Table 11.2 Cost Comparisions for Community College Education Abroad Programs: A National Sample 2007–2008

	Summer session: 2008	Fall 2008 or Spring 2008 semesters	Winter or spring break: 2007–2008
Low	$785 (Baja) $1,824–$2,199 (Mexico) $2,175 (England) $2,127 (Italy)	$2,600 (Costa Rica) $3,687 (Madrid)	$340 (Baja) $1,900 (Costa Rica) $1,670 (Mexico)
Average	$2,500 (Cambodia) $2,670 (Costa Rica) $2,995 (Vietnam) $4,900 (China)	$4,385 (Argentina) $4,600 (Japan) $4,800 (Vietnam) $2,550 (EU) $2,600 (Costa Rica)	$2,000 (Argentina) $2399 (Thailand) $2,400 (Mexico)
High	$3,697 (Japan) $3,999–$4,645 (France) $3,885 (Peru) $3,997 (Germany) $4,275 (China) $4,543 (Austria/Italy)	$5,650 (Costa Rica) $5,850–$5,950 (Florence) $5,550–$6,797 (Spain) $6,627–$7,045 (England) $6,327–$8,375 (Paris)	$3,000 (England) $3,395 (Ghana) $3,400 (Vietnam) $3,900 (Florence) $3,995 (New Zealand) $4,500 (Turkey, Morocco, Israel) $4,500–$4,955 (South Africa)

However, as a 2005 study of 110 California community colleges shows, that while administrators and faculty cite personal issues as the most common barrier, students instead cite their lack of knowledge of existing programs (Raby & Rhodes, 2005). Even when community colleges do offer education abroad, ad hoc marketing makes it such that students frequently learn of opportunities by chance. So when colleges complain that they can never get enough students to run a program, it is because information is not getting to the students, not because of lack of interest (Raby & Rhodes, 2005).

Reimagining Global Learning in Community Colleges

Community college education abroad remains on the periphery of most community college missions, with limited college support, and even less advocacy. Best practices in the field have, until very recently, been in the domain of universities, and rarely took into consideration the unique community college characteristics discussed above.[22] Thus, after 40 years of peripheral community college education abroad, the time has come to reimagine global learning possibilities. This chapter does so by looking at new patterns and the means by which education abroad can become institutionalized for the next generation of community college students.

Reimagining begins with education abroad offices holistically connected throughout the college, including student services, classrooms, curriculum, and evaluation processes. Unlike Hess, who simply advocated for a staffed office, we propose that this is but one piece of the globalizing puzzle. A truly community-centered model will include a transparent budget model that encourages diverse revenue streams to support the center including (1) direct fees for supporting programs and advising services; (2) direct links to the college foundation for scholarship funds and donor outreach; and (3) a community advisory board that supports both funding and the evolution of a center that meets the community's needs.

Similar to Hess's model, leadership for this initiative comes from both top-down and bottom-up models. Reimagined top-down reform is more than paper support by senior leadership. It begins with institutionalization of education abroad as a critical component of the college through campus committees, mission statements and college policies, and college budgets. Hence the many pieces of the project are shared by all administrative areas. Many successful community colleges in the field do have strong chancellor/presidential support for study abroad; however, since senior leadership does not work alone in the community college, success must also come from the bottom up with supportive faculty who envision and lead programs and staffing that daily counsels students living, traveling, working, retiring, or studying abroad. In this new construct, it is central that faculty-led initiatives link the abroad experience with existing course academic, technical, and vocational content, local international trade centers, thematic symposia offerings that are the center of a global learning community, and international students who bring first hand accounts to domestic classroom. But rarely can these be connected through volunteers. When diverse staff (admissions, counseling, faculty, community relations) are charged with meeting both student interests and community outreach components, then education abroad becomes much more than a program. Areas such as the provision of informal counseling for individuals traveling abroad; outreach to K-12 schools; networking with international students; offering career, short-term work, or retirement abroad help; and reviewing credit earned abroad all become part of a larger college–community goal. Such a crossroads of global activity produces inspiration for learning on the front-end, and wrap-around learning for the college and community, and a long-term vision for globalizing the college.

In a time of contracting resources, higher education increasingly connects programs into networks and expansive partnerships. This is partly due to application of management science to education, it is also due to the increasing individuality and power that students have through technology. For example, currently all education abroad credit is based on the principle that a student signs up for a program first and then learns. This eliminates the opportunity for students who have already lived, traveled, or worked abroad to apply that experience for college credit. Equal opportunities need to be in place between both programs and individualized learning plans; finding a formula to support faculty involvement across diverse learning formats (5 students = one equated credit hour, for example), and allow learning to be measured, connected with service, and credited through local demonstration of knowledge and skills acquired. This brief model exemplifies one way in which a college can create multiple pathways to global learning. It is critical to reimagine financing so that it can support the size of the service population. The model might include; direct fees for supporting programs, advising services, and transcript evaluation; direct links to the college foundation for scholarship funds and preapproved fund-raising activities as well as donor outreach; a mix of for-profit (noncredit) and at-cost (credit) programs; and a community advisory board with the mission to support both fund raising and continued evolution toward the community's needs. Moreover, the stability of revenue streams into the college are likely to play a much larger role in external outlook and programming than internal champions.

Reimagining opportunities provides the context for educational reform. A reimagined education abroad model includes several means to promote students and community members, learning outside the "local" boundaries, and then sharing the benefits of that learning in local contexts. Choice becomes critical in this process. Choice for students to enroll in college developed group programs (either alone or in consortia), in direct-enrollment programs, in independent study, or in work, internship, or volunteer programs. By embracing the many options that students have today, education abroad is connected with the total college learning environment and in so doing, connects colleges to more potential partners, which helps to expand their own recruitment base. In conclusion, integrated in this mix then are trustees who support education abroad policy and practice; administrators who initiate reforms; and faculty who teach internationalized curricula, on campus and abroad, and of course students who are the one element that connects all pieces of the globalizing puzzle. For colleges that offer education abroad, institutionalization, holistic integration, and expansions of opportunity are key targets. For colleges that do not offer abroad opportunities, and thus may have fewer entrenched interests, the possibility to employ an organic model may be even greater.

The chapter has outlined numerous examples of both historical shortcomings and college success stories to frame limits, challenges, and various avenues toward improvement. Given the vast diversity of community and technical colleges in the United States today, no one model prevails. However, because the history of education abroad in community colleges has been written as a peripheral program, today we need to reframe education abroad into a community and global context. The following 10 core principles shown in Table 11.3 were distilled from our research on many of the programs referenced in this chapter, and ordered as a framework for colleges to reimagine education abroad programs contextualized within the larger community college mission of global workforce development. These principles form the basis of the conclusions that follow.

By considering education abroad within the study of the whole organism (the college) it is not hard to see that few activities have the same potential to connect the college with great and distant resources. Rarely have colleges recognized the true value of education abroad programs as spanning local boundaries to attract future resources (knowledge, human, and economic resources)

Table 11.3 *10 Prerequisites to Re-Imagine Education Abroad in Community Colleges*

1. Support in word and deed for the college mission to provide a diversity of higher education global learning opportunities.

2. Diverse stakeholders are charged to prioritize the multiplicity of learning experiences, as take place in education abroad, that contribute to global workforce preparation.

3. Institutionalize education abroad as part of the global college experience that can happen alongside or through classroom, distance, service, experiential, individualized, and other modes of learning.

4. Budgeting, that weaves networks across general education curriculum, faculty professional development, student enrichment, department outreach, trustee orientation, and college-industry partnerships.

5. Staff with dedicated positions, with influence in administrative circles, and diverse skill sets to build instructional networks, including office support to address all student needs in the application process.

6. Consistent emphasis to bring in new faculty, staff and administrators to ensure growth and to provide sustainability over time.

7. Define education abroad as neither profit-making nor financial loss, but rather as a way to link the college to a series of knowledge communities.

8. Coalition-building with national and state-wide consortia to reduce costs and expand academic resources.

9. Assessment and evaluation components that measure comprehensive and complete learning experiences across orientation, pre-departure training, multiple learning experiences connected with intercultural and reflective activities, and re-entry components on campus.

10. Accept that results are similar to other small, yet labor intensive academic programs; education abroad is "life-changing" and thus a cost effective strategy for the knowledge and experience that later result in high-value community contributions.

back to the local setting. The framework provided above is designed for this purpose: to break down the notion that programs can thrive in isolation from larger college and community goals.

Students, faculty, staff, programs, partnerships, and networks are all part of something much larger than any college. They are all part of the swirl that is lifelong learning; colleges can only hope to be sending as many agents as possible into this swirl, because the only way to benefit the community is to actually return knowledge, ideas, and a productive global citizenry to the local community. In this context, education abroad is connected to the larger college's international education mission and hence the reform journey is framed not only in staff and dollars, but in the institutional, and human, mission of growth. Living systems theories (Senge, 1990) provide the framework for college leaders to reconsider why study abroad is valuable not just for students, but for the college community. How students, faculty, and international education administrators all contribute to this vision is a key element to sustaining education abroad beyond the programming crises that occur from time to time.

CONCLUSION

Organizations adapt and change as a result of influences from their external environment, rather than primarily from their own inspiration (Pfeffer, 2003). The community college, due to its local nature of district boundaries and often elected trustees, has adapted, albeit slowly, to over 100-plus years of national and global influences. Community colleges have long been valued for their ability to adapt to local economic and sociopolitical changes, and thereby serve their students. Certainly, community colleges will be rooted in their local community interests far into the future, particularly if a majority of their funds come from local taxes and tuition. However, the multicultural nature of the community, employment prospects in a globalized economy, and the highly mobile nature of students today have forever changed the mission of the community college. The world is knocking on our district doors.

George Zook wrote in 1947 in the Truman Commission Report that, due to an internationalized society, there was no more learning for a local context. Current globalization echoes these words, for we now intentionally need to learn on a global level to support our local environments. Few intensive learning experiences besides education abroad provide transformative learning to a level that causes reconsideration of one's own self as a learner, and with the impulse and even passion to share the benefits in the home community.

From the many questions posed in this chapter, it becomes clear that education abroad is not programs and places, but, like the community college itself, about *connections and processes between people.* These relationships expand the boundaries of the college and community to educational networks and resources far beyond the college district. The problem in the past had always been too few people engaged in the relationships to sustain and support student learning needs. In order for community colleges to meet students' needs and gain the benefits of global knowledge networks, they will need diverse funding streams, many stakeholders, and community networks to form the new global learning enterprise of the college.

This chapter has provided answers for how college leaders can address global learning needs alongside access, local mission orientation, and pressing financial limitations. Historical references and context were presented to demonstrate that the globalizing process began many decades ago by national education leaders, yet only through recent globalization have community colleges rediscovered this association with their mission. While responses will vary from college to college and state to state; where one place might add a fee, another will focus on space, students are increasingly seeking global learning opportunities. The time is right for community colleges to connect all of the elements associated here with education abroad into a network of global learning relationships. Through reimagining education abroad in the community college, it can be recreated as connecting community, through many passionate learners, to a rapidly globalizing society.

NOTES

1. AACC, 1998; ACIIE/Stanley Foundation, 1994; ACIIE/Stanley, 1996; Building Communities, 1998; Konrad, College of DuPage Annual Reports, 2002–2008; Edwards and Tonkin, 1990; Elsner, Tsunoda, and Korbel, 1994; Fersh 1993; Gerhart, 2004; Green, 1993; Green and Siaya, 2005. Greenfield, 1990; Guidepost, 1991; King and Breuder, 1979; King and Fersh, 1992; Levin, 2002; Raby, 2000, Raby, 2005–2007; Romano, 2004; Scanlon 1990; Sjoquist, 1993; Smithee, 1991; Tsunoda 1994.
2. Community college education abroad time line: 1969 Rockland Community College (New York) dedicated the first office to education abroad.

    1971 AACC established an office for international education whose mission mentioned study abroad.

    1972 U.S. Office of Education's Institute of International Studies Group Project Abroad Grants and in Section 603 of the Title VI National Defense Education Act first included community college applicants (Fersh & Greene, 1984).

    1973 College Consortium for International Studies (CCIS) pioneered a tristate cooperative consortium with Mercer (NJ), Harrisburg (PA), and Rockland (NY) Community Colleges.

    1976 Five California colleges, Orange Coast, El Camino, Glendale, L.A. Harbor, and Santa Monica offered the first state accredited, faculty-led, short-term programs which expanded in 1977 to the semester programs.

1984 California Colleges for International Education (CCIE), a nonprofit consortium, set a precedent that defined education abroad as including only credit-bearing classes that were transferable to the University of California and California State University systems, thereby distinguishing them from community service or field studies.

1987 Illinois Consortium for International Studies and Program (ICISP) was initiated.

1986 Maricopa Community College District (AZ) initiated programs.

1994 Northcentral Technical College (WI) initiated programs.

1998 College of DuPage (IL) initiated college-based programs.

1999 Howard College (MD) initiated programs.

1995 and 2001 AACC conducted the first two national surveys on the number of community colleges that offered education abroad. Between 1995 and 2001, although each survey had a different set of colleges, a 26% increase was noted (Blair, Phinney, & Phillippe, 2001).

2002 CCID Troika Program initiated with three participating colleges; Washington Consortium of Community Colleges for Study Abroad (WCCCSA) initiated programs; and Community College of Philadelphia.

3. In part, the low response rate may be related to limited community college staffing that makes completing, much less knowing about the annual IIE survey, a continual problem.

4. These were hosted by national organizations such as NAFSA, CCID, and ACIIE as well as by multistate organizations such as the Forum and CCIS and by state consortia, such as CCIE.

5. Passive trustee support is seen at all colleges since each legal abroad program must be approved by the Board of Trustees on an annual basis. Strong administrative support is seen at North Virginia Community College (urban), St. Louis Community College (urban), SUNY Broome Community College (NY, suburban), and Lake Tahoe Community College (CA, rural). Examples of holistic interaction in which traditional on-ground courses are linked to abroad experiences are seen at Mission College (CA, suburban) and Howard College (MD, urban).

6. See College of DuPage (IL), at http://www.cod.edu; Brookdale (NJ), at http://www.brookdale.cc.nj.us; Santa Barbara (CA), at http://www.sbcc.edu; and Miracosta (CA) http://wwww.miracosta.cc.ca.us.

7. See Frederick (MD) at http://www.frederick.edu, Georgia Perimeter at http://www.frederick.edu, Oklahoma City at http://www.occc.edu , Cabrillo (CA) at http://www.cabrillo.edu/academics/foreignlanguages/studyabroad, and Citrus (CA) Community College at http://www.citruscollege.edu.

8. Community college winners of the IIE Heiskell Awards in the award category of Study Abroad: (2006) Honorable Mention—Glendale Community College (CA); (2003) Winner—Fox Valley Technical College (WI) and Honorable Mention—Lake Superior College (IL); and (2002) Honorable Mention—Brookdale Community College (NJ). In the award Category of Internationalizing the Campus: (2008) Winner—St. Louis Community College at Forest Park, and Honorable Mention—Florence-Darlington Technical College; (2005) Winner—Santa Fe Community College, and Honorable Mention— Kapiolani Community College.

9. For example, Portland (OR) uses all international revenue to support all international programs while Highline (WA) uses grant revenues to support faculty development.

10. The National Center for Education Statistics (NCES) reports that less than 300 community colleges have over 10,000 unduplicated headcount; 501 colleges between 2,000 and 9,999 students; and 258 colleges with headcounts under 2,000 (Levinson, 2005, p. 4).

11. Of the top six community college education abroad programs listed by IIE *Open Doors*, all but two have administrators who have been in place for over a decade: College of DuPage (IL); Cabrillo College (CA); Santa Barbara City College (CA); Citrus College (CA).

12. Consortia exist in a multistate mode, such as College Consortium for International Studies CCIS; or on a state-wide mode, such as CCIE or WSIEAP. Some consortia also exist regionally, such as the Foothill consortium of California, which includes 14 geographically close community colleges.

13. Examples include, Community Colleges for International Development CCID "Troika" career-specific curriculum on nursing, alternative energy, or aqua-culture; Fox Valley Technical College (WI) German auto industry program; Kirkwood Community College (IA) Australian automotive program; St. Louis College England Mortuary Science program; or Napa Valley College (CA) wine production program in Australia. Other examples include the Mt. San Antonio College (CA) Global City program in London and Glendale College (CA) Muslim multiculturalism in France.

14. Tidewater Community College (VA), funded by the National Security Exchange Program NSEP, initiated a three-state consortium to offer on-campus and distance learning Vietnamese language and culture credit classes, followed by a field study course in Vietnam, and culminating with both on-campus classes and regional community forums. Santa Monica College (CA) 2008 policy creates global learning competencies

for Associate of Arts Degree requirements combine in-class internationalization with out-of-class education abroad.

15. These endeavors exist but are difficult to report due to above mentioned staffing issues.

16. Frost has developed assignments and educational plans with numerous students who have successfully carried out moves to Latin American, European, and Asian countries. Ordinarily, students who do this prefer to live for at least six months abroad and gain advanced language competencies.

17. Citrus Community College (CA) enables abroad students to simultaneously take online courses.

18. St. Louis Community College cultural resource management archaeology program in Macedonia provides six credit hours partially through service learning activities alongside Macedonian students (Fuller, 2008); Madison Area Technical College (2008) (WI) international service learning program in rural health care or rainforest conservation in Belize; Ann Arundel Community College (MD) offers internships in culinary sciences. Maricopa Community College District (AZ) offers independent travel to prearranged lectures and work meetings to enhance students' professional training; and several California community colleges include directed work/internships as a component of their credit study abroad in such areas as sports medicine, martial arts, wine production, and peace studies.

19. These bylaws defined supervision and administration of education abroad (faculty selection, legal contracts, registration of students, application, class size, Board approval); curriculum components (predeparture instruction, class evaluation, attendance, reentry); fiscal components (financial assistance for students, provider selection, logistical details, pricing); legal components (liability insurance, student insurance, instructor's responsibilities; health and safety guidelines); and marketing (brochures, promotion and student selection) (CCIE; www.ccieworld.org).

20. Middlesex and Borough of Manhattan Community Colleges use a portion of college fees for scholarships; Bellevue (WA) and San Bernardino Valley (CA) link service and fund raising to scholarships; DuPage (IL), Oakland (MI), Howard (MD), Parkland (IL), Maricopa (AZ), and Santa Barbara (CA) utilize endowments and specific fund-raising efforts.

21. Sample study abroad tuition range, 2007–2008. Summer and Winter break programs include three or four credit units. Most costs include visa, airfare, lodging, food, tuition, and local campus enrollment fees (Snap-Shot Survey, 2008).

22. Attempts to publicize community college best practices have been limited. AACC has supported education abroad in policy, yet only conducted their first workshop on this topic in 2008. Two other national community college organizations, ACIIE and CCID have limited advocacy with education abroad as their primary interests are in other areas of international education. In 2001, the NAFSA Knowledge Community on Education Abroad authorized a working group (EA-KC-CC) to emphasize the unique needs of community college education abroad. This group has since sustained an online discussion board, with over 350 members, SECUSSA-CC listserv, (SECtion on US Study Abroad-Community College) and a national committee which confers at the annual NAFSA conference.

REFERENCES

American Association of Community Colleges & Association of Community College Trustees. (2006). *Building the global community: A joint statement on the role of community in international education*. Retrieved January 24, 2008, from http://www.aacc.nche.edu/

American Council on International Intercultural Education (ACIIE) & Stanley Foundation. (1994, November 28–30). *Building the global community: The next step*. Conference proceedings, Warrenton, VA. Muscatine, IA: Stanley Foundation. Retrieved December 20, 2008, from http://www.stanleyfoundation.org/publications/archive/CC1.pdf

American Council on International Intercultural Education (ACIIE) & Stanley Foundation. (1996, November 15–17). *Educating for the global community: A framework for community colleges*. Conference proceedings, Warrenton, VA. Muscatine, IA: Stanley Foundation. Retrieved December 20, 2008, from http://www.stanleyfoundation.org/publications/archive/CC2.pdf

Bailey, T. & Morest, V.S. (Ed.). (2006). *Defending the community college equity agenda*. Baltimore: Johns Hopkins University Press.

Blair, D., Phinney, L., & Phillippe, K. A. (2001). *International programs at community colleges*. Washington, DC: American Association of Community Colleges.

Brockington, J. L., Hoffa, W. F., & Martin, P. C. (Eds.). (2005). *NAFSA's guide to education abroad for advisers and administrators* (3rd ed.). Washington, DC: NAFSA: Association of International Educators.

California Colleges for International Education (CCIE). (2009). Retrieved from www.ccieworld.org on January 21, 2009.

Clark, B. (1960). The "cooling-out" function in higher education. *American Journal of Sociology, 65*(6), 569–576.

Cohen, A. M. (1972). Community college growth. *Change, 4*(9), 32a–32d.

Cohen, A. M. (2009). Community colleges in the United States. In R. L. Raby & E. J. Valeau (Eds.), *Community college models: Globalization and higher education reform.* Berlin: Springer.

Cohen, A. M., & Brawer, F. B. (2003). *The American community college* (4th ed.). San Francisco: Jossey-Bass.

Community Colleges for International Development (CCID). (2009). Retrieved January 21, 2009 from http://www.ccid.org

Council on Learning. (1981). *Statement and recommendations on American responsibilities as a global power and appropriate educational directions: National Task Force Statement on Education and the World View.* New Rochelle, NY: Change Magazine Press.

Dellow, D. A. (2007). The role of globalization in technical and occupation programs. In E. J. Valeau & R. L. Raby (Eds.), *International reform efforts and challenges in community colleges* (pp. 39–47; New Directions for Community Colleges, 138). San Francisco: Jossey-Bass.

Dudderar, J. (2002). Developing and administering study-abroad programs. In R. M. Romano (Ed.), *Internationalizing the Community College* (pp. 45–58). Washington DC: Community College Press.

Edwards, J., & Tonkin, H. (1990). Internationalizing the community college: Strategies for the classroom. In R. Greenfield (Ed.), *Developing international education programs* (pp. 17–26; New Directions for Community Colleges, 70). San Francisco: Jossey-Bass.

Eells, W.C. (1931). *The junior college.* New York: Houghton Mifflin.

Fersh, S. (1993). *Integrating the trans-national/cultural dimension.* Bloomington, IN: Phi Delta Kappa Educational Foundation.

Fersh, S., & Green, W. (Eds.). (1984). *The community college and international education: A report of progress* (Vol. 2). Fort Lauderdale, FL: Brevard Community College Press.

Forum on Education Abroad. (2007). *Standards of best practice.* Forum on Education Abroad. Retrieved January 24, 2008, from http://www.forumea.org

Freeman, S. A. Task Force on International Education. (1966). *Undergraduate study abroad. International education: Past, present, problems and prospects,* H. Res. 527, 89th Cong., 2nd Session. Washington, DC: Government Printing Office.

Frost, R. A. (2007). Global studies in the community college curriculum. *Community College Enterprise, 13*(2), 67–73.

Fuller, M. (2009). Retrieved January 20, 2009, from.http://users.stlcc.edu/mfuller/macedonia.

Gleazer, E. (1980). *The community college: Values, vision and vitality.* Washington, DC: American Association of Community and Junior Colleges.

Green, M. F. (2007). Internationalizing community colleges: Barriers and strategies. In E. Valeau & R. L. Raby (Eds.), *International reform efforts and challenges in community* colleges (pp. 15–25;New Directions for Community Colleges, 70). San Francisco: Jossey-Bass.

Green, M. F., & Siaya, L. (2005). *Measuring internationalization at community colleges.* Washington, DC: American Council on Education.

Greenfield, R. K. (1990). *Developing international education programs.* San Francisco: Jossey-Bass.

Hess, G. (1982). *Freshmen and sophomores abroad: Community colleges and overseas academic programs.* New York: Teachers College Press.

Hollinshead, B. (1936). The community college program. *Junior Community College Journal, 7,* 111–116.

Institute of International Education. (2007). *Open doors.* Retrieved January 24, 2008, from http://opendoors.iienetwork.org/?p=25122

Institute of International Education. (2009). Gilman International Scholarships. Retrieved January 21, 2009, from http: www.iie.org/programs/gilman/index.html.

Kadel, C. (2002). Service learning abroad. In R. M. Romano (Ed.), *Internationalizing the community college* (pp. 59–70). Washington, DC: Community College Press.

King, M. C., & Breuder, R. L. (Eds.). (1979). *New directions for community colleges: advancing international education.* San Francisco: Jossey-Bass.

King, M. C., & Fersh, S. C. (1992). *Integrating the international/intercultural dimension in the community college.* Cocoa, FL: Association of Community College Trustees and Community Colleges for International Development.

Konrad, Z. (2002–2008). *College of DuPage annual reports, 2002–2008.* Unpublished documents.

Koos, L. (1924). *The junior college.* Minneapolis: University of Minnesota Press.

Korbel, L. A. (1998). *New expeditions: Charting the future of global education in community colleges.* Washington, DC: American Council on Education.

Korbel, L. A. (2007). In union there is strength: The role of state global education consortia in expanding community college involvement in global education. In E. J. Valeau & R. L. Raby (Eds.), *International reform efforts and challenges in community colleges* (pp. 47–57; New Directions for Community Colleges, 138). San Francisco: Jossey-Bass.

Levin, J. S. (2002). *Globalizing the community college: Strategies for change in the twenty-first century.* New York: Palgrave.

Levinson, D. (2005). *Community colleges: A reference handbook.* Santa Barbara, CA: ABC-CLIO.

Milliron, M. D. (2007). Transcendence and globalization: Our education and workforce development challenge. In E. J. Valeau & R. L. Raby (Eds.), *International reform efforts and challenges in community colleges* (pp. 31–39; New Directions for Community Colleges, 138). San Francisco: Jossey-Bass.

Pfeffer, J., & Salancik, G. (2003/1978). *The external control of organizations: A resource dependence perspective.* Stanford, CA: Stanford University Press.

Raby, R. L. (2000). *Internationalizing the community college curriculum: Theoretical and pragmatic discourses.* New York: NAFSA: Association of International Educators.

Raby, R. L. (2005, June 21). Study abroad in community colleges. *Community College Times,* 10–11.

Raby, R. L. (2007). Internationalizing the curriculum: On- and off-campus strategies. In E. J. Valeau & R. L. Raby (Eds.), *International reform efforts and challenges in community colleges* (pp. 57-67; New Directions for Community Colleges, 138). San Francisco: Jossey-Bass.

Raby, R. L., & Institute of International Education. (2008). Snap-shot survey. In R. Raby & Institute of International Education (Eds.), *Expanding education abroad at U.S. community colleges* (IIE Study Abroad White Paper Series, Issue Number 3). New York: Institute of International Education.

Raby, R. L. & Sawadogo, G. (2005). Education abroad and community colleges. In J. L. Brockington, W. F. Hoffa, & P. C. Martin (Eds.), *NAFSA's guide to education abroad for advisers and administrators* (pp. 151–173). Washington, DC: NAFSA: Association of International Educators.

Raby, R. L., & Tarrow, N. (Eds.). (1996). *Dimensions of the community college: International, intercultural, and multicultural perspectives.* New York: Garland.

Raby, R. L., & Valeau, E. J. (2007). Community college international education: Looking back to forecast the future. In E. J. Valeau, & R. L. Raby (Eds.), *International Reform Efforts and Challenges in Community Colleges* (pp. 5–15; New Directions for Community Colleges, 138). San Francisco: Jossey-Bass.

Romano, R. M. (Ed.). (2004). *Internationalizing the community college.* Washington, DC: Community College Press.

Russell, J. (1949). Basic conclusions and recommendations of the president's commission on higher education. *Journal of Educational Sociology, 22*(8), 493–508.

Scanlon, D. G. (1990). *Lessons from the past in developing international education in community colleges.* San Francisco: Jossey-Bass.

SECUSSA-CC (2009). secussacc@listserver.itd.umich.edu. Washington, DC: NAFSA.

Senge, P. M. (1990). *The fifth discipline: The art of the learning organization.* New York: Doubleday.

Sjoquist, D. P. (1993). Globalizing general education: Changing world, changing needs. In N. A. Raisman (Ed.), *Directing general education outcomes* (pp. 51–58; New Directions for Community Colleges, 81). San Francisco: Jossey-Bass.

Tsunoda, J. (1994). Address to the association of international education administrators annual conference at Tokai University at Honolulu. Unpublished document.

Vaughn, G. B. (2007, October 26). The community college's role in the community. *The Chronicle of Higher Education, 54*(9), B16.

Wheatley, M. (2006). *Leadership and the new science: Discovering order in a chaotic world* (3rd ed.). San Francisco: Berrett-Koehler.

Zook, G. (1947). *The president's commission on higher education: Higher education for American democracy.* Washington, DC: U. S. Government Printing Office.

Chapter 12

North of 49

Global Citizenship à la canadienne

Roopa Desai Trilokekar and Adrian Shubert
York University

INTRODUCTION

The concept of global citizenship appears to have a particular affinity for Canada and Canadians. Lloyd Axworthy, who was Minister of Foreign Affairs from 1996 to 2000, played a key role in the international ban on land mines and developing the doctrine of right to protect, began his recent book with a paean to his compatriots' vocation as global citizens:

> Canadians are on the road to global citizenship. Increasingly, in work, travel, education and in personal and political engagement, the world is our precinct, with international trade, technology and business driving much of our global interests. But there is also a political, cultural and even moral dimension to our emerging role in global society. (Axworthy, 2003, p. 1)

And when the distinguished professor of international law Michael Byers (2007) asked in the subtitle of his book: *What is Canada for?* his answer was that its role, as a country, is to be a global citizen:

> [Canada] achieves its greatest successes when it charts a path that is not determined solely by economic factors…a truly great country should be about… addressing global developments, such as climate change, that threaten the safety and well-being of all. And it should be about improving the lot of human beings everywhere for the simple reason that doing so is right and just. (Byers, 2007, p. 240–241)

For her part, Jennifer Welsh generally eschews the term *global citizenship*, but proposes that Canada aspire to something very similar: to be a model citizen:

> [F]irst, it must show others what a liberal democracy looks like in the post-September-11 era; second, it must work side by side with others in less stable parts of the world, demonstrating how they might create the foundations for healthier societies… [This model] also suggests activism: model citizens continually strive to make the commons more just. (Welsh, 2005, p. 26)

One particularly interesting aspect of Welsh's vision is that it goes beyond government to include individual Canadians, and particularly younger Canadians, whose international engagements demonstrate that they are "inherently internationalist" and "already at home in the world" (Welsh, 2004, p. 34; Welsh 2005, pp. 28, 239–240).[1]

These ways of seeing Canada's role in the world has deep roots, going back to Lester B. Pearson, a career diplomat who was Minister of External Affairs from 1948 to 1957 and recipient of the 1957 Nobel Peace Prize for creating the United Nations peacekeeping role during the Suez Crisis of 1956. Pearson's vision was for Canada, as a "middle power" to have an activist role in world affairs in an age, which he described in the 1950s,

> when different civilizations will have to learn to live side by side in peaceful interchange, learning from each other, studying each other's history and ideals and art and culture, mutually enriching each other's lives. The alternative, in this overcrowded little world, is misunderstanding, tension, clash and catastrophe. (1957)

Canadians routinely talk of the Pearsonian tradition, which was a kind of global citizenship avant la lettre.[2] This is more than self-congratulation—or self-delusion. Others see Canada and Canadians this way. That self-described "global soul," Pico Iyer, has called Canada

> the spiritual home…of the very notion of an extended, emancipating global citizenship…. Canada seems to have worked more than anywhere I know to build up a sense of global accountability and conscience, perhaps because (unlike its neighbors to the south and east) Canada has never been in a position to imagine itself the centre of the world. (Iyer, 2004, pp. 1–3)

Former UN Undersecretary General Brian Urquhart cites Canada as one of the few countries which "frame their foreign policies with regard to the larger international interest" (Urquhart, 2007, p. 27).[3] Coming from a very different direction, former adviser to President François Mitterand and international consultant Jacques Attali has described Canada as "one of the first examples of a successful multicultural, democratic country without borders, where everyone will be simultaneously a member of several communities that were formerly mutually exclusive" (quoted in Iyer, 2004, p. 4).

There is undoubtedly a connection between this approach to the world and Canada's distinctive approach to multiculturalism and national self-definition.[4] Iyer, 2004 Robert Latham, the director of York University's Centre for International and Security Studies (YCISS), suggested that Canadian society is too complex to be captured by categories of culture and ethnicity. People live their lives in an overlapping plurality of spaces and subjectivities within and across borders. A powerful first step toward recognizing itself as multiversal would be for Canada to proactively support dual and multiple citizenships. It could also take the lead in bringing other governments together to build an international regime for multiple citizenships (Latham, 2007).

Global citizenship as a notion is flawed given that there is no global state or global polity, yet the ideals of global citizenship hold a special place for Canada and Canadians as seen from the above discussion on foreign policy, and more recent attempts at building a modern democratic and multicultural society. But how exactly might global citizenship come to be defined within a Canadian context? How might it reflect Canadian values and promote Canadian interests, particularly when notions of national citizenship and what it means to be "Canadian" are undergoing dramatic changes? Michael Byers (2005) presents a universalistic definition for global citizenship.

Global citizenship empowers individual human beings to participate in decisions concerning their lives, including the political, economic, social, cultural and environmental conditions in which they live. It includes the right to vote, to express opinions and associate with others, and to enjoy a decent and dignified quality of life. It is expressed through engagement in the various communities of which the individual is a part, at the local, national and global level. And it includes the right to challenge authority and existing power structures—to think, argue and act—with the intent of changing the world.

The Association of Universities and Colleges in Canada (AUCC) proposes a definition of global citizenship that is close to the heart of the Canadian ethos.

Global citizenship can be seen as a continuum going from being aware of the interdependent nature of our world, to understanding how local and global issues affect the well-being of people around the world, to committing or taking actions to help create a more equitable world, or at least avoid actions that would generate inequity.[5]

The triad of knowledge, understanding, and action to create a socially equitable and just world seems to be at the core of the Canadian vision of global citizenship, one that influences educational and training initiatives for youth in Canada.

FEDERAL GOVERNMENT AND HIGHER EDUCATION

Canada's greatest challenge in international education has always been and remains the failure to develop a "vision and an agenda for international education, even though there is a growing awareness that both are urgently needed" (Farquhar, 2001, p. 1). To quote a recent article by John Mallea, "Put simply, no national agenda for international higher education exists. Nor, it seems, is this weakness likely to be remedied soon" (Barrow, Didou-Aupetit, & Mallea, 2003, p. 121).

International education is at an interesting intersection of two distinct policy arenas, foreign affairs and higher education, which creates a challenge for federal states such as Canada, where higher education is typically the responsibility of the state or provincial governments, while foreign policy remains the domain of the federal government. Given the importance of higher education to national development, in most other federations national governments have taken a lead policy role. The Canadian case is unique: Canada has never had a federal ministry of education or higher education, and there has never been a federal higher education policy framework.

This does not mean that Ottawa has no role to play in higher education. The federal government has specific areas of responsibility (Jones, 1996; Cameron, 1997) and has taken on specific policy and programmatic initiatives in an attempt to have a more direct role in supporting higher education from time to time (Axelrod, forthcoming). However, this approach has been ad hoc, fragmented, and can be best described as a string of initiatives developed in the absence of an overall policy framework (Fisher et al., 2006). Any possibility of a more defined role of the federal government in higher education or a national higher educational policy framework would draw strong and immediate reaction from the provinces, which fiercely protect their jurisdictional authority over education.[6] The situation in Canada is so extreme that the Council of Ministers of Education of Canada (CMEC)[7] refuses to act as a representative of the various provincial ministries in its consultations with the federal government. In its view, the federal government ought to approach each of the 10 provinces individually for any policy or programmatic input; it should not expect a centralized national response.[8]

Thus, although at the level of the individual institution there are many apparent similarities between the United States and Canada,[9] once we move beyond the level of the individual institution, the differences between the two systems immediately come to mind. Both Canada and the United States have federal systems, but constitutionally and in practice Ottawa and Washington have very different roles. With no national department or office for postsecondary education and minimal, if any, intermediary coordinating bodies and no Canadian higher education policy (Skolnik & Jones, 1992), the Simon Act, the National Defense Education Act (NDEA), or Fund for the Improvement of Postsecondary Education (FIPSE) would be impossible in Canada. Even though the American Council on Education's (ACE) *Promising Practices* speaks of "America's historic neglect" of international education and the low priority and modest funding of federal initiatives, they are major league compared to the situation in Canada (Green, 2002, p. 7).

FOREIGN POLICY, DEVELOPMENT TRADITION, AND INTERNATIONAL EDUCATION

Unlike higher education, the Canadian federal government has full jurisdictional responsibility for foreign affairs. And in this respect, Canadian foreign policy orientation and in particular, its relations with the developing world, have been influenced by Canada's history as a noncolonial middle power. In 1960, Canada established the External Aid Office, "to give Canada a clearer voice in the field—development assistance—that was of growing importance in international relations" (Bergbusch, 1999, p. 25). In a few years,

> [The] creation of the Canadian International Development Agency (CIDA) in 1968 symbolized a [further] commitment that led to expansion of the aid program to most parts of the developing world, making Canada one of the more generous donors among industrialized countries. (Morrison, 1998, p. 1)

A direct result of these new initiatives was the arrival of international students from developing countries in the 1950s and 1960s and more Canadians going abroad for travel, to volunteer, or for work opportunities. Canada's development aid funding undoubtedly reflects the, "ebb and tide" in policy focus; however, what is noteworthy is that Canada's liberalism found expression in "humane internationalism"—"an acceptance that the citizens and governments of the industrialized world have ethical responsibilities towards those beyond their borders who are suffering severely and who live in abject poverty" (Morrison, 1998, p. 2). This commitment to international development assistance is reflected in both Canadian foreign policy as well as Canadian public attitude toward development aid. Andrew Cohen in his book, *While Canada Slept*, suggests that development has been a priority agenda in Canada's external relations and receives overwhelming support from the Canadian public. In 1997, 94% of Canadians agreed that "we are [and continue to be] a very generous country when it comes to giving aid to poorer countries" (Cohen, 2003, p. 82).

There is a gap between perception and reality here. After an initial period of caution between 1950 and 1964 and one characterized by "humane internationalism" between 1964 and 1976, Canadian development policy became increasingly tied to the interests of national economic prosperity and broader foreign policy objectives. Starting in the late 1970s, the budget for development was cut severely, changing the Canadian International Development Agency's (CIDA) role in the university sector and resulting in a reduction of funding for university based projects (Pratt, 1996). Between 1980 and 1998, the percentage of GDP that Canada devoted to development assistance fell by a third, to 0.29%, leaving it in 11th place internationally.[10] By 2001, the Canadian percentage had fallen even further, to 0.22%, although by 2005 it had risen again, to 0.34%. Even so, Canada remained behind Denmark, Norway, Sweden, France, Germany, the Netherlands and the United Kingdom (University of Victoria, 2001).

The 2005 International Policy Statement (IPS) called for an increase in aid funding by 8% each year, resulting in a doubling of assistance from 2001 to 2010, although the Conservative government elected in 2006 did not adopt its predecessor's approach to foreign policy (Department of Foreign Affairs and International Trade, 2005).

This priority on development aid in the 1960s and 1970s affected Canadian universities. The first international office was created at the University of Guelph in 1967 to handle development activities. "This tradition also explains, at least in part, the emergence of the two major formative strands of internationalization in Canadian universities—development co-operation and international students" (Shute, 1999, p. 2). As early as the 1960s a number of Canadian universities took on international roles that foreshadow what we now call global citizenship, and did so, as James Shute has argued, as an extension of a tradition of outreach and community service that stretches back to the 19th century. "The explicit early adoption of international roles by some Canadian universities evolved directly from an orientation and commitment to the larger communities of which they were—and are—a part" (Shute, 1999, p. 1). Shute also argues that engagement in outreach and development has brought a range of benefits: ongoing links between Canadian universities and their partners in the Global South; the subsequent activities of Canadian academics as advisors to a range of international agencies; the production of scholarship on development issues; the import of international experience "back to their classrooms, labs and departments"; and the presence of international students, through development projects and, before that, through the Colombo Plan (1950) and the 1960 Commonwealth Scholarship and Fellowship Plan (Shute, 1999). This CIDA style of internationalization, however, Shute suggests was mainly dependent on the commitment and idealism of individual faculty members (Shute, 1999). The universities, as institutions, played a much smaller role. International offices were frequently separate from the universities' core functions and often dependent on external funding and their projects often had little impact on their home campuses, particularly in the realm of study abroad experiences for Canadian students, which is interestingly absent from the above list of international activities.

What should be noted, however, is the recognition of the importance of involving citizens in development assistance programs. CIDA's creation of the Non-Governmental Organization (NGO) Division within its organizational structure in 1968, made it the first development agency in the West to establish cooperation between the government and private development agencies, and provide financial support to the nongovernmental sector to promote development abroad, including core funding for volunteer-sending organizations (CIDA, 1986; Tiessen, 2007). The role of students in development finds expression in several nongovernmental volunteer organizational initiatives. Two organizations deserve special mention, particularly because their programs have had a long and strong purchase on Canadian universities.

Perhaps the first manifestation of global citizenship in Canadian universities was the creation after World War I of International Student Services, which, in 1957, became World University Services of Canada (WUSC). The original goal was to provide assistance to students on the war-ravaged campuses of Europe, but in the 1950s the organization expanded its concerns beyond Europe. Development projects were undertaken by WUSC, which launched its current flagship project, the Student Refugee Program in 1980 and in 2006 initiated its Students Without Borders program which offers placements to students at one of iits development projects. WUSC's activities are supported by an extensive network of more than 60 campus-based local committees (WUSC, n.d.).

The second organization is Canadian Universities Service Overseas (CUSO). Starting in 1957 as a volunteer program at the University of Toronto, CUSO was established in 1961 as "a non-profit organization for sending young Canadians to serve overseas." Although over time, CUSO's focus moved to development projects, and consequently the volunteers it sent abroad were much further removed from their university experience, the name recalls the deep connection between Canadian universities and their students and activities that now fall under the rubric of global citizenship (CUSO, n.d.). There are several other nongovernmental volunteer organizations that provide Canadian youth with international experiences, such as Global Citizens for Change, Canadian Cross Roads International, Canada World Youth, and Youth Challenge International.

Most CIDA sponsored international programs for Canadian youth were thus offered not through the university but through the nongovernmental sector via volunteer organizations. In additional to those offered through organizations such as WUSC and CUSO, another CIDA initiative is the International Youth Internship Program (IYIP) started earlier in 1997, as part of the Canadian government's youth employment strategy. The IYIP is a CIDA initiated employment program for young Canadians between the ages of 19 to 30 who are postsecondary graduates. The program is offered in partnership with several Canadian nongovernmental organizations, including universities, to provide youth with a, "chance of a lifetime to work in a developing country and contribute to Canada's international development goals." Under this program, CIDA funds over 400 internships per year (CIDA, n.d.). There is, however, one significant and new CIDA initiative that engages directly with Canadian university students, it is the Canada Corps University Partnership Program, now known as Students for Development. A creation of the government of Paul Martin (2003–2006), Canada Corps was first announced in 2004, as part of Canada's new International Policy Statement (IPS) which, "called for a new commitment to global citizenship and envisaged Canada Corps as an important way to achieve it" (Tiessen, 2007, p. 80). Within an overall goal of promoting democratic governance in the developing world, Canada Corps' mandate included putting "our idealism to work by helping young Canadians bring their enthusiasm and energy to the world." This eventually manifested itself in the Canada Corps Student Internships and the Canada Corps University Teams Partnership Program,[11] after much deliberate and focused lobbying on the part of Association of Universities and Colleges of Canada (AUCC) on behalf of the Canadian postsecondary educational community.[12]

The Canada Corps initiative is funded by the Canadian International Development Agency (approximately C$2 million/year) and administered by the AUCC.

> The internship program will consist of 100 four-month student internships, with each of AUCC's 92 member universities across Canada being allocated at least one. Universities will oversee the selection of the students, expected to be experienced third or fourth-year under-graduates or graduate students. Most internships will take place in a developing country where the university already has academic links, and students will receive academic credit for the internship. Universities will also be responsible for organizing an orientation pro-gram, and will work with returning students to raise public awareness of the results and

activities achieved by the interns…. The second [component of the] program would see teams of [three] senior undergraduate or graduate students, led by faculty members, working with developing country partners to strengthen governance capacity. (AUCC, 2004)

The programs ran this way in 2005 and 2006, but in 2007 the University Teams component was eliminated because the internship program was considered to be more effective in terms of its broader impact and coverage of a wider range of development issues. The number of internships available increased to 132, and 138 in 2008 given the success of the overall program to all stake holder groups, students in particular, who reported benefiting both personally and professionally from being given exposure to a wide range of career opportunities and a better understanding of complex global issues (CIDA, 2007).[13]

Tiessen (2007) suggests that global citizenship is, "a cornerstone of Canadian foreign policy on youth programs and features prominently in the IPS" (p. 80). Most certainly the Canadian development tradition leaves an imprint on the policy objectives and programmatic approaches of the government's youth initiatives, both targeted within and outside the university sector. Although the programs within the university sector are relatively small in number compared to those offered through the volunteer/NGO sector, most reflect the principle of the triad of building student/youth awareness, understanding, and action as it relates to global citizenship and the international promotion of Canadian values of social justice and equity.

FEDERAL STUDY ABROAD INITIATIVES

As stated above, CIDA's engagement with Canadian universities has had minimal *quantitative* impact on international education, in particular study abroad. With the exception of the latest Canada Corps Student Internships Program, which is a credit transfer program, study abroad has featured more prominently in other federal initiatives, but these have been limited and have not necessarily evoked the broader goals of global citizenship.

The responsibility for a range of policy areas that directly intersect with the postsecondary sector, specifically international education, are dispersed across several federal departments; however, the Department of Foreign Affairs and International Trade (DFAIT) is often identified as the key, and in some ways, the 'logical' federal department to provide leadership for international education.[14] The Department of Foreign Affairs (DFAIT) has had an established division of International Academic Relations since 1967, and the five major program categories for this division include Canadian Studies Program, Canadian and International Scholarship Programs, Youth Exchange Programs, Federal, Provincial, and Multilateral Relations, and the Marketing of Canadian Education (Trilokekar, 2007). The Division performs a dual function of providing, "a number of opportunities for Canadians to learn about the world and for international students to learn more about Canada." To support academic mobility among young Canadians the division offers a selected range of international scholarship programs for Canadians to pursue graduate study and research abroad. It also facilitates work abroad by negotiating reciprocal temporary work permits with close to 40 countries for Canadians between the ages of 18 and 35. These permits cover working holidays; student work abroad programs; international co-op placements; and young professional/young worker opportunities (DFAIT, n.d.). The Department of Foreign Affairs has often attempted to coordinate policy development in international education. For example in 1994, the Department conducted extensive consultations with various stakeholder groups and prepared a nation wide policy document on "The International Dimension of Higher Education in Canada: Collaborative Policy Framework," in which it strongly recommended increased facilitation of student and faculty mobility programs (Department of Foreign Affiars and International Trade, 1994). Unfortunately, DFAIT did not have any success in promoting this policy, and has continued to face constant challenges both in terms of funding cuts to its academic relations program as well as in coordinating any efforts in developing a national international educational policy.

Since the 1990s, another federal department, Human Resources and Skills Development Canada (HRSDC), has established a portfolio in international education through its support for international academic mobility programs (IAMs). The two most significant have been with the European Union and joint United States and Mexico program (in the United States, these programs are administered by the Fund for the Improvement of Postsecondary Education; FIPSE). The incentive to establish both these programs came from external sources. In 1991, the United States invited Canada and Mexico to explore higher education cooperation within a larger policy framework to promote North American free trade.[15] The result was the North American Cooperation in Higher Education, Research and Training initiative which provided funds to universities to incorporate mobility of students and faculty, build strategic institutional partnerships, support networking and the use of information technologies, and leverage existing resources. A second international mobility program was established as part of the European Community Education, Training and Youth initiative. Similar to the North American program, the Canada-EU program for cooperation in higher education and training promoted academic exchanges and collaborative activities with higher education institutions in Canada and Europe and supported activities such as joint curricular teaching, new educational technology and distance education, in a diverse range of fields (Joyal, 1994). This is the 14th year of the International Academic Mobility (IAM) initiative (HRSDC, 2008).

DFAIT was initially identified as the coordinating secretariat for both these initiatives; however, since HRSDC had the stronger resource base, given its access to funding under the government's prosperity learning initiative, both programs came to be funded and administered there. The Canadian government, through HRSDC, contributes C$1.6 million annually to the program. This enables nearly 200 Canadian students each year to undertake part of their studies in another North American country, with an equal number of foreign students coming to Canada. The IAM model was designed to develop skills, "which will allow young Canadians to find employment in a competitive and rapidly changing international marketplace and to excel in their chosen fields" (HRSDC, 2007, p. 24). Says Christiane Boulanger, coordinator of the program at HRSDC, "These experiences are an excellent indicator for future employers of students' ability to adapt to new circumstances—an important skill in today's global workplace." While, with the exception of a bilateral exchange program with Taiwan between 1995 and 2000, the government's plans to expand this model of cooperation to the Asia Pacific and the Latin American regions have yet to materialize, the two initial programs continue to function. The latest calls for proposals set out similar objectives as outlined above, interestingly, neither the phrase global citizenship nor its most significant contents appear (HRSDC, n.d./a, n.d./b).

Besides DFAIT and HRSDC, other federal departments such as Industry Canada, Citizenship and Immigration Canada, and the research funding councils are engaged in different aspects of international education with little, if any, coordination. Most programs are limited, both in terms of funding and outreach because they engage a relatively small number of participants. While a few programs offer study abroad and academic transfer possibilities, there is a stronger emphasis on volunteer work abroad, and this is the case for both development assistance programs offered through CIDA and programs offered through DFAIT. Skills development and training based programs to prepare Canadians for a global economy are beginning to garner more focus, even if the programs are delivered in developing economies. Thus, with the exception of CIDA, federal agencies are much more likely to invoke preparing Canadians for a global economy than stimulating a broader notion of global citizenship as a rationale for their programs. And when they do invoke the notion of global citizenship, while the focus remains on student/youth awareness and understanding as observed through program objectives and design, the notion of *action* as an aspect of global citizenship is missing. Global citizenship is more narrowly understood in the context of global economic relations and the advantageous positioning of Canada and Canadian business interests rather than as an ethical political, cultural, or social cause for the promotion of the values of global justice and equity.

PROVINCIAL INITIATIVES

Responsibility for postsecondary education in Canada lies with the provincial governments, and their attitudes toward internationalization and study abroad have been anything but consistent, both among the provinces and within individual provinces over time. Many see internationalization as a synonym for recruiting international students, although some provinces have taken a more wide-ranging approach.

The government of Quebec has been supporting internationalization since the 1970s, although the motives and approaches have changed over time. Until quite recently, the emphasis was on attracting international students, and particularly those from French-speaking countries, by offering reduced levels of tuition. In the mid-1980s, economic growth became an explicit goal of internationalization, leading to the extension of reduced tuition to students from Europe, Japan, and the United States. During the current decade, the government became convinced that other aspects of internationalization: sending Quebec students abroad and promoting international research collaboration, were important and should be supported (Picard, 2006).

Québec introduced the Programme de bourses pour de courts séjours d'études universitaires à l'extérieur du Québec (PBCSE) in September 2000. The development of global citizenship does not appear as one of the rationales for offering the scholarships. McGill University describes the aims of the program to be:

> motivate[ing] Quebec Residents to participate in an exchange, study away, or internship program outside the province in order to:
>
> enrich their learning experience;
>
> obtain a degree with an international component; and
>
> *contribute to the improvement of the Quebec labor market with the knowledge acquired overseas.* (McGill University, n.d.; Québec Government, n.d., emphasis added)

In November 2005, the Conseil Supérieure de L'Education submitted a report entitled "L'Internationalisation: Nourrir le Dynamisme des Universités Québecoises" to the Minister of Education, Leisure and Sport. For the members of the Conseil, internationalization constitutes a "strategic tool for the social, economic and cultural development of Quebec," and student mobility, for both Quebec students abroad and foreign students to Quebec, was one of four basic orientations it recommended (2005).[16] The report recognized that the government's scholarship program to support study abroad (PBCSE) had succeeded in increasing the number of Quebec students participating in mobility programs, but did not see student mobility as the primary vehicle for internationalization, and certainly not for creating "citoyens du monde." Here, pride of place went to internationalizing education at home:

> Internationalizing education is a central challenge to internationalizing the universities. This includes a number of measures including internationalizing the curriculum. This permits all students to receive an education which is rooted in the national culture at the same time as it is open to the world. The principal goal is to develop "global citizens," capable of resolving global problems as well as appreciating and valuing cultural diversity as a source of enrichment of the patrimony of humanity. (http://www.cse.gouv.qc.ca/fichiers/documents/50-0449F.pdf, p. 18)

Ontario has been much less consistent. At the beginning of the 1990s, the provincial government took some innovative steps in promoting study abroad through consortial agreements with Rhône-Alpes in France (ORA) and Baden-Württemberg in Germany (OBW), although the funding for these programs was soon eliminated as a result of severe budget cuts, and for about 10 years the province provided no support to study abroad or for international education in broader terms. This neglect was reversed in 2004, when the new Liberal government announced it would develop an international strategy aimed at promoting the province as an education destination for international students and increasing the opportunities for Ontario students to study abroad. With regard to the former, the government participated in the federal government pilot program to encourage off-campus work opportunities for students and has cooperatively worked with the postsecondary institutions within Ontario to participate in national and international recruitment fairs.

In supporting study abroad, in a very short time Ontario moved from being a laggard to being a national leader. In 2006, the government announced the creation of the $2,500 Ontario International Education Opportunity Scholarships: 272 for 2006 to 2007 and 800 for 2007 to 2008. It also restored funding to the ORA and OBW programs, as well as providing funding for a new exchange consortium with universities in the Indian states of Maharashtra and Goa (OMG) (York University, 2006), supporting the mobility of approximately 50 students under the ORA and OBW programs and 25 students under the OMG program in both directions. The new strategy's vision statement sets out the goal of having Ontario "recognized as a world leader developing tomorrow's global citizens through transformative learning opportunities for both domestic and international participants," but subsequent public statements have not continued this focus on global citizenship. Rather, the emphasis has shifted to the importance of study abroad for the province's economic health. In announcing the new study abroad scholarships, Chris Bentley, the Minister of Training Colleges and Universities, said that they would

> help students pay for international studies and help Ontario's competitive edge through the global knowledge they bring back with them.... Students, and ultimately Ontario's future prosperity, will benefit from the further expansion of knowledge and skills acquired across the globe.

Announcing the government's support for the OMG exchange program 3 months later, Bentley repeated the economic rationale (2007a, b). The "Backgrounder" that accompanied both these press releases reinforced the point: "International education enriches the experience of students and strengthens Ontario's competitiveness in the global economy. Students returning from an international opportunity also bring insight into new technologies and global processes that help enhance the province's industries" (Bentley, 2007a, b).

Like Ontario, the province of British Columbia has been inconsistent in its support to international education. Although it was one of the first provinces to establish a dedicated provincial international education consortium, the British Columbia Centre for International Education (BCCIE), in 1990, just a decade later, the government withdrew its funding (Savage & McKittrick, 2002). From receiving 90% of its budget from the province, BCCIE now functions as a nongovernmental organization based strictly on membership fees and business development activities (Savage & McKittrick, 2002). Interestingly, the BCCIE mandate seems to have narrowed considerably from "strengthen[ing] the internationalization of the public post-secondary system in B.C." to one that is more aggressively focused on promotion and recruitment (British Columbia Ministry of Advanced Education, n.d.).

In more recent years, the Ministry of Advanced Education has rekindled its interest in, "expanding the international reach of its post-secondary institutions by promoting British Columbia as a destination for international students and supporting study abroad by domestic students" This is in keeping with the initiatives of other provinces. However, a unique feature is that international education is seen as a key part of the Province's Asia Pacific Gateway strategy, which is illustrated by the type of scholarship programs established by the Ministry and its focus on recruiting international students from the Asia Pacific region. The two main initiatives of the Ministry include the Learn Live BC Web site as a portal to educational opportunities in BC and the Study/Work Abroad Web site providing BC students with an online access point for information on study or work abroad.

In 2007, Premier Gordon Campbell also announced the initiation of several new scholarship programs. Two of these are designated for British Columbia students to study abroad so as to "gain valuable knowledge and experience that will contribute to B.C.'s competitiveness and productivity." In setting up these scholarship programs, Advanced Education Minister, Murray Coell mentioned another objective, that they "increase students' cultural awareness and develop an appreciation for global citizenship." Four hundred One World scholarships worth $1,000 to $3,000 each and up to 50 Pacific Horizons scholarships of $1,000 each will be awarded annually to students to take part in postsecondary studies, co-op work experiences, internships, and other approved formal or experiential learning activities overseas. Interestingly, it is not the BCCIE, but the Irving K. Barber British Columbia Scholarship Society that is managing the endowment and distributing the funding to British Columbia's public postsecondary institutions.

This provides a snapshot of 3 of the 10 provinces within Canada. While international education is not a priority declared by all provincial ministries the trend is increasingly in this direction. These three major provincial approaches suggest that each of the provinces has had a different history regarding how and when they established international education portfolios within their respective government ministries. Some like Quebec have internationalization linked to broader cultural policy, while others like Ontario and British Columbia have their policies framed within provincial economic objectives. Some provinces like Quebec are making a concerned effort to broaden the scope of their policy approaches while others like British Columbia seem to moving from a broad to a narrower approach. Certainly over time, one can observe both a growing interest and a convergence in provincial policies and programs, with each focusing on an economic rationale and a two-pronged approach of attracting more international students and supporting more study/work abroad opportunities. Provinces link the notion of global citizenship to study/ work abroad; however, they do so primarily in the context of enhancing the global competitiveness of their respective economies and enhancing the required global competencies and skills of their future workforce, the only exception being Quebec. A broader notion of global citizenship, as defined by Byers and others, in context of the political, social, cultural, environmental, and economic realms or the notion of global citizenship advanced by AUCC as global awareness, knowledge, and action for an equitable world is certainly missing. While the promotion of Canadian values and interests is supported, it is only in the realm of economics and trade.

CANADIAN UNIVERSITIES, STUDY ABROAD, AND GLOBAL CITIZENSHIP

The concept of global citizenship has enjoyed a significant revival in the age of globalization that began in the 1990s, and has recently become a central part of the discourse of university internationalization in the United States (Carter, 2001). The strong development tradition in Canada means that it has an older and stronger purchase for Canadians, although it appears to be enjoying a new vogue in the world of international education. The theme of the 2007 annual meeting of the Canadian Bureau for International Education was "Citizens of the World: Making an Impact through International Education" and the theme for Canada's celebration of International Education Week that same year was "Citizenship for the World—Preparing Graduates for the Future" (Canadian Bureau of International Education, 2007).

But how far has this discourse penetrated Canadian universities? How do Canadian universities engage with notions of global citizenship? To what extent are these notions influenced by federal and provincial policy and programmatic approaches? And, how do these notions get translated into study abroad initiatives? The 2006 Association of Universities and Colleges of Canada's (AUCC) survey on internationalization offers the most up-to-date snapshot of study abroad, as well as permitting comparisons with the situation in 2000, when the previous survey was done. There can be no doubt that things have improved in many ways. The absolute number of Canadian students involved in an "out-of-country academic experience undertaken for credit," tripled from 5,058 in 1997–1998 to 17,850 in 2005–2006. This represented an increase from 1 to 2.2% of the total student body. Part of this increase derives from the greater support offered by Canadian universities: 81% now provide some type of financial support for international experiences, compared to 63% in the earlier survey (AUCC, 2007). The 2006 survey also revealed that universities saw developing "responsible and engaged global citizens" as by far the most important reason for promoting study abroad. Three quarters of the institutions responding put this among the three top reasons and 44% put it first (AUCC, 2007). Does this mean that there is a correlation between university objectives of promoting global citizenship and the increase in the number of student studying abroad? Is the connection between global citizenship and study abroad mutually reinforcing?

The first decade of the 21st century has seen the concept of global citizenship gain broad currency in Canadian universities. Just what this means and the level of commitment offered varies greatly from institution to institution, but there can be no doubt that the University of British Columbia has embraced global citizenship more thoroughly than any other. The university's

"Trek 2010," which was launched in 2005, includes in its Vision "prepar[ing] students to become exceptional global citizens" and states that part of its mission is to produce, "graduates who will acknowledge their obligations as global citizens, and strive to secure a sustainable and equitable future for all."[17]

The stimulus for making global citizenship so central to UBC's role came from then-President Martha Piper. As early as 2000, Dr. Piper was speaking about the meaning of civic society, citizenship, and the role of universities. Her 2002 Killam lecture, "Building a Civil Society: A New Role for the Human Sciences," argued that her goal of building a strong civil society required that we

> encourage knowledge and scholarship that will enable individuals to better understand themselves, their values and the roles they play as citizens... [and] pursue knowledge and scholarship that will assist us to define our Canadian identity and our role as global citizens.[18]

For Piper, global citizenship meant

> we need not give up our special affiliations and identities, whether national, ethnic or religious; but we do need to work to make all human beings part of our community of dialogue and concern, framing local or national politics within a broader structure of respect for all human beings.[19] (Piper, 2002)

Piper's vision underlay a wide-ranging consultative process at UBC that began with a major conference on global citizenship in September 2002. This was followed by a strategic planning discussion paper (October 2003); a Green Paper (March 2004), and a White Paper (September 2004) (University of British Columbia, 2006). The consultations included soliciting electronic feedback on the Green and White Papers; holding workshops and student forums; and, starting in January 2004, a

> Global Citizenship Project " organized by Student Services to engage students and alumni in discussions on the notion of "global citizenship" so that there would be significant student input into the understanding of this concept within the university and to ensure student and alumni contributions were incorporated into the University's Trek2010 strategic plan. (University of British Columbia, n.d.).

The result was Trek 2010: A Global Journey, which was adopted in November 2004 and launched on March 10, 2005 (University of British Columbia, 2006).

There is certainly no shortage of activity related to global citizenship at UBC. A Google search for "UBC global citizenship" generated 149,000 hits.[20] The "Global Citizenship" page on the university's internationalization Web site highlights several activities (University of British Columbia, n.d.). What is striking about this is the absence of any mention of study abroad. Indeed, the Global Citizenship Teaching and Learning rubric describes

> initiatives to help integrate what students learn in the classroom and enhance their acquisition of global competencies through experiential opportunities in the community like the Learning Exchange Trek Program, which enables students, staff and alumni *to provide community service in Vancouver's inner city.*

Many of the University's students do study abroad, of course, but the UBC approach suggests that cultivation of global citizenship does not require an enhanced commitment to study abroad and can be coherently pursued without it.[21]

It is interesting to note that the AUCC survey reports institutions ranking "responsible and engaged global citizens" as by far the most important reason for promoting study abroad, as the absence of any direct connection between study abroad and the goals of global citizenship is also illustrated by the experience of York University. Since 2000, York has aggressively promoted study abroad, and other forms of relevant international experiences, without incorporating the concept of global citizenship into its rhetoric or rationale. Not even the prize-winning York International Internship Program (YIIP), which was started in 2004, which in many ways is an ideal vehicle for promoting global citizenship, uses the term: "YIIP provides both York undergraduate and graduate students a non-credit opportunity to apply their academic knowledge to an international work environment and enhance their job-related skills in an international and intercultural setting" (York University, 2007).

This is also the case of York's Schulich School of Business. Even though Schulich brands itself as "Canada's Global Business School," it does not engage the term *global citizenship* or the preparation of global citizens' anywhere in its mandate or objectives. Explicit in its approach, however, is the preparation of students for a global economy and a global corporate world that extends to what is referred to as the "triple bottom line": economic, social impact, and environmental management (The Aspen Institute and the World Resources Institute, 2003). Schulich has been ranked the number one school in Canada and among the top three business schools in the world that lead the way in integrating issues of social and environmental stewardship into business school curricula and research. In many ways, Schulich promotes broader aspects of global citizenship (knowledge, understanding, and action) through its emphasis on corporate, social, and environmental responsibility and focus on sustainability as a cornerstone of management education.

Université Laval, in Québec City, is another Canadian leader in study abroad. With funding from a private donor, Laval introduced its *Profil international* (International Profile) in 1999 and since then the number students going abroad has skyrocketed, from less than 100 in 1998–1999 to almost 1,000 in 2007–2008. The program is based on bilateral agreements with other institutions, which number 420 in 66 countries. As a French-speaking university, Laval has had to face challenges that English-speaking institutions do not, and as a result has worked with what they call "asymmetrical exchanges": students from partner institutions study French at Laval's École des langues while its students take disciplinary courses at the partners. With many of its partners in developing countries, in 2002, Laval introduced the *Stage interculturel et international* (International and intercultural internship). In this program, students work for 8 to 10 weeks with an NGO or other local organization on a humanitarian project, mostly in medical fields, for which they receive financial assistance and credits toward their degree.

Laval is another university that does not use the language of global citizenship. Even with its *Stage interculturel et international*, it prefers to talk about "compétence en international" (global competence) and "formation sans frontière" (training without borders).[22]

The three case studies seek to illuminate the diverse ways in which Canadian universities have addressed internationalization, study abroad, and the project of global citizenship in the absence of any national or international education policy or program. It is important to note that there are a number of significant differences between study abroad in Canadian universities and those in their U.S. counterparts. Canadian universities are more likely to send students on semester to year-long exchange programs to partner institutions so that they take classes with the local students and students from the partner universities mix with their own students. Canadian universities are also less likely to establish their own "island" campuses and short-term study programs. And they are much less likely to use commercial third-party providers. But there are also a few commonalities shared: most importantly that only a miniscule number of students include study abroad as part of their university education.[23]

As in the case of the United States, the lack of funds has been identified consistently as the single most significant barrier for Canadian students to participate in study abroad experiences by AUCC (Knight, 2000). However, unlike the United States, there is no pan-Canadian large scale study abroad program such as the Lincoln Study Abroad Fellowship Program supported through the federal government. The AUCC has focused its efforts on lobbying the federal government since the 1990s encouraging an investment of approximately $25 million annually to target the sending of between 5 and 10% of Canadian students abroad. In its lobbying efforts it appeals to the federal government's commitment to access and national economic interests in having a skilled, knowledgeable, and experienced global workforce. To date, it has had limited success.[24]

Within Canadian universities, there does not seem to be a clear relation between study abroad and global citizenship, albeit both objectives are of importance. As institutions of higher learning, it is evident that Canadian universities see one of their many roles as preparing citizens for the service of the broader communities in which they are located—both local and global. The Canadian ethos of volunteerism and service and the values of social justice and equity undoubtedly penetrate the discourses of internationalization and global citizenship at the universities. However, it is equally true that since 2000, there is a penetration of provincial and federal government rhetoric of the importance of global skills for the competitiveness of the national/global economy which is reflected in several of the policy statements and programmatic objectives of the universities. Even so, there seems to be a balance between the political, economic, social, cultural, and environmental aspects of global citizenship within and across the university sector, but the question to consider would be how these priorities may shift in the near future as provincial interests in international education activities expand.

CONCLUSION

Is there a distinctly Canadian approach to study abroad and the making of global citizens? At the federal level, certainly Canada's place in the world as a middle power and its foreign policy tradition of humanitarianism, peacekeeping, and development assistance has provided the foundation for Canadian views on their role and place in the world as, global citizens. A broad notion of global citizenship is invoked through a public sentiment committed to democracy, civic engagement, and volunteerism.

However, translating this ethos into a national policy on international education continues to be a challenge as AUCC lobbies for a federal flagship program to boost the profile of study abroad within Canada. The history of international education in Canada, however, suggests that such a program is unlikely. While the halo effect from past foreign policy priorities continues to influence academic institutions, nongovernment organizations, and the public at large in their perceptions and attitudes toward Canada's role and place in the world, the federal government itself has moved in totally different directions in its foreign policy orientation, leading foreign policy experts to lament Canada's international commitment and declining influence in the world. The possibilities of a major national initiative appear even more remote in the context of the Conservative government of Stephen Harper which is wary of any strong federal framework, and has shifted foreign policy priorities away from international development assistance and human resource development to a more direct link between immigration and the recruitment of international students. At the provincial level, while there is a growing interest in support for study abroad, albeit provincial policies link the notion of global citizenship and study/work abroad to enhancing the global competitiveness of the labor force in their respective economies.

At the same time, Canadian institutions have increased their international engagements. Canadian universities are reporting internationalization as a core priority to their institutional missions, shifting from their earlier and more peripheral international developmental focused approaches, and are investing in new organizational structures, hiring of senior staff, and development of innovative student programs. With increased funding made available through private sources, reallocation of institutional funds, and new monies from provincial governments, they are providing a wider and innovative range of study/work abroad options to their students.[25] Yet, one has to question exactly how significant study abroad and the project of global citizenship are to the provinces and individual institutions as the percentage of Canadian students studying abroad remains at an extremely modest 2.2%.

Canadian institutions have begun addressing the needs of the 98% of Canadian students who do not study abroad through multifaceted on-campus approaches to internationalization focused largely on curriculum. Accompanied by increased attention to cocurricular activities, this may prove to be the most fertile ground for cultivating global citizenship as a generalized phenomenon. Perhaps Canadian multiculturalism might also offer new opportunities to reframe thinking on global citizenship and study abroad? There is evidence that the link between internationalization and Canadian multiculturalism has provided an impetus to universities to develop more inclusive curriculum and address the needs of a growing diverse student body. However, policy documents and program initiatives suggest that the link between multiculturalism, global citizenship, and study abroad remains at best tenuous (see Barndt, in press).

In conclusion, global citizenship *à la canadienne* illustrates that study abroad and global citizenship are not necessarily mutually reinforcing and that the promotion of meaningful global citizenship can take place in the absence of study abroad. It also suggests that work abroad programs, broadly defined through a range of federal government opportunities such as volunteering, internships, and co-op programs, which provide direct and demanding opportunity to engage with the international community and with issues of citizenship, are considered a more effective strategy to building global citizenship (knowledge, awareness, and action) than study abroad programs which provide less direct contact with the community at large, confine experiences linked with academic credit requirements, and are often expensive to pursue (more of a concentration on knowledge and awareness). One can also observe a shift in the definition of global citizenship as a concept built on a triad of knowledge, understanding, and action to one that is built on a triad of knowledge, skills, and economic competitiveness.

The absence of a national policy has enabled a diversified approach to the objectives of global citizenship, where a plethora of heterogeneous and uncoordinated programs at the federal, provincial, and institutional level—work and study abroad programs, internationalization of the curriculum, and local service learning initiatives—together build a broad concept of global citizenship and a wide range of meaningful opportunities for our students. Linking study abroad to global citizenship appears attractive, but it can potentially be a double-edged sword that may lead in a direction distinct from the one anticipated.

ACKNOWLEDGMENTS

The authors want to thank several of the interviewees that have chosen to remain anonymous for their valuable input in filling the gaps in the existing literature and with the interpretation of policy and program initiatives, as well as Stephen Dunnett, Simon Marginson, Monique Genereux, Pari Johnson, and Isabelle Legaré at AUCC for their detailed and helpful comments on an earlier draft of this chapter.

NOTES

1. Welsh's observation about young Canadians in the first years of the 21st century captures the widespread commitment to engagement and volunteerism that goes well beyond formal academic activities. An appetite for becoming involved in global issues is certainly abroad, and not just among university students. Craig Kielberger became a Canadian icon at the age of 12 when he founded Save the Children in 1995, and on October 19, 2007, his organization's "National Me to We Day" drew more than 7,000 high-school student leaders to an event in Toronto. Retrieved January28, 2008, from http://www.freethechildren.org/metoweday/event/index.html. At the university level, the 8 Goals Campaign has brought together a number of student organizations to "mobilize Canadian post-secondary students to champion the Millennium Development Goals. Once informed on the issues, we can work together and call for policies to strengthen Canada's contribution to global development." Retrieved January 28, 2008, from http://www.8goals.ca/site//node/2. There is student activism around global citizenship on campuses across the country.
2. Although Welsh explicitly proposes her idea of a "Model Citizen" as an alternative to the longstanding concept of middle power (2004, pp. 33–35).
3. The Liberal government's 2005 International Policy Statement, which was abandoned by the subsequent Conservative government, asserted global citizenship "reflecting Canada's desire to make a difference in the world" as one of its three priorities: http://geo.international.gc\.ca/cip-pic/ips/overview-en.aspx
4. for more on this, see also Michael Valpy (2008, June 28).
5. Based on discussions and e-mail correspondence with AUCC staff, January–February 2008.
6. In fact, even on matters of foreign policy that concern education, such as the signing of international agreements which have implications for educational exchange, or the representation of Canadian education interests at international venues, the provinces would question the legitimacy of federal government's role and function (Trilokekar, 2007).
7. An intergovernmental organization founded by the ministers of education to serve as a mechanism for policy discussions and means of cooperation with the federal government.
8. This is best illustrated in the government's attempts to enable international students to work while studying in Canada in 2005. Policies were established on a province by province basis, with each province signing a separate agreement with the federal government (CIC). At the same time, Ottawa used its power to unilaterally differentiate the length of time international students could work in the country after graduation: the longstanding policy of 1 year was increased to 2, except for those who had studied at universities located in Montreal, Toronto, and Vancouver. See *Canada Immigration News and Views*. Retrieved May 2006 from http://www.diycanadaimmigration.com/blog/index.html; see also Trilokekar, 2007.
9. For example, from the type and structure of the degrees we offer, to the divisions of knowledge we employ, to the way we administer ourselves, so much so that a professor from one country could walk into a university in the other and understand what was going on in a way that would not be the case with universities in Europe or other parts of the world.
10. Only the United States, Australia, and Germany cut aid more sharply in this period.
11. The university team's partnership program was a competition for funding toward a major international project to be carried out by a team of Canadian university faculty and students with partner institutions in the South. Teams of senior undergraduate or graduate students were to be led by faculty members to work in developing countries to strengthen governance capacity. Each of the teams would receive up to $50,000 and draw on the extensive network of international partnerships and the expertise on governance issues at Canadian universities.
12. AUCC was instrumental in convincing CIDA of the importance of situating the youth initiatives within Canadian university structures thus leveraging the already existing resources, networks, and community linkages

through faculty contacts and access to approximately one million students. AUCC proposed that given the very nature of universities as learning institutions, they are uniquely placed to facilitate global citizenship engagement within structured international learning experiences and also provide academic credit to students, a feature that would make this program unique compared to other volunteer opportunities. This information is based on discussions with AUCC staff, January–February 2008.

13. For descriptions of the actual internships and team projects, see http://www.aucc.ca/programs/intprograms/sfd/sfd_2005_e.html; http://www.aucc.ca/programs/intprograms/sfd/sfd_2006_e.html. For information on the program itself and the application process, see http://www.aucc.ca/programs/intprograms/sfd/sfd_2007_e.html (all retrieved July 2008).

14. This is in keeping with other developed countries where international education programs are often housed within their respective ministries of foreign affairs.

15. As a first step, a steering committee was created and a conference organized at Wingspread, Wisconsin in 1992. An important element of this cooperation was that representatives from different stakeholder groups, including government (both levels and CMEC), educational institutions, and the private sector participated in the proceedings. A consensus document setting out the principles and objectives of collaboration was prepared and a trilateral task force was created to move the process forward and arrange a major symposium in Vancouver the same year. The Task Force focused on means to reinforce national efforts in support of innovation and human resource development, identifying five interrelated issues of common interest (Joyal, 1994).

16. Our translation. The other three were supporting international research collaboration, consolidating partnerships with universities abroad, and internationalizing the curriculum.

17. On the UBC approach, see John R. Mallea, "The University's Role in Developing Global Citizens: An Innovative Canadian case-Study", paper presented at the Internationalizing Canada's Universities Symposium at York University March 2nd-3rd, 2006. Retrieved April 2007, from http://international.yorku.ca/global/conference/canada/papers/John-Mallea.pdf

18. In many ways, this emphasis on the role of the university to create social change and translate awareness into student action within their communities parallels the principles of the Clinton Global Initiative University, retrieved from http://chronicle.com/weekly/v54/i25/25a04001.htm; http://www.clintonglobalinitiative.org/NETCOMMUNITY/Page.aspx?pid=1399&srcid=-2 on June 2007.

19. In her address to the Canadian Club in Ottawa in May 2004, she added to this definition the phrase "who see themselves not simply as citizens of a local region but also as human beings bound to all other human beings by ties of concern and understanding." Retrieved October 12, 2007, from http://www.canadianclubottawa.ca/en/events/archives/speeches/03/piper.html

21. The Trek 2010 document does include "Increas[ing] opportunities for student participation in international projects and study abroad programs" but gives it no special salience.

22. We want to thank Richard Poulin and Monique Genereux, of the Bureau international at Laval, for their assistance. More information on the Stage interculturel et international, which won the AUCC-Scotiabank award for internationalization in 2004, is available at http://www.aucc.ca/programs/documents/preparing_students_e.pdf

23. As well, as the AUCC 2000 survey indicated 61% of study abroad participants in Canada are female. The top two destinations are Western Europe and Australia and New Zealand, and the reasons for this are cited as being language issues, western cultural orientation, quality of education, and number of institutional agreements. The next most popular countries include Mexico, the United States, and in the countries of Central and South America. Asia ranks lower, with the least popular destinations including Africa, Central and Eastern Europe, and the Middle East.

24. On one hand, it has worked closely with CIDA to develop the Canada Corps initiatives involving the university sector, and on the other it recognizes important initiatives such as the development of new graduate scholarships for international and Canadian students which include $6000 one semester study abroad stipends for up to 250 students, funded by the federal government. These programs are in addition to the two international academic mobility programs run by HRSDC. Put together however these programs represent a very small effort. There has not been any major federal funding or programmatic support for study abroad on the national scale as recommended by AUCC.

25. This is evident through the many applications made to the AUCC-Scotiabank Awards for Excellence in Internationalization at Canadian Universities, in fields ranging from health, law, environmental science, among several others, each focused on broader notions of global citizenship in context of the political, social, cultural, environmental, and economic realms. Retrieved February 22, 2008 from http://www.aucc.ca/programs/scotiabank_e.html

REFERENCES

Aspen Institute and the World Resources Institute. (2003, October 6). Beyond Grey Pinstripes Preparing MBAs for Social and Environmental Stewardship. Washington D.C.: The Aspen Institute and New York: World Resources Instiute. Retrieved 15 May 2007 from http://www.aspencbe.org/documents/bgps-2003-brochure.pdf

Association of Universities and Colleges of Canada. (AUCC). (2004). Retrieved January 29, 2008, from http://www.aucc.ca/publications/media/2004/12_21_e.html

Association of Universities and Colleges of Canada (AUCC). (2007 August). Canadian universities and international student mobility. Retrieved January 8, 2008, from http://www.aucc.ca/_pdf/english/publications/student_mobility_2007_e.pdf

Axelrod, P. (Forthcoming) Implementing the "innovation" strategy: Post-secondary education in the Chrétien years. In D. Anastakis & P. Bryden (Eds.), *People, provinces and power: Essays in honour of John T. Saywell*. Toronto: University of Toronto Press.

Axworthy, L. (2003). Navigating a new world: Canada's global future. Toronto: Knopf.

Barndt, D. (in press). Reframing internationalization in a (post)colonial and diasporic context: Two initiatives at York University. In A. Shubert, G. Jones, & R. D. Trilokekar (Eds.), *Internationalizing Canadian universities: Policies, practices and challenges*. Toronto: Lorimer.

Barrow, C. W., Didou-Aupetit, S., & Mallea, J. (2003). *Globalization, trade liberalization, and higher education in North America: The emergence of a new market under NAFTA?* Netherlands: Kluver.

Bentley, C. (2007a). Retrieved February 27, 2008, from http://ogov.newswire.ca/ontario/GPOE/2007/05/29/c6389.html?lmatch=&lang=_e.html

Bentley, C. (2007b). Retrieved February 27, 2008, from http://ogov.newswire.ca/ontario/GPOE/2007/02/23/c3940.html?lmatch=&lang=_e.html

Bergbusch, E. (1999). Development odyssey re-visited: How CIDA evolved. *Behind the Headlines: Canada's International Affairs Magazine, 56*(2), 24–27.

British Columbia Centre for International Education. (n.d.). Internationalizing teaching and learning. Retrieved February 5, 2008, from http://www.bccie.bc.ca/bccie/FSA/internationalizing_curriculum.asp

British Columbia, Ministry of Advanced Education. (n.d.). International education. Retrieved February 5, 2008, from http://www.aved.gov.bc.ca/internationaleducation/

British Columbia, University of. (2007). Trek 2010. Retrieved November 29, 2007, from http://www.trek2000.ubc.ca/index.html

Brown, D., Cazalis, P., & Jasmin, G. (1992). *Higher education in federal systems*. Kingston, ONT: Institute of Intergovernmental Relations.

Byers, M. (2005). Retrieved February 27, 2008, from http://thetyee.ca/Views/2005/10/05/globalcitizen/

Byers, M. (2007). *Intent for a nation: What is Canada for? A relentlessly optimistic manifesto for Canada's role in the world*. Vancouver: Douglas & McIntyre.

Cameron, D. M. (1997). The federal perspective. In G. A. Jones (Ed.), *Higher education in Canada: Different systems, different perspectives* (pp. 9–29). New York: Garland.

Campbell, G. (2007). Retrieved February 5, 2008, from http://www2.news.gov.bc.ca/news_releases_2005-2009/2007AE0018-000367.htm

Canadian Bureau for International Education (CBIE). (2007) CBIE Annual Conference 2007. Retrieved January 28, 2007, from .http://www.cbie.ca/conference/2007/index_e.html

Canadian Bureau for International Education (CBIE). (2008, February 27). International education gets a boost in federal budget (news release). Ottawa.

Canadian International Development Agency. (n.d.). Retrieved January 28, 2008, from http://www.acdi-cida.gc.ca/internships.

Canadian Universities Service Overseas (CUSO). (n.d.). Retrieved February 27, 2008, from http://www.cuso.org/about_cuso/since_61/index_e.php

Carter, A. (2001). *The political theory of global citizenship*. London: Routledge.

CIDA. (1986). *CIDA's NGO division: Introduction and guide*. Ottawa, Canada: CIDA.

CIDA. (2007, May). Evaluation of Canada corps university partnership program (CCUPP) and students for development (SFD). Partner with AUCC, Evaluation Division, Performance Knowledge Management Branch. Quebec. Retrieved from http://www2.news.gov.bc.ca/news_releases_2005-2009/2007AE0018-000367.htm

CIDA. (n.d). International Youth Internship Program. Retreived January 28, from 2008 http://www.acdi-cida.gc.ca/internships

Cohen, A. (2003). *While Canada slept: How we lost our place in the world*. Toronto, ON: McClelland & Stewart.

Conseil Superieure de L'Education. (2005). L'Internationalisation: Nourrir le Dynamisme des Universités Quebecoises [Internationalism: Nourishing the dynamism of Quebec universities]. Retrieved February 10, 2008 from http://www.cse.gouv.qc.ca/fichiers/documents/50-0449F.pdf, p. 3.

Department of Foreign Affairs and International Trade. (1994). The international dimensions of higher education in Canada collaborative policy framework [Draft Discussion Paper]. Ottawa.

Department of Foreign Affairs and International Trade. (2005). *A role of pride and influence in the world. Canada's International Policy Statement, Development*. Ottawa: Author.

Department of Foreign Affairs and International Trade. (n.d.). Retrieved February 8, 2008, from http://www.dfait-maeci.gc.ca/culture/iear/menu-en.asp

Dower, N. (2003). *An introduction to global citizenship*. Edinburgh, Scotland: Edinburgh University Press.

Dower, N., & Willims, J. (2002). *Global citizenship. A critical reader*. Edinburgh, Scotland: Edinburgh University Press.

Farquhar, R. H. (2001). *Advancing the Canadian agenda for international education*. Ottawa: CBIE.

Fisher, D., Rubenson, K., Bernatchez, J., Clift, R., Jones, G., Lee, J., et al. (2006). *Canadian federal policy and postsecondary education*. Vancouver: University of British Columbia .

Green, M. F. (2002). Internationalizing undergraduate education: Challenges and lessons of success. In D. Engberg & M. Green (Eds.). *Promising practices: Spotlighting excellence in comprehensive internationalization*. Washington, DC: ACE.

Human Resources and Skill Development Canada. (n.d./a). Retrieved November 27, 2007, from http://www.hrsdc.gc.ca/en/hip/lld/lssd/iam/mainpage.shtml

Human Resources and Skill Development Canada. (n.d./b). Retrieved November 27, 2007, from http://www.hrsdc.gc.ca/en/hip/lld/lssd/iam/anouncements.shtml

International Academic Mobility Initiative. Retrieved March 12, 2008, from http://www.hrsdc.gc.ca/en/learning/exchanges/na_iam_2008_en.shtml

International Education Branch. Retrieved January 28, 2008, from http://www.gov.mb.ca/ie/public/intl_branch.html

Iyer, P. (2004, November-December). Canada: Global citizen. *Canadian Geographic*.

Jones, G. (1996). Governments, governance and Canadian universities. In J. C. Smart (Ed.), *Higher education, handbook of theory and research* (Vol. 11, pp. 337–371).

Joyal, S. (August 1994). *International cultural affairs, higher education and scientific cooperation. Refocusing Canada's international cultural policy in the nineties: Issues and solutions* (Report to the Minister of Foreign Affairs, Department of Foreign Affairs and International Trade). Ottawa.

Knight, J. (2000). *Progress and promise: The 2000 AUCC report on internationalization at Canadian universities*. Ottawa: AUCC.

Latham, R. (2007). Retrieved February 28, 2008 from http://www.yorku.ca/yfile/archive/index.asp?Article=9267

McGill University. (n.d.). Retrieved February 10, 2008, from http://www.mcgill.ca/studyabroad/pbcse/overview/

Morrison, D. (1998). *Aid and ebb tide: A history of CIDA and Canadian development assistance*. Waterloo, ON: Wilfred Laurier University Press.

Office of the Premier, Ministry of Advanced Education. (2007, April 2). Scholarships support overseas learning for students [News release]. Retrieved February 5, 2008, from http://www2.news.gov.bc.ca/news_releases_2005-2009/2007AE0018-000367.htm

Office of the Premier, Ministry of Advanced Education. (2007, June 12). Pacific century scholarships to draw top grad students [News release]. Retrieved February 5, 2008 from http://www2.news.gov.bc.ca/news_releases_2005-2009/2007OTP0082-000775.htm

Ontario, Government of. (2005). *Internationalization of post secondary education in Canada and abroad*. Ottawa: Author.

Pearson, L. (1957). Retrieved November 14, 2007 from http://nobelprize.org/nobel_prizes/peace/laureates/1957/press.html

Picard, F. (2006, March). *The internationalization of Québec's universities*. PowerPoint lecture presented at Internationalizing Canada's Universities: Practices, Challenges, and Opportunities. Retrieved from http://international.yorku.ca/global/conference/canada/papers.htm

Piper, M. (2002). *Building a civil society: A new role for the human sciences*. Killam lecture. Retrieved 29 November, 2007, from http://www.fedcan.ca/english/pdf/fromold/2002killamlecture.pdf

Pratt, C. (1996). Humane internationalism and Canadian development assistance policies. In C. Pratt (Ed.), *Canadian international assistance development policies: An appraisal* (pp. 334–380). Montreal, PQ: McGill/Queen's University Press.

Québec Government. Retrieved February 10, 2008, from http://www.formulaire.gouv.qc.ca/cgi/affiche_doc.cgi?dossier=8326&table=0

Savage, C., & McKittrick, T. (2002, September 30–October 4). *Australian/Canadian state/provincial international education consortia: A comparative study*. Paper presented at the 16th Australian International Education conference, Hobart, Australia. Retrieved from http://www.idp.com/16aiecpapers/program/thursday/postersessions/McIttrick_p.pdf

Shute, J. (1999). From here to there and back again: International outreach in the Canadian university. In S. L. Bond & J. P. Lemasson (Eds.), *A new world of knowledge: Canadian universities and globalization* (pp. 21–44). Ottawa: IDRC. Retrieved from http://www.idrc.ca/en/ev-9400-201-1-DO_TOPIC.html

Skolnik, M. L., & G. A. Jones. (1992). A comparative analysis of arrangements for state coordination of higher education in Canada and the United States. *The Journal of Higher Education. 63*(2), 121–142.

Tiessen, R. (2007). Educating global citizens? Canadian foreign policy and youth study/volunteer abroad programs. *Canadian Foreign Policy, 14*(1), 77–84.

Trilokekar, R. D. (2007). *Federalism, foreign policy and the internationalization of higher education: A case study of the international academic relations division, department of foreign affairs and international trade, Canada*. Unpublished doctoral dissertation, University of Toronto.

University of British Columbia. (2006). Trek 2010. Retrieved on November 29, 2007 http://www.trek2000.ubc.ca/index.html

University of British Columbia. (n.d.). Global Citizenship Project. Retrieved on November 29, 2007. http://www.students.ubc.ca/current/global.cfm

University of Victoria. (2001). Canada vs The OECD: An environmental Comparison. Victoria: University of Victoria. Retrieved on February 27, 2008, http://www.environmentalindicators.com/htdocs/indicators/25offi.htm

Urquhart, B. (2007, October 11). Are diplomats necessary? *New York Review of Books, 54*(15). Retrieved from http://www.nybooks.com/articles/20671

Valpy, M. (2008, June 28). Our part-time home and native land. *Globe and Mail*.

Welsh, J. (2004). *Where do I belong? Exploring citizenship in the 21st century*. The Hart House Lectures, Hart House, University of Toronto, Toronto.

Welsh, J. (2005). *At home in the world: Canada's global vision for the 21st century*. Toronto: Harper Perennial Canada.

World University Services of Canada (WUSC). (n.d.). Retrieved February 27, 2008, from http://www.wusc.ca/en/about/about_us

York University. (2006). Retrieved February 10, 2008, from http://www.yorku.ca/ontbw/; http://www.yorku.ca/ontra/

York University. (2007). International Internships. Retrieved on January 28, 2007 http://international.yorku.ca/internships/index.htm

Chapter 13

Global Citizenship and Study Abroad

A European Comparative Perspective

Hans de Wit

Journal of Studies in International Education

INTRODUCTION

In general, international educators have a tendency to use the same language when they deal with meanings, rationales, approaches, strategies, and activities. International educators, though, tend to approach the internationalization of higher education from a rather narrow national and local perspective and are thus inclined to be as parochial in their approach as the students who are to be the beneficiaries of their work. This is based on the fact that higher education and its international dimension are still based primarily on the nation-state, even in this area of rapid globalization and regionalization of our economies and societies. Approaches to internationalization of higher education differ from country to country, and this also applies to the meaning attached to the terms *global citizenship* and *study abroad,* both of which are central to this publication.

In an 1998 essay on the occasion of the 50th anniversary of NAFSA, titled "Ducks Quack Differently on Each Side of the Ocean" (De Wit, 1998), I tried to explain the differences in approach to internationalization in Europe and the United States, referring in the title to Joseph Mestenhauser's comment that "everything that quacks must be international education" (Mestenhauser, 1998). Three characteristics were mentioned as driving U.S. internationalization policies: passion, ethos, and rhetoric; the emphasis on peace as a driving rationale; and overcoming parochialism.

Later (De Wit, 2002), I expanded my analysis:

- Immediately after World War II the internationalization of higher education was more dominant in the United States, and founded on arguments of foreign policy and national security. In Europe, the tradition is still rather young, only became more important as part of the European economic and political integration process, and was primarily motivated by arguments of economic competition.
- The international dimension of higher education has a longer tradition of organization and a higher level of professionalism in the United States than it has in Europe.

- In the United States, the objective of international education is more directed to global and intercultural awareness, in response to cultural parochialism; while in Europe the emphasis is more on the extension and diversification of academic performance.

- In the United States, the emphasis in study abroad activities is on undergraduate mobility, whereas in Europe priority is given to exchanges at the graduate level.

- The focus of international education in the United States is more directed toward globalization of the curriculum, area studies, and foreign language study, while in Europe the focus is more on networking and mobility.

- In the United States, study abroad and foreign student advising have a tendency to be seen more as different, unrelated activities, while in Europe they are seen as related parts of mobility schemes, with the emphasis on exchanges.

- In the United States, study abroad tends to take the form of faculty-supervised group mobility, whereas in Europe mobility is based more on mutual trust and is oriented toward the individual.

- In the United States, the push for internationalization comes more from the State Department and the Defense Department, from private foundations and professional associations, and from institutions of higher education and their representative bodies, contributing to an active lobbying and advocacy tradition. In Europe active advocacy and lobbying tradition have only recently emerged.

- In the United States, at both the policy and professional levels, there is a lack of a strategic approach and a tendency toward fragmentation. In Europe, the different programs and organizational aspects are more integrated into an overall strategy, and at the professional level one can see a higher level of integration. (pp. 76–77)

As possible explanations for these issues I mentioned:

- In the United States, internationalization is seen as part of general education, whereas in Europe it is seen more as an activity within academic specialization.

- In the United States, undergraduate education has to compensate for the lack of global and intercultural education and foreign language training in primary and secondary education. In higher education, this takes the form of international education. In Europe, general education, including global and intercultural education and, at least in some countries, active foreign language training, are an integral part of primary and secondary education. Higher education can undergo internationalization more as an integrated part of academic specialization.

- In the United States, area studies, foreign language training, the study of international relations, and development studies, are externally added and sponsored programs, whereas in Europe they have developed as regular disciplines, no different from, for example, law, economics, or medicine.

- In the United States, internationalization is more driven by political rationales of national security and foreign policy, while in Europe economic competition and academic quality are the main rationales for the internationalization of higher education. (p. 77)

Different cultures and structures in primary, secondary, and undergraduate education, as well as different emphases in foreign policy after World War II, play an important role, combined with a lack of national policy for higher education and internationalization in the United States, a lack of private initiative in higher education and internationalization in Europe, different leadership traditions and different funding mechanisms.

I also stated that it would be likely that the differences would gradually diminish, that Europe would enter a period of uncertainty and change, and that international education in the United States would have a comparative advantage because it has been based more on a diversity of funding sources, whereas the Europeans always could rely on state and EU funding, and that U.S. universities are more likely to use proactive strategies while the European institutions are more reactive.

I have quoted so extensively from my 1998 essay and my 2002 comparative study on internationalization of higher education in the United States and Europe because it will be interesting to see what has happened in the past decade. This paper compares the American perspective on internationalization of higher education and in particular global citizenship and study abroad with a European view 10 years later, in order to clarify the process of internationalization of higher education and the way it is embedded in national and institutional cultures, systems, and histories, even in this age of globalization. Have the two become closer in addressing international education, as I foresaw 10 years ago?

According to Peter Stearns in his book *Educating Global Citizens in Universities and Colleges* (2009) still "arguably the biggest challenge ... involves the tension between global education needs and goals, and a strongly parochial American Society" (p. 6). He argues that although not new this inclination to parochialism has become "more troubling as the global environment intensifies" (p. 6). He adds:

> In between the temptation towards excessive zeal and the resistance to anything that smacks of global, but centrally related to parochialism: an odd hesitancy to push very far, in fact, at least in some aspects of global education. Thus: send students for study abroad but in carefully sanitized, American-run institutions where they may not have to run into too many foreigners. Thus: teach modern languages, but make sure students don't get pulled away from English too fully, lest psychic balance be disturbed. (p. 10)

He acknowledges that these statements are caricatures, but they are strikingly consistent with my observations 10 years ago. So, has nothing changed on the American side and has "fundamental American-ness...not [been] challenged too abruptly" in the past decade? (p. 10). And what about Europe?

In answering these questions, it is important to keep in mind that in Europe the global perspective has always been different from that of the United States, given the fact that Europe has only recently established an identity of its own as a consequence of the development and gradual expansion of the European Union, and before was rather absent. The world started at the borders of each of the relatively small nations which made up Europe and had been fighting among themselves to conquer the rest of the world. Although much reference is made to the idea that universities are European institutions par excellence and that there has existed since the Middle Ages and Renaissance a free flow of students and scholars in Europe, higher education in Europe has been closely tied to the nation- state for a long time, and only in the later part of the 20th century can one observe a loosening of ties between state and university, as a result of the globalization of our economies and the process of economic and political integration in the European Union (e.g., Neave, 2001). Europeans have felt themselves to be global citizens to a greater degree than their American equivalents. Only in recent years has there been a drive to create a European citizenship, as in the policies for internationalization or Europeanization of higher education, but this development has arisen more from the European Commission than from the citizens themselves.

It is also important to keep in mind that study abroad in the European mind has a more expanded definition than in the United States. In Europe study abroad implies both the mobility of students as part of their home degree (exchanges with, study at, and credit transfer from another institution) and for a degree at another institution, either in Europe or beyond (international students or degree mobility). In the United States study abroad is used in a more narrow sense, focusing primarily on home degree mobility and taking place in most cases in American-run institutions and programs.

So, study abroad and global citizenship arise from a different context and different perceptions in Europe from the United States. Before returning in my concluding remarks to this question of how Europe and the United States in the present context of increasing globalization of our societies and economies perceive global citizenship and study abroad in comparison to a decade ago, it is relevant for the purpose of this book, which is primarily focused on global citizenship and study abroad in the United States to address the development of internationalization of higher education in Europe in some detail, with specific emphasis on citizenship and study abroad.[1]

THE INTERNATIONALIZATION OF EUROPEAN HIGHER EDUCATION

In Europe as a whole, there are approximately 4,000 institutions of higher education, of which around 3,300 are in the European Union. The number of students was over 17 million (12.5 million in the EU) in the year 2000, and the number of staff were 1.5 million, including 435,000 researchers. These numbers are more or less the same as for the United States.

On average, the member states of the European Union spend 5% of their GDP on public expenditure for education, which is comparable to the United States. Public expenditures dropped in the past decade, private expenditure did not increase, and the European Union now lags far behind the United States in overall spending: 1.1% compared to 2.3%. "This gap stems primarily from the low level of private funding of higher education in Europe. This stands at a meager 0.2% of European GDP compared with 0.6% in Japan and 1.2% in the U.S.A." (Commission of the European Communities, 2003, p. 12). On average, 80% of total expenditure on higher education in Europe comes from public sources.

In addition, higher education in Europe also uses its funding inefficiently: the European Union faces high dropout rates among students—an average of around 40%; a mismatch between the supply of qualifications and the demand for qualified people; a huge disparity in the duration of studies in the Union; a disparity in the status and conditions of recruitment and work for researchers; and lack of transparent systems for calculating the cost of research (Commission of the European Communities, 2003, pp. 14–15). These factors have been crucial for the development of the internationalization of higher education in Europe.

Macrohistorical changes affecting the international dimension of Europe's higher education over the past decades were: the emergence of nation-states in the 19th century and earlier; Europe's historical role in the world, in particular its role in colonization and in the process of decolonization; the impact of higher education in countries such as France, Germany, and the United Kingdom on higher education in the rest of the world; recent trends in European integration; the collapse of the former Soviet Union and associated East–West rapprochement;

recession and financial constraint; mass nature of higher education; the dissolution of some structures and blocs and the emergence of others.

THE 1950S AND 1960S: LAISSEZ-FAIRE

If we confine discussion to the macrolevel and the post-Second World War period, the 1950s and 1960s in Europe are not seen today as a period of internationalization, but it would be entirely wrong to believe that international student mobility was absent then. In general, the period 1950 to 1970 was, according to Baron (1993, p. 50), characterized by a foreign policy among receiving countries of benevolent laissez–faire: of open doors to foreign students—who to a large extent, came from the former and, at that time, still existing French and British colonies. Some elements of this are still seen in the pattern of student flow to these countries, although (in the British case especially) the impact of more recent policies has largely transformed the picture.

The open door and laissez–faire policy and the one-way dimension were the main characteristics of the process of internationalization of higher education, at a global level and in Europe in particular. The universities themselves played a mainly passive role as receivers of foreign students. The effects on higher education cooperation within Europe were marginal. International activity was mainly oriented toward the cooperation of European higher education with the United States (outward mobility) and with the Third World (inward mobility). A European policy for internationalization did not exist, and the same applies to the institutional level. At the national level, international cooperation and exchange was included in bilateral agreements between nations and in development cooperation programs, driven by political rationales. Institutions were passive partners in these programs.

If we look at student mobility in 1965, in outward mobility (West) Germany (7), Greece (8), France (9), the United Kingdom (13), and Italy (16) were among the top 20 sending countries with a limited number of 39,500 students. In inward mobility, in 1998, France (2), Germany (3), the UK (6), and Italy (10) were among the top 10 receiving countries, taking in 20.2% (87,500) of the total number of international students, together far less than the United States (28.3%) (Cummings, 1993).

THE 1970S: THE FIRST STEPS TO POLICIES OF EUROPEANIZATION

In 1973, the creation of a Directorate for Education, Research and Science (DG XII), under the first Commissioner for Science and Education, Ralf Dahrendorf, not only institutionalized education within the Commission structure but also linked EU policies for education and research. With this, the Commission was able to move away from having to base its rationales for an education and research policy on noneducational arguments—economic rationales primarily—to a proactive and integrated policy in these fields.

In 1974, the ministers of education of the European Community adopted principles for an education action program that was launched in 1976.[2] The action program included three measures for higher education: joint study programs, short study visits, and an educational administrators program. Although important in itself, the impact of the action program was marginal. In that sense, the period from 1972 to 1985 can be seen as a period of stagnation.

THE 1980S: THE GREAT LEAP FORWARD

The 1980s produced four distinct changes: first with a research and development policy for the EC; second in the open door mobility of individual students; third in student mobility as an integrated part of study; and fourth in the widening of scope to other regions—third countries in Western Europe, Central and Eastern Europe, third countries outside Europe. The last three changes are relevant for the purpose of this article.

With respect to the individual mobility of students, the European nations and universities began changing their benevolent laissez–faire policy to a more controlled reception and in some cases the active recruitment of fee-paying foreign students. At first, this applied nearly exclusively to the United Kingdom, notably the British decision in 1979 to introduce full-cost fees for foreign students. Higher education as an export commodity quickly became dominant in the United Kingdom.

For most people on the European continent, considering the education of foreign students as an export commodity was still anathema at that time. On the European continent, the reception of foreign students was and in most cases still is based more on foreign policy arguments than on considerations of export policy. At the end of the 20th century, the international movement of students as an export commodity had spread over the European continent and became a more important element of higher education policy than it had been in the past, both at the national and institutional level.

In the late 1970s and early 1980s the notion of study abroad, in the sense of sending students to foreign institutions of higher education as part of their home degree program, became an issue on the continent that overshadowed the developments in mobility of individual students. Since the 1980s, student mobility as a one-way, individual process stimulated by political or economic considerations has (with the exception of the United Kingdom) lost prominence as a policy issue. It has been marginalized by the greater attention given to student mobility in the framework of exchange programs, which have been among the top priorities in higher education policies of the 1980s and 1990s. Before this period, organized programs for the exchange of students and staff did exist, but these programs were limited in both funding and scope, stimulating mainly unrelated exchanges at the graduate level.

The 1976 joint study programs scheme of the EC aimed at the promotion of joint programs of study and research between institutions in several member states. The focus of this experimental program was primarily the stimulation of academic mobility within the EC. This scheme was replaced in 1987 by its successor, the European Action Scheme for the Mobility of University Students (ERASMUS). The action program of 1976 was the basis for future activities in academic cooperation and exchange within the European Community. Since the implementation of the ERASMUS program in 1987, significant results have been achieved in cooperation and exchange within higher education in the European Union. Thanks to ERASMUS, in the period from 1987 to 2008, more than 1.5 million students have been exchanged, and the program expanded to other European countries outside the EU.

In the 1990s, the creative and informal period of European Community educational policy came to an end. The Maastricht Treaty, which was signed in 1992 and ratified on November 1, 1993, included education for the first time in a European Community treaty. The importance of strengthening the European dimension in education was placed high on the agenda.

The role of the European Commission in higher education has not been limited to educational mobility and exchange within the European Union. It has impacted in the first place the opening-up of Central and Eastern Europe. The EC, through its so-called PHARE program, opened the way in 1989 for several forms of cooperation, both in R&D and in education. Thanks to TEMPUS and other programs supported by national governments and other international private and public organizations, a rapid improvement in the educational infrastructure and of the quality of education in Central and Eastern Europe has been achieved. Now most of these countries have become members of the EU or at least are accepted as participants in the EU programs. Also, all the countries, including Russia since 2003, have signed the Bologna Declaration and taken part in its development process (Confederation of EU Rectors' Conferences [EURC] & Association of European Universities [CRE], 1998).

But the cooperation programs of the EU go beyond Europe. The early fear on the part of some governments and academics outside Europe of the emergence of a Fortress Europe in international education has been proved to be unfounded by a booming number of exchange agreements and programs of cooperation linking institutions of higher education in Europe with counterpart institutions all over the world. This is reflected in the creation of the new ERASMUS Mundus program, started in 2004 and intended to create high level joint degree programs between EU institutions and those from elsewhere in the world.

THE PRESENT DECADE

This overview of the development of Europeanization of higher education in the period between the 1960s and the 1990s explains how these developments culminated in the 1990s in a broad range of programs and activities to stimulate a European dimension in higher education. The main focus lay on the Europeanization of higher education with an emphasis on R&D, mobility of students and staff, curriculum development, and network building.

A study of eight mobility programs (Waechter & Wuttig, 2006), of which six are part of the European Union schemes (SOCRATES/ERASMUS, Leonardo da Vinci, ALBAN, EU-US Cooperation Program, and the Marie Curie Program),[3] indicates that in 2002 and 2003 there were 141,229 students involved in these programs, approximately 10% compared to the total of 1.1 million foreign degree seeking students. Of these 141,229 students, 87% are ERASMUS students, indicating the importance of this program for short, organized, funded mobility as part of home degrees. The program grew from 3,244 students in its first year, 1987–1988, covering 12 countries to 123,897 in 2002–2003, covering 31 countries. Spain received the most ERASMUS students in 2002–2003, followed by France, the United Kingdom, Germany, and Italy, with numbers rising over the past five years. This finding, as Waechter and Wuttig (2006) state, "stands in a marked contrast to the pattern of mobility outside of programmes [diploma mobility], in which Spain does not figure as an important destination country at all" (p. 164). The United Kingdom, receiving the most foreign degree seeking students, is only in third place as the country of destination for ERASMUS students, mainly due to the limitations on the number of ERASMUS students that are placed by UK institutions. So far as countries of origin are concerned, the United Kingdom is only in fifth place after France, Germany, Spain, and Italy. If we compare inbound and outbound mobility in ERASMUS, the United Kingdom and Ireland have the highest net import each with a ratio of .47, followed by Sweden (0.50), Denmark (0.64), and the Netherlands (0.67). The highest net exporters are Bulgaria, Romania, and Lithuania, all 12 new EU member states being net exporters (Waechter & Wuttig, 2006, p. 165).

THE BOLOGNA PROCESS

At the turn of the century, Europe prepared for a big step forward in Europeanization, which manifested itself in the Bologna Declaration on European higher education.

The groundwork for what is already widely known in higher education as the Bologna Process was laid by the Sorbonne Declaration, signed on May 25, 1998 in Paris by the ministers of education of France, Germany, Italy, and the United Kingdom on the occasion of the anniversary of the University of Paris. The Sorbonne Declaration was surprisingly well received, both in the political arena and in the higher education community of the four countries and in the rest of Europe.

The positive reception of the Sorbonne Declaration set the stage for a broader initiative. At the invitation of the Italian minister of education, a meeting took place in Bologna, Italy. The debate was based on the Sorbonne Declaration and on a study prepared by the Association of European Universities (CRE), and the Confederation of European Union Rectors' Conferences on Trends in European Learning Structures (Haug, Kirstein, & Knudsen, 1999). The study showed the extreme complexity and diversity of curricular and degree structures in European countries. Whereas the Sorbonne Declaration spoke of *harmonization*, both the study and the resulting Bologna Declaration avoided this word—owing largely to the potentially negative interpretations. Instead, the study speaks of "actions which may foster the desired convergence and transparency in qualification structures in Europe."

The Bologna Process, directed to the realization of a European Higher Education Area by 2010, implies a substantial reform of higher education, beyond the borders of the 25 countries of the European Union. The Bologna Declaration was signed on June 19, 1999, in Bologna, Italy, by the ministers of education of 29 European countries, who based their declaration on the following understanding:

> A Europe of Knowledge is now widely recognized as an irreplaceable factor for social and human growth and as an indispensable component to consolidate and enrich the European citizenship, capable of giving its citizens the necessary competences to face the challenges of the new millennium, together with an awareness of shared values and belonging to a common social and cultural space. (1999)

Since 1999, the number of signatory countries has increased to 45. By 2010, every higher education institution in the signatory countries is supposed to be organized in conformity with the declaration, even though the declaration is voluntary and not binding for the countries and their institutions.

In the Bologna Declaration of 1999, the ministers aimed to reach the following objectives:

- Adoption of a system of easily understood and comparable degrees, including the adoption of a diploma supplement;
- Adoption of a system essentially based on two main cycles, undergraduate and graduate
- Establishment of a system of credits—such as the European Credit Transfer System (ECTS)—as a means of promoting student mobility;
- Promotion of mobility by overcoming obstacles to the effective exercise of free movement;
- Promotion of European cooperation in quality assurance; and
- Promotion of the European dimension in higher education.

The creation of a European space for higher education, the prime objective of the Bologna Declaration, should be completed in 2010. Every 2 years, the Bologna process is monitored to assess its progress.

THE LISBON STRATEGY AND THE EUROPEAN RESEARCH AREA

The Bologna Declaration should be seen in connection with another ambitious process, agreed upon by the members of the European Council at their meeting in Lisbon in March 2000, "to become the most competitive and dynamic knowledge-based economy in the world, capable of sustainable growth with more and better jobs and greater social cohesion." The Lisbon strategy intends to deal with the low productivity and stagnation of economic growth in the EU, through the formulation of various policy initiatives to be taken by all EU member states. It was adopted for a 10-year period in 2000 in Lisbon, Portugal by the European Council. There are eight dimensions of the strategy: creating an information society for all; liberalization by completing the single market and developing a state aid and competition policy; building network industries in telecommunications and transportation; creating efficient and integrated financial services; improving the enterprise environment for business start-ups and in the regulatory framework; increasing social inclusion by returning people to the workforce, by upgrading skills and modernizing social protection; enhancing sustainable development; and developing a European area for innovation, research, and development (World Economic Forum, 2004).

As the last dimension shows, the Lisbon strategy is, among other things, directed to the development of a European research area. "Research activities at national and Union level must be better integrated and coordinated to make them as efficient and innovative as possible, and to ensure that Europe offers attractive prospects to its best brains" (European Council, 2000). In 2002, the European Council in Barcelona underlined also the importance of education for the Union. The link with the Bologna process was established at the Berlin meeting in 2003, where the close link between education and research was confirmed. In its report *The Role of the Universities in the Europe of Knowledge* (2003) the Commission defined five main challenges for higher education in the European Union: increased demand for higher education; internationalization of teaching and research; cooperation between universities and industries; proliferation of institutions where knowledge is produced; and reorganization of knowledge (Commission of the European Communities, 2003).

The Lisbon strategy of 2000 was ambitious and generic, more an overview of important issues to address than a concrete action agenda. A renewed Lisbon strategy was formulated in 2005, pointed toward growth and jobs in Europe, and calling for increased investment in knowledge and innovation (European Commission, 2005). The ambition level for the EC was reduced to the level of becoming a highly competitive knowledge-based economy by 2010.

DEVELOPMENTS IN EUROPEAN STUDENT CIRCULATION

European trends in international mobility have been influenced by global, national, and regional perspectives. If we look at the situation with respect to student mobility in Europe in 2002 and 2003, we see that in absolute numbers, Germany, the United Kingdom, and France, which together also have 53% of the total number of universities in Europe, are still the major destinations for international students in Europe. Together with Australia and the United States they have a joint market share of 70% of all international students in OECD countries.

On average, according to UNESCO (2005), 6% of the students in Europe are internationally mobile students, but half of them come from inside Europe, which means that 3% are non-Europeans, similar to Canada and 1% less than for the United States. An exception is France, where only 28% of the students are European, and 51% of the students come from Africa. For that country, but also for many other European countries one has to keep in mind that many international students are second or even third generation immigrant students who have a foreign passport but have received most of their education in the host country. This applies to students from former colonies and to the children of immigrant laborers of the 1960s and 1970s.

According to UNESCO (2006), in terms of outward mobility, the number of mobile students from Western Europe has stagnated over the past 5 years, resulting in a drop in share of all internationally mobile students from 22% to 17%. In absolute numbers, Western Europe has the second largest group of mobile students abroad after East Asia and the Pacific (407,000, 17% of the global total). On average, European countries see 2.8% of their students engaged in outbound mobility. Fifteen out of every thousand people of tertiary age are currently studying abroad: 77% of Western European mobile students stay within their region of origin, 15% go to North America. The United Kingdom, Germany, the United States, and France are the main destinations. Central and Eastern Europe is following Western Europe as the region with the third-largest number of mobile students abroad, 300,000. Turkey and the Russian Federation in that region have the largest number of students abroad. The outbound mobility ratio (1.6%) is much lower though than for Western Europe (2.8%), and below the world average. The vast majority of students from Central and Eastern Europe study in Western Europe, in particular Germany, 20% stay in the region, and relatively few go to the United States.

Inward and outward mobility in Europe is very closely related, since neighboring countries in the region are the primary destinations. Among the top five destinations one also finds the United States, but only in the case of the United Kingdom as the number 1 destination. Australia is mentioned four times among the top five destinations, in two cases by English speaking countries (the United Kingdom and Ireland) and in the two other cases Scandinavian countries, where Australia in recent years has become a country of destination, also thanks to active marketing efforts by that country. The only other country of destination outside Europe mentioned once is Kazakhstan in the case of Russia. In other words, European student circulation is regional in the first place and oriented toward English speaking countries in the second place. This is less true for the countries in Central and Eastern Europe, where Germany is an important destination country.

A study conducted by the Academic Cooperation Association (ACA) at the request of the European Commission on perceptions of European higher education in third countries (ACA, 2005), shows among other things that the information about Europe and its higher education is limited primarily to the UK, Germany, and France. According to the study, students rank the United States first for issues such as innovation, competition, and dynamism and see Europe as a more traditional destination, notable for its universities, its cultural heritage, and its arts. In Russia and Latin America, Europe is better perceived than in Asia, where the United States and Australia are more favored. The study sees the potential for promoting European higher education as a distinct brand and to create a perception of Europe as a whole. But also it calls for improvements to enhance the attractiveness of European higher education, such as selection, scholarships, access to alternative sources of funding, recruitment of quality teaching and research staff, the implementation of more flexible immigration and visa policies, and the development of more programs taught in English.

What will be the future trends and issues concerning mobility in Europe? In the first place we observe under the influence of the Lisbon strategy a radical shift from a quantitative approach to a more qualitative approach to recruitment of international students: the brain gain argument. This implies a different approach to legal immigration in the face of a shrinking labor force: recruitment of the best students and scholars, not to train them and then send them back, but to prepare them to take the empty places in our research and industry. This search for the best students without border discrimination will be the most important factor in student mobility in Europe for the coming decade and one for which competition with the rest of the world will become the most intense. It is connected to efforts to stop the brain drain of the best European students and scholars, in particular to the United States, a growing concern for the realization of the objectives of the Lisbon strategy.

In the second place one should not be surprised if several institutions of higher education in Europe decide not to invest in recruitment of students from beyond the European Union. They may argue that there is still enough potential for recruitment of students from the countries that have just entered the EU and in the future will enter the EU, without the competitive disadvantage of higher tuition fees, without high recruitment costs, and with fewer obstacles to enter and to adapt. This would further enhance the trends of international student circulation within the European region, which already is present as the figures above indicate.

In the third place, it is important to note that there is relatively little information about the levels and fields of study. The further evolution of the Bologna process will provide more opportunities to collect information on student circulation by bachelor's, master's, and doctoral programs, and by fields of study. It would not be surprising if the growth levels for Europe and in particular the European Union will be at the master's and doctoral level, and that competition for the best students will concentrate more on the natural sciences and engineering at these levels.

Other countries, in particular the English speaking countries such as the UK will also continue their quest for international students beyond Europe. Concerned with dropping numbers in 2005—caused by growing competition and increased student charges, then Prime Minister Blair announced in 2006 plans to attract a further 100,000 foreign students to the UK, in addition to the current 300,000 (BBC, 2006). This was the second initiative in a few years by the UK government, but, although the initiative was supported by the university community, both academics and students were concerned about the increasing dependency of British higher education on overseas students' fees in an ever more competitive global environment.

Finally, there will be a slow but gradual trend toward cross-border delivery of programs by European institutions of higher education, primarily within Europe from the West to the East and Southeast, and also beyond Europe. Europe, with the exception of the UK, is still lagging behind in this area, but in particular in Eastern and Southern Europe, there is an increasing presence of foreign providers, both from Western Europe and elsewhere, and European universities are getting more active in franchising and twinning programs in Asia, Latin America, and Africa.

GLOBAL AND EUROPEAN CITIZENSHIP: INTERNATIONALIZATION AT HOME

Over the past decades the emphasis in European internationalization of higher education has been more on mobility of students—study abroad as part of their home degree and for full degrees—than on the curriculum. In response to this focus on mobility, a countermovement for internationalization at home emerged in Europe in the late 1990s, which focused more on the internationalization of the curriculum and the teaching and learning process asking a valid question about the 95% of students who do not travel abroad. As Luijten-Lub (2007) states: "At the beginning of 1990s the need was recognised to extend the analysis of [activities concerning] internationalisation from simply the physical mobility of students to the more complex issues of internationalisation for all faculty and students through curricular, co-curricular, and other institutional adaptation" (p. 39).

Jeanine Hermans (2005), addressing the issue of culture as part of internationalization of higher education in Europe, comes to a rather critical analysis on the way culture is included as an important dimension, both in staff and student mobility, enrolment of international students, curriculum, advising international students, internationalization of staff, internationalization of facilities and services, positioning in international networks, international accreditation, policy relating to international student affairs, and institutional intercultural policy development. She concludes, that

> Awareness in higher education institutions of cultural diversity as a critical factor in successful internationalisation, although well established in international offices and with staff working internationally, is largely lacking in other parts of the institution. The awareness that exists is fragmented, and competence in dealing with diversity is more an exception at the level of an individual than common practice. (p. 112)

Her conclusion that "intercultural issues are so far still largely unresolved in the process of European higher education," and that "intercultural learning in individuals and organisations tends to occur accidentally and haphazardly" (p. 113) gives a clear picture of the state of internationalization in Europe. Her use of primarily American authors, something she shares with other Europeans dealing with intercultural and global competences, is an illustration of the level of debate in Europe on these topics. A major study on internationalization of the curriculum in Europe, by Marijk van der Wende (1996), was an unpublished doctoral dissertation. The contributions by European authors on the topic of internationalization at home, such as Nilsson, Otten, Teekens, Waechter, and others (Nilsson & Otten, 2003) are either theoretical or case studies by institutions. Waechter (2003, p. 8) states correctly that intercultural studies have a much longer tradition in the United States than in Europe and that in particular in Europe the international and intercultural agendas have not yet been integrated.

OTHER CHALLENGES AND OPPORTUNITIES IN THE INTERNATIONALIZATION OF EUROPEAN HIGHER EDUCATION

Together, the Bologna process and the Lisbon strategy are the foundation for a reform agenda that will inevitably not only lead to more transparency and the removal of obstacles for internal labor and student mobility, but also serve to make education and research more competitive in the context of the global knowledge economy, and in doing so increase the focus on inward mobility from outside Europe.

The driving rationale behind the two reforms is the fact that Europe is lagging behind its competitors in research and development, innovation and change, in particular the United States. The challenge for European higher education is how to consolidate and enhance its quality, and in particular increase excellence, in the face of new regional but in particular global challenges. This is illustrated in the bottlenecks as mentioned by the Commission: uniformity leading to too few centers of world-class excellence, insularity, overregulation, and underfunding. To battle these, the Commission proposes to work on increasing attractiveness, for instance by some concentration of funding on present and potential centers and networks of excellence; strengthening system and institutional management; and encouraging higher and more efficient investment in higher education by governments, companies, and households (European Commission, 2005, pp. 3–8; see also Commission of the European Communities, 2006).

These bottlenecks must be overcome in the context of a presumed increase in global competition in higher education. In this competitive environment, quality will become more decisive than quantity; competition will require more cooperation, particularly in terms of strategic alliances; and competition will require new forms of cooperation, for instance joint and double degrees.

The Bologna declaration and Lisbon strategy are seen by the European governments and the higher education sector as the driving instruments to take up that challenge. The two processes not only look at the internal implications for higher education, but also explicitly refer to the need to increase the international competitiveness of European higher education and to make it more attractive to students from other continents. In that sense, the declaration follows the pattern visible everywhere, with competitiveness becoming a driving rationale for the internationalization of higher education. Van der Wende (2001, p. 249) described this as shift in paradigms from cooperation to competition. Creation of a European identity, a European citizenship, and the development of competitiveness with the rest of the world are the key catalysts for the political initiatives in education by the European Commission.

Van Vught, van der Wende, and Westerheijden (2002) though, in answering the question whether the Bologna process is an adequate European response to the wider challenges of globalization, came to the conclusion that

> In terms of both practice and perceptions, internationalisation is closer to the well-established tradition of international co-operation and mobility and to the core academic values of quality and excellence, whereas globalization refers more to competition, pushing the concept of higher education as a tradable commodity and challenging the concept of higher education as a public good. (p. 117)

In that respect, it would be a simplification to see the Bologna process as merely a response to globalization, it can be seen rather as a form of internationalization and Europeanization of higher education at a new level, moving from the casuistic toward the systematic, and in the end from the disconnected and specific to the core, toward an integrated internationalization of higher education (Teichler, 1999, pp. 9–10).

There are other issues, not directly part of these two processes but implied by them, which become more relevant, in particular:

- The development of a typology of higher education institutions in Europe.
- The debate about tuition fees in Europe.
- Higher education as a tradable service.

European higher education is very heterogeneous and minimally transparent. A report by a group of primarily Dutch higher education scholars states that

> A better understanding of the various types of higher education institutions, their mission and provisions will support the European aim of increasing student mobility, inter-institutional and university-industry cooperation, the recognition of degrees and hence the international competitiveness of European higher education. Consequently, the exploration and development of a typology of higher education institutions in Europe is directly linked to the aims of the Bologna process and the Lisbon strategy. (Van Vught et al., 2005, p. 5)

The Carnegie Classifications in the United States and the UK system of higher education serve as reference points. Such a European typology should reflect the diversity in European higher education, but at the same time provide transparency, now lacking. The typology, according to the report, should be inclusive for all European institutions that provide higher education; should be a tool enabling the development of institutional profiles; should not be prescriptive, exclusive, or rigid; and its ownership should rest primarily with the institutions. The next step in developing such a typology will be a pilot project.

The debate on tuition fees in Europe has recently become more open, a discussion that is inspired by the Bologna process and is influenced by EU regulations, but mainly is guided by national issues. As mentioned before, the United Kingdom had already moved to differential fees for international and national students in 1979. Austria, Belgium, Ireland, The Netherlands, Denmark, the Slovak Republic, Switzerland, Finland, and Sweden have recently followed the UK example for higher fees for non-EU students. In Germany, some of the states have been successful in demanding their own right to set tuition fees for national students. In that respect the landscape is rapidly changing as well. In the UK, after some intense debate, a government plan to allow variable and higher tuition fees was approved in 2004. Sadlak and de Miguel (2005), in the European contribution to the 2005 *World Report on Higher Education,* speak to this point: "Higher education as a 'public good' is still an important value in European higher education. At the same time there is a clear orientation towards a system based on charging tuition fees combined with a support system, inclusive of loans" (2009, p. 59).

There is also a move to cross-border delivery of education in Europe—higher education activities in which the learners are located in a host country different from the one where the awarding institution is based—in particular in Southern European countries such as Greece, Italy, and Spain, with the UK and the United States being the main exporters to these countries. Van der Wende and Middlehurst (2004) note that "the overseas delivery of education via PIM (Programme and Institutional Mobility) programmes is a major and growing market for the United Kingdom" (p. 117), with an annual growth of 10%. Overall, one must say though that higher education in Europe is not yet very actively involved in cross-border delivery of education.

CONCLUDING REMARKS

Peter Stearns mentions American parochialism as one of the biggest challenges for American society and international education. He added the need for "increasingly ample and explicit recognition of mutuality and reciprocity." Together they have resulted for instance in "the careful insulation of 'study abroad' students under the tutelage of American faculty using the same curricula as those back home" (2008, p. 239), but also in a geographical unbalance with "an excessive European focus" (p. 244). This focus results from American faculty's "emendations of Eurocentrism and unthinking commitment to American exceptionalism" (p. 247). Stearns is aware that there is a need for secondary schools in the United States to move "in a global direction," adding new foreign languages and serious world history, but for the foreseeable future he thinks that "universities must expect to need segments of general education to bring students more fully up to speed on basic global contexts" (p. 256).

So, at first glance, little seems to have changed in international education since the late 1990s. I noticed in 1998 "a nearly exclusive use of material from the 1980s from a limited number of US sources who appear in nearly all publications on international education from the US," and that remains unchanged (De Wit, 1998, p. 16). In 2007 I wrote on the occasion of the 10th anniversary of the *Journal of Studies in International Education* that "the literature base of nearly all manuscripts from the USA is limited to American literature" (De Wit, 2007, p. 257). American exceptionalism also seems to apply to the researchers in the field of international education.

But this would be a too narrow and negative view. Internationalization of higher education and the focus on global citizenship and study abroad have changed drastically on both sides of the ocean over the past decade, as indicated by other chapters in this book and my overview of developments in Europe. In the first place, internationalization of higher education has changed itself radically over the past decade as a consequence of globalization. There is the classic divide between student and staff mobility (study abroad, education abroad, academic mobility, foreign students advising, academic exchange, etc.) on the one hand and the more curriculum oriented approach (international studies, global studies, multicultural education, intercultural education, peace education, etc.) on the other hand. Today one can see a new divide emerging between internationalization at home, activities that help students develop international understanding and intercultural skills, and internationalization abroad in which all forms of education cross borders, with mobility of students, teachers, scholars, programs, courses, curriculum, and projects (Knight, 2005, p. 59). In the second place, one can observe an increasing concern about the attention paid to global issues in primary and secondary education in Europe, comparable to the United States; for example, in such areas as history and foreign languages. Since the late 1990s, unfortunately it has become necessary to include global issues in the curriculum of higher education, and one already sees the emergence of such programs, for instance the development of university colleges providing general education in The Netherlands (University College Utrecht, Roosevelt Academy, University College Maastricht, University College Amsterdam).

In Europe, the mainstreaming of internationalization in the agenda of higher education in recent years appears to lead in many cases to a more fragmentary approach, similar to that found in the United States. This might seem contradictory at first glance, but the trend to introduce the international dimension into all functions and activities of the institution and no longer concentrate them in international offices, together with the increasing importance of recruitment of international students, might result in a divide between study abroad on the one hand and enrollment of international students on the other hand. In the United States one observes a counter trend toward a more integrative approach to internationalization, stimulated by programs of the American Council on Education, NAFSA, and other organizations to assess and support internationalization of the campus (ACE, 2008; Green & Olsen, 2003), and more attention to internationalization at the graduate level, in particular in law schools and MBA programs. Stearns (2009) notes that these changes are limited and tentative because "the graduate field may be more resistant to challenges to routine, less well organized to pick up new kinds of global signals" (p. 78).

Finally, the debate on and in particular the implementation of intercultural and global competences in the curriculum seem to be more advanced in the United States than in Europe. Based on a stronger history in this area (for instance Mestenhauser & Ellingboe, 1998), recent contributions from among others Deardorff (2006) on intercultural competences and Hunter, White, and Godbey (2006) on global competences, are examples.

One can add to these observations also the trend in European higher education to deregulation and privatization, and a change of funding mechanisms and leadership styles more similar to those in the United States, and it becomes clear that we are moving indeed more in each other's direction, notwithstanding the fact that, as I indicated at the beginning of this paper, higher education and its international dimension both in Europe and the United States are still based primarily on the nation-state, even in this area of rapid globalization and regionalization of our economies and societies.

NOTES

1. The analysis of internationalization of higher education in Europe is a revised and reduced version of De Wit (2008).
2. For an overview of 30 years of European cooperation in education, see European Commission (2006). See also K. de Wit and Verhoeven (2001).
3. The other two are the Nordplus program of the Scandinavian countries and the Ceepus program between 10 countries in Central, Eastern, and Southeastern Europe.

REFERENCES

Academic Cooperation Association. (2005). Perceptions of European higher education in third countries. Retrieved June 2006, from http://www.aca-secretariat.be/02projects/Perceptions.htm

American Council on Education (ACE). (2008). *Mapping of internationalization*. Washington, DC: Author.

BBC. (2006, April 18). Overseas students' plans unveiled. BBC News. Retrieved April 18, 2006, from http://www.bbc.co.uk

Baron, B. (1993). The politics of academic mobility in Western Europe. *Higher Education Policy, 6*(3), 50–55.

Commission of the European Communities (COM). (2003, February 5). *The role of the universities in the Europe of knowledge*. Retrieved January 28, 2009, from http://cur-lex.europa.eu/Notice.do?val=278315:cs&lang=en&list=278315,&pos=1&page=1&nbl+1&pgs=10&nwords

Commission of the European Communities (COM). (2006, May 10). *Delivering on the modernisation agenda of universities: Education, research and innovation*. Brussels. Retrieved January 28. 2009, from http://ec.europa.eu/enterprise/innovation/documents_en.htm

Confederation of EU Rectors' Conferences (EURC) & Association of European Universities (CRE). (1998). *Bologna declaration on the European space for higher education*. Retrieved June 19, 1999, from http://ec.europea.eu/education/policies/educ/bologna/bologna.pdf

Cummings W. (1993). Global trends in overseas study. In D. Craufurd Goodwin (Ed.), *International investment in human capital, overseas education for development*. New York: Institute of International Education.

Deardorff, D. K. (2006, Fall). Identification and assessment of intercultural competence as a student outcome of internationalization. *Journal of Studies in International Education, 10*(3), 241–266.

De Wit, H. (1998). Ducks quack different at each side of the ocean. In H. De Wit *50 years of international co-operation and exchange between the United States and Europe: European views* (pp. 13–20). Amsterdam: European Association for International Education.

De Wit, H. (2002). *Internationalization of higher education in the United States of America and Europe: A historical, comparative, and conceptual analysis*. Westport, CT: Greenwood Press.

De Wit, H. (2007, Fall/Winter). Ten years of editorial policy of the *Journal of Studies in International Education*: Overview, challenges, and opportunities. *Journal of Studies in International Education, 11*(3–4), 251–259.

De Wit, H. (2008). International student circulation in the context of the Bologna process and the Lisbon strategy In P. Agarwal, M. Elmahdy Said, M. Sehoole, M. Sirozi, & H. de Wit (Eds.), *The dynamics of international student circulation in a global context* (pp. 167–198). Rotterdam: Sense.

De Wit, K, & Verhoeven, J. (2001). The higher education policy of the European Union: With or against the member states? In J.Huisman, P. Maassen, & G. Neave (Eds.), *Higher education and the nation state: The international dimension of higher education.* (pp. 175–231). Paris: Pergamon/IAU Press.

European Commission (ECom). (2005, April 20). *Mobilising the brainpower of Europe: Enabling universities to make their full contribution to the Lisbon strategy.* Brussels: Author. COM 152 final. Retrieved January 28, 2009, from http://eur-lex.europa.eu/Notice.do?va;=398507:cs&lang=en&list=398507:cs,&pos=1&page=1&nbl=1&pgs=10&hwords=

European Commission (ECom). (2006a). 1976–2006: *Thirty years of European cooperation in Education.* Brussels: Office for Official Publications of the European Communities.

European Commission (ECom). (2006b, May 10). *Frequently asked questions: Why European higher education systems must be modernized.* Retrieved Retrieved June 25, 2006, from http://europa.eu/rapid/pressReleasesAction MEMO/06/190

European Council. (2000). Presidency conclusions, Lisbon European Council, 23 and 24 March 2000. Retrieved January 28, 2008, from http://consilium.europa.ueDocs/cms_Data/docs/pressData/en/ec/00100-rl.en0.htm.int/comm/lisbon_strategy

Greene, M., & Olsen, C. (2003). *Internationalizing the campus, A user's guide.* Washington, DC: American Council on Education.

Haug, G., Kirstein, J., & Knudsen, I. (1999, June 18–19). *Trends in learning structures in higher education.* (Project Report prepared for the Bologna Conference). Copenhagen, Denmark: Danish Rector's Conference Secretariat.

Hermans, J. (2005). The X factor, internationalization with a small "c". In B. Kehm & H. de Wit (Eds.), *European responses to the global perspective* (pp. 134–153). Amsterdam: European Association for International Education/European Higher Education Society.

Hunter, B., White, G. P., & Galen, C. G. (2006, Fall). What does it mean to be globally competent? *Journal of Studies in International Education, 10*(3), 267–285.

Kelo M., Teichler U., & Waechter B. (Eds.). (2006). *EURODATA, Student mobility in European higher education.* Bonn, Germany: Lemmens Verlag.

Knight, J. (2005). Higher education in the trade context of GATS. In B. Khem & H. de Wit (Eds.), *Internationalisation in higher education: European responses to the global perspective.* Amsterdam: European Association for International Education/European Higher Education Society.

Lanzendorf, U. (2006). Inward and outwards mobile students. In M. Kelo, U. Teichler, & B. Waechter (Eds.), *EURODATA, Student mobility in European higher education* (pp. 78–95). Bonn: Academic Cooperation Association (ACA)/Lemmens Verlag.

Luijten-Lub, A. (2007). *Choices in internationalisation: How higher education institutions respond to internationalisation, Europeanisation, and globalisation.* Unpublished doctoral disseration. University of Twente, Enschede, the Netherlands.

Mestenhauser, J. A. (1998, Spring). International education on the verge: In search of a new paradigm. *International Educator, 7*(2–3), 70.

Mestenhauser, J. A., & Ellingboe, B. J. (1998). *Reforming the higher education curriculum: Internationalizing the campus.* Phoenix, AZ: Oryx Press.

Neave, G. (2001). The European dimension in higher education: An excursion into the modern use of historical analogues. In J. Huisman, P. Maassen, & G. Neave (Eds.), *Higher education and the nation state: The international dimension of higher education* (pp. 13–73). Paris: Pergamon/IAU Press.

Nilsson, B., & Matthias O. (2003, Spring). Internationalisation at home. [Special issue] *Journal of Studies in International Education, 7*(1).

Sadlak, J., & Miguel J. M. de. (2005). Europe. *Higher education in the world 2006: The financing of universities* (GUNI Series on the Social Commitment of Universities 1, pp. 198–222). Barcelona, Spain: GUNI.

Stearns, P. (2009). *Educating global citizens in universities and colleges.* New York: Routledge.

Teichler, U. (1999). Internationalisation as a challenge of higher education in Europe. *Tertiary Education and Management, 5*, 5–23.

UNESCO. (2005). *Global education digest 2005.* Paris: Author.

UNESCO. (2006). *Global education digest 2006.* Paris: Author.

Van der Wende, M. (1996). *Internationalising the curriculum in Dutch higher education: An international comparative perspective.* Unpublished doctoral dissertation, University of Utrecht, The Netherlands.

Van der Wende, M. C. (2001, September). Internationalisation policies: About new trends and contrasting paradigms. *Higher Education Policy, 14*(3), 249–259.

Van der Wende, M. C., & Middlehurst, R. (2004). Cross-border post-secondary education in Europe. In *Internationalisation and trade in higher education: Opportunities and challenges* (pp. 87–135). Paris: Organisation for Economic Co-Operation and Development.

Van Vught, F., van der Wende, M., & Westerheijden, D. (2002). Globalisation and internationalisation: Policy agendas compared. In J. Enders & O. Fulton (Eds.), *Higher education in a globalising world: International trends and mutual observations: A festschrift in honour of Ulrich Teichler* (pp. 103–120). Dordrecht: Kluwers Academic.

Van Vught, F., Bartelse, J., Bohmert, D., Burquel, N., Divis, J., Huisman, J., & van der Wende, M. (2005). *Institutional profiles: Towards a typology of higher education institutions in Europe.* Enschede, The Netherlands: CHEPS.

Waechter, B. (2003, Spring). An introduction: Internationalisation at home in context. *Journal of Studies in International Education, 7*(1), 5–11.

Waechter, B., & Wuttig, St. (2006). Student mobility in European programmes. In M. Kelo, U. Teichler, & B. Waechter (Eds.), *EURODATA: Student mobility in European higher education* (pp. 78–95). Bonn: Academic Cooperation Association (ACA)/ Lemmens Verlag.

World Economic Forum. (2004). *The Lisbon review, 2004, an assessment of policies and reforms in Europe.* Geneva, Switzerland: Author.

Chapter 14

Strategy for the Development of a Global City

Study Abroad in Singapore

Peter Pang
National University of Singapore

INTRODUCTION

In universities across the globe, study abroad has now "gained new academic significance" (Marcum, 2001). Understanding the globalizing world is seen as a priority for higher education, and study abroad is recognized as a key strategy in preparing graduates for active engagement in the global community.

In the tiny island-city-state of Singapore, going global is a matter of survival. With an area of 700 square kilometers and a population of about 4.8 million (2008), Singapore recognized early on that its economy needed to develop a "second wing." This second wing was to go regional, with the objective being to "strengthen our domestic economy, expand our national economic zone and ratchet up our standard of living....The new wing is deemed necessary to take off from the flock of newly industrialising economies and fly in the league of developed economies" (Chia, 2000, p. 124; Lam, 1999). Since the launching of the "go regional" policy of 1992, Singapore now consistently ranks at or near the top in the A. T. Kearney/*Foreign Policy* Globalization Index. Singapore's Prime Minister Lee Hsien Loong called globalization "a given for Singapore" (H. L. Lee, 2005a).

As a country with no natural resources except people, Singapore places special emphasis on education, and its national strategies for survival and development can be seen directly in its education policies.

The objective of this paper is to look at the role study abroad plays in Singapore's national strategy. To provide a fuller background, I will give a few key examples of how education policy supports Singapore's development.

Modern Singapore traces its origin to 1819, when it began its transformation from a small fishing village to a vibrant entrepôt in the British empire. It gained self-rule in 1959. In 1963, it became part of Malaysia. In 1965, independence was thrust upon Singapore when it was expelled from Malaysia. At that point, survival of the tiny island-state with no natural resources or hinterland was far from clear (K. Y. Lee, 2000).

Singapore is a predominantly (ethnically) Chinese society in a multiracial country with significant Malay and Indian (mainly Tamil) communities. It is situated in the midst of large Malay–Muslim communities in the neighboring countries of Malaysia and Indonesia. Singapore went through a tumultuous period of racial tensions, resulting in racial riots in the 1950s and 1960s.

To mitigate racial tensions, one of the earliest educational policies adopted was bilingualism in schools, where English, the common colonial language, was adopted as the main language of instruction, and pupils learned their own ethnic tongue (mainly Chinese, Malay, or Tamil) as the second language. This resulted in a common curriculum for all Singaporean children (Gopinathan, 1974, 1997).

This language policy also served Singapore well because it enabled it to transform itself from an entrepôt economy into an industrial economy. Ease of communication with the common usage of English was important in bringing multinational investment to Singapore.

At the same time, education had the important responsibility of producing a well-trained workforce for industry. Primary, secondary, and tertiary education thus emphasized equipping students with the necessary know-how to function in particular industries. A manpower planning framework was also adopted to ensure that there was sufficient supply of manpower for the various industries. From its establishment in 1980 (while tracing its roots back to 1905) until the mid-1990s, the National University of Singapore (NUS) was mainly a teaching university with the mission to train manpower for Singapore's economic activities. In a period of less than three decades, Singapore grew from its premature birth with uncertain survival prospects to being a developed country. This is sometimes referred to as the "Singapore miracle." Green (1997) wrote that education played a key role not only in "miraculous economic development but equally as a vehicle for promoting a cohesive civic identity, based on the ideological tripod of multiculturalism, multilingualism, and meritocracy" (p. 147).

However, with the opening up of China, and later India (as well as other countries), the strategy of pursuing an export-oriented, multinational corporation-driven economy was no longer viable for Singapore. To keep ahead of the competition, which is global in nature now, Singapore needed to develop a knowledge-based economy, one that was focused on cutting edge research and high value-added development (Singapore Ministry of Trade and Industry, 1998).

To prepare Singapore for a knowledge-based economy, the education system needed to foster a citizenry that was less rule-bound, more explorative, and capable of higher order thinking skills. This involved the education systems in changing its philosophy. Instead of preparing students for specific functions in particular industries, education must now equip students with skills for independent inquiry as they engage in lifelong learning. Thus, in 1997, the Singapore government rolled out the "Thinking Schools, Learning Nation" initiative. When then Singapore Prime Minister Goh Chok Tong announced this new policy he said: "'Thinking Schools, Learning Nation' is not a slogan for the Ministry of Education. It is a formula to enable Singapore to compete and stay ahead" (Goh, 1997). We note that, in fact, "Thinking Schools, Learning Nation" has been adopted as the Singapore Ministry of Education's vision (2008).

In the meantime, global competition intensified at an unprecedented rate, and Singapore struggled to keep pace. To stay ahead of the competition, Singapore believed it had to be a global city, which attracted not only business and capital, but also talent and ideas (Sanyal, 2007; Velayutham, 2007). In his 2006 National Day Observance Ceremony speech then Minister for Education Tharman Shanmugaratnum said: "Our future lies in Singapore being a global city, a city whose people think beyond its borders, and which attracts foreigners and encourages them to settle into its midst." Singapore realized that to be a global city, it needed to cultivate a society that was more open, diverse, and in tune with global practices and norms than had hitherto been the case.

Shanmugaratnum further elaborated: "Our task in the Ministry of Education, and in our schools and tertiary institutions, is to prepare young Singaporeans to embrace this future with confidence. They cannot get by on old strengths. We must help them discover and build new strengths, and climb new peaks. That is what the new Singapore will be—many new peaks of excellence.... We will provide more opportunities for our students to gain global experience."

The Ministry of Education has embarked on many initiatives to provide greater breadth and flexibility in schools in order to nurture diverse talents. It recognizes that "we face the challenge of preparing students for a future of innovation-driven growth, and frequent and unpredictable changes in the economic and social environment" (Singapore Ministry of Education, 2002, p. 8; Gopinathan, 2007).

To provide multiple pathways for nurturing diverse talents, the Ministry has created "integrated programs" (in which students can bypass the standard O Level examinations), and has also set up a Sports School and an Arts School. There is also greater flexibility in school admissions that now take into account students' talents in nonacademic areas. There are parallel developments in the tertiary institutions.

In the face of unpredictable change, one thing is certain: central planning will be more and more difficult. While Singapore relentlessly prepares itself to thrive in the globalizing world and stay ahead of competition, it will need to think out of the box. Practices such as manpower planning are outdated. Nimbleness, adaptability, and a heightened entrepreneurial spirit are called for. As a nation, Singapore will have to rethink the notion of "meritocracy and elitism" (Tan, 2008). These ongoing developments will bring about a sea change in the educational landscape in Singapore.

Education has played a pivotal role in Singapore's development. As Singapore faces the challenges of the rapidly globalizing world, it sees its future as a hub that serves as an interface for many global activities. Just as its language policy and rigorous professional training have served Singapore well in a previous era, innovative global education that will produce a globally minded, globally savvy citizenry will be crucial for Singapore's future success.

While the verdict is still out on what exactly constitutes a global city, I believe we can readily agree that in the future it will become more and more important for people to be able to work in multinational teams (and adopt multidisciplinary approaches) to solve problems that will be increasingly global in nature. Thus, I believe a natural approach to study abroad is to create opportunities for students to work on global problems in multinational teams.

Below I will describe some of the study abroad programs of the National University of Singapore. For reasons of space, I will concentrate on a handful of programs offered by the University Scholars Programme (USP), which is the university's honors program. I will discuss the extent to which these programs serve the mission of the nation and the university, as well as challenges and shortcomings that they face. The programs that I will describe are based on transnational collaboration. Just as the Singapore educational system recognizes the need for greater breadth and flexibility, we realize that there is no single prescriptive approach to study abroad. What we need is more dialogue, more sharing, and more collaboration.

HIGHER EDUCATION IN SINGAPORE

Going global was so much in the Singaporean psyche that by the end of the 20th century "Singapore as a global city has become the dominant self-image of the city-state" (Kwa, 2002, p.121). However, in the earlier discussions from the 1970s to the late 1990s, the idea of the global city was in terms of economic activities and using the world as Singapore's substitute hinterland. It is only in the last decade or so that there has been a clear articulation that Singapore aspires to be globally competitive in attracting not only business and capital, but also talent and ideas, and that the nation's future lies in being a global "talent magnet."

All along, Singapore has realized that it has but one resource—people. Through government policies, and especially education policies, Singapore has managed to leverage on its sole resource to bring about economic growth at an average rate of 8.9% per year from 1965 to 1997 (Singapore Ministry of Trade and Industry, 1998).

As Singapore moves toward a knowledge-based, creativity-driven economy in the early 21st century, the demand on high level human resources becomes more acute. However, in recent years, like many other countries, Singapore has suffered from a low birth rate, which was 1.29 live births per woman in 2007. In spite of this, the population of Singapore grew 5.5% in 2007 (Statistics Singapore, 2008). This increase was largely the result of immigration. As these figures show, Singapore needs to attract immigrants who are highly educated and creative. In order to attract talent, Singapore has to be "a city which is full of life and energy and excitement, a place where people want to live, work and play, where they are stimulated to be active, to be creative and to enjoy life" (H. L. Lee, 2005b).

At the same time, Singapore needs to keep its citizens firmly rooted in the nation, and help them to realize their full potential. This is particularly important as immigration increases. A sense of rootedness will help build the nation, whose identity has been shaky from the time it decided to adopt the colonial language as its lingua franca (Wee & Bokhorst-Heng, 2005). It will also help make Singapore a "permanent talent magnet" rather than a "trans-national revolving door" (Yeoh, 2007).

Indeed, compounding the problem of low birth rate is the high rate of emigration. While Singapore is making up for the brain drain by attracting highly educated immigrants, the trend of emigration is "pretty serious" (K. Y. Lee, 2008). Every year, some 1,000 Singaporeans at the "top end" are giving up their citizenship, amounting to "4–5% of the top 30% of its population every year." It is noted that a major channel for the brain drain is through the pursuit of higher education overseas (many do not return to Singapore). To mitigate this, local universities had to change on two counts: First, they needed to offer more places. Plans are already underway to increase the cohort participation rate in local universities from 21% in 2003 to 25% in 2010 to 30% in 2015 (Singapore Ministry of Education, 2003, 2008). At the moment, there are four local universities in Singapore: National University of Singapore (NUS), Nanyang Technological University (NTU), Singapore Management University (SMU), and SIM University (UniSIM). A fifth university will open in 2011, and a sixth is being considered. Second, the universities have to offer more attractive programs. Local universities have recognized that a major appeal of overseas universities is their flexible curriculum, and consequently they have undergone major reorganization, starting with the introduction of the "modular system" at NUS in 1993–1994. More recently, a variety of double major and double degree programs have become available. There are also more joint and double degree programs with overseas universities (some of which involve study abroad). At the same time, there is a sharp increase in study abroad offerings. The idea is to offer the best of both worlds to local university students. While they are studying at a local university, they have ample opportunities to gain overseas education experience as well.

Thus, study abroad serves a variety of purposes. First and foremost, it helps students understand the globalizing world and prepares them for active engagement in the global community. Second, it fosters a globally minded citizenry to help Singapore realize its global city aspirations. Third, it figures in attractive programs that keep Singaporeans studying in local universities while they benefit from an overseas education experience. Last but not least, it allows local universities to gain from synergistic partnerships with overseas universities.

It is therefore hardly surprising that the two main public universities in Singapore both have overtly globally oriented vision statements: "Towards a global knowledge enterprise" (National University of Singapore, n.d., a), and "A great global university founded on science and technology" (Nanyang Technological University, n.d.). Both universities are building up a substantial portfolio of innovative study abroad programs and aim to have at least 50% of their students participate in them—NUS was well on its way to achieving the target in 2008.

Since it is so important to Singapore, the government invests heavily in education. Even as NUS and NTU were incorporated in 2006 as part of a move to grant greater autonomy to local universities so that they could become even more flexible, they continue to receive about 75% of their funding from the government (T. Y. Lui, 2008). To "provide assurance that Government funding for the universities is well-utilised and properly directed towards the achievement of national objectives," an accountability framework has been put in place (NUS, 2006b). In particular, the universities signed a policy and performance agreement with the Ministry of Education. The performance agreement covers study abroad.

THE NATIONAL UNIVERSITY OF SINGAPORE

The National University of Singapore (NUS) is a large public university. In 2007, NUS had 22,689 undergraduate and 6,616 graduate students, of whom 9,880 were international students (NUS, 2007). NUS plays a leading role in international alliances such as the Association of Pacific Rim Universities (APRU) and the International Alliance of Research Universities (IARU). It offers a variety of joint and double degree programs with universities around the world, and has more than 200 partner universities under its Student Exchange Programme. As such, NUS is a highly globalized university. For NUS, providing a globally oriented educational experience is a major strategic thrust; it is at the core of the University's mission (NUS, 2006a).

The 1990s saw significant changes in NUS on two fronts. First, in research, NUS made a conscious effort to transform itself from being a predominantly teaching institution to being a research intensive university. By 2001, NUS's research output placed it "within the top two universities in Australia, the top ten universities in UK, and the top sixty universities in USA…. NUS has made it to the prestigious league of Extensive Doctoral/Research Universities by the Carnegie Classification of Institutions" (Shih, 2001). Currently, NUS is ranked consistently among the top universities in the world. Second, in undergraduate education, NUS made a conscious effort to broaden its curriculum. The modular system put in place in the mid-1990s established a common credit system across the university, making possible a more flexible choice of courses. This fundamental move paved the way for NUS's shift from the British model of discipline-specific higher education toward the American model of broad-based undergraduate education. This shift reflects a change in philosophy in higher education in Singapore—from preparing graduates for specific industries to equipping students for lifelong learning.

An important initiative during that period was the Core Curriculum program, which was established in 1999 as a pilot to spearhead broad-based education. By 2001, Core Curriculum had spun off the university-wide General Education program, and transformed into the University Scholars Programme through merger with the earlier NUS initiative known as the Talent Development Programme. More will be said about the University Scholars Programme below.

Another important initiative, which began in 2001 and is still expanding, is the NUS Overseas Colleges. As mentioned above, the "frequent and unpredictable change in the economic and social environment" calls for nimbleness, adaptability, and a heightened entrepreneurial spirit. While the broad-based education initiatives help foster nimbleness and adaptability, the NUS Overseas College program was designed to promote entrepreneurship.

The NUS Overseas Colleges (NOC) are not physical colleges of the university located overseas. Instead, the NOC program allows NUS students to spend a year in one of five entrepreneurial hubs in the world—Silicon Valley, Philadelphia (Bio Valley), Stockholm, Shanghai, and Bangalore— to intern full-time with start-up companies while studying (entrepreneurship-related courses) part-time at NUS's partner universities—Stanford University, University of Pennsylvania, Royal Institute of Technology (Stockholm), Fudan University, and the Indian Institute of Science. The NOC thus combines study abroad with entrepreneurial development; it is a key strategy in the mission of developing NUS into a global university with a strong entrepreneurial spirit.

At the moment, NUS is embarking on perhaps its most ambitious educational initiative to date, and this is the University Town project. An integral part of NUS and in close proximity to its Kent Ridge campus, University Town will "pioneer an innovative model of learning and teaching integrated into residential colleges, creating a transformative educational experience that will prepare our graduates for a fast changing, globalizing world" (National University of Singapore, n.d., b). A cosmopolitan student body will live and learn in University Town, comprised of some 6,000 local, foreign, as well as visiting students, who will enjoy enhanced opportunities to engage in collaborative learning on topics of global importance with an Asian focus. Colocated in University Town will be graduate residences and world-class research facilities to create an "energizing intellectual hub" where there is vibrant interaction between undergraduates, graduate students, faculty, and researchers. According to the current plan, the University Town project will be implemented in phases beginning in 2010. Construction began in 2008.

THE NUS UNIVERSITY SCHOLARS PROGRAMME

The NUS University Scholars Programme (USP) was founded in 2001. Serving essentially as NUS's honors program (in the sense of those commonly found in American state universities), USP stretches the intellectual, leadership, and personal potential of exceptionally highly motivated students through its rigorous interdisciplinary curriculum and challenging learning-beyond-the-classroom activities. It places particular emphasis on fostering a global outlook in its students. Based on last year's figures, on average, during their 4 years at the university, each student in USP participates in an average of two study abroad activities that are organized (or coorganized) or facilitated by USP. These activities range from double degree programs that require 2 years study abroad, to overseas field trips and summer programs that last for a week or more. Many students also participate in study abroad programs outside of USP (organized by Singaporean as well as overseas institutions, including units of NUS other than USP).

This chapter focuses on USP's global education efforts. Before I present a few specific study abroad programs offered by USP, I will say a little about its philosophy for study abroad.

An immediate outcome of study abroad is that it exposes students to unfamiliar cultures and fosters an appreciation of the world's diversity. However, study abroad can achieve much more. At the individual level, study abroad should be a transformative experience that inspires new ways of thinking and new ways of acting. It should foster a proactive mindset that strives to acquire the skills to thrive in the globalizing world. At the global level, study abroad should cultivate an international network of people who are positive about working together to tackle global problems. Study abroad has to go beyond allowing the individual to experience the world. It has to create opportunities for substantive dialogues across national and cultural boundaries. We believe a good way to start is to facilitate meaningful interactions, both intellectual and emotional, with students from other universities, so that they can engage in real tasks to develop ideas and strategies to address global issues. Our goal is therefore not just to prepare individual students to perform in the new economic and cultural milieu, but to instill in them a way of thinking and acting that is founded fundamentally upon the interconnectedness of the globalizing world. This is important in helping Singapore develop the culture of a global city.

With this goal in mind, the concept that drives our study abroad programs is active engagement—intellectual and emotional. Our strategy is to: (1) structure learning in focused intellectual themes of global relevance with a strong reflective/comparative component, so that students can gain a deeper intellectual insight into global issues; (2) facilitate substantial intellectual and social interactions with students of one or more overseas partner universities, so that students can discover their place in the global network that is necessary to address global issues. For USP, study abroad is an integral part of our mission to stretch the intellectual, leadership and personal potential of our students. It strongly supports NUS's vision to foster "globally-oriented minds [that are] well-equipped to succeed in our fast-changing world," as well as the nation's aspiration to become a global city.

The University Scholars Programme has a wide range of study abroad programs, ranging from those that are "less formal" (the examples that I will be describing below fall into this category) to highly structured ones. Within the latter category is our Bicultural Immersion Programme. At the moment, three programs, in China, Japan, and India, are offered. They comprise a double degree program with Peking University's Yuanpei College; a double degree program with Waseda University's School of International Liberal Studies; and an exchange program with Lady Shri Ram College and Hindu College, both of which are affiliated with Delhi University. We also have two joint degree programs with the Australian National University's Bachelor of Philosophy programs in Science and Arts. There are also USP-specific exchange programs with honors colleges and liberal arts colleges.

STUDY ABROAD MODELS

Numerous study abroad models have been analyzed in the literature. Essentially, these models cover a spectrum of possibilities in the following aspects: (1) home university's involvement, and (2) students' independence. They range from the classic "island model," in which the study abroad program is designed, taught, and run by the home university, and conducted at an overseas location; to the "direct enrollment model," in which students study in a foreign educational system and take courses offered by the overseas host university. The advantage of the former is that there is consistent quality assurance for the students' education, while the advantage of the latter is that it provides for more intensive immersion. Clearly, the former does involve interactions with local guest speakers and local communities; whereas the latter is subjected to the rigor of the credit transfer process. The challenge, however, is to strike a balance between quality assurance and immersion. This is addressed by a plethora of hybrid models.

The right balance obviously depends on the desired objective. For many students, study abroad offers the first real chance of being independent. For them, student exchange is a good option. The disadvantage of student exchange, however, is its potential lack of intellectual focus. Students don't always receive thorough academic advice. To cope with the new environment, some students interact more with fellow exchange students from similar cultures than with local students at the host institution. The experience of student exchange hinges critically on the student's own initiative.

On the other hand, if the study abroad program is to fulfill a specific learning objective, say, to understand the workings of a particular local NGO, then a program organized by the home university could be quite effective. The shortcomings of such a program, however, are that it depends crucially on the faculty organizers' familiarity with local conditions and extent of local contacts. The scope and geographical location of such programs are therefore limited by the university's expertise.

In some cases, one finds a good match between two or more universities in different geographical locations or different cultural settings to collaborate in a study abroad project. The success of such a collaboration is predicated on compatible educational philosophy, student profile, and, most importantly, objective of the particular study abroad project. In the ideal case, "collaboration" means equal partnership and full reciprocity, where intellectual expertise, administrative support, and expenses are shared, and students from all partner universities participate fully in the entire study abroad program. This goes beyond the more common arrangement whereby the host university simply provides administrative and local logistical support, and some guest speakers. It is also different from the usual consortium model, which is essentially an arrangement to pool students for study abroad programs.

Such collaborations have most significance when the study abroad project takes on a transnational/cultural nature, where the project comprises two or more legs at different locations with the participants (composed of students from all partner universities) taking part fully in the entire project. A natural arrangement would be for each partner university to host one leg of the study abroad project.

The advantages of such collaborative projects are significant. (The challenges, which we will touch on later, are also severe, but first we will discuss the potential advantages.) Clearly, it addresses the restrictions of both the island and direct enrollment models. All partners are equal stakeholders, so there is incentive for all to contribute to the success of the study abroad project. Such projects make the most sense when the objective is focused and specific, such that the expertise and support required of the partner universities are clearly spelled out. Most importantly, from the start, such programs are designed to facilitate real interaction and collaboration between participants from the partner universities. They work best when the educational objective comprises a comparative dimension, which requires students from the partner universities to engage collaboratively in real tasks. For projects of a transnational/cultural nature described above, the advantage is particularly significant. While many study abroad programs that are conducted in one location also involve local partners, the relationship is usually asymmetrical. Also, while most study abroad programs naturally incorporate a comparative component and provide opportunities for participants to interact with the local students (as well as the wider local population), the local students often do not participate as equal partners because they may lack the background knowledge to understand the views of their visitors. Collaborative transnational/ cultural study abroad provides a more equal platform where all participants involved have the benefit of seeing for themselves multiple perspectives, however limited they may be, and thus experience a greater sense of active engagement in the project.

I will now illustrate USP's attempt to offer collaborative study abroad programs using a few examples. The first two programs that I will describe were initiated by George Washington University and the Chinese University of Hong Kong, respectively. We have indeed been very privileged to be invited to join these collaborations.

GEORGE WASHINGTON UNIVERSITY–USP
TWO CITY DIALOGUE PROGRAM

In 2004, George Washington University's Columbian College of Arts and Sciences initiated the Dean's Scholars in Globalization Program. It is a 2-year (freshman–sophomore) program that incorporates a study abroad component involving two partners —the University of Chile and the National University of Singapore. The program has a theme that changes from year to year which is selected for its global relevance and its amenability to comparative study, such as megacities (2005–2006), global health with particular emphasis on HIV/AIDS (2006–2007), and diaspora (2007–2008). Throughout the program, the students interact on cyberspace, as well as via videoconferencing. There are also exchange visits among the three destinations: Washington, DC, Santiago, and Singapore. (At the moment, NUS is only involved in the visit to Washington, DC. The plan ahead is to get both the Chilean and Singaporean students to converge on Washington, DC at the same time.) Below, I will only describe our experience from the perspective of NUS, and I will mostly concentrate on the global health program (2007).

The idea of collaboration was first explored in 2004, and subsequent discussions took place in Singapore in 2005. In 2006, GWU and NUS first collaborated in the "megacities" program. The main reason GWU and USP hit it off well was that there was good compatibility of objective. Both USP and the Dean's Scholars in Globalization Program are aimed at a small group (about 10 students from each side) of highly motivated students. The desired objective is to allow them to engage in cross-national and cross-cultural discussions on topics of global relevance, so as to achieve broad understanding of global issues.

In the following year, the topic of global health, with particular emphasis on HIV/AIDS, was decided jointly. As with all such programs, the key is the quality of the faculty drivers. For this particular program, we were fortunate to have exceptionally committed faculty champions, both from GWU and NUS. According to the expertise of the faculty champions, the focus of the program was to be on public education. Again, two videoconferences were held.

The Singaporean students visited Washington, DC for about a week in February 2007. During their visit, there were seminars by researchers, sharing by volunteers, and visits to local hospitals. There were also visits to the National Institutes of Health and the public health division of the RAND Corporation. On a lighter note, an additional excitement to the Singaporean students was that they experienced both Chinese New Year (and for some the first snow, which fell on that day) and President's Day in Washington, DC.

In May 2007, the GWU students visited Singapore. Besides seminars and discussions, there were also visits to the Patient Care Centre of Tan Tock Seng Hospital as well as the local NGO Action for AIDS.

These visit programs were large planned by the local host university, in consultation with the partner university. However, a success of the collaboration is that there is a high level of trust once the educational philosophy and objective of the yearly theme were thoroughly understood.

This program made an unmistakable impact on the Singaporean students. Some of them mentioned in particular that their eyes were opened to the substantial research done with men who have sex with men, a topic not normally discussed openly in Singapore. They also wrote:

> Student activists involved in AIDS awareness advocacy in GWU shared their experience with us over dinner in the evening. Other than promoting safe sex in GWU through posters, exhibitions, etc, they also try and get their message across using unorthodox methods such as protesting outside the White House and other government buildings. Their passion and enthusiasm in rallying others behind their cause was infectious and really rubbed off us. This led us to seek to do more for the AIDS patients in Singapore and culminated in the establishment of F.A.C.E., a student group that aims to decrease stigmatization and to raise funds for HIV patients.

This was an important step in cultivating a society that is more open, diverse, and in tune with the global practices and norms that are needed for a global city.

LEE SHIU SUMMER PROGRAMME

The Lee Shiu Summer Programme (LSSP) was an initiative of Chung Chi College, Chinese University of Hong Kong. In 2002, with a donation from prominent Hong Kong-based philanthropists Dr. Lee Shiu and Dr. Jennie Mui Lee, the Lee Shiu Centre for Intercultural Learning was formed at Chung Chi College. The objective of the Centre is to bring elite undergraduates from top universities in China to Hong Kong (and later also Singapore), to allow them to learn from the experiences and best practices of Hong Kong (and Singapore), and vice versa, and interact with their counterparts there. The vehicle is the Lee Shiu Summer Programme, a month-long residential summer program with the following four areas of focus: public governance, economic development, education, and social services. In 2002, about 80 students from Hong Kong and China (and a few from the United States) took part in the summer program that brought the participants to Hong Kong, Shanghai, and Shenzhen.

In 2004, USP was invited to collaborate with LSSP to inject an international dimension into it. As a predominately ethnic Chinese community, Singapore has a certain affinity to Hong Kong and China. Further, it shares many similarities with Hong Kong—both have strong anticorruption laws, both are port cities, both are financial centers, and both are up and coming global cities. At the same time, there are significant differences: Singapore is multicultural and does not have the hinterland that Hong Kong enjoys; politically, they are also distinct. Thus, Singapore is a natural complement to the summer program. For Singapore, it is clearly in its national interest to leverage on its majority ethnic Chinese community to enhance bilateral relations with China, whose rise is considered one of the most important phenomena of the early 21st century (Shee, 2005). China, therefore, has a special place in the globally oriented mission of NUS. It is worth noting at this point that NUS has numerous study abroad programs in China. Another important country for Singapore is India. Besides our exchange program with Lady Shri Ram College and Hindu College, in 2008, USP also conducted two study abroad programs in India, one on biodiversity and sustainable development in the Indian Himalayas, and the other on crafts and livelihood in Delhi and Rajasthan.

Again, USP is highly compatible with the philosophy of LSSP. Leadership development is an explicit aim of the summer program, and participants are brought together to discuss issues of public policy, with the specific aim of learning from each others' practices as well as understanding each others' thinking. Several meetings to discuss the collaboration took place in Hong Kong and Singapore.

In the 2004 program, which was held in July/August, about 80 participants came from the Chinese University of Hong Kong, National University of Singapore, a dozen universities in China, including Fudan, Peking, Tsinghua, Nanjing, Zhejiang, and Sun Yat Sen, as well as Princeton and Harvard. The quality of the participants was outstanding. Selection was particularly competitive in mainland Chinese universities; in some cases, about 200 applicants vied for three or four places. Selection was based on passion in China affairs and leadership potential. Some participants—Singaporeans and Americans—were not ethnic Chinese. The participants spent four intensive weeks living and learning together—2 weeks in Hong Kong, one week in Shanghai, and one week in Singapore. (In 2004, Fudan University was also a partner, in addition to NUS.) The speakers included prominent intellectual, government, business, and community leaders. There were also visits to government departments and nongovernmental organizations such as the Independent Commission against Corruption in Hong Kong, the Housing Development Board in Singapore, and the China–Singapore Suzhou Industrial Park, which is about an hour away from Shanghai. There was of course also plenty of time for students to interact and engage in group discussions (the students were divided into transnational groups—at first groups of 20, and later smaller groups of 5 as they worked on their group projects).

The program culminated in the Lee Shiu Young Leaders Forum in Singapore, in which participants presented their group findings as well as made policy recommendations to their governments in a fairly formal setting which attracted press coverage. The findings are also published. They cover topics ranging from "Developing anti-corruption strategies in modern China" to "English instruction in universities: Lessons from Singapore for China" to "Rising dragon/roaring lion: Suzhou industrial park as a successful collaboration?" (Ng, 2006).

At the close of the program, one Singaporean student reflected:

> We came to the program with a question mark above our heads: What is modern China? We now leave the program with many more question marks, some of which are: How can China alleviate social tensions due to the great disparity in wealth? How can China maintain economic development and environmental sustainability at the same time? How can China ensure government transparency and accountability under a one party system?... The Lee Shiu Summer Programme has motivated us to be not just onlookers, but rather participants of one of the most exciting events of this century—the rise of China.

The reflections of the Chinese students are also telling. One student wrote:

> Like many young people in China, I want to see my country grow prosperous and gain respect in the international community. But this will not happen by merely becoming more patriotic. We must think beyond our borders by broadening our minds to larger issues and building international networks. By participating in this program, we have already built a valuable network. This network will last and we can learn from each other and help each other in the days to come.

The next program was conducted similarly in 2006, this time with Tsinghua University as the third partner, and the places visited were Hong Kong, Singapore, and Beijing. Again, anticorruption, talent development, and youth development were major areas of discussion, as were the challenges of organizing the 2008 Beijing Olympic Games. The 2008 program concluded on August 5, three days before the start of the Beijing Olympics!

INTERFAITH DIALOGUE STUDY PROGRAMME

In 2006, USP initiated the Interfaith Dialogue Study Programme (originally started as the Islam Study Programme). The immediate objective was to look at contemporary issues of Islam, in particular how various societies with substantial Muslim populations dealt with the complexities of negotiating tradition and modernity. Singapore pays particular attention to religious harmony because of being a multicultural and multireligious society with about 15% Muslim population, and being surrounded by large Muslim societies (in Malaysia and Indonesia). Besides the official Maintenance of Religious Harmony Act, numerous policies and a comprehensive public education program, with an official Religious Harmony Day which is observed in all schools, the government further set up the Harmony Centre in 2006 to promote interreligious dialogue. In the past few years, USP has also organized a number of interfaith dialogue seminars (including assisting with the 2007 Building Bridges Seminar, which was convened by the Archbishop of Canterbury). The Interfaith Dialogue Study Programme, however, aims to allow students to observe firsthand how different societies address religious harmony.

The program was the brainchild of Professor Syed Farid Alatas, an NUS sociologist and Islam scholar. Following the three-location comparative study model of the Lee Shiu Summer Programme, Istanbul, Kuala Lumpur, and Singapore were chosen as the locations for the study program. All three cities have substantial Muslim populations, and yet are cosmopolitan, modern, and multireligious. Of the three societies, Singapore is the least overtly religious, while Islam is the state religion of Malaysia, and Turkey is a secular state as set out in its constitution. All three societies have manifestations of Islamic fundamentalism, to very different degrees, and struggle to balance their religious and secular desires. These three locations therefore provide fertile ground for comparative study which is relevant and informative for the three societies involved. For USP, in particular, dealing with religious harmony is of national importance and an essential aspect of leadership development.

For this program, we have multiple partners including Fatih University in Istanbul and the Centre for Intercultural Dialogue at the University of Malaya in Kuala Lumpur. Discussions for collaboration took place in Singapore, Istanbul, and Kuala Lumpur.

The original plan was that students from Fatih and the University of Malaya would participate fully in the program. However, due to various factors (in particular different academic calendars), in the end students from Fatih only participated in the Istanbul leg, while students from Malaya only participated in the Kuala Lumpur and Singapore legs.

The first study program took place in December 2006, with about 10 days in Istanbul, a week in Singapore, and a few days in Kuala Lumpur. In Istanbul, besides seminars at Fatih University, the students also visited mosques, churches, and synagogues, and had discussions with religious leaders. (Of course, they also took in the sights of the beautiful city.) At the conclusion of the program, the students presented their findings at a public forum at the Harmony Centre (Singapore), which was well received and attended by several religious leaders in Singapore.

The 2007 program was originally planned to include observing Kurban Bayrami as well as Christmas celebrations in Istanbul, among other activities, but was in the end postponed to the summer of 2008, from May 26 to June 14 (7 days in Singapore, 5 days in Kuala Lumpur, and 8 days in Istanbul). Among the places visited were the Centre for Islamic Studies, Foundation for Science and Culture, and Aya Sofya in Istanbul, and the Bangsar Lutheran Church and Soka Gakkai in Kuala Lumpur.

While a lot of the seminars and discussions centered on the social, political, and theological dimensions of interfaith dialogue, an interesting observation made by the students is that "dialogue doesn't necessarily mean literal discourse; rather, it can be metaphorical, carried out through art and architecture." They studied various facets of art and architecture in Aya Sofya (Istanbul), Soka Gakkai (Kuala Lumpur), and Church of St. Mary's Angels (Singapore) that show evidence of interfaith dialogue.

OUTCOMES

It is clear from the students' feedback and reflections that the study abroad programs mentioned above (as well as many others that we conduct) have made an indelible mark in the students' minds. Study abroad opened their eyes and stretched their imagination. However, if our aim is to change the way they think, act, and learn, then we need to go further. We need to track what students do after study abroad, and, much more problematically, try to tease out how their transformation (if any) is due to the study abroad experience. We have not yet embarked on this in any systematic way, but would just like to share a few observations that we find encouraging.

As we will discuss in the section on "Challenges" below, we have unfortunately (or otherwise) not been able to offer academic credit for some of our study abroad activities (all three examples given above are noncredit). What we do, however, is to encourage students to make use of this experience to formulate independent study projects that are for credit. For example, as a direct consequence of the GWU-USP program on global health, three USP students embarked on independent study projects on related topics. Also, as mentioned above, after the program, they founded F.A.C.E. In addition, some of them started volunteering at the Patient Care Centre, and some organized the StompAids Challenge.

Directly inspired by their experience at the Lee Shiu Summer Programme, three USP students participated in the "Ethical Leadership and its Challenges in the Era of Globalization" case competition organized by the Hong Kong Independent Commission Against Corruption and won the Overall Best Team Award at the Ethical Leadership for the New Generation Youth Summit held in Hong Kong in March 2007.

The Interfaith Dialogue Study Program of 2006 had piqued the interest in Arabic culture of a group of USP students, who subsequently founded the West Asian and North African Studies Interest Group at NUS. The Group has been active and has organized trips to Yemen as well as a language immersion program in Oman. One student also pursued independent study as well as her honors thesis research on related topics.

CHALLENGES

As anyone who has worked in this area would know, the challenges in organizing study abroad programs are severe, and I will only mention only four from the (institutional) point of view of USP.

Resources

I am not just referring to finance, which obviously is substantial once overseas travel is involved. Equally important is the strain on manpower. All the programs mentioned involve small numbers of students and yet they require high maintenance. The 2007 GWU–USP program involved 10 USP students, the 2004 Lee Shiu program 15 USP students, and the 2006 Interfaith Dialogue program had 19 students. Even though each program only spent a few days in Singapore, a serious amount of effort went into the planning and logistics. Obviously, we wanted the participants to learn as much as possible, in both formal and informal settings. We also wanted to present to them the most current state of affairs. Thus, for example, even for the Lee Shiu Summer Programme, which is held biennially, each program essentially is designed anew. For the 2008 program in Singapore, for instance, we focused on innovation, talent, knowledge, and environment because these are the four areas identified by Chinese Premier Wen Jiabao after his November 2007 visit to Singapore as being important for Hong Kong to enhance its competitiveness. ("Wen's 4 Ways for HK to Up Its Game" (2007)) The institution therefore must justify investing resources that may benefit only a small group of students.

Commitment

No study abroad program can be successful without the full commitment of faculty champions. For collaborative programs, in particular, there must be committed faculty drivers from all sides who must be able to work together in synergy as well as in complementary terms. They will also need to negotiate the framework of individual institutions, and that is particularly critical when academic credit is involved. This is one of the reasons for the main weakness of the three programs that I have described above: none of them carries academic credit for NUS students. I hasten to add that there is no institutional resistance at NUS to this (in fact, it has a lot of for-credit study abroad programs, including a very active Student Exchange Programme and the NUS Overseas Colleges program), but it does require much more careful planning and extra commitment from the faculty. I also find that our not-for-credit study abroad programs tend to attract students who are truly passionate about the topics. Those who are further motivated to deepen their study abroad experience can pursue for-credit supervised independent study. This way, students may engage at different intellectual levels; also, more faculty members (of more diverse expertise) can be brought in as supervisors (for independent study).

Timing

As different universities have different term times, it can be quite a daunting task to coordinate dates among partners. For instance, for the GWU-USP program, USP students go to Washington during their one-week break in February, but at that time GWU students have classes. On the other hand, GWU students come to Singapore in the summer, when many USP students have activities such as internships. To give another example: we also have a collaboration with Harvard students who come to Singapore during their Spring break in late March, which is close to our examination period. Our students do pledge to participate fully in both the outgoing (our students go to Harvard in February) and incoming portions of the programs, and they do greatly appreciate the learning opportunity, but it does put some stress on them (especially as examinations are looming). Inability to coordinate timing is also the reason why we have not yet managed to engage Chilean students (in the GWU program) and to attain full participation of Turkish students (in the Interfaith Dialogue program).

Finding the Right Partners

As I have already mentioned above, a successful collaborative study abroad program hinges on the quality of the partnership among the collaborating universities. It is crucial that there is compatibility in educational philosophy and student profile. Universities will need to engage in a lot of dialogue to understand each other to find compatibilities. My experience is that this is immensely worthwhile in terms of enriching the study abroad landscape of all parties involved.

CONCLUSION

In this paper I have described some of our attempts at creating opportunities for NUS undergraduates to work together intensively with students from other countries on issues of global importance through collaborative study abroad.

Study abroad plays a particularly vital role in NUS even as it is becoming increasingly important in virtually all universities around the world. In Singapore, study abroad is seen as a key strategy for the nation's continued well-being and, indeed, survival. When so much in Singapore hinges on education, it is imperative that all educational institutions work together toward national goals. I believe global education/study abroad is a case in point. One prominent study abroad director in a U.S. university said to me in private, referring to the NUS vision statement, "Towards a Global Knowledge Enterprise," "What university in the U.S. has a motto that is so much part of each and every aspect of the institution? That is, what university in the U.S. is as thoroughly branded as NUS? I don't think there's a single one, and that's what's so interesting to me about NUS."

I also argued in this paper that, to fulfill its calling to meet national goals, study abroad has to go further in NUS. I have tried to illustrate by using examples the ways in which our study abroad is shaped by four objectives: First and foremost, an educational objective: to help students understand the globalizing world and prepare them for active engagement in the global community. Second, a national objective: to foster a globally minded citizenry to help Singapore realize its global city aspiration. Third, a national/institutional objective: to support attractive programs that keep Singaporeans studying in local universities while at the same time they benefit from an overseas education experience. Last but not least, an institutional objective: to allow local universities to gain from synergistic partnerships with overseas universities.

In USP, we have adopted a particular approach that emphasizes active engagement. Our strategy is to offer study abroad projects that are tightly designed and sharply focused to allow a transnational team of students to engage in real tasks collaboratively and equitably to develop ideas and strategies to address global issues. Clearly, we have much to do to realize the full potential of this approach.

USP has only just begun building study abroad programs. We have much to learn from others who are way ahead of us. I would like to mention that in February 2008 a group of USP students and I had the good fortune to attend the EPIIC Symposium on Global Poverty and Inequality organized by the Institute for Global Leadership (IGL) at Tufts University. We were deeply impressed and inspired by IGL's achievements. Subsequent to the Symposium, our students have started working with Tufts students on two projects in Cambodia. There are many other successful programs that we should emulate. My purpose here is merely to further increase dialogue among universities interested in forming partnerships to offer collaborative study abroad programs. I believe these collaborative programs not only allow institutions to share resources and expertise, and enrich and diversify their study abroad offerings. In the long run, they create the people networks that are needed to solve global problems.

REFERENCES

Chia, A. (2000). Singapore's economic internationalization and its effect on work and family. *SOJOURN: Journal of Social Issues in Southeast Asia, 15,* 123–138.

Goh, C. T. (1997, June 2). *Opening address.* The 7th International Conference on Thinking, Singapore.

Gopinathan, S. (1974). *Towards a national system of education 1945–1973.* Singapore: Oxford University Press.

Gopinathan, S. (1997). Educational development in a strong developmentalist state: the Singapore experience. In W. K. Cummings & N. McGinni (Eds.), *International handbook of education and development: Preparing schools, students and nations for the twenty-first century* (pp. 587–608). New York: Elsevier Science.

Gopinathan, S. (2007). Globalisation, the Singapore developmental state, and education policy: A thesis revisited. *Globalization, Societies and Education, 5,* 53–70.

Green, A. (1997). *Education, globalization and the nation state.* Houndmills, UK: Macmillan.

Kwa, C. G. (2002). Relating to the world: Images, metaphors and analogies. In D. da Cunha (Ed.), *Singapore in the new millennium: challenges facing the city-state* (pp. 108–132). Singapore: Institute of Southeast Asian Studies.

Lam, P. E. (1999). Singapore: Rich state, illiberal regime. In J. W. Morley (Ed.), *Driven by growth: Political change in the Asia-Pacific region* (Rev. ed., pp. 255–274). Armonk, NY: M. E. Sharpe.

Lee, H. L. (2005a, April 22). Address. Asian-African Business Summit, Jakarta.

Lee, H. L. (2005b, August 21). Address. National Day rally, Singapore.

Lee, K. Y. (2000). *From third world to first: The Singapore story: 1965–2000.* New York: HarperCollins.

Lee, K. Y. (2008, February 8). Interview by Arnaud de Borchgrave. United Press International.

Lui, T. Y. (2008, March 4). Second reply on University Education by Minister of State, FY2008 Committee of Supply (parliamentary) Debate, Singapore. Retrieved October 19, 2008, from http://www.moe.gov.sg/media/speeches/2008/03/04/fy-2008-committee-of-supply-de-1.php

Marcum, J. A. (2001, May 18). What directions for study abroad? Eliminate the roadblocks. *The Chronicle of Higher Education,* B7.

Nanyang Technological University. (n.d.). Vision statement. Retrieved October 19, 2008, from http://www.ntu.edu.sg/AboutNTU/NTUataglance/Pages/visionmission.aspx

National University of Singapore. (2006a, January). *Creating the future: A strategy for NUS.* Retrieved October 19, 2008, from http://www.nus.edu.sg/corporate/about/strategies.htm

National University of Singapore. (2006b). *Annual report.* Singapore: Author.

National University of Singapore. (2007). *Annual report.* Singapore: Author.

National University of Singapore. (n.d., a). Vision statement: Towards a global knowledge enterprise. Retrieved October 19, 2008, from http://www.nus.edu.sg/corporate/about/vision.htm

National University of Singapore. (n.d., b). Integrated living, learning & discovery: nurturing one community. Retrieved October 19, 2008, from http://www.nus.edu.sg/utown/index.htm

Ng, H. (Ed.) (2006). *China's path to modernity and prosperity: A study of three cities—Hong Kong, Shanghai and Singapore.* Hong Kong: Chung Chi College, the Chinese University of Hong Kong.

Sanyal, S. (2007). *Singapore, the art of building a global city* (IPS Working Paper 17). Singapore: Institute of Policy Studies.

Shanmugaratnam, T. (2006, August 8). Address. 2006 National Day observance ceremony at Ministry of Education headquarters, Singapore.

Shee, P. K. (2005). Singapore-China special economic relations: in search of business opportunities. *Ritsumeikan International Affairs, 3,* 151–176.

Shih, C. F. (2001, July 30). *State of the University.* Address at the National University of Singapore.

Singapore Ministry of Education, Junior College/Upper Secondary Education Review Committee. (2002, October). *Report.* Singapore: Author.

Singapore Ministry of Education, Committee to Review the University Sector and Graduate Manpower Planning. (2003, May). *Report.* Singapore: Author.

Singapore Ministry of Education, Committee on the Expansion of the University Sector (2008, June). *Preliminary report*. Singapore: Author.

Singapore Ministry of Education. (n.d.). Vision. Retrieved October 19, 2008, from http://www.moe.gov.sg/about/#our-vision

Singapore Ministry of Trade and Industry, Committee on Singapore's Competitiveness. (1998). *Report*. Singapore: Author.

Statistics Singapore. (2008). *Population trends 2008*. Singapore: Author.

Tan, K. P. (2008). Meritocracy and elitism in a global city: Ideological shifts in Singapore. *International Political Science Review, 29*, 7–27.

Velayutham, S. (2007). *Responding to globalization: Nation, culture and identity in Singapore*. Singapore: Institute of Southeast Asian Studies.

Wee, L., & Bokhorst-Heng, D. W. (2005). Language policy and nationalist ideology: Statal narratives in Singapore. *Multilingua, 24*, 159–183.

Wen's 4 ways for HK to up its game. (2007, November 24). *South China Morning Post*. Retrieved October 19, 2008, from http://www.ddepot.org/news0711.htm

Yeoh, B. S. A. (2007). Migration and social diversity in Singapore. In T. H. Tan (Ed.), *Singapore perspectives: A new Singapore* (pp. 47–56). Singapore: Institute of Policy Studies and World Scientific.

Part Three

Institutional Challenges and Strategies for Fostering Global Citizenship Study Abroad

Chapter 15

It Takes an Entire Institution

A Blueprint for the Global University

William Brustein

University of Illinois at Urbana-Champaign

Confronted with a world that is strikingly different from what it was just a decade ago, higher education faces rapidly shifting economic, political, and national security realities and challenges. To respond to these changes it is essential that our institutions of higher education graduate globally competent students, that is, students possessing a combination of critical thinking skills, technical expertise, and global awareness that allow them "not only to contribute to knowledge, but also to comprehend, analyze, and evaluate its meaning in the context of an increasingly globalized world" (National Association of State Universities and Land Grant Colleges [NASULGC], 2004). For our students global competence is an indispensable qualification of global citizenship, that is, the ability to work cooperatively in seeking and implementing solutions to challenges of global significance (e.g., economic, technological, political, and environmental). Moreover, global competence is essential to our students as they enter an increasingly competitive global marketplace and to our nation as it addresses its global security needs. The skills that form the foundation of global competence include the ability to work effectively in international settings; awareness of and adaptability to diverse cultures, perceptions, and approaches; familiarity with the major currents of global change and the issues they raise; and the capacity for effective communication across cultural and linguistic boundaries. If our institutions of higher education are to be successful in equipping our students with the above-mentioned skills, they will need to pursue a comprehensive and a systemic approach to campus internationalization.

However, discussions of internationalization of our campuses rarely address the process in a comprehensive and systemic fashion. Rather, the prevalent tendency is to focus on one or another element of internationalization like global partnerships, recruitment of international faculty and students, or study abroad initiatives.[1] The benefit of a systemic approach to internationalization is that it allows us to comprehend how one decision, activity, custom, or structure can either inhibit or spur significant change in the overall process. Take for instance the case of a university seeking to increase its study abroad participation fivefold within 10 years. The prospect of reaching that goal will likely be influenced by factors such as internationalization being included in the strategic plans of all units, a requirement that all students complete an internationally focused minor or certificate, the elimination of financial and curricular barriers to study abroad, the establishment of incentives to faculty for developing and leading learning abroad programs, and the university setting up partnerships with foreign universities. To provide both scholars and practitioners with a blueprint for a comprehensive internationalization of our campuses, this chapter lays out what the author observes are the principal constituent components or pillars of a global university.

What is a global university? For the purposes of this chapter I employ language from the 2004 NASULGC Task Force report, *A Call to Leadership: The Presidential Role in Internationalizing the University*, which states that a global university is one in which international and multicultural experiences and perspectives are fully integrated into its teaching, discovery, and engagement missions. But what are the pillars or components required to attain the full integration of international and multicultural experiences and perspectives? The 12 pillars upon which a global university sits are (1) internationalizing strategic planning; (2) internationalizing the curriculum; (3) eliminating barrier to study abroad; (4) requiring foreign language proficiency; (5) creating international internships; (6) internationalizing faculty searches; (7) incorporating international contributions into the faculty reward system; (8) upgrading senior international officers' reporting relationships; (9) placing senior international officers on key councils and committees; (10) eliminating barriers to international student recruitment and retention; (11) drawing upon the expertise and experiences of immigrant communities; and (12) making global partnerships an institutional priority. Below I lay out what steps we need to take to set in place the 12 pillars of the global university.

Pillars enable buildings to stand but pillars are held erect by a strong foundation. The foundation in which the 12 pillars of a global university reside is comprised of two elements. First, full internationalization is not simply the creation of international "silos" or "stove pipes," that is, a college or school of international studies offering stand-alone degrees and possessing its own faculty tenure lines. Not that a school of international studies cannot be part of a global university but true internationalization calls for a *thorough infusion or integration* of international experiences and perspectives within the teaching, discovery, and engagement missions of each academic unit within the university. Second, successful internationalization requires that faculty, administrators, and staff perceive internationalization as *adding value* to what they do and helping them reach their goals. Internationalization efforts will eventually wither on the vine if they depend solely on altruistic motivations or top-down enforced compliance.

PILLAR 1: INTERNATIONALIZATION IS INCLUDED IN THE STRATEGIC PLANS OF ALL DEPARTMENTS, COLLEGES, AND SCHOOLS WITHIN THE UNIVERSITY

No one doubts the positive effects of including internationalization in the institution's strategic plans and goals. However, comprehensive internationalization is unlikely to occur unless every unit within the institution including academic departments, colleges, and schools also incorporate plans as well as benchmarks for internationalization within their own goals for its teaching, discovery, and engagement missions. I have seen this work most successfully where the chief academic officer of the university requests that each dean include international issues in his or her annual strategic planning and where each dean partners with the university's senior international officer (SIO) in an effort to facilitate the infusion of the international dimension within the college or school. In this process the extent to which the SIO is able to speak convincingly to the expected added value to the college or school that increased international activities will produce, the greater the likelihood of success. Furthermore, successful internationalization of college-based units may benefit from the establishment of an international advisory council chaired by the university's senior international officer and made up of each college's most senior administrator charged with the college's international portfolio. International advisory councils reporting directly to the SIO and comprised of those within the colleges' senior administration tend to be more active and effective as change agents than councils constituted by deans and chaired by the chief campus academic officer.

PILLAR 2: INTERNATIONAL ASPECTS ARE INTEGRATED INTO ALL MAJORS

It is essential for international aspects to be integrated into all majors or that all students (including those in the professional schools) complete a relevant internationally focused second major, minor, or certificate. If the training of globally competent graduates is accepted as one of the chief goals of our system of higher education, our curricula will have to be redesigned to ensure that outcome. Most of our institutions address the need for global competence by adding a diversity or international course(s) requirement—hardly sufficient to instill global competence in our students—or by offering degrees, minors, or certificates in area or international studies. However, there are major shortcomings in the way both area and international studies are generally carried out. Area studies programs tend to be highly descriptive and too often display an apparent abhorrence toward theorizing. The curriculum frequently resembles a cafeteria-style menu: one selection or course from this shelf, followed by selections from various other shelves. Somehow students are expected miraculously to pull together the disparate pieces into some coherent whole. Area studies fail frequently to take advantage of opportunities to generalize from their rich contextual findings to the broader world. International studies programs (particularly when they fall under the rubric of international relations) frequently manifest a lack of appreciation for the importance of the local and regional cultural contexts. There are few, if any, attempts at applying the theoretical approaches to the empirical context of the regions. As a result, American students often complete these programs without any competency in a foreign language or any knowledge of or any specific grounding in the culture of a society outside of the United States.

Additionally, our area and international studies programs often fail to give appropriate attention to such crucial steps as (a) integrating relevant learning abroad opportunities into the degree, minor or certificate; (b) incorporating critical thinking skills of knowledge, comprehension, analysis, synthesis, explanation, evaluation, and extrapolation into the learning experience (Caldwell, 2004); (c) assessing or evaluating global competence as an outcome; and (d) aligning the area of international studies concentration to a disciplinary major (e.g., biology, anthropology, history, engineering).

This last point deserves further examination and will likely engender controversy among international educators. We must continually ask ourselves if we are doing a disservice to our undergraduate students by encouraging them to spend their undergraduate years pursuing standalone degrees in area or international studies. I often meet with heads of multinational corporations, government offices, and NGOs. When I ask these leaders to describe to me what they look for when making hiring decisions they invariably begin by reminding me that they hire engineers, chemists, economists—in other words graduates with technical expertise. They proceed, however, to inform me of the enormous added value they see in graduates who combine a technical expertise with area and international studies knowledge, foreign language, and learning abroad experience. In particular, they highlight the benefits of global awareness, cultural sensitivity, and foreign language competency. It would appear that the assessment of these leaders is consistent with remarks advanced by Friedman (2005) in his best-selling book, *The World is Flat* and with the findings of the 2006 Committee for Economic Development's report, *Education for Global Leadership: The Importance of International Studies and Foreign Language Education for U.S. Economic and National Security*. Friedman suggests that companies of the 21st century will seek to hire graduates with technical expertise, especially in engineering, science, and business. But he notes that these same companies in an effort to come to terms with "glocalization," that is, the interface between global economic tendencies and local cultural values, will require that our technical experts possess a familiarity with regional and local cultures, for without knowledge of these cultures our companies are unlikely to be successful in understanding local consumer tastes. Even within the United States, according to the CED report, there is a great demand for globally competent workers who possess the skills to transcend cultural barriers and work together in global teams. The CED report notes that American affiliates of foreign companies employed more than 5.4 million U.S. workers in 2002. Inadequate cross-cultural training of employees in U.S. companies results annually in an estimated $2 billion in losses. To wit: the CED report cites the highly embarrassing incidents of the worldwide dissemination of Microsoft Windows 95 that placed the Indian province of Kashmir outside of India's geographical boundaries and the distribution in Arab countries of a video game in which Arabic chanting of the Koran accompanied violent scenes (Committee for Economic Development, 2006).

I proffer an additional criticism of stand-alone undergraduate degrees in area and international studies: if we are to achieve global competence then we are obliged to internationalize the educational experience regardless of the discipline. If we require students to select either a stand-alone major in area or international studies or a traditional disciplinary degree, students most likely will opt for the latter and we will be left with a situation where only a small number of students will have exposure to an international studies concentration. Global competence cannot be the preserve of only a few students. It is incumbent upon us as international educators to gain buy-in and participation in designing undergraduate programs that will let our students earn area studies certificates or minors truly linked and relevant to their disciplines, or carefully thought out disciplinary or international and area studies majors where *both* disciplinary expertise and area/international studies are fully integrated. The answer is not area studies *or* disciplines—it is developing a comprehensive and coherent curriculum that will train our students to become globally competent critical thinkers.

The University of Pittsburgh's Global Studies certificate provides a useful model of creating an international curriculum component available to all students. The Pitt Global Studies certificate provides undergraduates and graduate students across the entire campus with an opportunity for interdisciplinary training concurrent with academic or professional degrees in a major field. In consultation with an academic advisor, students design an individualized program of study requiring no less than 18 credits. Global Studies students choose one of the six global concentrations (sustainable development; globalized economy and global governance; changing identities in a global world; communication, technology, and society; global health; and conflict and conflict resolution) and unite it with the study of a particular region and a language of that region. In so doing, the program effectively integrates the study of major global issues with the study of their application in different regions and cultures, ensuring both the global relevance of area studies and the empirical grounding of globalization studies. The six Global Studies concentrations are thus designed to promote holistic learning while creating new and specialized forums for discussion and learning that break across disciplinary boundaries in order to better address the causes, consequences, and search for solutions arising from globalization. To ensure interdisciplinary learning, students take three courses in two departments other than their major. Each certificate student must complete a capstone research project as part of the coursework on a topic relating to chosen global and regional concentrations.

The University of Pittsburgh's Global Studies certificate is a major step forward toward providing students with a relevant international curriculum component open to all students. However, it falls short of a fully integrated internationalized curriculum because it is an add-on. To ensure a globally competent curriculum our colleges and universities need to rethink the contents of each academic department's major in an effort to infuse the international into each course required for the major and into the major's capstone experiences. Georgia Tech has made tremendous strides in this direction through its International Plan (IP). In the Georgia Tech International Plan international studies, language acquisition, and an overseas experience are integrated into the traditional bachelor of science degree for the various disciplines. Furthermore, upon completion of the undergraduate degree in the student's major and the IP requirements, the student's transcript and diploma state that the degree is a "Bachelor of Science with International Plan." The next step for schools like Georgia Tech should be to seek ways to internationalize each and every course within the major.

PILLAR 3: FINANCIAL, CURRICULAR, AND OTHER BARRIERS ARE OVERCOME

Financial, curricular, and other barriers must be overcome to make education abroad accessible and affordable for all students; education abroad offerings must be evaluated in terms of quality and relevance to the educational and career objectives of students. If we are to reach the Senator Paul Simon Study Abroad Foundation Act's goal of sending one million U.S. students abroad by 2017, we are obliged to rethink how we currently finance learning abroad opportunities. Most institutions rely chiefly on program fees (user fees) ranging from a few hundred to thousands of dollars to fund the operation of their study abroad offices and to provide scholarships to students. Frequently, the costs of program fees (on top of tuition) serve to place learning abroad beyond the reach of many students. Recently, a few institutions, including the University of Texas (system), Georgia State University, and the University of Illinois at Urbana-Champaign have seen efforts by campus student groups to levy upon themselves a general student fee to allow the funding of student scholarships for eligible students seeking to study abroad. In the case of the University of Illinois, the initiative originated with a group of passionate undergraduates working closely with the campus study abroad office and office of student affairs. These students went out and obtained the 2,000 signatures necessary to place the initiative for a student study abroad fee of $5 per semester on the student ballot. The measure passed overwhelmingly in February 2008 and has the potential to raise approximately $300,000 per year for study abroad scholarships. To put this in another way: an institution would need to receive a gift of $9 to $12 million to reach the figure of $300,000 per year. However, the student fees do not cover the operating costs of the study abroad office. Much like the University of Texas, Georgia State University, and the University of Illinois the schools of the Atlantic Coast Conference (ACC) have come up with an innovative model to assist in the funding of study abroad. The ACC presidents have agreed that a percentage of the revenues generated from their schools' participation in football bowl games will be used for study abroad and other international activities at their schools. Also, advancement efforts in support of study abroad scholarships have huge potential to become a means to raise funds for study abroad on our campuses. Over the years I have witnessed the tremendous appeal that contributing to study abroad scholarships holds for donors. Indiana University provides a recent example of an institution receiving a substantial gift for study abroad scholarships which the university agreed to match.

To reach the goal of the Simon Act (the United States in 2005–2006 sent approximately 200,000 students abroad), program fees, student fees, or bowl revenues may likely be insufficient. If our government and our campuses are truly committed to quality learning abroad opportunities for all students we need to move to a system where the costs of study abroad—including the costs of maintaining a study abroad office—are built into tuition (or in the case of public universities and colleges covered by tuition and state revenues) so that students attending institutions of higher education pay the same sum whether or not they participate in a learning abroad experience. Learning abroad is an academic priority and should be treated and funded no differently from other academic priorities.

Addressing the financial constraints of study abroad will certainly help move us closer to our goal of making study abroad accessible to all students. However, we will fall far short of our study abroad goals if we fail to address students' concerns that study abroad will result in additional curricular hurdles that potentially delay their graduation or that the study abroad offerings have little or no relevance to their educational or career objectives. In addition we must gain the buy-in of departments and their faculty, especially in terms of the faculty creating academically relevant study abroad opportunities. Both the University of Minnesota and Georgia Tech have made significant strides in working with departments to integrate relevant study abroad experiences into each major. These efforts appear to have reduced many of the perceived disincentives for students regarding curricular barriers to study abroad and both institutions have witnessed substantial increases in study abroad participation. However, efforts to reduce disincentives faced by faculty to initiate faculty-led study abroad experiences have been less successful. The perception of few benefits from faculty involvement in creating and leading study abroad programs often discourages faculty participation. Many academic departments continue to discount the importance of faculty involvement in study abroad for it is not seen as contributing to the priorities of teaching and research. On the other hand, when faculty perceives value to engaging in study abroad activities we see increased participation. Incentives to encourage faculty involvement in study abroad activities can take many forms including extra pay, fulfilling teaching requirements, and furthering research objectives.

Allow me to provide some innovative examples of which I have first-hand experience. The first is the Research Abroad Program (RAP), a jointly sponsored and funded program of the University Center for International Studies (UCIS) at the University of Pittsburgh and its University Honors College. RAP was created so that undergraduates interested in serious scholarship could engage in UCIS-faculty led research projects overseas. RAP gives faculty members and students the opportunity to work as a team to contribute to an existing body of knowledge rather than simply disseminating or absorbing information, as is the case in the traditional classroom. In RAP, the faculty members recruit undergraduate students for their research projects and faculty members and students work together as a research team. Faculty benefit from the research insights, skills, and assistance students bring, as well as the opportunity to pursue their own research during the summer. And students benefit from the hands-on, research-related experience in a real world situation that has an impact on the direction of their career path. Over the past several years RAP has funded teams from biology, public health, communications, engineering, history, religious studies, education, and French and Italian conducting summer research in India, Great Britain, France, Costa Rica, Peru, Italy, Tanzania, St. Kitts, and Ireland. Both faculty and students engage in predeparture training and postreturn collaboration. Upon return from overseas, faculty are strongly encouraged to collaborate on publishable papers with the student members of the team.

Another example from the University of Pittsburgh of an initiative to incentivize faculty to incorporate study abroad into their teaching and research is the Integrated Field Trip Abroad (IFTA) program. IFTA is an optional extension of a spring term course. It is a related three-credit course which exposes students directly to the content of the spring term course or enables them to apply directly what they learned in the spring term. Enrollment is limited to students who have taken the related spring term course; the faculty member of that course with grant funding from the university's Title VI Area Studies or Global Studies programs develops the IFTA and accompanies the group abroad. During the past few years Pitt has sponsored a large number of IFTAs. The 2005 Andrew Heiskell award-winning Plus3 program—for Business and Engineering freshmen—was Pitt's inaugural IFTA program. For the Plus3 program students complete the Managing Complex Environments course, including four mandatory spring workshops, in the spring term prior to departing. Students spend 2 weeks overseas (students select one country among Brazil, Chile, France, China, Germany, or the Czech Republic) where they will visit companies, hear talks about the country, sightsee, interact with local students, and enjoy ethnic meals. Students must keep a journal and will compose a written group report on one of the companies visited and orally present upon return. Additional IFTAs have included "State Reform in Finland and Estonia," "Islamic Culture in Sarajevo," "Czech Republic and Poland: Impact of the European Union and Globalization," and "Dublin and Belfast: Comparing Communication Science and Disorders across Cultures." Opportunities to add a comparative/international emphasis to their courses and to build collegial ties with foreign colleagues are two of the apparent benefits the faculty derive from sponsoring IFTAs.

The University of Illinois has also explored avenues to offer incentives for faculty participation in designing and leading short-term study abroad programs. One new initiative at Illinois is the campus-wide study abroad development grant program launched in winter 2008 which allows faculty to compete for funds for the purpose of designing and leading short-term study abroad trips. In addition to using the funds from the grant to design a study abroad course, the faculty member can employ the funds to cover the costs of a research trip overseas to the country or region in which the study abroad program will take place. There was an overwhelming faculty response to this initiative from across the campus. A new initiative at Illinois to offer further incentives for faculty participation in designing and leading study abroad is the Faculty Study Abroad Banking System. Under consideration is establishment of a campus-wide "banking system" for faculty to lead study abroad programs. The program would allow faculty to "bank" teaching credits in exchange for leading courses and other for-credit programs abroad, and exchange those credits at a later point for on-campus course releases. In turn, courses taught abroad will become part of the faculty's annual evaluation. The plan is that for study abroad courses taught during summer, winter, or spring breaks, faculty will receive 50% of credits taught toward course release during a regular term.

These study abroad initiatives at the University of Pittsburgh and the University of Illinois have offered incentives to faculty to design and lead study abroad courses and to students to participate in these faculty-led initiatives. The result has been a more creative menu of study abroad choices for students as well as leading to a dramatic increase in study abroad rates of participation at both schools. Illinois, for example, has reached a participation rate in study abroad of 30% which is quite admirable for a large, state-supported research university. At both schools the faculty buy-in programs like RAP have also created international opportunities that give students skills to solve global problems. The success of each of the programs mentioned above depends on the extent to which comprehensive internationalization becomes institutionalized within the culture of the college or university. Without the support of the institution's senior leadership and the belief that study abroad adds value to the teaching, research, and engagement missions of each academic unit within the institution, these programs are unlikely to succeed.

PILLAR 4: FOREIGN LANGUAGE PROFICIENCY

Foreign language proficiency is a requirement for all students and efforts are made to customize language instruction to fulfill the learning objectives of both majors and nonmajors of foreign languages. Among the challenges we face is the lack of adequate foreign language preparation for our students. Enrollment in foreign languages in U.S. universities and colleges has fallen from 16.5% (language course enrollments per 100 total student enrollments) in 1965 to less than 9% today; and between 1965 and 1995 the share of 4-year institutions with language-degree requirements for some students fell from roughly 90% to 67% while in 2001 only 27% of 4-year institutions of higher education required foreign language for all students (Howard, 2007). Most disconcerting is that among the foreign languages taught in U.S. institutions of higher education the percentage of students taught such critical languages as Chinese (3.3%), Russian (1.6%), and Arabic (1.5%) are wholly insufficient when compared to Spanish (52.2%), French (13.1%), German (6%), Italian (5%), and American Sign Language (5%) (Howard, 2007; Welles, 2004).[2]

Foreign language proficiency is a necessary component of global competence. If our institutions are to produce globally competent students, foreign language preparation has to extend beyond students matriculating in our departments of foreign languages and literature. The multicultural character of our societies and the globalizing trend of the workplace require foreign language competency for graduates in the social and natural sciences and in our professional schools. Too often at our institutions the primary responsibility for foreign language preparation falls upon faculty in language and literature departments who have few resources and limited interest to teach foreign languages to students, including both majors and nonmajors. In most research universities promotion and tenure for faculty in language and literature departments are dependent more on publishing articles and books on literature and producing marketable literature Ph.D. students than on teaching foreign language courses to nonmajors. Complicating matters further, foreign language departments have resisted efforts to allocate tenure track positions to language teaching specialists because the national reputation of a language and literature department correlates strongly with research publications in the field of literature rather than the teaching of foreign languages. Moreover, nonmajors in literature and language often find the content of foreign language courses irrelevant to their disciplinary interests and boring. Our challenge is to create a comprehensive and effective plan for foreign language preparation on our campuses that has as a primary objective the attainment of at least conversational proficiency in a second language for all our students. To that end, our campuses should strive to facilitate foreign language training for *all* faculty which, among other things, would spur the creation of new programs for languages-across-the-curriculum (Schneider, 2007). We need to do a better job of drawing on our international students and members of our heritage communities who have received training in the teaching of second languages to assist us in the foreign language preparation of our students. Responsibility for foreign language preparation may need to be placed under a campus-wide entity to ensure a more flexible approach and to allocate resources in a more effective way. Furthermore, institutions of primary, secondary, and tertiary education must work together to improve the foreign language preparation of students, especially in regard to proficiency in critical languages like Mandarin, Japanese, Korean, Arabic, Russian, and Farsi so that when students arrive on our campuses they have a solid footing on the way to advanced foreign language learning. These goals are totally consistent with the aims of the U.S. Department of Education's Title VI programs for international and area studies—programs which are an excellent source of funding for improving foreign language acquisition on our campuses.

There are some notable examples of universities which are piloting efforts to integrate the learning of foreign languages into the campus-wide curriculum. SUNY-Binghamton, the University of Richmond, the University of Mississippi, and the University of Iowa have been leaders in creating Cultures and Languages Across the Curriculum (CLAC) programs. At SUNY-Binghamton student tasks in many social science undergraduate courses include reading and research in a foreign language with the purpose of completing assignments and projects in which a non-U.S. approach and perspective to critical global issues is produced and presented to the class.

PILLAR 5: STUDENT INTERNATIONAL INTERNSHIPS

Opportunities for students' international internships must be made available. We can all agree on the value to students of combining educational and practical work experience while in school. Companies around the world are especially looking for future employees, and internships can serve as an excellent means for both the student and the company to evaluate each other for future employment opportunities. Our colleges and universities can play an instrumental role in increasing international internship opportunities through efforts by senior administrators to include internships as a priority item in discussions with the private sector and in the planning of high-level foreign travel missions. Furthermore, our faculty provides one of the richest resources for international student internships through their collegial networks and contacts with the private and public sectors. Since many of our international and domestic alumni work in multinational corporations and NGOs they are well positioned to open doors for international internship opportunities. Our institutions need to take advantage of this rich resource. Also, whether it is from a civic obligation or self-interests, I have found that locally based globally focused companies are often quite interested in creating international internships for students at neighboring schools. An excellent example of the role that locally based firms play in creating international internship opportunities is the newly established University of Illinois 3+2 program with Tsinghua University in Beijing, China. This program enables students at both universities to spend 3 years at their home university and 2 years at the partner university while earning an undergraduate degree from their home institution and a master's of science at the partner university. Built into the 2 years at the partner university is an internship at a locally based multinational corporation. The corporations find this arrangement quite attractive because they envision it as a vehicle to recruit well-trained graduates who already possess a good knowledge of the company and who they will likely place in their operations within the student's home country.

PILLAR 6: FACULTY SEARCHES ARE INTERNATIONAL

Faculty searches should be international and global experience is preferred. The market today for exemplary scholars is truly worldwide and our best universities seek the highest quality talent regardless of country of origin. All one has to do is to survey the top research journals and the most prestigious university presses to ascertain the extent to which authors represent all corners of the globe. We need to continue to advertise our faculty searches in outlets which are accessible to a worldwide audience and to make sure that we have adequate funding to invite in candidates from abroad. But there is still much more we can achieve in regards to highlighting the preference for hiring faculty whose teaching, discovery, and engagement involve international experiences and perspectives. On one level, a prominent scholar who lacks international experiences and perspectives would appear oxymoronic. Nevertheless, I frequently encounter directors of area studies programs bemoaning the fact that they can't get the history department or the political science department to hire someone with Brazilian or South Asian expertise, that there are no funds to hire a specialist of East Asian literatures, or the college of law has no one on its faculty able to cover European Union legal policy. A great university combines both disciplinary and area studies expertise, for each enriches the other. There are methods to ensure that our institutions continue to hire exceptional faculty who possess international experiences and perspectives. Several universities have committed to establishing international faculty lines for which the various colleges and schools within the university compete. The program is overseen by the campus senior international officer who is responsible for making sure that the overall international needs as dictated by the teaching, discovery, and engagement missions of the university are addressed. Tenure is held within the colleges and schools for these international lines. When the line becomes vacant, it reverts back to the senior international officer who can choose to continue the line in the same college or reopen the competition. Another means to ensure that faculty with international experiences and perspectives are hired which does not require the creation of new faculty lines is a program by which the university offers incentives to departments to include global experiences as a preference in its hiring. Here, for example, a department agrees to include in its ad for a faculty search a preference for an economist with teaching and research expertise relevant to Africa. If the department hires such an individual it receives extra funds to be utilized in the start-up package for the new hire or to use as it sees fit to address other departmental needs. A third avenue to enhance the hiring of faculty with global experiences and perspectives is to make it a priority of the campus capital campaign. Recently, the University of Illinois has created the new position of director of international advancement initiatives. The position oversees the efforts to raise private, corporate, and foundation funds for the university's international initiatives and will report to the university's senior international officer. It is important to note that this position is not envisioned to solicit funds to erect "international silos" within the university but to work closely with the development directors in each college and school to further their internationalization efforts. Having a designated development officer focusing on the international dimension should help in our efforts to recruit faculty with global experiences.

PILLAR 7: FACULTY REWARD AND TENURE INCLUDE RESEARCH AND TEACHING ABROAD

We have discussed above that faculty are more likely to engage in international activities if they perceive direct benefits from their participation. Attracting world-class students with whom to work, collaborating with non-U.S scholars on teaching and research initiatives, adding a comparative/international component to one's teaching, locating new sources of funding through internationally focused RFPs, or gaining access to important non-U.S. primary or secondary research sources are appealing incentives to faculty. Yet, if the faculty's commitment to international activities is not reflected in the annual merit review or tenure and promotion process, faculty are likely to discount the importance of international engagement. All of us have surely heard of stories where junior faculty who have led students on a study abroad program during an academic term were informed that such activities might hurt them when it comes to the tenure and promotion decision or where faculty who spent time abroad teaching on an exchange were chastised for abandoning departmental committee chores. A truly global university will require that the faculty's contributions to the internationalization of teaching, discovery, and engagement are fully appreciated and counted in both annual merit reviews and promotion and tenure decisions. Michigan State University is currently in the process of rethinking the requisites for promotion, tenure, and merit salary reviews by making faculty internationalization contributions one of the primary measures of research, teaching, and service. Our underlying assumption is that internationalization offers added value to the teaching, discovery, and engagement missions of the institutions and that our institutions should not diminish these contributions by discounting them in terms of the departmental incentive structure. To do so would be to create disincentives for an activity that benefits both the faculty member as an individual and the institution as a whole.

PILLAR 8: SENIOR INTERNATIONAL OFFICERS REPORT DIRECTLY TO THE CHIEF ACADEMIC OR EXECUTIVE OFFICER

At our most internationalized institutions the senior international officer (SIO) is charged with the task of maintaining and strengthening the comprehensive internationalization of the campus teaching, discovery, and engagement missions. This task is more likely to be accomplished when the SIO reports directly to those who are chiefly responsible for the university's teaching, discovery, and engagement missions (i.e., the Provost and President or Chancellor). There are unfortunately still too many situations in higher education where the SIO reports indirectly to the chief academic and/or executive officer of the campus. Obviously, the more doors there are between the SIO and the chief academic or executive officers, the greater the expenditure in time and the less likely the SIO's input will be presented as a priority or with the necessary conviction.

Recently, there has been notable upgrading of the SIO position at institutions like Indiana University, the University of Minnesota, and Emory University, and the creation of new positions of vice-president or vice provost at Brown University, Penn State University, Northern Arizona University, and the Ohio State University. Yet, we have also seen several instances lately where SIO's direct reporting lines have been downgraded from the provost or chancellor/president to a dean, an assistant vice president, or vice provost. Often, such downgrading appears to result from personnel changes at the provost or the chancellor level, administrative restructuring, or simply a desire by a provost to reduce the number of direct reports. If direct reporting of the SIO to the chief academic or executive officer is a necessary component for the establishment of the global university, what conditions can bring about that outcome? I propose that the following steps have to be in place:

a. a campus culture in which there is a consensus that internationalization adds value to the teaching, discovery, and engagement missions of the institution;
b. the mission statement and strategic plans of the institution firmly embed internationalization as a priority;

c. faculty and student senates and external advisory boards defend internationalization as an institutional priority;

d. international programs and studies offices are entrepreneurial in attracting extramural funding (successful fundraising seems to provide greater credibility to units);

e. SIOs are able to stay on top of the evolving aspects of the international dimension (e.g., growing importance in areas like export controls, strategic international partnerships, and corporate relationships) so campus units can turn to them to oversee these changes as well as to provide the comprehensive framework in which these changes reside.

PILLAR 9: SENIOR INTERNATIONAL OFFICERS ARE POSITIONED TO INTERACT WITH DEANS AND OTHER COUNCILS AND COMMITTEES

As important as it is for the SIO to report directly to the chief academic or executive officer of the university, it is equally important that he or she sits on the Council of Deans. Our campuses tend to be highly decentralized with much power residing in colleges and schools. The SIO sitting on the Council of Deans reflects the significance given to the international mission but also facilitates the critical collaboration required for the comprehensive internationalization of the academic goals of each college and school within the university. The SIO through his or her active cooperation with the members of the Council of Deans can be instrumental in furthering both the internationalization within each college or school and of a cross-fertilized internationalization, that is, international interdisciplinary collaborations across several colleges. It is paramount that the SIO becomes actively engaged in working groups and committees where much of the actual work of the Council of Deans is accomplished.

An international advisory council (IAC) chaired by the SIO and including each college's or school's most senior administrator overseeing the unit's international portfolio can serve as a very useful forum for developing and vetting proposals for consideration by the Council of Deans, enhancing the chances that those proposals will receive a prompt and favorable hearing. In addition to sitting on the Council of Deans and the International Advisory Council, the SIO should convene at regular intervals an external advisory board. An external advisory board comprised of influential individuals from the private and public sectors as well as academics not associated with the institution can perform a worthwhile role in the comprehensive internationalization of the university. During my years at the University of Pittsburgh I found our international studies' external advisory board a superb vehicle in providing a unique perspective on what employers seek in terms of our graduates' international skills, a powerful voice promoting internationalization to the university's senior administration, and a valuable conduit to gift prospects.

PILLAR 10: BARRIERS TO THE RECRUITMENT OF INTERNATIONAL STUDENTS ARE ELIMINATED

Barriers must be removed that make the recruitment of international students difficult or impossible and international students must be encouraged and given the opportunity to engage actively in the internationalization of the campus and community.

No institution of higher education can aspire to become truly global without an active strategy to recruit, retain, and integrate the highest quality international students. Our colleges and universities have for nearly a century attracted the best and the brightest from across the globe and have provided these individuals with a world-class education. Upon graduation many of these students have installed themselves in the United States and built exceptionally successful careers while at the same time they have, through their accomplishments, contributed to the improvement of the United States and the world. Others have returned to their home countries where they have made lasting impacts on their societies.

Currently the United States receives more than 500,000 international students a year—a number that has not grown substantially since the fateful events of September 11, 2001. Gaining entry to our colleges and universities remains a priority for students around the world for they perceive that a degree from a top-flight U.S. institution of higher education will not only equip them with a first rate education, but will likely position them favorably for the marketplace whether that be in the United States or elsewhere. Few will disagree that one of America's greatest exports is its system of higher education. But the long view of history teaches that those who hold a preeminent position one day are likely to be replaced by others in the future. For instance, between 1880 and 1920 the brightest students and scholars in the fields of medicine and science from the United States and other countries flocked to Germany to work in the great scientific labs and receive a rigorous education. By the 1930s that was no longer the case. U.S. higher education is now facing rather stiff competition for the best students by virtue of several factors including the emergence of excellent research institutes and universities outside of the United States particularly in East and Southeast Asia, a perception of heightened xenophobic attitudes within the United States, and the erection of immigration obstacles in the wake of 9/11. More specifically regarding this last point, the current quota on H-1B visas of 65,000 is far too small and is quickly reached, hindering our need for highly skilled researchers and professionals while the wait for green cards is typically more than 5 years. Individuals contemplating their future educational plans are likely to act in a rational fashion and weigh the costs and benefits associated with selecting an institution of higher education in which to pursue their studies. While the incentive to earn a degree from a U.S. university is likely to remain quite high due to the academic quality of the degree program, the increase in the disincentives like immigration hassles, affordability, and the perception of a lack of hospitality may alter the balance against applying to and accepting admittance from U.S. colleges and universities in the future.

For obvious reasons much attention vis-à-vis international students has focused on barriers to recruitment. Often receiving scant attention are the barriers to retention. Are our international students completing degrees in a timely fashion? If not, why? Are we doing enough to integrate our international students into the life of our campuses and communities? Are we underutilizing the potential that our international students have to help us internalize our campuses? Far too often international students self-segregate and interact rarely with domestic students. Think for a moment how helpful international students can be to inform other students about non-U.S. cultures or to provide new or different perspectives on issues especially in classroom discussions. Valuable interactions with international students on campus, whether in the classroom or dorm, may be the only exposure many of our domestic students will receive during their college years. Moreover, we are failing to take advantage of the value of international students in terms of internationalizing our neighboring communities. Many of our colleges and universities reside in suburban and rural areas typically lacking exposure to diversity. What if we were to create ambassador or (reverse) Peace Corps programs where admitted international students who met certain requisites could receive additional financial assistance for serving as international ambassadors to our surrounding communities including regular visits to K-12 classrooms? A program of this kind has distinctly great promise to educate our communities about cultures like those in the Middle East, about which much ignorance in the U.S prevails.[3]

Our campuses must develop a campus-wide strategy to eliminate the "ghettoization" of our international students by establishing international or intercultural living and learning communities and by sponsoring regular social and athletic opportunities bringing together international and domestic students. To achieve this end will require a coordinated effort involving the offices of international students and scholars, study abroad, and student affairs. I cannot think of any more appealing setting than a social or athletic event to foster dialogue across linguistic and cultural boundaries. At the University of Illinois the Office of International Students and Scholar Services works closely with the Vice Chancellor's Office of Student Affairs to organize twice-yearly World Cup indoor soccer tournaments where international students along with domestic students who have studied abroad or plan to study abroad form country teams. Teams march into the event with their country flags and the games provide opportunities for international and domestic students to compete as well as to interact with one another. The World Cup events have grown in popularity and receive significant news coverage on the campus and in the community.

PILLAR 11: AMERICAN IMMIGRANT AND HERITAGE COMMUNITIES ARE DRAWN UPON

American immigrant and heritage communities have their rich expertise and experiences to contribute to the institution's learning, discovery, and engagement missions.

The rich mosaic of American society provides us with a natural resource that our institutions of higher education often overlook. The many immigrant or heritage communities in our backyards offer a great resource to our schools in assisting our internationalization efforts. The perspectives of immigrants vis-à-vis their country of origin, the United States, and global processes are in many ways unique and would certainly enrich the classroom learning experiences of our students. In many parts of the United States and on many campuses I have observed the positive role that the Muslim immigrant and heritage community has performed in breaking down the stereotypes many non-Muslims have about Islam. A global university will eagerly utilize the valuable resource of heritage and immigrant communities and sponsor lecture series and conferences that draw upon the experiences and insights of these communities. Most importantly, immigrant communities can play a significant part in our desire to achieve foreign language proficiency for *all* students. To achieve foreign language proficiency for all our students—and there is no acceptable reason why that shouldn't be the case—we will need to vastly increase the number of foreign language instructors serving our campuses. Whether as aides to our foreign language instructors or instructors themselves, immigrants with the requisite language and teaching skills offer a logical and cost-effective means to fulfill our staffing needs. Moreover, in our desire to customize foreign language teaching to address the demand for second language acquisition by our students in the professional schools and science, we may find that many of our immigrants through their own professional backgrounds possess these particular language qualifications.

Our immigrant communities are also likely to contribute to our development efforts in terms of networking as well as gifts. In my years as a senior international officer I have found immigrant communities to be among the most receptive audiences to appeals to support campus international initiatives such as study abroad scholarships, international student fellowships, and area studies library collections.

PILLAR 12: GLOBAL PARTNERSHIPS AS AN INSTITUTIONAL PRIORITY

The last pillar of a global university and the one that has, with the possible exception of study abroad, received the greatest attention during the past few years are global partnerships as an institutional priority. The common wisdom is that in today's world if your institution is not engaged in cross-border education or does not have academic partnerships with foreign schools than your school is not global. The race among U.S. colleges and universities to set up partnerships (e.g., offshore campuses, joint or dual degree programs) with foreign counterparts is reminiscent of the California gold rush of 1849. Much like in 1849 I fear that this new gold rush has been undertaken without adequate strategic thinking about the expected benefits and risks and how these global partnerships contribute to the teaching, discovery, and engagement missions of the university. There is no question that global institutional partnerships constitute a major building block of the global university for they can buttress and enrich the three principal missions of a university. However, frequently valuable resources are expended on establishing a partnership with a foreign institution without the partners sitting down in advance and asking what does each expect to gain from the partnerships and how much does each partner expect to contribute. For the partnership to have a realistic chance of succeeding it requires that each side sees it as adding value.

What objectives should a university pursue in establishing global partnerships?[4] It makes little sense for our universities to attempt to set up institutional partnerships in as many countries as possible. It is much better to have a few substantial partnerships than to have many superficial ones. When deciding upon potential partners think of how that partner's research and teaching strengths could complement those of your institution. For instance, the University of Illinois and the University of Sao Paulo are planning a major collaboration in the study of biofuels alternatives and their social and economic implications. Illinois scholars are leaders in studying how to use corn crop residues, switch-grass, and *Miscanthus* in the production of biofuels while Sao Paulo scientists are prominent in the study of producing ethanol from sugar cane. Scholars at both Illinois and Sao Paulo believe that through their collaboration each will learn more about the field of bioenergy as well as develop policies to deal with the global social and economic implications of the adoption of biofuel alternatives. Faculty and administrators at both universities believe that by working together rather than alone the likelihood of obtaining funding for the research from their respective state governments and from the private sector is much higher.

Several U.S. universities are capitalizing on their membership in international consortia to establish multidimensional bilateral and multilateral relationships with like institutions. Two such consortia are Universitas 21 and the Worldwide Universities Network (WUN). Universitas 21 includes the University of Virginia which has used the network to develop exchange relationships and cohosted conferences with partners including the National University of Singapore, Hong Kong University, Waseda University, and the University of Melbourne. The WUN involving the University of Washington, Penn State, the University of Wisconsin-Madison, the University of California-San Diego and the University of Illinois at Urbana-Champaign on the U.S. side with several European and Asian universities has sponsored numerous research collaborations among the members and international conferences on international education. Members of the WUN each contribute $60,000 a year for the purposes of creating a pool of funds to be allocated on a competitive basis to fund international and interdisciplinary research initiatives involving WUN partners.

Once you have constituted a viable institutional partnership think of ways your institution can build upon the initial relationship both vertically and horizontally. Again, the primary motivation for expansion has to be based on mutual self-interests. A relationship initiated from complementary faculty research interests in chemical engineering can expand to include team-taught courses in chemical engineering and the development of a professional dual degree master's as well as become a good starting point to explore the possibilities of teaching and research collaborations in other fields, exchange of faculty and students, recruitment of international students, development of an alumni chapter, fundraising initiatives, a portal for study abroad programs for that world region, and dual or joint degrees. The essential point is to see how other institutional objectives might be fulfilled by expanding upon the inaugural relationship.

In thinking about global partnerships we are obliged to consider the tension between the desire of universities in the wealthiest countries to recruit the best and brightest from abroad and the realization that for the developing countries, where many of these students originate, the education of these students abroad is likely to reinforce a brain drain. We should allow partnerships where degree seeking, or even nondegree seeking international students have opportunities to return home and participate in capacity building in their home country. Dual or joint degree programs such as the University of Illinois's 3+2 specifying that students will return home upon completion of degree requirements and incorporating an internship with an NGO or a multinational company may provide a useful model for combining academic training and job experience that results in the placement of international students in attractive positions in their home countries.

Whether building partnerships with institutions in developed or less developed countries, the reality is that viable and sustainable partnerships typically evolve from collaborations where both partners believe that they are benefiting from the relationship. Helping institutions and governments in Africa to build their own science and technology programs offers the promise that such capacity may better equip them to solve the pressing problems in their societies—this type of collaboration is likely to be quite appealing to institutions in both developed and developing countries. The University of Pennsylvania's "Penn in Botswana" initiative is noteworthy. Each year Penn sends faculty, residents, and medical students to Botswana to work with their African counterparts in the care in public hospitals. For its efforts, particularly in combating and preventing HIV/AIDS, the Penn program has received funding from the Merck and Gates Foundations as well as from the President's Emergency Plan for AIDS Relief. In addition to the invaluable international experiences and knowledge that students, scholars, and staff at universities in the developed world will gain from such participation let us not forget that finding solutions to pressing problems in the developing world clearly benefits us all.

CONCLUSION

In conclusion, it has become eminently clear that the flattening of the globe and the events of 9/11 have altered the world in which we live. Achieving global competence at our institutions is not only desirable but a *necessity* if we are to remain competitive and adapt to our changing environment. The building blocks (students, faculty, staff, administrators, alumni, surrounding community, foreign universities, private and public sectors, etc.) for the global university are already within reach. Yet, if we are able to meld these blocks together, the collaboration will allow us to achieve true global competence by comprehensively internationalizing the teaching, discovery, and engagement missions of higher education. As is the case with all great edifices, the global university will not arise overnight. But by erecting the 12 pillars detailed in the global university blueprint, its construction is certain to be accelerated.

NOTES

1. Recent notable exceptions are McCarthy (2007), NASULGC (2004), Olson, Green, and Hill (2005).
2. I agree with many that Spanish should be considered a critical language for Americans given its widespread use within the United States and its predominance within the Western Hemisphere.
3. The concept of a "reverse" Peace Corps was initially brought to my attention by Jack Van de Water.
4. For a superb checklist of the important questions to consider when thinking about international institutional partnerships, see Green, Eckel, and Luu (2007, pp. 23–25).

REFERENCES

Caldwell, A. (Ed.). (2004). *Critical thinking in the sociology classroom.* Washington, DC: The American Sociological Association.

Committee for Economic Development. (2006). *Education for global leadership: The importance of international studies and foreign language education for U.S. economic and national security.* Washington, DC: Committee for Economic Development.

Friedman, T. L. (2005). *The world is flat: A brief history of the twenty-first century.* New York: Farrar, Straus & Giroux.

Green, M., Eckel, P., & Luu, D. (2007). *Venturing abroad: Delivering U.S. degrees through overseas branch campuses and programs.* Washington, DC: American Council on Education.

Howard, J. (2007, November 23). Enrollments in foreign-language courses continue to rise, MLA survey finds. *The Chronicle of Higher Education, 54*(13), A13.

McCarthy, J. (2007). A roadmap for creating the global campus. *The Chronicle of Higher Education, 53*(44), B12.

National Association of State Universities and Land Grant Colleges (NASULGC). (2004). *A call to leadership: The presidential role in internationalizing the university.* Washington, DC: Author.

Olson, C. L., Green, M., & Hill, B. (2005). *Building a strategic framework for comprehensive internationalization.* Washington, DC: American Council on Education (ACE).

Schneider, A. (2007). *Internationalizing teacher education: What can be done?* Unpublished paper.

Welles, E. B. (2004, Winter-Spring). Foreign language enrollments in United States institutions of higher education, Fall 2002. *ADFL Bulletin, 35*(2–3), 7–24.

Chapter 16

Turning Our Back on the World

Study Abroad and the Purpose of U.S. Higher Education

Riall W. Nolan

Purdue University

INTRODUCTION

Understanding something about how the rest of the world lives ought to be the mark of an educated person, but for all too many U.S. university students, it is not. Why this matters, why we're not giving students what they need, and what might be done about this, are the subjects of this chapter.

Study abroad, which is what I want to focus on here, is a blanket term covering a wide variety of international education experiences.[1] All of them can and should teach American students a basic but very important truth: that there are people beyond the shoreline who think just as well as they do, but who think somewhat differently.

This is not as simple a concept as it might appear at first glance. For some people, the encounter with another culture can be transformative, in both the short and the long term. If you can grasp the fact that people elsewhere can live productive, happy, and fulfilled lives on terms other than your own, you can also begin to imagine ways to live your own life somewhat differently. And, to paraphrase Aldous Huxley, once you get those doors of perception open, it's hard to shut them again.

I went to Senegal with the Peace Corps in 1965, and as a result of my time there, I began a career in international development and international education. In my work as an educator and international development specialist, I've tried to give that "out-of-culture" experience to as many students as I can, by enabling them to study abroad. The goal of getting more American students to go overseas is a challenging one, however, and I've spent the last 20 years trying to find ways to do it better. Whenever I get discouraged, I think of something that happened some years before 9/11, at one of my former universities.

I strolled out of my office one spring day to see a line of students across the quad, silently holding placards. As I looked at them, I realized that they were Muslim students. The placards said things like "Israel out of the West Bank," and "Stop Israeli settlements in Palestine." Interesting, I thought, a demonstration. We haven't had a demonstration on campus in years.

"What's going on? What are they doing?" The question came from beside me, and I turned to see two women looking across at the demonstrators. They were dressed in the standard undergraduate female uniform for our campus: running shoes, shorts, sorority sweatshirts, backpacks, and ball caps with their ponytails pulled through the back. One was White, one was African American.

"Well," I said, "they look like Muslim students, and they're protesting Israeli policy toward Palestine."

"But why are they doing it here? I mean, it's got nothing to do with us, right?"

Ah, a learning moment, I thought. "Not exactly," I said. "Don't forget, America's been a big supporter of Israel for quite a few years."

Silence. Then one of them said, "Oh, right, sure. We've gotta hang with Israel, 'cause that's who we get the gas from."

Whenever I need a reason to believe, I think of this story. My two young student friends were going to graduate, have families, vote, and pay taxes. And as far as I could tell, they would do all of these things knowing far less than they should about the world of which they are a part.

The cross-cultural experience that study abroad represents isn't just about individual transformation, however. In a broader and more significant sense, it's also about building a society capable of responding to the challenges of this century. And one of the most important of these challenges, as we know, is about learning to work with differently minded others across the globe to create positive and sustainable responses to the issues and opportunities we all face.

So in this chapter, I want to argue for looking at study abroad as a national educational strategy, and ask three key questions: What is it really good for? Why aren't more of our students doing it? And how can we change this?

WHAT IS STUDY ABROAD FOR?

The role and importance of study abroad in the education of our citizens needs to be seen against the backdrop of changes in the world we inhabit. Tellingly, most of the senior faculty and administrators in our universities grew up at a time when U.S. knowledge and power reigned supreme. The Second World War had left the economies of Europe in ruins, and we were the only economy capable of producing many of the things the world needed to buy. You bought American, you paid in dollars, and you spoke English while you were doing it. From everywhere on earth people came to us—for goods and services, for advice, and most of all, for education. It was at this time—the 40s, 50s, and early 60s—that our university system developed into what we have today. And although in many ways we dominated the globe, most of the rest of the world seemed very far away.

Today, we live in a vastly different world. Nowhere on earth is truly remote. We can go everywhere, and in turn, everywhere can come to us. Difference has moved in next door, and it's here to stay. Almost all of us now work for or with organizations with international connections. We have people from other countries as our bosses, as our employees, as our customers, and most importantly, as our competitors.[2]

On many of our most pressing issues—AIDS, terrorism, and global warming, to name but three—there is no longer a clear dividing line between "foreign" and "domestic," in terms of either the problem or the needed solutions. But we still know far less about the rest of the world than we should. Ahmad Sadri says, "Never before have so many lived so closely to so many of whom they know so little" (1994, p.169).

And we cannot assume that others in the world necessarily share our view of things. The philosopher Reinhold Niebuhr reminded us:

> The same [American] strength which has extended our power beyond a continent has also... brought us into a vast web of history in which other wills, running in oblique or contrasting directions to our own, inevitably hinder or contradict what we most fervently desire. We cannot simply have our way, not even when we believe our way to have the "happiness of mankind" as its promise. (cited in Kaplan 1997, p. 60)

To live—and succeed—in the world as it is today, we need to develop new ways of thinking and acting. And to do this, we need to develop new ways of learning.

It's no longer enough for our students to "know the material." They need to know *what to do* with the material in a changing, diverse, and often contradictory global environment. Today we speak of giving students "T-shaped qualifications," where disciplinary knowledge is integrated with an equally important understanding of how to apply that knowledge. This, in essence, means putting a *context* around the *content* of a particular knowledge area.

The shorthand term for this is *global competence*. The global competencies necessary for application are usually described in terms of knowledge of global events and affairs, attitudes of tolerance, curiosity and openness, and skill at learning and working across cultures. The definitive work on global competence was done by Lambert (1994), and global competence is a frequently discussed topic in international education circles.[3]

You can be a heck of an engineer, for example, but do you know how to work with the Germans, the Japanese, or the Brazilians to develop the next generation of fuel-efficient vehicles? You might be a whiz at growing corn or soybeans, but can you show the people in Africa how to do that? Individuals who have acquired this ability will have an enormous advantage in the coming years. They will not only be better at dealing with events and situations—they will be in a better position to shape and direct them from the outset.

In a sense, developing global competence is nothing more—or less—than adding an applied dimension to our teaching and learning, one which is global in scope. It is relatively easy to "teach the material" but much harder to help students understand the world in which they will be

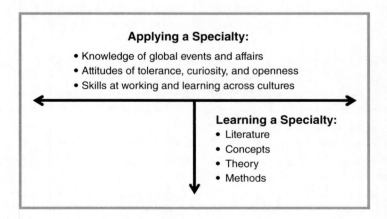

Applying a Specialty:
- Knowledge of global events and affairs
- Attitudes of tolerance, curiosity, and openness
- Skills at working and learning across cultures

Learning a Specialty:
- Literature
- Concepts
- Theory
- Methods

Figure 16.1 *T-Shaped Qualifications*

expected to use that material. Donald Schön (1985, 1987) would term this an instance of *reflective practice*: a negotiation between the practitioner and the world.

Schön has described the topography of practice as a wet and messy swamp, with a dry knoll rising out of it. On the dry ground, high above everything else, problems are solved in a relatively clean and smooth fashion, using research-based theory and technique. The problems on the high knoll tend to be technically interesting but relatively unimportant to humanity at large.

Down in the swamp, however, the problems are disordered, messy, and confusing, and usually resist purely technical solutions. But this is where the most important human issues lie, the ones which can't be solved by technique and theory alone, but through a combination of professional artistry and direct engagement with the issues. The scope and significance of the issues in the swamp are hardly ever clear at the outset, and few ready-made solutions are available. The stake-holders in such situations have differing and often competing interests, values, and perspectives.

In such situations, both the problems and solutions to the problems must be constructed; that is, built up through interaction and negotiation between the practitioner and the situation. Even where ends can be stated succinctly (e.g. *health, well-being, security,* or *profit*), the terms themselves may conceal important differences in meaning and interpretation. Each situation, in a sense, becomes a special one, and a fresh test of the practitioner's ability to frame and deal with the particularities of the case at hand.[4] We are training far too many of our students to sit on the knoll, when we really need to be training them for work in the swamp.

Developing this kind of global competence in our students matters tremendously, because the world's diversity isn't trivial. We may be more globally connected than ever before, and our issues may be global ones, but not everyone sees these issues in the same way. Helping our students learn to work together with people of different backgrounds to solve global problems is arguably our main educational challenge in the United States today. And in tomorrow's world, our economic or military power will be far less useful to us than our understanding. Indeed, most of our most pressing issues are what might be termed "adaptive problems" for which there will never be simple, fixed, and technically orthodox solutions. It will be through dialogue with differently minded others that we will make progress.

All of this has been clear to thoughtful people in academia for some time. And one would think that our institutions of higher education would be already focused on ensuring that their graduates are global in their outlook and capabilities. But with a few notable exceptions, they are not. As a result, many students graduate with no real idea of how the rest of the world lives or thinks. Worse, many of them have little curiosity about these different modes of life, except insofar as they interfere with what we consider our inalienable rights to life, liberty, and cheap gasoline. Why is this? Why aren't we doing better?

The number of U.S. students studying abroad is growing, but it is not growing very fast. *Open Doors*, the yearly report from the New York-based Institute of International Education (IIE), tracks the number of students moving in and out of the United States. Their 2007 report (the latest available as of this writing) showed that 223,534 U.S. students went abroad in 2005–2006 (the latest year for which figures are available). This was an increase of 8.5% over the previous year, an increase of 150% since 1995–1996, and an increase of 305% since 1985–1986 (Bhandari & Chow, 2007, p. 16).

For most of these students, Europe is their preferred destination. The UK, Italy, Spain, and France comprised (in that order) the top four, followed by Australia. Students in the social sciences, business, and the humanities made up over 50% of the total number studying abroad.

Engineering, health sciences, and agriculture were among the disciplines sending the fewest students overseas. Only 3.5% of study abroad students are African American, up from 3% in the late 1990s. Over 65% of study abroad students are women, a percentage that has held constant for a decade (Bhandari & Chow, 2007, p. 16).

So although the glass is half full, as we like to say, it is also very clearly half empty. Today, less than 2% of our students study abroad. Indeed, we have barely more students studying abroad than we do troops in Afghanistan and Iraq, and these students do not represent our student body as a whole. Far more women than men study overseas,[5] not many engineering students go abroad, and not many minority students.

And most of the students who do go abroad come from a very small number of universities. John Sunnygard, an international education consultant, notes that just 76 institutions in the United States sent at least half their graduates abroad, while 1,700 of them sent fewer than 10 students a year (Fischer, 2008a). The American Council on Education's (2008b) report on internationalization, noting that most U.S. institutions do not have a full-time person in charge of international education, also pointed out that in 2005, 27% of U.S. institutions sent no students abroad at all. The American Council on Education also found that the percentage of U.S. institutions which require an international or global course dropped from 41% in 2001 to 37% in 2006. Less than 20% of our institutions have a foreign-language requirement.[6]

So although some of the aggregate numbers are indeed rising, it is clear that study abroad remains marginal to the life of most universities, and as a consequence, to most of their students. If you ask on almost any U.S. campus why this is, you will get a remarkably consistent set of answers from most of the faculty. Students today, they will say, have neither the time nor the money to go overseas. Most of them aren't that interested in leaving home, and some of them are actually afraid to go overseas. Too many study abroad programs, they'll often add, are irrelevant, of low academic quality, or both. And if these faculty are from STEM disciplines, they may also mention—sometimes with pride—that there is no room for extras in their tightly packed, rigorous curriculum.

Those responses are plausible perhaps, but they are not strictly true. It is a fact, of course, that on most of our campuses, study abroad costs more, and it is also a fact that many students are heavily indebted and strapped for cash. It's also true that a significant number of our students have obligations, such as families and jobs that preclude overseas sojourns.

It may also be the case that for some of our students, there's anxiety or lack of interest. This would hardly be surprising. Students come to the university, for the most part, knowing little about other parts of the world and unable to speak a foreign language. Media coverage of international events, spotty at best, tends to focus on danger, disaster, and unusual happenings. As Ambrose Bierce once noted, war is how God teaches Americans about geography.

We're not, by and large, very interested in learning about the rest of the world. And the reason for that, I think, is rather simple. We don't learn, because we don't feel that we have to learn. A few years ago, Lewis Lapham (1996) said this about our political establishment, and it probably applies to American society in general:

> This [lack of interest in learning] is fairly common among people born to the assumptions of wealth and rank. They can afford to believe what they choose to believe, and they seldom find it necessary to revise the tests of the preferred reality. (p. 66)

But the claim that students are not interested in going overseas is demonstrably false. In 2000, for example the American Council on Education reported that nearly 50% of the students they polled entering college wanted to study abroad (ACE, 2000). And this desire is increasing. Fifty-five percent of the students polled in their latest survey (from 2007) say they are "certain or fairly certain" they will participate in study abroad, and another 26% have a "strong desire" to do so (ACE, 2008a, p. 1).

The authors of the ACE report comment:

> These data again raise the question considered in the 2000 report: Will students' desires for international learning experiences be satisfied, or will large numbers of students make choices, face barriers, or have concerns that prevent them from participating in study abroad and other international learning experiences once in college? (p. 2)

So to reframe our question: if over 50% of first-years say they'd like to go overseas, why do less than 2% of them actually wind up there?

The explanation for this dramatic fall-off lies in what happens to our students once they begin their studies. Put plainly, students in most of our universities enter a learning environment in which international study is neither valued nor encouraged. And although socialization at any university is accomplished through a variety of channels, the most influential element in this process is the faculty.

It is both an article of faith and a recognized fact in U.S. higher education that faculty are the lifeblood of the university. They are its energy, its creativity, and its imagination. But today they are also, I fear, the biggest obstacle to needed change. I will argue, therefore, that it is faculty attitudes toward overseas study, by and large, which discourage student participation.

Put plainly, students don't study abroad because their professors don't encourage them to do so. And their professors don't encourage them because they themselves don't consider the experience academically important, respectable, or valuable.

At most U.S. universities the faculty have control over two key things: who their colleagues are, and what is in the curriculum. And at almost all universities, faculty are not recruited for their international interests or abilities. They are recruited for their accomplishments in, or potential for, research, teaching, and publication. Once recruited, they are set on a tenure track which hardly ever recognizes international activity as important. The ACE report on "Mapping Internationalization on US Campuses" (2008b) reports that fewer than 10% of our colleges have guidelines for taking international activity or experience into account for tenure (ACE, 2008b; see also Fischer, 2008b).

So we begin, by and large, with a faculty that was not selected for either its interest or experience in matters international. And this faculty indifference is having serious consequences for our efforts to internationalize education.

Let me illustrate what I'm talking about with another true story. Several years ago, we were searching for a new dean of engineering. As is usual, candidates would come to campus and make presentations in open forums. My associate dean and I attended one forum in a large amphitheater. There were several hundred people in attendance, most of them engineering faculty.

The candidate came to the podium, cleared his throat, and said: "I want to talk to you today about educating our students to be global engineers. How many of you have heard of the Bologna Agreement?" Half a dozen individuals raised their hands. Two of them were my associate dean and myself.

The associate dean leaned over to me. "We're doomed," he whispered.

How different, I wondered later, were these faculty members from the two female under-graduates I began this chapter with?

We then add to this a tenuring system which provides real disincentives for international work. Although many younger faculty might be curious about what it would be like to lead a class overseas, they will almost certainly be warned—by their dean, by their department head, and by their colleagues—to avoid getting involved in anything other than the safe, predictable, tried and true activities which lead to promotion and tenure.[7]

It's not surprising, therefore, to find that 7 or 8 years later, relatively few faculty are interested in extending themselves globally. By this time, they have built a reputation in a particular field, they have a research program, publications being readied, grant proposals in the works. In other words, they now have a real career.

And we must acknowledge, after all, that there are some real risks for faculty in going overseas. Senior faculty have made their reputations on the basis of being expert in something. They owe their promotion and tenure to this expertise, and they are valued within their discipline for this.

Faculty suspect, and rightly so, that once they are overseas, they may no longer be so expert; no longer the main authority or gatekeeper. Students overseas are now likely to encounter raw reality instead of carefully bounded theory and case material. Whatever else international educa-tion is, it is about the applied aspects of one's discipline—about how the concepts discussed in the classroom work themselves out on the ground.

Overseas, faculty know or at least suspect that they will lose a measure of control over the learning environment. And while some are comfortable with this, many are not, and will prefer to remain in settings where they have more influence over their students, the material, and the learning which occurs.[8]

Not all faculty are indifferent to international matters, of course. For the language and lit-erature crowd, being international is their stock in trade. They travel overseas frequently, and they expect their students to do likewise. If students are going to be encouraged to explore other cultural worlds, it is these members of the faculty who will very likely encourage them.

The problem here is that in an odd way, such faculty may know too much. Most students, initially at least, do not learn about other cultural worlds directly; they learn a version of these worlds from their faculty mentors, who act as guides, gatekeepers, and interpreters. But a gate-keeper, let's remember, can close doors as well as open them.

Steeped in the minutiae of language, culture, and literature, some of these faculty have an unfortunate tendency to mystify their subject. By rendering another culture mysterious and com-plex, they remain guardians of the gates, so to speak.[9] In this way, cultural knowledge becomes an end in itself, rather than a means to an end. In practical terms, such faculty are apt to advise a student interested in learning about, say, the French, to (1) major in French; and (2) spend at least a year in France. Anything less than immersion, they will often maintain, is mere academic tourism. And by insisting on an all-or-nothing approach, they virtually guarantee the exclusion of most students.

Other faculty members, not necessarily opposed to study abroad, will nevertheless play the role of *advocatus diaboli* and require proof that study abroad "works" before they will "buy in." It is of course perfectly appropriate to ask questions about a specific program, and we have assessment instruments available for this on most of our campuses. But it is the value-added of international experience itself that is often being questioned, and this, I would argue, is fundamentally a waste of time. We have plenty of evidence that international experience is transformative, but we may never fully be able to "prove" why this is so.

Faculty are not the only culprits, of course. Equally to blame for our lack of attention to international education are the administrators in our universities—the deans, department heads, provosts, and presidents whose job it is to lead the enterprise.

At the level of upper administration, despite the rhetoric, there has been a generalized failure of leadership. The result is that international education is underresourced in general, and at most universities, not supported by policies that matter. Our deans, provosts, and presidents, with few exceptions, have declined to challenge the academic units they are responsible for to become more international.

If you ask them (and I do, every chance I get) why they don't push, you will once again get a consistent set of answers, which boil down to a reluctance to ask the faculty to do anything that they aren't already clearly in favor of. "It's easier," one university president explained to me, "to ride a horse in the direction it's already going."

Thus, changing policies for promotion and tenure to acknowledge international activity is, in the view of most upper administrators, something that should be left to the faculty. How exactly the faculty will make these changes is usually not explained.

If you ask faculty the same question, you also get an interesting similarity in response. It's the upper administration, they say, who really sets the course here. We're just trying to do what we think they want us to do. It would be foolish of us to change tenure and promotion policies in the absence of clear supportive signals from the higher-ups.

Interestingly, both groups are right. Faculty and administration at our universities are involved in an immensely complex set of relationships, the form, content, and dynamic of which differs significantly from one campus to another, but which is known generally under the rubric of "shared governance." When it works well, shared governance promotes creativity and synergy, but on all too many campuses, it simply means that each group can effectively prevent the other from getting what it wants.

And since the choreography of shared governance is delicate, neither side has much of an interest in altering the balance of forces. "If it ain't broke, don't fix it," could be the motto here.

In this situation, administrators, who theoretically control resources and therefore have a large say in what the rules are, have every reason not to irritate the faculty. They seek instead to enable faculty to do the creative work that they do, whether it be teaching, writing, or research. Faculty, in turn, have every reason to continue as before: it's the safe, established, secure way to build a career and a reputation, and to achieve a measure of security and protection that few other wage-earners in the world enjoy. And in the process, they will tend to hire, promote, and tenure people who very much resemble themselves.

The outlook is far from bleak, however, and change is on the way. Whatever we think caused either September 11 or the U.S. invasion of Iraq, it clearly wasn't a surfeit of cross-cultural understanding. Most people today understand, at some level, that we need to know more about who our new neighbors are in the global village.

But we also need to understand—and admit—that our universities aren't getting the job done. Indeed, in many of our institutions, we've somehow managed to create an environment in which the connections are largely missing between some of our best minds and some of the world's most pressing problems. So although change is happening, it is happening far too slowly.

Today, higher education in the United States is at a crossroads: the choices we make as educators in the next 10 years will determine, in large part, whether our educational system will thrive and continue to be a model for the rest of the world, or whether it will decline, fragment, and become increasingly irrelevant to the emerging needs of the new century.

WHAT DO WE NEED TO DO TO CHANGE?

The demand for more and better international education is clearly there, and it comes from students, from parents, and from employers. To an increasing extent, university administrations themselves have sensed that it's good to be "global," in very much the same way that it's good to be "green." We can expect, then, that more and more of our institutions will make some attempt, at least, to reorient what their faculty will do.

How they choose to do this will be very important. Except in very broad and general terms, there's no such thing as an overall "academic culture" in America.[10] Instead, there are academic *cultures*—many of them—and they vary not just from one institution to another, but within institutions, and across academic units. Any decision to "internationalize" must be made with a very clear sense of the specific institutional culture(s) concerned. To paraphrase the first line of Tolstoy's *Anna Karenina*, all successfully internationalized universities will be international in their own special way.

In like manner, however, we can also predict that universities which fail to internationalize will fail for a similar set of reasons. The Russian colleagues I worked with in the 1990s told me a fictitious anecdote which I think speaks to our present situation.

In the story, Stalin, Khrushchev, and Brezhnev are on a train, moving through the remote *taiga* forest in the dead of winter. Suddenly the train breaks down and stops. Stalin is the first to speak.

"Bring me the train engineer," he growled, unsnapping the holster on his pistol. "If he can't get us moving at once, I'll shoot the worthless dog. I'll shoot them all, one by one, until I find someone who can do the job."

"No, comrade." Khrushchev spoke in a soothing tone. "Let *me* try. Bring me the engineer, and I'll lecture him on the need to make every sacrifice for the good of the motherland. He'll be inspired, and will soon get the train going."

Both of them then turned to Brezhnev. "You've said nothing, comrade," they said. "What is *your* idea?"

Brezhnev thought for a moment. "Why don't we just pull the curtains," he said at last, "and pretend the train is moving?"

Few U.S. universities are going to try to internationalize at the point of a gun, so to speak. Few of them are set up for that kind of top-down management. And although some of our universities today have chosen to pretend, as it were, that the train is moving, this smoke-and-mirrors strategy won't work for very long.

Most universities at the moment, in fact, are trying Khrushchev's approach of talking the faculty into it, one professor at a time. This is effective, but only at the margins. It takes an inordinate amount of time and energy to internationalize this way, it is very piecemeal, and there is no guarantee that the faculty will stay bought, so to speak. Once they retire, lose interest, take a new job, or land a new grant, one may find that the program they championed simply disappears, like footprints on the beach.

As the pressures for internationalization mount, there is a fourth alternative that needs to be mentioned: outsourcing. This is already done by many institutions, to some extent at least, when they send their students on programs run by other universities, or by third-party providers. And this is well and good. Universities cannot be everywhere, and cannot teach everything, and it makes perfect sense to deal with specialized groups offering specialized programs. It makes even more sense if your institution has relatively low numbers of students wishing to go to a particular place, or to study a particular subject. By merging your students into a larger group from other institutions, everyone benefits, and everyone gets to go.

But some universities, unwilling to burden their faculty with the petty details of programming, and looking to wholesale the entire international education operation, will choose to hand most or all of its international education over to others, for a fee which will then be passed on to students. This already happens on some campuses, but I would predict, as the demand for international education continues to grow, that it will greatly increase at some universities, if not at all.

There are some opportunities here, as well as clear dangers. Third-party providers can offer programs, locations, and modes of learning (particularly in the area of community service) that would be difficult or impossible for some universities. They may in some cases offer pricing at levels below what the university itself could provide. And many of the better providers are willing to work with universities to develop what are in effect customized programs for particular needs.

But the dangers are there, too. Study abroad is becoming big business, but it is essentially an unregulated industry, and has only recently developed clear and broad ethical standards of practice. The flurry of subpoenas issued last year by New York's Attorney General were, in the view of many, a gross overreaction to a few relatively minor problems at a very few institutions. But in the future, as more universities look for ways to send more students overseas, the use of providers of all types is likely to increase, and with it, the potential for abuse and mismanagement on one side or another.

It is tempting, perhaps, for an overburdened president or provost to see an off-campus provider of study abroad programs as the answer to a prayer. But to the extent that campuses outsource international education, they fail to develop among their own faculty the internal capacity for international engagement that they so clearly need. Donald Hall (2007), in an op-ed piece entitled "Why Professors Should Teach Abroad," put this very clearly:

> My teaching and the experiences of my students here in the United States have been substantially enhanced because of my work abroad.... I can speak from firsthand experience about the culturally specific assumptions embedded in the materials I teach, rather than naïvely promote their transcultural truth or value. That type of humility is valuable but often sorely lacking in American classroom exchanges. Students will not learn the cultural limitations of their knowledge, which they must if they are to develop effective global-communication skills, if faculty members themselves are parochial in their vision and awareness. (p. B20)

If, as we are wont to believe, faculty are the bedrock and lifeblood of the university, what does it say about that university's regard for international education if its offerings in that area are neither part of its own curriculum, nor designed and taught by its own professors?

If we are to bring international education into the curriculum we must make it important to the faculty at most institutions in ways that clearly it is not important now. To do this, we will need to engage in a long-term and very intentional effort to bring about fundamental and far-reaching change in how our universities work as institutions.

This involves not just changes of attitude among individual faculty members, but changes in the character of the institutions within which these faculty work. Without such institutional change, nothing that an individual faculty member does will have much lasting impact.

The anthropologist Mary Douglas (1986) reminded us that our institutions are fundamental to how we perceive and approach problems and opportunities. In a very real sense, institutions think, and they direct our thinking:

Institutions systematically direct individual memory and channel our perceptions into forms compatible with the relations they authorize.... Any problems we try to think about are automatically transformed into their own organizational problems. The solutions they proffer come from the limited range of their experience. (p. 92)

One of our problems, however, is that we have a very imperfect understanding about how change in academic institutions actually happens. Academic receptivity at the faculty level clearly seems to be a necessary condition for curricular change, but an equally necessary condition appears to be faculty readiness to hear leadership's call. And in situations where either the political will of the leadership or the receptivity of the faculty is missing, efforts often fail, or fail to take root in a systematic or sustainable manner. Changing the way our faculty think and act with respect to international education will therefore require changes at multiple levels, over a period of some years.

Although each campus will promote change in its own way, experience with other broad social change efforts (the environmental movement comes to mind) suggests that four elements will need to be involved simultaneously: structural changes in policies and procedures; a set of champions; broad coalitions of supporters across the social and economic spectrum; and patient but relentless campaigning over an extended period of time. I'd like to look briefly at each of these here.

The single most important structural change relates to policies on recruitment, promotion, and tenure. A few universities—Michigan State and Minnesota, for example—have already made policy changes of this nature, and we can expect others to eventually follow. Although this change will be slow to come and difficult to achieve on many of our campuses—where these policies are considered by most faculty as the academic equivalent of scripture—change must happen, if we are ever going to make it possible for our energetic younger faculty to extend themselves beyond the classroom.

International activity should not and must not be viewed as displacing the traditional academic foci of teaching, research, and service. Rather, such activity wraps these in a global mantle, broadening their reach and heightening their relevance. Nor does the inclusion of international activity require all faculty to participate. It merely makes it possible, for those who do engage, to have their work counted when the time comes.

Other structural changes are also needed, including serious efforts to internationalize the curriculum, instead of relegating global or cultural issues to the margin, as so often happens now. Language learning, its place in the curriculum, its connections with other disciplines, and perhaps most of all, its pedagogy, needs to be seriously reworked.[11]

Finally, our best universities in the next 10 to 20 years will be those which have strong and permanent structural linkages with top universities overseas. Such linkages might take the form of joint or dual degrees, joint research collaborations, two-plus-two programs, or any of a number of other possibilities. This has already begun in some places, but much more could be done.

Developing champions on each campus for international education begins with the development of a cadre of trained professionals. We will always have—and have always had—champions and advocates among the faculty, but we need more and better people in the upper levels of administration whose job it is to promote internationalization across the campus. Most universities, as the ACE report referenced earlier noted, have no such person.

Our national associations for international education leaders (such as NAFSA and AIEA) are well aware of the need to promote international education, but have so far been reluctant to raise their voices to university provosts and presidents. These associations are, however, beginning to take seriously the issue of how international leaders on campus are recruited, trained, and supported. A recent study by NAFSA, which I coauthored (Lambert, Nolan, Peterson, & Pierce, 2007), looked at those qualities which seem to matter in a "senior international officer," whether that person be a dean, director, or vice-provost.

We found that successful international education leaders shared several key characteristics, among them a deep knowledge of their own campus culture, skills in promoting and managing change, and a high degree of competence in interpersonal interaction, particularly interaction across cultures.

Unfortunately, these are not characteristics common to the faculty at large. Nor are they necessarily the qualities sought by the search committees which seek to hire such people. So in addition to improving the opportunities for the professional development of international education administrators, one of the other main tasks awaiting us is the education of our presidents, provosts and other top university officials about the skills and abilities needed for success. The days are long gone when one could simply assign a retiring or burnt-out faculty member to the "international" job and be done with it. Indeed, individuals with strong academic records but no administrative experience to speak of are probably not the best candidates for these jobs.

Champions and networks of champions will serve as catalysts for the formation of coalitions and networks at other levels, involving other groups. Accrediting bodies, trustees, industry groups, and professional associations of all kinds have a direct stake in how well our graduates are prepared. So far, however, we have not really tapped these groups as a source of advocacy, pressure, or support. Our state and federal legislators, who have paid so much attention just recently to issues of accountability and outcomes measurement, need to be encouraged to turn their attention to international education, and to ask our universities what specifically they are doing, and how, to ensure that U.S. students are learning, not just about the past, but about what awaits them in the future. Herman B. Wells, a former president of Indiana University, saw this clearly when he said, "A university must do more than just stand guard over the nation's heritage, it must illuminate the present and help shape the future" (1967, p. 1).

Finally, of course, we need to campaign, patiently but relentlessly, on behalf of our cause. No one message is enough; no one approach works for everyone. Changing hearts and minds is easier when you have policies and procedures set in your favor, but we still need to think carefully about how to frame our messages, and to whom. Years ago, Edgar Schein (1985) reminded us that institutional culture comes from the top, and so I would suggest that we start with our presidents, provosts and trustees, and that we urge them to move beyond mere words. It's no longer good enough, in other words, to simply pretend the train is moving.

William Schowalter, an emeritus professor of engineering at Princeton, said this to his colleagues in an article in Chemical Engineering Progress (2007):

> Change can be hard, both for individuals and for organizations. Nevertheless, if U.S. universities are serious about retaining leadership positions through the 21st century, some of [their] core principles will require modification. It will be necessary to move from rhetoric to action. (p. 38s)

With university leadership "on board," and with sensible enabling policies in place, it will not prove that difficult to help faculty develop international competence. Indeed, my prediction would be that, freed from the artificial constraints of current tenure and promotion arrangements, many of them would jump at the chance to become more internationally engaged. And at that point, our real work can begin: developing a true cross-cultural pedagogy, using the world's diversity to enhance and illuminate the understanding and capacities of our students.

All of these activities, it need hardly be added, are works in progress which will continue far beyond the efforts of the individuals involved. For as the political journalist I. F. Stone once remarked, if you expect to see the final results of your work, you've not asked a big enough question.

It's not yet clear that we have the political will within the academy to change. But there are two powerful trends in our favor. The first we have already mentioned: the growing desire of students to go abroad. Universities will ignore this at their peril. The American Council on Education (2008a) pointed this out when it said:

> ...institutions that do not encourage and expand international learning experiences may find themselves increasingly at a disadvantage in enrolling the current generation of students and satisfying their strong desires for a truly global college education. (p. 2)

The second is the growth and development of universities overseas. The Bologna Agreement (which most of our engineers, please recall, knew next to nothing about) will very soon have the effect of transforming European higher education, and making it directly competitive with the United States. Australia already has some of the finest research universities in the world, and they are aggressively recruiting international students. In China, India, Korea, and elsewhere, world-class universities are taking shape, and they too are looking—as we have been—to enroll the world's best and brightest.

We will either change, or we will likely fail. Schowalter (2007) warns:

> Will the resistance to change, a trait well known among some of the best research universities, be their undoing in a globalized world?... [M]any will concede that permanence is one of the factors that made "prestigious" universities seem so prestigious. However, permanence should not be mistaken for excellence.... My opinion is that unless U.S. universities embrace globalization as a new opportunity, they will, within a generation, find themselves among the also-rans of the world's research universities. (p. 38s)

The next few years in higher education will present us with choices that the academy has avoided making for a long time. What is higher education for? How does it relate to the kind of society that we want to be? And most importantly, what should we expect, as citizens, taxpayers, employers, and parents, of the institutions we have created?

Change is already happening, of course, but not fast enough. Europe and Asia, as noted, have already begun to globalize their education systems in planned, comprehensive ways. In the years ahead, our universities will learn at first hand what we wish our students to learn: that there *are* other minds out in the world which think as well as ours. Our university system, once the only game in town, will face increasingly stiff competition from other countries.

In the meantime, however, several generations of U.S. students will be denied the opportunity to gain the global competence they need. As a result they will be less prepared than they might have been to seize international opportunities, and avoid international pitfalls.

Our universities cannot hope to contribute effectively to our national dialogue on globalization unless they can become global themselves, and are both willing and able to learn from that dialogue.

Internationalizing higher education is essential to America's future. We are unlikely to be able to sustain our way of life without a multiculturally aware citizenry: our economic growth, our security, and our democracy depend on this. International education should be empowering, liberating and transformational. Its goal should be to help develop citizens who are creative, morally and socially responsible, and engaged with the issues of our time.

Building global capacity in ourselves, our students, and in our institutions will be a process of continual renewal and reinvention, a dialogue and negotiation with the world surrounding us. It is our students who are our most eager and valuable allies in all of this. They are curious about the world beyond the shoreline, and they are anxious to engage meaningfully with the world's problems. Our job as educators is to connect with these impulses, and to direct them appropriately.

Increasingly, all of our students will be called upon to do two things: understand and manage difference; and devise innovative solutions to new problems. The ability to do the second will depend, to a large extent, on how well they learn to do the first.

Universities are where we begin to build the future, one student at a time. Some see the university as a factory, turning out a stream of precision products. Others see it as a garden, where each bloom is special. I see the university differently: I see it as a shipyard. We are building ships. And although ships are safest and most secure when they are at anchor in a snug harbor, we all know that this is not why we build ships. This is not what they are for. The ships we build will go to places we have never been, and face challenges we can only dimly imagine. And so we must build them well, with care and confidence.

NOTES

1. *Study abroad* is a catch-all term for a wide variety of educational experiences which take place in a different country from the one in which the home campus is located. At Purdue University, we define study abroad as any overseas educational experience (for credit or not) which counts as progress toward a degree. In addition to the traditional semester or year abroad exchange programs of various kinds, study abroad includes internships, practicums, clinical rotations, service learning, "intersession" programs of all kinds, independent study trips, and various types of dual-degree, joint degree, or "sandwich" programs.

2. One of the most recent—and to my mind, one of the most astute—discussions of this is Fareed Zakaria's *The Post-American World* (2008). The core issue we face, he argues, is not a decline in American power, but "the rise of the rest."

3. For a taste of this now voluminous literature, see, for example: Deardorff (2006), Gacel-Ávila (2005), Hunter, White, and Godbey (2006), Ruben (1989).

4. The knoll and swamp image comes from Schön (1987, p. 3).

5. Gore (2005) provides an extended analysis of gender issues in study abroad which are beyond the limited scope of this chapter, but well worth reading. Recent anthropological research (McKinney, 2008) has also shed considerable light on why we have gender imbalances in study abroad.

6. See the discussions of these figures in *Inside Higher Ed* (2008), the *Chronicle of Higher Education* (2008), and ACE (2008a, 2008b).

7. I hear this constantly in my work, and at every university I have ever worked at. Younger faculty, many of whom are keen to participate in international education, claim they have been explicitly warned against it by their elders. Their elders, in turn, are often indifferent. One response from a senior professor in my field seems typical. "I'm a tenured full professor with a fully-funded research agenda," she said. "Why should I care about this?"

8. Some recent stories in the *Chronicle of Higher Education* provide timely and poignant examples of how both faculty and students are in some cases fundamentally unprepared for what they encounter overseas. See, for example, Alles (2006), Barbour (2006), Hall (2007), Zemach-Bersin (2008).

9. Ambrose Bierce once defined an *interpreter* as someone who enables two people to understand one another by repeating to each one what it would be to the interpreter's advantage for the other to have said (Bierce, 1993, p. 93). This would seem to describe this kind of faculty person fairly well.

10. There are several good overall discussions of U.S. academic culture from several different viewpoints. See, for example, Bergquist (1992), and Birnbaum (1988).

11. Space does not permit me to do more than simply mention some of the more innovative approaches to language learning which have been in place for some time now, but are hardly ever incorporated into our mainstream academic repertoires. I would include here the work of people such as John Rassias at Dartmouth, the training approaches used by both the U.S. military and the Peace Corps, and the experiments being tried at Drake University now.

REFERENCES

Alles, G. D. (2006, November 17). Richer? Superior? Americans abroad. *The Chronicle of Higher Education, 53*(13), B13.

American Council on Education (ACE). (2000). *Student poll*. Baltimore, MD: American Council on Education and Art & Science Group.

American Council on Education (ACE). (2008a). *College-bound students' interest in study abroad and other international learning activities*. Washington, DC: Author, Art & Science Group, and the College Board.

American Council on Education (ACE). (2008b). *Mapping internationalization on U.S. campuses: 2008 edition*. Washington, DC: Author.

Barbour, J. (2006, October 6). The moral ambiguity of study abroad. *The Chronicle of Higher Education, 53*(7), B24.

Bergquist, W. H. (1992). *The four cultures of the academy,* San Francisco: Jossey-Bass.

Bhandari, R., & Chow, P. (2007). *Open doors 2007, Report on international educational exchange*. New York: Institute of International Education.

Bierce, A. (1993). *The devil's dictionary*. New York: Dover Publications.

Birnbaum, R. (1988). *How colleges work: The cybernetics of academic organization and leadership*. San Francisco: Jossey-Bass.

Deardorff, D. K. (2006). Identification and assessment of intercultural competence as a student outcome of internationalization. *Journal of Studies in International Education, 10*(3), 241–266.

Douglas, M. (1986). *How institutions think*. Syracuse, NY: Syracuse University Press.

Fischer, K. (2008a, April 18). Study abroad providers feel effects of growing public scrutiny. *The Chronicle of Higher Education, 54*(32), A40.

Fischer, K. (2008b, May 30). New report charts mixed results in colleges' internationalization efforts. *The Chronicle of Higher Education, 54*(38), A24.

Gacel-Ávila, J. (2005). The internationalization of higher education: A paradigm for global citizenry. *Journal of Studies in International Education, 9*(2), 121–136.

Gore, J. E. (2005). *Dominant beliefs and alternative voices: Discourse, Belief and gender in American study abroad*. New York: Routledge.

Hall, D.E. (2007, October 5). Why Professors should teach abroad. *The Chronicle of Higher Education, 54*(6), B20.

Hunter, B., White, G. P., & Godbey, G. C. (2006). What does it mean to be globally competent? *Journal of Studies in International Education, 10*(3), 267–285.

Inside Higher Ed. (2008, May 22). Not so international after all? Retrieved December 19, 2008, from http://insidehighered.com/news/2008/05/22/intl

Kaplan, R. D. (1997, December). Was democracy just a moment? *Atlantic Monthly, 80*, 55–60.

Lambert, R. D. (Ed.). (1994). *Educational exchange and global competence*. New York: Council on International Educational Exchange.

Lambert, S., Nolan, R., Peterson, N., & Pierce, D. (2007). *Critical skills and knowledge for senior campus international leaders*. Washington, DC: NAFSA: Association of International Educators.

Lapham, L. (1996). *Hotel America: Scenes in the lobby of the fin-de siècle*. New York: Verso.

McKinney, J. S. (2008). *Anthropological analysis: Why more females study abroad and how this can inform marketing efforts*. Presentation at NAFSA Annual Meetings, Washington, DC.

Ruben, B. D. (1989). The study of cross-cultural competence: Traditions and contemporary issues. *International Journal of Intercultural Relations, 13*, 229–240.

Sadri, A. (1994). Adjusting to the world according to Salman Rushdie. In C. Becker (Ed.), *The subversive imagination* (168–186). New York: Routledge.

Schein, E. (1985). *Organizational culture and leadership*. San Francisco, Jossey-Bass.

Schön, D. (1985). *The reflective practitioner: How professionals think in action*. New York: Basic Books.

Schön, D. (1987). *Educating the reflective practitioner: Toward a new design for teaching and learning in the professions*. San Francisco: Jossey-Bass.

Schowalter, W. R. (2007, January). U.S. research universities—Globalize or face demise? *Chemical Engineering Progress, 103*(1), 36s–38s.

Wells, H. B. (1967, Fall). A case study on interinstitutional cooperation. *Educational Record*. Washington, DC: American Council on Education.

Zakaria, F. (2008). *The post-American world*. New York: Norton.

Zemach-Bersin, T. (2008, March 7). American students abroad can't be "global citizens." *The Chronicle of Higher Education, 54*(26), A34.

Chapter 17

Faculty Beliefs and Institutional Values

Identifying and Overcoming These Obstacles to Education Abroad Growth

Joan Elias Gore

University of Virginia

THE OBSTACLES

Despite widespread mission statements committing U.S. colleges and universities to international education, a significant challenge for this mission comes from university faculty who are often responding to signals received from their institutional leaders. Identifying the obstacles presented by faculty and developing a strategy to overcome them is central to internationalizing American higher education and educating its citizens for an increasingly global society (Green & Schoenberg, 2006).

In recent years, the words *internationalization* and *globalization* have been frequently uttered on college campuses across the United States. Many leaders in the higher education community agree with increasing the international component of their curricula, and many schools have announced new initiatives to do so.

Indeed, the American Council on Education (ACE) has put internationalization high on its agenda since the 1950s. Intent on understanding how effectively this focus has influenced American undergraduate education over the past half-century, ACE initiated a study in 2000 titled *Mapping Internationalization on U.S. Campuses: Final Report 2003*, which was updated in 2008 (Siaya & Hayward, 2003; Green, Luu, & Burris, 2008). Both reports included mixed news. "Higher education has made some progress in internationalizing the undergraduate experience in the past 15 years," the first report stated, "but there is still much work to do." In the 2008 update, the authors observed: "Overall, internationalization is still not a major element of most U.S. colleges and universities" (Siaya & Hayward, 2003, p. viii; Green et al., 2008, p. xi). Biddle (2002) agrees: she writes, "'Internationalization' became a buzzword in academic circles," and "the rhetoric surrounding it ubiquitous" (p. 1). An earlier ACE report by Hayward and Siaya (2001), found that "Although college and university presidents express stronger commitments to international education than they did a decade ago, that commitment does not seem to translate into an action agenda on campus" (p. 5). Representative of the "weaknesses in internationalization" reported in *Mapping Internationalization 2008* (Green et al., 2008) was the observation that, while many "… institutions offer education abroad opportunities, and although student participation is increasing," enrollment remains low (p. x).

At the same time, educators hear more warnings that "the level of international knowledge and understanding" among Americans is "wanting in comparison with others" (NAFSA, 1990a, p. 1) and that "as a nation we suffer from a pervasive lack of knowledge about the world" (NAFSA, 2003, p. 5). The ACE survey confirmed in 2001 that "the overall level of Americans' international knowledge remains low" (Hayward & Siaya, 2001, p. 3). The National Geographic-Roper (2006) survey showed that American students demonstrated such a limited world knowledge that report writers declared they were unprepared for a "global future." Of college-age Americans surveyed, 63% couldn't locate Iraq on a map, 48% thought India was Muslim, and half could not find New York on a map (National Geographic-Roper, 2006). In 2003, a strategic task force on education abroad organized by NAFSA observed that, "As a nation we suffer from a pervasive lack of knowledge about the world. There have been periods, indeed entire eras, in our history when Americans have relished their isolation from the world. Some have made speaking only English a point of national pride instead of a disgrace" (p. 1).

The calls to increase support for education abroad ring through the halls of America's higher education community. Students who wish to study abroad are still predominantly female, as they have been for almost a century (Gore, 2005), and today they are choosing to study in sites that have not traditionally hosted many American undergraduates (Institute of International Education [IIE], 2008). Study abroad scholarship programs are receiving more applications. The U.S. Congress has proposed increasing expenditures on international education and foreign exchange programs (e.g., H.R. 5179 and the Simon Act; see NAFSA, 2008). All short-term indicators suggest a rise in student interest. But, despite public support and student interest, enrollments in study abroad, along with participation in other internationalization efforts, have been slow to increase over the past decades. In 2006, IIE President Allan Goodman observed that only 1% of all U.S. undergraduates study outside the United States for some part of their undergraduate career (Goodman, 2006, p. 7).

So, despite growing interest, international education remains at the margins of American postsecondary education. What is the problem and what can be done to overcome it?

FACULTY AND INSTITUTIONAL BELIEFS ABOUT EDUCATION ABROAD

Evidence indicates that faculty are part of the problem and that institutional policies, despite mission statements, do not encourage faculty to support education abroad. Among faculty, study abroad is often suspect because it is so heavily grounded in the liberal education tradition. That tradition is often linked with female students, resulting in suspicion about the serious intent of anyone—usually women—who study the liberal arts overseas. Foreign study is not valued in and of itself. Instead, faculty perceive it as a strategy to avoid challenging academic study or professional preparation. Marshall Gregory, professor of English, liberal education, and pedagogy at Butler University wrote, "A Liberal Education is Not a Luxury" (2003) in which he recognized that the liberal education discourse of the last century "implicitly concedes the strongest ground in any discussion of educational aims to faculty members from professional and pre-professional programs" (p. B16).

With regard to study abroad, Kathleen M. Reilly (1995), former foreign study director at Seton Hall University, observed that:

> Study abroad has long been considered a worthwhile, if only tangential, academic activity for the personal development and cultural exposure of college students. Usually associated with the affluent, study abroad was most often considered the domain of women in the liberal arts.... Students and administrators still frequently view study abroad as the cultural dabbling of dilettantes despite dramatically changed social, economic, and political conditions that are making international experience critically important. (p. 1)

Reilly encapsulated frequently expressed beliefs (Gore, 2005, pp. 25–78) that study abroad is considered a Grand Tour, for "personal development and cultural exposure"; that it is "considered the domain of women"; and it is "usually associated with the affluent." Reilly identified another related perception, saying that many consider study abroad "tangential," concerned only with liberal arts—an education considered "the cultural dabbling of dilettantes" (1995). Briggs and Burn (1985) summarized this view as well when they decried the reputation of study abroad as an elitist female pursuit and observed that this image derived in part from association with the study of humanities (p. 39).

Even when the liberal curriculum is considered important, it is still not viewed as useful. Speaking after 9/11, Jenkins and Skelly (2004) wrote that study abroad programs fail to encourage effective global citizens (p. 8). Engle and Engle (2002) denounced study abroad, especially its liberal arts content, as failed, frivolous, weak, and without serious professional purpose (p. 29; see also Citron, 2003, pp. 41–42).

For some faculty, education abroad is seen as being trivial and insignificant precisely because it is pursued by women. "The arts are tinged with effeminacy in the popular thinking," stated Newcomer (1959). Men apologize for their interest in the arts, while women find such an interest to be "natural" (pp. 240–244). Stimpson (1998), feminist scholar, observed "There may be a bias against the liberal arts, a feeling that real men don't speak French, that in the 20th century these are women's topics" (Lewin, 1998). Male and female alumni responding to a survey conducted of Sweet Briar Junior Year in France alumni (Gore, 2005), wrote, for example: "I found in studying French that most men find French to be a 'sissy' language," and "It is more accepted (culturally) for the female gender to have an interest in arts and culture" (p. 174).

These beliefs within the academy frame the valuation of foreign language and overseas study. Engle and Engle (2002) argued that U.S. study abroad is pursued as "the extension via field learning of classroom study in such domains as the arts, international relations, or archaeology; language study as much for liberal arts curricular breadth as for later professional use; enhanced cultural awareness through host culture interaction" (p. 29). They postulated that inbound students take their education much more seriously than do U.S. students (p. 37)—an opinion not altogether unsurprising given their view of what U.S. students encounter in study abroad programs.

> At this point an honest look at what "comes out" of most experiences abroad would make us blush...but then, as most study abroad is structured, we can hardly expect students to get much out of their experience when they are required to put so little into it: little academic work, to be sure, even less in the way of prior required language preparation, host cultural contact often restricted (literally) to pragmatic mini-conversations with waiters, post office workers, and train conductors. (Engle & Engle, 2002, p. 34)

In addition to these criticisms, employers seem to doubt the value of overseas education experience. "Currently, very few employers specifically recruit candidates with overseas study experience, unless they require either cross-cultural skills or a job specifically requires it," observed the authors of a recent study conducted by the J. Walter Thompson Institute of International Education (n.d.). For many faculty and employers the quality of liberal education abroad is suspect.

FACULTY BELIEFS: AMERICA FIRST

These doubts are reinforced by nationalistic biases that continue to pervade American higher education. As Philip Altbach (1998) observed, "American faculty seem to feel that U.S. higher education is at the center of an international academic system" (p. 77). William Hoffa (2002) commented, "If U.S. faculty assume that little of lasting educational value can happen outside of a classroom on their own campus, one can be sure that they are even more suspicious of such experiential doings on foreign soil" (p. 59).

The belief that serious academic work can best be done in the United States, not abroad, serves to marginalize international education. Even during America's postcolonial era, as the founders of educational institutions looked to Europe for models, a mistrust of the academic worth of Old World institutions was articulated. When Thomas Jefferson founded the nation's first full-fledged state university, the University of Virginia, he recruited five Europeans among his first seven professors. He explained that with so few American scholars to choose from in the young republic, he preferred hiring "foreigners of the first order to natives of the second" (Honeywell, 1931, p. 94). Despite this rationale, Jefferson received criticism from newspaper editors who accused him of insulting the American people by this act of intellectual "importation" (Malone, 1981, p. 409).

Beliefs as to the superiority of the American educational system are reinforced by the sometimes sparse amount of international research conducted by faculty at U.S. universities. Although ACE surveys of faculty attitudes are somewhat encouraging, indicating that a majority of faculty at surveyed institutions supported some type of international academic experience, the *Mapping 2003* survey (Siaya & Hayward, 2003) indicated that most faculty travel one month or less, most travel is to English-speaking countries (the same criticisms many faculty levy against students), and some travel only to countries adjacent to the United States; 80% had not submitted or published in a foreign journal during the past 3 years; 75% had not worked collaboratively with a foreign-born scholar; 73% felt international work would not be considered in their promotion and tenure reviews; and, although in the minority, 36% still felt that "The more time spent teaching students about other countries, cultures, and global issues, the less time is available for teaching the basics" (pp. 9–10).

Looking at institutional policies overall, the authors of *Promising Practices* (Engberg & Green, 2002) reported on the ongoing problem of marginal institutional support for international education across the board in American higher education:

> A recent survey…of more than 750 colleges and universities nationwide by the American Council on Education (ACE) suggests that the gap between national rhetoric and institutional policies and practices is also considerable. While around 75 percent of four-year institutions highlight their international education programs, activities, and opportunities in student recruitment literature, only four in 10 identify international education as one of the top five priorities in their strategic plans and only about one-third have formed a campus-wide committee or task force to work solely on advancing campus internationalization efforts. (p. 10)

The further survey revealed that only two out of five institutions required undergraduates to take courses focused on perspectives, issues, or events outside the United States. Queries about language requirements in 4-year institutions revealed that only 23% had a foreign-language entrance requirement, and 37% had a language requirement for all students in order to graduate. Especially disheartening was the finding that only 4% of the institutions surveyed have guidelines that specify international work or experience as a consideration in faculty promotion and tenure decisions (Engberg & Green, 2002).

INSTITUTIONAL VALUES: RESOURCES AND REWARDS

Judgments about the worth of international education are also expressed through resource allocation (Goodwin & Nacht, 1988, p. 55). The Association of International Education Administrators (AIEA) has reported that even when an international education office receives institutional funds, they rarely cover two-thirds of operating expenses, and the typical office has to generate "significant proportions of total revenue" (Hoemeke, Krane, Young, & Slavin, 1999, pp. 9–10; Engberg & Green, 2002, p. 16). And no survey has yet reported success in grounding education abroad in fully staffed and financially supported offices located within the heart of the academic world. Without resources or faculty support, education abroad continues to founder in comparison to domestic higher education.

Programs Are Academically Weak and Insignificant in Comparison to U.S. Education

The preference for domestic education can be found in some of the earliest discourse about modern study abroad. When Smith College began its program in the 1920s, the faculty objected vehemently, reports Patricia Olmsted, director emeritus of Smith's Office of Study Abroad. According to Olmsted (1987), the French department in particular questioned the feasibility of the junior year abroad model, given their students' inability to integrate into the French university system (p. 4). The Smith faculty voted against what they deemed a "wild" proposal. Olmsted reports a Smith College dean as saying:

> The Junior Year is in large part a tool of general educational experience; language, places, museums, general know-how; not the development of critical powers and fine discriminating judgment on literary questions. The French department at Smith can develop these powers for its students; in a comparable degree the Paris faculty cannot.... (Olmstead, pp. 15–16; Garraty & Adams, 1959, pp. 9–10)

A set of mutually exclusive values soon attached to the junior year abroad. John Bowman (1987) described these early programs as, "in part, a transformation of the European tour for young women into an academic experience" (p. 13). The junior year abroad soon became associated with an elite population studying less than serious academic subjects in the Grand Tour tradition.

Yet admiration was also expressed from early on. A junior year abroad provided a significant opportunity to immerse students in another culture and language. Richard Lambert typified this ideal when he noted in a speech at CIEE's 41st Annual Conference (1988), that the "relatively brief period of time" students devote to study abroad often becomes an obstacle for effective learning" (Lambert, 1988). Goodwin and Nacht (1988) reported that when faculty support foreign study, it has often been for the junior year immersion model, "defended with almost religious zeal by its supporters, who are mainly faculty members and study abroad directors at the institutions of origin… in prestigious highly selective colleges and universities" (p. 35).

Nonetheless, whether short-term or full-year, it is the quality of the experience that raises suspicions. As Benjamin De Winter stated (1995),

> The traditional partner universities in Europe place less emphasis on the results of a particular semester. In fact, there may be almost no work required to receive credit, and credits often do not even exist. European students are expected to study more on their own, in preparation for all-important comprehensive exams after 6 or 10 semesters. (1995, p. 59)

De Winter further observed:

> American students who enter such a system for just one or two semesters perceive a lighter work load. Unprepared as juniors for highly independent study methods, and distracted by the adjustment to a new environment, they appear to do less "academic" work than their friends back home. Professors, too, may share this perception, looking at education abroad programs as opportunities to get away from campus, with fewer responsibilities and a reduced workload abroad. (1995, p. 59)

Attitudes within American higher education toward the junior year abroad contradict one another. The model stands on the one hand as an example of valuable study and on the other as an academically weak and frivolous Grand Tour experience for wealthy women.

Host country faculty have contributed to these beliefs that devalue the junior year abroad as academically unchallenging. Historically, some have questioned the serious intent of these college juniors, younger than the majority of students at European universities (Briggs & Burn, 1985). As Asa Briggs and Barbara Burn noted, many professionals in U.S. and overseas higher education "remain convinced that graduate study abroad is far more important than undergraduate," because undergraduate study abroad does not involve the same focus, goals, or values (pp. 55–56). Green, Eckel, and Barblan (2002) note that "Rarely does an American student enroll at a foreign university in the same way that foreign students enroll at U.S. institutions." They observed that U.S. education abroad is primarily for undergraduates, three-quarters of whom study in English and many of whom are taught by American faculty with American classmates, all limiting their exposure to their host community (p. 22).

This dismissal of the quality of U.S. education abroad reveals that post-World War II changes in study abroad models have not necessarily improved its perception within the American academy. Since World War II, students have been offered choices for their length of study. During this period, though, the number of students going abroad for a semester or a summer has come to far exceed the number studying abroad for a full academic year, and almost half go on short-term programs less than a quarter of a year in length (Chin, 2003; Obst, Bhandari, & Witherell, 2007). Perhaps this is especially reinforced when these experiences last only a few weeks, as they often do today.

Although designed to encourage more American students to study abroad, English-language programs have been perceived as weakening the academic quality of offerings overall (Gore,

287 ■

2005). Briggs and Burn (1985) reported this suspicion in the early years of English-language programs, observing that "organizing special programs for American students in foreign language countries which are mainly conducted in English and also teach elementary or intermediate skills in the host country's language," they found, "has the basic deficiency of insulating the Americans from the local students and culture" (p. 45), a sentiment echoed more recently by Green and Schoenberg (2006).

Nevertheless, many worry that there continues to be insufficient language preparation for study abroad. Sheila Biddle (2002) observed that while there is great support for study abroad, little language learning is actually going on. Likewise, the members of the most recent NAFSA Task Force on Study Abroad (2003) focused on the lack of foreign language competency in their report. The report implicitly if not intentionally criticized the current state of study abroad, while at the same time it argued for the value of going abroad for language training. Engle and Engle included the increasing number of English language programs in their denunciation of the quality and worth of study abroad (2002).

In short, efforts to make education abroad appeal to more students have drawn criticism from a different direction (J. Pritchett, personal communication, May 12, 1997, October 3, 1997, October 6, 1997). By increasing English-language offerings, education abroad coordinators have inserted a new element in the discourse that draws disparaging comments from faculty about study abroad.

In addition to forms of study programs, those administering education abroad themselves may sometimes be viewed as exercising skills not central to the mission of the institution. Mestenhauser (2002) noted that American faculty rarely respected the skills of their international education colleagues. He observed that gender and credential evaluation of administrators could be another component in judgments about study abroad, paralleling William Hoffa's observation that the gender of study abroad advisers may discourage male prospects (2004). "We are a female-dominated profession numerically," said Mestenhauser, "but this doesn't mean we are a profession which supports women in senior positions" (Personal communication, April 1989).

His observation was confirmed by a NAFSA survey of its membership at the time (1990), reinforced in 2004 with a second survey (p. 31). Within the education abroad section of NAFSA, 64% of the membership was female; 21% held a bachelor's, 69% a master's, and 9% a PhD or JD (S. S. Tennies, personal communication, August 31, 2004). Regardless of the actual competence that education abroad practitioners may possess, the absence of the PhD prompts distrust from faculty about the judgment of these professionals and the programs they supervise.

Education abroad advisers often find themselves low on the higher education pay scale, further confirming their marginality in the eyes of their peers (H. Hensen, personal communication, April 30, 2004). As of 2004, the median salary for a study abroad adviser was $35,291 (Strout, 2004) lower than the lowest faculty rank salary ($38,501) (Wilson, 2004). Among median salaries for midlevel college student services administrators in 2003–2004, the category of study abroad adviser ranked only six positions from the bottom. Study abroad advisers earned less than food service unit managers (Strout, 2004).

Senior international educators present a somewhat different picture. At the start of this century, the Association of International Education Administrators (AIEA) reported that office heads most often held a PhD, and that more than 40% held faculty appointments, with reported salaries that were twice the size of education abroad advisors' salaries (Hoemeke et al., 1999, p. 12–13); at this most senior level, the majority were male (pp. 6–10). Still, the AIEA survey also revealed that international educators did not always hold positions of power. One-third held positions of dean or higher, but two-thirds were director level or other (p. 6). Even at this most senior level at most colleges and universities, in positions where the average age of the jobholder was almost 55 years old, salaries ranged widely from $40,000 to $150,000 per year (p. 12).

Even at institutions with a centralized office headed by a senior appointee, study abroad development itself may not be centralized. On many campuses, it is initiated by individuals acting on their own rather than by staff appointed and supported by the central administration (Siaya & Hayward, 2003, p. 74). Despite the contribution a faculty member might make, there is no guarantee of respect or reward from his or her colleagues (Briggs & Burn, 1985, p. 51).

This lack of institutional commitment is reflected in the tenure and promotion policies. Despite their avowed interest in things international, most faculty surveyed for *Mapping Internationalization,* in 2003 and in 2008, doubted that international work would count in tenure and promotion decisions (Green et al., pp. 21–22; Siaya & Hayward, p. 75). In the most recent study of the faculty role in internationalization, researchers argued for including international education in these decisions, noting: "Nothing speaks more clearly about an institution than its reward structure" (Green & Schoenberg, 2006, p. 25).

By definition, that which is excluded as important in tenure and promotion decisions quickly becomes peripheral to higher education practices. All of these structural factors—resource limitations, low salaries, gender- and credential-associated devaluation, and faculty anxieties about reward for international efforts—reinforce suspicions about short-term and English language programs, weak overseas institutional practices, and more broadly, perceptions that study abroad is a women's liberal education pursuit. All coalesce to perpetuate the perception of education abroad as inferior to domestic education.

OVERCOMING THE OBSTACLES

Without resource allocation and institutional support, education abroad programs will continue to be marginalized. Recognizing the obstacles and changing institutional practices to support education abroad will be essential to build faculty buy-in for study abroad programs. How can this be accomplished?

Transforming Belief

The American higher education community must be persuaded that education abroad is worthy of support. This is a difficult argument, challenging what we have observed to be long-held beliefs about education abroad, which discount the value of liberal education, distrust the women who have pursued it abroad, and distrust the value of foreign education itself. Looking at these beliefs through the mirror of discourse analysis can contribute to understanding how to overcome the hurdles of faculty and institutional suspicion about study abroad.

The Practice of Discourse Analysis

Discourse analysis examines how things are understood and how they come to be valued. Discourse, or rhetorical, analysis studies not events or things themselves but the discussion about them—how events or things come to be perceived, understood, and valued and how, in turn, those perceptions have an impact on the events themselves.

Rhetorical analysis has a long history. From Plato and Aristotle onward, it has been central to Western pedagogy (Bedford/St. Martins, n.d.). In modern times, the concept of discourse has broadened in scope to include text, dialogue, action, events, and symbols, as well as formal public speaking, according to the 1973 edition of the *Oxford English Dictionary*; the word *rhetoric* has come to encompass both language and action, including the interaction of public discourse, actual and symbolic, with values in broad social contexts (Wiener, 1973). Theorists include the interactions of language, perception, and culture as part of the process that not only individuals but also groups undergo as they create the beliefs that construct their shared sense of reality (Bennett, 1998).

This contemporary concept of discourse is nurtured in the work of Michel Foucault. Much of Foucault's work proceeds from the notion that discourse has the power to generate beliefs about people, things, events, and activities of common concern to the community (Foucault, 1972). These dominant beliefs (Gore, 2005), such as those examined in this chapter, are bound historically, and it is possible to explore the conditions that caused them all to be believed as descriptions of reality (Foucault, 1972). Shared within a social group, these beliefs can interact to form an "episteme"—a powerful and overarching definition that controls perceptions about events, institutions, and individuals—"...a definition that gains acceptance as a powerful 'truth'" (pp. 186–187; see also Barker, 1978, p. 7; Foucault, 1977, p. xix; Merquior, 1991, p. 34).[1]

Discourse does convey truth, but it is a socially constructed truth, unconsciously created by those who share it, Foucault argues. We have observed in this chapter that there are beliefs articulated about education abroad that are deeply held within the academic community. They define study abroad as academically irrelevant liberal education and with no serious intent or professional preparation.

Foucault's methodology draws attention to how beliefs are formed: whose voices are normalized and empowered as the dominant voices, and whose voices are excluded in an alternative discourse. In educational settings as well as in other settings, some discourses have been empowered while other discourses have been disenfranchised (Barker, 1998). For Foucault, identifying the foundations of empowered discourses and the existence of alternative voices offers the potential to introduce new concepts into the discourse and to transform existing beliefs and attitudes (R. Cohen, personal communication, September 1, 1999; Foucault, 1972, 1988).

In Foucault's vision, transformation cannot occur simply through calls for change. Transformation is possible only when the episteme changes that controls the fundamental perception of an activity (Merquior, 1991). Change, according to Foucault, can create the potential for a "sea change" by introducing new voices into the discourse, voices that challenge the episteme (Foucault, 1972, p. 209). Inquiry into the foundations of the existing episteme can expose in whose interest powerful beliefs developed, framing an opportunity for alternative discourses to be heard (Foucault, 1970, 1972, 1978a). Foucault argues that those best suited to create the conditions for transformation are members of the group affected by an episteme, because they speak the language, understand the issues, and therefore have the greatest opportunity to influence other group members with their dialogue. They also have the most to gain from the transformation, for it is their experience that is limited by the prevailing episteme (R. Cohen, personal communication, September 1, 1999; Foucault, 1972).

As advocates of overseas education, we must find ways to effect change. As members of the academy, we know its terminology and understand its concerns. We are members of the higher education community ourselves; nonetheless our calls to action have not succeeded in transforming the negative beliefs about education abroad. It is our work, our reputations, our futures, and our students who suffer. Clearly, there is a relationship between the power of the episteme and the ongoing obstacles that advocates for education abroad confront. The challenge is to create a "sea change" in the way education abroad is viewed by the higher education community.

The Power of the Episteme

The episteme that devalues study abroad as academically weak and functionally irrelevant perpetuates the prevailing negative valuation of education abroad and continues to empower domestic education. Calls to share respect and resources with foreign education programs threaten to undermine the benefits the episteme confers upon the larger academic community. Yet advocacy discourse sometimes inadvertently reinforces the community's damaging beliefs without introducing new discourse that might evoke epistemic change. In other words, we contribute to the problem.

In Spring 2002, Jaclyn Rosebrook-Collignon, director of Albion College's study abroad program in Grenoble, France, sent an e-mail message to the NAFSA online discussion list supporting opinions expressed by Ben Feinberg in a *Chronicle of Higher Education* editorial:

> "What Students Don't Learn Abroad" points to one of our greatest weaknesses as international educators. In our efforts to ensure a "safe" and "fun" study abroad experience (safety, excursions, and "fun" group activities, and positive evaluation forms—"Did you have a good time?"), we forget the true pedagogical objectives of our students…it is our job to confront, counsel, and guide our students before, during, and after their study abroad experience. Pushing them, prodding them, asking them how the overseas experiences they are having or plan to have enter into their educational objectives (usually, it should be linguistic and/or cultural understanding and proficiency). And often we forget to remind them why they are abroad—to experience and learn about another culture. And that only through the prism of another culture will they truly learn something new about themselves. Bungee jumping and swimming with the sharks will do nothing to further their immersion in and understanding of another culture. We aren't supposed to be like their parents and say: "Well, as long as it's fun and exciting for you, then it must be good." Study abroad experiences should be difficult and challenging to our students' identities, certitudes, and value systems. Students should be expected to come back with solid linguistic skills and a more profound understanding of the target culture and its history. Sadly, too many of them come back waving stamped-up passports and wearing t-shirts from the Haufbrauhaus or various Hard Rock cafés. They've merely transplanted their lives for a period of time in a new exotic decor.
>
> This perhaps is a relatively new problem in study abroad due to a broader-based student public. On the one hand, study abroad is not only for the "elite" classes and this is good. (Not to say that the "elite" classes did much better while studying abroad, there were just fewer of them.) On the other hand, we are encountering a student public whose understanding of the world is too often "superficial."… Students can't break free of their own cultural chains (relating to time, productivity, and consumption) to be able to truly carry, feel, and understand the cultural chains of others. (J. Rosebrook-Collignon, personal communication, May 3, 2002)

This statement encompasses so many of the beliefs that are part of the discourse even among some who support education abroad. Not every advocate of education abroad shares Rosebrook-Collignon's vision of the experience. Still, most of us lack a history to create an alternative conception of study abroad. Belief constrains perception, says Foucault (1988a), and it constrains our own perceptions as professionals in the field of education abroad. These perceptions can be manifest even in the policy we write or support (p. 14).

While members of a community may hold a vision that is not entirely circumscribed by the predominating episteme, nonetheless the power of any episteme is so pervasive that it is impossible to escape its influence (Burchell, Gordon, & Miller, 1991; Foucault, 1977, 1970, 1988b). In the case of education abroad, policy makers, while they may not agree with Feinberg or Rose-brook-Collignon, cannot fully escape the power of the prevailing episteme. Discourse analysis reveals that even as advocates ask the higher education community to recognize the value of study abroad, the advocates themselves repeat the devaluing beliefs about it. If transformation lies in the introduction of new discourse, policy that advocates change without challenging negative beliefs and providing evidence to the contrary will be ineffectual. Instead, the discourse perpetuates the episteme. Even if inadvertently, policy makers can contribute to reinforcing the episteme by repeating denigrating beliefs, by stating evidence that sustains the belief without countering it with research showing very different valuations of education abroad, thereby introducing new discourse to establish alternative conceptions (R. Cohen, personal communication, September 1, 1999; Foucault, 1970, p. xxii).

Three reports represent the discourse within the academic community. They include one by the Council for International Educational Exchange (CIEE, 1988) and two by NAFSA (1990a, 2003), which provide examples of strong advocacy for education abroad. Statements in these reports illustrate the inadvertent confirmation of negative beliefs about education abroad by even its strongest supporters.

Comments by policy advocates about the Grand Tour illustrate how denigrating beliefs are perpetuated. Both the CIEE and the first NAFSA reports reflect the belief that study abroad is a Grand Tour, ignoring research to the contrary. The CIEE report links the junior year abroad to the Grand Tour: "The traditional grand tour, part of the education of a small segment of young Americans in the past, and the more recent 'Junior Year,' focused on the European cultural heritage and was most applicable to the liberal arts and humanities students," the report read. From this association, it proceeded to a recommendation: "Now global competence for our citizens requires us to expand study abroad into other areas" (CIEE, 1988, p. 9). This statement implies that education abroad has not helped students develop global competence, and such statements reinforce the episteme that foreign education does not offer serious academic study.

Other links have the same effect. For example, the 2003 NAFSA report stated that, among students encouraged to study overseas, "We also need to look beyond the usual suspects—the language majors and the rest of those in the humanities" (p. 10). The derogatory phrase "the usual suspects" could be easily heard by those holding the demeaning beliefs about education abroad as confirmation that liberal study abroad is frivolous.

Beliefs about the Grand Tour intermingle with conceptions about women's education, reinforcing distrust about foreign education programs. The late Barbara Burn recognized the power of diminishing beliefs when she and Asa Briggs pointed out: "That more women than men study abroad as undergraduates and more in humanities than in professional fields may exacerbate the perception that undergraduate study abroad lacks in seriousness of purpose" (p. 52). Nonetheless, her statements conveyed the idea that only recent study abroad programs are different from earlier ones in that they no longer send women abroad to train them as "cultural guardians." But she reaffirms the suspicion that education abroad programs have been typically pursued in the past by women seeking spouses, not careers.

Suspicions that wealthy women without serious academic intent have been the audience for education abroad programs are inadvertently reinforced in the newest NAFSA policy statement (2003), when, with the best of intentions, the authors wrote:

> We believe that campuses and other study abroad program providers should make every effort to keep study abroad as affordable, accessible, and enticing as possible, especially for those who now consider it beyond their reach. We must go beyond the models and incentives that applied to a time when study abroad was the province of elite, liberal arts colleges. Higher education will never be truly democratized until all students can access the opportunity to build necessary skills through study abroad. (p. 7)

This statement explicitly reinforces the belief that study abroad was owned by the wealthy and implies a derogatory connection to liberal education. These intermingled themes persist in education abroad advocacy. There is an absence in the advocacy literature of research that demonstrates how female participants have successfully used education abroad to prepare for professional life (Gore, 2005). Nor do policy statements explore why, even when financial aid is made available—as to some extent it has been from the beginning in 1922—women continued to be the primary users of study abroad (Gore, 2005).

Policy statements continue to sustain the belief that education abroad is the domain of wealthy women who have no career intentions. Brown (1983), former deputy director of NAFSA, has written that U.S. students abroad have historically focused on language and culture rather than on career skills (p. 74), implying that these students were neither academically serious nor interested in a career path. Indeed, the authors of all the reports seem to assume that since education abroad remains primarily a liberal arts experience, it is unconnected to professional development.

The NAFSA reports, old and new, argue for increased corporate support for education abroad to help create globally competent students, suggesting that early programs had no professional foundation. Overlooked is the goal of the sponsors of the first education abroad program at the University of Delaware, begun in 1922, who established their program to train globally competent citizens to operate professionally throughout the world and who secured, from the start, corporate sponsorship (Munroe, 1986). Both NAFSA reports assumed that corporate concern for international competence was a new phenomenon, reflecting the beliefs that degrade the functional value of education abroad (1990, p. 15; 2003, p. 15).

These examples of policy discourse which unintentionally reinforce negative beliefs about education abroad also ignore an overlooked history of the faculty who created these programs and students who pursued them. Their view was that study abroad would be a vibrant, academically strong and professionally oriented experience built by faculty advocates for their strongest students, to educate them to understand and function in the world in all its aspects. For participants—led by the female majority—the experience has been pursued with serious intent and with courage in the face of war, terrorism, and hardship rather than in the lap of luxury and wealth (Gore, 2005).

Though not recognizing these alternative views, all three reports appreciate the detrimental effect of the common belief that education abroad is inferior to education at home. The CIEE report (1988) stated "Foreign academic systems and facilities may be perceived as inadequate, inhospitable or not matching up with their own structure, and therefore not conducive to an effective learning environment for American students" (p. 14). Indeed, the reports tried to counter this belief. The most recent report (NAFSA, 2003) is explicit in describing the marginalization

293 ■

of education abroad today in the higher education community. In a section titled "Barriers to Be Overcome," task force members concluded:

> The fault, as Cassius tells Brutus in Act I of *Julius Caesar*, is not in our stars, but in ourselves. College policies, albeit often unconsciously, discourage study abroad more than they encourage it. Colleges must take a hard look at the possible institutional barriers that stand in the way of study abroad…which may include: a lack of leadership on the part of senior campus officials, [and] faculty indifference…. (p. 8)

Despite inadvertently reinforcing negative views, advocates nevertheless assert the value of education abroad and the role it should play in higher education. Given the negative beliefs about education abroad held by their academic peers, however, this advocacy is received with skepticism. It is a discourse directed to the domestic educators, whose vision of the superiority of their institutions over those abroad derives from the episteme they are being asked to abandon. The policy reports assert the value of education abroad, but, as Foucault reminds us, change does not come by claiming its need; it comes by exposing the foundations of the episteme and by introducing new discourses instead. These steps are missing in contemporary policy discourse. There is no inquiry, research, or revelation of alternative views of education abroad, the processes Foucault said were necessary to transform an episteme.

What is likely to be heard in policy discourse are statements that confirm the suspicions embedded in the dominant beliefs. Statements describing study abroad participants as wealthy women, statements describing some programs as academically weak, and criticism of some curricula as cultural (meaning shallow)—reinforce the normal view. Regardless of why such statements may have been made, no matter how noble their purpose, they inhibit real change.

For education abroad to succeed, the American higher education community must be persuaded that education abroad is worthy of support. The episteme that devalues study abroad as academically weak and functionally irrelevant empowers the domestic academic community and perpetuates negative perceptions of study abroad. Calls to give up this power and share respect and resources with foreign education programs threaten to undermine the benefits the episteme confers upon the larger community. Advocacy discourse, as well intentioned as it is, sometimes inadvertently reinforces the community's dominant beliefs without introducing new discourse that might evoke epistemic change.

All of us who are committed to education abroad need to develop new strategies and introduce a new discourse that changes the negative beliefs in the American academy about overseas education.

NEW DISCOURSES, NEW POLICY IN U.S. EDUCATION ABROAD

Carl Herrin, chair of NAFSA's Strategic Task Force on Study Abroad, who authored *Securing America's Future*, works diligently to bring about change in international education. Herrin decided to chair the task force after recognizing that previous calls had failed (Herrin, personal communication, April 30, 2004). "Those who read these lines need to do more than nod in agreement," wrote the late Senator Paul Simon in NAFSA's preface. Addressing us, he declared, "This is a battle for understanding that you must help wage" (NAFSA, 2003, p. ii).

How are battles for understanding waged? According to Foucault, as discourse changes, belief changes (Mourad, 1997, p. 61), thereby changing definitions of what is accepted and what is marginalized (Foucault, "Intellectuals and Power," 1977). International education policy makers can help generate change by transforming the episteme that has marginalized education abroad.

Advocates are engaging in research that reveal alternative views about study abroad and expose the power of the prevailing episteme. More exploration of the alternative discourses and the evidence supporting them, presented by the administrators, faculty, and students who have engaged in foreign study, could make widely known within academia the value of study abroad, from its inception in the United States after World War I to the present day. Exploring not only the intent with which study abroad has been pursued, but also the uses—career, volunteer, political arena, or other—to which participants have put their education abroad experience, will help transform the frivolous image often held. Incorporating such approaches into policy formulation could introduce new discourse about education abroad. As we explore the history of the episteme that excluded alternative discourses, we may divest ourselves of the beliefs that may be constraining our own views. By introducing new discourse, we will find new ways to empower ourselves (Foucault, 1985, p. 8; 1972, p. 16).

Education abroad supporters are already urging research to understand the quality and function of study abroad. The authors of *Educating for Global Competence* called for such inquiry (CIEE, 1988) and so has the Forum on Education Abroad, on whose board NAFSA's policy chair, Carl Herrin, serves.[2]

If transformation is to occur, the researcher must introduce this new discourse (Foucault, 1988a). International education researcher Hans de Wit recognized that discursive power is not exerted by an authority from above or outside a community. Rather, power is exercised by everyone in the community as their shared discourse sustains an episteme (Foucault, 1980, p. 159). Together, the members of a group define what is believed and normalized and what is suspect and marginal (p. 212). The entire higher education community needs to participate in a new dialogue about education abroad. Such a model of inclusion cannot guarantee faculty support, but it may permit new beliefs to emerge. Herrin has addressed this need. "It is virtually axiomatic for an international educator to advocate that more U.S. citizens go abroad," he observed (2004), but the effectiveness of this advocacy "depends on the ability of international educators to work with these other decision-makers," namely campus decision makers, the business community, and government leaders (pp. 3–4).

The need for full community participation in the transformation of the episteme is all the more compelling because the democratic structure of American higher education means that no central authority—national, regional, or local—is able to mandate changes in education abroad activity. The power of curricular development usually rests with the faculty (Brubacher, 1977; Green & Schoenberg, 2006). These traditions are clearly understood by education abroad policy makers, for as Herrin reflected: "Unlike the central role the U.S. government has with regard to foreign student and scholar flows, in study abroad the government responsibility is secondary.... If anyone is waiting for Uncle Sam to make this happen, they're in for a long wait and a great deal of disappointment" (2004, pp. 3–4).

In other words, the transformation of education abroad will not occur by dictum in the American system. Change emerges from within the system itself. The 1990a NAFSA report identified steps that must occur for policy recommendations to be implemented and urged action on the national, state, and institutional levels. *"The goal is to create a grassroots mandate for study abroad"* (p. 17, emphasis in original).

Talking to Ourselves

While the reports call for the inclusion of many constituencies in the dialogue about education abroad, discourse about foreign education is rarely widely disseminated. For example, the most recent of the NAFSA policy statements, *Securing America's Future* (NAFSA, 2003), was posted on the NAFSA Web site, accompanied by e-mail, newsletter, and magazine announcements. Although the report was available in hard copy by request, printed versions of the report were distributed only to international education policy leaders identified by NAFSA. They were handed out at a press conference that announced the report and mailed to each member of Congress (C. Herrin, personal communication, May 6, 2004). Mailing the report to members of Congress did carry the report outside the circle of those who already support study abroad but U.S. Representatives and Senators are deluged with such documents and Congress is unlikely to become a savior of education abroad (to date, for example, it has not passed legislation establishing the Lincoln Fellowships proposed by the late Senator Paul Simon). (K. Lantos, personal communication to grassroots@nafsa.org, July 28, 2008). College presidents may represent a more promising audience, but a hard copy of the report was not sent to them. These reports do not circulate to the faculty who make curricular decisions. The vast majority of American faculty members are unaware of the existence of these reports or the arguments they contain.

To build grassroots support, all members of the academy need to join the discussion because it is they who hold the power. Recognition of this responsibility is building. "In order to be successful, involvement in internationalization must extend beyond the circle of true believers," argued Green and Olson (2003, p. 81). Green and Schoenberg (2006) argued that to ensure students engage in global learning one must convince the faculty "…that global learning is a compelling goal that requires wide faculty participation" (p. 3).

At issue is how to extend discourse about international education in ways that attract faculty attention. There has indeed been an increase in the number of venues that publish research that can help produce this discourse within academe about education abroad in particular and international education in general. The Association of International Education Administrators (AIEA) began publishing the *International Education Forum* and issued "A Research Agenda for the Internationalization of Higher Education in the U.S." (Burn & Smuckler, 1995). AIEA grants totaling $10,000 annually support research related to international education (M. Kidd, personal communication to http://aieaworld.org, April 13, 1998). In the fall of 1995, Boston University began publishing *Frontiers: The Interdisciplinary Journal of Study Abroad* (N. Quigley, personal communication, June 8, 1998). *Frontiers*, now housed at Dickinson College, is sponsored by a consortium of colleges, and is a strategic partner of the Forum on Education Abroad. While these organizations support and publish research, journals on study abroad rarely circulate in the broader education community. CIEE and AIEA reported this problem in their initial journal efforts (J. Grunwald, personal communication, June 19, 1998; J. McCarthy, personal communication, June 9, 1998). Today, *Frontiers* reaches only libraries and education abroad professionals, with about 500 subscribers and a total circulation of 1,200 per issue (A. Whalen, personal communication, May 21, 2004). Articles about internationalism and education abroad that might engage or challenge the views of the faculty members across academia are not reaching them.

To strengthen the voice of education abroad advocates, CIEE expanded its agenda in 2000 by planning joint research and publication projects with other international education groups. Ten of "the world's most prestigious international education organizations," according to the *Journal of Studies in International Education* (CIEE, 1997), have joined forces with CIEE to stimulate research in international education, an effort out of which a new publication, the *Journal,* is the first concrete product. The resulting new organization, the Association for Studies in International Education (ASIE; CIEE, 1997), claims as its mission "to encourage serious research and publications concerning international education and academic mobility, to stimulate interest in such work, and to develop and promote ways to disseminate this work in a cost-effective and accessible format" (CIEE, 1997).

In January 2001, ASIE partnered with Sage Publications, a decision that expanded the outreach of the *Journal of Studies in International Education* and increased its frequency from biennial to quarterly. This major commitment to an emergent discourse, however, continues to be noticed primarily within the community of true believers.[3] This fate is shared by two other magazines that encourage research: *International Educator,* published by NAFSA (J. Steiner, personal communication, May 17, 2004) and *IIENetworker,* published by the Institute of International Education (D. Obst, personal communication, October 28, 2004). In both cases, subscribers are members of the parent organizations, which already favor international education.

Panels and committees dedicated to research now also regularly appear at international education conferences (D. Comp, personal communication, May 14, 2004; M. Kidd, personal communication, April 13, 1998). These efforts project the voices of policy advocates but their audience remains largely within the boundaries of the international education community. The challenge is how to engage the audiences who distrust the value of education abroad and do so in a manner that might generate their support.

Building Grassroots Support

Empirical studies of successful study abroad programs indicate that one of the most effective methods for change is to "build widespread faculty support," says Ann Kelleher (Kelleher, Schachterle, & Lutz, 1996, p. 417). Success is achieved by engaging faculty across the entire curriculum, revising the episteme about study abroad, and thereby building grassroots support. Several publications in recent years have offered similar suggestions to promote internationalization, including ACE's *Internationalizing the Campus: A User's Guide* (Green & Olson, 2003); NAFSA's *Internationalizing the Campus: Profiles of Success at Colleges and Universities* (NAFSA, 2007); ACE's *Promising Practices* (Engberg & Green, 2002)*;* ACE's *Reforming the Higher Education Curriculum: Internationalizing the Campus,* the ACE Global Learning for All series (Green & Schoenberg, 2006, p. iii); and Sheila Biddle's *Internationalization: Rhetoric or Reality* (2002). The University of Minnesota won an Archibald Bush Foundation grant to make just such an investment in curriculum integration of study abroad specifically and reported on their results at the Foundation's April 2004 conference. These assessments share in the effort to engage new audiences in support of international programs in higher education. They share the strategies used at institutions where broader engagement has already occurred, offering models of ways to expand the discourse. What they demonstrate is that effective initiatives all move outside the international education community and engage others in the academy in dialogue about study abroad. Their results suggest that to persuade faculty outside the education abroad community, foreign education advocates must seek wide distribution of their policy statements and partnerships with faculty outside international education circles.

Models of this approach are emerging within many disciplinary associations in the United States. One pioneer example exists in the American Assembly of Collegiate Schools of Business (AACSB). Together with the Association of American Colleges, AACSB sponsored research and published *Beyond Borders: Profiles in International Education* (Johnston & Edelstein, 1993; Kelleher et al., 1996). *Beyond Borders* provides case studies showing how business and liberal arts faculties cooperated in planning innovative international education projects. The two organizations collaborated to disseminate all research to their joint constituencies, thereby extending their audiences. Each organization carried to its own constituency the credibility needed to give weight to the message. Today, AACSB continues to support curriculum internationalization and programs abroad (AACSB, n.d.; Hult & Lashbrooke, 2003).

Other academic organizations are today joining in the endeavor, linking their members with representatives in international education in order to identify the global interests within their disciplines. Initiatives include projects undertaken by the American Chemical Society and the Accreditation Board for Engineering and Technology (ABET), the accrediting agency for programs in applied science, computing, engineering, and technology (Gore, 2005, pp. 159–160).

The American Council on Education has recently launched a major project designed to bring new faculty into advocacy roles for education abroad. The Where Faculty Live project presumes that, for faculty, their peers within disciplinary associations "…are likely to carry at least as much weight as their institutions' curricular goals or the pronouncements of policy-makers and higher education associations" (Green & Schoenberg, 2006, pp. 1, 3). ACE authors quote Sven Groennings, who wrote "In colleges and universities the academic disciplines are often the gatekeepers of educational change….basic changes…do not occur until faculty in their disciplinary and departmental arenas are ready to implement them" (p. 4, as cited in Groennings & Wiley, 1990, p. 11). With this philosophy, ACE has partnered with the Association of American Geographers (AAF), the American Historical Association (AHA), the American Political Science Association (APSA), and the American Psychological Association (APA) to "articulate global learning outcomes for their fields and begin to develop plans of action to achieve them in individual departments" (Green & Shoenberg, 2006, pp. 4, 9–17). Each association has identified goals for its discipline avoiding "…prescriptive measures, suggesting only goals and outcomes to be achieved through whatever educational experiences faculty members may devise" Green & Shoenberg, 2006, p. 19).

NAFSA recognizes the importance of partnering with academic groups to achieve this transformation. During the review of its 1990 report, members of various disciplinary associations were invited to provide input. But, as in the most recent report, the first NAFSA report was not circulated to faculty in such organizations, nor was it a research report. The campus-based initiatives and academic association approaches offered in from *Beyond Borders* and *Learning from Success* to the most recent ACE efforts include joint research, strategic planning, and communication that reach an audience well beyond those already committed to international education.

If more education abroad advocates were to follow these collaborative models, not only would more faculty members be reached, but also their belief systems would be more vigorously challenged, since the message would be coming from within their own ranks (Foucault, 1972). The range of potential links and partnerships include professional associations in all disciplines. These professional societies can speak to colleagues in their own language and generate their own renovated discourse in support of study abroad. Education abroad advocates on individual campuses can also follow suit, reaching out to their colleagues across the curriculum, as the University of Minnesota model suggests, to generate interest from within the departments not from above or outside them.

CONCLUSION

Education abroad continues to be marginalized by an episteme which devalues it, excludes the discourses of those who do value it, and leaves policy makers ineffective to change its role. Policy makers, while arguing for the value of education abroad, at the same time are constrained by this powerful episteme. Policy discourse rarely reaches beyond the international education community and statements inadvertently echo the devaluing episteme rather than transform it.

The steps outlined above may bring about change by contributing new discourse from which new conceptions can emerge. This discourse can come from research that illuminates alternative views and provides new evidence about the value of education abroad. It can come from faculty previously indisposed to foreign study but excited by their peers to explore the possibilities for their discipline through international education.

Sources for new discourse can extend well beyond those described above. As Mestenhauser (2002) has observed, it is important now to institutionalize international education and to make it a bona fide part of higher education's mission (p. 167). Faculty members who support education abroad need to be rewarded for their efforts on its behalf (Green & Schoenberg, 2006; Mestenhauser, 2002). To gain acceptance for international education, Mestenhauser (2002) argues, requires much more research on what is going on in all aspects of the field. Indeed, identifying shared interests, concerns, and values among all in the academy—domestic educators who distrust education abroad as well as their peers who advocate it—opens up the possibility for new discourse. Action on these fronts will make it all the more likely that recommendations articulated by education abroad advocates will be better received. Education abroad advocates need to do more than prescribe change to the academy if they hope to be successful. To create an audience willing to hear new discourse, ready to engage in policy dialogue, and open to validating education abroad, advocates and policy makers must engage in acts of transformation.

Advocacy and policies that prescribe change are likely to be met with continued resistance within the higher education community if the prevailing episteme is left unexamined. The seedbed of change exists within discourse itself that confronts old beliefs and reaches out to engage the very communities that have denigrated education abroad. New research, new history about education abroad and new partnerships across the disciplines are fertile ground for transformation. Therein lies the possibility that education outside the United States might come to be understood as central in the life of the American academy. With such change, faculty and administrators who support foreign education can become empowered, share in the resources and rewards of the academy, and—with new partnerships among their peers—most effectively contribute to the growth of education abroad in American higher education.

ACKNOWLEDGMENT

Portions of this chapter have appeared in Gore, J. E. (2005). *Dominant beliefs and alternative voices: Discourse, belief and gender in American study abroad.* London: Routledge/Falmer.

NOTES

1. When statements coalesce with a common theme and become a "dominant" vision, they cross the "threshold of epistemologization" and together form an episteme—a definition that gains acceptance as a powerful

"truth." For definitions of "discourse formation" and "discursive formation" see (Barker, 1998, p. 7; Foucault, 1972, chapter 2, 1978, p. xix; Merquior, 1991, p. 34).

2. Stated among the Forum's top goals are "Encouraging outcomes assessment and other research" and "Facilitating data collection." Forum on Education Abroad (n.d.).

3. The Journal circulates primarily to an audience with international education interest, though it is promoted to a general education market and there may be some circulation beyond the international education community, according to Bernie Folan (senior marketing manager at Sage Publications, London), e-mail correspondence, January 27, 2005. Sage does not release distribution figures.

REFERENCES

Altbach, P. G. (1998). *Comparative higher education: Knowledge, the university, and development.* Greenwich, CT: Ablex.

American Assembly of Collegiate Schools of Business now The Association to Advance Collegiate Business Schools (AACSB). (n.d.). Retrieved August 13, 2008, from http://www.aacsb.edu/publications

Barker, P. (1998). *Michel Foucault: An introduction.* Edinburgh, Scotland: Edinburgh University Press.

Bedford/St. Martins. (n.d.). A brief history of rhetoric and composition. Retrieved December 11, 2008, from *The Bedford Bibliography for Teachers of Writing,* http://www.bedfordstmartins.com/bb/history.html

Bennett, M. J. (1998). Intercultural communication: A current perspective. In M. J. Bennett (Ed.), *Basic concepts of intercultural communication: Selected readings* (pp. 12–35). New York: Intercultural Press.

Biddle, S. (2002). *Internationalization: Rhetoric or reality?* (ACLS Occasional Paper No. 56). New York: American Council of Learned Societies.

Bowman, J. E. (1987, November). *Educating American undergraduates abroad: The development of study abroad programs by American colleges and universities* (Occasional Papers in International Education). Retrieved December 11, 2008, from: http://www.ciee.org/research_center/occasional_papers.aspx

Briggs, A., & Burn, B. (1985). *Study abroad: A European and an American perspective.* Paris: European Institute of Education and Social Policy.

Brown, M. A. (1983). U.S. students abroad. In H. M. Jenkins & Associates (Eds.), *Educating students from other nations* (pp. 65-85). San Francisco: Jossey-Bass.

Brubacher, J. S. (1977). *On the philosophy of higher education.* San Francisco: Jossey-Bass.

Burchell, G., Gordon, C., & Miller, P. (1991). *The Foucault effect: Studies in governmentality.* Hemel Hempstead, UK: Harvester Wheatsheaf.

Burn, B., & Smuckler, R. H. (1995). *A research agenda for the internationalization of higher education in the United States: Recommendations and report.* New York: Association of International Education Administrators.

Chin, H. K. K. (Ed.). (2003). *Open doors 2003: Report on international educational exchange.* New York: Institute of International Education.

Citron, J. L. (2002). U.S. students abroad: Host culture integration or third culture formation? In W. Grünzweig & N. Rinehart (Eds.), *Rockin' in red square: Critical approaches to international education in the age of cyberculture* (pp. 41–56). Münster: Lit Verlag.

Council on International Educational Exchange (CIEE). (1988). *Educating for global competence: The report of the Advisory Council for International Educational Exchange.* New York: Author.

Council on International Educational Exchange (CIEE). (1997). Association for Studies in International Education (ASIE). *Journal of Studies in International Education,* Spring, 1, 1. Retrieved from http://www.ciee.org/journal.cfm?subnav=journal/. Today available at http://jsi.sagepub.com/archive/1997.dtl

Darvich-Kodjouri, K. (1995). *International activity on state college and university campuses.* Washington, DC: American Association of State Colleges and Universities.

Davies, G. (1996). Experiential, cooperative, and study abroad education. *Journal of Chemical Education, 73*(5), 438–440.

De Winter, B. U. (1995). *Overcoming barriers to study abroad: A report of the New York State task force on international education.* Ithaca, NY: Cornell University Press.

Engberg, D., & Green, M. F. (Eds.). (2002). *Promising practices: Spotlighting excellence in comprehensive internationalization.* Washington, DC: American Council on Education.

Engle, J., & Engle, L. (2002). Neither international nor educative: Study abroad in the time of globalization. In W. Grünzweig & N. Rinehart (Eds.), *Rockin' in red square: Critical approaches to international education in the age of cyberculture* (pp. 5–22). Münster: Lit Verlag.

Forum on Education Abroad. (n.d.). http://www.forumea.org. Retrieved June 5, 2008.

Foucault, M. (1970). *The order of things.* (A. Sheridan, Trans.) New York: Random House.

Foucault, M. (1972). *The archaeology of knowledge* (A. M. Smith, Trans.). New York: Pantheon Books.

Foucault, M. (1977). Intellectuals and power. In D. F. Bouchard (Ed.), *Language, counter-memory, practice: Selected essays and interviews* (pp. 205–217). Ithaca, NY: Cornell University Press.

Foucault, M. (1978). *The birth of the clinic: An archaeology of medical perception* (A. Smith, Trans.). New York: Vintage Books.

Foucault, M. (1980a). *Power/knowledge: Selected interviews and other writings, 1972–1977* (C. Gordon, Ed.). New York: Random House.

Foucault, M. (1980b). Truth and power. In C. Gordon (Ed.), *Power/knowledge: Selected interviews and other writings 1972–1977*. New York: Random House.

Foucault, M. (1985). *The history of sexuality: Vol. 2. Uses of pleasure* (R. Hurley, Trans.). New York: Pantheon Books.

Foucault, M. (1988a). *Politics, philosophy, culture: Interviews and other writings 1977–1984* (L. D. Kritzman, Ed., & A. Sheridan, Trans.). New York: Routledge.

Foucault, M. (1988b). *Technologies of the self: A seminar with Michel Foucault* (L. H. Martin, H. Gutman, & P. H. Hutton, Eds.). Amherst: University of Massachusetts Press.

Garraty, J. A., & Adams, W. (1959). *From main street to the left bank: Students and scholars abroad*. East Lansing: Michigan State University Press.

Goodman, A. E. (2006, Fall). Message from Allan E. Goodman. *IIE Networker, 7.*

Goodwin, C. D., & Nacht, M. (1988). *Abroad and beyond: Patterns in American overseas education*. Cambridge, UK: Cambridge University Press.

Gore, J. E. (2005). *Dominant beliefs and alternative voices: Discourse, belief, and gender in American study abroad*. New York: Routledge.

Green, M. F., Eckel, P., & Barblan, A. (2002). *The brave new (and smaller) world of higher education: A transatlantic view*. Washington, DC: American Council on Education.

Green, M. F., Luu, D., & Burris, B. (2008). *Mapping internationalization on U.S. campuses*. Washington, DC: American Council on Education.

Green, M. F., & Olson, C. (2003). *Internationalizing the campus: A user's guide*. Washington, DC: American Council on Education.

Green, M. F., & Schoenberg, R. (2006). *Where faculty live: Internationalizing the disciplines*. Washington, DC: American Council on Education.

Gregory, M. (2003, September 16). A liberal education is not a luxury. *Chronicle of Higher Education, B16.*

Groennings, S., & Wiley, D. (Eds.). (1990). *Group portrait: Internationalizing the disciplines*. New York: American Forum for Global Education.

Hayward, F. M., & Siaya, L. M. (2001). *Public experience, Attitudes and knowledge: A report on two national surveys about international education*. Washington, D.C: American Council on Education.

Herrin, C. (2004). It's time for advancing education abroad. *International Educator, 13*(1), 3–4.

Hoemeke, T. H., Krane, M., Young, J., & Slavin, G. (1999). *A survey on chief international education administrators, their institutions and offices*. Buffalo, NY: Association of International Education Administrators.

Hoffa, W. W. (2002). Learning about the future world: International education and the demise of the nation state. In W. Grünzweig & N. Rinehart (Eds.), *Rockin' in red square: Critical approaches to international education in the age of cyberculture* (pp. 57-74). Münster: Lit Verlag.

Honeywell, R. J. (1931). *The educational work of Thomas Jefferson*. Cambridge, MA: Harvard University Press.

Hult, G., Tomas, M., & Lashbrooke, E. C. (Eds.). (2003). *Study abroad: Perspectives and experiences from business schools*. Amsterdam and Boston: JAI.

Institute of international Education [IIE]. (n.d.). Retrieved from http://www.iienetwork.org/?p=34243/

Institute of International Education [IIE]. (2008). Retrieved August 13, 2008, from http://opendoors.iienetwork.org/?p=131556

International Education Leadership Act of 2008, Retrieved January 29, 2009 from http://www.govtrack.us/congress/bill.xpd?bill=h110-5179

J. Walter Thompson Education for the Institute of International Education, the German Academic Exchange Service (DAAD), The British Council, and the Australian Education Office. (n.d.). *An exploration of the demand for study overseas from American students and employers: An analysis of how future employment considerations are likely to impact students' decisions to study overseas and employers' perceptions*. Retrieved December 12, 2008, from http://www.nafsa.org/_/File/_/study_by_iie_daad_bc.pdf

Jenkins, K., & Skelly, J. (2004). Education abroad is not enough. *International Educator, 13*(1), 8–9.

Johnston J. S. Jr. & Edelstein, R. (1993). *Beyond borders: Profiles in international education*. Washington, DC: Association of American Colleges and Universities.

Kelleher, A., Schachterle, L., & Lutz, F. (Eds.). (1996). *Learning from success: Campus case studies in international program development*. New York: Lang.

Lambert, R. (1988, November). Worcester Polytechnic Institute Studies in Technology and Culture, Volume 15.

Study abroad: Where we are, where we should be. Paper presented at the 41st Annual Conference on International Educational Exchange, Cannes, France.

Lewin, T. (1998, December 6). Colleges in the U.S. beginning to ask, where have all the men gone? *New York Times,* p. A38 .

Malone, D. (1981). *The sage of Monticello.* Boston: Little, Brown.

Merquior, J. G. (1991). *Foucault.* London: Fontana Press/HarperCollins.

Mestenhauser, J. (2002). In search of a comprehensive approach to international education: A systems perspective. In W. Grünzweig & N. Rinehart (Eds.), *Rockin' in red square: Critical approaches to international education in the age of cyberculture* (pp. 165–214). Münster: Lit Verlag.

Mourad, J. (1997). *Postmodern philosophical critique and the pursuit of knowledge in higher education* (H. A. Giroux, Ed.). Westport, CT: Bergin & Garvey.

Munroe, J. A. (1986). *The University of Delaware: A history.* Newark, DE: University of Delaware Press.

NAFSA: Association for International Educators. (1990). *A national mandate for study abroad: Getting on with the task, report of the national task force on undergraduate study abroad.* Washington, DC: Author.

NAFSA: Association for International Educators. (2002, July/August). Survey sheds light on members. *NAFSA Newsletter.*

NAFSA: Association for International Educators. (2003). *Securing America's future : Global education for a global age, report of the strategic task force on study abroad.* Washington, DC: Author.

NAFSA: Association for International Educators. (n.d.). *Understanding the Simon Act.* Retrieved from http://www.nafsa.org/knowledge_community_network.sec/education_abroad_1/year_of_study_abroad_3/practice_resources_15/understanding_the_simon

NAFSA: Association for International Educators. (2007). *Internationalizing the Campus: Profiles of Success at Colleges and Universities* (L. Schock, Ed.). Washington, DC.

National Geographic-Roper. (2006). *Survey of geographic literacy.* Retrieved from http://www.nationalgeographic.com/roper2006/findings.html

Newcomer, M. (1959). *A century of higher education for American women.* Washington, DC: Zenger.

Obst, D., Bhandari, R., & Witherell, S. (2007). *Meeting America's global education challenge: Current trends in U.S. study abroad & the impact of strategic diversity initiatives.* New York: Institute of International Education.

Olmsted, P. (1987, May). *Sixty years of study abroad: A backward glance at the profession.* Presentation at NAFSA Conference, Long Beach, CA.

Reilly, K. M. (1995). Unpublished paper.

Siaya, L., & Hayward, F. M. (2003). *Mapping internationalization on U.S. campuses: Final report 2003.* Washington, DC: American Council on Education.

Strout, E. (2004, April 2). Median salaries of midlevel college administrators by type of institution, 2003–4. *Chronicle of Higher Education online.* Retrieved April 2, 2004 from http://chronicle.com/weekly/v50/i30/30a03001.htm/

U.S. Congress. (2003). *House Report 108-10. Making further continuing appropriations for the fiscal year 2003, and for other purposes,* accompanying H.J. Res. 2. Consolidated Appropriations Resolution.

Wiener, P. P. (Ed.). (1973). *Dictionary of the history of ideas: Studies of selected pivotal ideas.* New York: Scribner.

Wilson, R. (2004, April 23). Faculty salaries rise 2.1%, the lowest increase in 30 years. *Chronicle of Higher Education,* p. A13.

Chapter 18

Selling the World

Study Abroad Marketing and the Privatization of Global Citizenship

Talya Zemach-Bersin

Yale University

From the moment they step onto the campuses of liberal arts colleges and universities, American students are inundated with advertisements promoting study abroad. In hallways and classrooms, glossy posters depicting faraway locations urge students to spend a spring break, summer, semester, or year encountering new people, places, and languages in a destination of their choice. By the time American undergraduates finally point to a program description in a seductively designed catalogue and declare their adventure of choice, they have both unconsciously and consciously been absorbing the images and rhetoric of international education advertisements for years. Although dedicated international educators often encourage global citizenship education with a focus on civic engagement and cross-cultural respect, program advertisements appeal instead to American students' sense of entitlement, consumerism, and individualism. This institutionalized commercial rhetoric influences how students approach international education, the quality of education in which they are prepared to engage, and, ultimately, the political and social foundations of our future.[1]

In recent years, America has been increasingly criticized for its cowboy diplomacy, poorly informed foreign policy, international ignorance, and arrogant insistence on asserting a global moral and political authority throughout the world. Educators and politicians have responded by citing study abroad and global citizenship education as valuable methods for countering cross-cultural incompetence and parochialism in American culture. The ways in which study abroad programs are promoted to students, however, undermines many of the goals that international educators endeavor to achieve. Even under the banners of global citizenship and cross-cultural understanding, advertisements endorse attitudes of consumerism, entitlement, privilege, narcissism, and global and cultural ignorance. This chapter identifies and critiques the major advertising tropes that help to inform the ways in which students conceptualize and approach an international education experience pre-departure. In an attempt to enroll students, advertisers have sacrificed defining study abroad in progressive and critical terms. To better understand the negative pre-departure effects of study abroad advertising, I will present an analysis of student interviews that illustrate the extent to which many students understand study abroad as a commodity, an entitlement, and a non-academic adventure. The second half of this chapter critiques the rhetoric of global citizenship and explores some of the reasons why the current state of global citizenship education is often insufficient to successfully counter the harmful narrative of study abroad promoted by advertisements. While contextualizing these challenges within the broader context of

American culture, I will suggest some possible methods for preparing students to approach study abroad critically and responsibly. By shifting the focus of pre-departure from global to local, students can be encouraged to un-learn, rather than enact, many of the problematic attitudes prevalent in U.S. culture that international educators seek to ameliorate

Advertisements are not benign; they influence how consumers understand and think about products, experiences, and even their own identities. Advertisements are also shaped by the cultures and societies from which they emerge. An analysis of study abroad advertisements therefore raises concerns about higher education practices that both inform and are informed by American culture and society. This multidirectional flow of influence blurs the relationships between ideas, perceptions, cultures, and advertisements, often making distinct origins impossible to delineate. Study abroad advertisements are only one of the many influences that students are exposed to predeparture. Other forms of mass media, as well as the attitudes and opinions of peers, politicians, families, and teachers also affect the ways in which students approach and understand international education. It is especially important and informative to explore study abroad advertisements, however, because of what they can tell us about the calculated, institutional, widespread, and commercial framing of international education with the specific goal of motivating students to study abroad. In what ways are students influenced by the commercial discourse of study abroad? To what extent do students reproduce this discourse in the language they use to describe their experiences of study abroad? Perhaps most importantly, what can be done to ensure that American students are prepared to engage responsibly and critically with the world beyond U.S. borders?

To help answer these questions about the relationships between advertising and the perceptions of students, I interviewed 25 juniors and seniors from Wesleyan University who studied abroad.[2] Interviews lasted between 30 minutes and 3 hours. I asked a series of questions about the initial process of choosing a program, predeparture expectations, personal thoughts on identity and travel, and hindsight wishes and critiques. The students interviewed had traveled to a wide variety of countries throughout the world, including Ghana, India, England, Greece, Argentina, Nicaragua, South Africa, Ecuador, Nepal, Morocco, and the Czech Republic. They had traveled abroad with a range of program providers, including the School for International Training (SIT), the Institute of International Education (IIE), the Council on International Educational Exchange (CIEE), and the International Honors Program (IHP). In terms of race and gender, this sampling of students was roughly proportional to national study abroad statistics. Seventy-five percent of those interviewed identified as women, and approximately 80% identified as White or Caucasian (Abraham Lincoln Study Abroad, 2006). However, in many ways the 25 students interviewed are not representative of all American students who study abroad. As students at an elite, private, and costly university, it is likely that the majority of students interviewed come from middle to upper class backgrounds, have had at least some travel experience prior to their semester abroad, and have enjoyed a rigorous, high quality academic education for most of their lives. From 2005 to 2006, approximately 40% of Wesleyan students selected study abroad destinations that are considered "developing" or within the "third world." Additionally, the majority of Wesleyan students study abroad with third party program providers such as SIT or CIEE.

While interviewees come from a diversity of backgrounds and traveled to a wide range of countries, they are all Wesleyan University students who have access to Wesleyan's study abroad ideology and participate in the Wesleyan campus environment. Both the academic and social cultures of Wesleyan are decidedly liberal, fostering a critical awareness of inequality, power relations, and systems of oppression. Wesleyan, like many private liberal arts universities, has in recent years engaged in a project of celebrating the globalization of higher education. Wesleyan considers "intellectually rigorous study abroad" to be an integral component of "the University's efforts to internationalize the curriculum and prepare students for global citizenship" (Wesleyan University Office of International Studies, Mission Statement, n.d.). Almost 50% of Wesleyan students study abroad for credit and they participate in approximately 150 programs in 50 countries (Wesleyan University Office of International Studies, About Us, n.d.). In 2005, Wesleyan introduced a strategic plan called "Engaged with the World," in which the university declared its efforts to "prepare our students to face a rapidly changing world with confidence and the sense of responsibility to want to make the world a better place" (Wesleyan University, 2005, para.1). Wesleyan's efforts are part of a national trend in which institutions of higher education are seeking to integrate the values of global citizenship into the liberal arts undergraduate experience. It is likely that the types of concerns raised by Wesleyan students are similar to those of students at other elite, private, liberal arts institutions where studying abroad is widely accepted. The Abraham Lincoln Study Abroad report (2005) on the status of study abroad in the United States asserted that "If participation rates by type of institutions are considered, liberal arts colleges come to the fore," noting that small liberal arts colleges send a larger proportion of their students abroad than other institutions (pp. 14–15). By locating Wesleyan students within a national, political, and social context, I address themes beyond the university campus, drawing attention to specific perceptions and experiences in order to shed light on some less recognized aspects of international education and the predeparture experiences of students.

Advertisements for study abroad are a distinct example of the commercialization of higher education, and the extension of consumerism into the field of international education. Wesley Shumar (1997) examines how education itself has become a product that is packaged and sold to student consumers. "The purchase of goods and services, once a metaphor for tuition and learning," Shumar (1997) writes, "is now the central reality of college life, with learning itself imagined as a purchasable service commodity" (p. 126). Instead of treating learning as an engaged and committed process, the education system often functions as though learning is a thing that can be purchased. Study abroad commercialization has in many ways paralleled the commodification of higher education, to such a degree that many people now perceive of international education as a prepackaged experience, in which students are passive consumers (Bolen, 2001). In this fantasy, foreign destinations and their citizens are products or commodities. It is likely that as study abroad providers have multiplied to service the growing numbers of Americans looking for an international education experience, the competition and commercialization within the industry has increased. Students are told that they can purchase not only international travel itself, but also cross-cultural understanding, global citizenship, personal advancement, and adventure. Countless study abroad advertisements actively and thoroughly communicate the idea that international education is a commodity. The desires and bodies of Americans are positioned as important and valuable, while the countries and the people being visited are depicted as backdrops, props, and products that can be purchased for the students' personal growth and development.

Proponents of international education regularly assert that students who study abroad will learn to see the world from new perspectives and gain deep respect and appreciation for cultural difference while cultivating mutual understanding across cultures. Advertisements for study abroad, however, tell a significantly different story. In *The Whiteness of Power: Racism in Third World Development and Aid*, Paulette Goudge (2003) identifies the extent to which advertisements for international travel focus "almost exclusively on the anticipation of personal achievement spiced up with the opportunity for adventure and a chance to experience the exotic" (p. 15). Goudge argues that advertisers of international travel seem to have determined that "directly hooking into a range of personal interests and desires will be more successful" than discussing larger and more complex pictures of cultural interactions (p. 15). By "successful," Goudge is clearly referring to higher rates of participation, not the quality of learning. "The needs and desires" of the traveler, Goudge writes, "are continually highlighted and are visually illustrated on every page through photos and drawings. Their greater importance is continually stressed" (p. 15). Frequently, advertisements for international education indulge in the same language as tourism or adventure travel. As Wally Olins, Chairman of a consulting firm that created a tourism campaign for Poland, told *Travel & Leisure* magazine, advertising a travel destination "boils down to…manipulation and seduction" (Chermayeff, 2007, para. 22). Advertisements for study abroad similarly seek to manipulate the thoughts and desires of students in an effort to seduce them into enrollment and participation. Program providers engage consumers by capitalizing on the ways in which aspects of U.S. culture value personal advancement, achievement, adventure, and individual success, regardless of the broader consequences of such actions.

Study abroad is positioned through marketing and popular discourse as an experience designed primarily for the individual consumer's self-improvement and personal fulfillment. Typically, study abroad providers spare little hyperbole when attempting to convince students of the profound and life-altering powers of a semester abroad. Cross-Cultural Solutions (2006) advertises their programs by luring students with the anticipatory statements, "It's an exciting and personally inspiring experience, and you'll develop memories that will be with you forever. It's the experience of a Lifetime!" (p. 9). This is echoed by the American Institute for Foreign Study (2006), which claims that they, too, can provide students with the "life-changing experience of study abroad" (p. 20). The School for International Training's (SIT) Web site (n.d.) encourages students to "transform your life and undergraduate education with a challenging semester or summer abroad" (home page). World Learning's home page (2008) claims to offer "culturally rich" undergraduate study abroad programs, and an SIT program brochure (2007) explains to students that their product "will prove invaluable to your future" (p. 1). Wesleyan's Office of International Studies (OIS, n.d.) similarly explains that by providing their students with study abroad options, they are offering students "a wealth of knowledge and experience that can enrich the personal, academic, and professional lives of participants" (About Us, para. 1). As shown here, advertisements often use words with strong monetary connotations, such as *enrich, rich, wealth,* and *invaluable.* In this way, study abroad is articulated as having a social currency or commercial value that students can both literally and metaphorically "profit" from. CIEE attempts to convince students that they are incomplete and in a state of hunger, want, and desire without the CIEE product. Study abroad, CIEE (n.d.) explains on their Web site, is "for anyone who wants to indulge in a passion" or "explore a fascination." By claiming to create "programs that fulfill students' academic hungers and adventurous desires," CIEE promises that their product will satiate and fulfill the needs of students. CIEE (2007) also asks boldly on their promotional brochures, "What will your story be?" (cover), doing little to disguise the sentiment that it is acceptable for students to think only of themselves and their own advancement. All of these advertisements explicitly position study abroad as a product serving the individual American student's quest for success, personal development, and social advancement.

While American students are depicted as active and adventurous, many advertisements describe the world outside of the United States as passive, submissive, and open. Oftentimes, study abroad destinations are represented as literally waiting to fulfill the needs and desires of American students. International Studies Abroad (ISA, 2006) advertises with the slogan "The

World Awaits…" (p. 2), and Lesley University's Audubon Expedition Institute (2006) runs study abroad programs with the motto "Let's wake up the world" (p. 25). These advertisements imply that countries across the globe are oblivious, sleeping, or passively waiting for American students. This depiction of a passive world "waiting" for a study abroad student's discovery is common, from James Madison University's (n.d.) study abroad Web site rejoicing in the statement "the world is waiting!" (para.7) to StudyAbroad.com's (2006) enticing exclamation "Study Abroad: because the whole world is waiting to be explored." Such rhetoric inadvertently evokes the sexual and gendered language of colonialism, in which foreign lands are characterized as passive, needy, undeveloped, and submissive as a justification for exploitation and domination.[3] Unfortunately, study abroad advertisements frequently fall into this historically informed trope, portraying American students as not just more important, but far more active, real, and powerful than the world beyond the borders of the United States. By assigning the qualities of passivity and unconsciousness to non-U.S. countries, study abroad advertisements portray program destinations as prepackaged commodities just "waiting" to be purchased and consumed.

Study abroad advertisements and promotional materials also depict a world that can be owned and controlled by the study abroad student. For example, the Glimpse Foundation (n.d.), a group devoted to "fostering cross-cultural understanding and exchange, particularly between the United States and the rest of the world," has developed the slogan, "It's your world, get acquainted" (para. 1). Similarly, SIT has named their "online community" for SIT alumni "Our-World," although 96.5% of SIT students during the fall 2005 semester were from the United States alone (SIT, 2006). These advertisements validate the idea that knowledge leads to power and ownership. They additionally espouse the notion that the entire world is preordained as the property of the American student. Student consumers are told that the world is already theirs to enjoy, regardless of how much they know. By claiming the entire world external to the United States as "ours," study abroad advertisements communicate the idea that Americans have a legitimate global authority, which can be enacted through a semester abroad. For example, CIEE (n.d.) tells their students to "make the world give up its secrets" (para. 1), and "make the world your laboratory" (para. 3). CIEE's advertising slogan both lauds and encourages imperialist desires for international control and coercion. The phrase "make the world" evokes the possibility of arm-twisting to ensure that students get what they want out of their semester abroad. Students are encouraged to believe that because they can purchase and consume the world as their "laboratory" for personal adventure and exploration, there is no secret they cannot obtain, no boundary they cannot cross. The expansion of U.S. power and hegemony throughout the globe is legitimized and naturalized by these ill-conceived advertisements that both audaciously and unconsciously assert that the entire world belongs to, and can be controlled by, the American student who studies abroad.

Descriptions of a waiting world are reinforced by a trope of "discovery" and expanding "frontiers." The United States is a nation built upon a narrative of discovery and expansion, and U.S. popular culture frequently uses the term *discover* to refer to places that are known and inhabited, refusing to relinquish fantasies of ownership and authority that follow the act of discovery.[4] The illusion of discovery is firmly rooted in the U.S. collective imagination, and study abroad advertisements often capitalize on this fantasy. Such advertisements place the study abroad student in the position of explorer and adventurer, bravely penetrating the depths of other lands to discover new knowledge. University of Virginia's study abroad Semester at Sea (2006), for example, is advertised as a means for students to "discover many cultures" (p. 13), while Lexia International (2005) encourages students to "Make your study abroad a personal discovery" (p. 1). CIEE taps into the American desire for discovery simply by placing the word *discover*, on the cover of many of their promotional materials and handing out stickers printed with the word at study abroad fairs. One of the leading academic journals on study abroad is called *Frontiers*, a name that inadvertently invokes the imperialist desires of figures in American history, such as Frederick Jackson Turner and Theodore Roosevelt, who viewed the American frontier as the line between civilization and savagery, in need of constant expansion outwards. Framing study abroad within the language of discovery grants the experience a status of mythlike proportion and glory with roots in frequently violent and destructive histories. Accordingly, indulging in the discourse of "discovery," has the effect of disregarding the lives, achievements, and histories of those who already inhabit host nations.

The full color photographic images found in study abroad advertisements and brochures provide consumers with visual representations of the proposed benefits and values of the abroad experience. Intended to sell study abroad as an easily accessible product, the images often depict scenes showing cross-cultural friendships between a happy White student and exotic non-White locals. This approach is ubiquitous in visual advertisements for study abroad. Pitzer College's advertisements use this type of image repeatedly in a single catalogue, nearly one for each of their advertised program locations. In one Pitzer College brochure (2007), a picture entitled, "Hamming it up with new Botswanan friends," depicts a White male student with blond hair in a clean, collared shirt surrounded by smiling African children in worn clothing who appear eager to be photographed (p. 9). As a symbolically paternalistic figure, he sits in the center of the image at a slightly higher elevation than the rest. The International Honors Program (2007–2008) advertises similarly, with an image of a smiling White female student, dressed in a beaded headdress and chest piece, standing in the center of the image surrounded by out of focus, blurry black bodies (p. 8). The viewers' attention is drawn in both cases to the White American student, as if to suggest that non-White locals are background props or passive scenery to be enjoyed by their guests. Local hosts are depicted as an undifferentiated group, apparently nameless and often unworthy of being shown in focus.

Some students reflect similar sentiments in their own photographs. A "self portrait" taken in Ghana, which was awarded an Honorable mention in SIT's 2006 Photo Contest, depicts a White female student in a bright yellow dress holding an open pad of paper and a pen in her hand (Walters-Bugbee, 2006). She is sitting with her legs crossed surrounded by a crowd of mostly male Ghanaians. The Ghanaians are watching her, eagerly leaning toward her as she writes. It is unclear whether she is teaching or being taught, listening or being heard. The only unambiguous aspect of this photograph, as with the others, is that the White study abroad student is happily the center of attention in a moment that highlights both amiability and difference. Despite the fact that over 10 people are shown in the photograph, it is resolutely titled "Self Portrait," clearly referring to the White student in the center of the image. While this particular image is a personal photograph, its endorsed position on SIT's Web site locates it within a more general theme of study abroad images in which the White American student is presented as a superior and powerful figure.

Other images in study abroad advertising use motifs of individual success and achievement to highlight the potential benefits of study abroad by focusing solely on the visiting American student. The cover of Pitzer College's study abroad catalogue (2007) shows a full-page photograph of a White female student in blue jeans and sneakers alone on a rooftop. As she performs a ballet arabesque, the Great Wall of China and the Chinese Himalayan mountain range are visible in the distance below her (cover). Reveling in this moment of "the view from above" (Pratt,

1992), the student strikes her pose with a smile. Her front arm and hand is extended higher than the mountains. Her study abroad location is depicted as a backdrop for her personal enjoyment, against which she occupies a position of superiority. She can survey her location from above and benefit from this symbolically privileged position. A similar image was awarded SIT's grand prize for their 2006 student photo contest for capturing "the heart of Study Abroad" (Richardson, 2005). In this photograph, a young man is shown with his back to the camera, against a mountain range in Ladakh, India. His right fist is raised high above his head in a sign of victory. The photographer's creative use of perspective creates an illusion in which the student's body is as tall as the mountain range. Once again, the student's personal photograph imparts values consistent with other motifs in study abroad advertisements, which promote discovery, personal ownership, advancement, achievement, strength, and success. The happy White student remains the most significant concern, positioned as even larger and more profound than the Himalayas.

Visual and rhetorical themes such as these work together to structure a narrative of study abroad intended to appeal to American college students. This chapter has so far imposed distinct thematic categories through which to understand advertisements, but the separate motifs found in study abroad advertising act in cooperation and conjunction with one another to define study abroad along specific lines. While attempting to enroll students, advertisements for international education often promote highly problematic, insensitive, and disingenuous ideologies. By describing study abroad as an experience primarily about the advancement of American students, study abroad advertisements sacrifice a commitment to mutual and respectful learning across cultures. Tropes of discovery, ownership, and the submissive accessibility of the world beyond U.S. borders devalue study abroad destinations while highlighting the power and importance of American students. Study abroad is advertised as an experience that is available to American students regardless of their motivations, actions, or degree of knowledge. Overall, the commercial discourse of study abroad fundamentally frames international education, study abroad destinations, and the citizens of foreign countries as commodities.

It is this problematic narrative that students described being exposed to most intensely prior to their departure, and before the realities, challenges, and complexities of a semester abroad set in. Advertisements are likely at the pinnacle of their influence at the moments in which students select program locations and develop story lines to explain their choices to educators, family, and friends. Most students subconsciously learn from advertisements long before international educators have the opportunity to frame study abroad in more critical and complex terms. Although the students interviewed for this research had already returned from their semesters abroad, this analysis focuses on predeparture experiences and thoughts. I asked students to "think back" to predeparture, understanding that they would inevitably bring a postprogram perspective to their analysis. With the comfort of public anonymity, students did not sugar coat their attitudes or defend their actions. The majority of students were self-critical, expressing disdain and embarrassment for their previous perspectives. Students spoke bluntly about their motivations and expectations. In retrospect, some students felt they had betrayed their own intelligence and ethical instincts while selecting programs and preparing to study abroad. Although they regarded themselves as media savvy and progressively self-conscious, students recall having had predeparture attitudes that were overwhelmingly in accordance with the commercial narrative of study abroad.

The responses of Wesleyan students who studied abroad are indicative of the beliefs held by many elite American college students who have come to see study abroad as a rite of passage that will foster their personal growth and development. The *New York Times* announced that many "students now believe that studying abroad is an entitlement" (Gordon, 2006). Thirteen out of 25 Wesleyan students interviewed explained that they studied abroad because it was simply something they "always knew" they would do. As Lucy stated, "I just always knew that I would…. So it wasn't a question of *if*, it was a question of when and where." For Kasey, "It just seemed like the thing to do," while Gloria similarly assumed she would go abroad from "whatever age" it was when she first "discovered that was an option." Lindsay's response is further illuminating: "I barely decided to go abroad. It was sort of always something I assumed I would do." As Dakota said, "It never even really occurred to me that I *wouldn't* go abroad." It is as if, for these students, the decision to study abroad has already been made for them. Their responses accurately reflect the language used by Wesleyan's office of international studies. Wesleyan's OIS (n.d./a) Web site explains that study abroad can greatly improve the lives of students, and then celebrates the fact that "Wesleyan students seem to recognize this instinctively" (About Us, para.1). By discussing an interest in study abroad as a natural "instinct," Wesleyan's study abroad rhetoric renders the powerful influences of culture, privilege, education, and advertisements invisible and unimportant. As passive consumers, students are not encouraged to ask why they have "always known" that they would study abroad, and as a result are not required to take responsibility for their attitudes or decisions.

Despite describing themselves as having submissively and inactively made the decision to study abroad, most students had explanations for why they ultimately wanted to participate in an education abroad program. For many students, this had to do with a desire to take a break from school. Lindsay described her motivations succinctly when she said, "It had nothing to do with anything besides the fact that I wanted to get outside of Wesleyan, I was ready for change, and I wanted to challenge myself. That was it." Ten other students likewise identified the desire to take a break from campus life as their motivating factor for going abroad. For Jason, the decision to study abroad was inspired "first and foremost by the desperate need to leave [Wesleyan]." Desdemona said she wanted to "go somewhere far away and do something different." Kendrah first started thinking about studying abroad when her older friends warned her, "you *have* to go abroad, you're going to get tired of Wesleyan." Dakota likewise expressed a desire "get off of campus," adding that "there were no cultural reasons or academic reasons. I just needed to have some time away." Ruby similarly said she wanted to go abroad because she "just really didn't want to be in school." As seen here, many students initially think of a semester abroad as a vacation and as a break from academic responsibilities. International educator Thomas V. Millington (2002) writes that study abroad application essays or statements of interest often make him "wonder if the student is really interested in study abroad, or are they expecting to take a glorified vacation that they can translate into college credit?" (para. 4). Millington, of course, understands "study abroad" and "glorified vacation" to be two different experiences. Advertisements, on the other hand, have described the two as virtually synonymous by employing touristic themes of adventure and discovery with little accent on rigorous academic learning.

While some students described their decision to study abroad much as one would explain the desire for a vacation, seven of the interviewed students had motivations and expectations that are more specific to international education, namely, an interest in learning and developing new perspectives. These students noted the general value of studying a different culture while they described learning as a form of self-improvement. For example, as a student of international politics and government, Tim believed, "being able to see interactions from a different perspective…was a very important thing to do" in the field of international relations. Stacy explained that she wanted to "go beyond the states to get perspective on my own life here in America," while Kasey viewed her time abroad as a search for knowledge: "I really don't like the feeling of not understanding the world at large." Statements such as these reflect the belief that study abroad is a quest for knowledge that will improve the lives and educations of the individual student. Only one student described her desire to study abroad as having to do with a larger picture of civic duty or community responsibility: Ruby wanted to be better prepared to be a "positive member of society and the rest of the world," and thought her abroad experience could provide such an education. With the exception of Ruby, the knowledge that students hoped to gain while abroad fits into a broader theme of self-improvement and personal fulfillment. Many students view international education as a commodity serving a dual purpose: providing a change or adventure, and providing the knowledge needed to personally succeed in the globalized world. Just like advertisements, predeparture understandings of study abroad focus almost entirely on the individual American student's consumer needs.

Advertisements are the medium through which many students are first introduced to specific program providers and study abroad destinations. Interviewed students reported literally shopping for their study abroad experience by reading through brochures and catalogues. A February 2006 Wesleyan student newspaper article warns "indecisive types" that "to explore the library" in the Office of International Studies "is to choose between 39 countries and over 150 programs" (Wollman, 2006). With so many options from which to choose, it does not come as a surprise that many students reported finding themselves bound for locations about which they knew little, if anything. Ten of those interviewed described their program selection process as a relatively random shot in the dark. Lindsay, for example, selected a Tibetan Studies program from the SIT brochure while admitting that she knew "nothing about Tibet. I knew nothing about the political situation there." Jason chose his program after not "much more than a glance at any of the programs, including the one I chose." On the day the applications to study abroad were due, Jason selected a program in Ghana, saying "Eh, what the hell. I knew nothing about Ghana other than, well, it sounded nice. It had a nice ring. That was about it. It was really serendipitous." Susan, who decided to go to South Africa, said that she "didn't have much of an understanding" of South Africa, but "was just like oh, I think it will be interesting, like more of a whimsical decision." Making the role of advertisements explicitly clear in this process, Molly said that she circled about half of the programs on the SIT brochure until she "fell in love with the Uganda program on the brochure," although she doesn't "really quite know why." Julie, having "decided that I wanted to go somewhere where I would be completely out of my comfort zone and really had to rely on myself," explained that her program choices "really came down to Kenya, South Africa, and Fiji, and what else…there was some other weird country in there…oh, Malta." Admitting her lack of direction, Julie believed that her final decision to go to South Africa was "just kind of happenstance." In line with what study abroad advertisements espouse, students assume the openness and accessibility of the rest of the world to their personal desires, "whimsy," and escapist dreams regardless of their cultural and historical ignorance. Furthermore, to Wesleyan students, many of whom have significant previous travel experience, it is as though "exotic" and "unknown" program destinations carry a greater social currency than more familiar countries such as France or England. The less students know about a country, the more "life-changing" their adventure and experience of discovery may be. In this way, selecting a "random" program destination from an advertisement signifies a contemporary and individualistic method of conquering the dark unknown. By acquiring knowledge in "exotic" locations, study abroad students can make the world beyond U.S. borders legible, knowable, and therefore both consumable and controllable.

As established repeatedly by educators and politicians alike, one of the primary goals of international education is to counter cultures of global ignorance in America. The Office of International

Studies at Wesleyan hopes that students will develop international awareness even before they begin their semester abroad. Once they are accepted into a program, students are encouraged to research their destination prior to departure. OIS faculty tell students that it is "incredibly important" that they know as much as possible about their host country, particularly contemporary history and current issues so that they are better able to understand their surroundings, avoid making uneducated cultural assumptions, and to learn more from the experience. Students are provided with a variety of educational resources, ranging from books, movies, Web sites, and the wisdom of professors and study abroad alums. The Office of International Studies at Wesleyan holds region specific and sometimes program specific predeparture programs, intended to prepare students for studying abroad. Nearly all students interviewed, however, did not understand the potential importance of such an event. Scott, for example, attended his predeparture program, but explained, "It was really useless. I don't even remember what was said." Dakota similarly asserted that she was only told "totally obvious and useless things" at her predeparture program. Most students appear uncommitted and possibly uninterested in learning a great deal about their program and destination prior to departure. After all, the experience has not been sold to them as a studious or serious one in which cultural ignorance is scorned, but as an exciting act of personal discovery, adventure, and success.

This attitude extends beyond the university's predeparture program, and into the realm of personal preparation. Eleven of the interviewed students reported having read one book or less about their host country. According to Julie;

> I read Nelson Mandela's autobiography. That's it. I went with like actually zero preparation in actually knowing anything about South Africa. I didn't even know what kind of food they had. I didn't actually know anything. When the plane was taking off I said oh my god what did I just get myself into. And that's when the panic set in, of like you just went, you just did something, and you have no idea really what you're doing.

Because Julie understood her experience to be primarily for her personal development, her anxiety ridden question "what did I just get myself into?" shows little regard for the bigger picture, in which her ignorance will affect not just her quality of learning, but also potentially the lives and experiences of the South Africans with whom she interacts. In preparation for her trip to Prague, Dakota "read a few books by Czech authors and freaked out about my clothes." Ellie "got a guide book and that was it." Scott "took a class on Spanish cinema…but other than that I didn't do reading or research. I just kind of went!" Before spending the semester at the University of Sussex, Jessica "watched some English TV shows." While some students, like Julie, experienced their lack of preparedness as a source of last minute anxiety, others reported having intentionally neglected predeparture research in an effort to preserve the excitement of "mystery" and to have a raw experience of discovery and adventure. According to Jason:

> We got this elaborate list of readings and Internet resources and all these disclaimers of like, "all the students who come back all say one thing: they wish they had read more, blah blah." But just the kind of person I am, I love to go in fresh. And I was going there to get kind of punched in the face. And I didn't want to have that mitigated by any media depictions, especially Western media. I wanted culture shock. I wasn't going to be a tourist. I was going to live there. I wanted to go in fresh and make it for myself as opposed to having it made for me.

Although Jason did not want his experience to be influenced by Western media, his statements are consistent with the narrative of study abroad found in advertisements. His belief that he could "go in fresh" and "make it for myself" reflects both an ahistorical naiveté and a false expectation of power and control. Ideas about the value of individualism, the lure of discovery, and the entitlement to travel to locations with no prior cultural knowledge are all present in Jason's comment, showing the extent to which students' expectations and values closely match those established in advertisements. Rather than committing to study abroad as an educational experience that begins prior to departure, many students wait until after their plane has landed in Ghana, South Africa, or the Czech Republic to begin the process of learning about a culture and society other than their own. Ironically, while international educators seek to ameliorate the stereotype that Americans are globally illiterate and cross-culturally incompetent, American students frequently indulge in global ignorance in order to have the life-changing adventure that study abroad advertisements have promised.

Though students often put little effort into their predeparture preparation and program selection, they expect to reap significant benefits from the experience in return. Just as advertisements promise, students anticipate "life changing" experiences. Patrick, for example, said:

> Part of the appeal of going to Africa was I felt like when I went there my whole thought process would be changed and skewed. I felt like by going to Africa I would start appreciating things a lot more...I thought it would make me a way better person.

As prescribed by study abroad advertisements promoting personal growth and advancement, destinations most significantly represent something from which students can personally benefit. As a passive consumer of the study abroad commodity, Patrick assumed that "Africa" would "make" him a "better person," as if he needed to do little more than arrive on Ghanaian soil for the product to work its magic. Julie identified study abroad as part of her search for "independence," and Dakota thought that by going abroad she would have the opportunity to "take care of myself, and get myself in shape" after a particularly difficult school year. In fact, when asked what their expectations were, every student spoke only of him- or herself. They expected to be challenged, to grow, to see new places, to gain language skills, to achieve independence, and to have an adventure. Even before students experience study abroad for themselves, they expect that their semester away will be, as Kent State University (2008) advertises, "adventure for a semester— experience for a lifetime" (p. 85).

Both study abroad advertisements and participating students discuss international education as an entitlement, a nonacademic adventure, and an experience primarily for personal advancement. Perhaps partly in response to the prevalence of such troubling attitudes, educators, politicians, institutions of higher education, and study abroad providers alike have been calling for global citizenship education. While global citizenship is often promoted alongside other major themes in study abroad advertising, it stands apart as an ideology that attempts to appeal to notions of global responsibility, community, mutual learning across cultures, and idealism, rather than simply personal advancement based on an understanding of the world as a consumable commodity. Experiential Learning (2007), for example, explains on their Web site that when "students develop an analytical and compassionate lens, and integrate themselves into a world community," they become "truly global citizens" (para. 4). In this way, it is hoped that the values of global citizenship education will counter the consumerist and self-centered attitudes that are rampant in both U.S. society and study abroad advertisements. Through various advertisements, articles on study abroad, university mission statements, and other international education promotional materials, students are invited to become global citizens by studying abroad. Although students are encouraged to view themselves as global citizens, many do not embrace, take seriously, or understand the meaning of global citizenship. The notion that study abroad creates global citizens is ridden with contradictions and shortcomings. For multiple complex reasons, the current state of global citizenship education does not effectively counter the negative predeparture framing of study abroad found in advertisements.

Many students are first exposed to the idea of global citizenship through study abroad promotional materials that employ the term without explaining what it is intended to mean. This vague and depoliticized rhetoric of global citizenship is often used as an umbrella term to describe both the goals and benefits of study abroad. Temple University's Office of International Programs' (n.d.) mission statement, for example, tells students: "Prepare yourself to be a global citizen. Study abroad" (para. 3). Wesleyan's OIS (n.d.) similarly explains in their mission statement that study abroad is "integral to the University's efforts to...prepare students for global citizenship" (About us, para.1). Before she studied abroad, Ellie recalled a professor telling her, "I think all students should go abroad because it's an experience you need to have in order to be a citizen of the world." In these three examples, global citizenship is described as an identity primarily obtainable through study abroad programs. While international education advertisements frequently tell students what they will gain from a semester abroad, this rhetoric of global citizenship goes so far as to tell students who they can *become* if they purchase a study abroad product. Scott, for example, explained that he was familiar with the phrase *global citizenship* because "companies will advertise this idea that you can be a global citizen maybe if you take their language class, or if you get certain travel experiences." Through advertisements as well as statements by educators encouraging international education, global citizenship is established as an undefined, privatized identity available to students if they purchase and consume a particular study abroad product or experience.

Although much critical and in-depth work has been done in the field of global citizenship education, little is said in advertisements or mission statements about what "global citizenship" might actually mean or look like. Because "global citizenship" is so rarely defined and does not reflect a global institutional reality, it is an idea that is not readily understood by American students. Desdemona confessed that although she was repeatedly called a global citizen by her study abroad provider, "I don't think that I really knew what that meant." When Stacy was asked about the term *global citizenship*, she responded with a series of questions: "I wonder what they mean by global citizens...I don't even know what I see as an ideal global citizen. What does it mean to be a global citizen?" While Stacy's questions are critical and valuable, the fact that this interview represented the first time she had asked herself these questions—a year after studying abroad in India—calls into question the assumption that she had become, or was prepared to be, a global citizen. Stacy's confusion is not unique. Christine said that while she "liked" the use of the term *global citizenship* in Wesleyan's OIS mission statement, "I don't know exactly what it means to be a global citizen." Overwhelmingly, interviews suggest that although global citizenship is repeatedly applied to students at Wesleyan University, they are rarely, if ever, engaged in critical and rigorous discussions about how to think about and how to be global citizens.

Interviewed students were able to offer only vague and speculative definitions of global citizenship. Ellie suggested that global citizens are "supposed to give priority to mankind and humanity over one nation's population." Christine proposed that educators use "global citizenship" to refer to "some kind of larger responsibility to everyone." Dakota thought that global citizenship was used to describe "someone quick witted, smart, educated, and really interested in learning about other cultures, and who could move comfortably in a variety of cultural settings." Together, these proposed definitions reflect the belief that global citizenship implies a sense of international awareness, allegiance, and responsibility. Even these vague understandings of global citizenship exhibit just how disparate global citizenship education and the dominant commercial discourse of study abroad truly are. The majority of study abroad advertisements typically do not encourage the qualities of global responsibility and understanding, favoring instead more commercial, easily accessible, and less academic themes. Proponents of global citizenship education are working against deeply ingrained commercial techniques for framing study abroad while simultaneously having not yet provided a clearly defined alternative. The efficacy of the language of global citizenship is thus severely limited. "Global citizenship" in study abroad promotional materials is often an empty signifier, symbolic of a broad yet vague sentiment and lacking in concrete information from which students can learn. Instead of providing a strong framework for progressive learning, the reckless employment of global citizenship rhetoric in the discourse of international education has opened the concept of global citizenship to speculation and assumptions that do not necessarily match the intentions of educators.

Some students actively and critically dismissed global citizenship in advertising and mission statements as empty and meaningless, reflective of a rhetorical ideology rather than an educational reality. Because they both do not understand and have not experienced *global citizenship*, these students understand the term as a mere buzzword. Dakota was particularly critical of Wesleyan's use of global citizenship rhetoric: "I think that [global citizenship] is part of the language that Wesleyan uses for itself to maintain its position as a top university. It's like they have to say that," Dakota faulted. According to this student, the term *global citizenship* is used for trendy self-promotional purposes, not to describe an educational reality. Similarly, Jessica described the University's use of *global citizenship*, as "just a lot of jargon that they think sounds nice." For students like Jessica and Dakota, "global citizenship" is merely a "feel good" institutional illusion with no relevancy to their own experiences abroad or academic studies.

Ill defined, insufficiently understood, and academically unrealized, the ideology of global citizenship often fails to reach students because of perceived problems with the phrase itself. Left to their own devices, many interviewed students struggled with a literal interpretation of the words *global* and *citizen* combined into a single, institutionally nonexistent identity. A common interpretation was that in order to be a citizen of the world, one must understand the entire world, not just one study abroad destination. Students often explained that it was faulty to assume they could become "global citizens" simply by visiting one non-U.S. country. As Jessica explained, "I'm definitely not a global citizen because studying abroad was the only time I've ever left the country. I know nothing about the Middle East or Asia, so I'm not a global citizen." Ruby, likewise, said: "I visited one country in Africa, and maybe like three in Europe, and not the rest of the world, so I don't know if I could count myself as a citizen of the world." Recognizing that the "globe" outside of the United States is not monolithic or singular, but complex and diverse, these students argue that study abroad cannot produce global citizens through a one-semester long program to a single country or region.

In many cases, students felt that global citizenship does not reflect what they learned or gained from their semester abroad. While global citizenship implies a sense of international belonging or universalism, students reported that their experiences abroad highlighted separateness rather than similarities. Differences of class, race, language, and culture between students and their hosts often led students to identify strongly as "American citizens" not "global citizens."

Indeed, for many students who study abroad, writes Nadine Dolby (2004), "an encounter with an American self...is the most significant component of the students' experiences" (p.151). Jessica, for example, said that while living in America she rarely thought about her nationality, but that spending a semester in England made her identify "very strongly" as an American. Jessica explained that her heightened identification with her American identity was the result of feeling like a cultural outsider throughout her program. When asked how they self-identified while abroad, none of the 25 interviewed students said "global citizen," while many referred to themselves as an "American," or a "foreigner."

Other students rejected the notion that they had become global citizens by studying abroad because they felt that they had not developed the skills of a global citizen in a complete or sustainable way. Several students viewed the cross-cultural relationships and intercultural skills that they developed abroad as both time and place bound, unable to transcend life beyond the semester abroad. Kara expressed a concern for the "semester fling" quality of her abroad experience, explaining, "as far as global citizenship goes, I was there for three months. It's such a small fraction of my life that I could just as easily not follow up on it and unlearn everything." Not only were her cross-cultural relationships unsustainable, Kara worried, but possibly so too was the knowledge she acquired abroad. Jason, likewise, worried about the prospect of unlearning his skills of cross-cultural competency, wondering if "maybe my competency has diminished since I have returned to the familiar." Ruby said that although she "would *like* to be a global citizen, I think right now I feel pretty confined to this campus and this environment." Because global citizenship is closely linked to foreign destinations rather than local cultures of difference, some students feel unable to maintain their fledgling identities as citizens of the world upon their return to America. If global citizenship education "is going to be successful," Kara averred, "you really need to be able to come home and channel whatever you got." Unfortunately, international education is frequently not integrated into campus life and the undergraduate curriculum. By describing global citizenship as an identity developed and performed overseas, advertisements and mission statements sometimes unintentionally render obsolete the importance of fostering cross-cultural understanding and responsibility within the United States.

Other students argued that is unethical for U.S. based education programs to claim they can produce global citizens when global citizenship should be an identity accessible to all people, regardless of education, privilege, nationality, or mobility. Students frequently raised the question, "Aren't all people citizens of the world?" As Ellie explained, "people can be global citizens without ever traveling because it wouldn't be fair if you couldn't." These students described "global citizenship" in the discourse of study abroad as an elite and exclusionary identity, which they found personally and ethically unappealing. Indeed, by asserting that global citizenship is gained through study abroad, mission statements and advertisements inadvertently establish global citizenship as a privilege available only to those who have access to higher education, mobility, and relative economic comfort. Stacy said she would not have selected her program if she had been aware of the organization's exclusionary global citizenship rhetoric, and Desdemona explained that she could only identify as a global citizen if all human beings were afforded that same privilege. The word *citizenship* implies more than civic engagement and community responsibility. It also evokes the rights, powers, and privileges that are afforded to members of a community. Especially when promoted alongside typical study abroad advertisements, this American privatization of world citizenship reinforces global systems of power and privilege while endorsing attitudes of U.S. international entitlement.

In fact, rather than representing an alternative to a discourse and society preoccupied with individual advancement and personal success, global citizenship frequently becomes another way of describing the many ways in which Americans can benefit from international education and travel. There is a danger that if promoted in conjunction with themes of personal advancement and consumerism, "global citizenship" will appear to be a commodity with the primary function of allowing Americans to succeed economically, socially, and politically in the globalized world. For example, Scott's interest in global citizenship only went so far as resume building. "I would identify as a global citizen," Scott said, "if it's ever useful to me, if I'm trying to sell my own experience in terms of trying to get a job." Global citizenship frequently appears to be a self-referential, U.S. based ideal, made by and for Americans. Responding to her study abroad provider's use of "global citizenship" in their mission statement, Ruby said, "I think their use of global citizenship is like global citizenship as something that's positive for Americans within an American context, rather than something that's positive or even exists for the world beyond our borders." The narrative of global citizenship promoted in advertisements and mission statements sometimes appears to be, as Stacy put it, "just another way for the United States to benefit" from the globalized world. Because global citizenship education is infrequently defined, promoted alongside study abroad narratives that accent personal advancement, and established as a privatized identity made available to a relatively privileged class of Americans, its effectiveness as a progressive international education model is severely curtailed. In many ways, the current rendition of global citizenship does not provide a viable or accessible alternative to the deeply problematic commercial narrative of study abroad.

There exists a great chasm between the goals of many international educators and the realities of the ways in which these goals are expressed and promoted to students during predeparture. Study abroad promises to aid in developing cross-cultural respect and understanding, yet advertisements suggest that American students are more important than their hosts. When global citizenship is privatized and sold to American students through study abroad, the right of less privileged and academically educated people to call themselves world citizens is at least discursively curtailed. While some proponents of study abroad assert that international education may help us achieve a more peaceful world, it is common for study abroad advertisements to employ unintentionally imperialist and colonialist themed rhetoric. International education ought to be critical and academic, yet it is undermined by being advertised with the same commercial tactics as tourism or adventure travel. When global citizenship is promoted in conjunction with advertisements that depict study abroad destinations as props or products, and express disregard for the damaging effects of cultural ignorance, one must question the narratives of global citizenship and international education as they are promoted to students. Simply attaching the goals of global citizenship to the current commercial narrative of study abroad is not only insufficient and ineffective, but doing so also promotes an international education model that is plagued by irreconcilable and harmful contradictions.

Changing the ways in which study abroad is advertised is one way that those working in the field of international education can begin to make positive changes. Concerned educators and students can pressure advertisers and study abroad providers to cease sanctioning cultural ignorance and disrespect, refrain from depicting the world beyond U.S. borders as passive and controllable, and avoid endorsing images that validate a hierarchy of people in which White Americans are most valuable. Advertisers can instead work to inspire enthusiasm for critical thinking, civic responsibility, cross-cultural understanding, humble cooperation, and committed respect toward others. Possible images to promote such sentiments might include photographs of students studying, listening to local experts and scholars teach, or working on a project and problem solving with community members. Rather than depicting local hosts as nameless and blurry, providers could make an effort to identify individuals by name. Study abroad can be promoted as "life-changing" not because it is a glamorous adventure or a powerful commodity, but because when students critically examine their place in a world of inequality and difference, they are bound to develop new and lasting worldviews. Advertisements could frame study abroad not as an entitlement, but as a phenomenal privilege and a remarkable opportunity. Ultimately, if study abroad is to be promoted to students in a way that encourages and fortifies critical global understanding, the commercial narrative of study abroad must break away from traditional tourism advertising while providing compelling and ethical alternatives. The problematic sentiments found in advertisements, however, extend far beyond the study abroad industry. Global entitlement, cultural ignorance, narcissism, consumerism, and unexamined privilege, are problems deeply ingrained in American culture. Therefore, even if study abroad advertisements begin to change, it is crucial that universities and educators take steps to combat harmful global assumptions and attitudes before students leave the United States through rigorous predeparture programming.

To achieve the goals of fostering sustainable global responsibility, civic engagement, compassion, advocacy, and understanding, the first step to international education necessarily calls for the unlearning and denaturalizing of damaging U.S. cultural assumptions. We must shift our attention from global to local in predeparture programming, by critiquing our own values and attitudes here in America. Before they unpack their bags in foreign destinations, students should be required to unpack their culturally and subjectively based assumptions about their role in the globalized world. Deconstructing America's global identity and examining inequality, race, privilege, and difference are just as critical to predeparture preparation as general packing concerns. Before being able to learn about non-U.S. people and places with commitment and respect, many American students will first need to problematize, confront, and change their own attitudes and behaviors. Posing challenging questions before the students depart will create a more cohesive and integrated international experience while simultaneously helping students to develop the necessary analytical tools with which to understand their experiences abroad. Critical international education is crucial, so that the expectations students have about study abroad are based in honest self-reflection and a sensitive worldview rather than brazen interest in consumerism and personal success. Bringing every step of international education truly in line with a critical and progressive engagement with the world will help students to have a clearer understanding of, and commitment to the goals and purposes of spending a semester abroad.

By improving the commercial discourse of study abroad and developing rigorous predeparture programming, a learning environment will emerge in which the values of a critical global citizenship education can flourish. The current state of global citizenship education is in need of a conscientious reevaluation, and a subsequent renovation. In order to better match the values of global citizenship with the ways in which the term is employed and understood, the definitions and principles of global citizenship will need to be just as prominent as the phrase itself. If nuanced, clear, and analytical articulations of global citizenship replace the current privatized, individualistic, and elite connotations, it is possible that the notion of global citizenship will be able to provide an alternative discourse to the current commercial narrative of study abroad. The Web site of Macalister College's Institute for Global Citizenship (ICG) offers several suggestions for how to do this. The ICG clearly defines all terms, consistently connects global citizenship to local U.S. communities, links global citizenship to social justice, provides students with materials to further their understandings, and acknowledges the complexities and contradictions of the phrase. For example, ICG (2005) clarifies that global citizenship "involves adopting a conception of citizenship that encompasses and integrates the local, national and transnational dimensions of public life and agency—and that [it] does so in a way that guards against the twin dangers of parochialism and utopianism" (para. 5). Global citizenship is not a simple, indisputable, or perfect ideology. We must therefore approach global citizenship education with caution, critique, and rigor if it is to become a viable and positive predeparture influence.

Changing the course of study abroad and global citizenship education requires that students, politicians, scholars, educators, and international education professionals engage in sustainable and critical dialogues about the goals and concerns we share in common, the differences that make us stronger, the mistakes we've made, our plans for change, and the futures we envision for ourselves and our country. Key to these conversations will be a commitment to forging new discourses while rejecting and critiquing the harmful beliefs and assumptions so pervasive in both American culture and study abroad advertisements. By allowing dangerous cultural assumptions to frame international education for students predeparture, educators are missing out on an opportunity to define study abroad in progressive and critical terms which would encourage students to develop an understanding of their place in the world. Study abroad still holds the potential to guide students toward worldviews that are not based in unchallenged power, consumerism, entitlement, narcissism, or privilege—but in a nuanced sensitivity and commitment to learning and understanding across cultures. The field of international education needs to combat the problematic structures, attitudes, and assumptions within American culture that have played key roles in the proliferation of anti-Americanism abroad and international misunderstandings. This change does not occur merely by sending American students abroad as "goodwill ambassadors" to consume foreign destinations and return home with increased self-confidence and pride. Rather, the change begins with our own discourses and ideologies here in America, through the critical, conscientious, and committed reeducation of both American students and U.S. culture.

NOTES

1. Portions of this research were first presented in "The World Awaits: The Politics of Study Abroad and Global Citizenship," Talya Zemach-Bersin's undergraduate honors thesis written in 2007 at Wesleyan University.
2.. All names have been changed. Because of the limited number of students interviewed, this analysis is decidedly qualitative and does not purport to provide conclusive quantitative data.
3. For more on the gendered discourse of imperialism, see *Imperial Leather: Race, Gender, and Sexuality in the Colonial Contest*, by Anne McClintock (1995). McClintock writes that colonized land was gendered female by male, European explorers as a way to rationalize the assertion of patriarchal authority.
4. For a more detailed account of the importance of discovery and the frontier in U.S. history, see Richard Slotkin's Trilogy on the "Myth of the Frontier": *Regeneration through Violence* (1975), *The Fatal Environment* (1985), and *Gunfighter Nation* (1992). See also Frederick Jackson Turner's "Frontier Thesis," *The Significance of the Frontier in American History* (1899), and Theodore Roosevelt's *Rough Riders* (1902).

REFERENCES

Abraham Lincoln Study Abroad Fellowship Program, Commission on the (2005). *Global competence & national needs: One million Americans studying abroad*. Retrieved February 7, 2007, from http://www.nafsa.org/_/Document/_/lincoln_commission_report.pdf

Abraham Lincoln Study Abroad Fellowship Program, Commission on the (2006). *Trends and barriers in study abroad*. Retrieved February 5, 2007, from http://www.lincolncommission.org/docs.html

American Institute for Foreign Study. (Fall 2006). Advertisement. *Abroad View, 9*(1), 20.

Bolen, M. (2001). Consumerism and U.S. study abroad. *Journal of Studies inInternational Education, 5*(3), 182–200.

Chermayeff, I. (2007, January). Packaging a nation. *Travel and Leisure Magazine.*

Council on International Educational Exchange (CIEE). (n.d.). Study abroad with CIEE international study programs. Retrieved July 26, 2008, from http://ciee.org/study.aspx

Cross-Cultural Solutions. (2006, Fall). Advertisement. *Abroad View, 9*(1), 9.

Dolby, N. (2004). Encountering an American self: Study abroad and national identity. *Comparative Education Review, 48*(2), 150–173.

Experiential Learning. (2007). Services. Retrieved October 15, 2008, from http://experientialearning.org/services.html

Glimpse Foundation. (n.d.). *Mission statement.* Retrieved December 12, 2006, from http://www.glimpsefoundation.org/about.php#mission

Gordon, J. (2006, April 23). Studying abroad, safe or not. *New York Times.* Retrieved from http://www.nytimes.com

Goudge, P. (2003). *The whiteness of power: Racism in third world development and aid.* London: Lawrence & Wishart.

International Honors Program. (2007–2008). *Comparative study around the world* [Brochure]. Boston, MA: IHP.

International Studies Abroad. (2006, Fall). Advertisement. *Abroad View, 9*(1), 2.

James Madison University Study Abroad. (n.d.). *Studying, interning, and volunteering abroad.* Retrieved December 12, 2006, from http://www.jmu.edu/international/abroad

Kent State University. (2008, Spring). Advertisement. *Abroad View, 10*(2), 85.

Lesley University Audubon Expedition Institute. (2006, Spring). Advertisement. *Abroad View, 8*(1), 25.

Lexia International. (2005, Spring). Advertisement. *Abroad View, 8*(2), 1.

Macalister College, Institute for Global Citizenship. (2005). Definitions. Retrieved July 31, 2008, from http://www.macalester.edu/ globalcitizenship/proposal/definitions.html

McClintock, A. (1995). *Imperial leather: Race, gender, and sexuality in the colonial contest.* New York: Routledge.

Millington, T. V. (2002, March–April). Consumers study abroad: International education is not a commodity. *Transitions Abroad, 25*(5).

Pitzer College External Studies. (2007*). Study abroad with Pitzer College* [Brochure]. Claremont, CA: Pitzer College.

Pratt, M. L. (1992). *Imperial eyes: Travel writing and transculturation.* New York: Routledge.

Richardson, D. (2005). This is the moment. Image. Retrieved January 5, 2007, from http://ourworld.worldlearning.org/site/PhotoAlbumUser?view=UserPhotoDetail&PhotoID =40711&position=1&AlbumID=8261

School for International Training (SIT). (n.d.). Homepage. Retrieved January 7, 2007, from http://www.sit.edu

School for International Training, Study Abroad (SIT). (2006). *Class profile: Fall 2005.* Retrieved November 5, 2006, from http://www.sit.edu/class_profile_fall05.html

School for International Training, Study Abroad (SIT). (2007). *Europe.* [Program brochure]. Brattleboro, VT: World Learning.

Shumar, W. (1997). *College for sale: A critique of the commodification of higher education.* London: Falmer Press.

Study Abroad Semester at Sea. (2006, Fall). *Abroad View, 9*(1), 13.

StudyAbroad.com (2006). Homepage. Retrieved December 12, 2006, from http://www.studyabroad.com

Temple University International Programs. (n.d.). Why study abroad?. Retrieved October 31, 2007, from http://www.temple.edu/studyabroad/ students/index.html

Walters-Bugbee, E. (2006). *Adwoa: Self Portrait at Elmina Harbor boatyard.*. Image. Retrieved December 26, 2006, from http://ourworld.worldlearning.org/site/PhotoAlbumUser?view=UserPhotoDetail&PhotoID=40733&position=6&AlbumID=8263

Wesleyan University. (2005). *Engaged with the world.* Retrieved July 28, 2008, from http://www.wesleyan.edu/about/strategy.html

Wesleyan University Office of International Studies. (n.d./a). *About Us.* Retrieved July 5, 2008, from http://www.wesleyan.edu/ois/aboutus.html

Wesleyan University Office of International Studies. (n.d./b). *Mission statement.* Retrieved July 5, 2008, from http://www.wesleyan.edu/ois/

Wollman, D. (2006, February 17). Vast number of study abroad options made simpler. *The Wesleyan Argus, CXLI*(28). Retrieved February 20, 2007, from http://www.wesleyanargus.com/article/2686

World Learning. (2008). *Welcome to world learning.* Retrieved July 26, 2008, from http://www.worldlearning.com

Chapter 19

Global Citizenship for All

Low Minority Student Participation in Study Abroad—Seeking Strategies for Success[1]

Earl Picard, Farrah Bernardino, and Kike Ehigiator
Georgia State University

INTRODUCTION: CONTEXTUALIZING THE PROBLEM

In spite of the disruptions and challenges that confront study abroad programs in the post-9/11 era, student study abroad participation rates in the United States have continued to grow steadily. This is true in spite of heightened security restrictions, family and student safety and security concerns, and the increased expense of studying abroad coupled with tight family finances. In academic year 2005–2006, there was an 8.5% increase in the number of students going abroad to 223,543. From 2001 to 2006, the number of study abroad participants grew by a minimum of 13,000 students annually (Figure 19.1).

The trend is steady and upward but these are modest numbers and larger challenges lie ahead. In 2005 there were almost 17.5 million students enrolled in U.S. colleges and universities (U.S. Department of Education, 2008, Table 179). That figure is expected to increase to 20 million by 2016 (U.S. Department of Education, 2008, Tables 11, 181, Projections of Education Statistics to 2016). At just more than 223,000, the number of students who study abroad represents less than 2% of the total national student population. Even if we eliminate institutions with little potential to facilitate study abroad, there is still considerable distance between current study abroad levels and even a modest 5% participation rate. If external circumstances were to remain unchanged and the total continues to grow by 8.5% through 2016, a bit more than a half million students will study abroad, still less than 3% of the total number of students. Greater numbers are required to truly meet the goals of global citizenship.

By global citizenship we refer to students who, variously and in combination, have had exposure to other cultures, possess foreign language skills, have tolerance for those whose cultural backgrounds are different from their own, display a sense of curiosity about the world beyond their immediate experiences, are adept at navigating in unfamiliar circumstances and show empathy for others.

Indeed, study abroad is only one component of what should be a broad based program to provide students with global knowledge, skills, and experience. But it is an important component and its benefits must be realized broadly in the student population. According to the Institute of International Education (IIE, 2007), for more than a decade women have constituted 65% of the total study abroad pool. During that same period Whites averaged almost 84% of students who studied abroad. A profile of prototypical study abroad students probably would center on middle

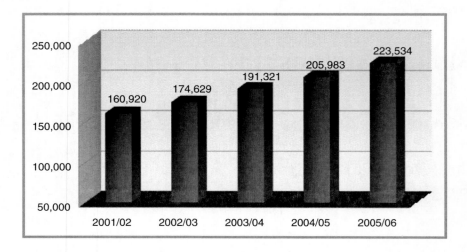

Figure 19.1 *Study Abroad Totals by Year 2001–2006*

Source: *Open Doors,* 2007: Online Report on International Education Exchange.

to upper middle class White females who are majoring in the humanities, social sciences, or business. This is where questions arise. Is the typical study abroad student truly representative of the college age population?

Focusing on university enrollment generally, the U.S. Department of Education (2008) observes that "much of university growth between 1995 and 2005 was in female enrollment; the number of females enrolled rose 27%, while the number of males rose 18%" (U.S. Department of Education, 2008, Table 216). Female enrollment stood at 10 million in 2005 while male enrollment numbered 7.5 million. In 2005, 57.4% of university students were female, up from 55.5% in 1995, while 42.6% were males, down from 44.4% in 1995. Females represent more than 65% of the study abroad totals and males constitute only 35% (U.S. Department of Education, 2008, Table 179). In spite of their flagging ratio in the nation's institutions of higher education, males of all races still are not studying abroad in numbers proportionate to their numbers in the student population. Steps should be taken to bring greater gender balance to the study abroad experience.[2] Indeed, at present, military service probably represents one of the main opportunities that college age males have to experience international travel. It would be disappointing if that were to remain the case.

A similar case could be made for widening the socioeconomic range of study abroad participants since, at present, mainly middle and upper middle class students participate. Students from more modest socioeconomic backgrounds also can, and should, greatly benefit from international exposure. Beyond the anecdotal, which is widely respected in the case of study abroad, it is difficult to pinpoint the distribution of study abroad participants by socioeconomic status. Study abroad professionals can attest to how many of their potential world travelers fail to participate because of compelling financial circumstances. And, they know how many have to struggle to fulfill their aspirations but do so in spite of the odds. They also know of the magic they have worked, often at great personal and professional sacrifice, to help make things happen for students with really long odds financially.

It is the case that the narrow socioeconomic profile of study abroad students is moderating to a certain extent. There is more available financial aid and study abroad offices are making greater outreach efforts aimed at students from more modest socioeconomic backgrounds. Nevertheless, we are on safe ground in saying that broad based global citizenship continues to necessitate greater socioeconomic diversity in study abroad.

Again, and more tellingly for our purposes, while study abroad numbers are going up, data and anecdotal information suggest that minority student participation is stagnant at what only can be considered woefully low levels. [3] Increases in total study abroad numbers obscure an ongoing disparity where race and ethnicity are concerned, which is evident when we look at study abroad totals. In 2005–2006 minority groups represented 17% of students who studied abroad, divided as follows: Asian/Pacific Islanders—6.3%; Hispanics/Latino—5.4%; African Americans—3.5%, Multiracial—1.2%; and Native Americans/Alaskan Natives—.6% (IIE, 2007) (Figure 19.2).

As Figure 19.3 illustrates, there was little variation in these ratios over the 5-year period from 2002 to 2006.

In 2005, according to the U.S. Department of Education, African-American students represented 12.7% of students in degree granting institutions. Hispanics represented 10.8%, Asian/Pacific Islanders stood at 6.5%, and American Indian/Alaskan Natives represented 1% (U.S. Department of Education, 2008, Table 216). When we compare those participation rates for the four minority groups to their numbers in the overall student population we clearly see the extent of disparity (Figure 19.4).

Asian/Pacific Islanders at 5.9% of the study abroad pool, and Native American/Alaska Natives at .8% are the only minority groups that come close to matching their numbers in the overall national student population. However, the number of Native Americans/Alaska Natives in the national student population is so low that parity between their enrollment numbers and their

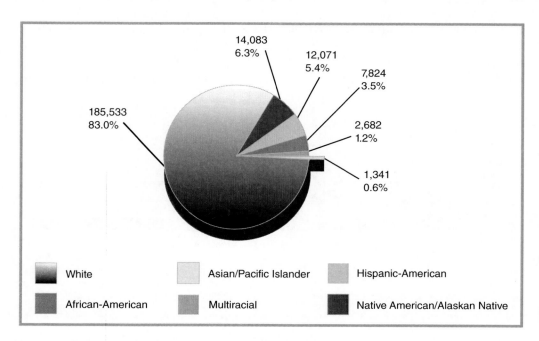

Figure 19.2 *2006 Study Abroad Totals and Percentages by Race/Ethnicity*

Source: *Open Doors,* 2007: Online Report on International Education Exchange.

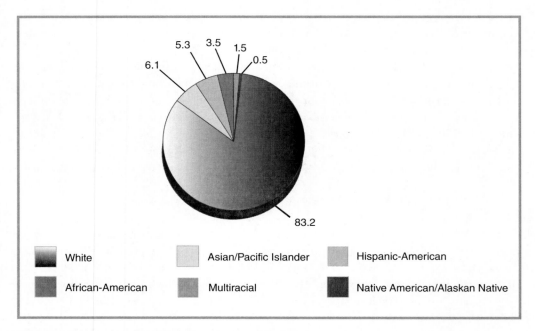

Figure 19.3 *Study Abroad Averages 2002–2006 by Race/Ethnicity*

Source: *Open Doors,* 2007: Online Report on International Education Exchange.

study abroad percentages is nothing to celebrate. At first glance, one might conclude that Asian Americans represent an exception to the unrepresentative minority participation rates because they are studying abroad in numbers reasonably close to their percentage of university enrollment. That conclusion only is true if we consider their current participation rates against their current total enrollment in universities and colleges. If we consider enrollment projections to 2050 when the three major minority groups are expected to represent 14% each of the total student popula-

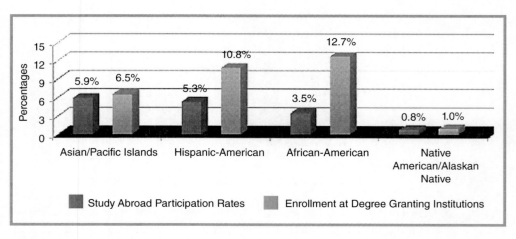

Figure 19.4 *2005 Minority Group Enrollment at Degree Granting Institutions and Study Abroad Participation Rates*

Sources: *Open Doors,* 2007: Online Report on International Education Exchange, and U.S. Department of Education, National Center for Education Statistics (2008). Digest of Education Statistics, 2007.

tion, that conclusion is less compelling. Since many students in the Asian/Pacific Islander population group, especially the Asian component of that group, come from relatively more privileged socioeconomic backgrounds, there is good evidence to suggest that their study abroad numbers will increase at a similar pace to their percentage of the total student population. However, it would be a dubious accomplishment if privileged Asians join privileged White Americans as the most likely students to study abroad. There is a need to broaden the Asian socioeconomic pool as well. Efforts should be ongoing to boost participation rates for the Asian/Pacific Islander, particularly those from less privileged backgrounds. The real challenge for this group going forward is to build on the modest study abroad success achieved to date while encouraging broader horizons where heritage travel and cultural reengagement, which might be more prominent in this group, is complemented by travel with fellow students to diverse destinations and language settings.

MINORITY STUDENTS AND STUDY ABROAD

The Paul Simon National Study Abroad bill, if it is signed into law will make high quality study abroad programs available to larger numbers of American students. The Simon bill authorizes $80 million for grants to individual students, colleges and universities, nongovernmental organizations, and other institutions that promote study abroad. While controversial in some quarters because of its indirect funding mechanism, the Simon bill includes a commitment to help at least 1 million undergraduates study abroad annually within 10 years. This important and historic legislation will have profound impact if it is signed into law. It will be important for the international education community to remain committed to its passage in spite of the legislative challenges that it faces initially.

The Simon bill promotes access to study abroad opportunities for U.S. students at diverse institutions of higher education, including 2-year institutions, institutions that serve minorities, and institutions that serve nontraditional students. The Simon bill specifically targets creative grant making, and promotes access to study abroad opportunities for diverse U.S. students—a group that includes minority students, students of limited financial means, and nontraditional students. The Simon bill also focuses on longer-term study abroad programs that maximize foreign-language learning and intercultural understanding and shorter term programs that might appeal to nontraditional students. If it is signed into law, it will represent a public policy initiative that should help to accelerate study abroad totals.

As illustrated above, in the coming years we can expect that overall participation rates will continue to rise, albeit modestly, even without the Simon bill and without a drive to have more minority students going abroad. The Simon bill's objective of sending one million students abroad also can be achieved readily without much variation in group participation rates. But would that represent real progress if the goal of global citizenship is to proceed beyond elite participation to achieve study abroad with diversity? The numeric target has to be accompanied by a spirited commitment to realize the program's remaining objectives that are focused on broadening access and realizing greater diversity.

The Simon bill seeks to expand study abroad opportunities for students who are underrepresented, so it is timely for the effort to substantially increase minority study abroad totals in light of the fact that there is a steady increase in the percentage of American college students who are members of racial minorities. In 1976, only 15% of university students were minorities. That number had increased to 31% by 2005. As the U.S. Department of Education indicated, "During that time period, the percentage of Asian or Pacific Islander students rose from 2% to 6% and the Hispanic percentage rose from 3% to 11%. The percentage of Black students was 9% at the beginning of the time period and it fluctuated during the early part of the period before rising to 13% in 2005" (2007, chapter 3).

Janet Lopez, in *The Impact of Demographic Changes on Higher Education*, observes that "in coming years white students will continue to represent the majority in higher education, even more so at private and 4-year colleges nationwide" (Lopez, 2006, p. 11). However, she notes that by 2050 Whites will constitute only 57% of college and university students. When we compare 2006 participation rates to the 2050 student population projection it is clear that it will take substantial effort to close the gap (Figure 19.5).

Going forward, as the percentage of minority students approaches 50% they will represent a critical constituency in the quest to increase study abroad participation rates nationally. Since minority student study abroad rates fall well below their numbers in the projected student population, that 14% projection certainly can serve as an intermediate target given where rates are today.

Looking at public universities only, we see that White students currently represent about 61% of the student body, Latino students constitute 21%, the African-American student population is slightly over 10%, and Asian/Pacific Islanders represent 6.9%.

> In 2040 the demographic projections suggest that Latino students will account for over 44% of the student population, Anglo students will account for 32%, African Americans will account for 8.1% of the student population and Asians for slightly over 15%. By 2040 the public universities will likely serve a majority Latino population in their institutions. (Lopez: 2006, p. 12)

In light of these demographic shifts, Lopez continues, by 2050 "institutions will have to diversify their student body in order to serve the needs of their general state's populations" (2006, p. 13).

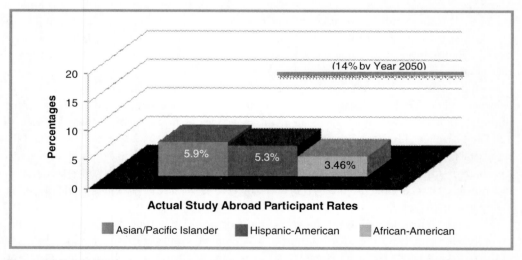

Figure 19.5 *2006 Minority Study Abroad Participation Rates and Projected University Enrollment by 2050*

Sources: *Open Doors*, 2007: Online Report on International Education Exchange, and U.S. Department of Education, National Center for Education Statistics (2008). Digest of Education Statistics, 2007.

This will not be diversification for the sake of diversification. The achievement gap that exists today between White and Asian students, on one side, and Hispanic and African-American students, can only be closed if African-American and Hispanic students participate fully in college life. They can make major strides in that direction by boosting their study abroad numbers and by becoming increasingly competent as global citizens. By doing so, they help to advance their own interests as well as those of the country in general.

Broadly speaking, low minority participation rates in study abroad may represent a missed opportunity for these students to realize many benefits such as enhanced personal development, refined interpersonal skills, employment readiness, preparation for graduate study, developed foreign language capabilities, broadened perspective, and other qualities often derived from studying abroad. The United States must educate more students of color if the country is to remain competitive in a global marketplace (Lopez, 2006, p. 19), and we must educate them as global citizens if they are to compete effectively in that marketplace.

Institutional benefits of minority study abroad might include enhanced campus harmony and understanding, richer classroom experiences, the benefits of peer influence for encouraging additional students to study abroad, and the positive impact on minority campus recruitment that could come from publicizing minority student experiences. Students who study abroad also tend to be more engaged in their studies and perform better academically.

Unless the current trend is reversed, the minority student population risks falling farther behind in the skills necessary for today's world and the global society will be deprived of potential contributions from this segment of the population. It is imperative, then, that strategies are found to increase their study abroad numbers.

Having said that, do we know what we need to know to develop and implement effective programs that bring minority students into the study abroad experience in representative numbers? Most of us know that minority students are not well represented but we probably do not know the true contours of the problem as it exists on our campuses nor do we know what might work or how to go about the task of boosting their numbers.

One way to better understand the problem, pinpoint challenges, and identify solutions is through programmatic stock taking in which an institution asks itself questions and answers them. We recommend that interested institutions undertake a structured self-assessment exercise to more sharply illuminate the contours of the problem, pinpoint challenges, and identify solutions to increase the number of minority students who study abroad and point the way forward. Many of the suggested categories and questions for such an assessment derive from findings that we identified in two case studies. Georgia State University and the University of Pittsburgh both have recognized the need to increase minority student participation in study abroad and have taken steps in that direction. A review of their efforts can help suggest focus areas and questions to ask of ourselves. Those cases also can suggest programmatic initiatives that might be adopted by others.

CASE STUDY: GEORGIA STATE UNIVERSITY

Georgia State University (n.d./a), founded in 1913, is a major public research university located in downtown Atlanta, Georgia, with an enrollment in 2007 of more than 27,000 undergraduate and graduate students and 1,054 full-time faculty members. Georgia State has one of the most diverse undergraduate student populations nationally and the most diverse in the University System of Georgia, with the minority student population at Georgia State representing 44% of the student body. The breakdown of minority students is as follows: African Americans—7,000; Hispanics—1,200; Asians and Pacific Islanders—3,100; multiracial—682; American Indians—68. Over 1,400 international students from 145 countries, representing every world region, matriculate at the university. Increasing minority student participation in study abroad is a matter of great importance to Georgia State as it should be for other institutions with relatively large minority student populations.

The institutional context is very promising because the university is committed to internationalization, developing its students as global citizens, and increasing its study abroad numbers. That commitment is reflected in the university's mission statement (Georgia State University, n.d./b) which, among other things, says:

> the goal of the university is …to provide access to quality education for diverse groups of students, to educate leaders for the State of Georgia and the nation, and to prepare citizens for lifelong learning in a global society.…a continuing **goal** is to be recognized (in Atlanta, nationally and internationally) as an institution with a strong global perspective and a center of international excellence in a number of areas.

In the university strategic plan, first articulated in the 2000 to 2005 period and reaffirmed for 2005 to 2010, Georgia State underscores this outlook by committing itself to "a core curriculum that promotes interdisciplinary, intercultural, and international perspectives" (Georgia State University, n.d./c, n.d./d).

The university's resolve is further reinforced by the strategic plan of the Office of International Affairs (OIA) which states that "Georgia State University's commitment to expanding its international involvement reflects an understanding shared throughout the University System of Georgia that a global perspective is essential to achieving institutional quality in today's ever shrinking world." The OIA's commitment is further reflected in the mission statement of the Study Abroad Programs (SAP) office which seeks to enrich the Georgia State University community "by promoting International Education and enabling students to engage in a global society." "Study abroad," SAP states, "is the principal and arguably the quickest means through which students can begin the journey of becoming global citizens. It is also one of the most effective means of internationalizing the university" (Georgia State University, n.d./e).

The commitment to increase minority student participation evolved as the university moved to increase its study abroad numbers across the board. The OIA's Study Abroad programs have expanded from 12 programs and 200 plus students in 1994 to some 40 programs and 582 students in 2008. The goal, as overall study abroad numbers increase, is to have the percentage of minority students studying abroad more closely mirror the percentage of minority students at Georgia State.

On average, between 2005 and 2008 White students comprised 45% of the student body and 60% of the study abroad pool; African Americans represented 27% of the total and 18% of those who studied abroad; Hispanic students made up 3% of the student population and 5%, respectively; 11% of Georgia State students were Asians and they represented 6% of those who studied abroad; American Indians stood at 1% and none studied abroad. Multiracial students were 2% of the student body and 4% of the study abroad pool. The remaining percentages fell into the "Other" category or did not respond (Figure 19.6).

Given the concern to boost minority student participation, in 2007 SAP undertook a random student survey to identify factors that deter minority students from studying abroad. From that

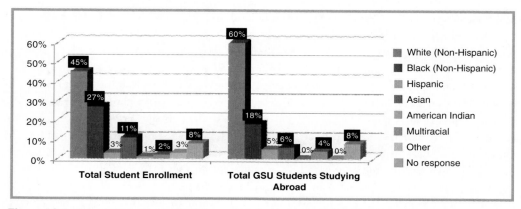

Figure 19.6 *Georgia State University Averages for Academic Years 2005–2008*

limited initiative Georgia State was able to identify insufficient information, indifference, lack of curiosity, limited or no travel experience, individual and family fear, lack of peer influence, financial challenges, and few if any mentors as some of the factors that deter minorities from studying abroad.

To address the problem, SAP implemented a Minority Outreach Initiative (MOI), spearheaded by an advisor, to improve marketing and outreach to currently underrepresented students, specifically students of color. The MOI includes a multitier approach and encompasses the following:

- Training staff
- Marketing and outreach
- Educating students about scholarships and aid
- Dispelling myths about studying abroad
- Soliciting funding for programming and scholarships
- Collaborating with offices on campus for events and projects

Georgia State developed several initiatives including a panel discussion "Broadening Horizons: Minority Students and Study Abroad" that includes minority students who have studied abroad and guest speakers, including, in one instance, a Fulbright Scholar from South Africa. The study abroad staff proceeded from the assumption that the best way to attract students is through their peers. The student panels are publicized heavily and strategically in places very likely to get attention and attract minority students.

Some of the topics addressed by the panel include initial hesitations about studying abroad, financial concerns, major-related issues, lack of family support, and uncertainty about how minority students may be perceived in other parts of the world. Student evaluations of the panel showed they wanted more but less formal programs. The office responded by holding a Broadening Horizons Meet and Greet every spring. This forum, a simple gathering of students with refreshments available, allows more conversation between students. While it is still too early to assess the impact of these programs, it is clear students are getting the message that the office wants to help. Many students start their advising sessions saying they have heard about Broadening Horizons and want more information about how to study abroad.

The SAP staff seeks to provide better resources to minority students so that they feel the experience is actually feasible for them. In addition to advising, providing funding information packets and workshops on how to afford study abroad, the office provides a page on its Web site that lists numerous scholarships for minority students. One scholarship that the staff heavily promotes and the students respond to is the Gilman Scholarship administered by the Institute of International Education. The Gilman Scholarship provides funding for undergraduates who are recipients of the Pell Grant and aims to support students who have been traditionally underrepresented in study abroad. Georgia State usually receives one or two Gilman awards per year.

It also has set up a mentor program that matches students based on ethnicity and desired country of study with those who have already studied abroad. The relationship gives mentors the opportunity to share their experiences in detail. It also allows those being mentored to ask questions and talk about fears and uncertainties and other matters they may not feel comfortable sharing with an advisor. As a precautionary note, SAP indicates that finding mentors is much easier than finding students for them to mentor but it is a good initiative to undertake. The following testimonial is from a mentee that demonstrates the value of students advising other students:

> Even when I began to seriously consider going overseas to continue with my academic studies, I had tons of doubts and questions at the back of my mind—questions that I felt were too delicate to discuss with my study abroad advisor. By developing a one-on-one relationship with a mentor, my doubts were quelled. My questions were answered with an insider's knowledge and understanding. Now, I cannot wait to study abroad!

African-American Student (Mentee)

SAP also makes use of a Study Abroad Squad which is a student assistant team that focuses on outreach and recruitment. These students are the face of study abroad on campus because the SAP staff does not often have the opportunity to get out of the office to recruit. With limited on-campus housing and a large percentage of the student body that leaves campus directly after classes, outreach becomes an even more difficult task. Prior to 2008 SAP received funding to support a two-member squad. The office was approved for four students in 2008 and achieved diversity in the Squad to increase outreach to minority students.

SAP knows the importance of outreach to freshmen. Educating students early about study abroad is important to get them to go abroad later. This gives them the time to plan their course sequence so they know when they can go abroad and what courses they will need to take beforehand. It also gives them the time to identify sufficient funding and persuade their parents to support the opportunity. At Georgia State, the SAP staff has taken advantage of the Freshman Learning Communities on campus by heavily promoting study abroad and publicizing events to these classes. In this way, the staff plants the seed for study abroad early on and will eventually see many of these same students studying abroad later.

The SAP office also was instrumental in developing the student fee-supported International Education Fee (IEF) Scholarship Program, one of only two or three in the nation and the first one in Georgia. The $5.00 fee per semester (slightly less in summer) funds the management of SEVIS (the international student tracking system mandated by the federal government), all international student orientations, some minimal support for new study abroad program development, and study abroad scholarships for students. In the 5 years since the inception of the fee, $515,000 has been awarded as IEF Scholarships. Given that many minority students at Georgia State must work to put themselves through college, the IEF Scholarship has helped to both increase and diversify the students studying abroad. However, there is still a critical need for a study abroad endowment for additional scholarships, which is an SAP priority. The IEF Scholarship only provides limited funding and many students still do not consider study abroad because they know the scholarship will not lower the cost enough for them to be able to afford to undertake international study.

Staffing is a major issue. During the 2008–2009 academic year SAP had five full- time staff members, one of whom was African American. The full-time staff is supplemented by four student assistants with three being students of color. Leigh Essex Walker, Georgia State Director of SAP says that the biggest impediment to greater involvement is an understaffed office. "Every member of the staff wants to better serve the minority students at GSU, but we can only do so much with the limited staff we have. Therefore, SAP has to plan strategically to identify what we can handle each year. In the end, though, we are more concerned with quality than quantity" (Walker, 2007–2008).

When asked if she thought increasing the number of minority group members in the office would affect recruitment of minority students and why there are not more minorities in study abroad offices, Walker noted the following:

> I do feel minority staff make a difference in reaching minority students, but I also think it's not always the race of the recruiter, but the enthusiasm/personality of the recruiter that can be just as important. My staff has shown dedication to the initiative, attending and leading sessions and workshops related to minority recruitment within their professional organizations, and collaborating on the topic with colleagues at other institutions. The next question is simple to answer…more minorities don't work in study abroad offices, because having studied abroad is usually a requirement to work in the field at almost every institution in the United States, and with so few minorities that have studied abroad, we only have a very limited pool from which to draw. The problem creates a domino effect. Nonetheless, we do try to publicize position openings in ways that will attract more diversity. For example, we e-mail our Broadening Horizons mentor database when there are student assistant positions open and we build largely on the relationships we have developed in our office. We recently hired an intern who had been a student on our first Broadening Horizons panel. (Walker, 2007–2008)

Georgia State has recognized the need to attract more minority students to study abroad through routine outreach efforts and new programmatic initiatives. They have taken a self-conscious approach to outreach that places minority students at the center of their efforts. The study abroad staff, though inadequate to the task, has been diversified. The SAP staff continues to look for opportunities to expand the effort. They would be the first to acknowledge that while what they have done to date was necessary and has produced early results, it is far from sufficient.

The SAP office also is concerned to know whether more minority students would be inclined to study abroad if a more diverse mix of majors, alternative destinations, minority program leaders, and targeted programs were available. These are questions that might be pursued through a more systematic assessment which the SAP office has committed to pursue.

CASE STUDY: UNIVERSITY OF PITTSBURGH

The University of Pittsburgh (Pitt) was founded in 1787 and is one of the oldest private institutions of higher education in the United States. Total enrollment in 2007 was 33,898. White students represented 73% of the student population. African Americans constituted 7%; Asian/Pacific Islanders made up 4.5%; 1.4% of the total were Hispanics; and American Indian/Alaska Native enrollment stood at .2%. The race/ethnicity of another 7.4% was unknown. International students represented 6.5% of the student population.

The University's mission statement sees its role as developing high-quality students to respond to the need of the state "and to the broader needs of the nation and the world." It also makes a commitment to "social, intellectual, and economic development in the Commonwealth, the nation, and the world." Internationalization is truly a mission of the university and the combined effort of the chancellor, the provost, faculty, and staff illustrates that where internationalization is concerned Pitt is a case where formal institutional rhetoric is far less important than actual practice. The university has a notable, globally oriented track record.

The mission of the Study Abroad Office (SAO) and the University Center for International Studies (UCIS) is precisely targeted. They are recognized as national leaders in fostering the inclusion of underrepresented groups in international education. The SAO commits itself to

advance the academic goals of the University by developing and promoting a variety of international educational opportunities; to augment students' intellectual, professional, and personal development through both formal and experiential learning in another cultural context; to enhance students' cross-cultural awareness and appreciation in an increasingly complex global environment; and to promote international opportunities to include under represented student groups.

Pitt, like most higher education institutions, initially lacked diversity in study abroad with most students who went abroad being predominantly White and affluent. Since 2002 the university has made a notable effort to attract minority students to study abroad based on their commitment to make study abroad a possibility for all students. Pitt recognized that, in line with national trends, the number of minority students studying abroad was unacceptably low and that they present a particular challenge. The initial focus was on increasing the rate of participation by African-American students who may not see study abroad as a realistic possibility. The university recognized that study abroad could be utilized as one tool to further integrate those students into the campus community. They also concluded that by studying abroad minority students could be provided impetus to be more competitive and develop core competencies to help them become more employable and succeed in the global marketplace. The SAO staff made it one of the central missions of the office to increase the number of underrepresented students studying abroad.

They concluded that in order to address the problem, SAO had to first build trust within the African-American student population. In line with that commitment, they developed the SAO office as a "safe zone" where minority students and people of any identity were welcomed and respected. They have developed an organizational culture where no topic is considered off-limits, and where SAO staff constantly seek to educate themselves on the needs of underrepresented students. The SAO also began reaching out to Black sororities and fraternities on campus, as well as to other underrepresented student groups and other units on campus for support on the premise that study abroad professionals have to make others on campus know what they are trying to do. Buy-in by other campus offices is essential; SAO has received strong support from the Student Affairs Office in particular. By reaching out to student groups and campus units SAO is able to dispel many misconceptions about study abroad such as the notion that many students think they cannot afford the experience and do not realize they can apply their financial aid to study abroad.

The university follows an "early and often" approach to reaching students. The SAO has developed an excellent relationship with the Office of Admissions. When students apply to Pitt, they are told about study abroad and that Pitt wants underrepresented students to go abroad. Again, when students are accepted to Pitt, they are told about study abroad. The premise is that reaching students early and multiple times is also important because you get buy-in on the part of parents. If parents are thinking about their child studying abroad early on, they can plan and it will not be as much of a financial shock.

After having worked with African-American students, SAO realized that there were very few resources that addressed their specific needs and experiences. Pitt pointed to a very active internship program as a key component of their outreach initiative. As their partnership with African-American students evolved, students who studied abroad became a part of the SAO intern program. They provide mentoring and advisory assistance to other students who wish to explore their study abroad options. Those students also help to educate SAO staff on their specific needs and concerns.

Pitt also has had great success using peer advising on the premise that the students relate well to each other. SAO developed the minority mentor program and makes designated scholarships available through the student affairs office. There is targeted outreach by study abroad office staff and there is an item on the Web site written by students for students which seems to work well in getting the attention of minority students.

The SAO feels it is important to present a diversified face to the campus. One approach they have used is to have the student newspaper do an article on study abroad using photos of underrepresented students. Pitt also is planning to work with the African-American Alumni Association to get quotes from minority alumni who studied abroad on how the experience impacted their lives. The expectation is that those quotes will help recruit other students.

In 2002 three African-American students at Pitt took it upon themselves to develop a comprehensive exploration of the African-American study abroad experience. The handbook, *The World is in Your Hands Student Guide*, which is updated periodically, has been a great success and is being used by study abroad offices and program providers throughout the country.

Perhaps one of the most innovative initiatives that Pitt has undertaken is their *Making It Happen* (MIH) documentary film.[4] The initial film focused on study abroad for students with disabilities and emphasized an individualized advising approach to address the needs of those students in study abroad. That film is available on the Web and as DVDs free of charge. A more thorough Web site, MySpace, and Facebook page have been developed for interaction, deeper exploration, and mutual support. The film was very well received and Pitt was encouraged to develop other vehicles focused on additional underrepresented groups.

Another *Making It Happen* film is now in the planning stages. This film will have the goal of increasing African-American participation in study abroad while showcasing African-American students who can serve as examples for prospective students who may be apprehensive about study abroad due to a variety of real and perceived barriers. It also will seek to educate faculty, university administrators, and study abroad programs on the specific needs of African-American students. The film will follow selected students through the entire process from initial contact with the SAO to their return from their study abroad experiences.

While programmatic initiatives are essential, SAO also believes that staffing is critical to success. In an interview with Farrah Bernardino on July 28, 2008, Carol Larson, Director of Management for SAO, noted that "there must be dedicated staff that see the mission of underrepresentation as a very serious goal and understand the meaning of 'diversity'" (Larson, 2008).

She goes on to say that, "it is absolutely imperative that the staff represent the students you are trying to reach. The credibility that we have gained has made such a huge difference and has been recognized by the students. Out of 12 full time professional staff in our three offices there are four males, eight women, one Gay, Lesbian, Bi-sexual, and Transgender (GLBT) staff, and three African Americans. This is not easy and takes a lot of work on the supervisory staff to make this happen and to work well, but the payoffs are tremendous " (Larson, 2008). During hiring interviews for new staff members the office also makes it clear that increasing minority involvement in study abroad is a central mission. This helps build a staff that is fully on board with the mission. As Larson noted, "It comes down to students and the passion of the staff. Our responsibility is to better prepare students to be abroad. Do I think we're perfect? No. But, we try." That level of self-awareness and deliberation is admirable and serves as encouragement to others who have most of their work ahead of them.

Pitt experienced a 30% increase in study abroad over a 5-year period (2002–2007), although the exact number and percentage of minority students is unclear because they have trouble getting students to self-report their ethnicity. Anecdotal information suggests that minority student participation is much higher than in the past. Trends definitely are moving in the right direction and the SAO staff is optimistic, realistic and committed.

SUGGESTED CATEGORIES FOR SELF-ASSESSMENT

The two preceding case studies have allowed us to identify several broad categories of concern that should figure prominently in a comprehensive self-assessment exercise focused on minority participation in study abroad.[5] One goal of the self-assessment exercise would be to identify factors that deter minority students from studying abroad in greater numbers. Another would be to identify challenges and impediments to increasing those numbers. A third would be to identify programmatic initiatives that can be targeted to minority students. Those initiatives then can constitute a set of best practices to the extent that participants share their stories and results. These may be some of the most important areas for investigation but, by no means do we suggest that they exhaust all possibilities that might yield useful information. We do maintain, though, that by interrogating these areas, study abroad officials will be pointed in the right direction and should be able to develop action agendas that can positively impact the problem.

Which institutions can benefit from this exercise? Any school would want to undertake an assessment if they recognize low minority participation in study abroad as a problem and want to do something about it. But, in general, institutions that just want to bring more balance to their study abroad programs will benefit as well.

The suggested self-assessment areas are: develop a profile of the minority student population; evaluate staffing and attitudes in the study abroad office; compare academic majors that study abroad with majors that attract the largest numbers of minority students; determine whether current destinations hold as much appeal for minority students as might others; develop a profile of program leaders who might have greater success in attracting minority students to study abroad; determine whether targeted programming might increase minority participation rates; and establish how greater funding support might impact the problem. In the discussion that follows, we identify salient considerations in each of those areas and suggest questions that can be explored.

UNDERSTANDING THE MINORITY STUDENT POPULATION

We start from the assumption that minority students should study abroad in greater numbers. Beyond that there are myriad answers to why they do not do so at present. A successful minority recruitment effort should begin with an attempt to understand the minority student population at your institution.

Beyond surveying minority students directly there also is a need to better understand who they are from the standpoint of their socioeconomic profiles, their majors, interests, and whether they work to support themselves and pay their educational fees. This task is arduous and will necessitate a multipronged approach that will require time commitments, broad based cooperation, diligence, and resolve. The institutional research office may be able to assist given the routine data that it collects on students. Under the best of circumstances the information that they collect will be of immediate use. More than likely, it may require that they revise their methods to include additional information that can be of use to the study abroad office in its minority recruitment effort.

The admissions office, the registrar, the student affairs office, minority service offices, and minority organizations potentially all can be data sources or can contribute to the research effort. Many students from underrepresented backgrounds may come from institutions with only a limited infrastructure to support study abroad students and limited institutional resources to support such an effort. This is particularly true in the case of many, but not all, Historically Black Colleges and Universities (HBCUs), Minority Serving Institutions (MSIs), and community colleges. That should be seen as a limitation but not an absolute barrier. For instance, it may be possible to interest an education or sociology professor in embracing this task as a research initiative where students can be recruited to conduct some of the research. Once a methodology is established and protocols and an initial data set have been developed, much of the ongoing work will be fairly routine.

Finally, it is important for study abroad staff to network and share experiences. They can attend events to educate themselves on the topic. Also, the entire study abroad staff and not just one individual should look for ways to improve minority student advising and programming. They also should share feedback they receive from minority students in their advising sessions that might help everyone better understand the problem and potential solutions.

STUDY ABROAD OFFICES: INSTITUTIONAL CONTEXT, STAFFING, AND ORIENTATION

There is a level of assessment that precedes an assessment of the study abroad office proper that focuses on the institutional context. Is there a clearly stated institutional commitment to this activity? What are the university's priorities where study abroad is concerned? Is it articulated in the university's strategic plan, its statement of goals and objectives, and its planning documents? Is study abroad viewed as a right or a privilege, an imperative or a matter of personal choice? What is the nature of the university's commitment? Are those commitments matched with resources, both human and material?

Only after the institutional commitment is established can one begin to assess the activities of the study abroad office. At that point the concern should be to establish how the office views study abroad. Is it an activity that is only limited to the elite few in select disciplines that traditionally study abroad or is it one that all students, irrespective of background or discipline, are encouraged to pursue? Does the office see itself as a proactive, aggressive, booster of study abroad or as one that takes a more passive approach? Are minority student numbers a real concern?

The concern, thereafter, is for the study abroad offices to ask and answer a series of questions of themselves. The operative question is whether organization, staffing diversity, attitudes, orientation, and processes impact this problem in any way and, if so, how? Concerns that study abroad offices might address include whether they have independently identified minority participation rates as a problem at their institution. If so, what is the staff doing in particular to address the problem? What are the perceived or documented impediments to greater involvement? What specific initiatives have been implemented or are being contemplated to attract more minority students? What support mechanisms are available to facilitate minority participation?

These questions assume that the institution tracks participation rates according to race and ethnicity so as to contribute to the annual *Open Doors* survey (IIE, 2007). However, all institutions might not contribute to the survey. Indications are that study abroad offices cannot easily calculate these figures since many students do not identify their race/ethnicity. For those that presently do not track minorities, they may choose to track these patterns going forward. Even in those cases where institutions are tracking minority participation, it still is possible to gather additional useful information beyond that required for the *Open Doors* survey.

We suggest that participating institutions ask and answer the following questions on staffing:

- What is the staffing pattern in the office and what, if any, is the number of minority staff members?
- Do you think minority staff do or might make a difference in reaching minority students?
- What reasons can you identify to explain why more minorities do not work in study abroad offices?
- Do you think more men would positively impact participation rates by minority males and, for that matter, males in general?
- What do you think might work, given sufficient time, personnel, and financial resources?

The question of minority staffing might prove to be controversial given, as indicated through anecdotal evidence, the relative paucity of minorities in study abroad offices. It may be that expertise in the field and being student centered are more important than ethnicity. However, that seems to beg the question. Professional expertise and empathy with students are necessary qualities for successful service in the study abroad environment, but are they sufficient for attracting larger numbers of minority students to go abroad? There are countless situations where dedicated study abroad staff meet that profile but still are not succeeding in attracting greater numbers of minority students to study abroad. Clearly, something more may be needed. A self-assessment can help identify that "something more."

In other cases one might argue that the attitudes of staff members are as important as, or more important than, racial or ethnic characteristics. A minority staff member may not be sympathetic and helpful to minority students. Another staff member may display more empathy, may be more conversant with the factors that impede minority participation, and may expend more energy helping minority students overcome obstacles. The operative question is: What staff characteristics and attitudes engender success? Are there particular staff characteristics that can prove effective? If those characteristics are ones that are not exclusive to minority staff members, they can be codified and included in hiring and promotion processes. What, if anything, can minority staff members bring to the task that might not be forthcoming from others?

Some would argue that minority staff members and student workers in the study abroad office do make a difference in encouraging minority students to study abroad, but what is the evidence? The research question is to know if, why, how, and to what extent the presence of minority staff members does impact the problem. We can proceed from the premise that having more minority staff members in study abroad offices cannot hurt and it might help. That statement can serve as a beginning point, a hypothesis, if you will, rather than as a firm finding. We begin with the question: Do minority staff members make a difference? Everything else flows from there.

Another line of questioning would be to ask why more minorities do not opt to work in study abroad offices. Do low pay and insufficient opportunities for advancement play a significant role? It would be useful to confirm that as one reason high quality minority candidates do not pursue employment in study abroad offices. It also would be useful to identify other factors that impact their decisions. Indeed, this may not be a race specific reason. Many people regardless of race choose not to enter the field for those same reasons. One very strong reason that minorities in particular do not enter the field is because studying abroad usually is a job requirement, so if fewer minorities are studying abroad, fewer of them consider the field. It becomes a self-perpetuating problem.

We propose that the self-assessment exercise take a hard look at information sessions and ask what is being done to address the concerns of minority students. Indications are that approaches are very uneven. Where some students might approach study abroad with a sense of adventure, minority students may do so with a sense of foreboding and fear of the unknown. They may have more concerns about the importance of studying abroad and what impact it will have on their graduation timetable and career prospects. They also may be concerned to know if racism will be a factor if they travel abroad and if they will be treated as objects of curiosity by people who, variously, have not encountered African Americans, Asians, or Hispanics before. They also may have to be convinced that studying abroad is not an activity mainly for White students of means and that there are ways for students of lesser means or those who work to support themselves to participate. Many of these are concerns that are voiced by students across the board. The point is to identify the particular or most compelling concerns that minority students have and to insure that they are addressed forthrightly in the information sessions and at various points along the way.

Some institutions address minority concerns in program-specific orientation sessions but some do not do so at all or only briefly in their general information and recruitment sessions. Others encourage program leaders to address minority concerns in their orientation sessions but are not actively involved and cannot say whether their advice is being followed. In other cases, the emphasis varies depending on the ethnic composition of the group being oriented. In still others, no distinction is made along lines of ethnicity although study abroad materials may suggest inclusiveness by displaying photos of minorities and their testimonials. Is that sufficient? We are aware of one case where staff in a study abroad office talked about doing something specifically targeted to minorities but they have not been able to determine what would be helpful. That uncertainty might have been encouraged when that office sponsored an optional predeparture workshop for minority students and no one showed up.

Some institutions opt to address minority concerns in one-on-one sessions but this approach does not allow other minority students to benefit from the insights and advice that might be shared with an individual student.

337

There is a need to ask whether study abroad offices are organizing information sessions that address the fears, misrepresentations, and funding obstacles that might bring minority students to write off study abroad. It will not be possible to get to the predeparture orientations if minority students bail out of the process before making a firm commitment to study abroad.

ACADEMIC MAJORS AND STUDY ABROAD

A question to ask in the self-assessment is whether the current majors that predominate in your campus' study abroad activities are the majors where the greatest numbers of minority students can be found. The 2007 Open Doors data base lists the social sciences (21.7%), business and management (17.7%), humanities (14.2%), foreign languages (7.8%), and fine or applied arts (7.5%) as the top five academic disciplines that send students abroad. Those disciplines together represent 69% of all students who studied abroad (Figure 19.7). The physical or life sciences follow closely behind at 6.9% and education is a distant seventh at 4.1%. All other disciplines combined account for just over 20% of the total (IIE, 2007).

A legitimate question to ask, in any given institutional setting, is whether the greatest number of minority students can be found in the disciplines that predominate in study abroad. Which are the disciplines where minority students can be found and to what extent do those disciplines participate in study abroad programs? Should the study abroad office attempt to broaden the range of academic majors that study abroad with the expectation that more minority students will do so because their majors feed increasing numbers of students into the study abroad pool? The answer will be different for each institution. Questions that flow from this one are which of those disci-

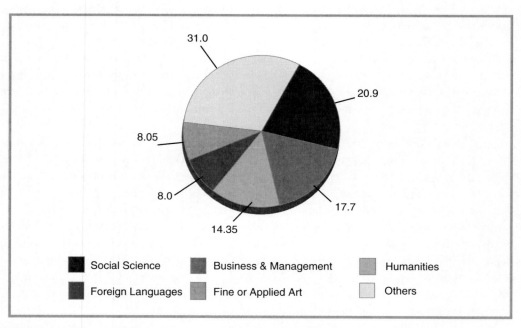

Figure 19.7 *Top Five Study Abroad Fields of Study for 1999 and 2006*

Source: *Open Doors*, 2007: Online Report on International Education Exchange.

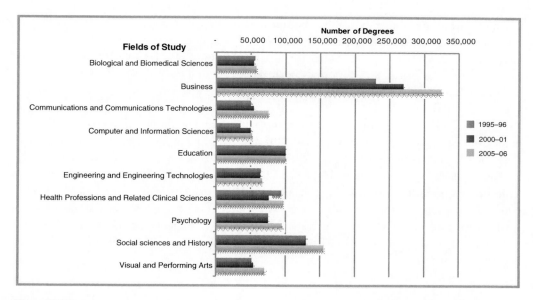

Figure 19.8 *Trends in Bachelor's Degree Conferred by Degree-Granting Institutions in Selected Fields of Study: 1995–96, 2000–01, and 2005–06*

Source: U.S. Department of Education, National Center for Education Statistics, 1995–96, 2000–01, and 2005–06 Integrated Postsecondary Education Data Systems, "Completions Survey" (IPEDS-C: 95–96), Fall 2001 and Fall 2006.

plines offer the most promise for developing new study abroad programs; which faculty in those disciplines are more likely to develop study abroad programs; what resources can be marshaled to assist them in that effort; and, what sort of appeal can be developed to attract minority students in those disciplines to participate?

There is no easy way to organize this task, especially for currently enrolled students. Since the data that should be gathered would come from the institutional level, it is possible that it might be available in the office of institutional research. The U.S. Department of Education tracks graduation trends by fields of study and has developed a useful way of grouping those disciplines for all students at all institutions while avoiding unnecessary detail (Figure 19.8).

It is possible, although not easy, to generate similar information on minority students at individual institutions. Indeed, the institutional research office ought to collect that information on the entire student body as a matter of routine. The question is whether data is generated for minority student subgroups. If not, they should be approached with an appeal to begin doing so.

DESTINATIONS AND MINORITY PARTICIPATION

Much has been made of the need to diversify study abroad destinations. Indeed, The Simon bill includes this as one of its objectives and is committed to increasing the number of students who study abroad in nontraditional destinations. There is a genuine need to put more regions, countries, and cultures in play in the quest for true global citizenship. For more than a decade the leading study abroad destinations, as reported by *Open Doors,* changed very little from year to year. The United Kingdom, Italy, Spain, France, Australia, Germany, and Ireland, all European or Anglo, always are among the leading destinations. Mexico, China, and Costa Rica are the only non-European, non-Anglo countries that manage to break into the top 10 year in and year out. Given the current study abroad student profile, this circumstance is perfectly understandable. But, this is not destination diversity, and it may point to one of the problems that impact minority student participation. Would more destination diversity attract greater numbers of minority students to study abroad?

This certainly is a question for investigation, a probe that might be included in a self-assessment exercise. Indeed, because of their day-to-day involvement and participation in the *Open Doors* surveys, many institutions already know their major destinations for study abroad. The research agenda is to determine whether and to what extent those destinations are or are not appealing to minority students. Are there destinations that might be more appealing? If so, which destinations are they and why are they more likely to attract minority students? If you are in a situation where most of your students are minority students, as in the HBCU and MSI environment, what might you do where destinations are concerned to kindle greater interest among your students?

PROGRAM LEADERS

How central are program leaders to the recruitment effort generally and in the case of minority students? Most would agree that, generally, they are the face of study abroad for students; they make initial appeals and often seal the deal by encouraging and supporting students in ways that often go beyond the call of duty. They have invested time and energy to develop the programs and their success depends on having students sign on to their initiative. We should be concerned to know what factors or characteristics program leaders may have that make for success in recruiting minority students. Would more minority program leaders produce better results? They might, but others may argue that nonminority faculty members also have been successful in recruiting minority students. Still further, a case can be made that the program's focus and its location are as important, if not more important, than the race of the program leader. Some faculty, because of the care and deliberation that they bring to the task, are popular program leaders regardless of their race or ethnicity. Those faculty members are enthusiastic and much of their influence on students is related to their personalities. Still, we need to ask whether having more minority program leaders might influence more minority students to study abroad? And, if so, how specifically is that accomplished? If minority status is less critical, then what characteristics might a program leader display that will be appealing to minority students to attract them into the study abroad fold?

TARGETED PROGRAMMING

One of the concerns that the self-assessment might address is whether the study abroad office organizes targeted initiatives to increase minority participation. Many institutions do. Others may feel that it is not necessary to target specific subgroups. For HBCUs and other MSIs all of their appeals are targeted to minority institutions. Still other institutions may not have considered the matter. Is it necessary to develop targeted programming specifically focused on minority students? And, if so, what sort of programming works and why? Both Georgia State and Pitt have developed and implemented targeted programs to good effect. Their examples might be instructive for other institutions.

FUNDING

The challenge of increasing minority participation rates comes on the heels of the most significant economic downturn since the Great Depression of the 1930s. The idea of designating funding for programs targeted to discrete student populations, when the overall need is so great and available funding is so tenuous, is one that must be defended. Yet it must be confronted because so many of the initiatives that might make a difference are closely tied to available funding. A question to ask in the self-assessment exercise is whether the institution has or can have funding set aside specifically to support efforts to recruit minority students and to support their study abroad programs. The Simon bill would certainly buttress this concern.

We know of some encouraging examples. One institution has set aside some of their language scholarships for African-American students. They announced those opportunities through their Black Studies program. In another instance, a university used scholarships to attract Native American students to study abroad. In other cases, external funding is used for this purpose. In still others, the universities have themselves identified funding that is targeted to minority students. To be successful, institutions of higher education should look to fund minority students with regular and substantial institutional resources and not just with soft, ephemeral external funding. Each of us needs to know what funding is potentially available, what has to be done to secure those resources, and how to put them to the best use. Finally, and for all students, but especially to boost minority student numbers in study abroad, universities will have to identify affordable programs that are or can easily be within financial reach for more students. Solving the financial problem clearly will go a long way to increase study abroad totals.

STRATEGIES FOR SUCCESS

One important potential result that can come from several institutions completing their self-assessment exercises is that they can share success stories. Some study abroad advisors admit that they lack ideas about what to do to promote greater minority participation. This is why sharing is important. If we establish what works and share best practices, others then can draw on those experiences and improve their minority outreach efforts. Some strategies that work already have been identified and to attack head on those factors that deter minority students from studying abroad in greater numbers one must first know their student body and understand as much as possible the racial/ethnic breakdown and profile. Take advantage of minority students who have returned from their study abroad experiences because they can serve as effective recruiters given their enthusiasm and the growth that they display once back on campus. We should be encouraged to develop peer-to-peer mentoring and student recruitment opportunities that involve returned minority travelers. One advisor at New Mexico State University (NMSU) encourages her colleagues to concentrate on building a strong campus-wide support network, support student-centered innovations and faculty developed initiatives, and fight for increased institutional support generally and especially to assist minority students to study abroad.

A self-assessment helps to pinpoint strengths, opportunities, and challenges. It can lay the foundation for programmatic vitality and improvement, help identify areas, and devise strategies for intervention. It need not be limited to concerns about minority participation. It can subsume those concerns while addressing myriad other issues of importance to your institution. The answers to some questions already may be clear for your institution. Others may be less relevant. The key is to structure the exercise to give your institution the information it needs to boost study abroad generally, and, more particularly, on the part of minority students.

RECOMMENDATIONS FOR THE FUTURE

Clearly there is much work to be done if we are to positively impact this problem. To achieve success, institutions will have to undertake a self-motivated, introspective approach to this task. We will need to better educate ourselves on the motives, fears, interests, and potential of our students. We probably will not be able to implement one idea or program and expect success. A searching, multipronged, and evolving approach is likely to produce the greatest sustained results. Although we pose these questions for research, it probably will be necessary to broaden the range of majors and the number of destinations in order to appeal to wider segments of the student population. With deliberation and hard work those changes can take place so that they appeal to minority students in greater numbers.

There are organizations that promote study abroad among minority students. The National Association for Equal Opportunity (NAFEO) certainly has a more than passing interest in this topic. Member institutions should continue to draw on its resources and push it to expend greater effort. The Center for Global Education, located at Loyola Marymount University, has initiated a Project for Learning Abroad, Training and Outreach (PLATO), a national consortium of some 22 partners, some of which are consortia themselves. PLATO provides comprehensive support resources for study abroad—with special support for underrepresented students.[6] This limited initiative points in a positive direction by bringing diverse entities together to solve a common problem. Other similar groupings also can be identified.

In conclusion, it is imperative to bring greater international awareness to the American public. The commitment to make every student a global citizen is an integral part of that quest. Study abroad is one of the critical components in the drive for global citizenship. For study abroad to realize its potential larger numbers of students must participate and there must be greater diversity in the population of students that do so. In short, the study abroad population has to look more like the general national population. Study abroad must broaden beyond the middle class White, female demographic to include more socioeconomic representation, greater gender balance, and sharp increases in minority student participation. Only then can we expect to truly achieve the lofty goals that are well within our grasp.

NOTES

1. We would like to thank our colleagues in the Office of International Affairs at Georgia State for their considerable support and encouragement as we pursued this research project. In particular we thank Wilma Newkirk for developing the graphics for this article. Adrienne Smith, in the Office of Institutional Research, provided invaluable survey research assistance. We could not have completed this project without her contribution.

2. While male participation in study abroad is not a focus of this study, it does represent a formidable problem and it underscores the need for a separate study that should be approached with some urgency.

3. By minority students we mean native born and naturalized students from racially and ethnically underrepresented population subgroups. That category would include Hispanics/Latinos, African Americans, Asian Americans/Pacific Islanders, Native Americans/Alaskan Natives, and persons of mixed backgrounds, but it would not include visa holders, irrespective of nationality.

4. http://www.youtube.com/watch?v=ECEhO16ycrQ

5. A Self-Assessment Guide can be found at Attachment A below.

6. The consortium includes organizations such as the American Association of Community Colleges, American Council on International Intercultural Education, California State University System, University of California System, Consortium on North American Higher Education Collaboration, National Association for Equal Opportunity in Higher Education, Hispanic Association of Colleges and Universities, and the University of Hawaii System.

REFERENCES

Georgia State University. (n.d./a). RetrievedJune 6, 2008, from http://www.gsu.edu

Georgia State University. (n.d./b). Mission statement. Retrieved June 6, 2008, from http://www.gsu.edu/24676.html http://www2.gsu.edu/~wwwoia/StudyAbroad/mission.html

Georgia State University. (n.d./c). Strategic plan. Retrieved June 6, 2008, from http://www2.gsu.edu/~wwwact/univ_strategic_plan/2000_2005_strategicplan.pdf

Georgia State University. (n.d./d). Strategic plan. Retrieved June 6, 2008, from http://www2.gsu.edu/~wwwact/pdf_plan_archive/2005_strategicplan.pdf

Georgia State University. (n.d./e). Study abroad mission statement. Retrieved June 6, 2008, from http://www2.gsu.edu/~wwwoia/StudyAbroad/mission.html

Institute of International Education (IIE). (2007). Open doors online report on international education exchange. Retrieved June 6, 2008, from http://opendoors.iienetwork.org/?p=89220

Larson, C. (2008). Interview by Farrah Bernardino.

University of Pittsburgh (n.d/a). Retrieved June 6, 2008, from http://www.abroad.pitt.edu/publications/world-inyourhands.pdf

University of Pittsburgh (n.d/b). Retrieved June 6, 2008, from http://www.abroad.pitt.edu/makingithappen/film.html

Lopez, J. K. (2006). *The impact of demographic changes on United States higher education 2000–2050*. Chapel Hill, NC: State Higher Education Executive Officers, North Carolina.

Murdock, S. R. (2006). *Population change in the United States: Implications for human and socioeconomic resources in the 21st century*. San Antonio, TX: Institute for Demographic and Socioeconomic Research, University of Texas San Antonio.

U.S. Department of Education: National Center for Educational Statistics. (2007). *Digest of educational statistics: 2007*. Retrieved June 6, 2008, from http://nces.ed.gov/programs/digest/d07/ch_3.asp

U.S. Department of Education, National Center for Education Statistics. (2008a). *Digest of education statistics, 2007* (NCES 2008-022). Retrieved on June 6, 2008, from http://nces.ed.gov/fastfacts/display.asp?id=98).

Walker, L. (2007–2008). Interview by authors.

ATTACHMENT A

Self-Assessment Guide: Minority Student Participation in Study Abroad

Potential Users:

Institutions that recognize low minority participation in study abroad as a problem and want to do something about it or institutions that just want to bring more diversity to their study abroad programs.

Self-Assessment Goals:

1. Identify factors that deter minority students from studying abroad in greater numbers.
2. Identify challenges and impediments to increasing those numbers.
3. Identify programmatic initiatives that can be targeted to minority students.

Understanding the Minority Student Population:

1. Which unit/entity is responsible for gathering institutional data on students? Is that data comprehensive enough to provide detailed information on the minority student population including their financial profiles, distribution among academic majors and participation in study abroad? If not, is it possible to enhance the data set to include those concerns?

2, If that option is not possible, does the Study Abroad Office collect that data or does it have any other avenues for securing that information? What are they?

   Considerations: Assuming the Study Abroad Office is leading this effort, collaboration with the Office of Institutional Research, Admissions and/or Office of Student Enrollment and Retention, Student Financial Aid, Student Services, might be very useful in securing the needed information. Are there opportunities to further engage minority students? Are there institution-specific issues that surfaced during this review that would need some attention?

3. Does the Study Abroad Office collect and sort data on study abroad destinations so that you can establish where minority students tend to study abroad?

4. What does the data reveal about the distribution of academic majors among study abroad students at your institution?

5. Are the academic majors that normally study abroad consistent with the most popular academic majors of minority students?

6. Where study abroad destinations are concerned, if there is no disparity in study abroad destinations between minority students and students in general what other conclusions can be drawn from the comparison between these two study abroad populations?

   Considerations: Are there opportunities to further engage minority students? Are there institution-specific issues that surfaced during this review that would suggest a need to diversify destinations?

7. If there is disparity in destinations, does the evidence point to a need for targeted intervention? Is there need for the Study Abroad Office to seek formal input from minority students to establish the reasons for the disparity? Can you determine if an effort should be made to work with faculty/program leaders to develop programs in the majors of interest to minority students?

8. What does the data reveal about funding and its accessibility for study abroad students at your institution?

   Considerations: Does your institution have an institution-specific scholarship for study abroad? Have you identified other scholarships/grants that support study abroad for minority students? Do you promote these scholarships?

   Is there need to increase funding to enable minority students to participate in study abroad? Is there need to increase efforts to identify scholarships and grants for minority students to take advantage of? Is there need to develop interventions directed at assisting minority students to identify funding for study abroad?

Study Abroad Offices: Institutional Context, Staffing, and Orientation:

1. Is there an institutional commitment to study abroad at your institution and is it clearly articulated the university's vision/mission statement/strategic plan?
2. Is institutional commitment to Study Abroad matched with human and financial resources (staff hiring, program funding, etc.)?
3. Has the office independently considered minority participation as an area for study abroad growth? If so, what programming has been created to tap into this area of growth and/or what are the outcomes so far?
4. Is the Study Abroad Office staffing pattern geared towards engaging minority students to study abroad?
5. Would or does the Study Abroad Office engage minority students in its programming efforts?
6. Would you agree that Study Abroad Offices should proactively encourage/mentor minority students to consider study abroad as a professional choice?

Profile of Study Abroad Program Leaders:

1. Are faculty program leaders actively engaged in recruiting minority students to study abroad?
   Who conducts specific program recruitment and outreach? Does the Study Abroad Office or the faculty advise students on destinations, funding, and program experience?
2. Could collaborative efforts with program leaders help minority students overcome issues and challenges to studying abroad? Could it, for example, help alleviate fears of traveling abroad, address hesitations around going to certain countries, or deal with the matter of racism?
3. Is there evidence to show that programs led by minority faculty leaders are of more interest to minority students?
4. Is there an annual evaluation of study abroad programs and does it include considerations of minority issues and feedback from all students, including minority students?

Chapter 20

Understanding the Challenges of Assessing Global Citizenship

Darla K. Deardorff

Duke University

"The educated American of the twenty-first century will need to be conversant with at least one language in addition to his or her native language, and knowledgeable about other countries, other cultures, and the international dimensions of issues critical to the lives of all Americans," states a report of the Committee on Economic Development (2006, p. 2). With globalization driving the demand for global-ready graduates, it becomes crucial for administrators to assess the outcomes of education abroad experiences to determine exactly what our students are learning while abroad and how effective our programs are in achieving stated learning outcomes. Some meaningful outcomes of such international experiences include greater proficiency in a foreign language, the development of global citizens, which includes enhancing one's intercultural competence and sensitivity, and the improvement of one's ability to live and work successfully in another culture (Herrin, 2004). The Institute of International Education reports that 95% of study abroad alumni noted that their experiences abroad had a lasting impact on their worldview which impacted their career paths (Akande & Slawson, 2000). Despite the growing numbers of students studying abroad, the overall percentage within the United States remains at around 1% of the total student population who actually go abroad. And within that number is an increasing number that go abroad for shorter and shorter periods. This current context of education abroad in the United States gives rise to several questions regarding the assessment of such experiences: How do we specifically define the terms used in stating learning outcomes, terms such as *global citizenship* and *intercultural competence*? How effective are short-term education abroad experiences and what are some realistic outcomes that can be measured from these programs? What are the best ways to assess these learning outcomes? What challenges will we encounter in trying to assess global citizenship development as an outcome of study abroad? How can we best use the data collected from assessment efforts? And how do we even get started in trying to assess learning outcomes? What do education abroad professionals need to know about assessment in general in order to adequately assess the outcomes of their programs?

ASSESSMENT IN INTERNATIONAL EDUCATION

Assessment in international education, particularly within education abroad, is a recent phenomenon, driven largely by the trends in greater assessment and accountability within higher education in the United States. When we take a closer look at outcomes assessment efforts in the field of international education, there is some progress being made. For example, a survey conducted in 2003–2004 indicated that 38% of responding schools were assessing intercultural competence (Deardorff, 2004), a key component to global citizenship. A follow-up survey in 2006–2007 showed an increase to 47% of schools assessing students' intercultural competence (Deardorff, 2007). According to the American Council on Education's report on *Mapping Internationalization* (Green, Luu, & Burris, 2008), 45% of the over 2000 institutions in the study had articulated global student learning outcomes, and 30% were formally assessing progress on internationalization.

International education organizations are focusing increased attention on assessment. The American Council on Education conducted a multiyear project on learning outcomes in international education called "Global Learning for All" in which the following institutions participated: California State University–Stanislaus, Cleveland State University (OH), Kennesaw State University (GA), Montgomery College (MD), College of Notre Dame of Maryland, Portland State University (OR), San Diego Community College (CA), and St. Louis Community College at Forest Park (MO). Through this project, participating institutions explored best practices in "setting international learning goals, reviewing their internationalization activities, aligning international activities with learning goals, partnering between institutions, and developing strategic internationalization plans that best serve their constituents" (American Council on Education [ACE], 2007). The project focused on learning that occurred through a variety of experience, on campus and abroad.

The American Council on Education also initiated a 3-year project funded by FIPSE to "advance the assessment of international learning with the long-term goal of improving student international learning at U.S. higher education institutions" (ACE). Six institutions participated in this project: Dickinson College (PA), Kalamazoo College (MI), Kapi'olani Community College (HI), Michigan State University (MI), Palo Alto College (TX), and Portland State University (OR). Learning outcomes were assessed using an e-portfolio and a self-report instrument. From this project emerged Web-based assessment resources that other institutions can use within the international education field. Specific learning goals addressed in this project related to the development of global citizens and included goal statements such as "Demonstrates knowledge of global issues, processes, trends and systems" (with a specific objective such as knowing principles, theories, and models that underlie global issues, processes, trends and systems) and "Understands his/her culture in a global and comparative context" (with a specific objective such as understanding history of his or her own culture in relation to the history of other cultures) (ACE, 2007).

Other organizations specifically within the international education field have also become more focused on assessment. The Forum on Education Abroad has increasingly focused on outcomes assessment within education abroad, producing a *Guide to Outcomes Assessment in Education Abroad* (Bolen, 2007). At the writing of this chapter, the Forum is spearheading a research project funded by the U.S. Department of Education and conducted through the University of Minnesota that is examiningways in which study abroad participants have become globally engaged during their lives following their experience abroad. The project is called "Beyond Immediate Impact: Study Abroad for Global Engagement", and involves 22 institutions and study abroad providers as well as 6,000 former study abroad participants in researching the long-term impact of education abroad experiences. Another key organization, The Association of International Education Administrators (www.aieaworld.org), a professional organization for senior leaders in international education, has offered specific workshops and sessions at its conferences that address assessment within the field, focusing primarily on student learning outcomes abroad.

In reviewing specific education abroad programs that are actively assessing student learning outcomes, the following patterns emerge:

1. A variety of assessments are being used before, during, and after the education abroad experience including e-portfolios, self-report surveys, embedded course assessment, focus groups, interviews and observations by others including host families and internship supervisors.
2. Intentional and adequate preparation (offered in such forms as predeparture courses), as well as intentional intervention in student learning during and after the experience, are necessary in order for students to maximize their intercultural learning and global citizenship development and to articulate learning outcomes.
3. Existing surveys and course assessments are being adapted to obtain more specific evidence of student learning, so as to move beyond the basic satisfaction surveys to include more relevant data on actual student learning.
4. Given the complexity of assessing global citizenship development, adequate support (leadership, financial, time, commitment, and training) is provided for efforts to be successful.

These patterns provide guidelines for future assessment efforts within the international education field, especially in education abroad programs.

CHALLENGES IN ASSESSING GLOBAL CITIZENSHIP

There are several challenges inherent in assessing global citizenship, the first of which begins with defining terms.

Definitions and Focus

There are currently numerous definitions and models for global citizenship, many of which suggest the following common threads: (1) global knowledge; (2) understanding the interconnectedness of the world in which we live; (3) intercultural competence, or the ability to relate successfully with those from other cultures; and (4) engagement on the local and global levels around issues that impact humanity. Of these components of global citizenship, intercultural competence is often considered the most ambiguous. And while it is possible to have intercultural competence without global citizenship, one could argue that it is not possible to decouple global citizenship from intercultural competence. However, there is currently no consensus among international education administrators on the terminology that can be used to describe this phenomenon. Various terms used to describe this concept include *global competence*, *international competence*, *cross-cultural competence*, *multicultural skills*, and so on.

In defining terms, it is important for professionals to consult the existing literature in the field. For example, one study (Deardorff, 2006) that is the first to document consensus among leading intercultural experts on what constitutes intercultural competence defined this rather ambiguous concept through the model shown in Figure 20.1.

As indicated by this model (Figure 20.1), intercultural experts reached consensus on the specific aspects of knowledge, skills, and attitudes that comprise intercultural competence which ultimately lead to visible behavior and communication that is both effective and appropriate in intercultural interactions. The one element that was agreed upon 100% by these experts was the

Table 20.1 *Terminology Used by Institutions to Refer to Intercultural Competence*

Terminology	# of institutions
Cross-cultural competence	6
Global competence	5
Intercultural competence	3
Global citizenship	3
International competence	2
Global awareness	2
Cross-cultural understanding	2
Other	2

ability to see the world from others' perspectives, a crucial element to the concept of global citizenship. Even given such a consensus definition of intercultural competence, there is still much work that needs to be done in honing very specific outcomes related to this construct, as well as those related to the overall construct of global citizenship. Such definitions and models can provide frameworks for guiding the thinking about assessment but further work must be done on articulating specific objectives and indicators which then provide more concrete statements which are actually assessable. So, for example, using the intercultural competence model here, a program would need to determine which intercultural competence aspects are most important to emphasize both programmatically and in assessment efforts (as determined by program mission and goals). If culture-specific knowledge is deemed a priority, then there would be specific

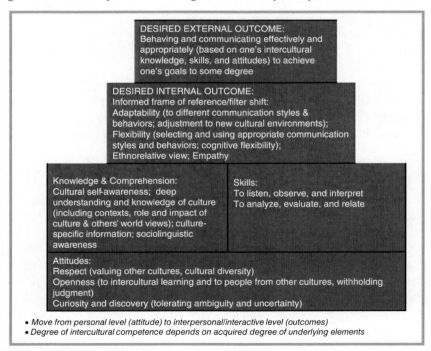

Figure 20.1 *Pyramid Model of Intercultural Competence*

Source: Deardorff, 2006

outcome statements around culture-specific knowledge and these outcome statements would point to specific assessment measures of these outcomes, perhaps through some actual tests of knowledge which may include culture-specific case studies.

Defining terms and priorities help lead to more focus within overall programmatic goals. Stating that a program goal is to develop "global citizens" is very broad and needs further specificity before assessment can begin. A study conducted by the American Association of Colleges and Universities (Musil, 2004) found that while all majors and fields of concentration identify global knowledge, engagement, and intercultural competence as essential outcomes, the study found that there is a disconnect between stated intentions and realities. This study also found that

> the goals for global learning at too many colleges and universities are unfocused.... Moreover, too few colleges and universities offer structured education opportunities for students to acquire knowledge, both theoretical and experiential, about the rest of the world, about America's place in the world, and about the inequities and interdependencies that mark current geopolitical relationships. (Musil, 2004, p. 1)

Thus, a primary challenge for education abroad professionals is in defining and then focusing on what specifically needs to be assessed within global citizenship, given that the concept itself is too broad for general assessment.

In defining global citizenship goals and outcomes, it is important to work with faculty in the disciplines to ascertain how these goals and outcomes manifest themselves within the different disciplines. What does it mean for an engineering student to be a global citizen? What does it mean for a social worker to be a global citizen? Such goals can most often be stated through specific courses and should address how global learning goals apply to particular courses. Faculty also need to take into consideration the teaching strategies that will enhance students' global learning in the course as well as the cocurricular activities on campus that complement the stated global learning goals in the course. One example of this cited in the AACU study (Musil, 2004) is a set of courses created at Pacific Lutheran University that align with institutional and programmatic goals of the study abroad program and connect with an initiative involving the local immigrant community. "The learning goals include understanding the impact of colonialism and immigration as well as identifying, describing, and acting on global issues in pursuit of justice and equality" (p. 10).

Realistic Outcomes

Another challenge in assessing global citizenship outcomes within education abroad is aligning realistic outcomes with the duration and type of experience abroad. What can a student reasonably be expected to learn in a week-long experience versus a 6-week summer program versus a semester abroad? The outcomes should be matched appropriately to the length of the experience. Much also depends on how the program is structured abroad. For example, if students remain in a "bubble" with other American students and American faculty with little opportunity to engage in the local community beyond going to a local pub or store or attending a cultural event such as a concert, then the learning outcomes would differ significantly from those programs whose students are engaged in direct service learning activities in the community or living with host families who are actively engaged in the cultural learning of the student.

■ **350**

Preparation

Adequate preparation is another key issue in assessing students' global citizenship. How well does a program adequately prepare students before sending them abroad? Unfortunately, interculturally competent global citizens generally do not occur naturally. If this phenomenon were naturally occurring, programs would not need to address this. However, this is unfortunately not the case and it is incumbent upon programs to intentionally address how to prepare students for experiences abroad, and to provide them with adequate intercultural training (generally beyond the few hours of a workshop that is often the case) and knowledge of world issues from a variety of perspectives, beyond the U.S. perspective. We cannot expect students to articulate the learning outcomes of their experiences if they have not been adequately prepared and given the concepts and language to articulate their learning.

Alignment and Integration

Integrating a comprehensive program to address and assess global citizenship, beyond a one-time course or education abroad experience, is essential if postsecondary institutions are to be truly successful in graduating global citizens who can make a difference in this world. The challenge is moving beyond that one course or one education abroad experience to truly integrate the learning across courses and cocurricular experiences on campus (Bok, 2006). And as the Association of American Colleges and Universities study found, learning outcomes in regard to social responsibility and civic engagement "are poorly defined and not well integrated into global components of the curriculum" (Musil, 2004, p. 3). So, the following questions arise through the observed disconnect on American campuses: How do the stated learning outcomes demonstrate cumulative learning throughout one's college education, especially in regard to global citizenship? How can the learning that is achieved through education abroad be integrated into coursework upon a student's return to campus? How can students' local/global engagement be integrated into coursework? How can we continue to track a student's global citizenship and engagement over time? Intentional practice as well as assessment is one suggested strategy for addressing integration of global learning throughout the institution and for ensuring the alignment of an institution's mission and goals with reality. Another strategy for greater integration and alignment is through an interdisciplinary approach to global issues such as environmental sustainability, poverty, and global health issues.

As we have discussed, there are several specific challenges to assessing global citizenship that include the greater clarity around definitions and specific focus needed, the statement of realistic learning outcomes given a program's duration and type, the adequate preparation of students in going abroad, and the alignment and integration of global citizenship throughout an institution's curriculum. Another basic question to ask is what a successful global citizen looks like? In other words, how will schools know if they have been successful in developing global citizens? Other key questions to explore in assessing global citizenship development include: How will commitment to global citizenship be assessed? How can students' motivation be assessed? What evidence (and from whom) is needed to determine if these goals and objectives have been met? What are the best methods/tools for collecting this evidence, as determined by the goals and objectives? How will the evidence be used? To whom will the evidence be communicated? Education abroad administrators need to reflect carefully upon these questions as they put together a comprehensive assessment strategy to assess global citizenship as an outcome of their programs.

THE NEED TO UNDERSTAND ASSESSMENT BASICS

Another major challenge to assessing global citizenship is that education abroad professionals often lack knowledge of assessment (or even feel uncomfortable tackling the assessment part). It is important for education abroad professionals to have a basic knowledge of assessment when they collaborate with others on campus in regard to assessment.

There are numerous ways in which to define assessment. The Higher Learning Commission of the North Central Association of Colleges and Schools (2006) defines assessment of student learning broadly as a participatory, iterative process that provides information on students' learning. Angelo (1995) defines assessment as an ongoing process aimed at understanding and improving student learning that involves explicit expectations and appropriate criteria which matches performance to those expectations. Evidence of learning is systematically collected, analyzed, interpreted, and used to document, explain, and improve student learning. Assessment also engages faculty and others in analyzing and using this information to improve teaching and learning, produces evidence that students are achieving the intended outcomes, guides faculty and administrators in making educational and institutional improvements, and evaluates whether implemented changes at the institutional, programmatic, or course level impact student learning. When one defines assessment, it is important to recognize the purpose of assessment, namely that it is not just for program improvements but ultimately for improvement of both teaching and learning, which impacts faculty and students. Providing feedback to students on their learning is an essential reason why assessment is undertaken. Thus, administrators need to reflect upon why such assessment is needed and desired, as well as how it will be used.

FRAMEWORKS FOR ASSESSMENT

There are many models and approaches that can be used to frame assessment efforts. Knowledge of such frameworks can help one in better understanding the overall context of assessment and such frameworks can help guide one in actual assessment efforts. One of the foundational approaches in the field of evaluation and assessment was developed by Tyler (1949) who advocated an objective-based approach through the framework of four main questions related to the objectives an organization should seek to attain, the learning experiences needed to achieve those objectives, the organization of the learning experiences for effective instruction, and the evaluation of the effectiveness of the learning experiences (Tyler, 1949). Tyler's work stresses the connection of students' learning experiences to the objectives and measuring whether those have been achieved. When applied to global citizenship assessment, one learns the importance of connecting experiences abroad to the specific objectives. Popham's (1993) later work reiterated Tyler's seminal work and emphasized the myriad of evaluative measurements that can be used in educational settings. He advocates the use of triangulation of methods (use of multiple methods) to provide evidence of greater validity of the measures. From Popham, we can learn the importance of using multiple methods (such as tests, observations, portfolios, focus groups, interviews, etc.) in assessing global citizenship, depending on our specific objectives. Stark, Shaw, and Lowther

(1989) offer a variation on the objective-oriented approach by emphasizing the utilization of student goals. This leads to the question of the nature of students' goals in relation to global citizenship. This will be discussed further in the section on learner-centered assessment. Boone (1985) also emphasized an objective-oriented approach in developing a conceptual programming model in which the evaluation and accountability subprocess is an integral and ongoing part of the entire programming process. Boone (1985) defines this subprocess as "making informed judgments about the effectiveness of the planned program and plans of action based on established criteria and known, observable evidence" (p. 73). From Boone, we can learn the importance of establishing specific criteria and matching it with observable evidence, primarily through students' work. Astin's (1991) classic model of assessing outcomes is known as the I-E-O model which provides a framework for assessing input-environment-outcomes of student development. Astin encourages administrators to start with the anticipated outcomes component first and then determine what is needed in the way of input and environment to achieve the outcomes. He also cautions against isolating any one of these variables during assessment; rather, he suggests that administrators should view all three components as interrelated. This perspective is very similar to Boone's and others in that assessment and evaluation are ultimately part of a complex whole. This stresses the importance of integration of assessment throughout what we do, with a caution not to view assessment in isolation from the program as a whole—in other words, assessment is not something that is done solely at the beginning and end of a program. From Astin, we can also learn the importance of beginning with the end in mind—that of graduating global citizens—and then determining what is needed to make this happen. Baird (2003) notes a more recent shift in the literature from individualistic goals set and assessed by institutions to more community-oriented outcomes negotiated between students and institutions, with active student engagement in determining specific outcomes. To that end, administrators may find themselves serving as negotiators or brokers in this process of negotiating student outcomes. This discussion has highlighted only a few of the many approaches that have informed the assessment and evaluation processes, and ways in which such approaches may influence our thinking about the assessment of global citizenship.

The one model which provides a concise framework for addressing outcomes within a program context, regardless of the field, is the program logic model (Rogers, 2000; Wholey, 1979), also known by other variations of "logic model." This model takes into account the inputs as well as the overall impact and includes the following dimensions: inputs, activities, outputs, outcomes, and impact. It is widely used in the private, public, and nonprofit sectors and by such entities as the U.S. Department of State, the Kellogg Foundation, and United Way. This model also incorporates definitions of assessment as both being integral to student learning as well as the broader program evaluation definitions around a systematic collection, analysis, and reporting of program information that informs decision making.

Let's take a closer look at the program logic model and how this framework can be used to not only provide a road map for clarifying intended outcomes but lead ultimately to lasting change within the program or organization. The model ultimately addresses three basic questions: Where are we going? How will we get there? How will we know when we've arrived? Here are the specific components of the model:

> **Inputs:** What is needed to achieve the stated goals? Stated goals and objectives can be written in the SMART Goal format (Specific, Measurable, Action oriented, Realistic, and Time delineated). Inputs are the resources and can involve people, time, money, partners, or other items available to the program.

Activities: What are the specific activities undertaken to achieve the goals? In the case of international education, activities can involve learning opportunities that occur through curriculum, education abroad experiences, research, involvement of faculty abroad, and so on.

Outputs: Who is involved and being reached? In other words, who are the participants? Outputs often include participation numbers such as the number of students in education abroad programs.

Outcomes: What do participants know, think, feel, or can do as a result of being in the program? How has participant behavior changed as a result of the program? Measuring outcomes involves both short-term learning outcomes as well as more medium-term action-oriented outcomes, including student engagement related to social action.

Impact: What is the long-term impact (consequences/results) of the program on participants; other learners on campus including international students and scholars; faculty; the campus and institution; the community—both the domestic community and the community abroad? Longitudinal studies are often necessary to assess long-term impact.

Figure 20.2 illustrates the program logic model adapted to international education. Utilizing the program logic is often one of the first steps in assessment and implementing change. This model helps to move programs beyond counting numbers to providing the meaning behind the numbers such as the student learning outcomes that result from student participation in experiences leading to their development as global citizens. Change occurs when the specific aspects of the logic model are understood, in particular the outcomes that are expected and then assessed.

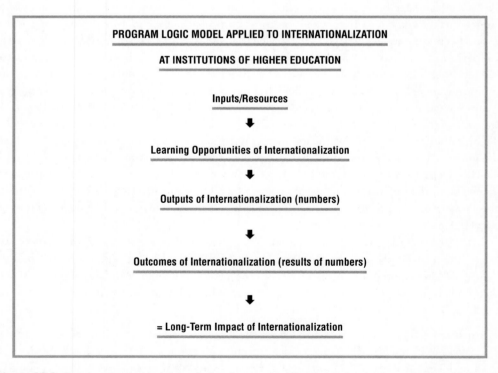

Figure 20.2 *Program Logic Model Applied to Internationalization at Institutions of Higher Education*

Source: Deardorff, 2004, p. 58

Limitations of the program logic model include the challenge of causal attribution since there are many factors that may influence outcomes, especially in education abroad experiences, as well as in the long-term impact which may not be addressed in the initial assessment efforts.

In recent years, the call for accountability within higher education has increased with accreditation bodies now focusing more on institutional assessment endeavors, particularly in regard to outcomes. Furthermore, assessment within higher education has shifted to a more learner-centered approach. This focus on the learner-centered approach has led to the relatively new field of the scholarship of teaching and learning (SoTL) and shifts the assumption of faculty being necessary for student learning to faculty as facilitators of student learning. To state it another way, the faculty paradigm has shifted from the "sage on the stage" to the "guide on the side," meaning that while faculty expertise and knowledge is still crucial, the transference of such knowledge is different. Huba and Freed (2000) summarize the following implications of this paradigm shift within higher education for learner-centered assessment:

They note that learner-centered assessment

1. Promotes high expectations for learning;
2. Respects diverse talents and learning styles;
3. Engages students in learning;
4. Promotes coherence in learning;
5. Synthesizes experiences, fostering ongoing practice of learned skills, and integrates education and experience;
6. Provides prompt feedback;
7. Fosters collaboration;
8. Depends on increased student–faculty contact. (pp. 22–24)

There are numerous points in the learner-centered approach that encourage students' development of global citizenship, including the integration of learners' education and experience abroad, which can result in students' active engagement in the community (both their own and their host community) and the world. In engaging students in learning, students are empowered to take responsibility for their own learning, thus promoting high expectations for the learning that will occur through education abroad.

A criticism of the student learning approach is that it focuses exclusively on the learning that occurs for the student, thus leading to dependence on student learning outcomes as the sole measure of success. Another criticism is that the focus on student learning may not address or assess unintended outcomes that could occur, nor does it provide as much specific data for program improvement. Ultimately, though, the purpose of postsecondary institutions is to facilitate learning in students. Thus, it is incumbent upon administrators and faculty in education abroad to move programs and courses beyond surface learning to the deeper learning and engagement of participants, which will ultimately lead toward the development of global citizens.

GENERAL ASSESSMENT CHALLENGES AND POSSIBLE STRATEGIES TO OVERCOME CHALLENGES

Having briefly explored some of the challenges inherent specifically within global citizenship assessment, what are some of the key assessment challenges in general and how can one begin to circumvent those? Some of these challenges such as alignment and clarity of definitions have already been discussed within the context of global citizenship assessment while others such as evidence of student learning, faculty resistance, and utilization of results exist regardless of the context of assessment.

Alignment

As already discussed earlier in this chapter, a challenge in initial assessment endeavors is in ensuring that mission, goals, pedagogy/curriculum/program, and assessment methods/tools are aligned. Often, a program may use an assessment method/tool because it is being used by another similar program or institution, which means that the tool may not inherently fit the program's actual mission and prioritized goals. Taking time to map these specific elements of mission, goals, curriculum/program, and appropriate methods/tools is essential to address the "alignment challenge." There are tools that can be used to aid in strategically mapping these elements to ensure alignment, including a technique called the Balanced Scorecard in which four different perspectives (Customer/Participant, Internal, Innovation/Learning, Financial) are reviewed in terms of goals and measures to gain a balanced strategic view of the program and track continuous improvement (Kaplan & Norton, 2005). Traditionally used in the corporate world, this tool can be used to view goals and needs from different perspectives (in the case of education abroad programs, such perspectives can not only include students, but also institution, program, and community perspectives) to see how these map strategically.

Clarity of Definitions

In assessment efforts, core concepts are often not defined clearly or if there are definitions, the scholarly literature has often not been reviewed as a basis for the definitions. Why is it important to define core concepts such as global citizenship or intercultural competence? Such clear definitions, based on scholarly work, help to bridge gaps and provide clarity and a foundation for clear objectives and indicators, thus moving beyond misperceptions and ambiguities. As discussed earlier in the chapter, it is important to consult literature and scholarly research on seemingly ambiguous concepts in order to provide theoretical frameworks upon which to build one's definition. Another key strategy is to facilitate on-campus dialogues around these concepts. Following literature reviews and on-campus dialogues, consensus can be reached on specific definitions to use which can then provide the foundation for the delineation of more specific indicators and measurable criteria regarding such broad concepts as global citizenship. This process often occurs over several months and involves inputs from all relevant stakeholders (including students), dialogues among stakeholders, and eventual consensus on definitions, goals, and specific objectives.

Expectations of Student Learning

Another challenge in assessment is moving students beyond surface learning to deep learning and engagement (Driscoll & Wood, 2007) within the realistic confines of the length of an education abroad experience. One strategy that can be used to respond to this challenge is an engaged pedagogy that outlines clear and realistic expectations, contains application to important issues and problems, and empowers students to make a difference in the world. In addition, criteria, often developed through dialogue with students, are clearly articulated and are well understood by students. In so doing, it is important to explore assumptions made about student learning including how students learn. The Scholarship for Teaching and Learning (SoTL) field provides many valuable resources in this regard.

Adequate Preparation and Support of Participants

Often, students are not able to understand or articulate the learning that occurs in their education abroad experiences because they have received inadequate preparation. In some cases, some programs have too much or too little support so that learning does not occur to the extent that it could. The challenge–support theory (Sanford, 1967) concurs with this in stating that too little or too much support can inhibit student learning. Thus, it is important for programs to achieve an adequate balance of challenge and support in education abroad experiences. One strategy to do this is to build in adequate predeparture learning and ongoing, balanced support for participants to maximize their intercultural learning while abroad. Feedback to and from students throughout the experience (before, during, and after) is essential for optimal learning. Projects such as the *Maximizing Study Abroad* curriculum developed by a team from the University of Minnesota addresses this issue. The *Maximizing Study Abroad* project, funded by a U.S. Department of Education grant and developed over a 4-year period, consists of a textbook which can be self-paced or used as part of a course. An initial research study that examined the impact of the materials found that the qualitative data indicated a positive impact on students using the *Maximizing* materials (Cohen, Paige, Shively, Emert, & Hoff, 2005).

Evidence of Student Learning Outcomes

Another challenge in assessing students' global citizenship development and intercultural learning is in obtaining and validating actual evidence of this learning. And even when evidence is collected, it may be from only one source—such as a student prepost instrument. Given the complexity in assessing global citizenship and intercultural competence, it is imperative that evidence be collected from multiple perspectives (beyond a student perspective) using multiple methods. Evidence of student learning can be obtained through direct and indirect means. Direct methods indicate what a student has learned or how the student performs based on application of knowledge and skills. Performance-based evidence such as supervised internships, community-based projects and comprehensive capstone projects can be utilized as direct methods to document student learning and growth (Hart, 2008). Other direct methods of collecting evidence include portfolios, observations by supervisors, faculty, and host families, and embedded course assessment such as research papers, essays, exams, and so on. Indirect methods are related to perceptions of learning or factors that predict learning; indirect methods of collecting evidence include surveys, self-report tools, interviews, focus groups, document analysis (of syllabi, transcripts), retention data and job placement data. Evidence can be both quantitative and qualitative and research recommends having both, as well as using a combination of direct and indirect measures. Triangulation of evidence (thus the collection of more than one piece of evidence) is critical given that it can provide validation (similar to a second opinion) of the data collected.

Resistance

In assessment in general, faculty and student resistance can become an issue which is often the result of the lack of trust, ownership, and resources/time, and especially if assessment is not viewed as integrated into the program but is rather something that is "extra." In addressing resistance, it is first important to ensure that assessment is integrated into student learning and is viewed by faculty and students as integral to the learning process. Engagement by both faculty and students is the key to countering such resistance. Involve students through negotiation of learning outcomes, feedback, and integrated self-reflection. Involve faculty through dialogue and partnership, so that they can adapt what they are already doing in terms of assessment (for a more thorough discussion on classroom assessment techniques, see Angelo & Cross, 1993). Recognizing and rewarding faculty efforts in assessment can also help ease resistance.

Getting Started, Putting It Together

In many cases, international education administrators have not been trained in assessment and thus are often challenged to even know how to begin in developing and implementing an assessment strategy, especially as it relates to such amorphous and complex concepts as global citizenship and intercultural competence. The first step is to explore your own institutional context of assessment and discover resources that are available, including those on campus who are already engaged in assessment. Once potential resources and on-campus partners have been identified, it is important to put together an assessment team. Assessment is too complex an undertaking to be implemented by only one office. In addition, more professional development in assessment may be needed for international education administrators and others involved in assessment endeavors. Once an assessment team has been identified, work on developing a comprehensive assessment strategy can begin.

KEY POINTS AND QUESTIONS IN DEVELOPING AN ASSESSMENT STRATEGY

Given the discussion on general assessment challenges and possible strategies to overcome those, what does this all mean? Synthesizing the key points in assessment, here are some questions to consider in developing a comprehensive assessment strategy:

A comprehensive assessment strategy is one that is:

Aligned & Articulated: Are mission, goals, objectives, and assessment measures aligned and articulated? As discussed earlier in this chapter, the assessment measures must fit with the stated goals and objectives. In using such tools, it is crucial to understand what the tool measures. In the case of global citizenship or intercultural competence, it is not possible to find one tool that measures the complex whole of these concepts. Thus, what is the specific focus or purpose of the tools under consideration? How does this fit with the stated goals and objectives?

Intentional: Is assessment intentionally addressed? If assessment is not intentionally addressed through the creation of an assessment team and through the articulation of a comprehensive assessment strategy or plan which is reviewed at regular intervals, then

Table 20.2 *Questions to Analyze when Assessing Intercultural Competence and Global Citizenship*

1. Have terms such as intercultural competence and global citizenship been defined utilizing existing definitions in the literature? From whose cultural perspective?
2. What are the cultural biases of the evaluator? Of the assessment tools and methods?
3. Who is the locus of the evaluation?
4. What is the context of the assessment?
5. What is the purpose of the assessment?
6. How will the assessment results be used? Who will benefit from the assessment?
7. What is the time frame of the assessment (i.e., one point, on-going, etc.)?
8. Do the assessment methods match the working definition and stated objectives of intercultural competence and global citizenship?
9. Have specific indicators been developed for the intercultural competence and global citizenship assessment?
10. Is more than one method being used to assess? Do the methods involve more than one evaluator's perspective?
11. In regard to intercultural competence, are the degrees of intercultural competence being assessed? What is to be done with those not meeting the minimal level of intercultural competence?
12. Has the impact of situational, social, and historical contexts been analyzed in the assessment of intercultural competence?
13. How do the assessment methods impact the measurement outcomes? Have the limits of the instruments/measures been accounted for?
14. Have student/participant goals been considered when assessing intercultural competence and global citizenship?

Source: Adapted from Deardorff, 2004

assessment may occur more randomly without becoming integral to student learning and program improvement.

Developed: Have assessment issues been carefully analyzed before a plan is implemented (see Table 20.2 for specific questions)? For example, have assessment measures been examined for inherent bias? Carefully thinking through such issues from the outset can greatly aid in the implementation of the overall assessment strategy.

Integrated: Is assessment integrated throughout the program and not viewed as an "add-on"; that is, implemented only as a prepost exercise? While prepost surveys are popular among administrators, assessment needs to be implemented comprehensively throughout a program. Faculty are key in integrating assessment into the curriculum.

Focused: Is assessment realistic, with two to three outcomes being assessed per program per year? An assessment plan can help prioritize specific goals and objectives which can vary from year to year in terms of priority.

Shared: Is assessment shared with others on campus through partnerships or as an assessment team? Assessment is a complex process and thus it becomes important to partner with others on campus including faculty, assessment specialists, senior administrators, and so on.

Supported: Is the senior leadership supportive of assessment efforts? Senior administrative support is crucial to the success of assessment efforts and without such support, assessment efforts have often been less than successful. Moreover, are faculty supportive of assessment efforts? Since faculty play a large role in assessment efforts (through embedded course assessments), it is crucial to engage faculty in this process throughout.

Resourced: Is there adequate time and funding for assessment efforts and have administrators received sufficient training and knowledge in assessment, with ongoing professional development? Successful assessment efforts require adequate financial resources as well as trained staff and faculty to undertake such efforts.

Analyzed: Have the assessment tools, results, process been analyzed and evaluated? This can include taking into account the limitations of the assessment tools and the process. It is also important to think through who will do this analysis.

Communicated: Have the results been communicated to all stakeholders? In the case of education abroad, stakeholders include students, parents, faculty, program directors, academic advisors, administrators, advisory groups, alumni, and possible funders/funding agencies. Communication mechanisms include direct student feedback, summaries and reports on Web sites, alumni magazines, and so on.

Used: Have the results been used for program improvement as well as for student feedback? Program improvement is not synonymous with student feedback. Referring back to definitions of assessment, the purpose of assessment is primarily for improvement of teaching and learning, as well as program improvement. It is important to use the data collected through assessment and to only collect what will actually be used. In providing feedback to students, it is important to consider such questions as how the feedback can promote their learning instead of merely providing an indication of the monitoring of their learning. Further, how can the feedback help students redirect their learning to achieve intended goals such as global citizenship development, if these goals have not been achieved? Is feedback mutual, allowing students opportunities for sharing information and reflecting on the experience? How often and how is the feedback communicated to students? Rubrics (rated scales) are often a more precise way to document student learning and provide specific feedback to students. In regard to program improvement, what do assessment results indicate in regard to needed program changes (this can include procedural, personnel, learning experience itself, experiential/curricular services, etc.)? What do the data say about the teaching strategies being used? Consider how the assessment data can be used to revise the current goals and objectives of the program and explore what students are doing well and what areas need to be strengthened to improve their learning in those areas.

Reviewed: Has the assessment process and strategy been reviewed on a regular basis and improved upon? Regular, planned review of the assessment team, process, and strategy is important in improving the overall assessment efforts.

These points can be used as a checklist (see Table 20.3 below) on assessment and coupled with the program logic model, can provide a solid framework within which to develop and implement assessment strategies toward empowering interculturally competent global citizens.

GETTING STARTED IN ASSESSMENT

Once on-campus resources have been identified and an assessment team has been put in place, the first key question to explore is the following: Based on the overall mission, what are the goals and objectives to be assessed?

Goals provide broad direction, purpose statements and even expected outcomes. Objectives provide the roadmap for achieving the goals. Given that the development of global citizens may be an oft-stated goal in education abroad programs, this goal can be further operationalized through the delineation of specific objectives related to this overarching goal of global citizenship

Table 20.3 *Example of Aligned Goals, Outcomes, Assessments*

Goal:	Outcomes:	Assessments:
To generate new knowledge about global studies	Students can identify some of the processes through which civilizations, nations, or people are defined historically and in the present	Pre/post test essay requiring students to demonstrate mastery of the desired outcomes Focus group discussions
	Students develop new abilities to describe the host country from the inside out	Documentation of classroom discussions Student portfolios
Goal:	Outcomes:	Assessments:
To spur greater civic engagement and social responsibility	Students acquire a heightened sense of global interconnections and interdependencies	Documented questions and issues raised in course assignments
	Students can describe a social problem requiring collective remedies that transcend national boundaries	Reflection exercises and activities about experiences in civic participation
	Students are more likely to believe their individual intervention in a global social problem is both possible and consequential	Journal entries or writing assignments about involvement in social advocacy groups and programs

Source: McTighe Musil, 2004

development. There are four different types of objectives to consider with the context of global citizenship (Clayton, 2008):

1. Personal growth objectives—such as meeting learners' expectations and learners' personal skill development. Question to consider: What are the learners' expectations and personal goals as they relate to global citizenship development?
2. Group process objectives—such as how learners may function within a group or community including the roles played, approaches to tasks, and issues around teamwork. Questions to consider: What specific roles do participants have as they function within the host community? How do participants approach teamwork in working together with those from the host culture and others from diverse backgrounds?
3. Civic learning objectives—such as greater understanding of underlying issues, taking action, of being global citizens. Questions to consider: How do participants demonstrate understanding of global issues? What is the evidence of this understanding? To what extent do participants take action on global issues?
4. Academic learning objectives—such as relating specific theories or academic concepts to a particular experience/situation. Question to consider: How do participants apply intercultural learning concepts and theories to their experience abroad and beyond their experience abroad?

Given the time-intensive nature of good assessment practice, it is often quite difficult and overwhelming to assess all goals and objectives each time in every program. This leads to the importance of prioritizing which goals and objectives to assess in a given program and the priorities can certainly change from year to year. Even given the larger goal of developing global citizens, the specific objectives as outlined here may be prioritized differently by administrators or even by participants.

APPLICATION: ASSESSING GLOBAL CITIZENSHIP

Given that global citizenship consists of the common threads of global knowledge and understanding of the world's interconnectedness, of intercultural competence, and of engagement, what are some actual examples of stated learning outcomes within these areas?

The Association of American Colleges and Universities developed a sample matrix, part of which is cited (McTighe Musil, 2004, p. 16), and provides some sample global citizenship goals, specific outcomes, and aligned assessments (see Table 20.4 below).

A note about engagement: There is a growing trend toward measuring engagement on U.S. college campuses and includes a variety of aspects such as students' engagement in learning, on-campus engagement, faculty engagement with students, engaged pedagogy including service learning, and students' civic engagement. One of the longest running surveys is The Cooperative Institutional Research Program (CIRP) Freshman Survey administered by UCLA's Higher Education Research Institute (HERI), which has been collecting data from institutions since 1966 on such areas as students' values and beliefs about civic engagement; for example, the results of its fall 2008 survey found that student political interest is at an all-time high (Pryor et al., 2009). The National Survey on Student Engagement (NSSE), initiated in the late 1990s and widely used in postsecondary institutions in the United States, measures student perceptions of their educational experiences and their involvement on campus. According to scholars involved with NSSE,

Table 20.4 *Checklist for Assessment*

_____Aligned & Articulated – Are goals, objectives, assessment measures aligned and articulated?

_____Intentional – Is assessment intentionally addressed?

_____Developed – Have assessment issues been carefully analyzed before a plan is implemented?

_____Integrated – Is assessment integrated throughout the program and not viewed as an "add-on" i.e., implemented only as a pre-post phenomenon?

_____Focused – Is assessment realistic, with 2-3 outcomes being assessed per program per year?

_____Shared – Is assessment shared with others on campus through partnerships?

_____Supported – Is the senior leadership supportive of assessment efforts?

_____Resourced – Is there adequate time and funding for assessment efforts and have administrators received sufficient training and knowledge in assessment, with ongoing professional development?

_____Analyzed – Have the assessment tools, results, process been analyzed and evaluated?

_____Communicated – Have the results been communicated to all stakeholders?

_____Used – Have the results been used – for program improvement as well as for learner feedback?

_____Reviewed – Has the assessment process and strategy been reviewed on a regular basis and improved upon?

Source: Darla Deardorff, 2008

"student engagement is generally considered to be among the better predictors of learning and personal development" (Carini, Kuh, & Klein, 2006). Such CIRP and NSSE data can be used as further documentation in regard to engagement outcomes related to global citizenship.

CONCLUSION

So, how do we know if we are graduating interculturally competent global citizens? There is no easy answer. The assessment process, when intentionally integrated strategically into education abroad programs, involves the dedicated efforts of all stakeholders, including the students and faculty. There are challenges, as discussed in this chapter, in assessing global citizenship but there are also ways in which we can respond to those challenges through intentional, integrated, and informed efforts. The emphasis on accountability, on student learning, and on assessment seems here to stay. Thus, it is incumbent upon education abroad professionals to hone their assessment knowledge and work with others on campus to develop a successful assessment strategy. In so doing, education abroad programs document evidence of developing global citizens, and more importantly, guide students toward fulfilling their responsibilities in our global community.

REFERENCES

Akande, Y., & Slawson, C. (2000, May 28–June 2). *Exploring the long term impact of study abroad: A case study of 50 years of study abroad alumni.* Paper presented at NAFSA: Association of International Educators, San Diego, CA.

American Council on Education. (2007). *Assessing international learning outcomes.* Retrieved May 14, 2008, from http://www.acenet.edu/Content/NavigationMenu/ProgramsServices/International/Campus/GoodPractice/fipse/index.htm

Angelo, T. (1995, November). Reassessing (and defining) assessment. *The AAHE Bulletin, 48*(2), 7–9.

Angelo, T., & Cross, P. (1993). *Classroom assessment techniques: A handbook for college teachers.* San Francisco: Jossey-Bass.

Astin, A. W. (1991). *Assessment for excellence: The philosophy and practice of assessment and evaluation in higher education.* New York: American Council on Education.

Baird, L.L. (2003). New lessons from research on student outcomes. In S. R. Komives, D. B. Woodard, Jr., & Associates (Eds.), *Students services: A handbook for the profession* (4th ed., pp. 595–617). San Francisco: Jossey-Bass.

Bolen, M. (2007). *A guide to outcomes assessment in education abroad.* Carlisle, PA: Forum on Education Abroad.

Bok, D. (2006). *Our underachieving colleges: A candid look at how much students learn and why they should be learning more.* Princeton, NJ: Princeton University Press.

Boone, E. J. (1985). *Developing programs in adult education.* Englewood Cliffs, NJ: Prentice-Hall.

Carini, R. M., Kuh, G. D., & Klein, S. P. (2006). Student engagement and student learning: Testing the linkages. *Research in Higher Education, 47*(1), 1–32.

Clayton, P. H. (2008). *Where's the learning in experiential learning?* Paper presented at the North Carolina State Undergraduate Assessment Symposium, Raleigh, NC.

Cohen, A. D., Paige, R. M., Shively, R. L., Emert, H. A., & Hoff, J. (2005). *Maximizing study abroad through language and culture strategies: Research on students, study abroad program professionals, and language instructors.* Retrieved May 14, 2008, from http://www.carla.umn.edu/maxsa/documents/MAXSAResearchReport.pdf

Committee on Education Development. (2006). *Education for global leadership: The importance of international studies and foreign language education for U. S. economic and national security.* Washington, DC: Committee on Education Development.

Deardorff, D. (2004). *The identification and assessment of intercultural competence as a student outcome of internationalization at institutions of higher education in the United States.* Unpublished doctoral dissertation, North Carolina State University, Raleigh, NC.

Deardorff , D. K. (2006). The identification and assessment of intercultural competence as a student outcome of internationalization at institutions of higher education in the United States. *Journal of Studies in International Education, 10*(3), 241–266.

Deardorff , D. K. (2007, April). *Assessment methods and tools in international education.* Presentation given at Undergraduate Assessment Symposium, North Carolina State University, Raleigh, NC.

Driscoll, A., & Wood, S. (2007). *Developing outcomes-based assessment for learner-centered education: A faculty introduction.* Sterling, VA: Stylus.

Green, M. F., Luu, D., & Burris, B. (2008). *Mapping internationalization on US campuses: 2008 edition.* Washington, DC: American Council on Education.

Hart, P. D. (2008). *How should colleges assess and improve student learning? Employers views on the accountability challenge.* Washington, DC: P.D. Hart.

Herrin, C. (2004, Winter). It's time for advancing education abroad. *International Educator, 13*(1), 3–4.3.

Higher Learning Commission. (2006, July 26–28). *Student learning, assessment and accreditation: Criteria and contexts.* Paper presented at Making a Difference in Student Learning: Assessment as a Core Strategy workshop. Retrieved May 11, 2008, from http://www.uni.edu/assessment/definitionofassessment.shtml

Huba, M. E., & Freed, J. E. (2000). *Learner-centered assessment on college campuses: Shifting the focus from teaching to learning.* Boston: Allyn & Bacon.

Kaplan, R.S., & Norton, D. P. (2005, July–August). The balanced scorecard: Measure that drives performance, *Harvard Business Review, 83*(7),172–180.

McTighe Musil, C. (2004). *Assessing global learning: Matching good intentions with good practice.* Washington, DC: Association of American Colleges and Universities.

Popham, W. J. (1993). *Educational evaluation* (3rd ed.). Boston: Allyn & Bacon.

Pryor, J. H., Hurtado, S., DeAngelo, L., Sharkness, J. Romero, L. C., Korn, W. S., & Tran, S. (2009). *The American Freshman: National norms for fall 2008.* Los Angeles: Higher Education Research Institute, UCLA.

Rogers, P. J. (2000). Program theory: Not whether programs work but how they work. In D. L. Stufflebeam, G. F. Madaus, & T. Kellaghan (Eds.), *Evaluation models: Viewpoints on educational and human services evaluation* (2nd ed., pp. 209–232). Boston: Kluwer Academic.

Sanford, N. (1967). *Self and society.* New York: Atherton Press.

Stark, J. S., Shaw, K. M., & Lowther, M. A. (1989). *Student goals for college and courses: A missing link in assessing and improving academic achievement.* Washington, DC: School of Education and Human Development, George Washington University.

Tyler, R. W. (1949). *Basic principles of curriculum and instruction.* Chicago: University of Chicago Press.

Wholey, J. S. (1979). *Evaluation: Promise and performance.* Washington, DC: Urban Institute.

Chapter 21

Here to Stay

Increasing Acceptance of Short-Term Study Abroad Programs

Lisa Chieffo and Lesa Griffiths

University of Delaware

BREAKING WITH TRADITION

When University of Delaware French professor Raymond Kirkbride set sail for France with a group of eight students on July 7, 1923, there was no question that the men would be spending an entire academic year taking courses alongside French students at the Sorbonne in Paris. The newly established junior year abroad was thus named with good reason at a time when international travel was not only time-consuming, but also reserved for an economically elite segment of the U.S. population. Even 80 years later, despite the decline in popularity of the classic year overseas, the majority of U.S. students who studied abroad did so for at least one academic term (a semester or quarter).

More recently the tide has shifted, marking a turning point in mobility patterns of American college students. According to the most recent annual *Open Doors* data published by the Institute of International Education (IIE), since the 2003–2004 school year more than 50% of students who study abroad do so as part of a short-term program, defined here as a program lasting less than a standard academic semester or quarter (Institute for International Education [IIE], 2006, 2007b). This gradual but steady increase in the popularity of such programs (from 38 to 53% of market share since 1993) has come at the expense of traditional year-long programs, which now represent only 5.5% of all study abroad students (compared to 15% in 1993).

One can posit many reasons for this shift. For example, students who go abroad for a semester or more must consider seriously the loss of income resulting from an extended period of unemployment. According to the National Center for Education Statistics (NCES), 54% of attendees at 4-year institutions and 44% of those at community colleges define themselves as "students who work," with an additional 35% of community college students considering themselves "employees who study" (NCES, 2006, pp. 13–14). For these students, being away for one month, or even less, may be the only financially viable study abroad option. At the University of Delaware, the growth of January short-term programming, in particular, has far outpaced that of summer programs, which may be attributable to the longer period of time summer affords for students to earn income to pay for college. A typical January session is much shorter and can be accomplished without detracting from summer earning potential. January also appears to be a more appropriate time for many faculty to direct such programs, as summer may be reserved for family vacations and other personal commitments.

Although the number of traditional-age students enrolled in postsecondary education has been growing more rapidly than the number of older students, this pattern, too, is shifting: "From 2005 to 2016 NCES projects a rise of 15% in enrollments of people under 25, and a rise of 21% in enrollments of people 25 and over" (NCES, 2007). Older students are more likely to be working or self-supporting, and hence are less likely to engage in longer-term education abroad opportunities.

The appeal of short-term programs applies to a number of other student demographic groups as well. Students in majors with rigid curriculums such as engineering or nursing, for example, and those attempting to complete double or even triple majors, may find it difficult, if not impossible, to study abroad for a semester and still finish their degrees on time. A short program offered outside of the standard academic term gives these students the opportunity to enrich their education while keeping on track with their courses. In addition, students who have little travel experience or who are extremely close to their families may find it emotionally impossible to commit to being away from home for an extended period. A shorter program allows for a more developmentally appropriate challenge for this group. Finally, students who have already studied abroad for a semester or more may wish to do so again but cannot be away for an extended period; for this population a short-term program satisfies their desire to explore without derailing graduation plans. In sum, short-term education abroad programs meet the needs of a wide array of students; therefore their popularity shows no sign of diminishing and is likely to increase for the foreseeable future.

CHARACTERISTICS AND CONCERNS

As already mentioned, short-term study abroad programs have been defined traditionally by their duration: anything less than a standard academic semester or quarter. But this definition is in fact too simplistic to describe the wide variety of programs offered. In its 2006–2007 *Open Doors* data-gathering survey, IIE asked responding institutions to distinguish between summer programs lasting less than 2 weeks and those lasting 2 weeks or more (IIE, 2008). January term programs are listed as a separate category, as are those offered during the academic year and lasting less than 2 weeks, versus those lasting from 2 to 8 weeks.

Just as important as the length of such programs are the characteristics of their structure and content. Although there are many models, typically a short-term program abroad consists of one or more faculty members from a U.S. institution traveling to one or more locations with a group of American students. (It bears mentioning that many universities outside the United States now offer short programs designed especially for foreign students, with or without accompanying faculty leaders, though these are not the focus of this chapter.) The group may have contact with a host institution abroad, with local instructors teaching special courses or delivering some lectures, or they may be completely self-contained, residing in hotels or apartments and receiving instruction only from the U.S. faculty leaders, who play a significant role in program development. Like semester and year programs, short-term programs may include components such as service learning, fieldwork, research, and even internships, but, unlike their longer counterparts, short-term programs seldom allow for the option of direct enrollment at a foreign institution. Due to time constraints, students enroll in just one or two courses, usually through the sponsoring U.S. institution, and these often focus on a specific theme or academic discipline relevant to the host site(s). Sometimes the program is actually an extended field trip for a course offered during the regular term on campus (e.g., an embedded spring break program). Group excursions and local visits of academic, historical, and cultural relevance are normally built into the program costs. Students are left with comparatively little free time and often spend the vast majority of their waking hours together.

For some, the model described above represents the worst-case scenario of U.S. study abroad, not far removed from educational study tours which emphasize adventure and experience over academic rigor. Those who have managed short-term programs abroad for any length of time surely have encountered the thinly veiled disapproval of senior-level administrators as they discussed programs based in sunny locales where, it is assumed, no real learning could ever take place. It is an unenviable position to be obliged to defend the academic merits of what should be an academically unassailable endeavor. But not all of the criticism of short-term programs has been undeserved. Institutions have sought to increase study abroad opportunities for their students (and enrollment numbers for their national rankings) with little oversight or attention to quality. Unlike traditional exchange programs, which often require lengthy institutional negotiations, or other longer-term programs, which may involve hiring local staff or renting space, establishing a short-term program abroad can be quick and easy, with little or no long-term institutional commitment. The university or college simply needs a faculty member willing to teach a course and able to find students interested in going abroad to take it. But how much meaningful academic and cultural learning can take place in a 4-week period as students surf and snorkel their way in groups along Australia's Gold Coast, listening to their American professor lecture on a bus, and stopping to pet kangaroos at the next wildlife refuge? At what point does the faculty director's claim to academic freedom prove inadequate to mask a lightweight program that could do more to damage the institution's reputation than not offering the program at all? Questions such as these frame a larger, ongoing discussion about whether short-term programs abroad can contribute in a meaningful way to an institution's goal of creating global citizens; and, if they can do so, then under what conditions?

A DEEPER DEFINITION

The models for short-term programs are diverse and abundant. And, just like semester- and year-long programs, the thousands of existing short-term programs vary tremendously in quality and, subsequently, in the resultant amount of student learning and cultural immersion. One can argue that, all other things being equal, the learning that can take place during one month must be less than what can occur over the course of one semester or one year. This contention is partially supported by the findings of a recent large-scale survey of nearly 4,000 participants in semester, year, and summer programs sponsored by the Institute for the International Education of Students (IES) over the past five decades (Dwyer, 2004). Results of this initiative revealed that students who had studied abroad for one year reported that their experience had a greater impact on their career than those who were overseas for just a summer session (Dwyer, 2004, p. 159). Perhaps more importantly, 29% of students on IES year-long programs reported still being in contact with host country nationals, and 63% with U.S. friends they met abroad, while just 7% of those on summer programs maintained contact with individuals from their host country, and only 26% were still in touch with fellow American program participants (Dwyer, 2004, pp. 158, 160).

Though these data indicate some greater benefits from longer programs, one must note that very similar, and overwhelmingly positive, results emerged from respondents on year, semester, *and* summer programs for most measures of intercultural development and personal growth. For example, between 92% (summer participants) and 97% (full year participants) of respondents

367

claimed that study abroad "continues influencing my interactions with people from different cultures" and "has had a lasting impact on my world view" (Dwyer, 2004, pp. 158, 160). It is clear, then, that short-term programs can and do have great benefits for students; the precise added value of longer programs remains the object of intense debate and research.

But it is ultimately not the length, but rather the characteristics and goals of a study abroad program that contribute to student learning. In their instructive essay that addresses this topic, Engle and Engle note that "focused and reflective interaction with the host culture is finally what separates study abroad from study at home" (2003, p. 4). Under this credo, a 4-week program with homestay lodging, courses in the host language, structured interaction with host country students, and academic assignments requiring journaling and community-based interviews, contributes more to students' cross-cultural competence than a semester-long program in which students are housed together in apartments and have self-contained classes and tours, with most host culture interaction left to serendipity. This scenario challenges the traditional view that "longer is better" with regard to sojourns abroad and recognizes that questions of program design demand at least as much attention as the consideration of length.

Of course, it must be recognized that not every program has cross-cultural competence as its explicit, overarching goal. For example a 2-week program for MBA students may be designed primarily to introduce students to the business practices and issues of a particular country or region and contain no or few opportunities for cultural immersion in the traditional sense. The faculty director's task is to schedule as many company visits as possible to complement the course content presented before and after the embedded trip abroad. Such a program can nevertheless contribute to campus internationalization by sheer nature of the fact that the students' coursework is infused with an international component which is lacking in a comparable course on campus. Further, by inviting only host country guest speakers, arranging e-mail partners with host country business students or working professionals, and including a weekend homestay, even such a short, discipline-focused program can be enriched to provide students with a broader, more meaningful experience. Spencer, Murray, and Tuma assert that "the best short-term programs balance the experience itself with processing the experience" but rightly point out that since time in country is so limited, "students tend to focus on what they see or do, and do not take time to reflect on what they are learning" (2005, p. 376). Therefore it is incumbent upon the instructor to foster intercultural reflection through assignments which encourage detailed processing of that which was observed abroad; this can even be done immediately upon return home.

Indeed, the notion of meaningful cultural immersion can be redefined in terms of the discipline-based nature of many short study abroad programs. While the MBA students in the example above cannot have the same kind of long-term personal experiences with members of the host culture that students abroad for a semester might have, their program could include purposeful encounters to expose them to the business culture of that country. In the same vein, a program designed specifically for majors in elementary education that includes visits to schools in various cities in England can challenge students to learn about the culture of schooling and childhood education in that country, which is quite different from the United States. Though these students may not return home with the deep immersion experience associated with a year-long, direct enrollment study abroad experience, they have, nevertheless, had a meaningful cultural learning experience very relevant to their academic discipline and future career.

Thus we begin to move toward a more appropriate definition of short-term programs that emphasizes less the length of sojourn and more its characteristics and structure. Additionally, we thereby recognize that the goals of programs will vary and that semester- or year-long programs do not necessarily represent the ideal arrangement, certainly not for all students. Viewing short-term programs in this way allows them to more easily be seen as part of an overall campus internationalization movement in which the vast majority of students and faculty can participate.

STRATEGIES FOR ACCEPTANCE AND SUCCESS

In the discussion above we argued that a purposeful strategy in program design is a primary contributor to program quality, independent of length of sojourn. Nevertheless, it is true that semester- and year-long programs have more of one resource than do shorter programs, namely *time*. Acknowledging this fact and the inherent benefits and drawbacks is a crucial step toward integrating short-term programs into the mainstream of an institution's study abroad offerings.

Recognizing the Trade-Offs

As has been mentioned before, students who are abroad for just a few weeks have less time to process their learning and their impressions than do those who are abroad for a longer period, and they have less time for lengthy reading and writing assignments, making strategic adaptations of traditional pedagogies necessary. On the other hand, since students on shorter programs typically take just one course, or perhaps two related courses, these programs can be academically very focused, concentrating on one specific theme related to the program site (e.g., ecotourism in Costa Rica or wildlife conservation in Tanzania). There is undoubtedly academic benefit to such a model, not the least of which is the potential for linking a faculty member's area of research to the specific topic of his or her program abroad, perhaps ultimately leading to future funding opportunities that combine research and study abroad in new and exciting ways.

While we recognize that students who participate in a short-term program do not have as much opportunity for cultural immersion and foreign language practice as they would on an equally well-structured longer program, it is necessary to realistically consider that many students would not study abroad *at all* if no shorter options were available. While it may be the case that some students choose a short-term program in lieu of a longer program because it is the more comfortable choice, it is also the case that for many more students the choice is between going abroad for one month or staying home. The fact is that the net number of students abroad is higher due to the existence of shorter programs. At the University of Delaware the vast majority of majors are represented among short-term study abroad students annually, including dozens of students in the fields of nursing, engineering, animal science, and more. Part of the trade-off in offering such programs is recognizing that their existence contributes to a democratization of internationalization across the campus. Internationalization, then, is not the purview of particular academic disciplines, but rather pervades virtually all colleges and departments, which then have significant ownership and pride in their study abroad offerings.

In the same vein, faculty members who would not be willing to make the commitment to lead an existing semester-long program, perhaps due to family or professional obligations, may find the idea of developing a short-term program more appealing. Many faculty directors offer their programs multiple times and are then themselves better positioned to educate students as global citizens. At the University of Delaware approximately 70% of academic departments have at least one faculty member directing a short-term study abroad program on a regular basis, including, for example, physics and astronomy, accounting, and mechanical engineering. This level of internationalization of the professoriate across disciplines, and its subsequent influence on future courses and research on campus, would not exist without the teaching opportunities offered through such programs.

Creative Diversity Under a Central Umbrella

Most U.S. colleges and universities have an office that manages at least some aspects of the study abroad programs available to its students. At some institutions faculty-led short-term programs have existed partially or wholly outside of the structure of this office, marginalized conceptually and in practice, often at the insistence of the faculty directors who are content to continue with the status quo without the meddling of pesky administrators. Since short-term programs can be established with little or no in-country infrastructure, it is theoretically possible for one individual to single-handedly develop a program until shortly before departure—typically when bills have to be paid. Fortunately this scenario has changed quite a bit over the past several decades, as campus risk managers realized the need for oversight and adherence to institutional policy.

But liability is not the only reason to have a centralized structure for managing all aspects of study abroad. If part of an institution's mission is to graduate global citizens, it follows that there should exist some measure of uniformity in procedures (e.g., how student scholarships are awarded), structural and academic standards (e.g., how course contact hours are accounted for), and data collection (e.g., how many computer science majors participate). Institutions which require experiential learning for graduation would do well to centralize program approval as a form of standardization and quality control. At the least, a proposal should pass before the relevant department chairperson(s) and college dean, with some schools even convening a faculty oversight committee to examine program proposals. Moreover, a centralized office reporting to the provost or other chief academic officer is more advantageously positioned within the organization to demonstrate need (for more staff, space, or funding), and to collaborate with other campus units to create offerings abroad that are well-integrated into the campus curriculum (e.g., service learning programs, programs designed for first-year students, and those with internship components).

Despite the need for centralized management of short-term programs abroad, one must recognize that such programs are most often conceived, developed, and run by faculty, for whom *standardization* and *uniformity* are frequently anathema. Hence colleges and universities must nurture faculty creativity and be flexible enough to accommodate their diverse programs, while at the same time maintaining institutional standards and policies. A certain level of "academic decentralization," then, serves to foster a sense of ownership and an entrepreneurial spirit among faculty, especially when they are well-supported in their program director role. This, in turn, coupled with strategic recruitment efforts from the study abroad office, can lead to involvement by faculty from traditionally underrepresented disciplines.

The Fruits of Their Labors: Faculty as Program Leaders

Unlike on campus, where faculty see students for a just few hours per week, while abroad faculty and students interact on an almost continual basis, at all hours of the day and night, during the week and on weekends. Furthermore, teachable moments extend far beyond a faculty member's academic discipline, as students are confronted with unfamiliar surroundings and new ways of doing things. In addition to being instructors teaching their courses, faculty traveling with students also fill the roles of disciplinarian, tour director, conflict resolution expert, accountant, and substitute parent, usually for no or little compensation beyond what they would receive to teach in relative peace at home. Additionally, they sacrifice time with their families as well as progress on their own research agendas. From a purely economic standpoint, then, assuming the responsibilities of a faculty director does not make much sense, and, from a personal and professional standpoint, may even be detrimental.

Yet, since short-term programs at most institutions depend on faculty involvement, motivating the professoriate is essential for growth and stability. This can be done in three ways: increased financial compensation, increased logistical support, and professional recognition. Most campuses will be hard-pressed to compete with corporate consulting fees when attempting to woo faculty in certain disciplines (e.g., engineering and business), but they can perhaps offer to cover some expenses more generously (such as a per diem), or provide stipends to compensate for some of the nonteaching responsibilities that a directorship entails (e.g., budget development or handling a sick student on site). In order to entice faculty to take a larger number of students than the minimum, travel-savvy program assistants (who may be graduate students) can be provided to accompany the group and manage many of the simple yet stressful tasks which the directors must otherwise perform. Perhaps most important, developing a study abroad program must be viewed campus-wide as a valid professional contribution toward promotion and tenure. While standards and procedures will vary across institutions and disciplines, the suggestion to include study abroad course development in a departmental promotion and tenure document can normally be made by any member of the unit. Deans, provosts, and department chairpersons who speak supportively about study abroad in the context of faculty professional development set the stage for discussions to move the leadership of short-term programs from the margins of faculty activity to the center of academic life.

Providers as Partners

As the study abroad field has grown, so, too, have the number of organizations, many commercial in nature, that offer in-country support to colleges and universities; for example, homestay coordinators, bus companies, travel agents, and even well-connected freelance individuals who, for a fee, will arrange guest speakers and behind-the-scenes tours. Some of these provider entities offer comprehensive services and work with colleges and universities to custom-design programs and meet all of their logistical needs. Others, including some universities outside of the United States, advertise ready-made programs to which American schools can simply send their students. Indeed, this latter option can be particularly attractive for smaller institutions with an infrastructure too small to support in-house programs, as long as the provider programs (including their courses) have been appropriately vetted and approved.

Similar to the issues surrounding the length of study abroad programs, the decision of whether or not to use providers, and, if so, what type, raises questions about ensuring program quality and about maintaining institutional integrity. Certainly the convenience of communicating with only one individual and of paying only one invoice can make employing one provider a very attractive option from an administrative perspective. For institutions with small study abroad offices unable to manage the myriad aspects of program organization, a third-party provider who can handle everything from finding classroom space to hiring guest lecturers may represent the only viable means by which such schools can sustain programs over which they have ownership. For others, the best alternative is to provide students with a comprehensive list of vetted, approved, preexisting programs to which they may apply and be assured of receiving credit at their home school.

College and university involvement with such third-party providers received unwanted attention in the summer of 2007 when the attorney general of the State of New York opened an investigation into the relationship between particular institutions and some of the major providers in the United States. The inquiry focused on "whether cash incentives and other perks that study abroad agencies give universities influence their decisions about where students may study" (Schemo, 2007). Alleged perks included free and subsidized travel for college study abroad staff, institutional rebates, marketing stipends, and more, and were in some cases tied to the number of students schools sent on a provider's program. It goes without saying that even the appearance of a conflict of interest with a program provider will not only immeasurably harm an institution's reputation, but such practices are also in conflict with the Code of Ethics for Education Abroad established by the Forum on Education Abroad (2008, pp. 10–12). For institutions able to do so, working directly with a postsecondary institution abroad on logistics and other program arrangements ensures closer alignment of goals and expands the possibilities for academic collaboration beyond that of the short-term program. In either case, the U.S. college or university must choose the most appropriate type of provider in light of its own needs and capabilities, all the while maintaining academic integrity and keeping costs in check.

OUTCOMES ASSESSMENT OF SHORT-TERM PROGRAMS ABROAD

Despite the increase in study abroad participation by 150% in the past decade (IIE, 2007a), neither academia nor the education abroad profession can supply a comprehensive answer to this question: "What do students learn while studying abroad that they do not or cannot learn as well at home?" As more and more campuses seek to include study abroad opportunities in their internationalization strategies, and claim as a goal the creation of global citizens among their graduates, there exists a greater demand for data on how students are changed (if at all) by these sojourns. Given the vast diversity in the types of programs offered (direct-enrollment at a foreign institution versus insular courses for U.S. students, homestay versus dormitory housing, longer versus shorter sojourns, English-language versus host-country language instruction), and hence the diversity in the experiences of the students involved, this question will occupy researchers for years to come.

Despite the fact that short-term programs represent more than half of U.S. study abroad participation, published work concentrating specifically on these programs is limited, often focusing on smaller, discipline-based groups of students and neglecting preprogram baseline data or a comparison group of peers on campus. Additionally, the main body of scholarly work has traditionally been in the arena of second language acquisition, not intercultural competence. Therefore, while isolated studies continue to shed light on various aspects of learning during short-term sojourns abroad, no consensus exists regarding how such programs benefit students, how they contribute to an institution's global citizenship goals, and how their impacts differ from those of longer programs.

Nevertheless, several current studies bear mentioning which investigate specific aspects of student learning. An article by Shames and Alden (2005) addresses the largely neglected topic of students with learning disabilities on study abroad. The authors conclude that their 13 subjects experienced "considerable developmental leaps" and "increases in their intellectual and social curiosity" as a result of 3- to 6-weekprograms (p. 22). Harrison (2006) investigated the impact of "international study tours" on 62 business majors and determined that those with high self-monitoring traits (ability to adjust one's behavior to situational factors) reported a higher level of engagement with the host culture. McLaughlin and Johnson (2006) address the assessment of academic work done during a 3-week field study, a popular pedagogical model for programs rooted in the natural sciences. They created a rubric to assess students' cognitive learning levels based on their writings in field journals, and also asked students to self-assess their learning gains. The authors concluded that students reported making strong gains in knowledge, skills, and conceptual learning, and they asserted that "integrating curricular design and assessment provides an avenue to promote disciplinary learning gains in short-term study abroad courses" (p. 75). Finally, Cubillos, Chieffo, and Fan (2008) compared listening comprehension gains and strategies of 48 students on month-long language programs in Spain and Costa Rica with those of 92 students taking the same Spanish course on campus. Surprisingly, the students abroad reported higher confidence levels about their language skills, even though there was no significant difference in test score gains between the abroad and on-campus groups.

The largest published study to date concentrating solely on the impacts of short-term programs was conducted among 2,336 University of Delaware students during January 2003 and 2004, 1,509 of whom studied abroad for the month, and 827 of whom took similar courses on campus during the same period (Chieffo & Griffiths, 2004). At the end of the term students were asked to reflect over the past 30 days and respond to questions regarding their perceived changes in globally related attitudes and knowledge, as well as their frequency of engagement in globally related activities (e.g., looking up a non-U.S. location on a map). Among other things, the study found that "students in the abroad group were generally more cognizant than their peers at home of varying national and cultural perspectives" (p. 170), "were more disposed to communicating in a foreign language and considered themselves more patient with people who do not speak English well" than their on-campus peers (p. 171).

Perhaps even more telling than the quantitative data were the students' responses to the open-ended question, "What do you think is the most important thing you have learned in the past month?" The students who went abroad wrote twice as much as those who remained on campus and stated that they learned about an entire range of topics, including (among others) knowledge/appreciation of another country or culture, tolerance/patience/understanding, course-related knowledge, differences between home and host country, and language/communication issues (Chieffo & Griffiths, 2004, p. 173). The on-campus group, on the other hand, was undeniably focused on classroom knowledge, with 45% of their responses subsumed under this category (compared to just 8% of the responses from the students who went abroad). "About 27% of the comments from the abroad group included responses related to personal growth and development, such as adaptability, flexibility, patience, responsibility, respect for others, and appreciation for the arts" (p. 173). Nearly 30% of the abroad group wrote that they "learned to view the U.S. differently, acknowledging their position of privilege in the world, noting differences between the U.S. and their host countries, indicating a greater awareness of global interconnectedness, and in some cases openly criticizing U.S. policy" (pp. 173–174). Although this large-scale study did not include any presojourn data collection, the sheer number of respondents, mass of quantitative and qualitative data, and the fact that a control group was present, provide compelling evidence that students are changed by even a month-long study abroad experience in ways that contribute meaningfully to campus internationalization efforts.

A Systematic Assessment Model

Recognizing an overall dearth of studies on the impacts of short-term programs, particularly those involving large numbers of students and pre- and posttreatment data sets, the University of Delaware (UD) has embarked on a systematic, long-term, large-scale data collection effort to learn more about how students perceive changes in their knowledge, skills, and attitudes as a result of participation in such a program. The development of this initiative was prompted by the establishment by UD's Faculty Senate of a three-credit Discovery Learning Experience (DLE) requirement for all undergraduates beginning with the entering class of 2005. The DLE is defined on the Web site of the University's Office of Undergraduate Studies as "experiential learning which involves instructional experiences out-of-class and beyond typical curriculum courses... [and] under the supervision of a faculty member. Discovery Learning Experience includes internship, service learning, independent study, undergraduate research, and *study abroad*" [emphasis added] (University of Delaware, n.d./b; see also n.d./a).

Concurrent with this requirement was the establishment of UD's Office of Educational Assessment (OEA), which itself was a response to the requirement of the institution's accrediting agency, the Middle States Association of Colleges and Schools (MSCHE). The OEA's Web site states, "MSCHE expects that accredited institutions will implement comprehensive institutional assessment plans that employ student outcomes assessment measures in general education and in all undergraduate and graduate majors." With the DLE now forming part of every undergraduate student's curriculum, it became clear that not only traditional on-campus courses, but also the entirety of study abroad programs, fall under the assessment mandate.

With approximately 15,000 undergraduates at UD, how to easily track students' fulfillment of the DLE requirement became an issue. Although students on UD's study abroad programs enroll in courses with particular section numbers reserved for classes offered abroad, there existed no common enrollment element among the institution's approximately 80 programs which could easily identify the DLE on the transcripts of nearly 1,700 study abroad students annually. Therefore a zero-credit, pass/fail course was developed with the overarching "University" (UNIV) rubric, which exists apart from all of the academic colleges. All students who participate in any UD study abroad program must enroll in this UNIV 370 course in addition to their other regular study abroad courses. The course title is "Study Abroad," plus the country or city where the program takes place. In this manner all study abroad experiences appear on a student's transcript and are automatically noted as DLE in UD's online student records system.

Because UD already has a system in place for online course evaluations which has been used for years by many academic departments, it seemed a logical next step to make use of this system to develop an online "evaluation" which is in essence an assessment tool to ask students about their learning during their term abroad. Just as they would log on to complete an online evaluation for a course on campus, study abroad students log on to UD's secure, Web-based system and complete a questionnaire which includes Likert-scale and short-answer questions; responses are released to faculty directors and after course grades have been submitted. For example, students are asked to rate how frequently they are able to ascertain whether a member of the host culture is annoyed with them, whether they are aware of how their appearance would be accepted at their program site, and whether they can give examples of at least two cultural taboos in that country. In addition, they are asked about the degree to which they agree with statements such as, "I was able to adapt at my program site with less access to a cell phone and/or e-mail than I am used to at home"; and "I can discuss with confidence at least two historic events that are important to the population of my host sites." Those studying in countries where the prevailing language is not English are asked to respond to specific statements such as, "I know how to greet, thank, and bid farewell to inhabitants of my host country in their local language"; and "I am able to recognize and clear up a misunderstanding in the language of my host site(s)." And finally, all students are asked to provide short narrative responses to questions about their perceived learning, both in and out of the classroom. Those who complete the online assessment receive a "pass" grade in UNIV 370, while those who do not receive a grade of F, which does not impact their grade point average but which, nevertheless, is not desirable on a transcript.

In order to collect baseline predeparture data from outbound students, the same assessment instrument was built into the multi-part online orientation which students already must complete in order to meet their obligations to the program. In addition to short online quizzes on health, safety, and behavioral matters, students complete the assessment questionnaire. Hence, pre- and postsojourn data can be compared to measure student changes in knowledge, skills, and attitudes, and responses among programs and student majors can be analyzed as well.

At the time of this writing the first group of students to have completed the predeparture piece is currently abroad; therefore no data yet exist to demonstrate what changes, if any, students claim to have undergone during their sojourn. Nevertheless, with an infrastructure in place, the groundwork is set for continued data collection for years to come.

In order to further link the study abroad DLE with institutional assessment initiatives, and to ensure academic quality of short-term programs, UD faculty who propose such a program must state in their proposal what products they expect from their students in order to demonstrate that stated learning goals have been met (see University of Delaware, n.d./d for the online program proposal). Learning goals are a combination of the standard DLE learning goals, campus-wide goals focused on intercultural outcomes, and program or discipline-based goals developed by each individual faculty director. One of the tools for assessment must address the DLE requirement for reflective learning. In this way short-term study abroad is conceptualized from the beginning as a supervised Discovery Learning Experience with specific outcomes related to students' global knowledge, skills, and attitudes, which are then assessed both before and after the program.

GROWING PAINS

As student interest in short-term study abroad grows, so does demand for program options that offer geographic and academic breadth, and institutions are scrambling to meet this demand. Students who intend to study abroad for a semester or year are likely to have more limited programmatic choices and to reserve the experience for their junior or senior year. On the other hand, in the short-term world, having just one or two program options in a particular academic discipline or target language is no longer acceptable; students want to choose among several locations and courses. The proliferation of programs in response to this demand is enormous. An online search of the short-term program offerings of just the top two research/doctoral institutions appearing in the 2007 *Open Doors* survey, Michigan State University and the University of Georgia, yields a list of programs available on all seven continents, including Antarctica (IIE, 2007c).

From London to Lima

This proliferation of locations and programs has resulted in students incorporating multiple and diverse overseas experiences into their academic careers. A student minoring in Spanish but majoring in elementary education, for example, may choose to study in Spain for the summer as a sophomore, taking lower-division courses, followed by second or even third short-term study abroad experiences in South America during future years, enrolling in advanced Spanish courses. At the University of Delaware, approximately 20% of students on short-term programs are repeaters, up from 11% just a few years ago. At St. Olaf College, a national leader in short-term programs among liberal arts institutions (IIE, 2007c), approximately 35% of graduates participate in more than one study abroad program (Lund, personal communication, June 24, 2008). Students such as the recent UD graduate in Environmental Studies who spent January terms in London, Tanzania, China, and Antarctica (not to mention a full semester in Costa Rica) demonstrate the view of study abroad as an ongoing component of one's undergraduate education, rather than as a culminating, one-time experience. Students are seeking opportunities to add depth *and* breadth to their academic pursuits, and short-term study abroad offers a full range of possibilities to fulfill this goal.

Come to Campus and Go Away: Programs for First-Year Students

At the University of Delaware, we consider ourselves fortunate in that studying abroad has become part of the culture of the institution, with the participation rate for study abroad surpassing 40% among undergraduates (IIE, 2007c). Increasingly, students and parents remark that the opportunity to study abroad was an important part of the decision to come to the University, and they therefore expect to have many program options available to them. Just a few years ago, that demand came from juniors and seniors. More recently, however, first-year students are exploring options before they arrive on campus and are completing applications for January-term programs within just a few weeks of settling into their dorm rooms in September. With upperclassmen historically given preference for spaces, the challenge now includes the design of short-term programs specifically for freshmen.

In order to better understand the factors that motivate freshmen (as opposed to more advanced students) to engage in study abroad, researchers at UD asked freshmen and sophomore study abroad participants what influenced them to go abroad, how they thought they grew and changed while abroad, and whether they intended to study abroad again. Over a 2-year period data were collected from 86 freshmen, 111 sophomores, and 32 sophomores who had also studied abroad the previous January as freshmen (referred to here as repeaters). Not surprisingly, freshmen reported being influenced less by their peers in their study abroad decision than sophomore first-timers did, and sophomores claimed that the relevance of a program to their major or career played a bigger role in their decision than it did in the case of freshmen (Chieffo, 2006, 2007). Apart from those two factors, the motivations of freshmen and sophomore first-timers to participate in short-term study abroad were statistically identical, and virtually no differences in self-reported learning outcomes were found between the two populations.

There were, however, major differences among the groups with regard to travel and interactions with other cultures. One of the most interesting findings was that 75% of students who studied abroad during their freshman year, as well as nearly 70% of sophomore repeaters, expressed intent to study abroad again, compared to just 25% of sophomore first-timers. This statistic may be linked to the fact that 44% of the freshmen described their prior international travel experience as "substantial," while only 20% had never been abroad before; on the other hand, 45% of sophomore first-timers had never left the U.S., and only 27% of that group described their international travel as "substantial." In the same vein, freshmen reported a statistically higher level of interaction with non-U.S. cultures than sophomore first-timers (57% vs. 41% claiming "substantial" or "extensive" experience). When the sophomore first-timers were asked whether they wished they had studied abroad earlier in their academic careers, 81% responded negatively; the vast majority were apparently satisfied with their decision.

In addition, all students reported learning a vast amount during both first and second study abroad experiences, demonstrating that participation in multiple short-term programs is indeed worthwhile. For example, 85% of all respondents stated that they learned a moderate or great amount about the people of another country, the history and culture of another country, and current political or social issues outside of the United States, just to name a few. First-timers, both freshmen and sophomores, reported higher levels of learning than sophomore repeaters in the areas of international travel logistics and how Americans and the United States are perceived abroad. However, virtually no differences in learning emerged between freshmen and sophomore first-timers, which indicates that class year played no significant role in the students' in-country experiences. In sum, it appears that those who study abroad as freshmen represent a unique population of already well-traveled students who are then more likely to study abroad again, and to benefit from doing so, while most of those who wait until their second year are either not ready or not interested in pursuing this opportunity as freshmen.

It is worth noting that, even though first-year study abroad may not be the best choice for most students, successful models for building on-campus community for freshmen have proven equally successful when transplanted overseas as part of a short-term study abroad program. Since winter of 2002 UD has offered one or two freshman-only programs every January, modeled after the first-year experience which exists on campus (Chieffo & Griffiths, 2006). These programs typically limit group size, restrict the population of participants to freshmen, and feature common courses. Faculty directors are highly engaged and work with a peer mentor, typically an advanced student with study abroad experience who travels with the group. Because parents have not yet recovered from the first round of college tuition bills, designated scholarship support may increase program participation.

Balancing Growth with Risk

As the demand for short-term programs increases, so, too, grows the need for willing and qualified faculty to develop and lead such programs. While it may not be problematic to find someone in the English department willing to teach Dickens in London, the need for program options in underrepresented locations and academic disciplines may require incentives such as exploratory trips, additional support in the form of salary or program assistance, and a willingness to support an underenrolled program on its first outing. In cases in which the leadership of short-term programs may not be strongly supported (e.g., among junior faculty with high research expectations), non-tenure-track faculty or even qualified senior professional staff could be considered, depending on an institution's policies. Senior faculty members not engaged in a heavy research agenda are crucial candidates, since they can represent long-term allies for the study abroad office. And finally, never underestimate the energy, life experience, and contacts that a recently retired faculty member can bring to a short-term study abroad program.

A different type of challenge occurs when several faculty in the same discipline embrace the opportunity to develop and direct a short-term program and suddenly find themselves in competition for the same pool of students. At an institution where study abroad is conceived as a key component of global citizenship, the study abroad office may not be in a position to discourage enthusiastic faculty from proceeding with program planning, despite the potential difficulties that could ensue if minimum enrollment levels are not met. Options to reduce the competition include rotating programs biannually, offering programs in different locations, developing programs that offer courses appropriate for distinctly different subpopulations of a major (freshmen and sophomores versus juniors and seniors), and combining a discipline-specific course with a general education or language course to further distinguish one program from the others. If there is a requirement that program proposals be approved by the department chairperson, college dean, and perhaps even a faculty committee approximately one year before travel, this helps ensure against multiple underenrolled programs because the particular issues of competition can be discussed openly far in advance.

Keeping "Study" In Study Abroad

Because the design of a short-term study abroad program is often associated with an individual faculty member, each and every program can be unique. Programs may take place on a cattle station on the south island of New Zealand, in an elementary school in Panama, or in the corporate headquarters of the CFOs of companies in four different countries, and hence provide students with quite different, but equally valid, academic experiences. Nevertheless, academic rigor must be the guiding principle in the development of all programs, regardless of their location or structure. Professional staff in the study abroad office are not in a position to judge the appropriateness of a program's academic components. These aspects can only be assessed at the departmental and college level by peers who are familiar with the expertise and qualifications of the faculty director and the course expectations within their discipline. This is why an established, multilevel review process for program proposals is crucial, including the presentation of a course syllabus and a day-by-day program calendar.

As more and more faculty in a wider range of disciplines begin to propose new models for programs, and program design becomes more complicated (e.g., including stops in multiple countries in a very short period of time), study broad faculty and staff can quickly realize they need the help of seasoned travel professionals. The use of commercial travel agents can greatly reduce the time faculty and staff invest in program organization. Although there are many travel agents who claim to offer "educational" services, such agents must be vetted carefully because their educational excursions are often intermixed with standard tourist hot spots, and for faculty trying to create a program that is attractive to students, the lure of including must-see tourist destinations is strong. It is important to keep in mind that commercial entities have a raison d'être that may conflict with the goals of an educational institution. A persuasive tour provider may be able to convince a faculty director to include a host of interesting and exciting yet nonacademic excursions into his or her travel package, thereby not only increasing program costs for students, but also contributing to the "fun in the sun" image problem under which these programs often suffer. Maintaining the appropriate balance between educational/cultural excursions and recreational/tourist excursions is critical. In addition to adding significant costs to a program, activities for recreation and tourism can quickly become the focus of student journals, blogs, and postprogram presentations, thereby contributing fodder for criticism of short-term programs as academically lightweight and culturally superficial.

As the number of well-designed, academically challenging, short term program options grows to include a myriad of offerings across disciplines, the image problems associated with short-term study abroad are likely to diminish, but this will require the combined efforts of campus academic leaders and study abroad professionals. Programs with stated academic objectives in which student learning is assessed in multiple ways will necessarily establish a reputation of quality and rigor. As more and more institutions incorporate short-term programs into their core study abroad offerings as part of larger internationalization efforts, presidents, provosts, and faculty governing bodies will be obligated to implement systems to ensure the same level of academic oversight that prevails on their campuses.

LOOKING AHEAD

Despite the increase in research initiatives and outcomes assessment specifically concentrating on short-term programs abroad, the profession has barely scratched the surface to discover what impacts these programs really have on students. And given the unique nature and variety of the programming, assessment will continue to be a challenge. A number of questions loom large for the future:

- How do students who participate in short-term programs compare to those who study abroad for a semester or longer with regard to cross-cultural competencies, knowledge of global issues, or other important goals?
- What are the long-term impacts of such programs on students' careers and other life decisions?
- How are the impacts different for those who study abroad multiple times in a variety of locations?
- How short can a program be and still have meaningful influence on student learning?
- What characteristics of program design and structure contribute most to intercultural competency?
- How does teaching on a short-term program influence the faculty's teaching on campus or their research interests, or even their own international perspectives?

These and many other questions remain unanswered.

As study abroad continues to gain in popularity among U.S. college students, short-term programs are likely to remain their most common choice. In fact, as more older, working individuals pursue higher education, demand for such programs is certain to increase. An attitude shift away from semester or year-long programs as the gold standard in education abroad may be necessary across the profession if we are to accept students' choices and facilitate meaningful overseas experiences for them. With this in mind, colleges and universities can begin to build infrastructures and implement systems to support such programs, ensure their academic quality, and incorporate them into larger strategic plans for campus internationalization.

REFERENCES

Chieffo, L. (2006). *The freshman factor: Outcomes of short-term education abroad programs on first-year students.* Retrieved June 1, 2008, from http://international.udel.edu/studyabroad/assessment/freshmen-abroad-outcomes.pdf

Chieffo, L. (2007). *LIFE abroad: A short-term study abroad experience for first-year students.* Presentation at conference of NAFSA: Association of International Educators, Minneapolis.

Chieffo, L., & Griffiths, L. (2004, Fall). Large-scale assessment of student attitudes after a short-term study abroad program. *Frontiers: The Interdisciplinary Journal of Study Abroad, 10,* 165–77.

Chieffo, L., & Griffiths, L. (2006, Fall). LIFE abroad: A unique model for study abroad. *IIE Networker,* 49–50.

Cubillos, J., Chieffo, L., & Fan, C. (2008). The impact of short-term study abroad programs on L2 listening comprehension skills. *Foreign Language Annals, 41*(1), 157–185.

Dwyer, M. M. (2004, Fall). More is better: The impact of study abroad program duration. *Frontiers: The Interdisciplinary Journal of Study Abroad, 10,* 151–163.

Engle, L., & Engle, J. (2003, Fall). Study abroad levels: Toward a classification of program types. *Frontiers: The Interdisciplinary Journal of Study Abroad, 9,* 1–20.

Forum on Education Abroad. (2008). *Code of ethics for education abroad.* Retrieved June 1, 2008, from http://www.forumea.org/documents/ForumonEducationAbroadCodeofEthics.pdf

Harrison, J. K. (2006, Fall). The relationship between international study tour effects and the personality variables of self-monitoring and core self-evaluations. *Frontiers: The Interdisciplinary Journal of Study Abroad, 13,* 1–22.

Institute of International Education (IIE). (2006). *Study abroad duration selected years.* Retrieved June 1, 2008, from http://opendoors.iienetwork.org/?p=89222

Institute of International Education (IIE). (2007a). *Americans studying abroad at record levels: up 8.5%.* Retrieved June 1, 2008, from http://opendoors.iienetwork.org/?p=113744

Institute of International Education (IIE). (2007b). *Duration of study abroad by institutional type.* Retrieved June 1, 2008, from http://opendoors.iienetwork.org/?p=113284

Institute of International Education (IIE). (2007c). *Leading institutions by duration of study abroad and institutional type, 2005/06.* Retrieved from http://opendoors.iienetwork.org/?p=113300

Institute of International Education (IIE). (2008). *2006–2007 open doors survey.* Retrieved June 1, 2008, from http://opendoors.iienetwork.org/?p=studyabroad2007

McLaughlin, J. S., & Johnson, D. K. (2006, Fall). Assessing the field course experiential learning model: Transforming collegiate short-term study abroad experiences into rich learning environments. *Frontiers: The Interdisciplinary Journal of Study Abroad, 13,* 65–85.

National Center for Education Statistics (NCES). (2006). *Profile of undergraduates in U.S. postsecondary education institutions: 2003–04, with a special analysis of community college students.* U.S. Department of Education 184. Retrieved June 1, 2008, from http://nces.ed.gov/pubs2006/2006184.pdf

National Center for Education Statistics (NCES). (2007). Postsecondary education. *Digest of Education Statistics: 2007.* Retrieved June 1, 2008, from http://nces.ed.gov/programs/digest/d07/ch_3.asp

Schemo, D. J. (2007, August 16). Study abroad is new focus of inquiry into perks. *New York Times,* A13. Retrieved June 1, 2008, from http://www.nytimes.com/

Shames, W., & Alden, P. (2005, August). The impact of short-term study abroad on the identity development of college students with learning disabilities and/or AD/HD. *Frontiers: The Interdisciplinary Journal of Study Abroad, 11,* 1–31.

Spencer, S., Murray, T., & Tuma, K. (2005). Short-term programs abroad. In J. Brockington, W. Hoffa, & P. Martin (Eds.), *NAFSA's guide to education abroad for advisers and administrators* (3rd ed., pp. 373–387). Washington, DC: NAFSA: Association of International Educators.

University of Delaware, Faculty Senate. (n.d./a). Retrieved June 1, 2008, from http://www.facsen.udel.edu/sites/DLE.aspx

University of Delaware, Office of Educational Assessment. (n.d./b). Retrieved June 1, 2008, from http://assessment.udel.edu/The%20Assessment%20Office/manual.html

University of Delaware, Office of Undergraduate Studies. (n.d./c). Retrieved June 1, 2008, from http://www.ugs.udel.edu/#DLE

University of Delaware. (n.d./d). Retrieved June 1, 2008, from http://international.udel.edu/ipssdb/proposal/submit.asp

Chapter 22

Going Global in the Sciences

A Case Study at Emory University

Philip Wainwright, Preetha Ram, Daniel Teodorescu, and Dana Tottenham
Emory University

As colleges and universities respond to the need to produce students who have better cross-cultural skills and who can function in a globalized economy, there is no greater area of need than in the sciences. In fact, the sciences are arguably the most international of all fields of intellectual endeavor. The universal languages of mathematics and science allow scientists to share their work even when they cannot speak each other's language. This same universality, however, has made study abroad in the sciences seem less important, or at least less intuitively logical, than in the humanities or the social sciences, where mastery of place-based knowledge and cultural difference has been a compelling motivator of programming. With ever greater numbers of students studying abroad and with the globalization of economic systems plain to see, the need and desire of undergraduates in the sciences to have international exposure and to learn about working in the global context has became more evident.

This chapter makes the case for the centrality of science education abroad in any comprehensive international education strategy. As the number of U.S. students pursuing science and engineering (S&E) degrees declines and the cutting edge of science research becomes global rather than national, U.S. educational priorities and international trends in science education highlight the importance of training scientists who understand science in a cultural context and who can succeed when collaborating and competing with scientists from all over the world. Though there are some differences, many of the same educational motivations for study abroad that apply in other disciplinary areas are increasingly important in the training of scientists.

This chapter also describes structures that one institution, Emory University, has put in place to increase access for science students to meaningful international experiences in the sciences and suggests techniques that could be used broadly for strengthening undergraduate science programming abroad. Emory University is a midsize private research university with the majority of its undergraduates enrolled in a liberal arts bachelor's program. Emory has comprehensive offerings in the arts and sciences, but unlike many of its peers does not have an engineering school. Many of its students are preprofessional in orientation and many science students identify themselves as premedical. The formal structures of majors and minors focus on disciplines and are not organized by preprofessional track.

With study abroad as an important part of Emory's internationalization efforts, the main study abroad office, the Center for International Programs Abroad (CIPA), has adopted a strategy of broadening access to and participation in study abroad programs. The Science Education Abroad at Emory (SEA) program creates a multipronged approach to establishing opportunities for science students to pursue their scientific studies abroad, while also learning about cultural difference in general and within the science community in particular. The SEA program provides science majors with opportunities to study abroad as part of faculty-led science programs, at internationally recognized institutions of excellence in the sciences, and to conduct research in labs overseas that complement a student's academic experiences at the home campus. The chapter will describe the goals, successes and limitations of each of these approaches, both in terms of science education and cross-cultural education.

SCIENCE IS A GLOBAL ENTERPRISE

Today's scientific enterprise is overwhelmingly international: international teams of scientists collaborate on traditionally defined problems and on emerging problems that have a global impact. This new landscape of science, described in detail in National Science Foundation (NSF) Indicators of Science and Engineering report (National Science Foundation, 2006) views the changes in science and technology in the last 2 decades and provides data to support the growing need for internationalization of science. In the 1990s, the United States clearly dominated the scientific and technological enterprise by all the common metrics. The United States was *the* destination for science research and for scientific education, at both undergraduate and graduate levels. The scientific education community saw no reason to send its undergraduates and graduates outside the United States, when in fact the United States was a clear leader in all things scientific.

All this has changed within the last 2 decades. New players have appeared on the field, including Asian countries like China, South Korea, Taiwan, Singapore, and India. Their role is clearly evidenced by the NSF in the report cited above. For example, international research and development (R&D) spending has seen robust increases worldwide, while the share of the United States has dropped from 93% to 84% in the last 10 years. This drop in the share has come about because of the emergence of Asian countries as R&D spenders. When comparisons of R&D performance are made, China has moved up to the third position behind the United States and Japan (National Science Foundation, 2006).

The NSF also reports that Europe and Japan are losing market share in high technology manufacturing while the high technology shares of Asian markets are expanding. Growth in the number of high-tech patents from Asia is now at about half the U.S. patents filed. Japan and China have shown a surge in applications attesting to increases in technological sophistication in these parts of the world. Research articles published worldwide demonstrate the growing importance of the European Union and Asian countries relative to the United States in scholarly production in the sciences (National Science Foundation, 2006). While the output of articles has grown worldwide, U.S. production has remained flat and has led to a decrease in the U.S. share of the output. In terms of citations or acknowledgment of research by the scientific community, while the share of U.S. scientists still dominates, the non-U.S. fraction is rising. More collaboration is also evident in these publications. Overall, about 20% of published articles had authors from two or more countries compared to 8% in 1988 (National Science Foundation, 2006).

In today's scientific enterprise, players come from many different countries and collaborate across national borders on problems that do not respect state boundaries. Science is truly global and the new scientist has to be equipped to succeed in an international and intercultural environment.

National and International Trends of Science Education

When compared with international institutions of higher education, U.S. colleges and universities are doing poorly in the area of science education. While the U.S. S&E workforce has grown, there are still not enough qualified scientists to fill the available S&E jobs as reiterated by Bill Gates to the Congress on March 17, 2008. The National Science Board (2003) noted that there was a flat or reduced domestic interest in engineering and mathematical sciences. The S&E workforce suffers also because decreasing numbers of students are attracted to the field and of these, not many are retained in the sciences. Attrition from the sciences is a well documented problem (National Science Board, 2003). By contrast, in many countries, particularly in Asia, the number of first university degrees in S&E awarded around the world has risen rapidly. Worldwide there was an increase from about 6.4 million in 1997 to 8.7 million in 2002. Particularly strong increases occurred in Asia and Europe, with large numbers and strong gains in engineering and the natural sciences.

These trends in the global distribution of science graduates point to a need to strengthen science education at home. To summarize, educators need to prepare their students for a very different scientific milieu than the one they were trained in. The new scientific enterprise is aggressively international, with a predominantly multinational workforce, working on global problems in academic and industrial research labs all over the world. Funding for scientific research may be diminishing in the United States, but it is increasing in other countries. To capture these resources, U.S. scientists will need to build professional networks and career connections. The National Science Board recommends that: "Federal agencies should encourage and support policies and programs that provide incentives for expanding participation in international cooperative research and education activities by younger scientists and engineers" (National Science Board, 2003).

STUDY ABROAD AS ENGAGED LEARNING AND GLOBAL EXCHANGE

Study abroad plays an important role in the motivation and retention of students in the sciences. U.S. science educators are constantly exhorted by NSF and other policy making organizations to improve these statistics by attracting increasing numbers into science, by improving retention in the sciences, and by improving persistence to a S&E graduate degree. Systematic studies of interventions and measures that help students stay interested in science and attract them to careers in the sciences point to the importance of research, field study, and other out-of-the-classroom experiences that situate students in a close professional and mentoring relationship with faculty. As established in educational reform literature, students' interest in science, motivation to study, and retention in the field correlate with interventions that provide opportunities for faculty–student engagement and mentoring. Other interventions such as providing small-group experiences in courses, contextual science content, and connecting science content with the student's own experience and interests also lead to an increased interest in the sciences. Study abroad provides one avenue for engaged learning by providing these kinds of experiences and thus leads to stronger interest in science.

The development of international professional networks is an important aspect of empowering young scientists to succeed in a globally competitive landscape. The National Science Foundation recognizes the importance of professional networks. This vision statement of its Office for International Science and Engineering declares "Because science and engineering are increasingly global, NSF's Office of International Science and Engineering (OISE) seeks to ensure that U.S. institutions and researchers are globally engaged, are able to advance their research through international collaboration, and will maintain U.S. leadership within the global scientific community" (National Science Foundation, 2008). This clearly articulated vision has led to several NSF supported undergraduate programs where science students are given an opportunity to learn about cultures other than their own, to develop international professional networks, and to initiate collaborations that may span different continents. When students work in research labs, and interact with faculty and research groups, they not only learn new science skills, but return with new professional networks that are sure to benefit them later. Exposure to these professional networks is another benefit that study abroad can bring to the developing scientist.

Study abroad also places a high value on the process of global exchange of knowledge. Successful cross-cultural encounters encourage students to widen their perspectives and respect cultural differences. In the context of science study abroad, this process may also include respecting and acknowledging the scientific contributions of others in research communities worldwide. With the explosion of science and technology worldwide, the United States can no longer be a leader in all the areas of science. For example, Germany leads the way in alternative energy fuel research. A young scientist seeking to explore this field would benefit from a research experience in a German lab. Broader policies regarding cloning or stem cell research have led to several non-U.S. labs pioneering approaches and research in these areas. In some countries like Singapore, government backing of science and technology has led to aggressive growth in some sectors like biotechnology and urban planning concepts such as Biopolis. Students can learn much from visiting these different cutting edge areas of excellence in science and can bring back knowledge that will enhance and empower science in the United States.

Finally, as the United States, one of the most technologically advanced nations in the world, faces the prospect of declining numbers of American born scientists, other educational systems are churning out scientists with mysterious ease. When sending future scientists, educators, and science professionals to study abroad in these successful institutions, we can hope that they will integrate these elements into the science education of the future. This educational endeavor truly benefits American science education and the science students of the future.

The Institute of International Education *Open Doors* data shows that 15.1% of the students studying abroad declared a major in science, math, or engineering (IIE, 2007). Clearly there are obstacles, real or perceived, that prevent more science students from participating in study abroad. As the following case study suggests, confronting these obstacles and transforming them into opportunities proves a valuable enterprise in promoting the global exchange of scientists.

SCIENCE EDUCATION ABROAD: A CASE STUDY AT EMORY

Within the backdrop of trends in science education, Emory's science departments and CIPA established SEA in 2005. Science Education Abroad, based in close collaborative relationships, seeks to internationalize the undergraduate curriculum in an effort to improve the retention and engagement of science majors and to provide greater access to study abroad across all majors. The resulting SEA programs were designed specifically to address the needs of students in the sciences and the educational priorities of the science departments.

Table 22.1 *Summer Science Faculty-Led Programs*

1. Chemistry Studies Program in Siena, Italy
2. Ecology and Evolutionary Biology Program in Queensland, Australia
3. Interdisciplinary Global Health Program in Cape Town, South Africa
4. Neuroscience and Behavioral Biology Program in Paris, France

Table 22.2 *Recommended Direct Enrollment Institutions for Science Semester Programs*

1. James Cook University, Australia
2. University of Melbourne, Australia
3. Imperial College, England
4. King's College London, England
5. University of Sussex, England
6. University of Paris VII (advanced French language required), France
7. University of Siena (Italian language required), Italy
8. University of St. Andrews, Scotland
9. National University of Singapore
10. University of Cape Town, South Africa
11. Bogacizi University, Turkey
12. University of the Virgin Islands

Table 22.3 *Partnerships with Program Providers Specializing in Environmental Studies*

1. Organization for Tropical Studies / Duke University (Costa Rica)
2. School for Field Studies (Mexico, Kenya)
3. School for International Training (Panama, Mekong Delta, Tanzania)

Science Education Abroad includes a three-tier approach to programming: (1) semester and year-long study abroad opportunities including 12 direct enrollment institutions distinguished in the broad-based sciences and three program providers specializing in environmental studies; (2) faculty-led summer study abroad programs representing chemistry, biology, environmental studies, global health, and neuroscience and behavioral biology; (3) and independent research in partner laboratories and internships overseas. Collectively, the current SEA program offerings in 2008 include programs in 15 countries representing the major world regions: Africa (Kenya, Tanzania, South Africa), Australia, Asia (Mekong Delta, Singapore), Europe (England, France, Italy, Scotland), Latin America and the Caribbean (Costa Rica, Mexico, Panama, Virgin Islands), and the Middle East (Turkey) (see Tables 22.1, 22.2, 22.3). The increase in participation rates for science students serves as one indicator of the success of SEA programs. From 1997–1998 to 2005–2006, participation of science majors studying abroad increased from 54 students to 125 students, representing 12% and 21% of the total number of students studying abroad in those respective years (see Table 22.4). Furthermore, in 2005–2006, 140 students, or 23% of all study abroad participants, had either a major or minor in a science field (see Table 22.5). Since 25% of Emory University undergraduate students are science majors, the SEA initiative is close to reaching a similar target representation of science study abroad students compared to overall students engaged in study abroad. Approximately one-fifth of majors in biology and physics are studying abroad, whereas one-fourth or more of majors in chemistry, math, and computer science are studying abroad (see Table 22.6). Despite the structured nature of science curriculum on

Table 22.4 *Study Abroad by Major in the Sciences on All Programs (Semester, Year, and Summer)*

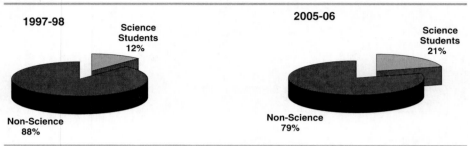

Year	Science Students	All Students
1997–98	54 (12%)	452
2004–05	107 (17%)	625
2005–06	125 (21%)	610

25% of Emory students are science majors.
This data excludes visiting students from other institutions who attended Emory University study abroad programs.

campus, demanding schedules, pressures of completing laboratory research, and perceived barriers among students and faculty alike, SEA programming at Emory has made significant strides in internationalizing the undergraduate science curriculum.

Collaboration and Incentives

In order to be successful, Emory undergraduate science programming abroad had to fit into existing educational priorities within the liberal arts curriculum, existing curricular priorities for science departments, and existing structures for international education at Emory. This ambitious project also required the creation of programmatic structures to accommodate science students and of advising resources to support them in making the decision to have an international experience. Success in both these areas was made possible because relevant administrative and academic units collaborated closely.

Collaborations between study abroad professionals and scientists provide an avenue for study abroad professionals to reevaluate some basic assumptions about study abroad. The traditional priorities given to cultural immersion and language study for undergraduates are not necessarily a given focus of science faculty members. Science faculty can be direct, practical, and bottom-line driven. Their ambitions and constraints may be different from faculty members in the humanities and social sciences. Science faculty want their educational programs to be as effective as possible,

Table 22.5 *Study Abroad by Majors and Minors in the Sciences 2005-06*

Year	Students with a Science Major	Students with a Science Minor	Total with Major/Minor in the Sciences	All Students
2005–2006	125	15	140 (23%)	610

25% of Emory students are science majors.

Table 22.6 *Participation of Science Students by Academic Major 2005–06*

Major (Av. Majors/yr)	Semester	Summer	Total	Percentage Study Abroad Compared to Average Majors/yr
Biology (200)	11	27	38	19%
Chemistry (60)	1	22	23	38%
Neuroscience and Behavioral Biology (250)	19	22	41	16%
Physics (10)	0	2	2	20%
Environmental Studies (50)	6	2	8	16%
Math/Computer Science (50)	5	8	13	26%

and they want their students to be well-trained and to compete well for admission to graduate and professional schools. Science faculty are passionate about their disciplines, research, and teaching interests. They want to profile the quality of their graduate programs abroad, to attract international students, and to connect with researchers abroad who have complementary interests. An outsider may perceive a "what's in it for me?" approach here, but a closer look at their work conditions and priorities may result in new, innovative programming on campus.

Science faculty are also not a monolithic category of professors, teachers, and researchers. The most powerful faculty members are usually active researchers who run labs and rely on grant money to be successful. They must use their limited resources and time judiciously. Semester-long faculty exchanges do not work well for science faculty. Thus, short term exchanges are generally more practical and useful for science faculty than semester exchanges, as long as they foster deep and useful connections with scientists at other universities. On the other side of the faculty spectrum are those who are primarily responsible for and dedicated to undergraduate education. At Emory these faculty members are generally lecturer track faculty, rather than tenure track faculty. These are the faculty members who will probably actually organize and execute programs as well as use their connections to students to convince them to participate. Due to this disciplinary context, it is much less likely in the sciences than in other areas to have a senior faculty member who is interested or available to direct a study abroad program. The study abroad office needs allies in both of these faculty groups.

A number of things can fire the imagination of science faculty members for study abroad. It is very attractive for research scientists to have opportunities to visit each other's labs, to exchange students to work in labs, or to send or acquire bright graduate students. The most compelling opportunities of this kind will flow out of existing connections between faculty members where there is a high degree of respect that the partners do "good science." Science faculty members will also be excited by the enriching opportunities that study abroad provides for their students.

For study abroad professionals to appreciate and to work effectively with science faculty, they must acknowledge departmental priorities, and be willing to adapt an existing range of approaches to create programs that address scientific, cultural, and educational priorities. There are a number of ways in which these priorities can align and complement each other. In lieu of a compromise, the resulting programming emerges as meaningful and valid study abroad which has broad-reaching benefits for student and faculty engagement.

TRANSFORMING OBSTACLES INTO OPPORTUNITIES

The effort to strengthen Emory's offerings in science study abroad began with a systematic review of obstacles and opportunities in the undergraduate curriculum as well as existing perceptions among faculty and students. Science education abroad programming had to meet a diverse variety of needs and reduce perceived barriers to study abroad that ranged from student reluctance to take risks to faculty indifference. Data were gathered about each problem area to help develop approaches that would lower the barriers to science study abroad and win the approval of faculty. Data collection involved focus groups, interviews, questionnaires, and postprogram evaluations. The process included asking both faculty and students to respond to questionnaires, hosting periodic meetings with relevant faculty to brainstorm and to advocate for new programming, and collecting information specifically about the experience of science students through postprogram evaluations. Student feedback was critical in providing key information to advocate for the value of science study abroad. The analysis of this data yields five broad obstacles to science education abroad programming. The SEA program has actively articulated the common assumptions and barriers to study abroad and devised strategies to transform these obstacles into opportunities for future science students.

> **Obstacle:** Science students do not study abroad because of crowded schedules and the need to make progress in order to major. There is some validity to the argument that science students' college careers are typically more crowded and more structured than those of the nonscience majors. Courses are sequential and year-long and often cannot be taken out of sequence. Many Emory students enroll in double majors which creates further complications for their schedules. When students participating in summer study abroad programs were surveyed, science majors chose a study abroad program primarily because of the course offerings (88.4% vs. location 86.1%). Nonscience majors on the other hand chose programs based on location (89.6% vs. 87.5% for courses).

These results led SEA to focus on developing summer study abroad programs with specific curriculum niches, identifying key institutions for viable semester programs for science students, and designing outreach initiatives led by student leaders. In faculty-led discipline-based summer programs, students are required to take two courses taught by Emory faculty. Faculty directors design the programs to include one course that is required for a science major, thus ensuring students' progress toward their degrees and enhancing recruitment and enrollment efforts. The design of the second course on these programs reinforces disciplinary context, satisfies general education college requirements, or offers an experiential learning content in order to successfully attract science students (see Table 22.1). For example, the Chemistry Studies Program in Italy offers "Analytical Chemistry," a required course for all chemistry BA and BS majors, and a second elective in the same major. The Ecology and Evolutionary Biology Program in Australia offers a required major course and a second course that serves as an elective for both majors in Environmental Sciences and Biology. Faculty often establish prerequisite courses to ensure that students have adequate preparation for the summer courses.

The SEA program has also integrated semester-based options for students with the capacity in their schedule to engage in a longer-term study broad option. Semester programs pose challenges for science students due to the sequential courses required for majors, the timing of premedical MCAT examinations, and application cycles to graduate and professional school. However, faculty support, informed advising, and advanced planning enhance students' opportunities for success in participating in a semester program. In some cases, the programs expand the on-campus course offerings for a student with a particular specialty. For example, a student desiring to focus on marine biosciences would be well advised to spend a year at the National University of Singapore or James Cook University in Australia because the Emory Biology Department does not offer these courses.

Science students are guided toward a small group of semester programs in international institutions that are highly ranked, have undeniably excellent science programs, and offer science courses in English (see Table 22.2). These conditions ensure that students continue to make progress toward their major uninterrupted and offer opportunities for science students to participate in undergraduate research during their semester abroad. The establishment of these programs involves close screening by Emory faculty, site visits by relevant science faculty to ensure curriculum compatibility, and proposals vetted through the CIPA Education Abroad Committee. In addition to these direct enrollment universities, Emory also maintains affiliations with three program providers that specialize in environmental studies programs through intensive fieldwork components and field station infrastructures (see Table 22.3).

To address students' reservations about study abroad and scheduling, the SEA program found that word of mouth was the most effective way to disseminate information. Survey data indicated that half the science students found out about study abroad from their friends. Students value the opinion of residence hall advisers, orientation leaders, Student Government Association leaders and other advanced level science students. The establishment of a formal student advis0ry board with premed sciences students who studied abroad informed us about student concerns, the members were good advocates of the programs, and helped popularize the programs through campus outreach. From 2004 to 2008, the demand for the summer Chemistry Studies Program rose from 18 to 35 applicants this year. Thus, efforts to use student networks for outreach successfully raised the profile of new summer programs designed specifically to meet the scheduling needs of science students.

> **Obstacle:** Premedical sequence courses, MCAT preparation, and medical school interviews prevent students from studying abroad.

At Emory, 23% of the incoming class of 2005 said they would like to become physicians compared to 11.7% for all private universities in the annual freshman survey conducted by the Higher Education Research Institute (Teodorescu, 2005). Following graduation, an alumni survey in 2003 that sought feedback from alumni who graduated with a science major between 1992 and 2002, found that 12% of the respondents had completed an MD program and another 15% were enrolled in medical school (Teodorescu, 2003).

Emory's premed students' academic decisions and actions are largely guided by what is "acceptable" for medical school. Students on a premed track usually take chemistry and biology in their freshman year, followed by organic chemistry in their sophomore year, and physics during the junior year when most study abroad occurs. There is a prevalent perception that science courses taken abroad do not count or even worse, disqualify students from applying to medical school. Typically students with excellent performance are willing to take the risks, but most other students are not.

To counter this concern, SEA developed a multifaceted approach that included talking to premed student organizations, meeting with premed advisers and faculty advisers, preparing literature for freshmen and potential science majors that included information about study abroad, providing information on the CIPA Web site that would facilitate the task of program selection, and working with directors of undergraduate study in science departments to establish lists of Emory course equivalencies for coursework overseas.

Programs can be designed to provide experiences that premed students value. The Interdisciplinary Global Health Program in South Africa couples a core course with a service-learning, experiential-based course. This program attracts a diverse group of science majors, including premed students, due to its curriculum of one course required for the Global Health minor and a second service-learning course that places science students in schools in the townships surrounding Cape Town. Service-learning projects range from working with adult learners and K-12 students, learning about the AIDS epidemic, to engaging in ongoing public health initiatives. Such summer study abroad experiences are extremely engaging and attractive to our premed science majors.

> **Obstacle:** Anecdotal evidence suggested that science faculty do not actively encourage study abroad or perhaps even discourage study abroad.

In 2006, when asked whether faculty in the major encouraged them to apply for study abroad only 42% of the science majors were inclined to say "Agree" or "Strongly Agree" while 56% of the nonscience majors did so. In addition when asked, "Were faculty members in the major knowledgeable about study abroad?" once again there was a clear difference in the responses of the science (30.6%) and nonscience majors (44.7%). To address this issue we organized a series of meetings, with different formats, including luncheons, seminars, receptions, departmental faculty meetings, and communicated via e-mail and one-on-one meetings to educate faculty about study abroad opportunities and the value of study abroad. Science Education Abroad also engaged faculty responsible for teaching the introductory courses that students most often take when studying abroad. When faculty in introductory courses are knowledgeable about study abroad options and are enthusiastic proponents of study abroad, then they transmit this enthusiasm to their first-year and second-year students. When students hear about study abroad early in their college careers, as first-year or second-year students, particularly from their science faculty, they tend to be more successful in developing a plan that will include a study abroad experience. Through close collaborations with faculty who teach these foundational courses, SEA engages them in our efforts and educates them by arranging faculty site visits whenever possible. While many faculty have traveled abroad, few have familiarity with other educational systems, resources, or teaching practices. Science Education Abroad targets faculty who teach general chemistry, introductory biology and physics, and organic chemistry because they teach the large enrollment first and second year courses. The strongest advocates of study abroad are faculty who have visited the program sites and are therefore assured of the quality and rigor of the academic experience in that international institution. In the next iteration of the survey in 2007, the responses of nonscience and science majors responses were similar to both questions demonstrating that the program succeeded in some measure to close the gap.

Science Education Abroad also pursued a targeted strategy to engage faculty by discovering their interests and by strengthening relationships and building programming at institutions where the Emory faculty were already connected and which had world class reputations for excellence in the sciences. This targeted strategy resulted in program development in new summer programs, establishment of affiliations with International Institutes of Excellence in Science, and encouraging innovative partnerships in summer research.

The International Institutes of Excellence involved a list of premier direct enrollment universities where the quality of science is unquestioned and where course equivalences are listed in the database (see Table 22.7). Emory's first success was the creation of a neuroscience track for students in the neuroscience and behavioral biology major at Emory to study at the University of St. Andrews in Scotland. Emory was fortunate to have preexisting ties to St. Andrews and funding available to support a series of 2-week faculty exchanges to help coordinate curriculum and advising for the exchange. The connections between departments that these exchanges fostered

Table 22.7 *Emory Course Equivalence Database for Semester Programs*

Discipline	Courses established as Emory Course Equivalences	Percentage of Total Courses
Sciences	271	13%
Other Disciplines	1747	87%

Country	Program	Number of Science Courses established as Emory Course Equivalences
Australia	James Cook University	6
Australia	University of Melbourne	15
Australia	University of New South Wales	28
Australia	University of Queensland	19
Australia	University of Sydney	5
Australia	University of Western Australia	1
Costa Rica	Duke Organization for Tropical Studies*	3
England	King's College London	7
England	Lancaster University	5
England	London School of Economics and Political Science	5
England	Queen Mary, University of London	3
England	University College London	27
England	University of Sussex	56
Italy	University of Siena	2
Kenya	School for Field Studies*	4
Korea	Yonsei University	1
Mekong Delta	School for International Training*	2
Mexico	School for Field Studies*	4
Panama	School for International Training*	3
Scotland	University of St. Andrews	42
Singapore	National University Singapore	29
South Africa	University of Cape Town	1
Tanzania	School for International Training*	3
	Totals	271

*The curriculum for these programs focuses on Environmental Studies.

and the ongoing student programming has led to numerous collaborations, including the estab-lishment of a dual-degree program and specific research collaborations. The full involvement of the relevant departmental faculty was essential to this success, as was the prospect of benefits, not only for students but also for the research interests of the faculty.

While it is not always possible to replicate this kind of multilevel collaboration, we have also had success in expanding the list of Institutes of Excellence through less labor intensive and expensive coordination of curriculum. The expansion of this list coincided with careful exami-nation of course offerings and the establishment of a course equivalency database system. The Center for International Programs Abroad (CIPA) compiled information about courses at the targeted institutions and in a single meeting with the directors of undergraduate studies of the science departments identified and approved the most relevant courses at a number of partner universities. This review and preapproval of courses has been very important for recruiting and advising students, as well as for increasing the knowledge of faculty and study abroad advisers.

An important planning and advising tool for semester programs involves the course equiv-alency database. By maintaining a comprehensive list of approved courses suitable for science majors and preprofessional students, students and faculty work together to find a suitable plan of study that complements the students' academic goals on campus. The course equivalency database

INTERNATIONAL RESEARCH EXPERIENCE FOR SCIENCE (IRES)

Students with prior research experience identify an international research adviser who is either known to their Emory research adviser or is already a collaborator. The Emory research adviser is thus involved in both the choice of the adviser and helps define the summer research project in close collaboration with his or her international colleague. Not only does this program provide an international experience to the Emory student, it encourages international research collabo-rations between Emory faculty and their international counterparts. This mechanism engages science faculty in internationalization efforts in a sustainable way. Faculty see a direct benefit to their research agenda, especially when the student returns to the Emory lab and continues the research with a new skill set or a new perspective.

Emory faculty working with student researchers and an international collaborator can pro-pose new exploratory projects. If funded, the students perform the research in the international location, jointly advised by the Emory researcher and the international host. Emory research-ers prepare the student prior to departure and jointly advise the student during the project. Communication between the two research advisers during the course of the project leads to more fruitful collaboration, new projects, and maybe even grant proposals.

Since 2006, we have sent about 8 to 10 students a year. Students are required to enroll in a one credit course the spring before their departure. The course provides both preparation for the research that lies ahead and orientation to the new country and culture. Speakers who are knowledgeable about international science and work with the Emory research advisers provide lectures to prepare students for the lab. Students conduct a minimum of 10 weeks of research abroad, maintain a blog while they are away, communicate with others in the cohort even though they may be in distant countries, and conduct presentations upon return to their faculty and fellow students. In the last few years several of the students have published papers based on their research abroad and have gone on to graduate school in their field. The program is funded by funds from different internal Emory sources, as well as funding from the Howard Hughes Medical Institute and external scholarships such as DAAD.

includes 271 science courses (13% of all courses) with an established Emory course equivalent, representing 23 programs in 12 different countries (Table 22.7).

> **Obstacle:** Some departments with strong existing commitments to study abroad and strong place-based rationales for supporting study abroad resisted science programming abroad.

Perhaps one of the most surprising obstacles to establishing science programming abroad has been the uneven response of departments that perceive themselves as having an existing proprietary interest in particular world areas or countries. As Emory has defined its study abroad priorities internally, cross-cultural and linguistic learning has been at the core of what is considered a legitimate and academically supportable study abroad experience. Given the primacy of cultural learning in study abroad, the cross-cultural relevance of science study abroad has been open to challenge, precisely because of the "universality" of science. But science occurs in cultural, institutional, economic, and political contexts. Well-designed and implemented study abroad programming can open new perspective and insight to science students about their own studies and future careers. Fortunately the discussions about the science initiative and its relationship to place-based learning have played out productively with the guidance and mediation of the faculty Education Abroad Committee. The deliberations of this committee have created ground for cooperation, understanding, and have resulted in stronger programming.

The persistent question for the study abroad professional, and the potential source of criticism from faculty members in other fields is whether science based study abroad programming is sufficiently place-based to be justified as study abroad. Even though the primary standard for science departments is that study abroad programs have an uncompromising emphasis on "good science," most science faculty members who engage with study abroad recognize the important of cross-cultural education. All Emory programs involve considerable contact with members of a local institution. Where appropriate they involve language training and coursework relevant to the location, and in most instances the science coursework itself draws on local resources and circumstances to address practical applications of science.

New programs designed to join science related subject areas with research and practical experience have been very promising. The Interdisciplinary Global Health Program in South Africa focuses on Global Health issues as experienced in the South African context. It also provides ample opportunity for contact with the local culture through a substantial service-learning component. Furthermore, many environmental studies programs draw upon the natural environment in locations such as Australia, Costa Rica, Tanzania, and the Mekong Delta to engage students in hands-on fieldwork unavailable in land-locked Atlanta.

> **Obstacle:** Science faculty are not convinced of the educational benefits of study abroad.

The benefits of any educational intervention have to stand up to the scrutiny of assessment. The benefits for language or area studies majors are more intuitively apparent, with the increased opportunity to practice a language or learn about a culture in depth leading to improvements in disciplinary skills. Our conversations with faculty both in science departments and outside the sciences indicated that we would need to demonstrate the disciplinary benefits of study abroad for science students at Emory. So in our survey we asked students who had participated in study abroad (2006 and 2007) to rate their agreement with the following statements: "The study abroad experience increased my **skills** in my major" and "The study abroad experience increased my **interest** in the major."

Five years after the launch of the SEA programs our surveys of science students indicate that study abroad has addressed a number of educational priorities. Students were generally enthusiastic about the time they had spent abroad, but in their postprogram evaluations a couple of interesting patterns emerged. In both 2006 and 2007, science majors noted that the study abroad experience increased their interest in their academic major and we documented an increase in their self-reported interest (from 53% to 72%).

Students also reported gains in skills related to their major. In 2007, approximately four-fifths of the science majors noted that their study abroad experience taught them skills that are highly applicable to their studies. The level of agreement was comparable to that of all CIPA participants. Student comments from the chemistry and environmental studies/biology program were even more compelling.

- "Our studies directly corresponded to field trips we were taking. Having a smaller group allows for better relationship building with professors and fellow students."
- "Eight credit hours, connections with students abroad, understanding of instruments that Emory does not have, lab time, and tours from actual chemists that show what chemistry is capable of on a day-to-day basis as well as how it is routinely applied."
- "When else can you LIVE in Tuscany and learn how all the chemistry you have been studying in a classroom in Atlanta can actually be applied to the things around you—like the vineyards, glass making, or art restoration? It's pretty amazing when you think about the application of all the things you've learned and then actually see them and to use them."
- "This was an excellent opportunity as a biology major to really go out and see what they were talking about in class. The classes made you more aware of what you were seeing, and made you appreciate it more, and be more knowledgeable talking about it at home."
- "I fully enjoyed the group of students I went with and the experiences we had. It is difficult for many PREMED students to travel abroad, so this was an amazing opportunity that added to my Emory experience."

These results and comments were shared with faculty in several different venues and communications and have spurred greater interest in faculty for developing new programs.

SUSTAINABLE LANDSCAPES IN SCIENCE EDUCATION ABROAD

The success of the SEA programs in part lies with the multi-tier approach of the program design, the active science faculty engagement, and the diversity of program offerings. Diversity and flexibility of program offerings is a pivotal tool for meeting the distinct needs of science students. The Center for International Programs Abroad places a high emphasis on offering a wide array of programs, from faculty-led to direct enrollment to hybrid programs through program providers to experiential courses, in order to closely match the academic needs of the prospective student with the best program. The development of science programming falls in line with the study abroad office's overarching priority on program diversity, and offers another dimension to integrating study abroad into the undergraduate education.

As described throughout this case study, the SEA programs fall into three broad-based categories: (1) faculty-led summer programs; (2) semester-based programs in direct enrollment universities and with select program providers; and (3) independent research and internship

FROM ITALIAN VINEYARDS TO THE LAB: THE MAKING OF AN ENGAGED SCIENTIST

Nicholas Justice is a chemistry major who went on the summer Chemistry Studies program in Siena, Italy and stayed for the fall semester. In between the two programs, he also spent 3 weeks during the harvest season, as an intern in a historic vineyard in the Chianti region. During his semester at Siena, he took courses and participated in a research project with one of the faculty at the University of Siena, Professor Renzo Cini.

The Siena experience was extremely valuable for my education and for my development both as a chemist and a person. I have had the opportunity to learn not only an enormous amount of chemistry one-on-one with a fantastic professor, but I have been able to grow and mature in a challenging environment where the language barrier was a constant obstacle. I have seen my horizons grow quite literally outside of the United States as this experience has opened my eyes to the opportunities and joys of studying or working abroad.

If I focus on only the chemistry studied, I will be unable to describe the massive amount of material I learned. I do not have space here to describe in depth everything I learned of inorganic chemistry in general, of instrumentation, of how to invent solutions quickly, of how to work in a small research group, of how a wine business is run, of how to differentiate different types of vine species, of how to behave respectfully and independently in a foreign environment, of how to meet and get along with very different people, and most of all of the Italian language.

My 3-week internship in the vineyard was "intense." Between really learning to speak fluently in Italian and the 12-hour work days, I found myself with little time even to think. However, the workload did not prevent me from enjoying the experience and the language barrier did not prevent me from learning. I worked in the labs at the vineyard but also in the fermentation unit and outside with the vines. I stayed with other interns from many different countries. That was an incredible experience.

I continued to work with grapes in Dr. Cini's research labs at University of Siena on developing a method for the detection of polyphenols in wine using RP-HPLC and isocratic elution with a UV-VIS detector. I made four presentations to Dr. Cini's group, two were in English and two in Italian. I then took a course offered by the university and taught by Professor Cini. I enjoyed how he interacted one-on-one with the students. I was also able to attend the seminars given by other students' thesis work within the university. The opportunity to see how their chemistry education differed from ours, and how their didactic approach differed from ours, was almost as interesting as the material itself. They all were performing interesting research in relatively new areas, and were usually much more specialized than their American counterparts. Professor Cini took at least several hours a week in addition to teach me some of the basics of inorganic chemistry, a course I have not yet had at Emory. I cannot express enough how important this program has been to me in terms of my development as a young researcher. I had the opportunity not only to work as a technician in a high-throughput industrial laboratory at the vineyard, but also to work in a small group of talented researchers and students in a university. With Dr. Cini, I felt at home, welcomed, appreciated, and respected. I felt that I was part of the team and that my ideas were important. I enjoyed his company and teachings immensely, and will always cherish the days I spent here. When I went to Siena, I was not sure of what I was doing next. I had so much fun with chemistry in Siena that when I came back, I enrolled in the BS MS program at Emory and am applying to graduate schools here in the United States and abroad.

EAST MEETS WEST: THE EMORY TIBET SCIENCE INITIATIVE

The Emory Tibet Science Initiative is an ambitious undertaking to develop a science curriculum for Tibetan monastics. This initiative is a positive outcome of an ongoing exchange relationship established between Emory University, the Institute of Buddhist Dialectics (in Dharamsala, India), the Drepung Loesling Institute (in Atlanta, GA), and the Drepung Loesling Monastery (in South India). Though its initial goal involved exchanging Emory students and Tibetan students, the partnership has evolved to embrace a bold new research agenda in the sciences.

At the request of His Holiness the Dalai Lama, now a Presidential Distinguished Faculty at Emory, Emory faculty have taken the lead in this effort. One of the goals of this program is to build bridges of communication between practitioners of Western science and Buddhist science so as to create new knowledge in areas such as cognitive neurosciences and mental health. This multifaceted and interdisciplinary effort brings together faculty, staff, and students from all units of the campus and captures the essence of the new Emory. Emory's semester study abroad program in Dharamsala, India, long recognized as a leading program in Tibetan Buddhist studies has influenced many Emory undergraduates and contributed to His Holiness's request. Emory's South Asian studies program is top ranked and attracts many top scholars in Tibetan studies. However, it was only recently that the scientists at Emory joined hands with Tibetan scholars, faculty in religion, philosophy and other disciplines to work on the unique curriculum development project.

In 2008 the first group of faculty offered a 4-week intensive introductory session with lectures and activities in cosmology, life sciences, and neurosciences. We plan to offer Emory undergraduates an opportunity to participate in a unique summer study abroad program learning not only about science and Tibetan culture, but also contributing to this unique dialog between Western science and Eastern philosophy. The program will seek science majors and will offer an interdisciplinary science course with a hands-on component. Students will participate in the science lectures with the monastics and work with them in the labs and during field trips. They will also benefit from a course in Tibetan culture, and their learning will be considerably enhanced by their stay in a vibrant Tibetan community.

opportunities. The compelling story of an Emory science student, Nicolas Justice, illustrates the impact of combining summer study abroad with intensive research collaboration in an Italian laboratory.

Establishing a strong science study abroad program on any campus requires creativity, flexibility, collaboration, and appreciation of diverse needs and outcomes. From the initial discussion of the process to the implementation stage, the Science Education Abroad program proves to be in a continual state of evolution. As new intuitional partners emerge, so do new faculty members and incoming freshman arrive on campus eager to participate in the initiative. The recent announcement of His Holiness the XIV Dalai Lama as a Distinguished Presidential Faculty at Emory University has propelled an existing exchange partnership into new dimensions of exploring Eastern and Western scientific approaches.

In order to successfully capture the energy of science education programming, key steps must be taken to ensure that a sustainable landscape is built for future students, faculty, and study abroad administrators engaged in science study abroad.

The study abroad office plays a pivotal role in student outreach and marketing of study abroad programs. For science students, the importance of reaching students in the first year of college is imperative in order to provide ample time for planning and design of integrating study abroad into the 4-year plan. Freshmen faculty advisers and first-year students are advised to introduce science majors to study abroad. The SEA Web site includes planning documents with a semester by semester worksheet that students can use to plan out their college career. The planning documents have suggestions for study abroad sequences, locations, and courses.

In the initial phases of the initiative, CIPA dedicated one study abroad adviser who served as the liaison to the Office of Undergraduate Education in developing strategies for success in advising students about science programs. As the initiative has expanded to programs in all world regions, CIPA has integrated science advising into the preexisting geographic world advising areas. The Center for International Programs Abroad has dedicated staff that focus on advising students holistically by world area, from initial marketing and outreach, individual advising sessions, pre-departure meetings, crisis management while abroad, and reentry initiatives and outreach to prospective students. The integration of science advising by world area requires cross-training of CIPA staff. The inclusion of CIPA advisers in special presentations with science faculty members enhances the overall collaboration between the study abroad office and science departments. Study abroad advisers are encouraged to participate in professional conferences and workshops designed to enhance their skills in advising underrepresented students. The CIPA advisers hold weekly meetings to discuss special advising issues, address barriers that arise for students, inform staff of new programs on the horizon, and share knowledge and best practices from conferences. This cross-training approach ensures that any science major that walks into the office is able to meet with an informed staff member who can point the student in the right direction.

While study abroad advisers assist students with logistics of program selection, they also place a priority on directing students to department academic advisers for planning. Sustainable practices in science study abroad require having informed faculty advisers and strong academic advising allies. Faculty can guide students in their early explorations, recommend specific programs, and help them navigate the process. They help resolve course equivalency issues, advise students about majors courses, maintain informal or formal data about students and their feedback, and share their experiences with other faculty in departmental and college meetings. Faculty advisers are extremely influential and have contributed in a major way to the success of the Science Experience Abroad programs.

As faculty grow more confident of the established alliances between Emory and high-ranking universities abroad, academic departments have demonstrated greater flexibility in awarding course equivalencies while ensuring the intellectual content and the academic rigor of international courses. Course equivalency databases are also a very important component of planning. The database plays a central role in documenting international course options and suggested Emory course equivalents from relevant departments. The database includes a diverse array of courses, including preapproved introductory level courses and some upper level electives. Sequential science courses are also included in this list. Most science programs in the United States and abroad offer fairly similar introductory chemistry, physics, biology, and math courses. A typical science major at Emory takes one or two of these courses in their first 2 years and often has to take one of these subjects in the junior year when they are studying abroad. The two-semester physics sequence that is required for most science majors at Emory and required for medical school admissions, is most often the subject that students take in their junior year. When students search for semester options, it often comes down to where they can take physics. Thus a comprehensive database serves as a key resource for planning science study abroad.

Continual assessment and postprogram evaluations ensure administrators and faculty are actively meeting the needs of today's science students. Routine evaluations should be provided to faculty advisers leading programs as well as to faculty committees reviewing programs on the recommended list. Establishing key connections with graduating seniors and young alumni also generates networking opportunities for students. Through formal and informal networks, the myths and barriers associated with science study abroad begin to fade as a new generation of students embraces now-established global opportunities.

CONCLUSION

At Emory we have found that when structured opportunities are available for science students to study abroad, students will study abroad in considerable numbers. Science students may have special considerations, but when the science faculty and the study abroad office work together, appropriately structured programs and advising can meet the needs of the science students, the educational priorities of science departments, and the cross-cultural learning goals of international educators. As science education globalizes and the relative strength of science education in the United States diminishes, the need for an internationalized science curriculum is clear. The SEA program provides some examples that have worked at one institution, but its success has been based on collaboration, flexibility, and the creation of carefully designed programming that can be broadly replicated.

REFERENCES

Gates, W. (2008). Testimony before Congress. Retrieved February 2, 2009, from http://www.forbes.com/2008/03/12/bill-gates-innovation-tech-sciences-cx_bw_0312gates.html

Institute of International Education. (2007). *Open doors report.* Retrieved June 2008, from http://opendoors.iienetwork.org/

National Science Board. (2003). *The science and engineering workforce: Realizing America's potiential.* Retrieved June 2008, from http://www.nsf.gove/nsb/documents/2003/nsb0369/nsb0369.pdf

National Science Foundation. (2006). *Science and engineering indicators.* Retrieved June 2008, from http://www.nsf.gov/statistics/seind06/c0s1.htm

National Science Foundation. (2008). *Toward a globally engaged workforce: A vision for the Office of International Science and Engineering.* Retrieved June 2008, from http://www.nsf.gov.od/oise/vision-doc.jsp

Teodorescu, D. (2003). *Emory College science baccalaureatre alumni survey.* Unpublished report.

Teodorescu, D. (2005). CIRP 2005 freshman survey: Selected findings. Retrieved February 2, 2009, from http://www.emory.edu/PROVOST/IPR/documents/researchonstudents/CIRP05_FreshSurvey_rpt.pdf

Chapter 23

Undergraduate Research During Study Abroad

Scope, Meaning, and Potential

Bernhard T. Streitwieser[1]

Northwestern University

INTRODUCTION

This chapter addresses the question of how undergraduate research during study abroad supports the development of global citizenship. Building in students the capacity to understand and appropriately conduct research is one of the goals of a high-quality undergraduate education. Providing study abroad students with opportunities to further engage their research interests to learn deeply about an aspect of a foreign culture—whether the investigation deals with a historical matter or is concerned with present-day issues, or the methodology is archival, field-based, or observation-driven—is a fundamental way of developing the skills we can broadly ascribe to global citizenship. Students who have meaningful learning experiences gain the tools of wider knowledge and greater cultural understanding that after a study abroad experience can translate into active civil engagement. When carefully prepared, guided, and focused research is undertaken it augments the important personal and academic development that takes place during study abroad and allows students to engage in a form of intellectual activity that can promote the broad goals of civic education: open-mindedness, critical thinking, and the willingness to constructively advance society and its diverse membership. This kind of global citizenship is fostered in study abroad generally but made explicit through research abroad.

The aim of this chapter is to encourage a vigorous dialogue among study abroad practitioners and those who are uniquely positioned to most effectively harmonize the benefits of undergraduate research abroad with current programming in order to manifest this important form of civic global engagement. To encourage the discussion, this chapter offers a brief sketch of the development of the undergraduate research movement in higher education over the last several decades and, more recently, its limited headway into study abroad; discusses current challenges the field faces in fostering undergraduate research; and offers a new definition for undergraduate research abroad that addresses student learning needs, institutional priorities, and administrative realities. The chapter concludes with a review of some of the currently existing study abroad research opportunities, successful program models, examples of student achievement, and recommendations for program planners who seek to incorporate study abroad research opportunities into their future programming

Higher education today faces a challenging paradox: On the one hand, some observers are concerned that undergraduates seem self-centered and apathetic about civic engagement (Paul,

2006) and, on the other hand, some observers posit that college students today are in fact more interested than ever in serving their communities (Colby, Ehrlich, Beaumont, & Stephens, 2003). While one can debate which specific activities and personal motivations qualify under the broad umbrella of civic engagement, or how community service fits into the goals of study abroad, educators taking up these questions clearly care deeply about developing in their students a civic mindedness that can translate into meaningful action both in local and global terms. While discussions of civic engagement and accompanying pedagogies abound in secondary and higher education, in study abroad there has so far been less focus on how best to translate civic mindedness through study abroad into globally engaged activism during and following the experience. This transformation of experience to action is essential in the development of global citizenship. The challenge is to make the lofty goals of intellectual civic engagement more tangible and lasting, and one way to begin that process is through promoting active and focused research by students during their time abroad.

For generations, study abroad has provided students with opportunities to expand their educational and intellectual horizons. However, in today's globalized world with its rapid advances in travel and technology, students now have unprecedented opportunities that not only enable global activism but indeed require them to translate genuine understanding of foreign "others" into action as constructive agents of change on an international level. Study abroad allows students to engage in real world settings where experiential learning truly provides the first tools to becoming empowered as agents of change, not only in the foreign communities in which they spend time or their own communities to which they return, but more importantly in infinitely broader ways as deeply informed and newly empowered citizens who leave undergraduate education with infinite ways to help others besides themselves.

THEORETICAL FRAMEWORK

The work of Colby, Ehrlich, Beaumont, and Stephens, *Educating Citizens: Preparing America's Undergraduates for Lives of Moral and Civic Responsibility* (2003), lays out a powerful argument for the critical responsibility that higher education institutions bear in guiding students to lead lives of social responsibility and civic maturity. They write,

> A fully developed individual must...possess the moral commitment and sense of personal responsibility to act, which may include having moral emotions such as empathy and concern for others; moral and civic values, interests, and habits; and knowledge and experience in the relevant domains of life. We are concerned with the development of the whole person, as an accountable individual and engaged participant in society—local, state, national, and global. (pp. 17–18)

The authors advocate that the curricular and extracurricular activities that students engage in during their undergraduate years are critically important in educating students to seek out new ways of interpreting their world, developing new frameworks for understanding themselves and others, making contributions to society, and providing leadership at a variety of levels. Civically responsible students, they argue, recognize their role within "a larger social fabric," see society's problems as shared, and know they must venture beyond their "immediate sphere" and learn to "understand how a community operates, the problems it faces, and the

■ 400

richness of its diversity" to make the community—and in the case of study abroad, the *global* community—a more habitable place (pp. 17–18). In short, Colby et al. recognize that what we do to improve life on a small scale within one community intrinsically also has the broadest possible ramifications for others elsewhere. Elizabeth Paul has also written compellingly about the undergraduate research movement but focused attention on community-based research as a way to effectively combine undergraduate research and service-learning. While she does not directly address research abroad, Paul's observation that students who engage in meaningful research partnerships with local communities are "public scholars" is cogent (2006, p. 13). Utilizing the skills of scholarship to genuinely and openly improve the lives of others—and in the case of study abroad to develop in the process a civic mindedness that is global rather than local—embodies the kind of moral development that Colby et al. espouse and which is critical for developing students as global citizens.

In this vein, we know that the highest ideal that motivates the work of international educators is intercultural exchange that enables participants to expand their intellectual and personal horizons and become empowered to act with a heightened sense of responsibility, sensibility, and understanding. Inherent in this belief is that the opportunity to rethink one's assumptions and develop new understandings and skills will inspire a more visceral appreciation of the importance of working to overcome world wide political and social divisions (Altbach, 2004, 2006b; Bok, 2006; Byers, 2007; Colby, Ehrlich, Beaumont, & Stephens, 2003; Lutterman-Aguilar & Gingerich, 2002; Shubert, 2008; U.S. Department of Education, 2006). There is broad consensus today that a rich educational experience in another culture can ideally and at minimum provide students with a meaningful academic and personal learning opportunity. This goal lies at the very heart of the underlying mission of global exchange and is directly and unequivocally related to the philosophy of global citizenship.

Indeed, if study abroad is accepted as a critical facilitator in the process of developing global citizens, we must ask ourselves what kinds of initiatives and activities in particular in study abroad programming can have the greatest impact in advancing this goal. Undergraduate research is one such activity in that it provides a powerful vehicle for more deeply exploring what global citizenship means through immersing students in the intensive study of an issue of personal interest in another culture. Our institutions of higher education and the planners and practitioners of study abroad opportunities have the obligation to create the models and provide the frameworks, training, and guidance that will make this exploration possible and meaningful for students.

POTENTIAL AND OPPORTUNITIES

However, the challenges to the creation of high-quality undergraduate research opportunities on study abroad are many. One of the field's biggest challenges is to overcome the perception by some that study abroad is little more than a vacation from academic work or, worse, an opportunity for vacuous tourism or voyeuristic exploration that sidesteps deeper cultural learning. A spate of recent criticism of a variety of activities associated with study abroad, largely from the media but also from within the field itself, has forced the study abroad industry to vigorously reevaluate itself. For example, an inquiry in 2007 by New York State's Attorney General into some of the billing policies of institutions and "third party providers" generated a spike in meetings, panels, papers, and discussions and eventually led to the publication of a set of standards

401

of ethical conduct (Forum on Education Abroad, 2008; Lewin, 2006; Schemo, 2007a, 2007b). However, beyond even the business of study abroad, the philosophy behind much of the current programming has also come into question, again prominently in the media (Pappano, 2007), but perhaps more importantly from within the academic community itself. For example, some scholars have rightly pointed out the dangers of rapid program expansion without attention to the implications for program quality (Dobbert, 1998; Ogden, 2007–2008; Woolf, 2007). Looming over scrutiny by those who are directly engaged in study abroad activities are also warnings that have come from astute observers of American higher education, among them Derek Bok, who writes in *Our Underachieving Colleges* (2006):

> The preparation given to students both as citizens in a country deeply affected by world events and as professionals likely to be engaged with foreign cultures seems haphazard at best.... It is a safe bet that a majority of undergraduates complete their four years with very little preparation either as citizens or as professionals for the international challenges that are likely to confront them. (pp. 232–233)

Despite healthy skepticism from study abroad consumers through their legal authorities and the media, and justified soul searching by scholars and practitioners in the field, the core ideals of study abroad hold out higher promise. Quality undergraduate research abroad has the great potential to give study abroad as an academic endeavor a more serious profile. In the recent climate, however, it can seem that the most promising aspects of the endeavor are being neglected; for example, carefully structured undergraduate research and its potential for critical learning. By its very purpose, intellectual inquiry and the search for answers to meaningful questions provides a way to more profoundly engage through intensive contact with a host community. Tony Ogden makes a similar observation: "As international educators, we should not be satisfied with simply exposing students to different experiences. Rather we should be satisfied only when our students are engaged and motivated to pursue experiences that lead to transformative personal growth" (2007–2008, p. 50).

A quality research project provides a tangible artifact of one's learning and potentially gives meaning to an accomplishment that can have a dramatic personal and academic impact. It is no secret that today there is intense competition for the best students. Globalization and the rapid internationalization of higher education confront all institutions that seek to be world class with unprecedented challenges (Altbach, 2006a). An independent research project that gives students autonomy and yet holds them accountable to high standards of scholarly excellence abroad can go far in training responsible global researchers and shoring up a cadre of well-trained and culturally aware professionals in the future.

Undergraduate research abroad also has the potential to uniquely frame the overall 4-year undergraduate experience if predeparture preparation, on-site guidance, and integration upon return to the home campus curriculum are thoughtfully considered (Whalen, 2007b). We should think about time spent abroad in terms of its continuity within the larger narrative of the undergraduate experience; how what students do abroad is part of developing a global awareness and civic mindedness that also has a bearing on what they do upon returning (W. Murphy, personal communication, December 4, 2007). Student development during study abroad is thus a critical part of the larger intellectual and personal developments that research has already shown takes place during the 4-year experience (Pascarella & Terenzini, 2005).

UNDERGRADUATE RESEARCH DURING STUDY ABROAD

While there is much that overlaps between domestic undergraduate research and research under-taken abroad, there are also many important differences. Students still need training on proposal development, data collection and analysis methods, adviser guidance, and articulation of project goals to make the effort feasible and worthy of scholarly attention. Among some of these, students who plan to research abroad need to adequately understand the foreign context that dictates cultural norms about appropriate inquiry and behavior and how to present oneself as a credible researcher. Students need to be careful about sensitively honoring the integrity of their research subjects and knowing what questions, behaviors, or assumptions might be deemed offensive or even have the potential to put them in a dangerous situation. Students also need to be mindful of the degree to which research subjects in the given political or religious context can even share their opinions with an outsider. And finally, among the many additional concerns to consider, students must be aware of the difficulties involved in articulating questions and understanding answers in a foreign language or through an interpreter without losing their intended meaning.

Increasing numbers of U.S. colleges and universities actively support undergraduate research opportunities today, regardless of their mission as research or teaching-focused institutions (Garde-Hanson & Calvert, 2007; Hu, Kuh, & Gayles, 2007). Some institutions require comple-tion of a research project as an undergraduate thesis, while others support students in a myriad of ways to carry out an independent research study. However, within current study abroad program-ming, helping students conceive of a research project, collect and analyze data, and complete an academic paper is an activity that lacks strong support in study abroad programming (Houlihan, 2007). Despite the important national data gathered annually by the Institute of International Education (IIE) through its *Open Doors Report*, no comprehensive studies or other databases exist that provide systematic documentation of how many students in fact take advantage of a research abroad opportunity each year (Bolen & Martin, 2005). Currently, according to IIE, only slightly over half of the existing study abroad programs offer an independent study or field research com-ponent at all. Of the 7,682 study abroad programs in the current IIEPassport database, 1,884 offer an "independent study" component, and 1,474 offer a "directed field study component" (personal communication, IIEPassport).[2] These data, however, are grossly unspecific and pose a number of important further questions, which will be addressed below.

What today can truly be called an undergraduate research movement (Taraban & Blanton, 2008) represents the development over time of a scholarly, interdisciplinary debate and the vari-ety of initiatives by institutions, foundations, funding agencies, and visionary individuals about what elements within the undergraduate experience make learning personally meaningful and academically rigorous. Traditionally, research at the university level has been conducted almost exclusively by faculty and graduate students (Bauer & Bennett, 2003; Gonzalez, 2001; Lopatto, 2004). However, support for and opportunities to engage undergraduates in research has been available and vocalized for decades. In fact, examples abound of scholars historically, particularly in the sciences, who have produced important research in their early college years (Blanton, 2008). While the 1998 Boyer Commission report, *Reinventing Undergraduate Education: A Blue-print for America's Research Universities* is often cited by scholars as critical in the development of today's undergraduate research movement, interest in promoting this kind of learning existed well before the late 1990s (Katkin, 2003). Boyer's report made a very powerful argument that research universities should expend greater effort to more actively engage undergraduates in

403

serious independent and collaborative research (Boyer Commission, 1998). Programs and organizations that enable undergraduate research have grown steadily over the years, as have the numbers of conferences, journals, and other outlets that disseminate the work of young scholars (Blanton, 2008; Gonzalez, 2001). The 2006 U.S. Secretary of Education's Report, *A Test of Leadership: Charting the Future of U.S. Higher Education*, called for a number of reforms and accountability measures in higher education that are likely to have further impact on the development of undergraduate research opportunities in the future. All of this activity has led over time to a growing cadre of students who by now have had an opportunity to conduct research through their program of study, with the help from a faculty adviser or simply by articulating their interest in making an independent project possible.

Since Boyer's report, studies produced by a diverse array of institutions of higher education have indeed demonstrated an active and continuing response to his call for changes in undergraduate education and, specifically, the creation of more intensive research opportunities (Hakim 1998; Hathaway, Nagda, & Gregerman, 2002; Kardash, 2000; Katkin, 2003; Lopatto, 2004; Mogk, 1993; Rauckhorst, Czaja, & Baxter Magolda, 2001; Tomovic, 1994). These studies have shown that research opportunities for undergraduates are valuable and offer an array of benefits, including cognitive, personal, and professional development (Hunter, Laursen, & Seymour, 2006; Lopatto, 2003, 2004). Undergraduate research has been justified as important for meeting degree requirements, building the kinds of academic excitement that can increase persistence toward graduation, and, by extension, fostering an interest in graduate education (Lopatto, 2004; Hathaway et al., 2002; Kremer & Bringle, 1990; Nagda, Greggerman, Jonides, von Hippel, & Lerner, 1998). While in the natural sciences there has been a long tradition of undergraduates working on faculty research projects as a way to acculturate them to the profession (Fitzsimmons, Carlson, Kerpelman, & Stoner, 1990; Zydney, Bennett, Shahid, & Bauer, 2002), more recent years have also seen greater collaboration in the humanities between undergraduates and their faculty mentors. Trends in the expansion of undergraduate research have also included the distribution of these opportunities more widely across the curriculum in order to utilize the expertise of a wider segment of the faculty, not just from the sciences but more widely from within the humanities as well (Fortenberry, 1998).

CHALLENGES

Despite the growing enthusiasm for greater undergraduate research opportunities, some significant challenges remain. First, compared with available funding for graduate level research, funding for undergraduate research remains comparatively modest, although signs indicate that the trend is changing. A quick Internet search reveals that existing undergraduate research opportunities are still provided by a fairly small number of funding agencies when compared with grants available to graduate or faculty researchers.[3] Second, where study abroad is concerned, finding support to finance study abroad in general, and in research abroad in particular, remains a major challenge, particularly for minorities (Dessoff, 2006; Green, Hesel, & Bartini, 2008; IIE Passport, n.d.). Third, generally there has always been more undergraduate research funding available for students in the sciences than for those in the humanities. Fourth, many of the most prominent grants steer to relatively few places internationally. For example, Germany offers a very generous slate of research funding opportunities whereas Latin America and Africa offer many fewer. Some of this variation can be explained by simple economic realities between the respective governments and their abilities to offer grant assistance to foreign visitors. Fifth, supporting student engagement in research abroad requires the dedication and expertise of a variety of people to train and monitor students throughout their research. Unfortunately, many of the administrators in the field of study abroad woefully lack the time, resources, and expertise to appropriately prepare and train students to undertake a research project abroad. Sixth, while there is no clear and agreed upon definition of what undergraduate research is, although definitions have been proposed, there is even less clarity about how such activity can be part of study abroad. This ambiguity has important implications for knowing how to support undergraduate research during study abroad because it leaves wide gaps about what we should expect it to be, how we can structure, prepare, and support it, and how in the end we should be evaluating its impact. These are critical questions the field needs to address. And seventh, a final challenge and perhaps one of the hardest to overcome is that most scholars do not consider undergraduate research to be "real" or authentic in the sense that original or generalizable findings will substantively contribute to the established literature (Kalgren & Tauber, 1996). In fact, many faculty regard how they learn through their research to be distinctly different from the way students learn as undergraduates (Light & Calkins, 2007). Attempting to view undergraduate research in the same light as faculty or graduate-level research misses, however, the fundamental point that first-time independent research should be a formative and critical learning experience for students. While most undergraduate research may, indeed, not be original, this fact does not mean that it cannot have distinctive value. I would argue that if undergraduate research during study abroad is to be taken seriously as an academically meaningful experience, then standards for judging it must approximate those of any other kinds of research we regard seriously.

Despite the above challenges, undergraduate research opportunities are now slowly making their way into study abroad programming by institutions and for-profit and nonprofit organizations. Recent, large-scale studies of faculty and students make it clear that there is growing enthusiasm for undergraduate research opportunities. Data in the 2007 National Survey of Student Engagement report, *Experiences that Matter: Enhancing Student Learning and Success*, and in the 2007 report by the American Association of Colleges and Universities, *College Learning for a New Global Century* (2007), show undergraduate research and study abroad each ranking among the most promising "high impact" experiences. Additionally, the latest report from the American Council on Education and the College Board, *College-Bound Students' Interest in Study Abroad and Other International Learning Activities* (2008), shows 55% of respondents not only planning to study abroad but also seeking international experiences that will include internships and volunteer opportunities—activities that include research possibilities. Although Boyer's report did not discuss study abroad specifically, its description of the potential for deeper learning through internships arguably captures many of the same advantages of a study abroad research opportunity, which also includes the application of research training to real-life contexts and the need to work in interdisciplinary ways in a nonclassroom setting (Boyer Commission Report, 1998). And finally, the Forum on Education Abroad's *State of the Field Survey* (2006) showed 56% of students agreeing that opportunities to conduct independent or directed research during study abroad were important, and 64% of administrators agreeing that more programs were needed that include opportunities for undergraduates to conduct research abroad within their curriculum.

Despite all of this enthusiasm, however, the relative scarcity of research opportunities abroad should not be surprising given that preparation of students for international learning remains relatively weakly supported. Derek Bok in *Our Underachieving Colleges* laments that current overseas education inadequately increases our students' global understanding and many study abroad programs fall far short of the mark in providing opportunities for "a deep engagement with a different culture" (2006, p. 237). According to the most recent report by the American Council on Education, *Mapping Internationalization of U.S. Campuses* (2008) in which more than 1,000 colleges and universities were surveyed, still only 37% require at least one course with an international or global focus, and only 45% require undergraduate foreign-language proficiency for some undergraduates while a mere 16% require it for all undergraduates (Green, Luu, & Burris, 2008).

A NEW DEFINITION OF UNDERGRADUATE RESEARCH DURING STUDY ABROAD

As the above discussion points out, to move forward in making undergraduate research during study abroad an important part of mainstream programming the field needs to come to some consensus on what it is and what it should entail. Having a definition those in the field can turn to is important so they will know how to better integrate the activity into regular study abroad programming and realistically accomplish research-related learning goals. Some of these questions address the philosophy of undertaking research during study abroad, some address the procedural aspects of a research project, and some look at the purely administrative factors that need to be considered.

In terms of philosophical considerations, we need to be clear about what we believe lies at the core of the research experience and what we expect our students to gain from the experience as learners. In that regard, we need to be clear about how we structure the preparation before, guidance during, and reflection afterwards, to ensure the experience has meaning and in the end substantive educative value. While there is a range of literature on global engagement, one compelling way to consider the transformative power of study abroad and research comes from Jack Mezirow's theory of "perspective transformation" (1983), and the extension of his work by Edward Taylor on intercultural competency (1994). Both theories suggest ways in which study abroad can also ideally be seen as a transformative intellectual and personal experience and develop the kind of sensibility commonly associated with global citizenship. This type of transformation can also develop the kinds of outcomes the field regards as important: language learning; intercultural competence defined as culture-specific knowledge, self-identity and attitude toward other cultures; skills like tolerance for ambiguity or strategies for more effectively acquiring new information; disciplinary knowledge; and social and emotional growth (Myer-Lee & Evans, 2007). These theories resonate in particular for students who undertake research abroad. The study of a question that can only be studied in another culture enables, and in fact requires, a deeper engagement and integration of activities with reflection during time abroad. But this benefit is not confined only to the finite period of studying abroad.

In terms of the procedural aspects, we need to ask ourselves what we expect students to learn through the steps of doing research and learning about ethical principles, following an established methodology, and placing findings into the appropriate scholarly context. And, in terms of administrative considerations, we need to ask ourselves if we are ensuring appropriate research preparation and training and if we are training students properly to go through the stages involved in formulating the purpose of the study, collecting the data, and learning how to analyze and write up their findings. Further, we need to ask ourselves where the opportunities for conducting undergraduate research are coming from and if we are making them available to our students. We need to know whether a university or college, a study abroad provider, an individual or institutional grant, a professor, or the student on his or her own is making the opportunity happen, and what the implications of each source of support are. If the research is mentored, we need to know whether the oversight is by a faculty member, a granting agency, the program provider, on-site faculty, or no one at all. If the project is with a faculty member, we need to be clear what the student's role is and whether he or she is merely serving in an administrative capacity or actually doing substantive work through which learning occurs and a meaningful contribution emerges. We need to be clear whether or not students are held accountable for their work upon completion, and how it is assessed for quality and academic creditworthiness. Ideally, the excitement and momentum of the research can be sustained and some recognition and support for further development of the product is provided. Finally, we need to be clear whether or not the product is worthy of serious scholarly attention or has merely been an esoteric exercise that was "fun" but accomplished little else. In many ways all of these considerations boil down to the questions of whether or not the current opportunities the field and individual providers are making available are indeed adequate or need to be further developed, improved, or perhaps replaced with new types of offerings, and where to set the bar for undergraduate research achieved during study abroad.

To begin to address some of the above challenges, and in particular how to evaluate undergraduate research produced abroad, we first need to think about how and when this research can take place, in what form, and with what kind of support. The following figure illustrates the variety of ways in which undergraduate research during study abroad can currently be conducted. The model illustrated in Figure 23.1 below is not meant to be prescriptive but rather descriptive of the current situation.[4]

The above model, influenced by what is currently known and what the preliminary study discussed in the following section will support with data, proposes a way to contextualize undergraduate research during study abroad by looking at three phases during the undergraduate experience: (1) the preparation; (2) the time during study abroad; and (3) what can come of the research upon return. The phases show that there are a variety of scenarios involved in preparing students before they venture abroad; two primarily different ways of undertaking the research while overseas; and several ways the end product can be further developed upon return.

A second way of addressing the challenge of how to best support undergraduate research during study abroad is to know where it fits into the context of higher education research generally. At the first level, faculty and professional researchers conduct funded, basic, and applied research that is generally expected to make a substantive, original, and generalizable contribution to the wider scholarship. At the second level, doctoral and postdoctoral research represents the entry of new scholars into academic or professional inquiry on the expectation that they will contribute to existing scholarship, if not necessarily striking out on new paths of discovery or producing basic research (Lovitts, 2007). At the third level, undergraduate research can incorporate domestic or international independent study, include assisting a faculty member on a project, and even in some cases include gathering data and performing analysis for a major class assignment. This third category ideally provides opportunities for undergraduates to learn the fundamentals of research design and methodology and then utilize these skills in real-life settings such as science laboratories, fieldwork, archives, or any number of other venues (Healey & Jenkins, 2006).

A variety of definitions already exist that have attempted to generally explain what undergraduate research is, although the interpretations differ significantly. Some definitions stress the authenticity of the research experience for first time learners,[5] some place the emphasis

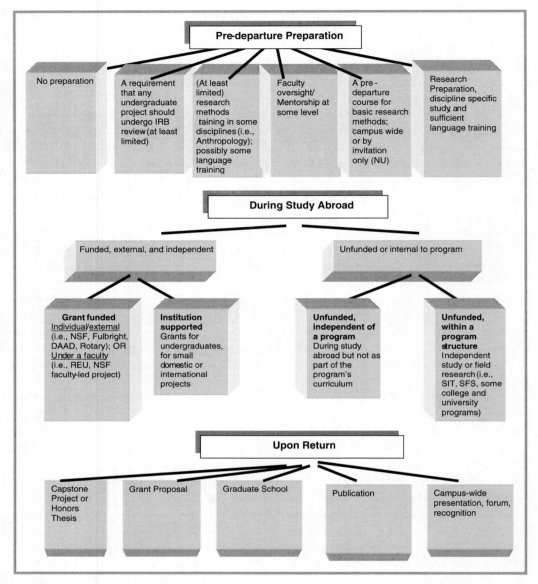

Figure 23.1 *Undergraduate Research During Study Abroad*

on the opportunity for creative exploration,[6] some highlight the importance of mentorship,[7] and still others stress the importance of originality.[8] Each definition regards the experience through a different lens. Stressing originality implies far different expectations for achievement than stressing authenticity of experience or opportunity for creative exploration. A focus on originality is closer to the general standard for doctoral-level dissertation research; a focus on creative exploration and authenticity of experience implies a more student-centered focus; and a focus on mentorship highlights the educative value of the experience and the exchange of experience from expert teacher to novice learner.

Taking each of these definitions and turning our attention now to study abroad in particular, we have further interpretations we should consider. Houlihan (2007) describes three kinds of research abroad: "independent field-based research" conducted by the student for a grade; "collective field-based research" where a student works under the guidance of a faculty member and does research either for a course or for the faculty member's project; and "client-focused, directed, field-based research" where the research serves a community, NGO, or other entity (2007, p. x). Although he does not explicate a direct educational goal with each type of research, Houlihan's focus is clearly on research as experiential, hands-on learning—a ubiquitous theme in the study abroad literature. Neal Sobania and I have previously argued (Streitwieser & Sobania, 2008) that undergraduate research should be guided inquiry prepared with the help of faculty and ideally overseen by a campus institutional review board, monitored throughout, and in the end held accountable for a product such as a presentation, a paper, or some other tangible achievement. Taking each of the above definitions into account and further reflecting on them in light of study abroad being transformative learning toward the development of global citizenship, I propose the following new definition for undergraduate research that is undertaken as part of study abroad:

> Undergraduate research conducted during study abroad should be motivated and led by the student, prepared and assisted with guidance from faculty or on-site program mentors, sanctioned by an institutional review board, and aimed to educate students about rigorous academic inquiry while also allowing them to explore questions of personal interest that contribute to their academic and personal development and potentially advance a relevant scholarly literature.

This definition provides an answer to the important philosophical, procedural, and administrative questions I have posed above. It places the independence of the novice researcher at the core of the research undertaking abroad. However, it also respects and incorporates the important role that institutional oversight and expert mentorship plays in the process. The definition regards the learning experience as the most important focus of research activity abroad, and only secondarily cites making a contribution to the advancement of scholarship as a desired but not required outcome. Indeed, this definition sets the bar high for institutions and program providers and holds out the expectation that work produced will be in the currency of scholars. It expects them to expend considerable effort and take serious responsibility to facilitate a powerful and genuine learning experience abroad, but it does not hold novice learners to the same standard expected of scholars who come to the task with more experience.

THE CURRENT STATE OF THE FIELD: OPPORTUNITIES FOR UNDERGRADUATE RESEARCH DURING STUDY ABROAD

The data that currently exist on the availability of opportunities to engage in research during study abroad, and the kinds of preparation offered, is uneven at best and in many cases nonexistent. The IIEPassport data cited at the beginning of this chapter indicate that a fairly healthy number of respondents to their annual survey offer some form of research opportunity. Of the 7,682 study abroad programs reported, over half (4,324) indicate that they offer an "independent study" or "directed field study" component. These data, however, leave a number of critical questions unanswered: (1) Of the programs that offer "directed field study" or "independent study," how many students in each program actually take advantage of the opportunity? (2) Do any of the programs reporting data (whether university-based or third party provider) offer predeparture research training or on-site guidance for the student conducting research abroad? (3) And, if some kind of predeparture or on-site training or guidance is offered, of what does it consist?

In an effort to get beyond these data, I conducted two preliminary studies to investigate more deeply the issue of support for undergraduate research during study abroad. (1) A short survey was sent out with the assistance of the IIEPassport.org Prospecting Services Division via Survey Monkey in January 2008 to 1,115 study abroad advisers at a large range of U.S. institutions.[9] (2) The Web sites of the U.S.-based membership of the Forum on Education Abroad were also reviewed to tabulate and categorize the type and degree of support each offers for students who wish to conduct research during study abroad.

THE SURVEY STUDY

Four close-ended and one open-ended item were sent out to collect data on (1) how many study abroad programs (university-based or provider) offer research opportunities; (2) how many students take advantage of these opportunities; (3) what the field study or independent study consists of; (4) if students who do this type of research abroad are offered any predeparture training or on-site guidance; and, (5) if so, what that training consists of. In the survey, "research," was explained as any inquiry conducted by the student during time abroad, whether within a program, under a faculty member's project, supported by an individual grant, or even undertaken for credit or noncredit, as long as it is likely to result in some kind of tangible product that provides meaning to the experience, such as an honors thesis, a grant application, a student publication or a formal presentation.

Among the respondents to the survey, 28% represented large public universities or colleges; 22.5% small private universities or colleges; and 14% small public universities or colleges. Twenty-one percent classified themselves as nonprofit "third party" providers and 5.6% as for-profit study abroad providers. The "other" category accounted for 2.8% of respondents. While the survey was not successful in gleaning answers to the question of exactly how many students from each responding institution conduct research abroad among the total population studying abroad, the information about research training that came back and what it consists of was very interesting indeed.

In terms of the survey item, "How is the research your students undertake conducted?" the data revealed that where and how students conduct research varied considerably. The largest percentage of students (62.8%) who conduct research abroad do so within a program that supports research as part of the general program curriculum. After that, 48.7% conduct research with the backing of their home institution but not within the program's curriculum itself. That finding is supported by later data in the survey, which find accompanying faculty mentorship to be the most prevalent type of institutional support that students receive. A total of 33.3% of students conducts research with the approval of their program provider; but, again, not as part of the program's regular curriculum and not for regular program credit. A smaller percentage (16.7%), conducts research as part of a faculty member's project. Finally, the same percentage of students (11.1%) conducts research with individual funding as do those without it. Figure 23.2 below shows the variety of ways in which students undertake their research.

The survey item asking, "If your institution supports undergraduate research during study abroad, what form does this support take?" found that faculty mentorship provides by far the most prevalent form of institutional support for students who plan to conduct research abroad

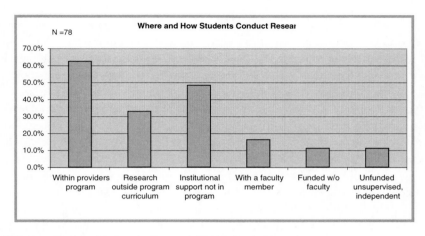

Figure 23.2 *How Students Undertake Research During Study Abroad*

(67.9%). The second two most likely sources of support—research information provided via Web links versus institutional review board (IRB) oversight—were reported in the same magnitude (26.9%), which is ironic in that the type of assistance they provide differs so dramatically. This finding is particularly interesting given that the first source of support lacks any oversight component while the second embodies the most rigorous type of oversight an institution can provide. In terms of more active training provided to students, 23.1% of respondents indicated that a research methods course is one of their study abroad prerequisites; 20.5% indicated offering a predeparture course of several class meetings that includes training for research abroad; and 10.3% indicated offering one workshop aimed at research preparation. Finally, 16.7% of respondents indicated that they currently do not offer any research training and have no plans to do so in the future, while a much smaller percentage, 2.6%, indicated having nothing at the moment but planning to offer some type support (unspecified) soon. Figure 23.3 below shows the variety of preparation offered for conducting research during study abroad.

Finally, the last survey item, "If any kind of predeparture or on-site training or guidance is offered please briefly describe," found a range of ways that responding institutions support independent research. Among the 51 responses to this open ended item, the following categories

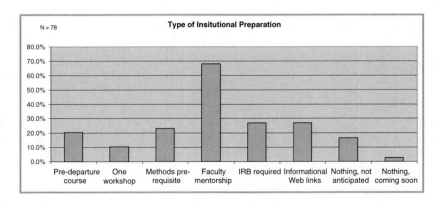

Figure 23.3 *Variety of Preparation Offered for Conducting Research During Study Abroad.*

emerged. A predeparture research preparation course involving several sessions; a single prede-parture workshop or seminar addressing research interests; home institution or on-site faculty mentoring; a discussion of research issues included in the on-site orientation (although how thor-oughly was not clear from the data); research opportunities through a program course; meeting one-on-one with students interested in research; and providing research resources. In terms of the last type of support—research resources, these take the form of online information, hand-outs, reading materials, or even e-mail consultations and in one case an "online response system." Unfortunately, the data did not specify how detailed the e-mail consultation or online response system was in terms of research guidance.

The answers to the open ended items also revealed some more unique arrangements for ways that respondents indicate supporting student research. In some cases institutions require that outbound students fulfill certain predeparture requirements, and choosing a research methods course if they intend to undertake research abroad is one way of doing that. At other institutions, support for students who are interested in research abroad is offered on a customized basis or under special circumstances as solicited by the student him- or herself. In such cases, the data indicates that the director of the campus international or study abroad office may provide the consultation or support. In other cases, study abroad programs may offer "research internships" in which some training will be provided at the local organization hosting the intern interested in research of the organization. This activity would likely be characterized as participant–observer research or action research, in which the student plays both the role of intern working in the organization and also outside objective observer (Patton, 2002). Finally, some support offered by institutions seems to suggest that it is dependent on essentially preexisting factors, such as whether the research has secured funding or the project is deemed to require preparatory train-ing. Along those lines, in another case a more careful approach dictates that students are not permitted to embark on a research study directly upon arrival but only after several months of acclimating to the setting, selecting a research site, and gaining permission for the project after the plans have been assessed.

Unfortunately, the overall response rate to the survey was relatively poor: 95 respondents out of a potential pool of 1,115; less than 10%, which may indicate that many may simply have noth-ing to contribute or, worse, have no interest in supporting undergraduate research. Also, those surveyed only represent a small number of the entire IIEPassport database that is surveyed on an annual basis, thus many potential respondents were not contacted. Even so, considering the fact that this type of data has not been collected previously may provide some useful insights of value to those considering incorporating a research component into their programming in the future.

THE WEB SITE STUDY[10]

In order to further mine the numbers suggested by the IIEPassport, a second small study was conducted in the winter of 2008 to look at stated support for research abroad among the study abroad and international office Web sites of the 191 U.S. Members of the Forum on Education Abroad.[11] The Forum's total 275 members represent roughly 75% of students who study abroad each year (Whalen, 2007a). Specifically, we looked at the types of research opportunities avail-able for undergraduates based on the information provided on each institution's Web pages.[12] After reviewing all sites we classified the information into three general categories: (1) institu-tions or providers that do not appear to offer any information for conducting research abroad;

(2) institutions or providers that appear to offer only limited information and links to information about research abroad but do not include detailed language about such opportunities; and (3) institutions or providers that offer extensive information for students who wish to conduct research abroad.

Among the 191 sites studied, 48% (91) did not include any language for students interested in study abroad research; 34% (66) included limited information or links to research information but often it was only geared toward graduate students or faculty but did not include information for undergraduates about preparatory courses or research training; and 18% (34) provided what I considered to be extensive information on policies, research resources, and preparatory courses. There was considerable variation among the sites providing some information. Sites with extensive information included downloadable pdf documents with detailed instructions and policies for conducting research abroad, links to the names of students who could be contacted for information, extensive and relevant information about grants and scholarships for undergraduates, and information about specific workshops or preparatory courses available. Sites with limited information often only noted that research was possible and then provided links to external grants and scholarships, or sometimes provided an official statement that research could be approved and then simply guided students to an office or contact person. In the least informative cases, some funding sources might be listed but these often were only for faculty or graduate students.

This modest review and snapshot of U.S. Forum member study abroad or international office Web sites indicates that nearly half of the institutions and providers studied do not provide any information at all for students interested in conducting research abroad and only one fifth provide extensive information. That is, only a relatively small number of institutions appear to aggressively promote undergraduate research abroad and make the necessary and relevant information available. Finally, the provision of specific training workshops or research courses for study abroad students still only seem to be rarely offered (Streitwieser & Leephaibul, 2007).

CONCLUSION

Research opportunities for undergraduates during study abroad—if prepared carefully and guided throughout—can have a positive impact on increasing the academic rigor and profile of current study abroad programming. The growth of these opportunities should be encouraged in the future. The discussion and data presented above illustrate that undergraduate research opportunities during study abroad exist, are regarded as important, and have the potential to become a more regular part of study abroad programming but at the moment remain relatively uncommon. The field should ask itself what this component of study abroad has the potential to become in the future and what its further development implies for undergraduate education in general and study abroad in particular.

Supporting undergraduates to succeed in carrying out appropriate research during study abroad involves numerous challenges of which the field should be aware, including the responsibility to provide the necessary training and institutional support. Those in the field who promote undergraduate research during study abroad need to be aware of what is involved to do it correctly. The field also needs to consider the potential liability institutions and providers may face if it is not done appropriately. It is irresponsible and potentially damaging to all involved to put students into a foreign context to conduct research without providing them with the necessary preparation first (Streitwieser & Sobania, 2008). In that vein, undergraduate research abroad should not become an opportunity for voyeurism or be seen merely as a chance to shock or provoke through misguided projects that lack the necessary preparation (Streitwieser, 2007). And conducting a research project during study abroad should not be a blanket requirement of all students. Indeed, having all students undertake carefully prepared and guided research abroad is neither logistically possible nor advisable as a learning goal. Paul Houlihan notes from his experience as President of the School for Field Studies that many on-site faculty and staff report that their main challenge is helping American students prepare for and understand the steps involved in a research study since many of them appear to lack quantitative or qualitative research training (2007). Many institutions today proudly and publicly tout goals of internationalizing their campus and transforming students into empowered "global citizens," but the framework for bringing about the outcomes they seek through rigorous campus programming seems often to be missing. Thus, what really lies behind this grand advertising rhetoric is far from obvious and infrequently supported by substance (Horn, Hendel, & Fry, 2007). If we are to successfully develop global citizens it is implied that we must teach and prepare students to successfully and respectfully interact with cultural Others, but this takes concerted effort and dedication.

As alluded to earlier in this chapter, several hurdles currently challenge the field to create more opportunities for responsible research within general study abroad curricula. One of the most important of these is the need for greater oversight from upper-level administrators and their financial and moral support to improve study abroad programming and synthesize it better with the core academic mission of the institution or organization. This argument has been made repeatedly and on several fronts. In a paper published in the study abroad journal *Frontiers: The Interdisciplinary Journal of Study Abroad*, Bolen and Martin in 2005 argued that:

> If undergraduate research is endorsed by the highest academic officers of our institutions, our Presidents, Provosts, and Academic Deans, faculty are more likely to provide encouragement and support, and then students will be more likely to pursue these options. International educators can assist these efforts by creating programs that offer research options, advertising such programs, and, most importantly, finding funding sources for such efforts. (p. xiii)

A similar statement was made more recently by NAFSA: Association of International Educators, in its 2008 report, *Strengthening Study Abroad: Recommendations for Effective Institutional Management for Presidents, Senior Administrators, and Study Abroad Professionals*:

> Like any other rapidly expanding activity, study abroad needs the attention of top campus leaders to ensure that it is integrated into the academic program; operates in a fashion that is consistent with sound business practices related to contracting, risk management, and accountability; and serves the needs of students. Getting that balance right is ultimately the responsibility of institutional leadership. (p. 1)

However, the call to more actively facilitate research opportunities for undergraduates must in fact emanate not only from the top but ideally from all levels, the highest administrative cadres down to the thousands of academics and practitioners who are employed on a daily basis with creating programs and opportunities that ensure study abroad stands up to scrutiny as a serious academic undertaking.

All of the points raised in this chapter lead to the obvious question, then, of how the field should move forward with regard to appropriately fostering quality undergraduate research opportunities during study abroad. Some suggestions for developing appropriate and high quality undergraduate research abroad include the following:

- Help students to propose manageable projects. A chronic tendency of undergraduates proposing projects that will be longer than the standard term paper is that ideas tend to be grand and over ambitious, and the framework and literature within which to place the study is ill conceived if stated at all, and little consideration is given to cost, resources, and timeline. Advisers of undergraduate research projects thus need to assist students in crafting a project proposal that will be manageable in scope given the time they will spend abroad, the time they will have to undertake research amidst all of their other activities, the material and human resources they will have available, and their level of experience as beginning researchers collecting data for the first time. Manageability of the project is also important so that students do not feel overwhelmed by the task since making cultural adjustments by themselves will already present challenges.
- Provide predeparture training on proposal development, research methodology, and research ethics. This is essential if we are to expect quality work and hold students to academically rigorous standards of excellence.
- Require students to answer a series of questions that will help them articulate how their research will be relevant to others besides themselves.
- Require students to conduct a literature review and learn as much as possible about the research setting and the specific question(s) they plan to investigate before they leave.
- Require that students have their projects vetted before departure through some form of institutional review. Having students go through this process gives them an opportunity to learn about research, to carefully think through their projects, and to form a relationship with a faculty member or other adviser who can advise them throughout.
- Provide students with a faculty mentor from their home institution, open communication with their study abroad office or third party provider, and on-site mentoring.
- Especially if the topic is of a potentially sensitive nature, urge students to work with the help of an organization or expert in the country who can provide on-the-ground support, guidance, and if necessary protection.
- Give students the chance to publicly share their research upon returning home as a way to build in accountability, support the further development of the research, and provide affirmation for their effort.

Finally, some very strong study abroad program models already exist that either have research components at their core or offer carefully structured research opportunities within or alongside their general curriculum. Among a number of laudatory programs are many of those run by the School for International Training (SIT), the School for Field Studies (SFS), and some of the programs run by the Council on International Educational Exchange (CIEE), in addition to enterprising college and university-run study abroad programs that have built-in research opportunities. Unfortunately, it is not within the scope of this chapter to review these laudatory programs in detail, nor to share the noteworthy accomplishments of many of its students. However, these models are worth careful study as templates for future research programs. The arguments I have been making in support of increasing undergraduate research opportunities during abroad are illustrated best by a brief review of some of the eclectic student research projects published annually in special issues of the journal, *Frontiers*. [13]

- Haba na Haba and the Use of Drama for Community Use and Development
- Uruguay's Choice: Boost the Economy or Bust the Environment: An Investigation of the Various Aspects of Botnia
- Nipe Nikupe: Dependency, Reciprocity, and Paradoxes of Food Aid in Lugufu Refugee Camp
- France says "Non": Elites, Publics and the Defeat of the EU Constitutional Treaty
- The Faces of Globalization

These projects give but a mere glimpse into the diversity of subject matter that students who have chosen to conduct research abroad have addressed. As supporters of undergraduate research, scholars and practitioners of study abroad have much to consider in deciding how to most effectively facilitate the type of undergraduate research that will lead to transformative learning experiences for students and their development as global citizens. This chapter has made the case that there are clear links between undergraduate research abroad (the deep study of an aspect of a foreign culture), civic engagement (learning about and sometimes becoming involved in issues of importance to communities), and global citizenship (developing a commitment to acting as future agents of change within society's larger social fabric). Even if undergraduate research during study abroad may not be appropriate or possible for every student, it can make an important difference for those students who seek deeper engagement experiences. Dedicated planners, administrators, faculty, and researchers engaged in facilitating study abroad for students share the opportunity to build the essential skills of the next generation. It lies within their power to help students lucky enough to have a study abroad learning opportunity come to better understand the world, interact more harmoniously with other cultures, and together respond in innovative ways to the daunting challenges we will all face in the future.

NOTES

1. Special thanks to Gregory Light, Marina Micari, Amy Knife Gould, and Nick Seamons for feedback on earlier drafts.
2. Please note: these figures do not include campus-based initiatives open only to students at a given university, nor increased numbers of students who enroll directly in foreign university degree programs.
3. Some examples of grants supporting undergraduates domestic or international research include, among others: Research Experiences for Undergraduates (REU) grants from the National Science Foundation; Howard Hughes Medical Institute grants through individual colleges and universities; Science Undergraduate Laboratory Internships (SULI) at the Ames Laboratory; the Summer Research Opportunities Program (SROP) grants from the Committee on Institutional Cooperation (CIC); the Freeman Asia Scholarships for study in Asia; National Security Education Program Boren Scholarships for study of regions critical to U.S. national security interests; German Academic Exchange Service fellowships for study in Germany; Research Internships in Science and Engineering (RISE) grants from the German Academic Exchange Service; European Undergraduate Research Opportunities (Euroscholars) grants; Critical Language Scholarships for Intensive Summer Institutes.
4. Special thanks to Dr. Bradley Zakarin for his help discussing and developing the model.
5. "The undergraduate research experience [is] a concept that integrates the authenticity of research with the education of novice students" (Lopatto, as cited in Taraban, 2008, p. 4).
6. "Any creative effort undertaken by an undergraduate that advances the knowledge of the student in an academic discipline and that leads to new scholarly insights or the creation of new works that adds to the wealth of the discipline" (East Tennessee State University, retrieved February 29, 2008, from http://www.etsu.edu/honors/research/what.asp).
7. "Excellent undergraduate opportunities in discovery-, inquiry-, and creativity-based scholarship through mentored research experiences with NC State faculty and other national and international scholars and

8. "An inquiry or investigation conducted by an undergraduate student that makes an original intellectual or creative contribution to the discipline." Retrieved July 14,2007, from http://www.cur.org/about.html

9. The survey was also distributed via the SECUSS-L listserv to its 3,200 subscribers; posted on the Forum on Education Abroad's "Discussion" page and distributed to the members of the Forum on Education Abroad's Outcomes Committee for wider dissemination to colleagues.

10. Special thanks to Matthew Nusko and Sasha Hempel for their help with the data collection.

11. Since the Forum adds new members on a regular basis, only the sites of members listed as of the end of December 2008, could be studied. Nine institutional sites were excluded because they were under construction at the time.

12. One obvious limitation to this data is that while support for undergraduate research may not have appeared on the institution's study abroad or international office Web site, the institution itself may still in fact support undergraduate research activities abroad through a research office, academic department, or even individual faculty member. This study only tabulated information as it appeared on the given institution's international education office Web site.

13. For full project descriptions and supporting programs, see special issues 12, 14, 16 of the journal, Frontiers and the latest 2008 Forum on Education Abroad Undergraduate Research Award winners: Retrieved February 3, 2009, from http://www.forumea.org/research-awards.htm

---

REFERENCES

Altbach, P. G. (2004). Higher education crosses borders: Can the United States remain the top destination for foreign students? *Change, 36*(2), 18–24.

Altbach, P.G. (2006a). The costs and benefits of world-class universities. In P. G. Altbach (Ed.), *International higher education: Reflections on policy and practice* (pp. 71–76). Boston: Center for International Higher Education.

Altbach, P. G. (2006b). Internationalize American higher education? Not exactly. In P. Altbach (Ed.), *International higher education: Reflections on policy and practice* (pp. 63–67). Boston: Center for International Higher Education.

American Association of Colleges and Universities. (2007). *College learning for a new global century: A report by the National Leadership Council for Liberal Education and America's Promise*. Washington, DC: Author.

American Council on Education. (2008). *College-bound students' interests in study abroad and other international learning activities*. Washington, DC: Author, Art & Science Group, and the College Board.

Bauer, K. W., & Bennett, J. S. (2003). Alumni perceptions used to assess undergraduate research experience. *Journal of Higher Education, 74*, 210–230.

Blanton, R. L., (2008). A brief history of undergraduate research, with consideration of its alternative futures. In R. Taraban & R. L. Blanton, (Eds.), *Creating effective undergraduate research programs in science* (pp. 233–246). New York: Teachers College Press.

Bok, D. (2006). *Our underachieving colleges: A candid look at how much students learn and why they should be learning more*. Princeton, NJ: Princeton University Press.

Bolen, M., & Martin, P. (2005). Undergraduate research abroad: Challenges and rewards [Special Issue]. *Frontiers: The Interdisciplinary Journal of Study Abroad, 12*, xi–xvi.

Boyer Commission on Educating Undergraduates in the Research University. (1998). *Reinventing undergraduate education: A blueprint for America's research universities*. State University of New York, Stony Brook, NY. Retrieved February 3, 2009, from http://naples.cc.sunysb.edu/Pres/boyer.nsf/webform/contents

Byers, M. (2007). *Intent for a nation: What is Canada for?* Vancouver /Toronto: Douglas & McIntyre.

Colby, A., Ehrlich, T., Beaumont, E., & Stephens, J. (2003). *Educating citizens: Preparing America's undergraduates for lives of moral and civic responsibility*. San Francisco: Jossey-Bass.

Dessoff, A. (2006, March/April). Who's not going abroad. *International Educator, XV*(2), 20–27.

Dobbert, M. L. L. (1998). The impossibility of internationalizing students by adding material to courses. In J. A. Mestenhauser & B. J. Ellinboe, (Eds.), *Reforming the higher education curriculum: Internationalizing the campus* (pp. 53–68). Phoenix, AZ: American Council on Higher Education.

Fitzsimmons, S. J., Carlson, K., Kerpelman, L. C., & Stoner, D. (1990). *A preliminary evaluation of the research experiences for undergraduates (REU) program of the National Science Foundation*. Washington, DC: National Science Foundation.

Fortenberry, N. L. (1998). Integration of research and curriculum. *Council on Undergraduate Research Quarterly*, *XIX*(2), 54–61.

Forum on Education Abroad. (2008). *Code of ethics*. Retrieved October 14, 2008, from http://www. forumea.org/documents/ForumonEducationAbroadCodeofEthics.pdf

Forum on Education Abroad. (2006). *State of the field survey*. Carlisle, PA: Dickinson College.

Garde-Hanson, J., & Calvert, B. (2007). Developing a research culture in the undergraduate curriculum. *Active Learning in Higher Education*, 8(2), 105–116.

Gonzalez, C. (2001). Undergraduate research, graduate mentoring, and the university's mission. *Science, 293*, 1624–1626.

Green, M. F., Luu, D., & Burris, B. (2008). *Mapping internationalization on U.S. campuses: 2008 edition*. Washington, DC: American Council on Education.

Green, M. F., Hesel, R. A., & Bartini, M. (2008). *College-bound students' interest in study abroad and other international learning activities*. Washington, DC: American Council on Education.

Hakim, T. (1998). Soft assessment of undergraduate research: Reactions and student perceptions. *Council of Undergraduate Research Quarterly*, *XVII*(4), 189–192.

Hathaway, R., Nagda, B., & Gregerman, S. (2002). The relationship of undergraduate research participation to graduate and professional education pursuit: An empirical study. *Journal of College Student Development, 43*, 614–631.

Healey, M., & Jenkins, A. (2007). Strengthening the teaching–research linkage in undergraduate courses and programs. *New Directions for Teaching and Learning, 10*(107), 45–55.

Horn, A., Hendel, D., & Fry, G. (2007). Ranking the international dimension of top research universities in the United States. *Journal of Studies in International Education, 11*, 330–358.

Houlihan, P. (2007). Supporting undergraduates in conducting field-based research: A perspective from on-site faculty and staff [Special Issue]. *Frontiers: The Interdisciplinary Journal of Study Abroad, 14*, ix–xv.

Hu, S, Kuh, G. D., & Gayles, J. G. (2007). Engaging undergraduate students in research activities: Are research universities doing a better job? *Innovative Higher Education, 32*(3), 167–177.

Hunter, A-B, Laursen, S. L., & Seymour, E. (2006) Becoming a scientist: The role of undergraduate research in students' cognitive, personal and professional development. *Science Education 91*, 36–74.

Institute of International Education (IIE). (2007–2008). *IIEPassport academic year abroad, 2007–2008* (36th ed.). New York: Author. Retrieved February 3, 2009, from http://IIEPassport.org

Institute of International Education (IIE). (n.d.). *IIEPassport study abroad funding*. Retrieved February 3, 2009, from http://www.studyabroadfunding.org/articles/scholarship_release.html

Kallgren, C. A., & Tauber, R. T. (1996). Undergraduate research and the institutional review board: A mismatch or happy marriage? *Teaching of Psychology, 23*(1), 20–25.

Kardash, C. M. 2000. Evaluation of an undergraduate research experience: Perceptions of undergraduate interns and their faculty mentors. *Journal of Educational Psychology, 92*(1), 191–201.

Katkin, W. (2003). The Boyer Commission Report and its impact on undergraduate research. *New Directions for Teaching and Learning, 93*, 19–38.

Kremer, J., & Bringle, R. (1990). The effects of an intensive research experience on the careers of talented undergraduates. *Journal of Research and Development in Education, 24*(1), 1–5.

Lewin, T. (2008, March 9). Lawsuit takes aim at college's billing practices for study abroad. *The New York Times*. Retrieved July 29, 2008, from http://www.nytimes.com/2008/03/09/education/09studyabroad.html

Light, G., & Calkins, S. (2007, April). *Academic learning: Integrating faculty conceptions of research and teaching*. Paper presented at the American Educational Research Association Annual Conference, Chicago, IL.

Lopatto, D. (2003). The essential features of undergraduate research. *Council on Undergraduate Research Quarterly, 24*, 139–142.

Lopatto, D. (2004). Survey of undergraduate research experiences (SURE): First findings. *Cell Biology Education, 3*, 270–277.

Lovitts, B. (2007). *Making the implicit explicit: Creating performance expectations for the dissertation*. Sterling, VA: Stylus.

Lutterman-Aguilar, A., & Gingerich, O. (2002). Experiential pedagogy for study abroad: educating for global citizenship. *Frontiers: The Interdisciplinary Journal of Study Abroad, 8*, 41–82.

Meyer-Lee, E., & Evans, J. (2007). Areas of study in outcomes assessment. In M. Bolen (Ed.), *A guide to outcomes assessment in education abroad* (pp. 61–70). Carlisle, PA: The Forum on Education Abroad.

Mezirow, J. (1983). A critical theory of adult learning and education. In M. Tight (Ed.), *Adult learning and education* (pp. 124–138). London: Croom Helm.

Mogk, D.W. (1993). Undergraduate research experiences as preparation for graduate study in geology. *Journal of Geology Education, 41*, 126–128.

NAFSA: Association of International Educators. (2008). *Strengthening study abroad: Recommendations for effective institutional management for presidents, senior administrators, and study abroad professionals* (Report of the Task Force on Institutional Management of Study Abroad). Washington, DC: Author.

Nagda, B. A., Greggerman, S. R., Jonides, J., von Hippel, W., & Lerner, J. S. (1998). Undergraduate student-faculty research partnerships affect student retention. *Review of Higher Education, 22,* 55–72.

National Survey of Student Engagement (NSSE). (2007). *Experiences that matter: Enhancing student learning and success.* Bloomington: Indiana University Center for Postsecondary Research.

Ogden, A. (2007–2008). The view from the veranda: Understanding today's colonial student. *Frontiers: The Interdisciplinary Journal of Study Abroad, 15,* 35–56.

Pappano, L. (2007, November 4). The foreign legions. *The New York Times Education Life.* Retrieved July 29, 2008, from http://www.nytimes.com/2007/11/04/education/edlife/studyabroad.html

Pascarella, E. T., & Terenzini, P. T. (2005). *How college affects students: A third decade of research.* San Francisco: Wiley.

Patton, M. Q. (2002). *Qualitative research and evaluation methods* (3rd ed.). Thousand Oaks, CA: Sage.

Paul, E. L. (2006 Winter). Community-based research as scientific and civic pedagogy. *Peer Review,* 12–15.

Rauckhorst, W. H., Czaja, J. A., & Baxter Magolda, M. (2001, July). *Measuring the impact of the undergraduate research experience on student intellectual development.* Paper presented at Project Kaleidoscope Summer Institute, Snowbird, UT.

Schemo, J. D. (2007a, August 13). In study abroad, gifts and money for universities. *The New York Times.* Retrieved July 29, 2008, from http://www.nytimes.com/2007/08/13/education/13abroad.html

Schemo, J. D. (2007b, August 16). Study abroad is new focus of inquiry into perks. *The New York Times.* Retrieved July 29, 2008, from http://travel.nytimes.com/2007/08/16/education/16abroad.html

Shubert, A. (2008, February). *Global citizenship and study abroad: North of 49.* Presentation at the annual meeting of the Association of International Education Administrators, Washington, DC.

Streitwieser, B. (2007, November). *Shock value vs. academic value: Undergraduate study abroad research.* Presentation at the Council for the International Exchange of Students (CIEE) Annual Conference, Toronto, Canada.

Streitwieser, B., & Leephaibul, R. (2007). Enhancing the study abroad experience through independent research in Germany. *Die Unterrichtspraxis-Teaching German, 40*(2), 164–170.

Streitwieser, B., & Sobania, N. (2008). Overseeing study abroad research: Challenges, responsibilities, and the institutional review board. *Frontiers: The Interdisciplinary Journal of Study Abroad, 16,* 1–16.

Taraban, R. (2008). What is undergraduate research and why should we support it? In R. Taraban & R. L. Blanton (Eds.), *Creating effective undergraduate research programs in science* (pp. 3–10). New York: Teachers College Press.

Taraban, R., & Blanton, R. L. (Eds.). (2008). *Creating effective undergraduate research programs in science: The transition from student to scientist.* New York: Teachers College Press.

Taylor, E. (1994). Intercultural competency: A transformative learning process. *Adult Education Quarterly, 44*(3), 154–174.

Tomovic, M. M. (1994). Undergraduate research—Prerequisite for successful lifelong learning. *ASEE Annual Conference Proceedings, 1,* 1469–1470.

U.S. Department of Education. (2006). *A test of leadership: Charting the future of U.S. higher education.* Washington, DC: Author.

Whalen, B. (2007a). The management and funding of US study abroad. *International Higher Education, 50,* 15–16.

Whalen, B. (2007b, November). *Shock value vs. academic value: Study abroad and undergraduate research. Introductory remarks.* Presentation at the Council for the International Exchange of Students (CIEE) Annual Conference, Toronto, Canada.

Woolf, M. (2007). Impossible things before breakfast: Myths in education abroad. *Journal of Studies in International Education, 11*(2), 496–509.

Zydney, A. L., Bennett, J. S., Shahid, A., & Bauer, K. W. (2002). Impact of undergraduate research experience in engineering. *Journal of Engineering Education, 91,* 151–157.

Part Four

Innovative Global Citizenship Study Abroad Program Models

Georgia Tech's Comprehensive and Integrated Approach to Developing Global Competence

Howard Rollins[1]

Georgia Institute of Technology

In 2003, a group of faculty and administrators at the Georgia Institute of Technology (Georgia Tech) began to discuss and plan for a new more comprehensive and coherent approach to international education for undergraduates. The goal of this initiative was to produce globally competent undergraduates. We had in mind a program that would prepare our graduates as global citizens but also, and importantly, prepare them for global careers within their disciplinary major. This disciplinary emphasis reflects the belief that, in the future, all career paths will of necessity involve working in a global context. After more than 2 years of discussion and planning and with the approval of all faculty committees and all levels of the administration, Georgia Tech launched this new initiative, the International Plan, in the fall of 2005. The International Plan has received significant national recognition. It earned Georgia Tech honorable mention for the Heiskell Award in 2006 (Thompson, 2006) for Innovation in Internationalization and in 2007, it was a central piece in receipt of the Senator Paul Simon Internationalization Award by NAFSA (Schock, 2007).

Of course, a major component of the International Plan is the requirement that students study abroad or engage in other international activities outside the United States. However, the International Plan is a more comprehensive approach to developing global competence that includes additional requirements beyond study abroad prior to departure, while abroad, and upon return to campus. It is the view at Georgia Tech that study abroad alone is an important but not sufficient component to prepare globally competent graduates.

The present chapter provides a comprehensive description of the International Plan in four parts. First, we explore the problems with alternative efforts to prepare globally competent students. Why launch an entirely new program and why include study abroad as a necessary but not sufficient element of that new program? Second, we examine the definitions of "competence" in general and "global competence" in particular. What constituent elements are required to prepare globally competent students? Third, the International Plan is described and its components tied systematically to the global competencies we wished to achieve. In this section, the development and implementation of the plan is also discussed. How was the international plan developed and implemented? What issues surfaced and how were these addressed? Finally, in the fourth section, the preliminary outcomes of the International Plan are reported. Are we attracting students to the plan? To what extent have the colleges and schools at Georgia Tech joined the plan? Are student participants obtaining the required international coursework and experiences? What can we say at this early stage about whether International plan students are developing global competence? Are there less direct ways that the International Plan has impacted the broader community of Georgia Tech students –broader interest in study abroad for example? Is Georgia Tech attracting a different group of students as a result of the international plan–students with higher qualifications or with broader interests? What are the lessons for future efforts like the International Plan?

RATIONALE FOR INTERNATIONAL PLAN

At the time that discussions began in 2003 about establishing a new international education program, Georgia Tech, like many other universities in the United States and elsewhere, had already established a variety of international education programs, including study abroad, and these programs were very successful. In academic year, 2002–2003, a total of 877 Georgia Tech students participated in overseas programs representing almost 34% of the undergraduate degrees awarded that year. This record placed Georgia Tech among the top research universities in the country in percentage of students studying abroad (Institute of International Education [IIE], 2003). We have an even loftier goal going forward that 50% of graduates have overseas experience. We believe that the International Plan will help us achieve this goal.

However, the fact that Georgia Tech has respectable numbers of students studying abroad does not guarantee that any are becoming globally competent. There are several reasons for this: First, 79% participated in faculty-led short-term, mainly summer study abroad programs lasting 6 to 11 weeks. Such short-term programs, while documented to have some beneficial effects (Dwyer, 2004; Sutton & Rubin, 2004), may not develop the deep understanding and sensitivity about another culture that we believe is the hallmark of global competence. Many of these programs follow the "island model" where the students live together, are taught by faculty members from Georgia Tech, and thereby have limited contact with the local cultures. Many of these programs are offered in English-speaking countries. With the exception of language-based programs, faculty-led programs in non-English-speaking countries are also taught in English with no requirement for learning the language of the host country prior to study abroad.

Second, the programs in which most students participate are not well integrated into their disciplinary major. Students are not learning much about their own discipline as practiced in the host country. For example, a course in mechanical engineering taught by a U.S. faculty member to U.S. students does not necessarily instill knowledge about the practice of that discipline in the host country. Students also do not usually gain hands-on experience with their major as it is practiced within the host country either from host country faculty or by interning in host country offices, labs, or industries. In 2002–2003, for example, only a handful of students participated in a work abroad experience in their discipline.

Finally, students in many majors (e.g., science and engineering) often cannot afford to interrupt the rigorous curriculum in their major in order to take courses abroad that are not relevant to that curriculum. A survey of 417 of our first and second year students undertaken in 2004 indicated that 91% of students would like to study abroad but 66% indicated that there were no courses available in the major, 61% indicated that study abroad was too expensive, and 42% indicated a concern for an increase in time to graduation (Georgia Institute of Technology, 2005, p 16). In summary, Georgia Tech students, like the students at many other U.S. institutions, preferred short-term programs to semester- or year-long programs and felt that there were significant barriers to study abroad including the failure to integrate study abroad into the curriculum of the major. We came to the conclusion that simply sending students to spend a period of time studying in another country, especially as it is typically done, is not sufficient, in and of itself, to produce graduates who are globally competent.

Georgia Tech, much like many other U.S. universities, also offers students many on-campus international programs such as international minors and certificates (e.g., in international affairs and Asian affairs), second language instruction (eight foreign languages), and hundreds of courses with international content. However, students are offered this large menu of international options with no coherent explanation about how or what to choose. Students seeking a minor or certificate in international affairs are not required to study a foreign language or to study abroad and students in most disciplines are offered opportunities to study abroad, learn a language, take international courses, or obtain a minor or certificate in international affairs without regard to how these activities would relate to, or integrate with, studies within the major. Before the development of the International Plan, there was no general consensus across colleges and even among disciplines within a college about what such a coherent and integrated program should include.

GLOBAL COMPETENCE

The advisory committee that considered how Georgia Tech might develop globally competent graduates recognized early that an important first step in this process was to come to a consensus about our understanding of the term *global competence*. Georgia Tech has a long-standing culture that emphasizes the importance of learning outside the classroom. This concept of "learning by doing" is reflected in the fact that Georgia Tech has more students involved in optional co-op (alternating semesters of work and study) than any other university in the country (Mathews, 2007), by the strong emphasis on undergraduate involvement in research collaborations with faculty, and by participation in internships. The underlying rationale for this approach is that knowledge alone is not sufficient to prepare a student for implementing that knowledge in the real world. According to psychologists Wagner and Sternberg (1985), developing expertise in a domain requires tacit knowledge that "usually is not directly taught or spoken about, in contrast to knowledge directly taught in classrooms" (pp. 438–439). According to Sternberg et al. (2000), tacit knowledge is action oriented, is acquired by everyday experiences, and is used to solve practical problems in which the information needed to solve the problem is incomplete. Regardless of discipline, hands-on experience designed to develop the necessary disciplinary skills must be added to the base of knowledge.

In addition to knowledge and skill acquisition, competence within a domain often also requires the student to develop certain attitudes and beliefs about that domain. Humanities students must understand the theoretical underpinnings of their discipline. Social, physical, and biological scientists must maintain a strictly objective approach to research. Engineers must learn how to approach solutions to practical problems given the complexities of the real world in which those solutions must work. A person fully competent in any domain, then, would be expected to demonstrate all three of these aspects of competence: knowledge, tacit knowledge based on appropriate skills developed from practice, and appropriate attitudes and beliefs relevant to successful practice in the real world. While three characteristics of competence

425

might vary in importance across different disciplines, each component is necessary within any academic discipline.

These general characteristics of competence should also apply to the particular domain of global competence. A number of authors have described global competence in ways that are consistent with this analysis. Hunter, White, and Godbey (2006) provide an excellent recent review of efforts to define global competence. As Hunter et al. point out the term *global competence* is a contested concept (Gallie, 1956), one which has many definitions, each of which depends on the particular context (Hunter et al., 2006, p. 268). Indeed, most publications on the topic and most universities interested in global competence have developed unique definitions. Recent efforts have also been made to define global competence based on research with international experts in which a Delphi technique or surveys are used (Deardorff, 2006; Hunter et al., 2006). While there are many approaches to, and definitions of, global competence, most share common elements. Most include various types of international knowledge such as understanding globalization and world history (Hunter et al., 2006, p. 279); "familiarity with the major currents of global change" (Brustein, 2007, p. 1); "general knowledge of history and world events—politics, economics, geography" and "expertise in another language, culture, country" (American Council on International Intercultural Education conference, 1996, p. 3) or "knowledge of culture, geography, history, and language" (Barker, 2000, p. 3). Most definitions also prescribe the acquisition of global skills such as "awareness and adaptability to diverse cultures," "capacity for effective communication across cultural and linguistic boundaries" (Brustein, 2007, p. 1); and "intercultural skills and direct experience" (American Council on International Intercultural Education conference, 2006, p. 3). And finally, most definitions include the need for appropriate global attitudes or beliefs. Hunter et al. (2006, p. 279), suggest that globally competent students have a "nonjudgmental and open attitude toward difference." Deardorff (2006, p. 254) suggests that intercultural competence requires that one "value other cultures and cultural diversity," "have openness to intercultural learning and to people from other cultures," and "tolerance for ambiguity and uncertainty." The American Council for International Intercultural Education conference (1996, p. 3) called for "...openness to other cultures, values and attitudes...."

Finally, a number of the recent efforts to define global competence have indicated a new element: the critical role of discipline-specific global competence. Rollins, Lohmann, Long, and Griffin (2004) argued for the importance of integrating global competence into degrees in science and technology. More recently, Brustein (2007) suggests that the globally competent person must be able to work effectively in international settings, and Hunter et al. (2006) suggest that global competence includes the ability to collaborate across cultures and to "effectively participate in social and business settings in other countries" (p 283). While the inclusion of work-related global competence may be obvious within disciplines such as international affairs, political science, or business, there has been a growing recognition of the importance of global competence in the science and engineering disciplines given the rapidly growing need for scientists and engineers to work on international teams and to solve problems facing different countries and cultures. Lohmann, Rollins, and Hoey (2006) discuss the specific needs and challenges of developing globally competent engineers. Sigma XI (2007) has published an important report that develops the case for global competence among scientists and engineers. In this report, Sigma XI recommends that scientists and engineers have the knowledge, skills, and ability to: "...frame scientific questions and seek answers with people who have perspectives different from their own... work with scientists and engineers from other countries and to understand their social and intellectual approaches to science and discovery and how they bound problems differently... pursue knowledge in different contexts and cultures…work in dense networks that are evolving around the globe to share experiments, equipment, and results" (Sigma IX, 2007, pp. 22–23).

DEVELOPMENT OF GLOBAL COMPETENCE: THE INTERNATIONAL PLAN

While it is certainly interesting and informative to develop an understanding of the critical elements involved in establishing global competence, it is another thing entirely to figure out what programs universities should implement to instill global competence in students. For example, Adelman (1999) suggested that "global preparedness" should include a minimum of two international studies courses and two advanced language courses in addition to a period of study abroad. In its 1988 report, the Council for International Educational Exchange recommended second language learning and at least 3 months of deep immersive study abroad in which the second language is used. It is sufficient here simply to indicate that far more is involved than study abroad if the goal is to prepare students with the knowledge, skills, and attitudes that the above analysis suggests are all key elements in global competence.

The development of the International Plan began well before much of the research on global competence described above was published. Nevertheless, the development of this new approach to global competence required incorporating the core competencies described above as necessary ingredients. At Georgia Tech, global competence was defined as

> the product of both education and experience to include proficiency in a second language; knowledge about comparative international relations, the world economy, and the socio-political systems and culture of at least one other country or world region; intercultural assimilation such as appreciation for different cultures and interacting comfortably with persons in a different cultural environment; and the ability to practice the student's discipline within an international context. (Georgia Institute of Technology, 2005, p 12)

It was important, from the beginning, that the program be available to students in all colleges and academic majors at Georgia Tech including all disciplines in the humanities, social sciences, and sciences as well as in the professional colleges of architecture, computing, engineering, and management. This was not to be a program for engineers or a program developed by social science and humanities disciplines for others. A general template of requirements was needed that would be followed across the entire university. However, each academic discipline was expected to tailor the International Plan specifically to prepare globally competent students in that discipline (and do so in the standard 4-year program).

The details of the program were developed by a university-wide committee with participation by a faculty representative from each of the 12 interested academic units, representing all six colleges, as well as two university-wide administrators (within the provost's office). All participants were equal partners in this developmental process. The committee members were, for the most part, the faculty members with primary responsibility for undergraduate education within their discipline with an obvious interest in, and commitment to, undergraduate education. The committee met once or twice per month for 18 months to establish the general campus-wide requirements for the International Plan. These requirements were approved early in the spring semester, 2005 by all appropriate university committees.

427

REQUIREMENTS FOR THE INTERNATIONAL PLAN

One of the unique characteristics of the International Plan is that it is not a new degree, a comajor, a minor, or a certificate program. Instead, it is a modification to each disciplinary degree in which a "designator" is added to the student's transcript and diploma indicating that a significant component has been added to the disciplinary degree. The student must meet the same requirements in the major as all other students in that major. However, a strong international component is integrated into the degree. The designator for a mechanical engineering major's diploma would state "Bachelor of Science in Mechanical Engineering: International Plan."

Providing students with an International Plan designator serves two important purposes. First, it signifies that the international experience is integrated into the student's major discipline approved by the faculty in that discipline, the appropriate college, and the university as such. Second, it offers the student a coherent rationale for participating in the International Plan that ties to the student's future career plans; and it rewards the student by recognition on the diploma and on the transcript that this additional knowledge and expertise was successfully acquired.

The International Plan has three major components: international coursework, second language proficiency, and international experience. These three components are described in Table 24.1 (For a more detailed description see: Georgia Institute of Technology, 2005, p. 14; passages in quotes are directly from Table 5, p 14).

Table 24.1 *International Plan Requirements*

Requirement Type	Requirement
Coursework	
International Relations	"One course focused on international relations," "including topics such as the role of state sovereignty and nationalism and non-state actors in the international system; international conflict, peace, security, intervention, and nation-building," among other issues.
Global Economics	"One course that provides a historical and theoretical understanding of the global economy, including topics such as international trade, finance, investment, and production," among other issues.
Country/Region	"One course that provides familiarity with another country or world region that allows systematic comparisons of society and culture" and in which the student will gain international experience.
Disciplinary Capstone	One course that "integrates knowledge of the discipline and the international experience in a global context." This course "may be offered within a specific discipline or in a multidisciplinary context."
Second Language Competency	Demonstration of "competency in a language other than English at an appropriate level." The foreign language requirement depends on the language spoken in the country where the international experience will occur.
International Experience	Two academic terms, totaling twenty-six weeks, of residential international experience are required which involves "living among and immersed within the local international academic, research, or work community." "The terms may consist of full-time academic study involving coursework" earning academic credit, "internship or work experience, and/or research."

Required Coursework

As shown in Table 24.1, the first three required courses involve participants choosing at least one course from each of three categories. Academic departments submit courses for consideration within each category for approval by relevant college and university committees. Students are expected to meet these three requirements either before or during their overseas experience.

The first two categories are designed to provide students with significant knowledge about globalization. Given the interdependencies among nations and regions brought about by globalization, it seemed only natural that the first category selected was designed to insure that students have significant understanding of international relations—among governments and industries at local, regional, and world-wide levels. The principle idea here is that students should come to understand some of the complexities of globalization given local differences in how governments, businesses, and industries function. Equally important, the global economics requirement resulted from the committee consensus that globalization is intricately tied to the interdependencies of the world's economies. Virtually all national economies are now interconnected and interdependent. Economic changes in one part of the world impact economies in other parts of the world, often with shocking speed (witness what happened in mid-2008). The third category was designed to develop more in-depth knowledge of the particular country or region where a student would gain international experience. While the term *global competence* implies a more general knowledge focused on the interconnections and interdependencies of nations and regions, it is equally clear that knowledge about at least one local country other than one's own country is an important component of global competence. In *The World Is Flat*, Friedman's uses the term *glocalization* to refer to this connection between global trends and local cultural values. According to Friedman, one must understand both the global and the local and their interconnectedness in order to be successful (2007, pp. 400–426).

As of May 2008, the International Plan Committee has been relatively selective in approving courses for the first two categories: For the international relation's category, 27 courses have been approved (from history/sociology, international affairs, and public policy). For global economics, only seven courses have been approved (three from economics, including one developed specifically for the International Plan; the other four are from international affairs and management). The country/region category has substantially more available courses as might be anticipated by the fact that various countries and regions must be covered. This category includes 106 courses mainly from history, international affairs, and modern languages (upper division courses).[2]

The fourth course requirement is entirely different. Each participating discipline (or several disciplines working together), is required to develop a culminating course that integrates a student's international study and experience into the major. This course must be taken during, or upon return from, the overseas experience. The following statement was established by the central committee to guide academic departments in the development of this course:

> Globally competent graduates, generally speaking, should be able to shift cultural frames of reference to solve problems in the discipline, should be able to function effectively in multicultural work environments, and should have knowledge of global systems. The capstone course should be developed such that students have to demonstrate those competencies.[3]

Obviously, the purpose of the internationally based capstone course is to develop the participants' practical skills at putting the disciplinary knowledge into practice in different cultural contexts. The culminating course varies widely from one discipline to the next but is particularly different

429 ■

for the different colleges. The disciplines within the colleges of architecture and engineering require their students to take one or more studio or design courses respectively in the final year. These senior courses are intended to integrate the student's knowledge of the discipline with the practice of the discipline. For the International Plan, these two colleges have modified existing studio or senior design courses to incorporate international aspects of the discipline. Mechanical engineering, for example, requires their participants to develop a design project, as part of an existing design course, in collaboration with a company in the country where the student obtained international experience. The student interacts directly with the company to develop a design solution and writes a report in the language of the country as the final report for the design course. Architecture students complete their senior design course in Paris working side-by-side with French students. Schools in the College of Science tend to focus on research in collaboration with faculty at universities outside the United States. This research collaboration is intended to expose the science major to approaches to thinking about, planning, and executing research projects as these processes are practiced in another culture. Students in biology, for example, are expected to prepare a lab/field notebook; a poster or PowerPoint presentation of the research in the host country language; and a reflective essay comparing how biology is practiced in the host country and the United States. The College of Management capstone course uses case studies of various corporations to give majors some experience with putting theories and approaches into practice. This capstone course was redesigned to incorporate international cases and to include discussion of the relevance of the local culture, government, laws, and taxes into the solution to a particular case. The College of Computing offers students three alternative capstone options that are similar to the ones described above. Last but not least important, social sciences and humanities disciplines have typically enhanced an existing capstone course with a heavier international emphasis. These disciplines view integration of international elements with the discipline as obvious and critical. Most require the student to write a term paper within the existing capstone that integrates the student's international experience detailing how the discipline is practiced differently including theoretical underpinnings and approach to scholarship.

Foreign Language Competency

As shown in Table 24.1, students must demonstrate competency in a language other than English. Second language learning is considered one of the leading criteria for global competence (Deardorff, 2006; Hunter et al., 2006). It involves the development of all components of global competence. Students acquire linguistic knowledge including vocabulary, syntax, and grammar all of which often differ significantly from one's first language. Learning a second language also involves acquiring skills—particularly communication skills that enable one to converse comfortably with others in their language. The elements of pronunciation, style, tone, inflection, as well as culturally accepted forms of conversation are all essential to effective oral communication. All of these involve tacit knowledge which is acquired primarily by practice. Finally, second language learning provides insight into the culture of countries where that language is spoken. The way sentences are composed, the way gender is treated, the importance in the language of the relationship between the speaker and listener all convey information about the culture. Of course, language is the primary mode of communication among members of a culture and so learning to communicate in the language opens new and direct pathways to learning the nuances of that culture.

The second language requirement was one of the most difficult issues facing the steering committee. There were heated debates about whether participants could study in an English-speaking country. In the end, study in English-speaking countries was allowed but discouraged. There were three reasons for this decision. First, a number of English-speaking countries are important to globalization (e.g., Australia, Great Britain, Ireland, India). Second, there are a number of important countries where English is a primary language of discourse but where the cultures are very different from the United States (e.g., South Africa, India, Singapore). Third, all of these countries have cultures that are different from U.S. cultures and so students could be expected to develop global competence by spending significant time in them.

The form of the second language requirement was also an issue: Credit hours in language courses or proficiency testing. The program requires language proficiency for students who gain international experience using their second language. While these students must prepare linguistically for the international experience, their second language proficiency is assessed upon return to the United States. The Association of Certified Teachers of Foreign Languages (ACTFL) proficiency test is given by independent testers with the requirement that they reach a minimum of "Intermediate High" for European languages and "Intermediate Mid" for the more difficult Asian languages, Arabic, and Russian.

In contrast, students gaining international experience in an English-speaking country are required to learn a second language by taking 2 years of college-level courses with a B grade point average. This requirement may also be met by taking a proficiency test—for example, if the student gained the proficiency outside the classroom.

International Experience Requirement

As shown in Table 24.1, participants are required to spend at least 26 weeks (6 months) outside the United States gaining one or more of three types of international experience: Full-time academic study that involves coursework counting for credit toward the degree, work experience related to the discipline, or research collaboration in the discipline. Academic study may occur at Georgia Tech overseas sites, at Georgia Tech foreign partner institutions, or in a faculty-directed program so long as the student is immersed into the local community. International Plan required courses may be taken during the period of study overseas if these courses are deemed acceptable and equivalent to the required courses by the appropriate academic unit(s).

The international experience may involve a combination of two of these three types of international experiences. In fact, the consensus of the committee is that the best path to global competence includes study and then either work or research collaboration so that students are exposed to both the academic community and to the work environment. The international experience is also expected to be an immersive experience in which students live in and also study, work, or collaborate in research among the citizens of the host country. Overseas experiences of this nature also involve significant learning of knowledge, skills, and attitudes/beliefs. Knowledge is acquired in the courses taken abroad and as students learn how their discipline is practiced. However, speaking the language and interacting both socially, in the university environment, and at work all provide new communication skills and also foster intercultural awareness and understanding. Finally, students who study or work abroad for a significant period of time go through a process of assimilation and acculturation to a point where most become comfortable and accepting of the cultural differences between the host country and the United States. This acculturation is likely to be critical in producing the attitude changes to achieve intercultural competence such as acceptance and respect for other cultures, openness to intercultural learning and to people from other cultures as described by Deardorff (2006).

The international experience requirement also generated significant debate within the International Plan Committee. There was concern over whether Georgia Tech's faculty-led summer study abroad programs could be counted toward the 26 weeks of international experience. While many of these programs are taught by Georgia Tech faculty in English, the students sometimes live with local students or have local students in their classrooms thereby gaining some exposure to the local culture. Moreover, several of these programs offer students opportunities to learn or improve their second language skills in the appropriate second language. The committee decided to allow no more than one such program per student to count for the international plan so long as the students then spent the remainder of the time abroad fully immersed in the local culture. Moreover, disciplines offering short summer programs were expected to develop an optional bridge experience in the host country between the end of the summer program and the beginning of the fall semester in which students would continue their immersive experience. Often the bridge program involves a work experience or a research collaboration project with faculty at the university where the student will enroll in the fall.

Another area of concern arose over whether students might gain their international experience in more than one country. This is a particularly important issue for some disciplines such as international affairs where cross-country comparisons of governments, public policies, and industry practices are an essential part of the preparation of students. While the consensus was that most students should have a residential, immersive international experience in one country, the committee did allow some relaxation of this general rule in cases where there was "linguistic" or "intellectual content" consistency to justify a student gaining experience in multiple countries. For example, students might argue for obtaining international experience in both Spain and Argentina given that Spanish is spoken in both countries. Or, an international affairs major might make a case that international experience in both France and Germany is important given the importance of the European Union to that student's particular program of study. All such exceptions to the 26 weeks in one country rule require approval of the International Plan Committee.

ASSESSMENT

The assessment of the International Plan involves two components. First we wish to determine whether the program has been successfully and fully implemented. Are participation benchmarks by academic programs and by students being achieved? Are participants making progress toward completion of program requirements? The second component involves determining whether student outcomes have been achieved. The overarching assessment plan is not near completion. The first cohort of participants entered Georgia Tech in fall 2005 and most will not graduate until spring semester, 2010 (the average time to graduation is just under 5 years); so most student outcome data will not become available until 2010. However, we do have some early outcome data relating to impact on the student participants. We also have data reflecting the impact on the broader population of students who are not participating in the International Plan.

IMPLEMENTATION SUCCESS

Participating Disciplines

Table 24.2 presents data on the growth in the number of participating academic disciplines from 2005 to 2008. It also provides information about the number and percentage of the total under-

Table 24.2 Disciplines in International Plan in 2005 and 2008

College	Total Number of Disciplines	2005 Number of Disciplines In Plan	2008 Number of Disciplines In Plan	2008 Percent Disciplines In Plan	2008 Total Students Eligible	2008 Percent Students Eligible[1]
Architecture	4	1	2	50%	556	73%
Computing	1	1	1	100%	724	100%
Engineering	12	5	8	67%	6,408	89%
Humanities-Social Sciences	9	3	7	78%	665	75%
Management	1	1	1	100%	1,302	100%
Sciences	9	1	5	56%	879	74%
Totals	36	12	24	67%	10,534	86%

[1]Percentage of total student population in relevant college.

graduate population eligible to participate because they have declared one of the participating majors. Two important facts emerge from Table 24.2. First, the number of participating disciplines had doubled from 12 at the outset in 2005 to 24 in 2008, representing two-thirds of the 36 undergraduate degrees offered. Second, 86% of our entire undergraduate student body is eligible to participate. Clearly, the majors with the larger enrollments are participating. It is also clear in Table 24.2 that the growth of disciplines has taken place in all four colleges having more than a single disciplinary major. It is interesting to note that much of the growth in participating disciplines was driven by students in a discipline demanding access.

Student Participation

Table 24.3 presents data on student enrollment in the International Plan for the years 2005–2006 through 2008–2009, including those who dropped out or graduated. As depicted in the last column of Table 24.3, a total of 704 students have enrolled in the plan over the first 3 years. Of this total, 589 participants, or 84% have either continued in the program or graduated.

We had very ambitious goals for this program. Our goal was eventually to recruit 300 students per year with a rapid ramp up over the first 4 years from 100 to 300 participants. This final goal

Table 24.3 Student Participation in the International Plan for 2005–06 through 2008–09

	2005–06	2006–07	2007–08	2008–09[1]	Total across Years
Total Participants	138	156	163	247	704
Graduated with Plan	16	5	1	0	22
Remaining in Plan	50	122	148	247	567
Total with Graduates	66	127	149	247	589
Drop outs	72	29	14	0	115
Program Goals	100	200	250	300	850
Percent Goal Met	138%	78%	65.2%	82%	83%

[1]2008–09 data for first 8 months of year (June 1, 2008 to January 31, 2009).

represents about 12% of each graduating class. We exceeded our goal for the first year but fell short of our goal in the second through fourth years. Total student involvement for the fourth year is at 82% of our final goal (247 of 300). Clearly, student participation is well below our expectations. On the other hand, combining participation across all 4 years, we managed to reach within 83% of the total participation goal. We were also concerned from the start about the dropout rate given that most students sign up in their first year and must remain involved through graduation. One might anticipate that students would drop out in the first 2 years when they take courses but have no international experience. In fact, as shown in Table 24.3, the dropout rate is quite low, representing less than 10% of the total number of participants. It is also important to note that the highest number of dropouts took place in the first year when the program was new and when some of the details of the program were still being worked out.

We are concerned about the final level of enrollment in the program and have introduced some new programming to attract new students and to facilitate retention of students over the first 2 years. We now recruit high school applicants who express interest in study abroad, explain our program to high school advisers, and then engage in a second round of recruiting as admitted students arrive on campus. In addition, a number of activities have been generated to maintain interest in the program for first and second year participants such as presentations from industry about the importance of international education and experience.

International Activities of Participants

The implementation of the International Plan can also be assessed by the number of required international activities in which plan students have participated. Table 24.4 provides information on the types of international activities in which these students have been engaged since joining the program. Participants are supposed to be enrolled in language courses during their early years. As shown in the first row of Table 24.4, 332 students, representing approximately 85% of the participants, have taken at least one language course while at Georgia Tech. Moreover, 68% have taken two or more language courses. Participants are also expected to take one course from each of the three international categories of courses during their early years. The next four rows of Table 24.4 confirm this expectation. The percentages of participants who have taken at least one of the required courses since enrolling at Georgia Tech is 48, 20, and 39% for the international, global economics, and country/region categories respectively.

Table 24.4 also provides evidence about the various types of international experience in which participants have been engaged. As shown in Table 24.4, a total of 120 of the 389 participants studied or worked abroad in 2007–2008 representing 31% of the participants. Of this total, 68 studied on summer programs with the vast majority of these students on faculty-led summer programs and 38 studied on semester or year-long immersive exchanges—most with overseas partners. Participants are strongly encouraged to study, work, or collaborate in research in non-English-speaking countries. The third column of Table 24.4 provides direct evidence of the success of our efforts. For summer programs, 66 of 68 International Plan participants studied in non-English-speaking countries. Thirty-four of these students participated in our own overseas language programs called "Language for Business and Technology" where the emphasis is on language learning combined with learning about the practice of business and technology in the host country. Thirty additional students studied in Georgia Tech faculty-led programs in non-English-speaking countries some of which involved opportunities to learn the host language, or

Table 24.4 *Number and Percentage of International Plan Students Gaining Various Types of International Study and Experience in 2007–08 Academic Year*

Type of Experience	Number of IP Students	Percentage of IP Students	Number in Non English Speaking Countries
Courses Taken			
One or More Language Courses	332	85.3	
One or More International Courses			
International Relations	187	48.1%	
Global Economics	78	20.1%	
Country/Region	152	39.1%	
Study Abroad			
Summer Programs			
Georgia Tech			
Faculty Led	65	16.7	64
Summer Exchanges	1	0.26	0
Non Georgia Tech	2	0.51	2
Total	68	17.48	66
Semester Programs			
Georgia Tech Immersive	6	1.54	6
Exchanges	32	8.23	29
Totals	38	9.77	35
Totals Studying Abroad	106	27.25	101
Work Abroad	14	3.60	13
Grand Totals (study & work)	120	30.85	114

had immersive experiences such as living with host families or taking classes with host country students.

An important finding within Table 24.4 is that 38 participants (about 10%) participated in semester or year-long study abroad programs—six at one of the two Georgia Tech off- shore campuses[4] and 32 on exchanges at partner universities. Thirty-five (of 38) studied in non-English-speaking countries.

One would predict that the students in the program for more years would be likely to participate in semester abroad programs while students in their first or second year might be more inclined to take summer, faculty-led programs. This expectation is also supported by the data. The majority of students studying abroad for a semester or year in 2007–2008, enrolled in the program in 2005–2006 whereas the majority of students studying on a faculty-led summer program enrolled in the program in 2007–2008. Finally, a total of 14 International Plan participants worked abroad in 2007–2008. While this number is not large, it does reflect growth since inception of the International Plan. It is worth noting that 13 of these students worked in non-English-speaking countries.

OUTCOME ASSESSMENT

Three types of outcome data were available as this chapter was being prepared. First, we have important data describing ways in which the International Plan participants differ on the national first-year student survey, entitled "Cooperative Institutional Research Program" (CIRP), and on various admission criteria. These data address the question of whether the International Plan attracts different students to attend Georgia Tech. Second, we have some data on the academic performance of plan participants in comparison to other Georgia Tech students in the first 2 years of participation. Finally, limited survey data are available on the first graduates of the International Plan.

Entering Freshmen

Each year Georgia Tech gathers data on various demographic and performance indices of its incoming class. Comparisons were made on these variables between students participating in the International Plan and the entire first-year population collapsing over the years 2005–2006 and 2006–2007. These data are presented in more detail in a paper presented by Jonathan Gordon (2007). The data in Table 24.5 include only those variables on which there was a statistically significant difference between plan participants and the general student population. As shown in Table 24.5, there were significantly more females in the International Plan than in the general population of students. It is generally the case that more women than men study abroad (IIE, 2007). These data suggest that more comprehensive programs like the International Plan also are valued more by women than men. However, it is also important to note that over one half of the participants in the International Plan are men, which suggests that international programs that are tightly integrated with the discipline, provide students with a coherent degree-long program, and practical international experience may well attract male students well beyond what one would expect for typical study abroad programs.

International Plan participants also score higher (statistically significant) on the verbal section of the Scholastic Aptitude Test (SAT). This finding is not caused by the larger number of women among plan participants. Plan participants have statistically significantly higher verbal SAT scores even with gender statistically controlled. Math SAT scores are almost identical for plan and nonplan participants and do not differ statistically. The fact that verbal SAT is higher for plan participants provides some evidence that the International Plan is attracting students with higher initial preparation and ability. On the other hand, as shown in Table 24.5, high school GPA scores are nearly identical and do not differ significantly between plan participants and the general population.

It is also important to note that there were no statistically significant differences between plan participants and the first year population in the percentage of U.S. versus non-U.S. citizens, or among racial and ethnic groups. Moreover, while international students do participate in the International Plan, they are not allowed to gain international experience in their home country since this would not be a culturally different experience.

All incoming first-year students at Georgia Tech are given the CIRP survey. This self-report survey is designed to gather information in a variety of areas including socioeconomic status, information related to perceived student ability, and reasons given for college choices. Each participating university can also ask a limited number of its own questions. Since the survey is given by many universities, it is possible to compare survey responses of a given university's incoming

Table 24.5 *Demographic and Performance Characteristics of Incoming Plan Participants and the General Population of First Year Students*

Characteristic Measured	International Plan Participants (n=293)	First-year Populations 2005–6 & 2006–07 (n=6480)	Difference
Gender**			
Female	44.6%	30.0%	14.6%
Male	55.4%	70.0%	−14.6%
Admission Characteristics			
Mean SAT Verbal **	660	645	15
Mean SAT Math	686	690	−4
Mean High School GPA	3.76	3.72	.04

**p<.05 two tailed by chi-square test for gender and t-test for SAT.

class to that of various other groups of universities. Table 24.6 presents the data from this survey for International Plan participants and nonparticipants for the combined 2005–2006 and 2006–2007 academic years. Table 24.6 includes only those variables that yielded statistically significant differences between plan and nonplan participants. A more detailed report of these findings that includes all variables on the survey was presented earlier (Gordon, 2007).

The first thing to note in Table 24.6 is that plan participants score higher on variables that should be high for students who show a strong interest in international education. Plan participants are significantly higher on improving their understanding of other countries and cultures, ability to work with others from different backgrounds, and importance of taking 4 years of foreign language in high school. However, International Plan students are also significantly higher on a variety of other variables related to achievement. They have higher drive to achieve and higher perceived writing ability but lower perceived math ability. They also appreciate more highly than nonparticipants some of the higher level, more conceptual advantages attributed to higher education such as achieving self-understanding, gaining a general education, and appreciation of ideas. They also seek to become more cultured persons. Finally, plan participants show greater interest in being active U.S. and world citizens. They think it is important to influence the political structure, participate in community action, and to keep up to date with political affairs. The above characteristics represent attitudes and perspectives that would be essential preconditions for students to become global citizens.

The final two columns of Table 24.6 provide data in the CIRP survey from a group of 17 high selectivity public universities (no very high selectivity public universities were used) and 17 very high selectivity private universities. It is notable that the International Plan participants' responses are not only higher than other Georgia Tech students but also higher than the incoming students at the group of highly selective public universities and comparable to the incoming students at very highly selective private universities. The only exception to this finding is that plan participants have lower perceived math ability than other groups in the comparison.

How well are International Plan participants doing academically at Georgia Tech? Table 24.7 provides data on the GPA of the first two classes of plan participants in comparison to the population of all students in this 2-year cohort. The data in Table 24.7 clearly indicate that plan participants in both the first and second years are earning significantly higher GPA's than nonparticipants. While plan participants are expected to reach an overall GPA of 3.0 by the time

Table 24.6 *CIRP Survey Performance for International Plan (IP) students, Non-Plan Students, Students at Public Selective Universities, and at Private Highly Selective Universities*

Characteristics	IP Students	Non-IP Students	Private Highly Selective	Public Selective
Socioeconomic Characteristics				
Parental Income Over $150,000	36.5*	24.4	40.6	22.8
Ability Self Ratings				
Drive to Achieve – Highest 10% only	55.6**	36.3	51.4	33.9
Mathematical Ability – Highest 10% only	15.6**	33.0	33.2	17.8
Self Understanding	74.2**	59.6	66.8	61.0
Writing Ability	67.5**	49.9	67.1	52.5
Objectives considered "Essential" or Very Important"				
Influencing the Political Structure	34.4**	16.8	27.5	23.4
Participating in a Community Action Program	36.0*	22.0	36.2	28.2
Keeping up to date with political affairs	51.1*	38.6	55.0	41.9
Improving my understanding of other countries/cultures	85.6**	48.0	68.0	54.4
Reasons "Very Important" in Deciding to Go to College				
To Gain a General Education and Appreciation of Ideas	81.8**	65.7	80.1	68.1
To make me a more cultured person	64.8**	35.4	58.4	47.0
Georgia Tech Optional Items				
Ability to Work with Others From Different Backgrounds Extremely Important	71.3**	46.9	n/a	n/a
Interested in Participating in Leadership Training	77.2**	66.6	n/a	n/a
Four Years of Foreign Language Courses in High School	56.8**	31.6	n/a	n/a

*p<.05; **p<.01 two tailed t-test

they undertake international experience, there is no GPA requirement for admission to the plan.

International Plan Graduates

Our final outcome measure on plan participants comes from a survey of the first graduates of the program. All 19 graduates of the program were sent a short survey to determine the degree to which they found this program to be of value. We received completed surveys from 10 of them. The results of the survey are shown in Table 24.8.

Table 24.7 A Comparison of Plan Participants and Non Participants on Grade Point Average in the First Two Years

Academic Year	Plan Participants (n=293)	Non Plan Participants (n = 6,480)	Difference
First Year Cum. GPA***	3.30	2.90	0.40
Second Year Cum. GPA***	3.30	2.95	0.35
Combined Years ***	3.30	2.925	0.375

***$p<.0001$ two tailed F-test

As shown in Table 24.8, participants intend to take advantage of their international knowledge and experience. One half of the graduates plan to work in their disciplinary major and 80% plan to work outside the United States. All graduates intend to continue their language study and 90% plan to go on for an advanced degree. Second, all participants indicated that the International Plan improved their understanding of global issues and of a particular country/region. Eighty percent believe that their admission to graduate school or obtaining of a job will be enhanced. However, only one half of this group thinks they have better understanding of how their discipline is practiced in the country/region in which they studied or worked and only one half believe

Table 24.8 Survey of International Plan Graduates on Impact of the Program

Within the next five years, I plan to:	Percent Yes
Work in position related to field of study?	50
Work in a position in another country?	80
Pursue/continue foreign language proficiency?	100
Pursue graduate or professional advanced degree?	90
Do you think at this stage that the international plan:	
Helped you determine a career path?	50
Helped in the obtaining of a job or admittance into graduate school?	80
Improved your understanding of global issues?	100
Improved your understanding of the particular country/region in which you lived?	100
Improved your understanding of how your discipline is practiced where you studied, worked, or engaged in research?	50
Which elements of the International Plan do you now deem important?	Mean Score (1-5)[1]
International coursework	3.8
Capstone Course	2.4
Language Learning	4.8
Study Abroad	5.0
Work or Research Experience	3.7

[1]Likert scale from 1 to 5 with categories of unimportant, somewhat important, important, very important, or exceptionally important

the program helped them choose a career path. Finally, participants thought that the language learning and study abroad experience were exceptionally important, that the international course work and work or research experience abroad were very important, but that the capstone course was relatively unimportant. This latter result may due to the fact that the capstone course was in development when most of these students graduated and so these first students did not benefit from later improvements to these courses. It is worth noting that 50% of the graduates are working for global companies. Seventy percent are currently attending or plan to attend graduate school—two are simultaneously working overseas and in graduate school. All anticipate that they will eventually move into work involving global travel or living in another country.

BROADER IMPACT OF THE INTERNATIONAL PLAN

The International Plan is viewed by Georgia Tech as the signature program for international education. Given its extensive requirements, the program is not an option for many students. However, we anticipated that the prestige and visibility of the International Plan might result in greater student participation in all aspects of international education. Students who cannot participate in this program might be more inclined than prior to the International Plan to study or work abroad or to take more second-language courses. Table 24.9 provides data indicating the extent to which these indices have increased between 2003–2004 and 2006–2007 or 2007–2008.

As shown in Table 24.9, there were major increases in the number of participants in all areas of international education between years before and years after the launch of the plan. Language enrollments increased by almost 29%, which far exceeds the contribution of the International Plan students. This increase occurred without the addition of any new languages. There were also increases in study abroad participation that go well beyond the contribution of the International Plan student participation. Note that summer enrollments are up modestly which is an important result given faculty concern about a possible negative impact of the International Plan on faculty-led summer programs. However, there was a substantial increase in the number of students on semester- or year-long programs. The number of students on longer term programs jumped from 78 to 167 representing a 114% increase overall and a 65% increase excluding plan par-

Table 26.9 *Student Participation Changes in International Education Programming between 2003–04 and 2007–08*

Area of International Education	Number Pre International Plan	Number Post International Plan	Change	Percent Change
Language Course Enrollments (03-04 to 06-07)	3,714	4,526	812	21.9%
Study Abroad				
Summer (03–04 to 07–08)	664	701	37	5.57
Semester (03–04 to 07–08)	78	167[1]	89	114.10
Totals	742	868	126	16.98
Work Abroad (03–04 to 07–08)	14	74[2]	60	428.57

[1] 38 of these students are in the International Plan. Excluding the 38, growth is 65.38%
[2] 14 of these students are in the International Plan. Excluding the 14, growth is 328.57%

ticipants. Nonparticipants are also more likely to seek work abroad experiences. These numbers were very low in the years before introduction of the International Plan and rose dramatically by 2007–2008 for an increase that exceeds 400%. Again, the increase is not entirely accounted for by the participating International Plan students since only 14 of the students working abroad in 2007–2008 are plan participants. The remainder represents an increase of 46 students or 329% growth. It is important to note that the trends for short-term programs and long-term programs are opposite to what is happening across the United States. According to Open Doors (IIE, 2007), the percentage of students participating in short-term programs is increasing dramatically while participation in longer-term programs is declining.

SUMMARY AND CONCLUSIONS

The International Plan is a unique program because it offers students a comprehensive, coherent, degree-long program that integrates international education programming into each disciplinary major. It is also unique because the plan was developed and implemented university-wide under the supervision and control of a central faculty committee but at the same time with local disciplinary control and buy-in from the faculty within most disciplines. It is a demanding program that is not intended for all students but for a subset of Georgia Tech's best students. We anticipated that this signature international program would attract top students with a different set of interests and a broader perspective on the purpose of undergraduate education. We also anticipated that it might generate greater interest among students in all of our international programs thereby increasing the international education of a much wider group of students than those who participated directly.

As of the writing of this chapter, it has been just over 5 years since the planning for the International Plan began and near the end of the fourth year since the launch of the program. As the above assessment section demonstrates, the launch of the plan has been largely successful. All colleges are participating and the number of disciplines has doubled in the first 3 years. We are now at 82% of our goal of 12% student participation in each entering class—not quite as far along as we hoped but still sufficiently far along to feel comfortable that the goal is reachable. We need significant additional student participation in order to reach our goals and believe that the overall goal of 300 students per year will be reached as the disciplines that have joined the program in the last year or so begin to attract significant numbers of students. It is also important to note that the first large cohort of participants is just now beginning to obtain their long-term overseas experience. When this group returns to campus in 2008–2009, we anticipate a major increase in interest as the returning students talk about the impact on their lives and careers. Finally, it is also very evident that participants are actively engaged in meeting the plan requirements. Most are enrolled in required language and international courses and significant numbers are studying or working abroad.

There is also strong evidence that we are attracting students that are different from our usual first-year students. The International Plan participants are more capable, more interested in global and international issues, have higher first- and second-year grade point averages, and have loftier expectations for their undergraduate studies. Thus, preliminary data suggest that because of the International Plan, we are attracting a group of students with desirable characteristics who enhance the quality and range of our student population.

The International Plan has also significantly impacted participation in all of our international programs. Students not in the International Plan are taking language courses as well as gaining international experience in record numbers that we believe are directly linked to the launch of this program. Thus, this program will not only generate a significant number of globally competent students, but also, by virtue of this spillover effect, increase the international knowledge and intercultural awareness of a much larger group of Georgia Tech's students.

Unfortunately, at this stage, we cannot provide strong data to support our goal that International Plan graduates have developed global competence. There are some suggestions in support of this claim based on limited self-report data available from the first small number of graduates of the program. These graduates generally believe that the knowledge and experiences they obtained through the International Plan are important to them, facilitated their career choices, and for some landed them jobs with a strong international focus. What we don't have now are large numbers of students or data that go beyond self-assessment to determine whether students actually have greater international knowledge, have greater intercultural sensitivity, and can comfortably practice their discipline in other cultures. However, within the next 2 years, we should be able to document in clear and unambiguous terms whether our students have met these goals.

As with any new program, the implementation of the International Plan has generated a number of issues that required modifications and adjustments. For example, the original plan assumed that each student would gain 6 months of international experience in a single country. Some academic units, especially International Affairs, argued that this requirement was too restrictive. For some students interested in comparative government, spending time in two or more countries would be valuable. Also, modern languages faculty argued that it would be very valuable to spend time in two countries using a common language in order to broaden the cultural context. These pressures resulted in a new policy that enabled students to petition for spending time in more than one country if justified by common language or if the two countries are linked in an academically coherent way. A second serious concern surfaced as the International Plan Committee began to worry about whether the 6 months of international experience, in and of itself, would be sufficient to produce intercultural sensitivity. Other universities such as the University of Minnesota and Wake Forest University have added programming that engages students in reflection about the cross-cultural experience before, during, and on return from the international experience. At the end of the second year, we added such a program modeled after the program developed at the University of Minnesota. There have also been some issues raised about the culminating course developed by each individual discipline. In the second year of the program, the International Plan Committee developed a written description of the principles to be followed in developing this course and a new and more thorough review of each capstone proposal was undertaken. Finally, we have rediscovered how clever students can be at finding unique ways to meet the requirements of the plan, particularly the international experience component. We have had far more petitions for exceptions to the rules than we anticipated. While many of these petitions have been rejected, a few ingenious students have succeeded in persuading the committee to grant them.

What important lessons have been learned through the development of the International Plan that might be beneficial to others? First and foremost, it is critical to have the support of the university leadership. The president, provost, college deans, and academic department chairs must be receptive to new initiatives generally and to international initiatives in particular. This commitment is becoming progressively easier as incoming students and their parents demand international preparation, as accreditation bodies include international education in their criteria, and as college advisory boards consisting of alumni and business and professional leaders stress the demand for global competence in the workforce. The senior leadership must also be prepared to fund major campus-wide international initiatives. The International Plan would have fallen far short of its goals had the provost and president of Georgia Tech not agreed to provide generous funding for this program prior to its launch.

It is also critical to the success of campus-wide international initiatives that all academic units (colleges and academic departments) have the opportunity to participate in the plan as equal partners. Campus-wide initiatives should not be developed by one college or a few disciplines in one college and then offered out to students in other departments. If an international program is to be offered to all students, then every discipline should have an equal opportunity to have a say in what that program will be like and to tailor the program to the specific needs of its own students. The goal should be an overall template with significant flexibility to enable each discipline to meet its own specific international needs.

Finally, it is important to create a balance between high expectations for the program and what is a reasonable set of goals that can be achieved. Expectations should be sufficiently high to create a program that is worthy of implementation. Setting high expectations also enables the program to continue to have worth when implementation leads to compromises that challenge the quality of the program. On the other hand, it is important not to set expectations so high that academic departments cannot really implement the program or that students find it too onerous for participation. This is one reason it is so important to have wide participation from all colleges so that special issues within individual colleges or disciplines can be addressed.

NOTES

1. The International Plan was a collaborative effort involving the central administration, the deans and staff of each college, as well as faculty. Special thanks to: Jean-Lou Chameau, former Provost; Jack Lohmann, Vice Provost for Faculty Development; Robert McMath, former Vice Provost for Academic Affairs; Amy Henry, Executive Director of the Office of International Education; Jonathan Gordon, Director, Office of Assessment; Sandi Bramblett, Director of the Office of Institutional Research and Planning and to the following school chairs and faculty who served on the planning committee: William Long, Chair, International Affairs; Patrick McCarthy, Chair, Economics; Phillip McKnight, Chair, Modern Languages; James Foley, Computing; Paul Griffin, Industrial and Systems Engineering; Laurence Jacobs, Civil and Environmental Engineering; Christopher Jarrett, Architecture; Charles Parsons, Management; Lakshmi Sankar, Aerospace Engineering; David Sanborn, Mechanical Engineering; Terry Snell, Biology; Douglas Williams, Electrical and Computer Engineering.
2. A complete list of the available courses may be found at the Georgia Tech Web site, http://www.catalog.gatech.edu/students/ugrad/special/international.php#cr
3. Full capstone course guidelines may be found at http://www.oie.gatech.edu/internationalplan
4. Georgia Tech has a campus in Metz, France that offers undergraduate courses in engineering, computing, management, French language, and French culture year round. In addition, a year-long program is available in Architecture in collaboration with a Grand Ecole.

REFERENCES

Adelman, C., (1999). *The new college course map and transcript files: Changes in course-taking and achievement, 1972–1993*. Washington, DC: U.S. Department of Education.

American Council on International Intercultural Education Conference. (1996, November). *Educating for the global community, a framework for community colleges*. Paper presented at the Stanley Foundation and the American Council on International Intercultural Education Conference, Warrenton, VA.

Barker, C. M. (2000, January). *Education for international understanding and global competence* (Report of a meeting convened by Carnegie Corporation of New York). Retrieved from: http://www.carnegie.org/pdf/global.pdf

Brustein, W. I. (2007). Paths to global competence: Preparing American college students to meet the world. *IIENetwork.* Retrieved May 1, 2008, from http://www.iienetwork.org/page/84657/

Council on International Education Exchange. (1988). *Educating for global competence: The report of the Advisory Council for International Educational Exchange.* Retrieved May 30, 2008, from http://www.ciee.org/research_center/archive/Global_Competence/1988GlobalCompReport.pdf

Deardorff, D. K. (2006). Identification and assessment of intercultural competence as a student outcome of internationalization. *Journal of Studies in International Education, 10,* 241–266.

Dwyer, M. (2004). More is better: The impact of study abroad program duration. *Frontiers: The Interdisciplinary Journal of Study Abroad, 10,* 151–164.

Friedman, T. (2007). *The world is flat: A brief history of the twenty-first century.* New York: Farrar, Straus & Giroux.

Gallie, W. B. (1956). Essentially contested concepts. *Proceedings of the Aristotelian Society, 167,* 130–131.

Georgia Institute of Technology. (2005, March). *Strengthening the global competence and research experiences of undergraduate students.* Retrieved May 1, 2008, from http://www.assessment.gatech.edu/SACS/QEP/

Gordon, J. (2007, October). *Integrating global competence into undergraduate engineering degrees: Assessing the Georgia Tech International Plan.* Paper presented at the Sixth Annual Colloquium on Engineering Education, Istanbul, Turkey.

Hunter, B., White, G. P., & Godbey, G. C. (2006). What does it mean to be globally competent? *Journal of Studies in International Education, 10,* 267–285.

Institute of International Education (IIE). (2003). *Open doors on line: Report on international education exchange: Estimated participation rate.* Retrieved April 30, 2008, from http://opendoors.iienetwork.org/?p=35946

Institute of International Education (IIE). (2007). *Open doors on line: Report on international education exchange: U.S. student profile.* Retrieved April 30, 2008, from http://opendoors.iienetwork.org/?p=113282

Lohmann, J. R., Rollins, H. A., & Hoey, J. J. (2006). Defining, developing and assessing global competence in engineers. *European Journal of Engineering Education, 31,* 119–131.

Mathews, M. (2007). *Directory of cooperative education programs.* Washington, DC: Cooperative Education Division, American Society for Engineering Education.

Rollins, H. A., Lohmann, J., Long, W., & Griffin, P. (2004, November). *Integrating international competence into baccalaureate degrees in science and technology disciplines.* Paper presented at the Annual Meeting of the Council for International Education Exchange (CIEE), Santa Fe, NM.

Schock, L. (2007). Internationalizing the campus: Profiles of success at colleges & universities, 2007. *NAFSA: Association of International Educators,* 26–39.

Sigma XI. (2007). *Embracing globalization: Meeting the challenges to U.S. scientists and engineers* (Sigma XI report), 22–23. Retrieved April 30, 2008 from http://www.sigmaxi.org/about/news/2007GEW.shtml

Sternberg, R.J., Forsythe, G. B., Hedlund, J., Horvath, J. A., Wagner, R. K., Williams, W. M., et al. (2000). *Practical intelligence in everyday life.* Cambridge, UK: Cambridge University Press.

Sutton, R., & Rubin, D. (2004). The GLOSSARI project: Initial findings from a system-wide research initiative on study abroad learning outcomes. *Frontiers: The Interdisciplinary Journal of Study Abroad, 10,* 65–82.

Thompson, H. (2006, Spring). The "global campus": Andrew Heiskell Award for international education, *IIE-Networker,* 17.

Wagner, R. K., & Sternberg, R. J. (1985). Practical intelligence in real world pursuits: The role of tacit knowledge. *Journal of Personality & Social Psychology, 49,* 436–458.

Chapter 25

Holistic Student Learning and Development Abroad

The IES 3-D Program Model

Joan Gillespie
IES Abroad

Larry Braskamp
Loyola University Chicago

Mary Dwyer
IES Abroad

INTRODUCTION

Education abroad offers an ideal setting for students' significant learning and development because they encounter new places and people, take in new ideas and information, test themselves, and, in the process, discover something new about themselves and their potential. The holistic model of education abroad capitalizes on the richness of this setting and students' openness to new experiences to develop their intellectual and social lives in an international context. Premised on the theory of intentional program design to create meaningful educational opportunities, this model sees the classroom and community as contiguous spaces in the learning environment and asks students to share this vision. The goal to expand students' global perspective is embedded in such a model through cultural integration, and students' adaptation is supported in the program details.

This chapter brings together the theory and practice of the state-of-the-art holistic model of education abroad. Two complementary theories of human development support the framework of this structured learning environment. One theory is holistic student development, the perspective that students' intellectual, social, and interior lives are inextricably linked. The second theory draws from intercultural communication and its focus on cultural adaptation. These two theories share the cultural and narrative metaphor of the journey as personal change—in holistic student development, development apropos to 18- to 24-year-olds; in intercultural communication, the cognitive, attitudinal, physical, and behavioral change required by the sojourner in a new culture, regardless of age. The relevance of these theories goes beyond program design to program implementation. They suggest program goals, activities, and an appropriate sequence for them, and they enable the creation of assessment measures.

The following discussion is organized into four sections. The first section describes the theoretical components of holistic student development and intercultural communication that directly apply to the holistic model of study abroad. The second section integrates these perspectives in a conceptual framework for intentional program design with the specific goals of advancing students' intellectual growth and facilitating the development of skills in intercultural competence and their application. The third section reviews assessment measures at programmatic and individual levels. The final section presents IES Abroad/The Institute of the International Education of Students as a case study of an educational system with holistic programs.

The educational philosophy of the model described in this chapter is pluralist: it subscribes to a curriculum of liberal education in the humanities, social sciences, physical sciences, and fine arts and supports cross-disciplinary studies according to the scholarship of the host country. The model recognizes pedagogy as a cultural construct and embraces multiple teaching practices and assessment methods. The program described in this chapter enrolls students for a semester, full-year, or summer term for academic credit and is operated as a not-for-profit educational organization.

THEORETICAL CONSIDERATIONS

Two fields in the social sciences, educational psychology and human communication studies in intercultural communication, find common ground in their exploration of personal growth and the challenges of human interactions across cultures. Theorists of holistic student development and intercultural communication competence focus their research on the domain of cognition and also on one's affective condition to understand how change occurs and how it is expressed. They use the same word to describe the process of personal change and cultural adaptation—the metaphoric *journey*, the story of personal discovery in the tradition of the epic quest. The following overview of these theoretical frameworks is confined to their relevance to the holistic model of study abroad and explains the rationale for drawing on the total environment to advance the global learning and development of young men and women.

The holistic view of student development embraces the depth and breadth of the human mind and spirit—the whole person—and proposes that an educational setting should address the individual's intellectual growth as well as her personal growth to enable the student to mature and become a full participant in civil society (Baxter Magolda, 2001; Braskamp, Trautvetter, & Ward, 2006; Kegan, 1994; Pizzolato & Ozaki, 2007). It is not a new idea, but colleges in the United States are revisiting the theory particularly in terms of envisioning the campus community as one that is intentionally designed to simultaneously challenge and support students as they reflect on and make choices not only about their intellectual life, but also about social and civic engagement, ethics, and spirituality. In this view, faculty and staff are all called upon to contribute to this community and its inherent challenges by providing support. In short, the relationship and balance between challenge and support is a central theme in fostering human development, especially in young persons.

The theory identifies three key questions that men and women of traditional college age, 18 to 24 years, ask themselves: How do I know? Who am I? How do I relate to others? (Braskamp, 2007). Whether contemporary college students complete their degree requirements on campus or enroll in a program of study abroad to fulfill a portion of college credits, they begin to articulate the answers to these three questions in a globalized world. They learn about global issues and meet other members of the campus community with different cultural backgrounds, perspectives, religious beliefs, and customs; they respond intellectually and personally to ideas, concepts, and characteristics that surround them.

During the past decade, a number of terms have entered the vernacular to describe students' learning in this global context. *Intercultural maturity* is a term now used in student development theory (King & Baxter Magolda, 2005). Interculturalists speak of *intercultural competence* as a behavior, resulting from a combination of learned skills and natural aptitude (Chen & Starostra, 1996). Neuropsychologists advocate for *global consciousness*, a state of awareness of ourselves and others, of situations and events, in a worldwide context (Mansilla & Gardner, 2007). The term *global learning and development* is used in the model for study abroad described in this chapter to convey the equal importance of a student's intellectual, social, and interior life, and the developmental nature of the educational process. This model is action-oriented in both its goals and its means. It applies the principles of learning-by-doing to specific outcomes such as understanding the intersection of local, national, and global issues; recognizing and tolerating cultural diversity; and deepening one's awareness of the self in society and hence, of one's social responsibilities. Educators in the broadest sense of the term provide challenge and support to students who are newcomers to the global stage and are eager to create roles for themselves on this stage in the present and future.

Global learning and development adapt the same three dimensions of human nature as holistic student development—cognitive, intrapersonal, and interpersonal (King & Baxter Magolda, 2005). Together these dimensions create an understanding of self and others and enable a person to act on that understanding. "Dimension" is used purposely to create a visual image of a triangle with three interrelated sides.

The question "How do I know?" reflects the *cognitive* dimension, which expands with the mental exercise of becoming aware, reflecting on new information, and integrating it into existing knowledge. When students' capacity for complex thought is directed to global learning, they can identify different cultural perspectives, beliefs, social customs, and systems, and they can recognize the importance of cultural differences in societal and global relationships. Students

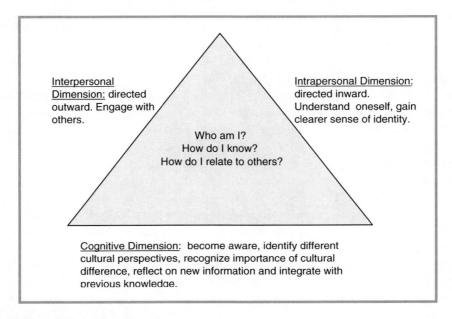

Figure 25.1 Holistic Student Development

begin to interpret their own cultural background and the characteristics of other cultures with a greater level of specificity. Breaking from the confines of dualism, they may draw on multiple perspectives and complex analysis to debate contemporary social, economic, and political issues. Their level of intellectual sophistication increases with knowledge and experience as they are able to understand and analyze global challenges presented by course material and experience outside the classroom.

Thoughtful students, particularly those whose strengths lie in language and mathematics, subject areas that correspond to the structure favored by the traditional classroom setting, are likely to reach the same intellectual maturity in a sequence of courses taught by dedicated faculty on the home campus. The difference in moving toward this maturity in a contemporary holistic program of study abroad is the role of direct experience in constructing and applying new learning. The classroom is only one venue in the total learning environment that invites students to see themselves and their own culture in the broad global context.

These multiple and broad venues present learning opportunities that are both challenging and rewarding because they require a range of aptitudes and learning styles to negotiate. These aptitudes and styles intersect with the multiple intelligences (MI) identified by Howard Gardner (1983/1993, 1999, 2007). Multiple intelligences theory presents an approach to thinking about individuals and the intellectual competence on which they rely to negotiate the world and use information to solve problems. Thus, for example, persons with linguistic intelligence might learn by observation and intellectual reflection. In the study abroad environment, they are drawn out of their learning "comfort zone" to test another form of intelligence, such as bodily-kinesthetic, and to use other styles such as direct experience and experimentation to reach an intellectual understanding. Those individuals whose preferred learning styles already rely on learning-by-doing quickly realize that the total environment in the holistic program is a classroom, that every experience and interaction is a lesson moving them toward cultural understanding.

The other two dimensions, *intrapersonal* and *interpersonal*, represent one's affective life of feelings about self and others and relationships with others. The intrapersonal dimension is directed inward, to understand oneself, and to gain self-possession and a clearer sense of identity. The interpersonal dimension is directed outward, toward relations with others and willingness to engage with others. Howard Gardner awarded these two dimensions the status of intelligence in his MI theory. Paired as "personal intelligences," these capacities do not simply represent the affective life of feelings and emotions but the life of the mind (Gardner, 1983/1993, 1999). Gardner's description of these two intelligences in particular carries resonance with the hybrid model of study abroad because they address the total student experience in a total learning environment.

The three dimensions, as the sides of a triangle, connect and together propel the student to a self-conscious confrontation of the values and beliefs that supported her or him through adolescence. Students simultaneously entertain the three questions asked in holistic student development theory, "Who am I, how do I relate to others, and how do I know?" By questioning, they begin to construct a set of ideals, purposely aligning themselves and identifying with a community, a process referred to as the key to socialization (Kegan, 1994). Restated as an educational goal, this process enables the student who is attuned to diverse culturally informed viewpoints and issues of international concerns to advance toward becoming part of the international community.

Interculturalists and theorists of intercultural communication consider the same three dimensions of human development—cognitive, interpersonal, and intrapersonal—as educational psychologists. However, the trajectory of their investigation of the role of communication in cultural adaptation examines the ways that a shift in attitude regarding cultural difference translates into action. On this trajectory, they identify personal strengths that predispose the sojourner to successful adaptation. A familiar list of attributes includes descriptors of the cognitive, intrapersonal, and interpersonal dimensions such as flexibility, open-mindedness, tolerance for ambiguity, self-confidence, resourcefulness, resilience, gregariousness, persistence, hardiness, and optimism (Gudykunst & Kim, 2003). Proponents of student development, by comparison, would argue that some of these traits are precisely what individuals will acquire during a term of study abroad, particularly during the first experience in a new culture, and that the development of these personal strengths signals exactly the appropriate direction for self-definition.

Whether students are predisposed to cultural adaptation because of personal strengths or are able to develop these strengths as they negotiate culture shock, they need to be psychologically healthy. Interculturalists identify a lack of intercultural communication competence as a significant source of psychological stress. The lack of competence may be the result of poor verbal and nonverbal skills in the host language or low self-esteem and social isolation (Gudykunst & Kim, 2003). Language skills can be improved with guidance, practice, and motivation. However, if the lack of competence reveals the student's diminished sense of self and negative feelings about others, the strategies for improving intercultural skills are not as clear as they are for language learning. What is clear in such a case is the need for programming for students' health and safety in the holistic model of education abroad.

The theory of intercultural communication contributes to the dialogue about models of study abroad programming by identifying the details of the communication process, verbal and nonverbal skills, and one's self-presentation as the most basic steps in the sojourner's cultural adaptation. Even students who lack language skills in the host country language should be able to perceive nonverbal cues and moderate their behavior in the cultural context. Similarly, American students in English-language countries quickly realize they must relearn English to use the language appropriately in the host country. American students who are learning and using a second language adopt new rhetorical strategies as they begin to understand that cultures define communication differently. For example, respecting the relationship between the speaker and the audience may be more important than transmitting information. Hence, a native speaker may never disagree with a conversation partner or say No, because taking such a stand would violate the personal relationship (Jandt, 2001).

Interculturalists are beginning to examine the role of physical sensory experience in explaining how the sojourner makes the leap from greater cultural awareness and acceptance of cultural difference to more effective and appropriate behavior and action across cultures. This line of thinking concentrates on the cultural concept of space and how the sojourner reacts to physical space—horizontal and vertical dimensions and the proximity of others. Becoming aware of this feeling in physical space and learning how to control a negative response through breathing exercises can serve as a means of adaptation (Bennett & Castiglione, 2004). This thesis promotes the development of the bodily kinesthetic intelligence, an intellectual capacity shared by athletes, dancers, and actors, among others, in MI theory (Gardner, 1983/1993, 1999). In the context of a holistic program of study abroad, the idea suggests an interesting line of research on cultural adaptation among student athletes who join local teams to maintain their training regime as well as students who patronize local health clubs, join an outing club, or test themselves in a new physical activity such as dance or drama to support their psychological well-being and cultural learning while they are abroad.

The theorists of human development and learning discussed in this section write from the perspective of Westerners, although their trajectory is international. Their multiple viewpoints coincide at the critical axis of global learning and development, which refers to both a process and a goal of the holistic program of international education. The inevitable changes that accompany students in their journey abroad in self-concept, awareness and understanding of another culture and subsequent relationships in that culture are the starting points of global citizenship. Students abroad expand their knowledge and sense of self in a global context.

THE HOLISTIC MODEL AND 4X3 FRAMEWORK

In the past, the "hybrid" model of an American program of education abroad referred to the administrative and academic structure: an American-based sponsor arranged for students to enroll in courses that it created and hired instructors to teach, and it registered them in courses at the local partner university. This model with two academic options was designed to reflect the best of U.S. and host country academic traditions. Today, the application of the hybrid concept to the design of a program of education abroad has expanded in both purpose and scope to include the delivery of a broad range of educational services, particularly in student affairs, paralleling the expansion of such services on American campuses. Nevertheless, through the expansion, one programming goal remains constant: the academic design meets the needs of students who intend to transfer credit for courses they take abroad to fulfill their undergraduate requirements toward graduation from their home institutions in the United States. The expanded holistic model provides significant support by building opportunities for students' global learning and development into the complete student experience.

The holistic model of education abroad respects the totality of human learning and development, based on the theories of holistic student development and intercultural communication. The model builds on these theories with its premise that two other areas of student growth—intellectual and linguistic—proceed apace with cognitive, interpersonal, and intrapersonal development. This premise originates from the IES Abroad Model Assessment Program (Institute for International Education of Students [IES], IES Abroad MAP), a comprehensive set of guidelines for program planning and development that directs the design of the holistic educational system discussed in this chapter. The operating principle of the design is one of student challenge and support: everyone who comes into contact with students is potentially an educator and cultural interpreter.

The core of this group consists of the administrative and teaching staff members who are responsible for establishing student goals. Once they identify these goals, or desired ends, in fostering student learning and development in study abroad, they can focus on the appropriate means that will direct a student toward those ends. They intentionally plan and implement the details of a program that are documented to be effective and to test new ideas that hold promise.

Earlier research involving 10 U.S. campuses with a strong mission for fostering holistic student development identified a "4-C" framework for classifying four important means: culture, curriculum, cocurriculum, and community in the educational setting (Braskamp, Trautvetter, & Ward, 2006). The 4-C framework and the three dimensions of student learning and development—cognitive, interpersonal, and intrapersonal—serve as a taxonomy for classifying the learning environment. This taxonomy was adapted for conceptualizing education abroad and establishing links between program goals and activities in each category and across categories (Braskamp & Braskamp, 2007). The framework was found to be useful in helping administrative and teaching staff members engage in strategic planning and program evaluation.

Many programmed activities and interventions transect categories. For example, a course

Table 25.1 *Framework for Connecting Student Learning and Sociocultural Environment*

ENDS	MEANS			
	Culture	Curriculum	Co-Curriculum	Community
Cognitive				
Interpersonal				
Intrapersonal				

taught at the program site (curriculum) reflects and elucidates the culture, and it may require a self-guided museum visit (cocurriculum) and a personal interview with a homestay host (community). Students' development as they are engaged in such a course includes their ways of knowing (cognitive), their intrapersonal growth as they draw on their own resourcefulness to locate the museum and find their way to the appropriate exhibit, and their interpersonal skills to conduct an interview. The key to this chart is intent: it encourages educators to be purposeful in creating an educational environment that connects the desired ends of global learning and development with the means—the activities, courses, and experiences in and out of the classroom—that guide students' progress toward those ends. Examples are presented in the final section, using Institute for the International Education of Students (IES) as the case studies.

The key characteristics of each of these four domains of the learning environment of students at a holistic program of study abroad are as follows.

Culture

Culture is defined narrowly here as the identity and character of the education abroad program. It is imbedded in the habits and behaviors of staff and faculty who are host nationals or long-time residents of the host country. Their face-to-face interactions with students offer frequent, continuing insights into the cultural context of verbal and nonverbal communication. Culture also is reflected in the program's location, facilities, and daily rituals—the dimensions of space and time that are manifested by allocation of offices, classrooms, and public areas, and the daily and weekly calendars. The sojourner eventually comes to recognize these cultural cues and ideally learns the appropriate response.

Curriculum

Curriculum includes the courses, the content of what is taught to students, as well as pedagogy, the ways in which faculty teach the subject matter. In a holistic program, the curriculum may offer a number of tracks, depending on the program focus and student profile. One track is designed specifically for American students and the common disciplines in liberal education at American institutions of higher education. Within this framework, courses that fulfill academic credit meet requirements in terms of content, reading, and methods of assessment. These requirements may be set by a faculty committee for study abroad at the home institution, the academic governing board of a consortium of institutions, or a combination of both. However, topics vary widely from courses that focus on the national history and culture of the host country to courses that address contemporary global movements in such areas as immigration, financial markets, political theory, and artistic expression, particularly in film and literature. Internships and community-based learning may be options in this curricular track, depending on the location, language requirement, and student profile.

Instructors who are hired as host country nationals to teach these courses generally reflect the local style of teaching and common assessment measures. The student may be challenged not only by the content of courses but also by how the content is delivered. For example, an academic culture may emphasize the lecture, supplemented by independent reading, self-directed primary research, and sophisticated rhetorical skills for constructing an argument in a lengthy essay that constitutes the only assessment of student learning.

An alternative pedagogical strategy that takes advantage of the total environment as a learning resource is field study, defined broadly as research in the location and with its host population in the form of site visits, personal interviews, and personal observation. Students in a Peace and Conflict Studies program in Dublin point to a 3-day field study in Belfast as first-hand experience that is essential to their learning. The neighborhoods that they visit, as well as meetings held with former paramilitaries, give students a firsthand view of the conflict and goes beyond what most Dubliners themselves are ever likely to experience. One student reported, "I had no idea how startling this program would be. We met a paramilitary who opened the conversation by saying, 'I was in jail for eighteen years for killing someone. I don't regret it. Now, what questions do you have?'" (IES, 2007b).

Another track may offer students the option of enrolling in one or more courses at a partner university as part of their course load. In this scenario, the holistic program staff facilitates academic advising and registration for the visiting student, who sits alongside local university students in the classroom and fulfills the same course requirements.

Training in the fine arts, most commonly in music or theater performance or studio art, may constitute a discrete track or a single course option taught at the program site or a partner university. The single course options that do not carry prerequisites are designed to attract the student who already is testing himself by placing himself in a new cultural environment and may want to test his skills further in a classroom environment that draws on a different intellectual competence. Such courses in which students learn to dance flamenco in Granada, Spain and tango in Buenos Aires, practice calligraphy in Tokyo, and use a second language to track down props for a theater production in Paris not only count for academic credit in the fine arts but also offer students a physical outlet for their creative energies.

A curriculum in the fine arts is essential to students in these majors who must pursue their training while they are abroad. They advance in their studies, and their talent acts as a bridge to the host culture, facilitating their adaptation. A student in Vienna, remembering her studio class in piano and the concert in which her teacher invited her to play, wrote,

> After we had all played, my piano teacher kissed me on the cheek and told me that I had played Mozart like a true Viennese.... Suddenly the anxiety and homesickness that had been lodged in my throat for the past few months vanished and I felt a wave of pure elation. I discovered I had somehow attained a decent mastery over the German language in the past months, and I was even able to engage with an erudite patron of the arts in a conversation about Schubert's youth. (IES, 2007c)

In countries where the first language is not English, required language courses at beginning, intermediate, and advanced levels and workshops on special topics such as creative writing and vocabulary for business and health care frequently are part of the curriculum. Students must develop their linguistic skills as well as understand appropriate contexts for language use. These classes also support cultural learning by creating content around popular culture and current events. The small number of students per class and importance of conversational skills are characteristics of the language classroom that supports holistic student development. The coordinator of a group of Spanish language instructors in Granada, Rosana Pinero said, "The holistic approach is necessary for learning another language. It's a mistake to think that if you know the grammar, you know the language. Language requires an intuitive approach, not a rational approach. We help them overcome their tendency to be competitive and instead to be supportive of their peers. We think it's essential to help them deal with the frustration of learning a language by building their self-esteem" (R. Pinero, personal communication, March 8, 2007).

Cocurriculum

The cocurriculum consists of planned activities that address program goals in furthering students' learning and cultural adaptation. The bookends of a holistic program's cocurriculum are an on-site orientation for students when they arrive and special preparation for reentry to their home, family, and friends as the term draws to a close. A common calendar of events may include creative activities such as workshops in music and dance, exhibits of student photography, cooking classes in the local cuisine, excursions to local parks and recreation areas, theater performances, and museum visits. Guided field trips to locations that students are unlikely to visit on their own are common to most hybrid programs. Organized sports and athletic outings also may figure into the cocurriculum as other means to support students in their new environment. The reentry program may consist of two sessions that bring closure to the experience. One session may be conducted with a professional psychologist who gives students the opportunity to reflect on their term abroad, themselves, friends, and family. A second session may be a scheduled special event such as a reception with an artistic performance by students who pursued music, dance, or theater during the term and an exhibit of student photography. An example of a cocurriculum at a language immersion program in Nantes, France is included below.

Community

Community for a holistic program of study abroad is visualized as a series of three concentric circles. One circle, the program itself, consists of administrative and teaching staff and enrolled students. The second circle is the local community whose members interact with the visiting students on a regular, organized basis, including faculty and students at the local university, the homestay families that host students and Resident Assistants in residence halls, and supervisors at internship placement sites. The third circle is the community at large in which students must learn to function, interacting with bus drivers, shopkeepers, and restauranteurs.

The distinguishing feature of the holistic program is the community comprised of its immediate circle. The staff and faculty give stability to this community and all of them contribute to building a sense of shared purpose, mutual respect, and program identity with the ever-changing population of enrolled students. Intercultural communication theorists point to the host environment and its openness to nonnationals as central to the sojourner's cultural adaptation (Gudykunst & Kim, 2003). The interactions that occur and relationships that develop in the program community between staff, faculty, and students are crucial to the students' cultural experience and learning. Ashley Taggart, the director of a program in Dublin articulated this concept:

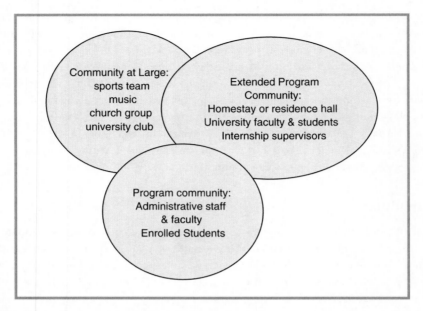

Figure 25.2 *Community Circles in the 4-C Program Design*

I wanted to create a relaxed and happy environment for both staff and students to work in. One of the most important means to achieving goals (of cultural knowledge and personal growth) is staff selection. Lecturers should be not only academically committed, but open to interaction, willing to be challenged, and sensitive to cultural difference.... The role of the Center staff cannot be overstated. Their ability to engage with the students as advisors and confidants as well as to provide structure and (occasionally) discipline is vital. (A. Taggart, personal communication, February 15, 2007)

Program activities may be designed to engage students in this community. One successful effort in a language immersion program is a language pledge, whereby students divide themselves into teams, set boundaries for the use of English and the target language, and monitor themselves. Another example is the recruitment of students to come together on a soccer team, practice, and compete against local students or other American students. In this community of staff, faculty, and students, codes of conduct for personal behavior and academic integrity apply. These codes suggest another reason why this circle is so important. It is a place of psychological and physical safety where rules are transparent to students as they make their adjustment in a new culture whose codes and cues may baffle them.

Interactions with the second circle may be planned only insofar as contracts have been exchanged for services. The university, homestay host family, and internship workplace exist as communities before the student's arrival; his integration requires mutual commitment to openness and understanding. This most promising integration occurs when partners in this second circle are committed to internationalization in a process of reciprocal learning. The homestay in particular also may become part of the new support system for the student. A student in Beijing wrote of this support:

> For my study abroad experience I was lucky enough to find myself living with a Chinese host family who spoke no English. While this did wonders for my language ability, the first two months I had a lot of trouble understanding what was going on around me.... [One] night [at dinner], as my [host] mother spoke with my [host] father, I listened intently.... Then something magical happened...when I heard my [host] mother [speak] I instantly understood.... As I reacted to this comment my [host] mother, eyes as big as saucers, turned to me, cocked her head, and asked, "You understand?" My host father, who is desperately trying to learn English by memorizing words and phrases from the dictionary, insisted I write down the English expression so he could later study it. My host mother looked fondly on me and told me how much my Chinese had improved. They were both so proud and excited that I had understood something on my own. (IES, 2008)

In this ideal scenario, the student is supported by his homestay family in language learning and he, in turn, supported his host in learning English.

The third circle, the greater community, lies outside any control of program administrators, yet this circle offers a constant round of integrative potential via daily routines and smaller existing circles such as a church congregation, musical group, or sports team. The staff of the holistic program of study abroad can assist students with their entry into these communities by keeping a database of contact information and experiences of former students. A student who played on a softball team at her home campus wrote of joining a softball team in Barcelona:

> I found a team and took probably one of the largest leaps of faith I have ever made.... The decision to let myself join a small community of people within my new culture was a decision that has transformed my life so completely; I don't even remember how it used to be. With softball I had something to break that awkward you-are-like-an-alien barrier that tends to be created between people of different nationalities.... Not only did softball break the ice socially, but it broke the ice linguistically for me. (IES, 2007d)

ASSESSMENT OF GLOBAL LEARNING AND DEVELOPMENT

The similarity between an assessment strategy for a program abroad and a campus community is the use of multiple sources to collect evidence of the effectiveness of the links between desired ends and appropriate means. However, the holistic model of study abroad presents a particular challenge to assessment because of the number of variables that impact student learning and development. These variables include: students' previous experiences with cultural difference and consequently the stages of cultural competence in which they begin their term abroad; their skills in negotiating a new environment regardless of previous experience; language competence in a non-English-language environment; and the hospitality and openness that host country nationals extend to sojourners. Further confounding these variables is that the long-term effects of study abroad on students' decisions about careers, graduate school enrollment, and political and social engagement might be implied but cannot be established.

Assessment in a holistic model is designed to reflect the two program priorities of students' intellectual growth and intercultural learning. One set of measures is directed toward the program characteristics—each of the 4-Cs—and depends on student input. Another set of measures focuses on the student and requires self-assessment and assessment of students by faculty and staff members to provide insight into student growth and development. Two terms applied to these measures are *direct* and *indirect*, the former focusing on what students learn and can do as a result of their engagement, the latter serving as indicators or proxies of student learning (Maki, 2004).

The holistic model relies on a number of common assessment methods, both quantitative and qualitative.

- Locally designed measures and tests—Assessments constructed by faculty for courses. Faculty teaching in study abroad programs may rely on a combination of student journals, critiques of reading assignments, analysis of a case study, an assignment linked to field study, written exams, and research essays to monitor student progress and assign grades.
- Standardized measures of content, skills, and values—Tests of content, reasoning skills, and language acquisition. Standard in-country language exams with an official sponsor such as the local Chamber of Commerce or a national cultural and language institute rate American students' progress against all international students seeking fluency in a second language and provide a reliable assessment of student language learning.
- Performance based methods—Student portfolios, group projects, artistic performances, oral examinations, and class presentations. These types of measures are more common in host countries whose pedagogical culture embraces active learning.

Students, in turn, assess teaching practice, usually through a survey whose items reflect research on how students learn. The premise of this assessment as an indirect measure of student learning is that effective teaching leads to learning. A standard set of questions in these assessments place responsibility on the student for his learning by asking about his motivation for taking the course and his commitment to the course material and course requirements.

An important indirect measure of student learning is the students' assessment of specific program characteristics, including details of the student learning environment, resources, and services, usually completed through a student survey. These large-scale assessments are significant to the hybrid program because the data identify which details in the learning environment were successful in achieving desired ends for students' learning and development and guides discussions of program improvement. Personal interviews of students, either random or targeted, by a third party, may be conducted to ascertain student response to specific program details and can be highly individualized.

Measures of students' intercultural development are largely indirect and include students' self-reports of their experiences using focus groups, surveys, and interviews to glean students' perceptions of their learning, attitudes, experiences, and reflections of development and change. Some surveys and focus groups assess student perceptions at different moments during their term abroad, most commonly, before they arrive at their study abroad site and just prior to their departure. This strategy may or may not indicate attitudinal change, since students become more sophisticated, and perhaps more modest, about their intercultural competence during their term abroad, and data can be inconclusive (Sutton, Miller, & Rubin, 2006).

One standardized survey that has recently been developed is the Global Perspective Inventory (GPI; Braskamp, Braskamp, & Carter Merrill, 2008). It has been specifically designed to provide self-reports of students' perspectives in the three dimensions of holistic student development—cognitive, intrapersonal, and interpersonal. Two scales of each domain have been constructed: one reflects the theory of cultural development and the other reflects intercultural communication theory. For example, the cognitive domain includes Knowing and Knowledge scales. The

Knowing scale stresses the complexity of thinking using cultural context in judging what is important to know and value. Knowledge refers to the degree of understanding and awareness of various cultures and their impact on the global society, and level of proficiency in more than one language. The Intrapersonal domain includes Identity and Affect scales. The Identity scale measures the level of awareness of one's unique identity and degree of acceptance of ethnic, racial, and gender dimensions of one's identity. The Affect scale measures the level of respect and acceptance of cultural perspectives that are different from one's own and the degree of confidence in living in complex situations. The Interpersonal domain includes Social Interaction and Social Responsibility scales. Social Interactions scale measures the degree of engagement with others who are different and the degree of cultural sensitivity in living in pluralistic settings. The Social Responsibility scale measure the level of commitment to interdependent living and the "common good." In short, the GPI is intended to provide a comprehensive portrayal of a student's global perspective following a term abroad.

Large-scale surveys of alumni have been conducted by IES Abroad to measure the longitudinal impact of study abroad and the specific impact of program elements. These longitudinal impact studies were conducted in 1999, 2002, and 2006. The largest of these surveys was administered in 2002 and sent to 14,800 alumni who enrolled in programs from 1950 to 1999. Three categories of questions addressed basic demographics, key study abroad program elements, and the impact of study abroad on select behaviors, attitudes, and accomplishments. A number of analyses of the survey data discuss the longitudinal effects of variables such as program model, study duration, enrollment in foreign university courses, student housing choices, participation in internships and field study, and language study on a variety of outcome measures (Dwyer, 2004a, 2004b; Dwyer & Peters, 2004; Norris & Dwyer, 2005; Norris & Gillespie, 2005; Ruhter & Opem, 2004; Steinberg, 2002). The data from alumni who were enrolled in hybrid programs and chose certain program options such as language study, an internship, or field experience correlates with responses concerning careers, such as the use of a second language in the workplace, work in an international capacity, and the development of professional contacts.

The broad topic of program evaluation was addressed by IES Abroad with the quality standards of the IES Abroad *Model Assessment Practice* (IES Abroad MAP, IES, 1999/2007a), first published in 1999, as a model framework for the design, development, and evaluation of programs of study abroad (IES, 1999/2007a). As the first document of its kind in education abroad, the IES Abroad MAP has benefited a wide audience, including faculty and administrators at U.S. colleges and universities and accrediting organizations who are charged with program assessment. The IES Abroad MAP also formed the basis for the standards of The Forum on Education Abroad adopted by the field. IES articulated this set of quality standards to guide them in their strategic planning and to advance the discussion in the field of program development and assessment. The IES MAP sets out guidelines for the student learning environment and the human and physical resources that are essential to the learning environment in a hybrid program. A new IES MAP for direct enrollment programs was published in 2007 (IES, 1999/2007a). The IES MAP defines five dimensions of student learning and development that constitute program goals. It is not a how-to manual but rather a philosophy of program planning whose premise is that the host country and culture are the starting points for creating the total learning environment (Gillespie, Braskamp, & Braskamp, 1999).

The guidelines of the IES MAP specific to student learning and development consist of five broad categories. The first two categories address students' intellectual development and, in a non-English-speaking host environment, language ability. In the holistic model, in the tradition of liberal education, the first essential learning outcome is knowledge—the mastery of texts and scholarship. In a program of study abroad designed to further students' progress toward their undergraduate degree, this goal must be explicitly stated. The category of language competence addresses correct use as well as appropriate use—the intersecting concerns of language instructors. Three other categories use the taxonomy of intercultural competence and holistic development defined earlier in this chapter—students' cognitive, interpersonal, and intrapersonal change and growth—to describe characteristics that IES seeks to develop and support in the challenging environment of a different country and culture.

The IES MAP implies a number of assessment measures as the means to promote program development by refining strategies to achieve goals for student learning and development. Every academic term, students are invited to complete a general program survey online when they return to the United States. These exhaustive surveys follow the categories of the IES MAP and include a self-assessment of language development, if applicable, and intercultural experience and adaptation. The format of the survey enables students to add narrative comments in the categories of curriculum, housing, and intercultural experience and to make general comments as well. Students complete other questionnaires and surveys specific to IES and university courses and instruction, housing, orientation, and field trips when they are on-site.

The second audience that conducts a program assessment is composed of representatives of the IES consortium and local faculty members who constitute an external review team. These reviews are held in the third year of a new program and follow a cycle of 8 to 10 years for existing programs. General charges to the review committee are drawn from the IES MAP and include all program details. A final report is drawn up by the review team, reviewed by the IES Curriculum Committee composed of U.S. faculty, and presented to the academic governing board for approval. The recommendations constitute a mandate for incremental program improvement to the administrative staff and faculty.

U.S. faculty who visit a program site as members of an external review team also assess teaching practice by observing the classroom, accompanying field study, and meeting independently with lecturers and students. One such team issued the following report about instructors at a program in Dublin:

> I was impressed not only by the caliber of the teaching but by the intelligence and poise of the students in class discussions and individual presentations. Lecturers clearly encourage students to develop good critical thinking skills, and this was especially apparent in courses where students were doing field studies. The emphasis on experience-based learning promotes a high level of engagement on the part of the students. (IES, 1999/2007a)

This assessment speaks to a holistic educational philosophy: students develop "poise," a social skill, along with "intelligence." Field studies offer the means whereby students become both intellectually and personally engaged. The report of the review team thus provides both a direct and indirect measure of student learning and development.

CASE STUDY, IES ABROAD/INSTITUTE FOR THE INTERNATIONAL EDUCATION OF STUDENTS

This case study examines IES Abroad/Institute for the International Education of Students, a not-for-profit consortium of more than 170 American colleges and universities that is incorporated in the State of Illinois as an educational organization. IES Abroad began in 1950 as the Institute of European Studies with a program in Vienna, Austria. Today it is a global educational system with 70 study abroad programs primarily for American undergraduates in Africa, Asia, Australia, Europe, New Zealand, and South America and enrolls more than 5,500 students annually in fall, spring, full-year, and summer terms and customized short-term programs. It is categorized as a "third party provider" whose administration and finances are independent of a college or university but whose academic governance is entrusted to elected representatives of the consortium. This academic oversight assures that the programs run by IES carry academic credit that transfers to the student's home institution and contributes to graduation requirements. The academic governance system also represents a check and balance on program quality control. The IES Abroad initiative in setting standards for hybrid programs of study abroad with the IES Abroad MAP is the reason to focus on IES as a case study.

A system-wide initiative for program development according to the guidelines of the IES MAP is IES 3-D Program Model, 3-D referring to the three dimensions of holistic student development. This model synthesizes the quality standards of the IES MAP and the philosophy of holistic student development that is visualized in the 4x3 matrix. The implementation of the IES 3-D Program Model consisted of two parts, a series of training workshops for administrative and teaching staff at several IES Centers with hybrid programs, and the publication of an internal *Sourcebook of Best Practices* based on the discussion of the 3-D model. These workshops occurred in the broader context of staff and faculty development at IES Abroad and can be viewed operationally as part of an ongoing dialogue on achieving learning and development goals in an intercultural context.

The audience for the workshops was the community of program staff and faculty who offer students their first interactions with the host culture and provide ongoing guidance and instruction. The workshops introduced the themes and vocabulary of holistic student development and encouraged instructors to think in terms of setting goals for students' personal development. Instructors may not articulate the connections between learning goals such as the mastery of course material and students' greater cultural awareness, although the content of their courses and teaching strategies may imply these connections. At some IES Centers, program staff members with advanced degrees also teach a course; they personify the idea that the educational administrator and classroom instructor are role models for intercultural understanding and share the responsibility for supporting students' learning and development. The training workshops succeeded in engendering a spirit of collaboration between administrative and teaching staff in planning the curriculum, cocurriculum, and community engagement with common goals for students' global learning and development.

After the workshops, many of the faculty and staff from each of the Centers volunteered to submit an entry for the IES Abroad *Best Practices Sourcebook* highlighting their course or a cocurricular activity. This internal manual extended the benefits of the workshops, engaging staff and faculty in reflecting on and planning for efforts to actively direct students' global learning and development, to broaden their perspective of the world and of their place in the world. The two case studies below follow the premise of the IES Abroad MAP that the program location—city, local culture, the historic and contemporary social, economic, and political state, and language— create the frame for the curriculum. They also represent a guideline of the IES Abroad MAP that the curriculum represents students' academic needs and interests.

The programs in these case studies are both language-immersion, in Nantes, France and Granada, Spain. IES Nantes requires advanced French for admission; most students enrolled in this program declare their major or minor in French. IES Granada offers an advanced Spanish curriculum for students at the advanced language level and an English curriculum for students at an intermediate language level. The IES Granada case study applies to advanced language students. As with students at IES Nantes, students at the advanced level in Granada are completing coursework for a language major or minor. Both program sites also host a high number of students in political science and international relations. This student profile—advanced language learners with knowledge of national and global politics—suggests that the curricula at these two sites are appropriate to their locations and for their intended student cohorts. The concurrent step to curricular development in program design is creating a complementary co-curriculum and identifying opportunities for community integration. The 4x3 templates indicate how these program details come together in the two case studies.

IES NANTES

Goals

Cognitive

- Improve U.S. students' ability to communicate in French, in particular with French youth.
- Discover, become aware of, and better understand the perspectives, worldviews, social interactions, values, and cultural practices of the French and especially young adults in France, which are different from those of the American student.
- Discuss openly cultural differences, current events, and social and cultural practices with French peers.
- Understand one's own cultural background when compared to another.
- Increase students' awareness of differences between people in general.

Intrapersonal

- Construct and trust in one's self-identity through comparisons with diverse others.
- Through new and different interactions and comparisons with French peers, become conscious of, analyze, and gain a new perspective on one's own worldviews, social and cultural practices, and behavior in social situations.
- Increase in self-confidence after being able to adapt to new and different social situations.

Interpersonal

- Increase students' ability and comfort in interacting with persons from different cultural backgrounds.
- Assist students in adapting to various social situations.
- Develop acceptance, tolerance, and respect of others with perspectives, values, worldviews, and social and cultural practices different from one's own.
- Support students' desire to socialize with the French, and eventually to form close social relationships.
- Create intercultural social situations that help to expand the student's sense of self.
- Develop students' ability to act appropriately, maturely, and with cultural sensitivity in social situations in France.

Means

- IES Nantes hires a social coordinator each academic year. This person is a Université de Nantes student who has been a student assistant at an American university through the IES student assistantship program. Her or his role is to organize a variety of activities that allow IES students to meet and spend time with French students.
- Several social activities per week are planned. Activities may include: dinner at a restaurant, meeting for a drink at a local bar or café, concerts, activities organized on the Université de Nantes campus by local student associations, accompanying students to university club and association meetings, sporting events, canoeing, bowling, student parties, karaoke.
- The social coordinator invites French students (personal acquaintances, students "recruited" at the University or via the Conversation Club). IES students may also invite their French friends. All IES students are invited to each activity.
- The social coordinator communicates with students through a weekly e-mail announcement of activities offered, and comes at least once a week to the IES center to talk informally with students about the week's activity.
- The IES Nantes associate director monitors the planned activities by requiring the social coordinator to give a weekly report on the activity, the date, and the number of participants. The associate director may give the coordinator suggestions about types of activities or how to attract students.

Assessment

- At the end of each semester, students receive an evaluation form in their mailboxes. Through open-ended questions, students are asked their opinions of the activities, suggestions for future activities, and if the activities enabled them to meet French students.
- Students may also make comments about the social activities in the more general program evaluation, which is also in paper format, and given at the end of the semester in each mailbox.
- Informal conversations might occur during staff interaction with students (IES staff eat lunch in the student kitchen and are very present in the Center) or during the regular meetings with the Student Council president and vice-president.

Special Considerations

- Conversation Club: The same goals may be met through the Conversation Club held at IES Nantes. Through a weekly 1½ hour French–English conversation group, French and American students have the opportunity to interact and create relationships. This activity is complementary to activities planned by the social coordinator.
- Safety: Social activities often take place at night. During the IES Orientation session on security, the Associate Director gives clear safety instructions to students regarding the best ways to return home (night buses or taxis), and in general to be safe at night. In addition, during orientation the associate director gives a presentation about French culture, social interactions, and the social behaviors of the French and how students should deal safely with possible problem situations.
- Financial Issues: Students note that social interaction in France often involves spending money. The IES Center allows interaction during open hours for the IES students; the Conversation

Table 25.2 *Holistic Student Learning in French Language Immersion Program*

		MEANS			
		Culture	Curriculum	Co-Curriculum	Community
ENDS	Cognitive	Understand perspective of French youth	Improve French language skills		
	Interpersonal	Act with cultural sensitivity	Improve communicative ability	**Conversation Club with French youth**	University activities and clubs
	Intrapersonal	Trust one's cultural identity	Increase self-confidence in language use		

Club is a free activity that takes place in the IES Center; the social coordinator must try to creatively plan activities that are inexpensive for students; students learn throughout the semester or year to be more creative in their personal social activities; IES sponsors some of the social activities (university-sponsored student parties, soccer games).

Discussion

The 4-Cs intersect in this project: the French culture, curricular goal for students' linguistic development, and a cocurriculum of planned activities through community integration. Program staff members note that this project is particularly successful in Nantes because of the small number of Americans in the city. French students are thus attracted to the planned activities in order to interact with American students. The end-of-term student questionnaire indicates the broad reach of the social coordinator; students report a high level of community involvement, participating in cultural activities and events publicized by the IES Abroad Center staff; the high importance of meeting local students and residence for learning about the host culture; their high level of success in meeting the challenge of being exposed to different perspectives; and their high level of success in using the language correctly.

The use of the 4x3 framework for a program in Nantes is illustrated above. A selected set of "desired ends" are included, with some "appropriate means" listed in bold (see Table 25.2).

IES GRANADA, THE SPANISH EXPERIENCE OF THE OTHER

Course Description

This course analyzes the different perceptions that Spaniards have about the towns and cultures that have coexisted and continue to coexist in modern day Spain. Students focus on three different populations living in 20th century Spain: the gypsies, Arabs, and Latin Americans. There is also reference to these groups drawing on the history of the Peninsula and during colonization. The course examines how perceptions about "the other" are constructed, including the repercussions of these ideas on multicultural societies, and the ways to manage cultural difference.

Goals

Cognitive

- Examine how perceptions about "the other" are constructed, including the repercussions of these ideas on multicultural societies.
- Examine problems derived from conflictive perceptions of "the other."
- Analyze ways to manage conflictive perceptions and cultural difference.

Intrapersonal

- Increased self-confidence in negotiating cultural difference.

Interpersonal

- Create a research project and pursue research as a member of a group.
- Learn interview techniques as a means of research.

Means

- Visit institutions, associations, and relevant neighborhoods in Granada.
- Final research project based on field work in multicultural neighborhoods of Granada, integrating local resources into students' training.

Assessment

Students keep a journal of field work, write a research paper, take an examination.

Discussion

The field research project is developed at the beginning of the term in consultation with the professor. As a group effort, it requires several steps and research using observation, interviews, and scientific resources. The professor monitors the progress of students throughout the term, meeting with them and reviewing the records of their research. The professor identified a number of factors that may determine the development of the students' research, including students' level of Spanish, students' level of motivation, and students' ability of observing, taking decisions, and coping with diverse situations.

The 4x3 framework in Table 25.3 lists a selected set of "appropriate means" in bold, and some "desired ends" (see Table 25.3).

CONCLUSION

The 4x3 template gives purpose and clarity to the principles of program planning that are established by the IES Abroad MAP. It creates a team of administrative and teaching staff by asking them to think of themselves as educators in the broadest sense of supporting student learning and development, with the additional responsibility to serve as role models for interculturalism.

Table 25.3 *Holistic Student Learning through Field Research*

		MEANS			
		Culture	Curriculum	Co-Curriculum	Community
ENDS	Cognitive		Examine perceptions of "the other"		Create a group research project based on field work
	Interpersonal		Learn interview techniques		Visit relevant sites in Granada
	Intrapersonal	Increased self-confidence in negotiating cultural difference			

A holistic program model also asks more of students; they must commit to engage the culture and people directly and respectfully, and to reflect on what they learn about themselves and their hosts from this engagement. While students may expect to be questioned on campus about their academic goals while they spend a term abroad, they may be caught off guard when asked about their goals for personal development. If the broad purpose of sending American students abroad is to give breadth and depth to their global perspective, as educators we should ask them to articulate these goals. These demands of administrative staff, teaching staff, and students extend to campus advisors. The results thus take time to effect.

The growing numbers of students going abroad and the increasing emphasis of U.S. colleges and universities on holistic student learning and development will place higher demands on education abroad to play an integral part in the total undergraduate experience. Education abroad programs that are intentionally designed to support students' global learning and intercultural development will meet this demand by contributing to the progress of students' journeys. In this dynamic field, the student profile represents an ever-increasing range of intercultural experiences, academic backgrounds, and interests. Additional research in a number of areas will contribute further to planning the learning environment in response to this range. For example, academic leaders will benefit from knowing more about the effect of students' prior experiences with multiculturalism and the openness of the host culture to the sojourner, the relationship between variable program lengths and specific program details in facilitating cultural learning, and stages of cultural adaptation for the beginning language learner and how these stages compare to those for advanced language speakers. The holistic program will continue to undergo improvements and refinements and represent an excellent alternative model of education abroad.

REFERENCES

Baxter Magolda, M. B. (2001). *Making their own way: Narratives for transforming higher education to promote self-authorship.* Sterling, VA: Stylus.

Bennett, M., & Castiglioni, I. (2004). Embodied ethnocentrism and the feeling of culture: A key to training for intercultural competence. In D. Landis, J. Bennett, & M. Bennett (Eds.), *Handbook of intercultural training* (pp. 249–265). Thousand Oaks, CA: Sage.

Braskamp, L. A. (2007, September). Three "central" questions worth asking. *Journal of College and Character, 10*(1), 1–7. Retrieved February 2, 2009, from http://www.collegevalues.org

Braskamp, L. A., & Braskamp, D. C. (2007, Fall). Fostering holistic student learning and development of college students: A strategic way to think about it. *The Department Chair, 5,* 118–127.

Braskamp, L. A., Braskamp, D. C., & Carter Merrill, K. (2008). Global perspective inventory (GPI). Its purpose, construction, potential uses, and psychometric characteristics. Retrieved Janaury 31, 2009, from http://www.gp.central.edu

Braskamp, L. A., Trautvetter, L. C., & Ward, K. (2006). *Putting students first: How colleges develop students purposefully.* Bolton, MA: Anker.

Chen, G. M., & Starosta, W. (1996). Intercultural communication competence: A synthesis. *Communication Yearbook, 19,* 353–383.

Dwyer, M. (2004a). Charting the impact of studying abroad. *International Educator, 13*(1), 14–20.

Dwyer, M. (2004b). More is better: The impact of study abroad program duration. *Frontiers: The Interdisciplinary Journal of Study Abroad, 10,* 151–163.

Dwyer, M., & Peters, C. (2004). The benefits of study abroad. *Transitions Abroad, 27*(5), 56–57.

Gardner, H. (1993). *Frames of mind: The theory of multiple intelligences.* New York: Basic Books. (Original work published 1983)

Gardner, H. (1999). *Intelligence reframed: Multiple intelligences for the 21st century.* New York: Basic Books.

Gardner, H. (2007). *Five minds for the future.* Boston: Harvard Business School Press.

Gillespie, J., Braskamp, L. A., & Braskamp, D. C. (1999, Fall). Evaluation and study abroad: Developing assessment criteria and practices to promote excellence. *Frontiers: The Interdisciplinary Journal of Study Abroad,* 101–127.

Gudykunst, W., & Kim, Y. L. (2003). *Communicating with strangers: An approach to intercultural communications* (4th ed.). Boston: McGraw-Hill.

Institute for the International Education of Students (IES). (2007a). IES model assessment practice. Chicago: Author. (Original work published 1999)

Institute for the International Education of Students (IES). (2007b). Report of the IES Dublin program review. Chicago: Author.

Institute for the International Education of Students (IES). (2007c). IES Vienna. Retrieved April 27, 2007, from https://www.iesabroad.org/IES/Programs/Austria/Vienna/Student_Profiles/viennaAlanaMurphy

Institute for the International Education of Students (IES). (2007d). IES Barcelona. Retrieved April 27, 2007 from https://www.iesabroad.org/IES/Programs/Spain/Barcelona/Student_Profiles/barcelonaDanielleLopez

Institute for the International Education of Students. (2008). IES Beijing. Retrieved January 18, 2008, from https://www.iesabroad.org/IES/Programs/China/Beijing/Language_Intensive/Student_Profiles/beijingGordon Hoople

Jandt, F. (2001). *Intercultural communication: An introduction* (3rd ed.). Thousand Oaks, CA: Sage.

Kegan, R. (1994). *In over our heads: The mental demands of modern life.* Cambridge, MA: Harvard University Press.

King, P., & Baxter Magolda, M. (2005). A development model of intercultural maturity. *Journal of College Student Development, 46,* 571–592.

Maki, P. L. (2004). *Assessment for learning: Building a sustainable commitment across the institution.* Sterling, VA: Sterling.

Mansilla, V., & Gardner, H. (2007). From teaching globalization to nurturing global consciousness. In M. Suarez-Orozco (Ed.), *Learning in the global era: International perspectives on globalization and education* (pp. 59–63). Berkeley: University of California Press.

Norris, E. M., & Dwyer, M. (2005). Testing assumptions: The impact of two study abroad program models. *Frontiers: The Interdisciplinary Journal of Study Abroad, 11,* 121–142.

Norris, E. M., & Gillespie, J. (2005). Study abroad: Stepping stone to a successful international career. *NACE Journal, 65*(3), 30–36.

Pizzolato, J. W., & C. C. Ozaki (2007, March/April). Moving toward self-authorship: Investigating outcomes of learning partnerships. *Journal of College Student Development, 48*(2), 196–214.

Ruhter McMillan, A., & Opem, G. (2004). Study abroad: A lifetime of benefits. *Abroad View Magazine, 6*(2), 58, 60–61.

Steinberg, M. (2002). "Involve me and I will understand": Academic quality in experiential programs abroad [Special Issue]. *Frontiers: The Interdisciplinary Journal of Study Abroad, 8,* 207–227.

Sutton, R., Miller, A., & Rubin, D. (2007). Research design in assessing learning Outcomes. In M. Bolen (Ed.), *A guide to outcomes assessment in education abroad* (pp. 23–59). Carlisle, PA: The Forum on Education Abroad.

Chapter 26

It Takes a Curriculum

Bringing Global Mindedness Home

Kevin Hovland and Caryn McTighe Musil
Association of American Colleges and Universities

Ellen Skilton-Sylvester
Arcadia University

Amy Jamison
Michigan State University

Talya Zemach-Bersin, a 2007 graduate of Wesleyan University, laments in a *Chronicle of Higher Education* opinion piece that her semester-long study abroad experience in Tibetan studies "focused on cultural and language studies while avoiding the very issues that were in many ways most compelling and relevant to our experiences." "Why," she asks, "had we not analyzed race, identity, and privilege when those factors were informing every one of our interactions?... Was there nothing to be said about the power dynamics of claiming global citizenship?" (Zemach-Bersin, 2008, p. A34).

Zemach-Bersin's critique serves as a reminder of three important lessons: (1) when working at the intersections of global learning and citizenship or civic engagement, colleges and universities must carefully define terms; (2) campuses should creatively and intentionally link the "big questions" that are always at the core of effective curricular design with multiple opportunities for global learning, including but not limited to study abroad and study away experiences; and (3) if institutions seek to improve student understanding of power, identity, and privilege, they must assess this learning and apply the lessons learned from assessment to the task of creating more effective pathways through the curriculum to these ends.

In 2001, The Association of American Colleges and Universities (AAC&U)[1] launched its Shared Futures: Global Learning and Social Responsibility initiative to engage colleges and universities in conversations about ways to envision and enact global learning models that would foreground the very issues that Zemach-Bersin found most compelling and relevant during her study abroad experience. *Shared Futures* supports faculty and administrators' efforts to create curricular and cocurricular strategies to help all students—those who study abroad and the vast majority who do not—approach the world's challenges and opportunities from multiple perspectives and wrestle with the ethical implications of differential power and privilege. The *Shared Futures* approach to global learning foregrounds questions of diversity, identity, citizenship, interconnection, and responsible action. It challenges all learners to explore the relational nature of their developing identities as they are variously shaped by the currents of power and privilege within a multicultural U.S. democracy and within an interconnected and unequal world (Hovland, 2005).

Global learning should provide opportunities for students to make progress in the following key outcomes. Students should:

- Gain a deep comparative knowledge of the world's peoples and problems;
- Explore the historical legacies that have created the dynamics and tensions of their world;
- Develop intercultural competencies so they can move across boundaries and unfamiliar territory and see the world from multiple perspectives;
- Sustain difficult conversations in the face of highly emotional and perhaps uncongenial differences;
- Understand—and perhaps redefine—democratic principles and practices within a global context;
- Gain opportunities to engage in practical work with fundamental issues that affect communities not yet well served by their societies;
- Believe that their actions and ideas will influence the world in which they live. (Hovland, 2005, p 16)

Colleges and universities are inventing and adapting multiple curricular and cocurricular strategies targeting these outcomes. Participants in the *Shared Futures* initiative, currently funded by The Henry Luce Foundation and the Fund for the Improvement of Postsecondary Education, are exploring the fundamental insight that responsibility for global learning cannot be isolated in one or two "global awareness" courses or reserved primarily for students who participate in a high quality study abroad program. Rather, responsibility for global learning must be shared *across* curricular and cocurricular activities in intentional and developmentally appropriate ways. In fact, AAC&U advocates that global learning become an organizing principle that provides coherence to the undergraduate learning experience, especially in general education, but also by linking general education with study in the major.

WHAT IS GLOBAL LEARNING?

Through *Shared Futures*, we have found it useful to align the goals and objectives of global learning to the powerful language of liberal education. In recent years, AAC&U and its member institutions have articulated a vision of liberal education designed around a set of learning outcomes we have identified as essential for engaged and knowledgeable citizenship at the beginning of the 21st century. These outcomes provide a framework in which it is possible to meld the theory and practice of global learning and liberal education and thereby open avenues for constructive conversations about the role of higher education in a complex and interdependent world. The desired outcomes for liberal education significantly overlap those of global learning; consequently, it is relatively easy to map global learning onto the best theory and practice of liberal education.

In *College Learning for the New Global Century: A Report from the National Leadership Council for Liberal Education and America's Promise*, the Liberal Education and the American Promise (LEAP) Council "calls on American society to give new priority to a set of educational outcomes that all students need from higher learning—outcomes that are closely calibrated with the challenges

Table 26.1 *The Essential Learning Outcomes*

Beginning in school, and continuing at successively higher levels across their college studies, students should prepare for twenty-first-century challenges by gaining:

Knowledge of Human Cultures and the Physical and Natural World

- Through study in the sciences and mathematics, social sciences, humanities, histories, languages, and the arts

Focused by engagement with big questions, both contemporary and enduring

Intellectual and Practical Skills, Including

- Inquiry and analysis
- Critical and creative thinking
- Written and oral communication
- Quantitative literacy
- Information literacy
- Teamwork and problem solving

Practiced extensively, across the curriculum, in the context of progressively more challenging problems, projects, and standards for performance

Personal and Social Responsibility, Including

- Civic knowledge and engagement—local and global
- Intercultural knowledge and competence
- Ethical reasoning and action
- Foundations and skills for lifelong learning

Anchored through active involvement with diverse communities and real-world challenges

Integrative Learning, Including

- Synthesis and advanced accomplishment across general and specialized studies

Demonstrated through the application of knowledge, skills, and responsibilities to new settings and complex problems.

---

of a complex and volatile world" (AAC&U, 2007, p. 11). These essential learning outcomes are described in Table 26.1.

It is the close calibration of the essential learning outcomes to the "complex challenges of the world today" that puts global learning in a generative relationship with liberal education. Global questions are, in fundamental ways, the context that provides relevance and urgency to liberal education. Liberal education has always been about big questions—both contemporary and enduring. If educational practices and ideas are a reflection of the priorities and concerns specific to a particular time and location, then today's reevaluation of liberal education cannot be fully appreciated without understanding its global context. As the LEAP Council argues,

> Global integration is now our shared context. The potential benefits of global interdependence are extraordinary, but so too are the challenges. Wealth, income, and social power are dramatically unequal within and across international boundaries. We are reminded daily of the clash of cultures, histories and worldviews. The globe itself is fragile and vulnerable as are our shared civic spaces. These global challenges will be with us for the foreseeable future. (AAC&U, 2007, p. 21)

The word *global* itself appears only once in the essential learning outcomes, in relation to civic knowledge and engagement within the personal and social responsibility outcome. This is consistent with common understanding and usage within higher education. Liberal arts colleges in particular, we found, link their vision of global learning to interdependence, social justice, leadership, and responsible citizenship in their mission statements (Hovland, 2006). However, the single location masks the fact that global concerns are infused throughout the entire set of essential learning outcomes.

The connection between the two is especially clear if we focus on the verbs: knowledge *focused* by engagement with big questions, both contemporary and enduring; skills *practiced* extensively, across the curriculum, in the context of progressively more challenging problems, projects, and standards for performance; personal and social responsibility *anchored* through active involvement with diverse communities and real-world challenges; and integrative learning *demonstrated* through the application of knowledge, skills, and responsibilities to new settings and complex problems. What this suggests, of course, is that global learning comprises complex and overlapping areas of development and that knowledge, skills, attitudes, and actions build upon each other, reinforcing each other across multiple contexts. By talking more specifically about global *citizenship,* certain elements in this mix are emphasized over others, but the fact remains that these elements need to be carefully defined and aligned as we try to design and assess developmentally appropriate learning opportunities.

Because global learning develops across these multiple contexts, comprehensive curricular pathways need to be designed in addition to the courses and study abroad programs that comprise the curriculum. Study abroad or study away is strengthened by opportunities for course-based preparation and reflection. The knowledge, skills, and experiences gained in study abroad or away, in turn, expand and deepen the insights that students bring to bear on what they are learning in the rest of their courses. Global learning, we argue, does take a curriculum.

ELEMENTS OF GLOBAL LEARNING

Colleges and universities are engaged in a great deal of work that usually falls under a broad definition of global learning. Because that larger category is not well understood, however, there remains confusion about the various ways the term *global* modifies different activities across multiple institutional contexts. As a consequence, it is often difficult to assess how (or even if) various manifestations of global work relate to other campus reform efforts. By differentiating between various elements of global learning, it may be possible to better match activities and programs with sets of learning goals. This will allow practitioners to better understand the appropriateness and effectiveness of various strategies for achieving global learning goals. It should also enable more productive conversations across both campuses and institutions about ways to link the goals of general education with robust study away programs like those at Arcadia University—study away that occurs both abroad and at home.

As described above, *global learning* is a contextualization of a liberal education intentionally designed to prepare students for a 21st century characterized by interdependence, complexity, and change. Global learning is a way to organize student learning outcomes across the curriculum. It integrates students' learning and challenges them to apply learning to complex real-world issues. But what do we mean when we talk about global knowledge, global literacy, global awareness, global mindedness, or global citizenship? Since there is not yet consensus on these questions, we encourage campuses to seek such agreement as a useful campus exercise. Below are some initial categorizations to stimulate discussion.

469

Global Knowledge

The complaint is often made that graduates do not know the basics of geography, economics, or languages, and that they are consequently unprepared for the realities of a global leadership and work (Hart, 2008). While basic levels of *global literacy* may be low, *global knowledge* aims higher. By global knowledge we mean to suggest certain ways of looking at the world—intellectual frameworks—that emphasize the complexity of our world, the dependence and interdependence of groups of people, and the relationships and systems that both connect and divide. Cornwell and Stoddard, in their influential essay, *Globalizing Knowledge: Connecting International and Intercultural Studies* (1999), argue that global knowledge is best understood as "newer paradigms of multiple belongings." These paradigms

> …use concepts such as globalization, diaspora, interculturalism, and hybrid identities to map new relations of politics and place, history and identity, economies and states. On these new multi-layered maps, it becomes difficult to separate the United States, or any other state, from complex embeddedness in historical and contemporary movements of people, capital, ideas, cultural forms, and even elements of the natural environment. (p. 10)

Again, these frameworks can provide students with fresh perspectives on the big questions—enduring and contemporary—that put knowledge into context.

Global awareness and *global mindedness* can be seen as developmental stages on the way to *global citizenship*. They can also be usefully understood, as Stoddard and Cornwell argue in "Peripheral Visions: Towards a Geoethics of Citizenship" (2003), as means to gauge a shifting vision or new perspectives within students. In choosing their title, the authors wished to

> invoke a cluster of related commitments. "Visions" alludes on a very concrete level to the need for knowledge on which to base judgments and actions. But it also suggests the more visionary or prophetic side of knowledge, called for as the world becomes both more dispersed and more interconnected, more visible and more mystified through rapid, global circulation of news, images, commodities, capital, and labor. "Visions" also suggests the perspectival element of knowledge, the way things look completely different from different locations or different points of view. (p. 44)

Global awareness and global mindedness both aim for one of the central goals of liberal education: a move away from provincialism and toward serious engagement with the perspectives of others.

Global Citizenship

Scholarly debate on the theory and practice of global citizenship is deep, growing, and interesting. In *Shared Futures*, we have been profoundly influenced by Martha Nussbaum's (1997) attempt to put the ideals and best practices of a liberal education to the task of developing in students a richer aptitude for humanity and thus a greater capacity for engaging in "dialogue that brings together people from many different national and cultural and religious backgrounds" in the search for "intelligent, cooperative solution[s]" to problems facing the world. Nussbaum goes on to describe three capacities "essential to the cultivation of humanity in today's world." They are: the "capacity for critical examination of oneself and one's traditions"; the "ability to see themselves not simply as citizens of some local region or group but also, and above all, as human beings bound to all other human beings by ties of recognition and concern" ; and "narrative imagination," the "ability to think what it might be like to be in the shoes of a person different from oneself, to be an intelligent reader of that person's story, and to understand the emotions and wishes and desires that someone so placed might have" (pp. 8–11). Nussbaum's cosmopolitanism is one compelling answer to the questions we pose in *Shared Futures*: "What does it mean to be a responsible citizen in today's global context? And how should one act in the face of large unsolved global problems?" (Hovland, 2005, p. 1).

In the context of developmental pathways to global learning, such questions of citizenship—global, local, or otherwise—can be even more broadly understood in terms of what Lee Knefelkamp has called "Civic Identity" (2008). Knefelkamp argues that civic identity has four essential characteristics. It "develops in the context of engaging the real social, political, and economic structures within any given society or culture." It is "deeply connected to, *complex intellectual and ethical development....*" "It requires an integration of critical thinking and the capacity for empathy. It challenges us to identify with others who may be significantly different from ourselves...." Finally, civic identity "requires active reflection, experimentation, and what Dewey called 'moral rehearsal.' Rehearsal for civic engagement requires multiple experiences and opportunities for learning" (Knefelkamp, 2008, pp. 2–3). In the case of global civic identity, we might amend the first of Knefelkamp's characteristics to emphasize how students can engage the real social, political, and economic structures across and between societies and cultures.

As institutions aim for complex developmental outcomes such as global citizenship, they need to design and assess clear pathways through which students can move through the curriculum toward that goal. Global citizenship involves knowledge, experience, and engagement with others. It is also essentially an integrative exercise, not an isolated experience. The curriculum then must be integrative (as do the assessment tools used to improve that curriculum) if we are not to be disappointed in student progress. Further, in Knefelkamp's definition of civic identity—and in the Shared Futures framework for global learning—the difference between engagement with local and global issues and communities is intentionally blurred.

ASSESSMENT

As we have suggested above, the cluster of values, knowledge, and experience that makes up global learning is complex. They are also, in some combination, increasingly viewed as essential learning outcomes for all fields of concentration and for all majors (AAC&U, 2004). Yet AAC&U research suggests that

> the goals for global learning at too many colleges and universities are unfocused. Moreover, too few colleges and universities offer structured educational opportunities for students to acquire knowledge, both theoretical and experiential, about the rest of the world, about America's place in the world, and about the inequities and interdependencies that mark current geopolitical relationships. (Musil, 2006, p. 1)

As Vande Berg points out in his introduction to a 2003 *Frontiers* issue devoted to study abroad assessment, the dearth of literature on study abroad assessment is largely due to a "unified vision" of such programs. This unified idea of study abroad was based on the traditional model of a junior year abroad, in which a small number of students—largely White and female—would spend their junior year attending a university abroad, likely in a Western European country, for the purposes of language acquisition or cultural immersion. The core elements of this model and the demographics of participating students held fairly constant through the 1980s even with variations in program duration.

Rust (2001) suggests that in the field of international education, there continues to be little discussion among educators of the methodological or theoretical issues that might define their work. They are often more concerned with administrative issues. This, however, must change dramatically if global citizenship is the outcome to be measured. Increasing numbers of students participating in study abroad programs has led to an increased diversity not only in students' backgrounds, but also their disciplinary interests. Many undergraduate institutions are adapting their mission statements to include references to the importance of global knowledge and understanding, which in turn has led to an increase in the number and type of programs offered. As study abroad has become a vehicle for developing global learning outcomes (in addition to language acquisition, for example) new assessment questions inevitably arise.

Growing interest in study abroad and its potential benefits for undergraduate students has led a few researchers to begin to address the methodological and theoretical issues neglected in the earlier literature. They are beginning to ask theoretical questions about the desired outcomes of study abroad programs and methodological questions on how best to achieve and assess those outcomes. Richard Sutton and Donald Rubin (2003) point out that institutions have in the past defined success through rates of participation or postprogram surveys of student satisfaction. They rightly argue that this not an effective way of assessing learning outcomes. To date, most work in this subject area has been done on the assessment of language acquisition programs, but as the prominence of other types of study abroad programs rapidly supersedes those designed solely for language study, researchers need to expand their exploration on this topic. As McTighe Musil has argued in *Assessing Global Learning* (2006),

> The concept of intentional practice...is especially useful as a framework for how to move global learning beyond the partial, episodic, and disconnected approach found on most campuses today. The concept of "intentionality" implies a close alignment between professed goals and actions taken to achieve those goals. This includes such things as how the faculty designs the curriculum, teaches the courses, and assesses learning, as well as how the institution fosters the success of all students, allocates resources, and rewards performance. (pp. 3–4)

GLOBAL CONNECTIONS AND ARCADIA'S UNDERGRADUATE CURRICULUM[2]

Arcadia University has been deeply engaged—through the *Shared Futures* project as well as other activities—in efforts to create and adopt intentional practices that would maximize the impact of its wide-ranging global learning agenda. Arcadia builds upon a foundation of leadership in study abroad; its Center for Education Abroad, celebrating a 60th anniversary this year, has been a national leader in providing excellent opportunities for Arcadia students and others in over 70 settings. Arcadia was chosen by the American Council on Education as one of eight institutions nationwide that exhibited promising practices in comprehensive internationalization, and received the Paul Simon Award for campus internationalization in 2006.

Despite this long-term success working in international education, project team members recognized in the *Shared Futures* network an opportunity to organize Arcadia's comprehensive educational priorities around global learning outcomes. In seeking to develop and assess greater levels of continuity within and across global curricular and cocurricular elements of undergraduate life, Arcadia designed and articulated a new undergraduate curriculum that prepares graduates for the complex realities of the 21st century by helping them "read back and forth between the local and the global, between multiple forms of identity and difference" (Cornwell & Stoddard, 1999, p. ix).

Study abroad and study away remain key to Arcadia's global learning vision because such experiences are central to institutional identity and mission. Yet, even as Arcadia celebrated the overarching success of study abroad, some administrators, faculty, and staff voiced concern that students too often see their study abroad experience as something separate from their time on campus or little more than a set of interesting courses alongside an extended tourism experience. The study away experience, they feared, can be an opportunity to reify assumptions and stereotypes rather than a time for engagement, reflection, and rethinking perspectives on the world. An Arcadia student's reflection provided some evidence of this danger:

> I don't think study abroad necessarily changes anyone.... I remember sitting on the bus and still hearing...[students] make racial jokes about Aboriginal people. So, it's like, just taking them out of a situation...isn't going to change how they think. (Shultz & Skilton-Sylvester, 2008, p. 21)

Of course, the goal of global learning and liberal education is to do precisely that—change how students think. Comments such as this reinforced the sense among Arcadia leaders that they needed to design more intentional ways to help their students put their curricular and cocurricular experiences into intellectual and educational contexts that would encourage them to see themselves as local and global citizens at home and away, and cultivate their capacity to empathize and gain insight into the lived experience of others.

Under the previous curriculum, Arcadia students were required to take a core global justice course and either study abroad or take one additional course with significant international content. The new curriculum (passed by the faculty in April 2007 with implementation beginning in September 2008) represents a systematic attempt to assist all Arcadia students in "bringing global mindedness home" in order to make these experiences a fundamental and required part of education at Arcadia, rather than something optional or peripheral. While perhaps subtle, the shift away from a *content* approach to a global requirement and toward a *practice* approach has had a profound impact on the curriculum. As several of the reform leaders explain the shift:

> It became clear to us that critical exploration of global interconnections, interdependence, and inequality across nations (including the U.S.) should be central to the global learning curriculum. Thus we defined "global connections" as an intellectual practice—an ability to take a global perspective—rather than as an area of inquiry in a particular field of study. Our new curriculum requires students to take courses that emphasize these global connections. (Shultz, Skilton-Sylvester, & Shultz, 2007, p. 5)

In addition to global connections *courses*, the new curriculum also requires students to participate in a global connections *experience*. This also represents a subtle shift from study abroad to study away, once again within the framework of interdependence and interconnection. These experiences were designed to represent

> ... an encounter with a cultural context different from the one in which [the student] grew up. Because we see global learning and U.S. pluralism as tightly interwoven, we do not require this global connections experience to take place abroad. We are eagerly planning several domestic options that allow students to cross racial, economic, and cultural lines without leaving the U.S. (Shultz et al., 2007, p. 5)

Taken together, the elements of Arcadia's global connections curriculum can be seen as parts of what AAC&U often calls "purposeful pathways" (Leskes & Miller, 2006). Students can move via purposeful pathways across a developmental continuum, building and reflecting upon the curricular and cocurricular experiences that have come before. Table 26.2 is a schematic chart of one such global learning continuum developed by Ann Kelleher at Pacific Lutheran University.

Purposeful pathways have become more feasible and more powerful in the new curriculum at Arcadia. Global connections course requirements are meant to span multiple semesters and to draw on intellectual, conceptual, and experiential dimensions of learning. The potential for developmentally appropriate integration is also enhanced by the multiple ways that students can fulfill requirements both inside and outside the major. In addition, all students will be formally reflecting on their experiences in a cross-cultural context, through electronic portfolios. Faculty members will respond to these reflections to gain insight into where the students are on the continuum and to encourage students to think about how their perspectives on global interdependence changes as they gain experience and as their own identities develop over time.

Paying close attention to student reflection allows curricular planners opportunities to gauge success in building coherent pathways. New connections can be established between elements of the whole, but those parts can also evolve to better serve the overarching global goals. Two cases from Arcadia serve as examples of such evolution.

FIRST-YEAR STUDY ABROAD EXPERIENCE

Beginning in the fall of 2003, Arcadia invited students to study abroad in the United Kingdom during their first semester of college. This First-Year Study Abroad Experience (FYSAE), initially a response to a housing shortage on campus, is now in its fifth year and has become a central reason why many students consider coming to Arcadia. The program started with a focus on London and has now expanded to Scotland.

An elective reentry course (ID 108: Study Abroad and Global Philadelphia) was designed for the spring of 2005 in response to some of the transition issues the first cohort of students faced in returning to suburban Glenside after an initial semester overseas. Now, in its fourth year, the course has gone through significant revisions as faculty have experimented with ways to assist students in developing global mindedness in relation to their experiences abroad and to invite students to see connections between the United States and the rest of the world, in this case, particularly in relation to the United Kingdom.

In its first 2 years, the course was designed to help students see the university culture itself as a "cross-cultural experience" by asking them to examine their own transitions from high school to college and by connecting them with others in transition, notably several immigrant commu-

Table 26.2 *Four-Phase Global Education Continuum: Pacific Lutheran University*

Learning Objective Categories	Introductory	Exploratory	Participatory	Integrative
Knowledge and Intellectual Skills	Explain, with examples, the origins of today's world, its trends, and its systemic interdependence.	Describe, with facts as well as generalizations, at least two major issues facing today's world. Analyze ample evidence about a significant topic related to a world issue.	Develop a clear mental map of the interrelatedness of global institutions, issues, and systems using ample examples.	Describe the world's economic, environmental, and political systems. Assess the complexities and contradictions in one of the world's systems based on ample information about one or more of the relevant issues currently facing humankind.
Cultural Knowledge and Skills	Describe, with examples, the world's cultural diversity. Communicate in a second modern language at a survival level.	Compare and contrast distinct behavioral characteristics of your own and one other culture. Communicate at a beginning level in a second modern language.	Analyze two cultures including their enculturation processes, worldviews, and economic/social/political patterns. Communicate at the intermediate level in a second language.	Reflect comparatively and in depth on one's own and a second culture. Adapt in a second culture by working effectively with a counterpart in that culture. Read, write, and speak at an advanced level in a second language.
Global Perspectives		Explain two ethical perspectives and evaluate the potential effectiveness of two relevant contrasting responses to one general world issue.	Assess your own perspective and locate it amid several philosophical, religious, ideological, and/or intellectual frameworks, taking into account their ethical assumptions.	Articulate the basic assumptions of two value-based perspectives (worldviews) and apply them in formulating alternative responses to one of the world's major issues.
Personal Commitment		Articulate a relationship between a global issue and your personal commitments and vocational choices.	Engage in creating a just and healthy world.	Demonstrate potential for distinctive leadership in a local community and internationally in the pursuit of a just, healthy, sustainable, and peaceful world.

Source: Kelleher, 2005

nities in Philadelphia. Opportunities for recognizing commonality were created through texts, documentary films, and field trips to Chinatown, a Korean Buddhist Temple, Italian/Mexican/Vietnamese South Philadelphia, and the Latino Corridor in North Philadelphia.

Some students were able to make connections between their own experiences of being newcomers and those of the immigrant communities where we visited:

> I can relate entirely with the [young Korean American woman who spoke to us at the Buddhist temple]. I experienced the culture shock of London, but also because I am a second generation [immigrant] woman with first generation parents, I struggle with acceptance both at home and in society. (Skilton-Sylvester, 2006)

The reentry course, as this student suggests, can tap into the power of culture shock as a tool to see connections as well as to challenge received ideas. Others saw opportunities to learn from diverse local communities as a fulfillment of their expectations as to what a college experience should be. As one student wrote:

> Going to communities and talking about what people have gone through in a different light is exactly what I thought of when I thought of college. I'm a very intellectual person so I like to try different learning experiences. If my academic career was laced with a lot more of these experiences, I would feel that I spent my money on something worthwhile. (Skilton-Sylvester, 2006)

Most of the first-year students in the course, however, were unable to articulate the ways that they saw the world as more interconnected, interdependent, or unequal as a result of this experience. The link between personal experiences, immigration trends, and ethnolinguistically diverse communities felt too abstract. Plotting the typical student experience on the Pacific Lutheran University schematic, while they often developed new knowledge and intellectual skills, and some dimensions of cultural knowledge and skills (although not modern language proficiency), it was quite rare for them to develop exploratory global perspectives or personal commitments in relation to global issues. It is not surprising that they remained at the introductory level.

On the other hand, one senior who took the course with first-year students spoke about interconnections and inequality both locally and globally in ways that we had hoped others would:

> We also don't realize that sometimes it's best to focus on events happening nationally. How many people know that billions of dollars were cut out of education to fund the war?... How many of us were in Philly protesting the possible passing of harsh immigration laws? It's extremely important for us to push past our isolationist past and become as globalized as the rest of the world—being in Europe showed me how truly behind we are. But sometimes, we have to concentrate on our own backyards before we think about fixing anyone else's. (Skilton-Sylvester, 2006)

Having the study abroad experience as a senior allowed her to move into the participatory and integrative ends of the continuum. As a senior and a student of color, she gained new insights about race in the United States through her time in the UK. Even as her experience demonstrated the potential of this course to enable transformative reflection, it also showed the need to think about ways to change the course to make it more effective for first-year students.

Working with colleagues and peers in the *Shared Futures* network, Arcadia faculty and administrators began thinking about how to help our first-year students develop a comparative, transnational perspective emphasizing interconnections, interdependence, and inequality. This required a significant overhaul of the course.

We now begin by actually talking about global learning goals with students. We articulate the goals, make expectations clear, and describe the kinds of work that we are looking for to demonstrate success. Then, we emphasize the process of exploring multiple perspectives. Upon returning from Europe, students spent time early in the semester reading and discussing two special issues of *Granta*—one titled "Over There" (Jack, 2003) that includes perspectives of Americans living abroad and another entitled "What We Think of America" that focuses on the perspectives of non-Americans on the United States (Jack, 2002). After having discussed these texts, students interview local, international, and immigrant members of the Arcadia community (or the universities where they studied in the UK) or Americans who have studied abroad. Through such practices, students are encouraged to think about how their experiences abroad have changed their perceptions of the world and their own global and civic identities.

In the second half of the course, each student selects a concrete part of everyday life that crosses national boundaries (such as food, water, soccer, petroleum, carbon, and technology) and through a common text, investigates the similarities and differences characterizing how these natural elements and human inventions are addressed in the UK and the United States. Students also compare how these commodities cross national boundaries, how they are regulated, and how citizens use them. We also ask them to think about how their own civic actions might shape commodity use.

Finally, we make explicit the connections between a course students take in the UK (ID 106: Cross Cultural Connections) and their reentry course (ID 108: Study Abroad and Global Philadelphia). These courses focus on complementary global learning objectives. Cross Cultural Connections focuses on what Musil terms "cultivating intercultural competencies," while Study Abroad and Global Philadelphia focuses primarily on those issues Musil (2006) calls "generating new knowledge about global studies" or "spurring greater civic engagement and social responsibility" (see Table 26.3 for a list of the complementary goals).

In their writing, as well as in classroom discussion, study abroad and global Philadelphia students show evidence of addressing these three core course objectives. It is also possible to see the ways they address not only intellectual and cultural knowledge and skills, but sometimes global perspectives and personal commitments as well—usually at the exploratory level.

For example, Wilson (2007)[3] writes about her deepening understandings of how others view her and the United States:

> I was speaking softly to an American student [in a Psychology class in London] when suddenly a British girl turned around and exclaimed "Where are you from!?" After telling her, I was pleasantly surprised at her reaction. Instead of shirking away from us, she proceeded to tell us how cool we and our hip accents were. She explained how American culture is all the rage here, and how she wishes she lived in America. She also asked us a few questions regarding our culture, like "Are there really cheerleaders and 'football' games?"; "Are you from New York or Hollywood"; "Do you know any celebrities?" This gave me a glimpse on how Americans look from afar.

But this deepening understanding did not only occur abroad, it also continued on the home campus, informed by the time abroad. Wilson continues:

Table 26.3 *Complementary Global Learning Course Objectives: Arcadia University*

Cross Cultural Connections students will:

Gain cross cultural awareness and sensitivity;
Interpret aspects of other cultures with greater sophistication and accuracy;
Traverse cultural borders with greater skill and comfort;
Reflect on how they are viewed, and how they view, the surrounding world;
Learn about the national and local cultures of the host country; and
Compare and contrast the host country culture with the student's own.

Study Abroad and Global Philadelphia students will:

Interpret aspects of other cultures with greater sophistication and accuracy;
Be able to pose critical questions about power relations as they investigate the dynamics of global
    and local transactions as applied to a social issue important to them;
Acquire a heightened sense of global interdependencies; and
Understand the need to address complex global issues across national and disciplinary boundaries.

An international student [at Arcadia] also gave me a helpful perspective. During an inter-view... when asked what he thinks it means to be American, he explains that "I only know what it is not to be American because I am reminded constantly that I am not." This is an unfortunate quote that shows another image of America.... Even though America is seen as a melting pot, it is hard for immigrants, especially of another race, to assimilate and be accepted as an American.

She goes on to say, "Americans need to resist stereotypes in the absence of personal experi-ence. After exposure and experience, these stereotypes dissolved as we saw foreigners as people, just as we are" (Wilson, 2007). In her analysis of her own experiences and the experiences of oth-ers, it is possible to see a shift from thinking in terms of absolutes to a more nuanced perspective. Wilson has developed what Stoddard and Cornwall (1999) have called a "perspectival element of knowledge." She is beginning to recognize "the way that things look completely different from different locations or different points of view." Although her perspective taking remains at the introductory level, it represents a real shift from where she started.

One of Wilson's classmates, Knight (2007) shows her ability to "pose critical questions about power relations" as she investigates "the dynamics of global and local transactions" by focusing on the war in Iraq and the "war on terror." She says:

Undoubtably [sic], the United States' position on foreign policy is a large part of the grow-ing dislike it faces in the world community.... Hopefully, the United States can change this "war on terror" from imposing our own views of democracy and freedom onto semi-willing participants into an opportunity to unite our fellow men and put an end to violence and intol-erance. The United States should not take how the world sees us and be angered or offended. Instead, we should take the criticism and learn to use the influence we have as a superpower to create a more stable, cohesive, and peaceful global community.

Although the depth of the analysis is not what one might expect from an upper-class student, her ability to think critically about America's power in the world in relation to her own study abroad experiences represents a shift in the depth of her understanding of how the United States is viewed by the rest of the world. Here first-hand experiences with UK residents who—as these students like to say, "hated America, but not Americans"—allowed her to see this in a more personal, nuanced way than she had before her time abroad.

Thompson (2007) illustrates a limited, but "heightened sense of global interdependencies" in her essay. Her analysis of America's consumption habits leads her to reflect on the economic interdependencies concerning production and the employment of undocumented workers. Unlike some of her classmates, she is able to articulate both the realities of U.S. immigration policy on the one hand and our simultaneous economic dependence on undocumented workers on the other. However, her use of the term *lazy* to describe Americans illustrates a limited analysis of race and class in the United States and shows evidence of her own privileged stance as a young, White American in college. She writes:

> …We produce next to nothing. We used to be one of the largest production and manufacturing nations in the world. We had Ford Model T factory lines, coal mines, and farms. Now we employ cheap labor from third world countries to do all of that dirty work for us…. While we are too lazy for assembly lines and farms, we continue to condemn illegal Mexican immigrants for hopping the border to work jobs that Americans would never compete for to begin with.

Although her level of analysis of interdependence remains at the level of knowledge and skills on the Pacific Lutheran University continuum and glosses over American inequality and privilege, her clarity and passion about the complexity and contradictions of our economic and immigrant policies shows some real promise. With our new curricular requirements, our hope is that she would have other opportunities to go deeper —to further examine the "we" of her statements above—by reading "back and forth between the local and the global" Cornwell and Stoddard (1999) suggest, and in particular, by paying attention to the ways that inequality shapes not only local/global interconnections, but diverse local experiences as well.

In each of these examples, students illustrate elements of our global learning goals. However, it is unclear whether or not we can claim that their experiences abroad or in courses that allow them to reflect on those experiences in relation to wider global issues actually help them to develop those competencies. One could argue that these students come to Arcadia with these abilities. Their essays, as well as their presentations about local and global food and water given in conjunction with a food and water forum they organized on campus as their final presentation, however, are markedly different from the final presentations just one semester before. At that time students remained focused on surface-level cultural differences (national flags, food, sports teams) and elements of tourism/vacation (drinking, beaches, clubs, and pubs).

In an effort to look at the ways FYSAE students' development may be different than others on campus, Dennis Gallagher, Arcadia's Associate Dean for Teaching and Learning has analyzed faculty perspectives on students (both those who did FYSAE and those that did not) and has some interesting things to say about general global awareness, student ability to view a single issue from multiple perspectives, and their comfort with complexity and ambiguity. Gallagher selected fall 2004 FYSAE students who were enrolled in fall 2007 semester and randomly selected non-FYSAE students enrolled in the same courses. He then asked faculty teaching these courses to rate each student on 17 different academically related characteristics. Faculty did not know who were or were not FYSAE students, nor even that FYSAE was an issue in the project. He found that:

FYSAE students were judged by faculty to be:

- More engaged in class
- Better academic performers
- Better speakers
- Better critical thinkers
- Better at integrative ability
- Somewhat better at having global perspectives
- Better at taking multiple perspectives
- More comfortable with complexity and ambiguity
- Better at applying learning to new contexts

There were no differences between the groups on ratings for the following characteristics. (Non-FYSAE students were *not rated higher* on any characteristics):

- General work ethic
- Academic maturity
- Personal maturity
- Ability to work independently
- Ability to work as member of group/team
- Respect for others
- Ability to work with others different from them
- General engagement with course. (Gallagher, 2008)

These results suggest that FYSAE students are developing at least some dimensions of global learning outcomes in ways that non-FYSAE students are not.

ACROSS THE OCEAN AND BACK AGAIN: STUDY ABROAD AND SERVICE LEARNING IN EQUATORIAL GUINEA

While assessment of Arcadia's First Year Study Abroad Experience has demonstrated some movement of students along the global education continuum, the goal remains to help students move from introductory learning, through exploratory, participatory, and finally, integrative stages (see Table 26.2). Consequently, curricular planners need to build on early experiences with opportunities to revisit key issues and developmentally more challenging levels.

One such example linking study abroad and service learning around global learning goals is Arcadia's program in Equatorial Guinea. When Ellen Skilton-Sylvester arrived on campus in 2004, Arcadia had been leading groups of students (mainly biology majors) to Equatorial Guinea to do conservation work related to sea turtles and various types of monkeys. Together with colleagues, Skilton-Sylvester developed a Fulbright-Hays Group Projects Abroad proposal entitled "Across the Ocean and Back Again: Study Abroad and Service Learning in Equatorial Guinea."

One of the central components of the new program was an education course entitled "Teaching & Learning in the Community." This course involved both a U.S. and Equatorial Guinea component. In the United States, students were matched with local K-12 schools to connect the work they would be doing in Equatorial Guinea with the social studies, environmental studies, or biology curriculum. In Equatorial Guinea, the course focused on their work tutoring local college students in English and learning Spanish from these same students at the Universidad National de Guinea Equatorial (UNGE). All of the elements of the course focused on sociolinguistics, language policy, language tutoring strategies, and issues of power and privilege in relation to their roles as predominantly White college students who speak English working with speakers of Spanish and local languages in Equatorial Guinea.

During the 2006–2007 academic year, students on their way to Equatorial Guinea did some intensive coursework predeparture that focused on issues of power and privilege and a crash course on teaching English as a second language. As part of the predeparture work in the fall of 2006, students also visited the schools and classrooms in the Philadelphia region that they would be returning to at the end of the program. These visits in September were opportunities to build relationships with kids and teacher. Students also wanted to find out what questions K-12 students and teachers had about Africa in general and Equatorial Guinea in particular so they could address them upon their return.

These visits were helpful in getting our students to imagine an audience for their experiences abroad when they came back. They also prepared students to investigate particular questions of students and teachers while away. However, some of the most striking insights from these visits came from White students who visited predominantly African-American schools located less than 5 miles from Arcadia's suburban campus. As one student said, "I had no idea there were schools where *all* of the students were Black." During a presentation at a school, another college student said, "I'm sure all of you have cars, but where we'll be in Africa, not everyone has a car." Students quickly corrected her saying "My family doesn't have a car!" This came as a complete shock to her as someone who grew up in a U.S. suburb. Here was a group of students on their way to study in Africa having assumption-shattering experiences just 5 miles from campus *before* their travel experience. In addition to providing a real audience for their learning while overseas, these local school experiences—both before and after (and sometimes via e-mail during) their time abroad also connected their local and global questions about economic inequalities and language diversity.

In addition to this course, the Africa program as a whole had a profound impact on students' understandings of how the United States and the world are interconnected and interdependent. Because Equatorial Guinea is an oil-rich nation, the role of U.S. oil companies is hard to miss and triggers student thinking about oil consumption on both a macro and a personal level when they return. The conservation work also disrupts their unexamined sense of right and wrong. In the fall of 2005, when Skilton-Sylvester visited the students in Equatorial Guinea, one student said, "When we first got here and I would see a trap set for a monkey, I would immediately disarm it. Now that I understand the economics of the bushmeat market and the limited choices people have here, I no longer know what to do when I see a trap" (student, personal communication). This level of understanding of local and global moral norms is something that he brought back to the United States as he struggled to figure out what role to play in conservation efforts upon graduation.

In a focus group about study abroad experiences, one student talked about how important local understandings are in relation to his experience in Equatorial Guinea:

> ...Yeah, that's like what we did with Equatorial Guinea, we went into local schools and did...presentations. But also, if we're going to talk about racism, we should talk about how it is part of people's everyday life in Cheltenham or Glenside or Philadelphia.

He recognizes the connection between what he learned doing conservation work in Equatorial Guinea and his campus-based environmental work. He says:

> I understood a lot more about…how people consume resources…and how people live off the land…and how a lot of environmental issues, if they don't take into consideration the… the indigenous or local populations…will affect the population. (Shultz & Skilton-Sylvester, 2008, p. 8)

The experiential work, he continues, was equally important as the knowledge gained:

> And then [it was valuable] just…getting out in the field and getting my hands dirty working and trying to negotiate very difficult situations of being in a different country and trying to communicate what's in your head and design a research project. So, I had to all in Spanish figure out what I was going to do so we could connect with our partner from the local university and explain and he contributed his ideas and we had to make some kind of hybrid research paper and then convey that to our guide to get him to take us where we needed to be…. It was a steep learning curve. But you know, I was able to do it and it gave me a lot of confidence and the stuff I do here around recycling and getting Philly Car Share on campus, you know, doing other stuff around campus. It's a lot of doing the same stuff; it's seeing where people [are], from their perspective, what their interests are, how does this help them, how does this hurt them? (Shultz & Skilton-Sylvester, 2008)

Because environmental issues were central to his study abroad experience and he investigated local issues with local people, he was able to look at the ways that these same kinds of issues appear in his efforts to make Arcadia more environmentally responsible. Although, this student was asking some of these questions before he went abroad, with the help of *Shared Futures* and a more intentional approach to global learning, the Arcadia curriculum was able to structure activities that expanded his understanding of interconnections, interdependence, and inequality and made them central to his understanding of the globe—including, but not limited to *both* Equatorial Guinea and suburban Philadelphia.

CREATING INFRASTRUCTURE FOR BRINGING GLOBAL MINDEDNESS HOME: NEW GLOBAL CONNECTIONS REQUIREMENTS IN THE CURRICULUM

As important as "Across the Ocean and Back Again, Study Abroad and Global Philadelphia" and its in-country complement "Cross-Cultural Connections" have been in shaping global learning outcomes and assisting students in bringing global mindedness back home, the courses have remained extra or elective courses rather than fulfilling any kind of requirement. The new Arcadia undergraduate curriculum changes that.

Starting in the fall semester of 2008, all students take a first-year seminar, complete two courses that fulfill the global connections intellectual practice criteria, and participate in the global connections experience and reflection. Each of these requirements will further institutionalize the global learning outcomes featured in the course—particularly an ability to connect the global and the local. These changes will not only influence FYSAE students, but will also continue to reshape study abroad—or what many of us are now calling *study away*—to include locations within the boundaries of the United States.

Making global/local connections will be further institutionalized through FYSAE students' participation in the in-country course fulfilling the global connections experience and reflection requirement. In addition, study abroad and global Philadelphia will move from a two-credit elective to a four-credit course that will satisfy FYSAE students' First-Year Seminar requirement. Because we also believe that developing global/local understandings needs to occur throughout their college career, students will also be required to take two additional courses that will fulfill the global connections intellectual practice during their sophomore, junior, or senior years.

Instead of being on the edges of the curriculum, these courses and either study abroad or study away are now both integral to our curriculum and foundational to more advanced global learning. Arcadia and its students will deepen ties to global Philadelphia through ongoing relationships with community organizations during the course. Such experiences ensure that all of our students who participate in FYSAE (as well as those who don't) will have multiple opportunities to develop as global citizens both at home and abroad.

CONCLUSION

Talya Zemach-Bersin is correct to suggest that study abroad programs that take global learning seriously must provide opportunities for students to study the power dynamics inherent in any claim of global citizenship. It is difficult to imagine a single course, however, that could address even some of the central questions of global civic identity—race, poverty, privilege, history, language, ethics, religion, gender, just to name a few. Global learning can be a useful way to organize pathways along which students can develop increasingly sophisticated ways of understanding their place in the world. While courses and study abroad are critical components of these pathways, it is the curricular design itself—intentional and developmentally gauged—that will allow students to make claims for global citizenship that are grounded in intercultural competencies, multiple perspectives, ethical awareness, and deep knowledge. Arcadia University and the other institutions in AAC&U's Shared Futures project have sought to better align existing general education designs with such important global learning outcomes. Such transformations of undergraduate curricula are critical to preparing students to live in an interdependent, interconnected, and unequal world.

NOTES

1. AAC&U is the leading national association concerned with the quality, vitality, and public standing of undergraduate liberal education. Founded in 1915, AAC&U represents the entire spectrum of American colleges and universities—large and small, public and private 2-year and 4-year. AAC&U comprises more than 1,150 accredited colleges and universities that collectively educate more than 7 million students every year.

2. At Arcadia, the curricular revision process began as a way of updating the General Education Requirements. However, because the new curriculum blurs the lines between the major and other requirements, we are no longer calling them General Education Requirements. Instead, we are calling the new curricular requirements The Arcadia Undergraduate Curriculum.

3. Students' final essays were published online through a campus publication entitled Global Matters. The link to the full text of the essays is: http://gargoyle.arcadia.edu/globalmatters/vol6no1/Home.html

REFERENCES

Association of American Colleges and Universities (AAC&U). (2004). *Taking responsibility for the quality of the baccalaureate degree*. Washington, DC: Author.

Association of American Colleges and Universities (AAC&U). (2007). *College learning for the new global century: A Report from the National Leadership Council for Liberal Education and America's Promise*. Washington, DC: Author.

Cornwell, G. H., & Stoddard, E. W. (1999). *Globalizing knowledge: Connecting international and intercultural studies*. Washington, DC: Association of American Colleges and Universities.

Gallagher, D. (2008, February). *Faculty rating study: Academic characteristics of FYSAE students*. Glenside, PA: Arcadia University. Unpublished report.

Hart, Peter D., & Research Associates. (2008). *How should college assess and improve student learning? Employers' views on the accountability challenge*. Washington, DC: Association of American Colleges and Universities.

Hovland, K. (2005). Shared futures: Global learning and social responsibility. *Diversity Digest, 8*(3), 1, 16–17.

Hovland, K. (2006). *Shared futures: Global learning and liberal education*. Washington, DC: Association of American Colleges and Universities.

Jack, I. (Ed.). (2002). What we think of America [Special issue]. *Granta, 77*.

Jack, I. (Ed.). (2003). Over there: How America sees the world [Special issue]. *Granta, 84*.

Kelleher, A. (2005). Global education continuum—four phases. *Diversity Digest, 8*(3), 10.

Knefelkamp, L. (2008). Civic identity: Locating self in community. *Diversity & Democracy, 11*(2), 1–3.

Knight, M. (2007). Conflicting images of the United States. *Global Matters, 6*(1). Retrieved July 28, 2008, from http://gargoyle.arcadia.edu/globalmatters/vol6no1/Thompson.html

Leskes, A., & Miller, R. (2006). *Purposeful pathways: Helping students achieve key learning outcomes*. Washington, DC: Association of American Colleges and Universities.

McTighe Musil, C. (2006). *Assessing global learning: Matching good intentions with good practice*. Washington, DC: Association of American Colleges and Universities.

Nussbaum, M. (1997). *Cultivating humanity: A classical defense of reform in liberal education*. Cambridge, MA: Harvard University Press.

Rust, V. (2001). The place of international education in the *Comparative Education Review*. *Comparative Education Review, 45*(3), iii–iv.

Shultz, J., Skilton-Sylvester, E. (2008). *Listening to student voices: Part one* (Report Prepared for the Internationalization Laboratory of the American Council on Education). Washington, DC: American Council on Education. Unpublished report.

Shultz, J., Skilton-Sylvester, E., & Shultz. N. (2007). Exploring global connections: Dismantling the international/multicultural divide. *Diversity & Democracy, 10*(3), 4–6.

Skilton-Sylvester, E. (2006, October). *Curricular strategies for combining the global and the local*. Presentation at AAC&U's Diversity and Learning Conference, Philadelphia, PA.

Stoddard, E., Cornwell, G. (2003). Peripheral visions: Toward a geoethics of globalization. *Liberal Education, 89*(3), 44–46.

Sutton, R. C., & Rubin, D. L. (2003). The glossari project: Initial findings from a system-wide research initiative on study abroad learning outcomes. *Frontiers: The Interdisciplinary Journal of Study Abroad, 10*, 65–82.

Thompson, J. (2007). Studying abroad: Expanding American tolerance one student at a time. *Global Matters, 6*(1). Retrieved July 28, 2008, from http://gargoyle.arcadia.edu/ globalmatters/vol6no1/Thompson.html

Vande Berg, M. J. (2003). Introduction. *Frontiers: The Interdisciplinary Journal of Study Abroad, 10*, xii–xxii.

Wilson, S. (2007). "I only know what it is not to be an American because I am reminded constantly that I am not." *Global Matters 6*(1). Retrieved July 28, 2008, from http://gargoyle.arcadia.edu/globalmatters/vol6no1/Wilson.html

Wright, M. (2007). Conflicting images of the United States. *Global Matters, 6*(1). Retrieved July 28, 2008, from http://gargoyle.arcadia.edu/globalmatters/vol6no1/Wright.html

Zemach-Bersin, T. (2008, March 7). American students abroad can't be "global citizens." *Chronicle of Higher Education, 54*(26), A34. Retrieved March 10, 2008, from http://chronicle.com/weekly/v54/i26/26a03401.htm

Chapter 27

Educating Globally Competent Citizens through International Service Learning

William M. Plater
Indiana University–Purdue University Indianapolis

Steven G. Jones
University of Scranton

Robert G. Bringle
Indiana University–Purdue University Indianapolis

Patti H. Clayton
North Carolina State University

EDUCATING GLOBALLY COMPETENT CITIZENS THROUGH INTERNATIONAL SERVICE LEARNING

If everyone were convinced that study abroad is good for all students and, more particularly, that we should all be global citizens, then this volume would be focused on best practices without an obligation for inquiry, documentation, explanation, or justification. Despite its long history (over 2,000 students were "studying abroad" at the University of Bologna in the early 13th century—to say nothing of the presence of international scholars in the ancient academies, from Greece to Persia to India and China), study abroad is not yet an ordinary learning experience for most American college students. As several chapters illustrate and most chapters allude, the idea of global citizenship is more problematic and less widely accepted than study abroad. Yet there seems to be nearly universal acceptance of the need within colleges and universities for greater global awareness, for deepened cross-cultural understanding, and for acceptance of the pragmatic value of experiential learning.

In the current environment of urgent attention to global interactions of all kinds—social, political, economic, environmental, religious—American higher education is faced with a need to engage immediately in "internationalization" across its diverse institutional missions even as it sorts out what is implied by global citizenship or its less inflected variant, globally competent citizenship. In the midst of these uncertainties, one proven pedagogy of engaged learning stands out as an effective means of increasing global awareness and knowledge, of deepening cross-cultural understanding and appreciation of diversity, and of experiencing some other part of the world first hand: *International Service Learning*. International service learning (ISL) meets all of these widely shared objectives while leaving to each institution the responsibility of articulating ISL's role within mission and its contextual framing in developing citizenship. And yet each individual participant in ISL retains the capacity to reflect on personal citizenship within a global community by whatever definition.

DEFINITIONS OF INTERNATIONAL SERVICE LEARNING

International service learning (ISL) is neither the addition of a service activity to a traditional study abroad experience nor the addition of an international experience to a domestic service learning course. Rather, ISL, when well designed and effectively implemented, is a transformative pedagogy that synthesizes the benefits of both study abroad and service learning. For example, integrating service learning and study abroad expands discussions of international reciprocity in study abroad programs and helps students value local voice and context as important components of the construction of knowledge. In return, study abroad moves the discussion of citizenship and engagement that characterizes domestic service learning from a typically local to a cross-national context, with accompanying major transformations in concepts of community and civic responsibility. While domestic service learning can, and increasingly does include cross-cultural learning and global conceptions of citizenship, international service learning inherently calls upon participants to reflect on the differences and similarities of locale and on their own sense of civic identity in a comparative, if not collective, framework.

The term *international service learning* has been used to describe a variety of international learning experiences, some of them curricular, others not; some organized by individual U.S. faculty or academic offices in U.S. universities, others organized by institutions in other countries or third party providers. The Ohio State University, College of Education and Human Ecology defines ISL as "an educational endeavor meant to enrich academic learning through participation in community service outside of the U.S....[that] provides students with opportunities to deepen their academic and intercultural understanding, begin to take global civic responsibility, and enhance their ability to work with people from different cultural and economic backgrounds" (2008).

Similarly, the University of Louisville International Service Learning Program defines ISL as "experiential education in which students engage in activities that address human and community needs together with structured opportunities intentionally designed to promote student learning and development" (2008). The University of Louisville lists the following outcomes for its ISL program: (1) critical thinking, problem solving, and communication skills; (2) personal growth; (3) social responsibility and appreciation for diversity; (4) different cultural perspectives on career choices; and (5) teamwork, balance, and relationship building (2008).

Indiana University-Purdue University Indianapolis (IUPUI) is currently developing a formal definition of ISL as a part of its overall review and reformulation of its global engagement and its enhancement of curricula through internationalization. IUPUI provisionally defines ISL as "a structured academic experience in another country in which students (a) participate in an organized service activity that addresses identified community needs; (b) learn from direct interaction and cross-cultural dialogue with others; and (c) reflect on the experience in such a way as to gain a deeper understanding of global and intercultural issues, a broader appreciation of the host country and the discipline, and an enhanced sense of their own responsibilities as citizens, locally and globally" (Bringle, Hatcher, Jones, & Sutton, 2007).

Not all institutions are equipped to develop their own ISL programs and may seek to partner with third party organizations to provide ISL opportunities for their students. One such organization is the International Partnership for Service Learning and Leadership (IPSL), which arranges short- and long-term international service learning experiences at partner universities around the world. All of their programs combine academic study with ongoing community service. Similar to the university definitions, IPSL (2003) defines ISL as the linkage of overseas academic study with community service. In addition to the outcomes identified in the previous definitions, IPSL also emphasizes the development of students' leadership skills and the importance of developing reciprocal relationships between academic institutions and the communities being served (IPSL, 2003).

However, not all third party providers have such comprehensive definitions of and approaches to ISL. Indeed, several use ISL to describe overseas volunteer opportunities with no overt academic content, which may include more tourism than service opportunities. Faculty and institutions seeking to partner with third party organizations should examine the degree to which academic studies are integrated with the service component, the nature of the service experience being offered to students, and the quality of structured reflection that is part of the experience.

In summary, for the purposes of this chapter, ISL is defined as

> an academic, curriculum-based course or a combination of courses in which students participate in meaningful, sustained community service; engage in regular, structured reflection activities that integrate academic content with real-world practice and that ask students to explore their own values, their sense of social responsibility, and their ability to work collaboratively with individuals and groups from diverse backgrounds; and have multiple opportunities to engage with residents of the host culture outside of an academic setting.

ISL can be structured in a variety of ways, as we will discuss below. However, before delving into the nuts and bolts of service learning programs, we discuss the context in which ISL programs can emerge.

CONTEXTUALIZING INTERNATIONAL SERVICE LEARNING

Earlier chapters have addressed both the urgency of globalization in American higher education and the alignment of this priority with institutional mission. In these chapters, the importance of study abroad—having both students and faculty travel to other nations and cultures as a part of the teaching and learning process—has been prominent as one of the most important means of achieving institutional objectives determined by mission and also of adding substance to the goal of preparing globally competent citizens.

Viewed principally as a variant of study abroad by many, ISL is also substantively more, as the preceding discussion of definitions illustrates. Although not necessarily the best means of achieving a particular institution's mission by itself, service learning has—with varying degrees of emphasis—the advantage of integrating teaching, research, and service within a coherent educational experience. It thus offers benefits, such as greater flexibility and utility, which enhance its efficiency and effectiveness.

As will be discussed subsequently, these considerations of efficiency and effectiveness are non-trivial. Most importantly, however, the issues of urgency and priority in meeting institutional mission related to preparing globally competent citizens argue for the integrative dimensions of ISL. These integrative dimensions are (1) internationalization and civic mission; (2) faculty teaching, research, and service; and (3) intentionality and outcomes.

INTEGRATING THE INTERNATIONAL AND CIVIC MISSIONS OF HIGHER EDUCATION

At a time when the Association of American Colleges and Universities (AAC&U) has been conducting the most extensive, sustained effort in decades to reform undergraduate education through its Liberal Education and America's Promise (LEAP) initiative, it has placed a particular emphasis on the goals and ends of liberal education, which it posits as the foundation for all baccalaureate learning. Schneider (2007), AAC&U's President, reports that the research the organization has conducted on its own or consulted "tells us that civic learning remains optional rather than essential for the majority of faculty, students, and employers" and concludes that "the apparent disconnect between the goals of college learning and democratic principles is an ominous sign" (pp. 1–2). Such realizations provide the impetus for the urgency reflected in the comments of the authors of earlier chapters, but they also reflect the inherent difficulties of making reforms to achieve worthy goals.

Undaunted, most of the nation's higher education associations have created initiatives specifically related to civic engagement and to internationalization. Few of them, however, are carefully related or integrated. Even AAC&U's program, *Shared Futures: Global Learning and Social Responsibility*, which is specifically designed "to provide students with the knowledge and commitment to be socially responsible citizens in a diverse democracy and increasingly interconnected world" (AAC&U, 2008), does not call for study abroad as a necessary or even preferential means to this end (although it certainly recognizes and supports study abroad in all its forms, including ISL).

Most of the associations representing colleges and universities appreciate the importance of study abroad. NAFSA: Association of International Educators (NAFSA), as one of the umbrella organizations for institutions of higher education, for example, has been promoting *An International Educator's Policy for U.S. Leadership, Competitiveness, and Security* (NAFSA, 2007). One of the four main points of the proposed policy calls for establishing study abroad as an integral component of undergraduate education. The Lincoln Commission's strong recommendation for one million American students to study abroad as a matter of national policy has been universally acclaimed as an intention, although yet without much movement toward funding and with some concern about the standards and quality of implementation (Commission on the Abraham Lincoln Study Abroad Fellowship Program, 2005). As significant as the realization of this goal might be, however, it is only a small step toward helping all college and university graduates become globally competent citizens.

Consider the American Council on Education's (ACE) Madeleine Green's observation in an interview with the *Chronicle of Higher Education* that only 1 percent of students study abroad. Rhetorically Green asks, "What are we going to do with the other 16,900,000" (McMurtrie, 2007)? The American Council on Education has done as much as any association to support study abroad in all its forms and has provided sustained guidance and support for institutions through its Center for International Initiatives (ACE, 2008), but the combined impact of internationalization and civic engagement has yet to be realized to any significant or widespread degree through ISL or other means (such as joint degree programs or social entrepreneurship internships) that intentionally target civic-minded learning abroad. The challenges are significant, and we need to be as effective as we can in reaching the now widely shared goal of preparing globally competent citizens. International service learning can help in specific ways.

A few national associations have dedicated themselves to this work by bringing together study

488

abroad and civic engagement programs. Innovations in Civic Participation (ICP) and IPSL are two of the more prominent organizations; ICP was formed in 2001 and works around the world to develop and strengthen policies and programs that focus on applying service as a solution to a wide range of social issues. In particular, ICP has supported the development of the Talloires Network (Tufts, 2008) as a collective of individuals and institutions committed to promoting the civic roles and social responsibilities of higher education internationally (see Innovations in Civic Participation, 2008). These organizations recognize that global citizenship is not the responsibility of only Americans. Global citizenship must also engage citizens of other nations. This principle of shared responsibility is important in many ways, especially in the preparation of globally competent citizens. This ideal cannot be American—or at least not imposed by America. It must be an international ideal born of mutual respect and a sense of reciprocity with interdependence. The opportunity to observe citizenship in play in other nations allows students to see, appreciate, and perhaps understand why behaviors, mores, and laws that are unacceptable or even illegal in their own nation or locale are acceptable, and in some cases appropriate in their host nation or locale, and vice versa. The experience of contrast calls upon the student to question why the differences exist, even if the perceived differences cannot be reconciled.

IPSL is more specifically focused on ISL. In 2003, IPSL issued a declaration of principles that both sets forth guidelines for effective and ethical programming and offers a set of learning outcomes that can be expected from successful ISL (2003). Both of these organizations—and others, such as Campus Compact (2007)—provide substantial, experience-based insights into the creation and management of ISL with the inherent goal of developing globally competent citizenship, both in the United States and abroad.

So, the twin goals of global citizenship and international learning experiences are widely accepted, even if difficult to achieve. Most of the national institutional membership associations have initiatives and resources available to support their member colleges and universities, and there are a few associations dedicated specifically to the integration of the two goals. With the alignment of these factors along with the nearly universal acceptance by higher education that it must be increasingly global in outlook, ISL offers a particularly powerful means of achieving these goals. It is likely that ISL's acceptance by colleges and universities is on the rise, although reliable data do not exist. Nonetheless, if this volume of essays is any indication, there is reason to believe this trend may accelerate as more academic leaders, faculty, and students act on their convictions by articulating learning objectives associated with global citizenship and by creating programs to achieve them.

INTEGRATING FACULTY ROLES: TEACHING, RESEARCH, AND SERVICE

Not only does ISL provide an approach for addressing institutional goals for internationalization and student civic development, it can also provide a mechanism for integrating the traditional faculty roles of teaching, research, and service. ISL is particularly effective when the faculty who are using this pedagogy base service learning abroad on their own research—including using the student experiences to extend, support, or enhance research. As research, especially scientific research, becomes more interdisciplinary and collaborative, the opportunities to work with colleagues in other countries open the door to service learning projects that may successfully engage students in the laboratories, field experiments, or settings of their counterparts in other countries. Moreover, the idea that research may better be construed as scholarship that has its applications in pedagogy and discovery opens the door for such opportunity even wider and helps promote flexibility in the conduct of faculty work in the traditional three areas (Boyer, 1990). Later in this chapter we will identify opportunities for research emerging from ISL. In principle, by applying the pedagogy of service learning to internationalization goals and by being intentional about the ways in which this pedagogy helps students learn and reflect on the responsibilities of citizenship in a global context, faculty who embrace ISL can find ways to use their time and limited resources even more efficiently and with greater personal control, especially given growing demands from administrative officers for more faculty involvement in an expanding range of activities. When widespread across a department or school, there can be still greater cumulative impact in attaining learning goals for students and in achieving more within resource constraints.

Many relatively new institutions that have been formed in this emerging era of global awareness, California State University Monterey Bay and California State University Channel Islands, for example, have adopted missions and supported approaches to learning that encourage the integration of faculty work to achieve institutional goals—explicitly including the goal of graduating globally competent citizens and using service learning as a principal means of achieving this end. Both of these institutions also reflect the efficiency and effectiveness of deploying service learning in the local community and abroad as a connected social continuum in which learning experiences are intentionally linked, conceptually and pedagogically. For example, when combining domestic service learning in a project that engages recent immigrants to a local community with short-term ISL, campuses have the opportunity to connect students to familial, religious, cultural, ethnic, linguistic, and economic social institutions in two (or more) locations and thus to multiply the learning opportunities. The ability to compound study abroad experience limited to only a few weeks by embedding it in a domestic but cross-cultural context through service learning brings a significant, even transformative, international experience within the range of most students (and faculty) who are constrained by money, work or family obligations, language, or apprehension.

The efficiency and effectiveness of this type of integration is certain to be more important across all institutional types as the transformation of the American academic workforce proceeds unabated toward a new model shaped largely by economic realities: since 1997, more than half of all new full-time academic appointments are for faculty who are ineligible for tenure and, more often than not, specialized in only one of the traditional areas of faculty work in research, teaching, administration (or other service), or client and patient services; nearly two-thirds of all recent academic appointments are for less than full time; and the overwhelming majority of both part-time and contingent faculty do not hold a doctorate (Plater, 2007). These changes— and others—are being forced by economic factors brought about by declining public support for higher education at a time of increased demand for access. The recent attention to the importance of global awareness and engagement only adds to expectations for faculty work and to demands on their time and expertise. Moreover, higher expectations for the productivity of institutions in areas such as economic development (typically fueled by research) and for public service in the form of contributed expertise to address local community issues intensify the demand on resources.

Service learning offers highly effective ways to organize, orient, and deploy the talent represented by this new and emerging academic workforce because the pedagogy can be taught, monitored, and assessed even when the faculty are mobile, contingent, and limited in their opportunities for integrating teaching, research, and service. When institutional goals for graduating globally competent citizens are clear and when work is effectively organized at the department or school level, ISL can provide a stable framework that accommodates the new and emerging academic workforce, as the next sections of this chapter explain.

Such an approach, however, requires the academic unit or institution to have long-term, strategic partners abroad with a strong, shared commitment to common goals. Mutuality and reciprocity build stronger programs not only because of ethical issues but because of practical ones. The key is in having clear learning and service objectives, a good plan for assessing outcomes, and a process of continuous improvement.

INTEGRATING INTENTION WITH OUTCOMES

Effective ISL, like service learning generally and, in fact, any teaching and learning strategy, is the product of intentional design. And the most effective design processes begin "with the end in mind," or with a good understanding of the goals or outcomes (Wiggins & McTighe, 1998), as well as with a solid understanding of the nature of the undertaking being designed.

The previous definitions of ISL identify a range of learning outcomes as well as meaningful community outcomes; and those outcomes are determined and influenced by all the partners in the process: the instructional staff (e.g., faculty), the community members (e.g., representatives of one or more community organizations), and the student(s). An important first step in designing ISL, then, is the careful articulation of the desired outcomes. What body of thought or content should students encounter in the community and in what ways should their understanding of it deepen? What aspects of the host culture, and of the home culture by comparison, should students come to understand more deeply? What issues or questions or concerns are important in the community and what changes would community members like to work on in collaboration with students? Answers to these questions help determine what type of service activity is best suited as both a "text" for learning and a useful contribution in the community.

Other important questions to consider in beginning to match educational goals to community activities involve the parameters (sometimes constraints, sometimes opportunities) that guide the design process. It is important to know who the students, faculty/staff, and community partners are; what knowledge and skills they bring to the project. What is their level of experience with service learning and with international education? What are their goals for learning and for cross-cultural and interpersonal interaction? What level of investment and participation can they commit to the collaboration and what roles do they envision themselves playing? It is also important to know the historical context of the community in general and of the service learning partnership in particular. What have been the nature and consequences of previous interactions in this community? What are its current needs and assets, how have they come to be, and what role do they play in this project? Investigating these characteristics of the people and places involved proceeds best when the focus is not only on deficits or needs (What do the students not know? What problems does the community need addressed?), but also, and perhaps primarily, on assets or abilities (What do the students bring in terms of knowledge and skills and interests? In what ways are community members addressing their own challenges and what do they have to teach?).

As the examples in the following section will show, service learning may take many different forms, with length and intensity of service, degree of institutional involvement, number of participants, and quality of orientation and reflection activities all being variables that are subject to design. Some of the design choices are determined by the institutions in question and are thus fixed as far as the participants are concerned; for example, in the alternative spring break model, the length of the experience is generally one week (the length of the break in the academic calendar). As another example, many programs preestablish community partnerships in the host country for students to step into on a rotating basis. In many cases, the students and faculty play a strong role in determining the academic content and learning goals and the approaches to reflection, even when they are not central in establishing community partnerships or negotiating the type of service the students will undertake. Another early step in the process of designing ISL, then, is to determine what elements are already given or predetermined and what elements remain to be decided upon.

The discussion that follows focuses on two important but easily underestimated challenges of designing for effective ISL programs: capacity building and the use of reflection to improve the quality of both learning and service. At the same time, we note that some or all of the elements of any particular service learning activity may have been preestablished by the institution or program in question.

CAPACITY BUILDING FOR INTERNATIONAL SERVICE LEARNING

Service learning in general often presents everyone involved with unfamiliar challenges (Clayton & Ash, 2004; Howard, 1998), and ISL arguably intensifies this situation. Students and faculty alike are, for the most part, accustomed to teaching and learning in traditional ways: inside the walls of a classroom, during finite periods of time, with the teacher and the texts understood as the sources of knowledge and the students positioned largely as passive recipients. Students and community members alike are, similarly, often more experienced with volunteerism than with the more complex service learning process, with its expectation of mutual benefits, its multifaceted objectives and relationships, and its integration of academic content with community knowledge. In the case of ISL in particular, in addition to these counternormative elements, all the participants are by and large much more familiar with their own cultures, language, and ways of being than with those of the other partners with whom they are going to be interacting. Capacity building—or, enhancing the ability of everyone involved to be involved effectively and to derive and generate maximum benefit from their involvement—is thus an essential aspect of well-designed service learning, including ISL (Clayton & Ash, 2004).

Capacity building most often takes place before the service learning experience begins and is most often focused on the student (and secondarily on the faculty) participants, although it is often key to appropriate and successful role-crafting among community members as well. It is important for the students to identify the ways in which the project will challenge them or push them beyond their personal zones of comfort, experience, and expertise. Such awareness can point them toward issues that they need to prepare themselves for prior to departure as well as issues they can focus their attention on in-country as an aid to their learning and growth. When students learn at least basic information about the host community (e.g., history, political and economic context, demographics composition, language, social norms), it can help them feel more confident living in the host community and can generate important questions for them to think about and investigate further both before departure and in-country. When they give careful thought to who they are interacting with as well as how and why, and about how they will themselves be served it helps them define an appropriate role for themselves in-country, avoiding both a "tourist" approach and a "technocratic" attitude—a sense of themselves as bringing needed expertise to people lacking the capacity to help themselves (Boyte, 2008).

Effectively designed service learning will attend carefully to these and other issues of preparation and to issues of entry and exit. How will students approach their initial interactions with members of the host community? What messages do they send by how they dress, what they do and do not say, when they do and do not ask questions, and to whom they address those questions? To what extent is it appropriate for students to approach their initial interactions as if they are seeking to establish personal relationships? How can they best enter into the community in order to build positively on any previous experiences the partnership may include, to convey respect and openness, to position themselves as collaborators in the process of learning and service that is about to begin?

Capacity building for effective partnering also includes anticipating issues related to exit, to leaving the community, and then returning home. How will expectations and relationships in-country be managed so as to avoid abrupt severance upon departure, which is potentially harmful to both students and community members? How can the service activities be undertaken so as to avoid creating inappropriate dependencies (physical, psychological, or emotional), again, for *any* of the participants? How can work be handed off smoothly and farewells made gracefully, so that all participants and the processes they have been involved in are left stronger, not more fragile? Even a relatively short period of immersion in another culture can generate transition difficulties for the participating students, not only the obvious ones associated with leaving home but also the less obvious ones that come with returning home having somewhat different perspectives and therefore seeing the familiar with new eyes. How can students who may for the first time see what they have taken as given at home, taken for granted in their day-to-day lives, manage the resulting dissonance and confusion? What should they expect in terms of how their family and friends, who may not have experienced such a change in perspective, will and will not readily understand their questions and their transition back to the norms of their everyday lives?

The issue of capacity building makes clear that ISL is not bounded by the dates of departure from and return to the home country. Significant preparation is required, for all partners, and must be built into any effective design. Transitions into and out of the experience require careful thought and management. And, especially given the likelihood that the greatest impacts of ISL, at least in terms of the student's learning and growth, may be experienced well after, perhaps years after, the completion of the project, an effective design process will include mechanisms to help the student anticipate and capitalize on its lifelong transformative potential (Kiely, 2005).

REFLECTION IN INTERNATIONAL SERVICE LEARNING

Meaning making before, during, and after the ISL experience is the function of reflection (Ash & Clayton, 2004; Ash, Clayton, & Atkinson, 2005; Bringle & Hatcher, 1999; Eyler & Giles, 1999; Eyler, Giles, & Schmiede, 1996; Hatcher & Bringle, 1997); and any well-designed ISL course or program will include effective reflection. Beginning with the end in mind, articulating objectives for learning and service, and designing reflection to help the learner and the partnership as a whole achieve those objectives are each important components of good ISL experiences. Reflection is a critical design component, regardless of how the ISL course or program is structured (Whitney & Clayton, in press).

Reflection and its central role in experiential education, including ISL, are often misunderstood (Ash, Clayton, & Moses, 2007). Reflection frequently connotes stream-of-consciousness writing, keeping a diary, or summarizing activities. Less often is it understood to be an analytical, evidence-based examination of the sources of and gaps in knowledge and practice, with the intent to improve thinking and practice. It is the latter understanding of reflection that is required if practitioners are to design reflection activities in ISL, to generate and document learning, and to improve the quality of service.

Using reflection maximally toward these ends requires a precise understanding of the learning and service objectives at stake in the ISL activity. As noted in our discussion of definitions of ISL, learning outcomes generally include academic, civic (e.g., global citizenship), cross-cultural, and personal (learning about oneself, one's values, one's growth processes). An important step in designing reflection so as to generate this learning is to express the desired learning outcomes in terms of specific, assessable learning objectives for each domain (Ash, Clayton, & Atkinson, 2005; Ash, Clayton, & Moses, in press; Jameson, Clayton, & Bringle, 2008).

For example, consider students studying nutrition and the general goal of understanding diverse cultures. More precise diversity-related learning objectives that are tied to the discipline of nutrition might include (1) identifying the nutritional requirements and dietary behaviors of a given ethnic group living in the host country; (2) describing the traditional diet of that ethnic group as well as the historic and contemporary influences on food selection; (3) analyzing the nutritional value of those traditional foods and contrasting that with the group's nutritional requirements; (4) evaluating the nutritional adequacy of the traditional diet and the role of food traditions relative to other behaviors in the diet of the group; and (5) applying this analysis of the relationship between nutritional requirements, dietary behaviors, and traditional foods to the student's own ethnic group or culture. This more precise articulation of objectives (in this case, at the interface of academic and cross-cultural learning) can guide the selection of relevant readings, the design of community experiences (e.g., to include participation in events during which traditional foods are consumed, in food procurement or meal preparation activities, etc.), and the crafting of reflection prompts that will support learners in attending to relevant dimensions of their experiences in the community.

Key here is the intention to design reflection so as to *generate* learning (Ash, Clayton, & Moses, in press; Bringle & Hatcher, 1999; Jameson, Clayton, & Bringle, 2008). Reflection strategies may include multiple opportunities for the students to reflect on their experiences, sometimes together and sometimes individually, sometimes in writing and sometimes orally. Multiple reflection activities that are carefully designed to build on one another and that include feedback (from peers, from instructor, sometimes from community members) are especially effective at deepening learning over time. Reflection that invites students to examine the service processes in which they are involved, with an eye to the effectiveness of their collaboration, can also be extremely useful in enhancing the quality of service over time, especially if the students are asked to set concrete, short-term goals for improvement and then are brought back to reflect iteratively on the consequences of taking action toward those goals.

Each reflection activity is guided by prompts that are carefully chosen in accordance with the desired learning outcomes (Ash & Clayton, 2004; Ash, Clayton, & Atkinson, 2005; Ash, Clayton, & Moses, in press; Jameson, Clayton, & Bringle, 2008). When the desired learning involves the students' own *personal growth*, then prompts may call their attention to their assumptions (What did they expect going into the experience? Why did they bring those assumptions? Which of them were and were not valid? Were any of them grounded in stereotypes?), their feelings

(How did they react emotionally to what particular elements of the experience? Why did they react that way? Are those reactions judged appropriate and, if not, what can they do to change it next time?), and the skills or abilities used or lacking but needed in the situation. When the desired learning involves *global citizenship*, then prompts may call attention to the similarities and differences in how a given sociopolitical phenomenon emerges in the host and the home community, to the ways in which students do and do not have a voice in shaping the resolution of a particular challenge, to the connections made between everyday choices at home or those of the home government and the lives of the people in the community that is being served, and to the dynamics of power and privilege as they are affected by intercultural exchanges. If the desired learning involves improved *group process*, then prompts may call attention to how decisions are being made, who is and is not assuming leadership roles, how individuals are and are not being held accountable for their contributions, whether tasks are adequately understood and distributed, and how progress is being assessed.

Maximizing the role of reflection in ISL, then, hinges on its intentional design toward desired learning and service outcomes. As noted earlier, students often find service learning in general an unfamiliar and challenging teaching and learning strategy, and this is especially true of its reflection component: learning how to learn through reflection is thus another important arena of capacity building in this process (Ash, Clayton, & Atkinson, 2005; Ash, Clayton, & Moses, in press; Jameson, Clayton, & Bringle, 2008). Instructional staff can effectively model learning through reflection for students, can provide thoughtful and constructive feedback that both supports and challenges them to deeper learning, can reward improvement in ways that make it safe for students to take the intellectual and personal risks that learning through reflection often evokes, and can make clear through the grading scheme that learning generated and documented through reflection is valued equally with other modes of evaluation.

STRUCTURING INTERNATIONAL SERVICE LEARNING EXPERIENCES

Thus far, we have argued that ISL can be an effective and efficient approach to integrating the international and civic missions of higher education; helping faculty merge their teaching, research, and service roles; and linking international learning and student development outcomes through intentional pedagogical design and critical reflection. In addition, we have presented ways of developing capacity for ISL and for designing reflection activities to reach learning objectives associated with ISL, noting that the particular design choices appropriate to any given ISL experience will vary. In this section, we more explicitly consider the variety of ways in which ISL experiences can be structured and the nature of the evidence on outcomes associated with these structures. This analysis is critical in order for institutions that are thinking about initiating or expanding ISL to understand the trade-offs involved in designing ISL courses and programs.

As a first pass at trying to achieve greater clarity, it is useful to make a distinction between ISL courses and ISL programs. The former are individual courses in which the content is at least partially delivered and the service at least partially conducted in another country. ISL *programs*, on the other hand, (1) integrate several courses, all of which are completed in another country; (2) last at least one academic term; and (3) incorporate a service learning component in at least one of the courses. Examples of ISL programs offered by third-party organizations include those offered

Table 27.1 *Course Structure*

	All in host country		Sandwich 1		Sandwich 2		Practicum		Competency-Based Service	
Foreign Faculty	S-H	S-L	S-H	S-L	S-H	S-L	S-H	S-L	S-H	S-L
Domestic Faculty	S-H	S-L	S-H	S-L	S-H	S-L	S-H	S-L	S-H	S-L

S-H = High level of contact with host country through community service.
S-L = Low level of contact with host country through community service.

through the IPSL, and the Amizade Global Service Learning Consortium. Examples of ISL programs offered by individual colleges include Augsburg College's Center for Global Education, the University of Minnesota's Studies in International Development, and the previously mentioned programs at the University of Louisville and The Ohio State University.

The intensity with which service occurs as part of a single course or a program may be a factor in identifying the community, partnership, or student learning outcomes of ISL. Table 27.1 reflects the high level of variability that is possible in designing ISL courses and identifies at least twenty possible variations in ISL course structure based on the locality of the course, whether the course is taught by host-country faculty or home-country faculty, the amount of service contact (S-H indicates a high level of contact, S-L indicates a low level of contact), and whether the course is content-focused or skill-focused (e.g., practica and competency-based programs). We will review each of these, provide examples of some, and summarize research on measuring outcomes from each type, when it is available.

ALL IN THE HOST COUNTRY

ISL courses that are taught in the host country in their entirety often have the advantage of providing students with greater contact with the host culture. However, since it is often the case that this is the only course completed by the traveling student, such courses tend to be of limited duration, generally lasting 6 to 8 weeks. The amount of service provided by the student may also vary, ranging from a single service activity to several hours of service per day throughout the duration of the course. Finally, whether students are taught by faculty from their home institution or from a local institution may have an impact on student learning, the nature of contact with the host community, and the students' appreciation of teaching and learning styles and strategies in the host community.

For example, Wessel (2007) describes a sociology course taught in Mexico by a home-country professor. Students also enrolled in Spanish-language courses taught by host-country faculty at a local university. The service component of the course involved eight hours per week at one of three community sites. Based on the subsequent analysis of participants' reflections and course evaluations, Wessel identifies the following challenges:

- The quality of students' experiences varies according to their proficiency in the host-country language, the length of their stay in the host country, and their prior knowledge of the host-country and the community in which they will be studying and serving (2007, p. 83).
- Culture shock not only affects students' ability to adjust to a new setting, but it also can hamper the nature of their interactions among themselves, especially when combined with group service projects (p. 86).

These challenges, once identified, can be addressed through predeparture orientation, but experienced study abroad and ISL coordinators know that they will rarely be eliminated.

Finding the proper balance between engaging students in academic study in a new country, engaging them with the community through service, engaging them with the host-country culture through field trips, and giving them time to reflect is another of the common challenges of ISL. Wessel (2007) cautions against trying to accomplish too much through ISL courses and reflects, "In retrospect, I think the program may have been too stimulating for some participants. The outside projects that were a part of the classroom course, which seemed interesting in the context of the course, were perhaps too much when combined with service learning and weekend excursions.... A course on intercultural communication could have been of use to the students" (p. 86).

In spite of these challenges, Wessel (2007) reports a high level of student satisfaction with the course. Many students referred to their experience as "life-changing" and reported gaining a better ability to understand and appreciate different cultures. Several students also reported that the experience provided them with intercultural communication skills that helped them in their career paths (p. 85).

Sandwich 1

As defined by Chisholm, a sandwich structure occurs when there is a "pattern of several weeks of full-time study followed by full-time service" concluding with another period of continued study, reflection, and examinations (2003, p. 280). One variation on the sandwich pattern emerges when the academic study occurs in the home country, with appropriate predeparture orientation to the host country, followed by a relatively brief stay in the host country and then a return to the home country for the conclusion of the course. In this structure, all of the service occurs in the host country. This pattern is likely to occur with courses in which the service occurs during a fall or spring break period.

Lewis and Niesenbaum (2005) conducted an assessment of the impact of a short-term (2-week) study abroad experience that was integrated into a full-semester course taught in the home country. They tested the hypothesis that the benefits of short-term study abroad would be similar to those of long-term study abroad experiences if significant community-based experiences were part of the host country experience (p. 254). For this particular course, the instructors combined community-based research with service learning to provide students with meaningful contact with residents of the host country. In addition, the first half of the course served as an extended predeparture orientation, with preparation related to research and language skills incorporated with the course content.

To test their hypothesis, Lewis and Niesenbaum (2005) conducted an online survey of students who had completed the course between 1998 and 2003. They found that the majority of the respondents reported that short-term study abroad was more attractive than long-term study; they had an increased interest in interdisciplinary study as a result of study abroad; and they had a better understanding of the costs and benefits of globalization (p. 257). Furthermore, nearly half of the respondents (42%) reported additional travel abroad after their study abroad experience (p. 257).

In general, the authors found that, in addition to producing outcomes associated with long-term study abroad, "STSA [short-term study abroad] helps students overcome the psychological barriers to study abroad and for some, leads to longer term study abroad" (Lewis & Niesenbaum, 2005, p. 258). The authors also report that the short-term study abroad experience, when combined with service learning, contributed to an improvement in students' critical thinking and research skills, personal development and growth, and an understanding of their "civic role in a globalized world" (p. 258).

Sandwich 2

This second sandwich pattern also involves academic study at home with service abroad, but here domestic service is integrated with service abroad. For example, a course on immigration issues may include domestic service with immigrant groups in the home community, followed by service work in the immigrants' home communities, ending with additional service with immigrants in the home country. This approach has the advantage of providing students with a comparative framework for analyzing an issue from different national perspectives. As beneficial as this variation might be, particularly in providing students with deep learning experiences in terms of analyzing social issues from a comparative perspective, no examples of this type appeared in a web scan of ISL courses and programs.

Practicum

Another variation on the ISL course is the international service-based practicum or internship, in which individual students study abroad as part of an intensive preprofessional learning experience. For example, some schools of education will allow students to complete student teaching in an international setting. Likewise, social work students might complete a bachelor's or master's level practicum in another country. Whether such experiences constitute an ISL program will depend on whether students are involved in community-based work that is linked to, but goes beyond, their practicum or internship requirements and the degree to which students are required to reflect on such experiences. The potential benefit of this type of experience is that it provides students with a broader perspective on their chosen profession as well as an opportunity to explore the service orientation of the profession in a cross-cultural setting.

Several studies had examined the role of international student teaching and service learning in developing cultural and global competencies among preservice teachers. Roberts (2003) and Cushner and Mahon (2002) found evidence of increased tolerance for cultural differences among participants. Cushner and Mahon also found evidence of participant-reported self-efficacy and the ability to incorporate cultural understanding and awareness into professional practice. Stachowski, Richardson, and Henderson (2003) found evidence that students participating in international student teaching were more likely to incorporate culturally appropriate materials into their planning and teaching than students whose student teaching was in the U.S. Stachowski and Visconti (1997) reported that international student teaching improved participants' abilities to adapt to new cultures and likewise become more tolerant of cultural differences.

Competency Based

Competency-based service learning occurs when the experience is part of the formal educational experience of the student but is not offered for credit. Rather, the experience is designed to allow students to meet required disciplinary or professional competencies. Such experiences are most common in the health science disciplines, such as dentistry, medicine, and nursing. Usually, such experiences are designed to provide students with opportunities to develop intercultural competencies related to their disciplines.

Studies of international clinical experiences for medical students have demonstrated that students who have these experiences are more likely to select primary care specializations (Gupta, Wells, Horwitz, Bia, & Barry, 1999; Pust & Moher, 1992; Ramsey, Haq, Gjerde, & Rothenberg, 2004); devote significant portions of their careers to provide medical care to underserved populations (Godkin & Savageau, 2003; Haq et al., 2000; Ramsey et al., 2004; Thompson, Huntington, Hunt, Pinsky, & Brodie, 2003); develop a greater understanding of global health issues and policies (Federico et al., 2006; Haq et al., 2000; Ramsey et al., 2004; Thompson et al., 2003); pursue public-health oriented career opportunities (Ramsey et al., 2004); and return to non-industrialized countries to provide care and/or engage in research (Miller, Corey, Lallinger, & Durack, 1995; Ramsey et al., 2004). Such studies have contributed to calls for not only increasing international learning opportunities for medical students, but for formally integrating international components into the core medical school curriculum (Drain et al., 2007).

PROS AND CONS OF EACH VARIATION

In general, ISL can add value to study abroad experiences by increasing students' contact with the host culture, requiring and structuring reflection, and providing opportunities for the development of global citizenship competencies through the provision of meaningful service. As we have shown, ISL experiences can be structured in multiple ways, with each variation possessing its own relative advantages and disadvantages. An advantage of the All-in-Host-Country approach is that it most closely resembles the "traditional" semester abroad program and the length of the experience, in theory, allows students to become more comfortable with and knowledgeable about the host country. Adding a concentrated service component intensifies the contact between the student and the host community. A disadvantage is that this approach is not widely accessible, particularly to the growing number of nonresidential students who rely on part-time or full-time employment to pay for their college education.

Because the time away from the home country is relatively short, the sandwich approaches make opportunities for overseas learning available to a larger number of students. Furthermore, as the studies cited above have attempted to demonstrate, the service component can, to a degree, compensate for the shortened length of the experiences by allowing students to engage in meaningful, reflective interaction with host communities. A disadvantage of these approaches is that the degree to which the service adds value to shorter experiences abroad, particularly with respect to intercultural communication and understanding, is not well established in the existing research.

The practicum and competency-based models, by offering students a comparative context in which to observe and practice their chosen professions, add a dimension to preprofessional training not available in the host country. In addition, the service component allows them to adopt a global, civic perspective on their profession that they might not otherwise have the opportunity to develop. A disadvantage is that, like the All-in-Host-Country model, they often require time and financial resources that are not available to the majority of students.

RESEARCH ON INTERNATIONAL SERVICE LEARNING

As we have already observed, the design of ISL experiences depends on a number of factors: the nature of the student population, the language skills of students, the history of prior contacts in the host country, the specific learning outcomes of the course or program, and the capacity of the higher education partners to provide desired services. As with any promising pedagogy, the practice of ISL should be informed by rigorous research and assessment to determine what works well and what does not, particularly with respect to improving students' intercultural and global competencies.

There are at least two compelling reasons for conducting research on ISL: (1) as responsible and reflective educators, practitioners look to research to provide a basis for expanding understanding, gaining confidence in, and improving educational experiences; and (2) research provides a means for conducting scholarship that can contribute to and evaluate discipline-based theories. Although research takes many different forms and is undertaken within both qualitative and quantitative paradigms, there is convergence among scholars on what constitutes good research. At the most general level, Shavelson and Towne (2002, p. 51) describe scientific rigor as being a function of six interrelated principles of inquiry:

1. Pose significant questions that can be investigated empirically.
2. Link research to relevant theory.
3. Use methods that permit direct investigation of the question.
4. Provide a coherent and explicit chain of reasoning.
5. Replicate and generalize across studies.
6. Disclose research to encourage professional scrutiny and critique.

For service learning in particular, there is consensus that good research will (1) be guided by theory; (2) involve clearly defined constructs; (3) control for or account for differences among groups; (4) use measures that have multiple indicators; (5) use multiple methods when appropriate; (6) establish converging results across different methods; (7) use designs that result in confidence in the conclusions that are reached; and (8) have implications for teaching and learning in general (Gelmon, Furco, Holland, & Bringle, 2005). These prescriptions for what constitutes rigorous, high quality research transcend distinctions of quantitative versus qualitative methods and suggest that either strategy can possess or be deficient in these attributes.

A review of many of the studies cited in the previous section demonstrates that past research does not measure up well to these criteria (see also Kiely & Hartman, in press). For example, most of these studies (Lewis & Niesenbaum, 2005; Porter & Monard, 2001; Smith-Paríolá & Gòkè-Paríolá, 2006; Wessel, 2007) are single-case studies and are not grounded in theory. There is little, if any, attempt to control for individual characteristics within groups and no attempt to test assumptions or make comparisons across like and different groups. In addition, given the idiosyncrasies of the individual cases, their research conclusions are not generalizable. Although such studies are valuable in terms of providing lessons-learned, they do not necessarily advance a cumulative body of knowledge on the effects of ISL. These studies, then, are consistent with a broader review of service learning research (Gelmon et al., 2005) which demonstrates that the pedagogy (variously defined, and with tremendous variability in implementation) is *associated* with many outcomes that:

- are based on the testimony and self-reports of students,
- come from small sample studies (e.g., single class or program),
- do not control for self-selection,
- only occasionally have appropriate comparisons,

- do not have multiple indicators or methods,
- have serious limitations on generalizability, and
- are based on a single experience and are measured at the end of the semester. (Bringle, 2006)

As Kiely and Hartman (in press) note, the research on ISL is also piecemeal (numerous isolated studies), for the most part not theory based, not cumulative across studies, and deficient in providing a rationale for the selection of methods and procedures.

The variety of types of ISL courses and programs, and the broad range of potential outcomes from these educational experiences, complicates the task of designing research to expand the knowledge base associated with ISL. Both service learning in general and ISL in particular present a complex yet rich collection of opportunities for research. Bringle and Tonkin (2004) and Tonkin (in press) provide a preliminary research agenda for ISL. As these analyses emphasize, and as our review of past research on various approaches to ISL illustrates, students are the central focus. In addition, however, research can examine the impact of ISL on institutions of higher education (locally and abroad), community (locally and abroad), faculty (locally and abroad), and the development of partnerships (Bringle, Hatcher, & Jones, in press; Bringle & Tonkin, 2004).

Most approaches to studying student outcomes in study abroad focus either on avoiding negative outcomes in the experience (e.g., importance of preparation and orientation, minimizing culture shock), on developing cross-cultural competencies and cross-cultural learning, or on a synthesis (e.g., Kim's stress-adaptation-growth model) of these approaches (see Kiely, in press, for a summary). The studies cited in the previous section illustrate that seldom have learning outcomes been addressed. For example, neither Wessel (2007) nor Lewis and Niesenbaum (2005) directly address the impact of ISL on academic or curricular learning outcomes. To the degree that Lewis and Niesenbaum explore the general effects of ISL on student learning, they rely on self-reports as opposed to replicable measures of student understanding or development. Because ISL involves travel abroad and usually study abroad, research on ISL should include these academic student outcomes. However, the defining characteristic of ISL, and the one that distinguishes it from study abroad and other forms of international learning, is the intentional goal of developing in students a set of knowledge, skills, and dispositions that are focused on global citizenship. Thus, ISL, like service learning in general, is not only about "serving to learn" but also "learning to serve" and the broader spectrum of civic outcomes (Battistoni, 2002). This set of civic educational objectives should be part of any definition of ISL, program or course design, and approach to critical reflection. It is both implied and enacted through the processes of well-designed ISL, which necessarily involve helping students learn to work *with* not just *in* the host community, in a manner that is democratic, respects alternative ways of knowing, and recognizes the community as a source of knowledge and those in the community as co-educators.

We view the core elements of being civic-minded to include:

1. *Academic Knowledge and Technical Skills*: In receiving a college education the civic-minded graduate will have acquired advanced knowledge and skills in at least one discipline, which can be applied to help solve problems in the community.
2. *Knowledge of Volunteer Opportunities and Nonprofit Organizations*: Civic-minded graduates will have a conception of the ways they can make contributions to society, particularly through nonprofit organizations.

501

3. *Knowledge of Contemporary Social Issues*: Civic-minded graduates will have an understanding of the complex issues and problems encountered in modern society, both at the local and national levels.

4. *Listening and Communication Skills*: In order to help solve problems in society, civic-minded graduates will need to have the ability to communicate well with others. This includes written and spoken proficiency as well as the art of listening to divergent points of view.

5. *Diversity Skills*: Civically minded graduates will have a rich understanding of, sensitivity to, and acceptance of human diversity in the pluralistic society in which they live. This can be fostered by students' interactions with persons in the community who are different from themselves in terms of racial, economic, religious, or other background characteristics.

6. *Self-Efficacy*: Civic-minded graduates will have a desire to take personal action and also a realistic view that the action will produce the desired results. Self-efficacy is a key component of personal empowerment.

7. *Behavioral Intentions* → *Civic Behavior*: Behavioral intentions can be viewed as predictors of behaviors. Civic-minded graduates will demonstrate that they value civic engagement by stating intentions to be involved in community service in the future and by displaying forms of civic involvement. One of the clearest ways that students can manifest these attributes is by choosing a service-based career or enacting civic responsibilities in a career in any sector. (Bringle & Steinberg, in press)

In comparison to most domestic service learning, ISL adds a cross-cultural component to each of these civic goals. Thus, research should focus on how the knowledge, skills, and dispositions of students are changed by the ISL experience from the perspective of both their home and their host culture and country.

Because of the centrality of the civic educational objective to ISL, future research needs to develop mechanisms for measuring its components. Strategies might use reflection products (see Ash & Clayton, 2004; Ash, Clayton, & Atkinson, 2005; Parker & Dautoff, 2008; Wessel, 2007); focus groups (Tonkin et al., 2004); academic artifacts in electronic portfolios (Cooper, 2008); or surveys (Bringle, Phillips, & Hudson, 2004; Lewis & Niesenbaum, 2005; Steinberg, 2007). Furthermore, this research needs to be situated within appropriate theoretical contexts (Kiely, in press; Merrill & Pusch, 2007) and must develop designs that explicate why and for whom any given outcomes occur.

CONCLUSIONS

ISL provides a powerful means for helping to achieve higher education's mission to prepare students as globally competent and globally aware citizens. Unfortunately, its potent nature can lead to complacency about fine-tuning the design of these educational experiences in order to meet particular learning objectives and about accumulating evidence on best practices to guide the development of the pedagogy. We have offered an overview of the nature of ISL and its rationale, provided some guidance on how to design ISL experiences structured to fit a variety of circumstances, and suggested guidelines for generating scholarship associated with the work that contributes to our understanding of the intersection of international education and the civic education of students. High-quality scholarship on and through ISL has the potential to improve all of higher education, in the U.S. and abroad. Such research and scholarship will inform, but transcend both service learning and study abroad as it deepens our collective understanding of teaching and learning—and, potentially, research and professional service. This scholarship can inform the respective agendas of both individual institutions and the several national (or international) associations that have made internationalization and civic engagement priorities in achieving their missions. Furthermore, this work can provide models that can be evaluated for their relevance to institutions of higher education around the world similarly engaged in determining how their graduates will most effectively and responsibly act in a world of greater complexity and interdependence.

REFERENCES

American Council on Education. (2008). *ACE—Center for International Initiatives*. Retrieved April 18, 2008, from http://www.acenet.edu/Content/NavigationMenu/ProgramsServices/International/index11.htm

Ash, S. L., & Clayton, P. H. (2004). The articulated learning: An approach to reflection and assessment. *Innovative Higher Education, 29*, 137–154.

Ash, S. L., Clayton, P. H., & Atkinson, M. P. (2005). Integrating reflection and assessment to capture and improve student learning. *Michigan Journal of Community Service Learning, 11*(2), 49–60.

Ash, S. L., Clayton, P. H., & Moses, M. G. (2007). *Learning through critical reflection: A tutorial for students in service-learning*. Raleigh, NC: Center for Excellence in Curricular Engagement, NC State University.

Ash, S. L., Clayton, P. H., & Moses, M. G. (in press). *Teaching and learning through critical reflection: A guide for service-learning instructors*. Sterling, VA: Stylus.

Association of American Colleges & Universities. (2008). *Shared futures: Global learning and social responsibility—Guiding principles*. Retrieved April 18, 2008, from http://www.aacu.org/SharedFutures/guidingprinciples.cfm

Battistoni, R. (2002). *Civic engagement across the curriculum: A resource book for service-learning faculty in all disciplines*. Providence, RI: Campus Compact.

Boyer, E. L. (1990). *Scholarship reconsidered: Priorities of the professoriate*. Princeton, NJ: The Carnegie Foundation for the Advancement of Teaching.

Boyte, H. (2008). A new civic politics. [Review of Lee Benson, Ira Harkavy, and John Puckett. *Dewey's dream: Universities and democracies in an age of education reform*. Temple University Press, 2007]. *Journal of Higher Education Outreach and Engagement, 12*(1), 107–112.

Bringle, R. G. (2006, April). *Service learning research*. Paper presented at the conference on How Do Civic Engagement Efforts Impact Students? Creating a Nexus between Research Scholars and Practitioners, Madison, WI.

Bringle, R. G., & Hatcher, J. A. (1999). Reflection in service learning: Making meaning of experience. *Educational Horizons, 77*(4), 179–185.

Bringle, R. G., Hatcher, J. A., & Jones, S. G. (Eds.). (in press). *International service learning: Conceptual frameworks and research*. Sterling, VA: Stylus.

Bringle, R. G, Hatcher, J. A., Jones, S. G., & Sutton, S. B. (2007). *International service learning: A preliminary definition*. Unpublished manuscript.

Bringle, R. G., Phillips, M., & Hudson, M. (2004). *The measure of service learning: research scales to assess student experiences*. Washington, DC: American Psychological Association.

Bringle, R. G., & Steinberg, K. (in press). Educating for informed community involvement. *American Journal of Community Psychology*.

Bringle, R. G., & Tonkin, H. (2004). International service-learning: A research agenda. In H. Tonkin, S. J. Deeley, M. Pusch, D. Quiroga, M. J. Siegel, J. Whiteley, & R. G. Bringle (Eds.), *Service-learning across cultures: Promise and achievement* (pp. 365–374). New York: International Partnership for Service-Learning and Leadership.

Campus Compact. (2007). *Campus compact*. Retrieved April 18, 2008, from http://www.campuscompact.org/

Chisholm, L. A. (2003). Partnerships for international service-learning. In B. Jacoby & Associates (Eds.), *Building partnerships for service-learning* (pp. 259–288). San Francisco: Jossey-Bass.

Clayton, P. H., & Ash, S. L. (2004). Shifts in perspective: Capitalizing on the counter-normative nature of service-learning. *Michigan Journal of Community Service Learning, 11*(1), 59–70.

Commission on the Abraham Lincoln Study Abroad Fellowship Program. (2005, November 14). *Global competence and national needs: One million Americans studying abroad*. Retrieved April 18, 2008, from http://www.nafsa.org/_/Document/_/lincoln_commission_report.pdf

Cooper, G. (2008). Assessing international learning experiences: A multi-institutional collaboration. *Phi Kappa Phi Forum, 88*(1), 8–11.

Cushner, K., & Mahon, J. (2002). Overseas student teaching: Affecting personal, professional, and global competencies in an age of globalization. *Journal of Studies in International Education, 6*(1), 44–58.

Drain, P. K., Primack, A., Hunt, D., Fawzi, W. W., Holmes, K. K., & Gardner, P. (2007). Global health in medical education: A call for more training and opportunities. *Academic Medicine, 82*(3), 226–230.

Eyler, J., & Giles, D. E. (1999). *Where's the learning in service-learning?* San Francisco: Jossey-Bass.

Eyler, J., Giles, D. E., & Schmiede, A. (1996). *A practitioner's guide to reflection in service-learning.* Nashville, TN: Vanderbilt University.

Federico, S. G., Zachar, P. A., Oravec, C. M., Mandler, T., Goldson, E., & Brown, J. (2006). A successful international child health experience: The University of Colorado Department of Pediatrics experience. *Archives of Pediatric and Adolescent Medicine, 160*, 191–196.

Gelmon, S., Furco, A., Holland, B., & Bringle, R. G. (2005, November). *Beyond anecdote: Challenges in bringing rigor to service-learning research.* Paper presented at the 5th Annual International K-H Service-Learning Research Conference, East Lansing, MI.

Godkin, M., & Savageau, J. (2003). The effect of medical students' international experiences on attitudes toward serving underserved multicultural populations. *Family Medicine, 35*(3), 273–278.

Gupta, A. R., Wells, C. K., Horwitz, R. I., Bia, F. J., & Barry, M. (1999). The International Health Program: The fifteen-year experience with Yale University's Internal Medicine Residency Program. *American Journal of Tropical Medicine and Hygiene, 61*(6), 1019–1023.

Haq, C., Rothenberg, D., Gjerde, C., Bobula, J., Wilson, C., Bickley, L., et al. (2000). New world views: Preparing physicians in training for global health work. *Family Medicine, 32*(8), 566–572.

Hatcher, J. A., & Bringle, R. G. (1997). Reflections: Bridging the gap between service and learning. *Journal of College Teaching, 45*, 153–158.

Howard, J. (1998). Academic service learning: A counter normative pedagogy. *New Directions in Teaching and Learning, 73*, 21–29.

Innovations in Civic Participation. (2008). *Innovations in civic participation: A resource for ideas and action.* Retrieved April 18, 2008, from http://www.icicp.org/

International Partnership for Service-Learning and Leadership. (2003). *Declaration of principles.* Retrieved October 20, 2008, from http://www.ipsl.org/pdfs/DeclarationofPrinciplesEnglish.pdf

Jameson, J. K., Clayton, P. H., & Bringle, R. G. (2008). *Investigating student learning within and across linked service-learning courses: Vol. 8. Advances in service-learning research.*

Kiely, R. (2005). A transformative model for service-learning: A longitudinal case study. *Michigan Journal of Community Service Learning, 12*(1), 5–22.

Kiely, R. (in press). What international service learning research can learn from research on international learning. In R. G. Bringle, J. A. Hatcher, & S. G. Jones (Eds.), *International service learning: Conceptual frameworks and research.* Sterling, VA: Stylus.

Kiely, R., & Hartman, E. (in press). Qualitative research methodology and global service learning: Concepts, methods, approaches, and best practices. In R. G. Bringle, J. A. Hatcher, & S. G. Jones (Eds.), *International service learning: Conceptual frameworks and research.* Sterling, VA: Stylus.

Lewis, T. L., & Niesenbaum, R. A. (2005). Extending the stay: Using community-based research and service-learning to enhance short-term study abroad. *Journal of Studies in International Education, 9*, 251–264.

McMurtrie, B. (2007, March 2). The global campus: American colleges connect with the broader world. *Chronicle of Higher Education,* A37.

Merrill, M., & Pusch, M. (2007). Apples, oranges, and kumys: Multiple methods, matrices, and models for research on students doing intercultural research. In S. B. Gelmon & S. H. Billig (Eds.), *Service-learning from passion to objectivity: International and cross-disciplinary perspectives on service-learning research* (pp. 21–40). Charlotte, NC: Information Age.

Miller, W. C., Corey, G. R., Lallinger, G. J., & Durack, D. T. (1995). International health and internal medicine residency training: The Duke University experience. *The American Journal of Medicine, 99*, 291–297.

NAFSA: Association of International Educators. (2007, October). *An international education policy for U.S. leadership, competitiveness, and security.* Retrieved April 18, 2008, from http://www.nafsa.org/public_policy.sec/united_states_international/toward_an_international

Ohio State University, College of Education and Human Ecology. (2008). *International service-learning: What is international service learning?* Retrieved April 18, 2008, from http://ehe.osu.edu/diversity/international/what-is.cfm

Parker, B., & Dautoff, D. A. (2008). Service-learning and study abroad: Synergistic learning opportunities. *Michigan Journal of Community Service Learning, 13*(2), 40–52.

Plater, W. M. (2007). Background paper for consideration of a project on the future of the professoriate. Unpublished manuscript.

Porter, M., & Monard, K. (2001). Anyi in the global village: Building relationships of reciprocity through international service-learning. *Michigan Journal of Community Service Learning, 8*(1), 5–17.

Pust, R. E., & Moher, S. P. (1992). A core curriculum for international health: Evaluating ten years' experience at the University of Arizona. *Academic Medicine, 67*(2), 90–94.

Ramsey, A. H., Haq, C., Gjerde, C. L., & Rothenberg, D. (2004). Career influence of an international health experience during medical school. *Family Medicine, 36*(6), 412–416.

Roberts, A. (2003). Proposing a broadened view of citizenship: North American teachers' service in rural Costa Rican schools. *Journal of Studies in International Education, 7*(3), 253–276.

Schneider, C. G. (2007). Civic learning in a diverse democracy: Education for shared futures. *Diversity and Democracy, 3*, 1–2.

Shavelson, R. J., & Towne, L. (Eds.). (2002). *Scientific research in education*. Washington, DC: National Research Council, National Academy Press.

Smith-Paríolá, J., & Gòkè-Paríolá, A. (2006). Expanding the parameters of service learning: A case study. *Journal of Studies in International Education, 10*(1), 71–86.

Stachowski, L. L., Richardson, J. W., & Henderson, M. (2003). Student teachers report on the influence of cultural values on classroom practice and community involvement: Perspectives from the Navajo Reservation and abroad. *The Teacher Educator, 39*(1), 52–63.

Stachowski, L. L., & Visconti, V. (1997). Adaptations for success: U.S. student teachers living and teaching abroad. *International Education, 26*, 5–20.

Steinberg, K. (2007, April 19). *Easy techniques for assessing service-learning programs*. Presentation at the Annual Conference of Indiana Campus Compact, Indiana State University, Terre Haute, IN.

Thompson, M. J., Huntington, M. K., Hunt, D., Pinsky, L. E., & Brodie, J. J. (2003). Educational effects of international health electives on U.S. and Canadian medical students and residents: A literature review. *Academic Medicine, 78*(3), 342–347.

Tonkin, H. (in press). A research agenda for international service learning. In R. G. Bringle, J. A. Hatcher, & S. G. Jones (Eds.), *International service learning: Conceptual frameworks and research*. Sterling, VA: Stylus.

Tonkin, H., Deeley, S. J., Pusch, M., Quiroga, D., Siegel, M. J., Whiteley, J., & Bringle, R. G. (2004). *Service-learning across cultures: Promise and achievement*. New York: International Partnership for Service-Learning and Leadership.

Tufts University—The Talloires Network. (2008). *Tufts University—The Talloires network*. Retrieved April 18, 2008, from http://www.tufts.edu/talloiresnetwork/

University of Louisville, International Service Learning Program. (2008). *What is the UofL International Service Learning Program*. Retrieved April 18, 2008, from http://louisville.edu/student/islp/

Wessel, N. (2007). Integrating service learning into the study abroad program: U.S. sociology students in Mexico. *Journal of Studies in International Education, 11*(1), 73–89.

Whitney, B. C., & Clayton, P. H. (in press). Research on the role of reflection in international service learning. In R. G. Bringle, J. A. Hatcher, & S. G. Jones (Eds.), *International service learning: Conceptual frameworks and research*. Sterling, VA: Stylus.

Wiggins, G., & McTighe, J. (1998). *Understanding by design*. Alexandria, VA: Association for Supervision & Curriculum Development.

Chapter 28

Creating Deep Partnerships with Institutions Abroad

Bard College as Global Citizen

Susan H. Gillespie
Bard College

with Jonathan A. Becker, Bryan Billings, Sergey Bogdanov, Christina Davis, Fazela Haniff, Ayesha Kajee, Thomas Keenan, Nikolay Koposov, Tawana Kupe, and Valery Monakhov

INTRODUCTION

The notion of global citizenship is not simple or uncontroversial. Where is such citizenship rooted? What criteria do we apply to judge the quality of its realization? How do we know whether it is effective? Who decides? Without international norms or established forums for discussion and debate, the notion of global citizenship can be manipulated by powerful interests, or remain diffuse and fail to make a lasting contribution. In this respect, global citizenship and the institutions that support it may come to resemble foreign aid. Many people would agree that foreign aid is a necessary and a good thing in general, and yet its results are sometimes doubtful and can even be harmful—for example, by creating dependencies that discourage local populations from mastering their own development, by distorting economies, by introducing technologies that are unsustainable, encouraging corruption, or allocating too many resources to interests tied to donors or aid agencies.

In the field of education, global citizenship seems more anodyne. What can be wrong with teaching young people to know the world better, and to develop loyalties that go beyond their "national interest"? Certainly, there's nothing wrong in principle, but we should be careful how we structure and manage the programs we offer, and whom they serve. By and large, American study abroad programs are conceived for the benefit of "our" students. We may create and offer the programs ourselves, as college administrators who are in day-to-day contact with partners abroad; or we may rely on independent providers, whose goals range from the idealistic to the frankly commercial, and whose actual engagement with institutions and faculty abroad may be largely invisible to us. Either way, international exchange and study abroad involve collaboration with people and institutions in foreign countries.

It is the contention of this chapter that if we aspire to act as global citizens, we and our institutions must take conscious responsibility for the nature of these interactions—explicit or implicit. A corollary of this contention is that we need to take seriously the project of creating international partnerships, and to apply our very best thinking to the partnerships we create. In seeking to realize new forms of international education, institutions are themselves acting as global citizens—good ones or bad ones. If we wish to make the world a better place, we should strive to model the ethical standards that we seek to impart to our students, and that must ultimately characterize meaningful global citizenship.

I maintain that the ethical standards that should inform global citizenship are to be sharply distinguished from the project of "cultural competence"[1] that is now popularly accepted as a goal of international education. In its exclusive emphasis on mastery and effectiveness, "cultural competence" can be detrimental to the openness and self-questioning that are essential to effective partnerships. In other words, "cultural competence" is not a sufficient basis for global citizenship. It lacks the crucial ethical and philosophical elements of mutuality and equality.

The Institute for International Liberal Education (IILE) runs Bard's major international partnerships, or joint ventures. We are most active in Russia and South Africa, where we have extensive partnerships with St. Petersburg State University and the University of the Witwatersrand.[2] IILE's mission statement commits us explicitly to entering into partnerships based on the principles of mutuality and equality. These are, notably, principles that attempt to structure the dynamics of the relationship, not just its legal or administrative form. Partnerships can take many shapes; they may differ according to the needs of the partners, their size and status, the specific goals of the collaboration, etc. Whatever the details, committing ourselves to a relationship based on mutuality and equality helps assure (1) that we all make a conscious attempt to listen, to be aware of the needs, goals, feelings, and ideas of our overseas colleagues; and (2) that we consciously seek to work in ways that serve not only our own personal or institutional or national ends (though these are all important), but those of our partners as well. There is also a more pragmatic angle to our idealism—we believe these principles to be the only foundation on which we can build relationships that will be sound and long-lasting.

IILE's collaborative projects are buttressed by the fact that Bard and its partner institutions agree to provide a dual degree or shared (dual) credit to students who complete our joint academic programs. After 4 years of study, Smolny graduates, 90% of whom are Russian, earn a dual bachelor's degree in arts and humanities (from Smolny College of St. Petersburg State University) and liberal arts and sciences (from Bard College). IHRE students, approximately half of whom come from North American colleges and universities, and approximately half from the University of the Witwatersrand (Wits) or other African universities, earn regular credit from Bard and Wits for completion of IHRE's semester-long, intensive, humanities-based human rights program. The commitment to the dual degree or dual credit is the central, most far-reaching, and important foundational feature of these academic partnerships. Institutions are jealous of the capacity to award their degrees; they cherish and protect this right. Thus, by its very nature, dual accreditation assures a high level of academic co-ownership and administrative involvement. It requires the participating institutions to realize a common set of educational goals and to apply formal assessment and evaluation criteria. Thus, it gives both partners the leverage to insist on academic quality.

Recently, we have come to think of Bard's most developed links with our university partners abroad as *deep partnerships*.[3] This seems like an excellent term for describing relationships that go beyond the achievement of short-term goals for our institutions or our "own" students. Partnerships are "deep" to the extent that they engage our ethical, intellectual, and philosophical capacities, as well as our well-honed professional skills. In Bard's case, the deep partnerships we maintain can be defined as long-term shared endeavors that include the exchange of students, faculty, and curricular elements.

507 ■

Creating deep partnerships, in which we attempt to live up to the principles of mutuality and equality, also suggests an interest in the reform of educational practices and institutions both abroad and at home. We openly acknowledge this interest, which we share with our university partners abroad, and which means applying progressive political, namely democratic principles, to an area of activity—education—that is too often viewed as largely exempt from such concerns. At Bard, the reform aspect of our partnership activities has mainly to do with changes in the way we approach and integrate international or global issues on our campus. Deep partnerships challenge and enable us to be more effective in learning with and from, not just about people in other countries. In practice, this is not easy. It requires an ongoing effort of imagination, dialogue, and administrative finesse, not to mention stubborn persistence.

We have found that we need to be continually alert to assumptions that "our way is the right way" (or indeed the only way). It has been instructive to observe that this attitude is by no means unique to the U.S. liberal arts college. African and Russian universities can be just as convinced as we are that their way is the only good way. This frequently forces us to reexamine our assumptions—something that in some ways is more difficult for us at Bard, since the partnership programs, for financial and other reasons, take place primarily on our partners' campuses. On the other hand, our major partners are very large institutions, and they can find it hard to change even when the will is there. Our presence then helps them implement the changes to which they aspire.

At Bard, we have found that universities in "countries in transition" can be especially open to change. Our partner institutions in Russia and South Africa have taken advantage of just such a period of "transition" to introduce elements of liberal education into their curricula. The appeal of liberal education is based in the greater liberty that it affords teachers as well as students. Thus, the introduction of liberal arts curricula and pedagogy, in partnership with Bard, has been a tool that opens up new spaces for multidisciplinary study, critical thinking, and a more student-centered pedagogy.

In concluding this introduction, I would like to pose a number of questions, the answers to which may serve to determine whether our international programs live up to the promise of global citizenship:

- Do the international programs in which we are engaged also benefit students and other citizens of the countries where the programs take place?
- Do institutions and colleagues abroad have a significant voice in the initiation, design, and administration of these programs?
- Are our institutions acting as global citizens by treating our partners abroad as rights-bearing entities that are philosophically our equals?
- Do the partner institutions and our colleagues abroad also benefit, and are we conscious of the impact, both objective and subjective, that our involvement has on them?
- Do we acknowledge and welcome the fact that this partnership has the capacity to change us, and our institutions?

The answers to these questions can only be found in practice. We can answer them in the affirmative only if we are willing to enter into genuine partnerships. On this basis, we can engage our colleagues abroad in an ongoing conversation that involves assessment and analysis as well as program development and delivery.

INITIATING A GLOBAL CONVERSATION

To give a sense of the nature of such a conversation, to model it, as it were, I asked a number of individuals involved in Bard's international partnerships, as well as several of my Bard colleagues, to respond to a series of questions. Each of the 10 contributors was asked to comment on one or all of the following questions:

- What is the principal value to your institution, and to you personally, of the partnership with Bard (Smolny, Wits)?
- What have been the most important benefits?
- What is the biggest challenge?

In addition, the contributors were invited to name their favorite metaphor for the partnership in which they are involved. The following comments are intended to give a flavor of the conclusions and reflections that accompany these joint ventures. I will follow them with some very brief reflections on the nature of the dialogue, drawing especially on my colleagues' choice of metaphors, as expressive of a domain of feeling and imagination that sheds a prospective and more personal light on our experiences and hopes.

For Smolny College of St. Petersburg State University

Sergey Bogdanov, Dean, Philology Faculty, St. Petersburg State University[5]

The Smolny project is the most serious and important experiment to take place in the Russian higher education system in recent years. It has not only helped the university to bring in new educational technologies, but it has also brought us new content. Essentially, Smolny is a point of growth for St. Petersburg State University—in fact, not only for this university, but for the system of higher education in Russia as a whole. What is most important is that the Smolny project, from its inception, has been multidisciplinary in its essence. As a result, the program has given birth to a new curriculum, new pedagogical technologies, and a new type of students; and we are also seeing new types of faculty. All these changes are built not so much on bringing in new resources or people who can provide the content of education—we had those here already. Rather, the joint venture allows us to develop those resources in a new form.

To enumerate the concrete benefits, it is enough to look at photographs of our graduates. There are already more than 300 young people who have successfully graduated from Smolny, and each year we see more and more students who find something useful in this program. It helps them to find their way in life.

In addition, there are quite a few officials in the Ministry of Education and Science, the Ministry of Finance, and elsewhere who recognize the benefits of Smolny's educational program. The support of these officials has helped us do very important things. For example, we are in the midst of renovating the Bobrinskiy Palace, which already serves as Smolny's main campus.

Smolny has also brought other important things to the university. This is what I meant when I spoke of Smolny as a point of growth and innovation. Many individuals who made contributions at Smolny are now serving the whole university. An example is Philip Fedchin, who is the chief technology expert at Smolny and who is simultaneously heading up the university's distance

509

education program and the large project "Innovative Technology in a Traditional University." People like this are obviously very beneficial to the university, so we don't lack specific benefits.

Like any large enterprise, Smolny also involves some risk. The fact that this new program is occurring within the framework of the university makes it easier from one point of view. We have the university structure to support it, and powerful intellectual resources. On the other hand, the fact that Smolny is a multidisciplinary program means that it touches on the sphere of interest of other departments and faculty members. For this reason it has required a lot of communicative work with colleagues. That's the first challenge.

The second challenge is not so much that we had to apply new standards to the Russian type of education, but is rather related to the saying that "big trees take the light from others." This caused quite a lot of problems within the Philology Department and other parts of the university—difficulties that sometimes prevented us from doing other things and led to conflicts. I remember very well the explanation I had to provide to the public prosecutor's office in 1999. There was a crisis within the university. While we were admitting students to Smolny, people came from the public prosecutor's office to check the procedure for accepting students, and there was quite a row. That was 10 years ago. But I suppose the difficulties that we encountered existed for many other new programs that got started at the same time in Russia.

For me personally, there are many positive memories of a personal nature. The most difficult thing, personally, has been having to serve as a medium joining two very different spaces—the problem of realizing the idea of liberal education in the concrete conditions of the university, without losing it.

My favorite metaphor is the tower. A tower connects heaven with earth and the subterranean world. It is a "stairway to heaven." In my dream, the city of St Petersburg is surrounded by seven towers. One of them is the Tower of Babel, which I see as something positive. It represents Smolny, too, in a way, and the seven towers are meant to protect our city, including Smolny, which is part of it.

Valery Monakhov, Professor of American Studies, Director of Smolny College[6]

It is not easy in a few words to describe the most important value in our partnership. One of the main values for me is the chance to be free and creative. For me personally, it is very important to have a chance to make something new and unusual. In addition, the partnership allows me to gain a broader view of the world—not just of the educational space, but a broader awareness of human life in general. This broader scope is extremely important when it comes to creating a new educational program, for to do this we need to understand not just the role of education, but the cultural and educational traditions in each particular country. The partnership with Bard embodies the possibility to enrich our educational practice, and the possibility to become more professional in our field.

It also creates a space for creativity for our teachers. Professor Yuri Kuperin, who is a distinguished physicist and the head of Smolny's new natural sciences program, came to my office after a recent visit to Bard. As we talked, I understood that he was, well, perhaps not exactly reborn, but certainly inspired by his visit to Bard and by the possibility of discussing new programs with his American colleagues. The chance to create something new is important for him in his own life. It is good to see our teachers feeling like this and it is a result of our partnership.

This is just one example of how important it has been for our teachers to be able to have a direct experience of liberal education as it is practiced in the United States. A critical quantity of people needed to know what liberal education really looks like and how it works, what its means and methods are. Over time, we were able to organize visits where they could see American universities close up. It would have been absolutely impossible to do this without support from the American side. We have also had very many visits from faculty and administrators from Bard—probably more than 20 visits a year, back and forth.

When we were young, as students, our own experience of education gave us some impressions, and we developed some different ideas and dreams about possible ways of changing the educational system. When we began to collaborate with our colleagues from Bard, we had in our hands, from this moment on, a real instrument to achieve our dreams, to modernize the system of education in Russia in a way that was essential to bringing about this modernization, as we understood it.

Fundamentally, I would say that we wanted to be freer. One way in which the partnership helped us achieve this goal is that we were no longer dependent on only one source of power and financing. We had a chance to choose not only among ideas but also among the sources of support for our activity.

The biggest challenge initially was resolving misunderstandings. At the very beginning, few people at Smolny really understood what liberal education means. We even had to invent a word for it. Thus, it was quite difficult to find people who were able to feel what it could be and to join us in trying to understand and implement it. We were fortunate to find some excellent faculty members at the very beginning of the process.

We also encountered hostility. This came not only from people who didn't know anything about education or about the real goals of our partnership, but also from people who were suspicious of us and our partners. Very often I had to answer questions such as: Why do your American colleagues want to participate in these programs? What are their real goals? A lot of people tried to find some hidden ambition, some devious purpose on the part of our American colleagues, because there had been a long tradition of hostile relations between our two countries. This was a difficult element from the past, which made it necessary to explain what the real goals were—my own as well as those of my partners—and to explain this repeatedly to very many people. This was one of the real challenges and it was very important to create a space of understanding, over a long period.

After we had come some distance, and Smolny was beginning to be successful, we began to feel increasing interest in our program from people not only at our university, but at other educational institutions in Russia. We began to find friends and supporters not only at the university, but also in the Ministry of Education and Science. We were open to other people; we invited them to our retreats, our seminars and conferences, and we had a real dialogue with other people. And dialogue, as we very soon discovered, was a very effective instrument for building bridges of understanding.

Another challenge was competition. Sometimes our competitors were not honest in their arguments and they tried to use misunderstanding of our real goals to achieve their own ends. They tried to say that we were going to destroy the national system of education, that we are some kind of traitors. But these attempts ended, for the most part, because it became evident that these were not our real goals. Our practical achievements convinced people over time.

In the context of our partnership, what is very important is that I know my partners are very cautious, very tolerant. They try to understand the other side, the other people involved. I am not sure I can express it very well in English, but whenever you do something you feel you must be careful not to make any mistakes because you are not sure you understand the other person. Eventually, this approach helps to create a huge space for real understanding. The key thing is to have tolerance, and understanding, and real good will to make something new and important and useful for our students and for the future.

Another aspect that is absolutely important for me—through the partnership I have found not only colleagues, but friends, too. I have had a real human experience of another country, another university. Today our partnership is a part of my life and of my own personality. In my feelings now, Bard College is the same as my own college, my own university; it is just as close to me. The space in which I live and work—my friends—this is my space too. From this point of view, our partnership is a very effective instrument for increasing understanding of other cultures, other peoples. I am sure that very many people from the Russian side who participate in this project, and who have participated during these 10 years of collaboration, share this feeling with me.

When I try to explain to other people what the difference is between the traditional system of Russian higher education and liberal education, I frequently compare it with the difference between Rubik's cube and the usual wooden cube with pictures. The system of liberal education, our curriculum, makes it possible for students to construct very different courses of study in different combinations. The usual wooden cube does not create so many possibilities.

Another metaphor that I like to use is to tell people that we are not buying a suit from a factory for our students, but instead we are at the tailor's and are trying to make something specially for each person. Each person is unique, so we are a personal tailor, not a factory that tries to fit everyone to the same standard.

Nikolay Koposov, Professor of History, Dean of Smolny College[7]

In describing the value of the collaboration with Bard, I would distinguish two things: first, the advantages of collaboration itself, and second the substantive advantages of this particular collaboration.

First of all, this type of partnership, which is very extensive and broad, allows one not only to know more about a different tradition, but also to better articulate one's own tradition—whether one identifies with it or not. In our case, there was a certain degree of dissatisfaction with the system that we inherited from the Soviet times, but this was precisely the context in which we came of age. The encounter with a different tradition enabled us to understand what the tradition we had inherited was about—its limitations and even some of its advantages. From this point of view, I would say there is a great value in being able to gain a better understanding of what one is looking for, and what the available resources are abroad. This can't be done without collaboration.

The kind of collaboration in which we are engaged at Smolny—what our colleagues there are calling "deep partnership"—has a rather different logic than the logic of exchange programs in the usual sense. Many of us, including myself, have passed through such exchange programs. Having spent several years at university in Paris, during the 1990s, I know quite a bit about the French system of higher education, but I know a great deal more about the American system. In the American case, I know many more details, including minor technical problems that would otherwise escape attention.

It might seem strange that I mention minor technical details, but there is a reason for this. Solving small problems often raises big issues. Now that St. Petersburg State University and Bard have combined to form Smolny College, and we are more or less one institution, I have come to understand that in fact minor issues can conceal very considerable cultural meaning. This kind of understanding is not always something one arrives at spontaneously—it can only happen through close collaboration that lasts for a very long time.

The major challenges I see are two. First, there was the challenge of creating the College as a social subsystem. This meant acculturating the model in Russia. We all expected that something would change when liberal education was transplanted to Russia, but that the core would sur-vive—a recognizable version of liberal education. However, liberal education is only a subsystem of the larger system of social relations in general. The most difficult case and ongoing challenge is how to make sure that a subsystem can be adapted into a society whose overall system is very different from the American one. Building a system of relationships within Smolny is one thing. We can do this, but the environment is different and this environment is not absolutely separable from Smolny itself.

There is a joke from the Soviet times that illustrates this problem. It so happened that Gor-bachev visited London once and had a look around. He came back to Moscow and reported to the Central Committee, "I have seen England and now I know why their economy is so much more flourishing than ours—it is because they drive on the left side of the road!" The Central Commit-tee discussed this report and decided that they would implement the measure too. But since there were some reservations, they decided to introduce left-hand driving on only some of the roads.

There is also a kind of institutional challenge, meaning that the very sense of what an institu-tion is differs in the United States and in Russia. The distinction between public and private, function and person, and so on, is somehow different in the American case. Even now, it is not so easy for me to function according to the strict sense of what an institution is, as understood in the United States. In Russia, many things are done in a more informal way. In the United States, democratization is much more linked to the idea of formalization. Democracy there seems, to a very considerable extent, to be a matter of very complex formal institutional relationships. Without these formalities, along with a very highly developed legal system and mentality to back it up, democracy, as it stands now in the United States, the United Kingdom, and Europe gener-ally, would have been very different. Russia does not have this longstanding legal situation. Hence many things are being done in a very different way. The American system of separation of powers is paradigmatic for the whole system. In Russia, things tend to merge and be perceived in a less formal, more private way, which allows for violations of the rules by everyone.

This extends into every part of life. Students need to learn to use institutional means when they want to ask for new courses, for example; to go to the student government instead of just coming to me and asking for something to be done. We are trying to institutionalize processes at all levels, but it takes time and the environment is not always conducive to this.

For the University of the Witwatersrand (Wits)

Tawana Kupe, Dean of the Faculty of Humanities[8]

I think the first value of our joint program, the International Human Rights Exchange (IHRE), is the cross-fertilization of ideas that occurs between the faculty, as well as the students, because the two systems are fairly different in certain ways. The system in place in South Africa is derived from the British system, whereas the American system—although it also has some elements of the British system—is not exactly the same. The result is a conversation between the two, which I would call cross-fertilization.

One aspect of this cross-fertilization has to do with how classes and interactions are con-ducted. I understand that when the IHRE program started here at Wits last year there was some kind of clash of cultures. Our faculty members found the American students a bit more disruptive. The South African students are more used to a lecture mode. Normally they listen to the lecture, which is delivered by the professor, and then the lecture is discussed in the tutorial, which is a smaller group that meets separately. The IHRE program seems to be a mixture—a small group discussion that is also a lecture. I think both have their particular strengths, and if they are mixed together in the same class you derive maximum value from paying attention and listening, but also not just listening; and from students listening to each other and not just to the professor. The whole exchange is more dialogic and participative.

The IHRE program also has a particular value in terms of its knowledge area. IHRE revolves around human rights, and human rights are not necessarily always contextually the same. So there is also an exchange of knowledge. Here the details are important—what is actually contained in the course outlines. I hope that the model that is being followed in the individual courses is not one where American professors and students come to learn about South Africa, meaning that the content is about South Africa and not about South Africa and the United States. For me that is problematic, in that one group becomes the object of study while the other group is both the object and subject of study. That to me is not a genuine exchange. There are challenges to this approach—if you approach a subject comparatively it could mean that you might lose depth. But if it is a comparative situation, then that is wonderful. It means that for both groups there is an exchange of roles—both groups become the object and subject of consideration. The result is that there is an ethical and moral balance, where both groups are studying each other, and themselves. This is one of the things that can genuinely improve understanding for people coming from different contexts. They will gain understanding both of other people's context, and of themselves and the context they come from. You understand yourself better if you take yourself out of your normal context and try to look at the same issue in a different context. It challenges your assumptions, your blind spots, your prejudices, the things you didn't problematize.

What these particular challenges do, among other things, is that they force you to begin to question your own system. This can be a good thing. One of the benefits of exchanges like this can be to force a curriculum review. It makes you rethink what you are offering and you might think—ah, I can include that too.

Some other positive benefits that can result from such collaborations come about when they actually develop into lifelong exchanges and relationships. An American professor and a professor from the partner university, having taught together in the same class, might create joint research projects, or write papers together. This is very beneficial. Of course the students also develop personal relationships, and they form academic relationships, too. Their experience may lead them to change their ideas about their future career, or about graduate education. For a university like Wits this can mean that we gain students who come back long-term to earn their master's, or that one of our students may go to the United States for postgraduate studies.

Then there is the very practical and direct benefit in the fact that the visiting students are charged fees to participate. In this way, they contribute to the general income of the host institution. There can be a downside to this as well; if the program is not properly costed, resources can be diverted to one program at the expense of others.

One of the challenges of the IHRE program is that it raises issues about the value of small-group teaching, and who benefits. Some people would look at this and complain that the benefit goes only to those students who are part of the exchange, but not to the institution as a whole. The other side of this is that in our other programs, where we have lecture courses that may have hundreds of students, our students complain that the courses are too large and they don't get individual attention. A special program like IHRE introduces imbalances, and this is something we need to deal with very carefully.

In general I like the exchange programs. It is of particular interest to go beyond the generalizations. That exchange is good is a slogan. We have to go beyond the slogan to see what is actually happening in the concrete realization of the program. Then we understand what it represents as a value system and as a practice.

Fazela Haniff, Head of the Wits International Office[9]

What is special about the kind of long-term, extensive partnership we have in IHRE is that our engagement allows new ideas to seep through slowly, in a positive way. It allows the system to be pliable and create space to found a more formal structure that accepts the richness of what an interdisciplinary program like IHRE can offer, as a complement to the existing menu of programs at the University. IHRE gives academics inside and outside of Wits a kind of approved tool, or vehicle, for introducing, challenging, and experimenting with possibilities to change and enhance the curriculum in ways that showcase the value of international education. There is an agreement that has been signed and sanctioned, so those faculty members who want to go in this direction but don't want to break the rules on their own have the freedom to explore these possibilities.

As for benefits, one of the most important is the dynamic of faculty from different cultures and traditions learning from each other—although we have our own international faculty too. In IHRE, the faculty dynamic happens primarily through team teaching. There are different teaching methodologies, different disciplines, and junior or senior people who can colearn from each other. This enriches both participants' experience. In the Wits case, it certainly also enhances the experience of our students, who normally would not have the opportunity to experience different ways of teaching the same subject matter, and don't have access to small seminars of this type. Engaging with the other students in a dialogue in the classroom brings a diversity of interpretation, ideas, responsibility, and attitudes that the students would otherwise not have experienced.

To cite one small example, IHRE offers an internship of 10 to 15 hours per week. The internship is not mandatory, and in the first year of the program a number of Wits students elected not to take it; perhaps they hadn't established the value of such a thing. Recently, though, some of these same students came to us and asked to take the internship this year, which we are allowing them to do. After seeing what their counterparts got out of it, they are developing a sense for the value of civic engagement that they didn't have before.

Administratively, we had to do a lot of work behind the scenes to manage the awarding of credits for students who belong to different Wits departments. This has led to heightened sensitivity and a greater understanding of the culture of exchange within the administration. Solutions are being sought that were previously outside the norm, and systems are being put in place that allow people to understand how different things can be done without compromising the system. Since IHRE is an integrated program, with more than one department involved, people don't see this as just an isolated problem, as they might if we were dealing with a few individual students coming or going. The fact that the Deputy Vice Chancellor, the Vice Chancellor, and the deans are all supporting the project lends seriousness and academic weight to the importance of finding solutions. This is a very big asset for my department, because one of our goals is to promote more exchanges in which Wits students can actively participate in the semester abroad program with our partner institutions and receive transfer credits. This actually fits very well within the institution's ambitions.

If I look at the academic richness that our Wits students, indeed all the IHRE students experience; the exposure of Wits faculty and administration to new people and ideas; what I see is that collaboration, in itself, can really act as a stimulus, or a spark. It's like opening a tap. The entire process has set things in motion. Collaboration, when it is in line with our ambitions, multiplies the impact, because it is happening at different levels of the supply chain and everyone sees how their link is important to the end result. Students, academics, and administrative systems are being fine-tuned because the achievement of the pilot year illustrated the value of this kind of change.

For Wits, I also see another future benefit. The success that IHRE achieved in the first year now allows us to further strengthen our engagement in Africa, for example with universities in East Africa and Southern African with which Wits maintains established relationships. We are now looking to engage them and get their students to participate. For this, we need to be able to exchange credits. The same is true domestically, where we are talking to other universities in South Africa about sending their students to Wits to do the IHRE semester. So the individual partnership can grow into a matrix of partnerships, which will result in a much richer experience not only for us, but for our other African partners who may not have some of what Wits has—or have opportunities like this one.

The last thing I would like to share is that the kind of engagement we have had with Bard's staff members has been extremely important to the success of my office and of IHRE. They were equally willing to shift gears, and when we visited Bard we became convinced that there is really a whole team of people there who are committed to making the program happen. This gave us a lot of needed confidence. If I had to isolate one key element in the whole collaboration, it would be trust. The personal things, learning to know each other personally, establishing trust—this is absolutely decisive in the end.

Ayesha Kajee, Director, International Human Rights Exchange (IHRE)

The creation of IHRE as a joint partnership between Wits University in South Africa and Bard College in the United States has many unique characteristics in the field of study abroad. IHRE aims to be a true exchange—it involves students, faculty, pedagogic methods, and curricular elements from both the North and South, with academic credit and institutional commitment on both sides. It is the only semester-long multidisciplinary undergraduate program with a human rights focus anywhere in the world. It incorporates a substantial internship component that infuses a real-world work experience component into the classroom.

Since human rights is a relatively young field of academic study, it also puts practitioners and students from various backgrounds on a more equivalent footing. This helps to avoid elitist bias and mitigates presumptions of intellectual superiority that may have tended to derail past partnerships in more traditional disciplines. IHRE's academic base in the South also reverses traditional notions of "benefit" and "beneficiaries." Significantly, IHRE has chosen to steer clear of study abroad models where students from the North live in specially designed accommodation and duplicate northern-style classrooms in a South African setting. IHRE students are Wits students in every sense—they live, eat, and study together with their South African counterparts, with no artificial concessions to separate them.

A thorough orientation is crucial. Even better is an orientation program that places local and international participants alike in an unfamiliar setting (as IHRE does during participants' first week in South Africa). This fast-tracks the establishment of a communal identity and breaks down artificial barriers of nationality, class, race, and gender. Providing opportunities to remain part of the IHRE community, even after the semester ends, and facilitating ongoing contact for both staff and students, where feasible, further strengthens the deep partnership aspect and the aim of building a transnational human rights community through IHRE.

The value to Wits of this partnership is manifold. IHRE makes a unique contribution to Wits's range of international offerings, since it is the only integrated undergraduate program offered by the institution. It also showcases Wits as a site for future postgraduate study. The opportunity to experience different teaching styles, and to interact with peers and professors from a wide range of cultures, experiences, and backgrounds, injects an unprecedented richness and depth into the Wits curriculum. In 2007, IHRE faculty came from several esteemed institutions, including Vassar College, University of California-Irvine, University of Connecticut, and New York University. Several IHRE faculty members from the inaugural (2007) program have been accorded honorary research status at Wits, and their published work enhances Wits' reputation as well as that of their home institution. Wits is a public institution, so the full body of published work associated with the university is an important consideration for the South African government.

The greatest challenges faced by the inaugural IHRE program have been those associated with integrating different academic and pedagogic styles, particularly as this relates to team-teaching. Where teams interpreted coteaching as sequential teaching, or where more than two lecturers cotaught a course, student feedback highlighted a degree of fragmentation and loss of coherence, prompting IHRE to move toward smaller teaching teams (two teachers per course) for the future. Feedback also indicated that students derived the greatest academic benefit in instances where coteaching was interpreted as team-teaching (i.e., with both teachers present simultaneously); thus this model has been mandated for the future. While most faculty expressed genuine appreciation for the pooling of perspectives and experience with a peer from a different pedagogic culture, there was an instance in which the team of teachers did not communicate well, both prior to and during the semester. To preempt such situations, IHRE requires teams to work together on syllabi and readings well in advance of the actual IHRE semester.

For Bard College

Jonathan A. Becker, Assistant Professor of History at Bard; Dean of International Studies, Bard Dean for Smolny College; and Academic Director, Institute for International Liberal Education

For Bard College, Smolny College primarily represents a willingness to discard norms of institutional conservatism, common in American colleges and universities, in order to pursue the better good. There is really little logical reason why Bard should be undertaking Smolny. It is located several thousand miles away from Bard's main campus, the vast majority of students at Smolny are Russian or from the former Soviet Union, and Bard expends significant energy on the project and does not generate revenue from it (although most of Bard's direct costs for the project are covered, partly through grants from individuals and foundations).[10] However, we pursued and continue to promote Smolny for the same reasons we have other innovative ventures—because it is consistent with our principles and represents an attempt to promote educational excellence, because it is fundamentally cooperative, and because we continue to believe that our efforts can make a substantial difference in a part of the world that is undergoing tremendous change.

The benefits that Smolny has provided to Bard have come in many forms. Working with our Russian colleagues to adapt the liberal arts model to a different environment has allowed us to reflect upon what we do at Bard. Why do we require students to take certain subjects as a part of our distribution requirements? Why do we place so much emphasis on written submissions instead of oral argumentation? What are accepted norms for providing feedback on papers? Being compelled to explain that which we normally do from habit or instinct has given us the opportunity to reflect and reconsider. For example, as a result of our discussions with our colleagues, and having observed Russian students' verbal abilities, I have substantially increased the number of oral assignments in my classes and have had discussions with Bard's dean about means of addressing students' verbal skills.

The greatest benefit to Bard from the Smolny project has been to inspire and reinvigorate faculty and administrators who see in Smolny the opportunities for engagement that led them to teaching in the first place, and who are motivated to work with colleagues who are genuinely interested in exchanging ideas and learning. Smolny represents the wonderment that one felt on first entering the university, and the limitless hope associated with the possible. The Bard faculty who have engaged in the project have become colleagues and friends, and gotten a dose of inspiration that they carry within them in Annandale and in St. Petersburg.

The biggest challenges for the Smolny project are in the classroom. It is no doubt a huge bureaucratic and legal challenge to change a curriculum, but the outlines of what we aspire to are fairly straightforward. However, suggesting that faculty alter their long-honored methods of teaching, and encouraging them to become more student-centric and not only to accept, but to encourage student challenges to their authority is something difficult to explain, and very challenging, especially for the older generation of teachers.

The biggest lesson that I have learned is that the project has paradoxically advanced much further and more quickly on the legal/bureaucratic front than I ever thought possible, but the challenges in the classroom, which I believed would be easy to address, are much more acute than I would have imagined more than a decade ago.

Thomas Keenan, Professor of Comparative Literature; Academic Director of IHRE at Bard; Director, Bard's Human Rights Project

One of the positive values I see is the fact that we have a program that in some sense belongs to us, that we are coauthors of, that our students can take, that we feel confident about, but that is not actually fully ours, and that is somewhere else and is about somewhere else. This has two upsides: it doesn't repeat what we already do, and it takes the students somewhere else that's interesting, while doing both these things in a mode that seems responsible.

For students in IHRE, the value of having the South African experience to draw on is obviously important. This involves both the South African experience itself and the experience of the South African students and faculty. In other words, there is both immersion in a place that seems to be oozing human rights experience, and also the fact that the faculty are more likely to know more about that experience. The students inevitably come back smarter and more committed. It's interesting how many of them want to go back there. This is probably about being abroad in a way that is more participatory. Whether because they are being integrated into other people's classrooms, or because the internships allow them to dig into particular local issues, or because of the friendships they have made—they come back feeling that they can't quite get South Africa out of them, that they haven't been able to stay the same person they were when they arrived. When they want to go back they are honoring that change that's happened within them.

The curriculum is unusual too. It is a kind of learning experience for the students that would be very hard for them to get at their own school—even setting aside the virtue of being in South Africa. IHRE is a very targeted, focused, and specialized curriculum over the course of an entire semester, in which all the courses are integrated with each other and are intended to make sense together. There are not many programs like this around—in fact one of the few other examples I am aware of is the Bard Globalization and International Affairs program in New York. You have a thoughtful package of classes that all go together, and then on top of that the benefits of internships, plus, in the case of IHRE, the proximity to that history and that present.

The benefits for faculty have to do mainly with the chance to work with other faculty there. The team-teaching requirement has proven to be unexpectedly popular. It may involve a bit more work and planning, but it seems to be a plus, an incentive even, for faculty who are drawn to teaching in the program because of the chance it gives them to exchange knowledge and perspectives with their peers from another place.

A less obvious, longer-term benefit for me comes about through the process of recruiting North American faculty to teach in the program. This is one of my responsibilities as Bard academic director of the IHRE program, and it is a good opportunity to find out about interesting people teaching at other schools, for the sake of recruiting them. If we had only our own school and its limited resources to work with we wouldn't have the same chance to make cross-connections with universities across North America. Although human rights is a limited field, it's not that limited, so it has meant discovering all kinds of people I wouldn't otherwise have discovered, in fields like Islamic law, for example, or literature and human rights. This was an unexpected benefit.

Since I have family ties in South Africa, just being there is not so new for me. However, for me, as for everyone, there is a difference between being somewhere as a visitor and being somewhere as a participant in a shared enterprise. You approach a place differently if you have a personal or institutional stake in the success of the enterprise in South Africa—or at Smolny for that matter. You are a member of the project, and it *is* a South African project, even if it's a partnership. I would like to emphasize this—for better or worse, it primarily belongs to them. This makes visiting a different experience, even it you're visiting in a professional way.

Clearly, there are some challenges. Again, because IHRE is located at Wits, because it turns out that it is primarily a South African institution, we are in the position of having to accommodate ourselves. Coming from Bard, which is very informal, we have to adjust to a much larger and more formalized bureaucratic and administrative regime. This is the biggest challenge. Then there is the challenge of filling the need for short-term faculty recruitment. Finding people who are good enough to have good jobs and yet are able to leave them for 7 or 15 weeks is complicated. Once we have found them, we have to address the other dimensions of recruiting them and trying to keep them happy. It is one thing to choose competent people with interest in the subject, who can teach in ways that are interesting. After that, we need to make arrangements for keeping them happy or at least minimally content in a foreign country that can sometimes be forbidding. If we are to keep them happy, we need to remember that they are not just working, but living in Johannesburg, with their families, perhaps living farther from campus than is convenient. This is important for the future—we want them to be interested in coming back and teaching in the IHRE program again.

Another challenge is more structural and concerns the program itself. We are trying, somewhat artificially, to create the effect of a relatively intimate, small campus in the middle of a big urban university. We have an intimate program, but not an intimate space—in a way we are airlifting in all these features of a small town and dropping it into the dispersal of a big place and a big city. Even if we are maximally efficient, it is hard to re-create the other things that go without saying on a liberal arts campus—people running into each other at dining hall, scheduling a talk on short notice, things like that. We can reproduce our liberal arts college atmosphere in the classroom, but not outside. From this point of view, the teaching in IHRE is probably more of a discovery for the South African students, because they get to experience a kind of intimacy in the classroom that is unusual for them. So the benefits for our students and the South African students are different.

I would say that the Rubik's cube actually rings true as a description of the administrative work. It seems like we have a large but finite set of pieces that we are moving around trying to find a satisfying configuration.

Bryan Billings, Bard Program Manager at Smolny College[11]

The key benefits for Smolny result directly from the combination of Russian academic life with the American idea of the liberal arts. This has brought in important new ideas in methodology and pedagogy—ideas like the interactive classroom and multidisciplinary curriculum. The College aspires to be a place of open dialogue both in- and outside the classroom, and students are expected to participate actively in the learning process. It's hard to overstress the importance of this attitude, or how different it is from the traditional Russian system, which is very hierarchical. This system, which relies overwhelmingly on large lectures and oral exams, in other words on rote learning, is still the norm in Russia.

I don't think the emphasis on liberal arts ideas means that we are exporting American values. There is a methodology and a pedagogy, but no ideology at all. In the classroom, at conferences or lectures, people put forth very many varying viewpoints. There is no American idea or Bard idea that is being pushed on students, except for the idea that students should be involved in the learning process and that everyone should be allowed to think freely. Maybe that's an Americanism. But we are not pushing any ideals other than democratic education itself. Our politics are limited to the politics of education. We want students to have the freedom to choose courses, to have their own opinions, to argue those opinions. Only a very few visiting professors come from the States, and a minority of Smolny faculty have trained in the United States. So to the extent that the faculty might have American ideas, they are in the minority.

I have been at Smolny 4 years, and in that time I would say that there has been a shift away from reliance on Bard and on the United States. Russians are more confident now, more sure of their country and themselves. When I came here 4 years ago there was more of a general feeling of subservience to Bard, or at least a sense that they felt they had to listen to Bard. Now our Smolny colleagues feel more strongly that Smolny as an institution can stand on its own feet and they may disagree with administrative decisions made by Bard. And Bard has generally been okay with this, as long as it doesn't affect the educational structure or the nature of the partnership itself. Bard remains very involved in issues of academic quality because of the Bard degree that students are getting.[12] But Smolny decides what majors it offers, what directions it is expanding in, and so forth.

At this point, about 7% of Smolny students are visiting American students. The rest are mainly Russian, with a majority coming from the Russian regions and some from the former Soviet Union. Because of the nature of the learning process, many of the Russian students seem very impassioned about the learning process and about Smolny itself. This does not apply to everyone, of course.

One of the obstacles Smolny faces is that some student expectations still relate to the old system, in which students—especially if they pay—can be pushed through their degree programs without preparing for class and without critical thinking. Even at Smolny, tuition-paying students may think that they can pass through whether they do the work or not. Smolny is working on this, focusing on first-year students. But students who don't commit to the new type of learning are still a problem; their old-fashioned ideas often hinder the learning process for others.

This is where U.S. students have a particular contribution to make. One of the greatest gains over the past 5 years is the increase in the number of U.S. students who are coming to study at Smolny, and the rise in the level of their Russian fluency. This has allowed more U.S. students to take general academic courses taught in Russian. They play a key role there; in fact, I often hear that the Americans are the best students in the class. They come to class, they do readings, they are willing to participate in topical discussions. They are not afraid to discuss something with each other or with other students. This opens up dialogue; once the Russians hear Americans speaking they realize they too have something to say. If they haven't done the reading, their comments are not so much to the point. But it represents a big change in the understanding of academics in Russia—students are becoming more interested in participating.

The personal benefits for me come primarily from working with students. American students who may have been coddled at home become very independent and learn to deal with many situations. Because at Smolny they are totally immersed in Russian society, they have to do a lot of problem solving on their own in a different culture. Meanwhile, their worldview and ideas are changing, thanks to their interaction with Russian students from completely different backgrounds. Their assumptions are challenged and they have to learn to think for themselves. An example would be gender identifications, a concept which is new to Russian students. There are also all kinds of different ideas that pop up in discussions of subjects like the Cold War or World War II (the Great Patriotic War in Russia), or the Holocaust.

It's amazing how many of the visiting North American students come back to spend more time studying or working in Russia. Last fall there we had 8 alumni of our program in St. Petersburg and another 5 in the former Soviet Union. Four more are returning this fall that I know of.

Personally, my time here has not been easy, but it has certainly given me a much greater understanding of Russia. Even though I had worked in Russian offices before, working with young people and professors at Smolny has given me a much greater understanding of Russian culture, of how things work here. I think being in this position has made me as close to being from two cultures as it is possible to be. I am ingrained in Russian culture, in a nonsentimental sense. The American pragmatist in me may once have had the attitude that says: "I see it. This is what we want to do, this is how we are going to get there." Now I say: "Let's wait, let's see what happens." It is not about memos. You have to go and speak to people personally, get a commitment, and follow through to make sure whatever it is actually happens. This also makes things more personal. When a new colleague comes from the United States, I see their American habits—this was me a few years ago.

Christina Davis, International Program Manager at Bard College[13]

Having studied in South Africa, served in the Peace Corps, and worked in rural development, I took the job at Bard precisely because the partnership programs of the Institute for International Liberal Education were aligned with the political and ethical values I hold. These are not island programs. They are real partnerships, and they engage students and faculty and even administrators on an intellectual and personal level. The more collaboration you have in the world, the more peaceful it will be. Fundamentally, this is about respect—it's the only way to encourage and foster peace. So you could say what I value most in this work comes from a human rights commitment. There is a broad human rights aspect to the educational programs we offer.

Of course the most important benefit of these programs is for the students. Collaborative programs of this type offer things that are just not available elsewhere. At Smolny, for example, the American students are directly involved in classes with their Russian peers. This is a very big asset and gives them insights into Russian life that they simply could not get in an island program. At the same time, it's not a program where we throw you in and don't give you any support whatsoever. So you have total immersion, but with personal support and the kind of interaction you would get at a small liberal arts college in the States.

In South Africa, in the International Human Rights Exchange (IHRE), there is something else as well, since all the courses except for one lecture course (the core course) are cotaught by pairs of faculty. The idea is to have one faculty member from the United States and one from Africa, although this year, for example, there are also faculty members from Israel, Egypt, Jamaica, and Zimbabwe. This means the IHRE students are going to find two very different people, sometimes from different disciplines and certainly from different countries and cultures, standing in the front of the classroom. As a result, there are opportunities to view first-hand different perspectives that the professors might have. As an example, the Islamic Law class this semester is being cotaught by a female professor from South Africa and a male JSD student from a U.S. college. Her perspective on Islamic law is very different from his. This already embodies an important lesson for the students, but when it gets really interesting is when they disagree in front of the class.

People with different cultural backgrounds are like people wearing different colored lenses. They see different things and they can say different things. The African literature class is taught by an American woman and a man from Zimbabwe. They were discussing the question of the responsibility of the writer. Is the text of a Zimbabwean writer meant for people in the West or for Zimbabweans? The Zimbabwean pointed out that during colonialism, being a writer often meant writing for the West, because at that time a lot of people in Zimbabwe were illiterate. Yet others would certainly see an obligation to write for the people of the country. These different perspectives can be surprising and make you think about things in ways you did not think about them before.

For me there is a lot of pleasure in seeing the students experience things like this and coming back changed. I am amazed at how open they are about this, and how much some of them have changed their perspectives. They say, "Wow, really. I never thought of it that way."

I myself experienced this kind of faculty dynamic and the incredible insights it can produce when I was a student at the University of KwaZulu-Natal. There was a course on Apartheid taught by an Afrikaner and a Zulu professor. The depth of their disagreement, and the extent to which their factual knowledge of what went on was really different, was extreme. This had a profound impact on me and encouraged me to study about this part of the world. I saw that you have to probe deeper to find answers. Truth emerges from different perspectives. Only when you are challenged and put in an uncomfortable situation, where your views are being directly challenged, do you grow. This is true for our students, as well—actually for everyone.

This kind of coteaching, the attempt to blend different educational principles and goals, also causes some difficulties. Faculty who come from small North American institutions tend to have the idea that teachers should encourage a lot of student engagement in the classroom, whereas a big university like Wits, in the South African tradition, is much larger, and faculty as well as students are used to a more formal, lecture-based style. This spills over onto the students, who come with their own expectations. U.S. students may be disappointed that there is not more discussion in some classes, and African students may feel that there is not enough raw information conveyed by the more dialogical style.

The language barrier is an issue in some countries, too, and cultural differences. It can be a challenge to overcome miscommunication. If you are not familiar with the culture, this can be frustrating. In the United States we tend to have a philosophy of "time is money." In other cultures, thank goodness, it's not that way. They might rather think that "what doesn't get done today will get done tomorrow." Bureaucracy can be frustrating, especially coming from Bard where there is not as much of it. At Smolny College, you have to go through many people to get something done. I think it's important to remember that they experience similar challenges when they are dealing with us—they don't understand why we need stuff *now*. Every time I get frustrated with another aspect of another culture, I realize that they are frustrated with me for the same reason, in reverse. Frustration is always two-way.

I have two metaphors that I think might apply to our "deep partnerships." The first is an orchestra. When you start out, people play in the wrong key, they may not be in tune. At the end, after practicing, you get a beautiful piece of music and a fantastic symphony. The second is an ocean. You are sitting on rocks and you see the waves crashing, but when you get out to sea the waves disappear; although there are still storms, you are stronger, and you can brave the storms.

CONCLUSION

The voices of colleagues cited above arise out of a multipoint dialogue that goes on monthly, weekly, daily, among different stakeholders[14] in Bard's "deep partnerships." The concepts and concerns emerging from this exchange have broadened and enriched all of our worldviews, and it is certainly safe to say that, for us at Bard, our knowledge of what it is like to work and live, teach and learn in Russia or South Africa is immeasurably enhanced. We believe the same holds true for "our" students, and that the Russian and South African faculty and staff have experienced similar benefits, although in different ways or with a different valence. My colleagues and I also have the satisfaction of knowing that the students, faculty, and staff members who have participated in our joint ventures now form part of an unusual global network that we have helped to create. We hope and expect that they will continue to make significant contributions to our common future.

It can be tempting to read our colleagues' comments as expressions of national or cultural character: Russian soul, South African sensitivity to rights issues, American pragmatism and focus on "results." Stereotypes almost always have something true about them. In fact, one of the principle benefits of deep partnerships, as reported by our colleagues, is the chance for all of us who are involved in them to confront not only our stereotypical views of others, but our incomplete and necessarily biased ideas about ourselves and our own societies.

To my mind, this change in the thinking of everyone involved in our "deep partnerships" is their most significant aspect. Education, after all, is about changing minds for the better. But how does the change occur? We can shed some indirect light on the question by taking a closer look at the metaphors our colleagues used in their interviews. Note that in the following I refer to metaphors introduced casually into the body of the interviews, as well as those specifically named in response to my question.

The dean in St. Petersburg sees our joint venture as a "tower of Babel," a structure that connects heaven and earth. This reflects an idealistic view of the structure and its "towering" ambition, although in this case, rather than calling down the wrath of an angry deity, the tower actually helps to protect the peaceful citizens of the city.

Smolny's director also chooses an architectural metaphor when he speaks of building "bridges of understanding." A bridge is the conceptual opposite of the so-called island programs that limit students' exposure to the surrounding society. Several times, Smolny's director praises the partnership as opening up "a space for creativity," a "space of understanding," and, again, "a huge space for real understanding." All these characterizations suggest that there are important structural aspects of the way the partnership is institutionalized, that the structures we build should be open-ended and connective, should permit movement in more than one direction, and should emphasize opportunities for movement, rather than constraint.

In a more sociological vein, Smolny's dean emphasizes that the partnership creates a "social subsystem" with a "separate system of relationships." These interlocking systems cause complex interactions that require careful management and may have unexpected effects—like a medical "transplant." The subsystem within which Smolny College exists is forced to interact with the larger university, a circumstance that further increases the need for communication and dialogue. It is another expression of the important ways in which our deep partnerships differ from "island programs."

The dean at Wits chooses the metaphor of cross-fertilization, which he describes (with a mixed metaphor) as a "conversation" between two different educational systems. Both of these terms suggest equality and two-way movement—movement that, in his view, is particularly valuable because it not only encourages, but actually enforces self-critique. He is leery of programs in which one partner is engaged in observing the other, who then becomes the object of a reflection that is not reciprocated. The IHRE academic director at Bard speaks of "airlifting" features of small town into a big city, and of the consequent difficulty of maintaining an intimate atmosphere that is conducive to informal conversations and exchange.

The head of Wits's International Office also speaks of "creating space to found a more formal structure," one that gives faculty members and staff "permission to introduce changes." Note that the changes she describes are not introduced from without, but are voluntarily adopted by individual faculty members who enter the new space and take advantage of the permission offered by the new structure. She also mentions that the long-term nature of the partnership allows changes to "seep" through, a process in that the collaboration is like "opening a tap," or striking a "spark." The fluidity of the process, the way a single action jumps across and sets ever more things in motion, multiplying its impact, suggests that a whole cascade of changes could follow.

Other metaphors refer less to the structure or quality of the exchange as a whole and more to its impact on individuals. The dean at St. Petersburg State University feels himself to be a "medium joining two very different spaces," as he works to merge new practices with existing ways of doing things at his institution. Bard's academic director for IHRE speaks of "membership" in the project, a quality that makes him approach the place differently, as a participant in a shared enterprise—someone who belongs. Our program manager at Smolny speaks of being "ingrained in Russian culture"—a phrase that suggests a true growing together, in which the experiences of the foreign have become integral to the very stuff of his identity—while also noting that the same experiences have caused him and the students he looks after to become more aware of their own cultural traits and biases. Another Bard colleague mentions "colored lenses," referring to emotional, cultural, or other variables that influence the ways we see that world. Like our Russian colleague, in his reference to the Tower of Babel, she turns this metaphor on its head, making a positive, productive benefit out of something that is conventionally seen as a deficit and a problem. The different colored lenses of our interlocutors are refracted in their dialogue with us, in a discourse that values contrasting perspectives and the emerging, confusing, and provocative blend of impressions. At the same time, the metaphor suggests that through these various glasses, we see more clearly.

Smolny's director's mention of Rubik's cube, while related to the complex of structural metaphors—Rubik's cube is a three-dimensional puzzle with many moving parts—also introduces an element of play, of the freedom and creativity that he values. His metaphor of the tailored suit, while it applies more to students than to the other participants in our joint venture, emphasizes Smolny's personal qualities, its attention to individuals and its capacity to fit different body types or personalities.

Two final metaphors, from Bard's international program manager, express the pleasures of collaboration, as reflected both in our joint performance and in the greater ease that comes with practice and experience. The members of the orchestra learn to play in key, in ways that harmonize and produce a beautiful concert.[15] Finally, there is the lovely metaphor of setting out to sea from the shore, with uncertain prospects and waves crashing all around, passing through the surf, and finding clear sailing ahead.

My own preferred metaphor for successful international collaboration, and for the deep partnerships in which we are engaged, is translation—if indeed it is a metaphor in this context, since the word *metaphor* also embodies the notion of carrying across. The ongoing international dialogue in which my colleagues and I are privileged to participate bespeaks a growing capacity of all the partners to translate experiences and ideas across cultures, disciplines, and histories. To my mind, this capacity, the mutual pleasure we take in it, and its reflection in our common practice are the real measure of whether our international education programs are actually creating "global citizens." If the concept is to be more than a catchword, it must involve the establishment of practical, human-scale frameworks within which we, as individuals, can listen attentively to each other and begin to see ourselves with those others' eyes, to hear and retell ourselves in their voices. This is both an essential precondition for resolving the global problems we all face, and an end in itself.

NOTES

1. Here is a typical definition of cultural competence:

   Cultural and linguistic competence is a set of congruent behaviors, knowledge, attitudes and policies that come together in a system, organization or among professionals that enables effective work in cross-cultural situations. "Culture" refers to integrated patterns of human behavior that include the language, thoughts, actions, customs, beliefs and institutions of racial, ethnic, social or religious groups. "Competence" implies having the capacity to function effectively as an individual or an organization within the context of the cultural beliefs, practices and needs presented by patients and their communities. (California Endowment, n.d.).

   http://www.calendow.org/uploadedFiles/managers_guide_cultural_competence(1).pdf, retrieved 8/30/08.

2. The program in Russia is Smolny College, which is Russia's first liberal arts college (http://www.smolny.org). The program in South Africa is the International Human Rights Exchange (IHRE. www.ihre.org).

3. The term first emerged in conversation with Ross Lewin, the editor of this volume.

4. The term is problematic, although we have not found a better one. It seems to imply that there is a natural progression from authoritarian to democratic societies; this can be a dangerous or misleading assumption.

5. Interview conducted on March 21, 2008.

6. Interview, March 19, 2008.

7. Interview, March 25, 2008.
8. Interview, March 16, 2008.
9. Interview, April 19, 2008.
10. Smolny is supported by a combination of tuition revenue (from both Russian and North American students), Russian state support, and philanthropic contributions; it is creating an endowment. Bard's role in Smolny College is supported by a combination of tuition revenue (from North American students), endowment, and philanthropic contributions. SPbU receives a percentage of Smolny's tuition and grants and participates in the large federal grants that Smolny has helped to obtain.
11. Interview, July 16, 2008.
12. Graduates of Smolny's four-year BA program receive a dual degree: a BA degree in arts and humanities from Smolny College of St. Petersburg State University, and a BA degree in liberal arts and sciences from Bard College.
13. Interview, July 30, 2008.
14. At Bard, the word stakeholder first entered our vocabulary through our collaboration in South Africa.
15. The word concert also means "mutual agreement; concord; harmony of action." Webster's New World Dictionary (1962).

REFERENCES

California Endowment (n.d.). *A manager's guide to cultural competence education for health care professionals.* Retrieved December 10, 2008, from http://www.calendow.org/uploadedFiles/managers_guide_cultural_competence(1).pdf

Webster. (1962). *Webster's New World dictionary of the American language, College Edition.* New York: World.

Chapter 29

Creating Study Abroad Opportunities for First-Generation College Students

Maria D. Martinez, Bidya Ranjeet, and Helen A. Marx
University of Connecticut

Never before in our nation's history has it been so imperative that our students become well versed in international affairs, understand their place in the global world, and learn how to successfully negotiate intercultural encounters. In *The World is Flat,* Friedman (2005) stresses the importance of preparing our students for the changing world that is unfolding in front of our eyes. He underscores the need for us, as teachers, to prepare our students for the fierce competition in the business world as a result of economic development in India and China. Citizens of the 21st century must develop commitments to social justice and environmental sustainability that reach beyond their personal and national boundaries to understand their roles as citizens of an interconnected world.

Many of us who work in higher education are aware of the tremendous importance of preparing all of our students to become global citizens who are committed and able to work within the intercultural, interconnected world. Study abroad experiences can and must play a critical role in such an education. The National Survey of Student Engagement (2007) posits that study abroad programs provide the types of "high impact" college experiences that teach the cognitive complexity and intellectual engagement necessary in today's increasingly sophisticated world. The survey reports that students who study abroad are "engaged more frequently in educationally purposeful activities upon returning to their home campus, and reported gaining more from college compared with their peers who have not had such an experience" (p. 17). The goals and educational value of study abroad experiences reach beyond the development of international perspectives or increased intercultural communication skills; these experiences influence students' personal development and elevate their intellectual maturity. Students often return from overseas experiences more engaged in their own education, confident of their interpersonal and intellectual abilities, and committed to exploring how they can become active members of their communities. Students go abroad expecting to learn about others and return home with new understandings about themselves and their place in the world.

Study abroad is a vital component of a 21st century education and must become more widely available to college students. In recognition of the important role that study abroad experiences play in America's future economic competiveness and national security, the Lincoln Commission (Abraham Lincoln Study Abroad, 2005) states that "[p]romoting and democratizing undergraduate study abroad is the next step in the evolution of American higher education. Making study abroad the norm and not the exception can position this and future generations of Americans for success in the world…" (p. 5). Toward this end, the Commission set a goal of sending one million college students abroad each year. We are, however, far from realizing this goal. Of particular concern to those who seek to increase the numbers of students involved in study abroad are the disproportionately low participation rates of first-generation college students, many of whom are from low-income families and from historically underrepresented minority groups. Study abroad opportunities can no longer be a luxury reserved for more affluent U.S. college students whose family backgrounds predispose them to seek out such experiences and whose income levels allow them to take advantage of such opportunities. Pascarella, Pierson, Wolniak, and Terenzini (2004) state that colleges and universities must insure that all students have access to "the full range of college experiences and to the personal, social, and economic benefits to which those experiences and degree completion lead" (p. 281). Participation in a study abroad experience has become one aspect of a vital undergraduate education and a rite of passage in students' global citizenship education, one that all students must have access to.

The need to provide equal access to study abroad opportunities for all students is not only an exercise in social justice; it has also become a necessity for universities. Diversity initiatives instituted over the past decade and the realities of a culturally diverse nation have led to a steady rise in the admission to college of students from increasingly different backgrounds, including low-income and first-generation college students. Such initiatives, however, cannot stop upon admission to the university or be solely focused on retention of students once admitted. In order to equitably serve these students, universities must design and promote programs that meet their needs and interests. Institutions have been moving beyond the myopic junior year abroad model. Some have seen the need to institute a range of policies and programs to provide an increasingly diverse student population with access to programming that is relevant and responsive to their unique backgrounds, interests, and needs. The diversity we seek in our universities must be matched by a diversity of options, destinations, and duration of study abroad programs (Obst, Bhandari, & Witherell, 2007).

There is, then, a moral and demographic imperative to provide equal access to study abroad programs for all students. Unfortunately, the reality is that universities are far from reaching this goal. To date, the participation rates of low-income, first-generation college and minority students in study abroad programs remain disproportionately low. Over the last decade, as interest in study abroad has increased nationwide, the characteristics of the "typical" study abroad student have remained relatively static. The National Survey of Student Engagement (2007) reports that those who study abroad are likely to come from elite colleges, be White and female, major in the arts and humanities, and have highly educated parents. Obst et al. (2007) in a report for the Institute of International Education indicate that minority students are underrepresented among study abroad participants: African Americans represent 4.0 % of study abroad participants, Hispanics 5.6 %, Asian Americans 6.3 %, multiracial students 1 %, and Native Americans only 0.4 %. These percentages are far below the rates of enrollment in college for these groups. The National Survey for Student Engagement (2007) reports that first generation college students are far less likely than their peers whose parents went to college to participate in high impact experiences, such as study abroad.

These statistics confirm what many of us know anecdotally from our work with low-income and first-generation students: colleges are not providing equal access to collegiate activities and experiences that are vital to successful work and life in a changing world. Obst et al. (2007) explain, "there remains a huge unmet need to expand American students' international experiences, and an even greater challenge to ensure that access to study abroad is available to all, including students of diverse backgrounds, low incomes, and underrepresented fields" (p. 5).

Providing the same access to admission to colleges is not enough. The commitment to provide equal opportunities must be accompanied by the ability to access the fullness of a college education, including study abroad.

RESEARCH ON FIRST GENERATION COLLEGE STUDENTS

To better understand how to provide equal access to a college education, researchers have sought to understand the college-level preparation, admissions, and retention of low-income and first-generation students (Texas Tech, 2008; Tym, McMillion, Barone, & Webster, 2004). Research on barriers to participation or the study abroad experiences of low-income or first-generation college students has been limited. Obst et al. (2007) state that in a review of literature they found "very little written about the lack of progress made in the last decade to increase the number of low-income and first generation college students, many of whom happen to be from minority backgrounds" (p. 5).

The void in the literature regarding study abroad policies, practices, and program models that meet the needs of first-generation college students presents a tremendous challenge for faculty and higher education administrators who are interested in developing study abroad initiatives for this population. The Council for Opportunity in Education (COE)[1] conducted one of the few studies related to access to study abroad opportunities for this population of students. The study sought to identify issues impacting participation in a survey of the college-level staff members who work directly with these students through the government sponsored TRIO[2] programs (Norfles, 2003). Staff members surveyed identified a number of barriers that inhibit student participation, which include: cost, lack of information about study abroad, family constraints, and individual limitations. The study also identified institutional barriers that play a vital role in the lack of participation of these students, including the lack of information and advocacy about study abroad among the staff people surveyed. These staff members may "discount the importance of study abroad for the students that they serve" (p. 17). The study found that a significant number of individuals who work directly with TRIO students did not have international experience themselves, lacked knowledge about study abroad options available to their students, and tended not to value or promote such experiences within their work with students. The study recommends that we pay more attention to removing institutional barriers to study abroad for these students and that programs that work directly with this population of students "get support from the international/study abroad program offices on their campuses so they may incorporate international educational opportunities within the information they provide to students" (p. 23).

These findings confirm the need for researchers and practitioners to move beyond the tendency to focus solely on identifying individual barriers to student participation. The study also suggests that we should focus more clearly on the institutional barriers that limit participation in study abroad and identify practices that increase access for all students. Research that examines successful study abroad practices and institutional efforts is vital.

A MODEL OF BEST PRACTICES: THE LIVERPOOL STUDY ABROAD PROGRAM

The University of Connecticut (UConn) has hosted TRIO programs since 1967. The Center for Academic Programs (CAP) was established in 1982 to bring these programs together under one umbrella. CAP's mission is to increase access to higher education for high potential students who come from underrepresented ethnic or economic backgrounds, and/or are first-generation college students. The CAP programs include Student Support Services (SSS), Educational Talent Search (ETS), Upward Bound/ConnCAP (UB), and GEAR UP (GU). The latter is a partnership grant also funded by the Department of Education. TRIO programs are different from financial aid programs and are intended to offer academic and social support to students to enable them to overcome class and cultural barriers to higher education. SSS works with low-income and first-generation college students.

The SSS program prepares low-income or first-generation students for successful entry into, retention in, and graduation from UConn. Students must apply to UConn in order to be considered for admission in SSS. Once admitted to the university, students receive academic and social support over the course of their college careers. Our SSS students participate in a 6-week summer precollegiate program before their freshman year. SSS serves approximately 1,100 students annually in Storrs and at the five regional campuses. As mandated by Congress, at least two thirds of the students we serve must be from families with low-income (income guidelines established by the U.S. government) and where neither parent graduated from college. Within the university, we work to ensure that program students have access to the full range of educational experiences offered to all college students. When necessary, we create dedicated programs to meet the unique needs of our students.

The Creation of the Liverpool SSS Study Abroad Program

In the late 1990s, as we sought to increase the number of SSS students traveling overseas, we realized the need to examine the complexities that were preventing their involvement in study abroad. Similar to the statistics that were being reported nationally, our students were participating in study abroad programs in significantly lower numbers than students in other categories. In conversations with students we discovered that they had become discouraged as they investigated the application processes to study abroad. Institutional programs and practices did not adequately address the needs of our low-income and first-generation college students.

At that time, at the national level, the COE was developing nontraditional alternatives in study abroad to provide greater access to TRIO students. In 1999, COE developed a series of study abroad programs for TRIO students with Michigan State University in South Africa and with the University of Wisconsin-Whitewater in Mexico. Two UConn SSS students participated in these programs in 1999 and 2000. We were encouraged by the success of our students' experiences and considered the viability of implementing a dedicated study abroad model for SSS participants at UConn. The ongoing goal is to use the SSS study abroad model as a vehicle to provide SSS participants with access to study abroad. Our motivation to find ways within our own institution to create such opportunities for more of our students led to our discussion with the Study Abroad Office regarding a potential partnership. Our ideas to examine new and innovative programs for SSS students were not well received. Fortunately, since that time and under new leadership, we have been able to develop extremely productive partnerships with the Office of Study Abroad. The Director of Study Abroad supports and consistently advocates for opportunities for SSS students.

Knowing that without a dedicated intervention strategy, SSS students would not participate in significant numbers in study abroad experiences, two of the authors of this chapter, Martínez and Ranjeet, designed and implemented a customized program. The SSS Study Abroad Program is intended to attract the participation of first-generation college students. The plan for the program was presented to the Center for Continuing Studies, which welcomed the idea and provided the necessary institutional structure. Since then we have created a culture and a critical mass among our staff and students within CAP that values and supports participation in study abroad programs through the internally run SSS dedicated program. This support has resulted in an increased interest in the SSS Study Abroad Program as well as the traditional programs. The findings from the COE study (Norfles, 2003), as discussed previously, reinforced our commitment and validated the need for such a program.

The description of this program is based on the years of experience Martínez and Ranjeet have had in designing, leading, and advocating for this and similar study abroad programs. In addition, the description of the SSS Study Abroad Program draws on responses from former participants surveyed. Twenty-five past program participants responded to an online survey which was anonymous and voluntary. The survey, part of ongoing assessment within CAP, sought to identify advising practices and programmatic elements that influenced SSS students' decisions to participate in these study abroad experiences.

The Liverpool Program

Based on our first-hand knowledge of the complexities of the issues facing this student population and using models fostered by the leadership from COE and the University of Liverpool Widening Participation, the program began in 2001 as a nontraditional, 3-week summer study abroad experience. Students in the Liverpool Study Abroad Program receive six credits upon completion. They take a three-credit course offered by the University of Liverpool on the historical and current effects of the transatlantic slave trade in Liverpool and a three-credit independent research project under the direction of UConn faculty. In an effort to augment the study abroad experience and instill in the students the importance of thinking globally, a series of educational tours to nearby cities and countries is incorporated into the curriculum. In the life of the program, students have visited Chester, London, Edinburgh, and Belfast in the United Kingdom, as well as other European cities including Berlin, Amsterdam, and Dublin. Since its inception, the program has taken an average of 10 to 12 UConn SSS students to Liverpool each May. In addition, SSS students have also studied abroad in South Africa, Cuba, and Mexico as part of similarly designed, dedicated SSS Study Abroad Programs. Plans are currently underway to make the SSS South Africa Study Abroad Program an annual opportunity offered to SSS students. In this description we will focus on the design of our Liverpool SSS Study Abroad initiative. The program and advising elements that we highlight have been, however, successfully implemented in all of our programs.

The design of this study abroad program and the customized advising and orientation practices we have developed take into consideration the unique needs and interests of many low-income and first-generation college students. A survey respondent clearly articulated the concerns and worries we found typical of many SSS students when they consider study abroad:

> Most of my inhibitions were taken away from simply talking to SSS counselors and receiving enough information before I made the decision. They assured me that any reason that kept me from not wanting to go (for example paying for the trip and getting a passport) would be completely resolvable. The encouragement from them also stimulated my interest and desire to study abroad.

This past participant clearly identifies areas that we have specifically addressed in our program:

the design of the program, the cost of the program, and the creation of a culture among our students and staff who value study abroad as an important educational experience. The description of the programs will discuss these important elements.

CREATING A CULTURE THAT VALUES STUDY ABROAD

One of the crucial aspects and one that we believe is often overlooked is the vital role advising and advocacy play in students' participation in study abroad experiences. There are barriers within the existing institutional practices and policies that must be addressed. At SSS, we have developed customized advising practices and an orientation program that overtly and specifically address our students' life circumstances, prior-knowledge and experiences, and personal academic interests.

"Marketing" Study Abroad

What is often not openly stated, but that we believe needs to be clearly examined, is that many of our students do not enter college with the intention to study abroad. We have found that, even though they are made aware of study abroad options by the institution, they still do not see these opportunities as relevant for them. The messages they hear fail to convey the importance of such programs within the context of a university education for global citizenship. Underlying our students' attitudes is a sense that study abroad is a privilege intended for White or rich students; they view study abroad as the "icing on the cake" of college and not an integral part of an education. Often, with the absence of family or peer role-models who have participated in study abroad programs, our students do not always understand that such experiences are not only academically and personally enriching, but can also prove to be the experience that opens doors to future employment and educational opportunities. It is often difficult for them to think about taking the time to study abroad for a semester or a year because their major concerns are their immediate needs to meet expenses and survive in college. Consequently, many of our students do not investigate or apply to available study abroad options.

Our first challenge, then, has been to institute advising practices that educate our students about the importance of study abroad experiences within a college education. While we "market" information about our programs heavily among our students—sending out e-mails, posting flyers, and holding information sessions throughout the year—we believe it is the consistent message our students hear from staff and past participants that is most significant in our efforts to generate the interest in study abroad. Our efforts begin in the first weeks when we meet with our students during the summer precollegiate program, prior to their freshman year. As part of the precollegiate experience former SSS students who have participated in an SSS Study Abroad Program give a presentation about their experiences. Here, the new SSS students are able to ask questions that relate to their own particular concerns about study abroad options. In this setting, where presenters share their first-generation and underrepresented status, study abroad becomes more tangible than it is when presented in the broader institutional context. Past participants of our study abroad programs have played a critical role in fostering a climate that is conducive to our efforts by communicating effectively with students and offering positive feedback. During mentoring and advising sessions in their freshman and sophomore years, we reinforce these initial presentations with more informal discussions of study abroad options. Our staff members routinely engage students in conversations about study abroad possibilities and advocate for their participation.

Dialogues about study abroad options, particularly our Liverpool program, have become part of the SSS advising practices. These advising policies and practices are overtly designed to create a culture within CAP that values study abroad experiences as vital to global citizenship. Many of our CAP staff members have participated in our study abroad program as faculty advisers and have witnessed the powerful effect of these experiences on our students. Clearly, building a critical mass within our program of students and staff members who have participated in study abroad is crucial in promoting an atmosphere that encourages such experiences.

We find that our students come to us with many uncertainties that prevent them from applying to study abroad. Often our students cannot clearly articulate their fears and concerns. Many of our students have not had significant travel experiences. Few of them have traveled outside the United States, and those who have done so for the most part have been abroad only with their families. These concerns and doubts regarding foreign travel are pervasive. For example, one respondent to our survey described her feelings:

> The biggest issue I had with applying for the study abroad program was my fear of flying…it was an eight hour trip across "the big pond" into a world that I have only read about or seen on television. I am not even the traveling type. Up until last December I had never been on the other side of Interstate 95. In other words, I had never ventured westward. My entire life I have clung to the east coast because that is where I have family.

Given their backgrounds and lack of exposure, our students' worries are not uncommon. While we encourage our students to tackle their personal fears and embrace the potential for personal growth that can come from facing such challenges, in our advising we respect their concerns and reservations as legitimate and worthy of attention. In response to this need, our advisers spend a great deal of time during the application and predeparture phases of our programs, assuring students that they can overcome any potential obstacles. We see it as our job to provide the support our students truly need to make their experiences a reality.

It appears that for our students the intervention instituted within our advising practices is the primary source of information and advocacy for participation in study abroad. We approach this role with energy and determination. We have concluded that the university cannot assume that students will seek out information from the traditional sources or that the students will necessarily enter the institution valuing such experiences. Most families of first-generation college students do not sit around the dinner table discussing study abroad experiences nor do they talk about global citizenship as an educational goal. Hence, there is a lack of or low level of participation among these students in study abroad fairs and similar events. We must institute advising practices that encourage and advocate for study abroad among low-income and first-generation college students and create a culture within our learning communities that values the importance of these experiences equally for all students.

Balancing Act: Intervention vs. Empowerment

> The SSS counselor that went with us had gone to that country previously (if my memory serves me correct) so if we had any questions she was great in answering them and guiding us. She also gave us space and trusted that we would make wise decisions, which was nice, because I never felt like I had a "babysitter."

In addition to the assistance we offer throughout the application process that we described previously, we continue to provide significant support once an application is submitted. The application procedure for a study abroad experience and the predeparture aspects of going overseas can be a daunting process, involving layers of bureaucratic paperwork and extensive planning. Teaching and empowering our students to negotiate these complex systems—finding the program that is right for them, applying to the program, obtaining their passports and other travel documents, learning how to deal with the consular system, and planning for their travel—are elements in our explicit goals within the SSS advising practices.

For example, our students often have complicated residency issues and other life circumstances that can be very stressful and create obstacles for their participation in a study abroad experience. We provide the level of support that our students need in order to address these obstacles, such as guiding them and providing them with the tools for obtaining passports, visas, and access to money (which requires a checking account, not something many of our students typically have). The usual assumptions about students' abilities to take care of these issues became clear to us when one of our students who had gone through the traditional advising cycle arrived at the airport to depart only to be turned back at the gate. She was not a U.S. citizen. Unfortunately, she had not been advised that she would need a visa to enter the host country (the other students, all U.S. citizens, had not needed a visa). Many might say that it was the student's responsibility to have known of this requirement and to have had the foresight to negotiate the system herself. Rather than assuming that students should have this information prior to college, we believe that acquiring this knowledge and these skills are vital elements of the SSS Study Abroad curriculum.

More than just encouraging students to seek out such opportunities, our advisers provide practical support and guidance. For instance, our staff is prepared to assist students in securing the necessary documentation for a visa or a passport, clarifying the hidden costs involved, and at times resolving difficult residency issues. One past participant recalled:

> [My SSS adviser] was beyond exceptional in assisting me with my passport and visa issues. She drove me to New York to the Jamaican consulate. She also drove me to New Haven to catch the train for New York. Once I encountered visa/passport issues, I wanted to give up. [My adviser] was very encouraging and supporting.

We provide students with the appropriate tools to solve their problems and to become self-sufficient. Our hope is that they will feel empowered to pursue other similar opportunities to explore the world. We propose that providing this level of support and assistance can make the difference in determining whether a student goes overseas or not.

Our supportive role intensifies as students get closer to their dates of departure. We have instituted elaborate predeparture orientation procedures to assure that our students are prepared for their trips. A past participant described it well:

> The staff was simply great. At the time I hadn't traveled outside of the U.S. by plane for about 17 years or so, and I had plenty of questions. The staff explained to us things to expect on the trip, safety measures at the airport, and things to pack. I remember having several meetings with the entire group going on the trip... we discussed all the things mentioned above and more. I did not even have to find a way to the airport as they picked me up from my front door and assured my mom that everything would be great and I would be very well taken care of.

In the weeks leading up to departure, we hold meetings with the group where we cover numerous details with students. As part of the curriculum we bring in currency from England and discuss the exchange rate. We also supply a detailed packing list and openly discuss issues of health and safety. During this time we routinely send out reminder e-mails and individually talk to students about their preparations. In the days before they leave peer advisers and counselors call each student to discuss any last minute issues. Since many of our students' families do not have cars, we arrange for transportation to the airport for any student who needs it.

The SSS staff deliberately cultivate relationships with the parents or guardians of our students during the summer precollegiate program. We continue this line of communication as our students apply to study abroad, with the understanding that getting family support among first-generation college students is critical in their decision-making processes. As our students apply to study abroad we both acknowledge and respect parental concerns. In particular, many family members are very worried about their children traveling and we have instituted a number of policies to address these issues. First, parents are invited to participate in all predeparture orientations and are encouraged to discuss any concerns they might have with the faculty adviser. We have found that having an SSS staff person accompany the students makes parents feel more comfortable about participation. When we meet students at the bus station or airport prior to departure, our faculty adviser communicates with families to put them at ease. A past participant stated: "They were there to greet my parents at the airport and assured them that I was in their hands for the trip." As soon as we land at our destination we leave a message on the Center's answering machine so that parents can call in to confirm that all is well.

About Finances

Funding is a concern for most SSS students when we discuss the possibility of study abroad, due to the high cost of these programs. Many of our students come from low-income families and study abroad seems frivolous, even selfish, to many of them. Furthermore, for first-generation college students, financing educational experiences is a new and often overwhelming commitment; these students do not necessarily see these commitments as investments in their futures but rather as immediate expenses. Survey respondents stated that financing for study abroad was a significant concern and identified this factor as one of the reasons they had not sought out traditional study abroad options. As we work within CAP and SSS to advocate for our students' participation in study abroad, we first acknowledge the realities of financing study abroad for a low-income first-generation college student and explicitly discuss the benefits of such an experience. In creating a culture that values study abroad we approach our students' reservations with the conviction that educational and personal growth result from these experiences and are worth the investment. We move toward this facet of our work with a similar mentality as that of well-educated parents who support their children's decisions to go on such programs with the financial assistance necessary to fund these experiences.

Thus, as we set out to design our program, we were determined to gain institutional financial support for our initiatives to guarantee that every student who was accepted into the program would receive a significant scholarship. We wanted to eliminate our students' concerns about costs from their reasons for not participating. Hence, we recruited key individuals and units within the university willing to supplement the funding from the U.S. Department of Education. As a result, the Financial Aid Office has allotted institutional funds to enable our students to study abroad. To date, we have been able to subsidize the program for every student, allowing us to significantly reduce the cost for participation.

The students' contribution is currently less than a thousand dollars, not an insignificant investment for our students. While we are pleased that we can provide a meaningful scholarship to our students, we also reinforce the notion that they are making an investment in their futures. A past participant explained:

> [It] was really inexpensive based on what was included but it was a lot of money for me being a full time student.... I was leaning more towards those three weeks to working back home and making some money…what really made the difference to me finally decid[ing] to go was that I was going to be getting some financial assistance.

Similar to many non-SSS participants who go on study abroad we have found that our students have to turn to their families for support, as a past participant explained:

> Money was the main issue for me, so once I applied and got accepted I sent out an e-mail to my family and friends letting them know how important studying abroad was to me and that I needed money to go. I asked for any amount that they could spare which would be more than I had and they all helped me out tremendously.

Throughout the application process SSS advisers openly discuss the costs of the program, the scholarship awards, and the expected student contribution. We find that presenting students with financial facts begins to debunk the myth regarding the prohibitive costs of study abroad. The conversations about finances are always positive because we feel confident telling our students that the SSS Study Abroad Program is an affordable, worthwhile investment.

Our ability to assure our students that we will provide significant scholarship has played a considerable role in our success. With the financial barrier addressed, students can directly confront other obstacles that might prevent them from applying. Despite the reasonable costs of the SSS Study Abroad Program, in the first years of operation we had to aggressively recruit students. Over the years the reputation of the program and the positive experiences of our returned students have dramatically increased participation. The program has been so successful that we find more students wanting to participate than we can accommodate. While the institutional support we receive is vital, we continue to make every effort to secure funding for our applicants each summer. We know that without financial support to defray the cost of our programs many SSS students would not be able to even consider participating. If we value study abroad we must make it financially accessible for first-generation low-income students.

CULTURALLY RELEVANT PROGRAMS

While it is crucial to create a climate that values and supports study abroad opportunities for first-generation students, creating programs they want to participate in is also vital. We must build innovative and nontraditional programs that take into account the different interests, curricular requirements, educational and developmental goals, and personal circumstances of an increasingly diverse student population. As we set out to design our study abroad program, we relied heavily on the models developed by the COE and their partner institutions. Our SSS Liverpool

Study Abroad Program includes three elements that we feel are particularly responsive to the interests and needs of our students: the fact that it is a short-term program, the content, and the role of the SSS staff person as faculty adviser.

Short-Term Program Design

Our program is a short-term summer program, a design decision that we believe is more responsive to the needs and interests of our low-income and first generation students. For many of our students the idea of leaving home for a semester or a year is neither practical nor appealing. As one respondent to our survey explained:

> Nothing prevented me from applying for a more traditional semester long study abroad program; I just wasn't interested in it. What drew me closer to the SSS study abroad was the time length. It was neither too long [n]or too short.

While this student explained that he was just not interested in semester-long programs, we have found that there are a host of reasons such programs do not appeal to our students, some related to their commitments to family, work, and academics.

One of the most important issues for students is the loss of income and the impact on their families. Part-time employment during the school year and full-time employment during the summer months is critical to our students' financial circumstances. In many cases, the income generated from working allows them to stay enrolled at the university. Furthermore, many of our students play multiple and significant roles in their families that they cannot neglect including monetary contributions. Often our students' families rely on them for language and leadership support and a long absence would be stressful for the household. Some of our students come from more traditional backgrounds where families are cautious regarding the development of a sense of independence that is often an expectation in mainstream American culture; a long-term experience away from home might be strongly discouraged.

In addition to these practical reasons for not being able to participate in longer programs, many of our students are intensely focused on graduating as speedily as possible and securing a job. We have found that our students have mistakenly believed that a traditional study abroad experience would set them back or take them away from their studies. While we work hard to advocate for our students' participation in other types of study abroad programs and help them understand how such experiences can work within their academic plan of study, a short-term study abroad program seems more appealing to many of our students and addresses the realities of their life circumstances. The choice to study abroad is then based on personal reasons rather than those related to their academic timeline.

The National Survey of Student Engagement (2007), which identified study abroad as one of the high-impact college experiences that lead to significant student, personal, and intellectual growth, concluded that "it appears that the amount of time one is abroad is not as important as whether a student has had such an experience" (p. 17). They advocate for the increased use of short-term study abroad options to meet the needs of students who cannot leave campus for an entire semester.

In addition to specific academic goals that we have for the program, centered on deepening our students' international perspectives of the transatlantic slave trade, our overarching goal is to instill in our students an understanding of the value of having a global perspective and of seeking other international experiences. A short-term program such as the Liverpool initiative can plant the seeds for our students' lifelong journey of global understanding, as the statements of these past participants reveal:

- After my SSS Study Abroad Program I want to apply to a semester-long program.
- I've no longer limited my career goals to remain in this country.
- I am actually thinking of going and continuing my graduate student studies abroad.
- This program changed my views on life….
- I believe that the goals were to help raise awareness about the experiences of different cultures. It served to help us understand some of the socioeconomic challenges that others face and how they strive through adversity.

We have found that many of our students return from the study abroad in search of other opportunities to go abroad and are also strong advocates for these experiences. Some students have secured summer internship opportunities at the University of Liverpool for the year after their participation in our program. Still others, bolstered by the confidence they gained in Liverpool, have sought to participate in more traditional study abroad options, ones they would not have considered previously. Just as one learning experience builds upon earlier ones, we hope that our students use their Liverpool SSS program experience as a vehicle for future international and intercultural experiences.

Program Content

Study abroad programs must be academically relevant and meaningful to students. Our 3-week program at the University of Liverpool is titled "Black Roots in Liverpool." This program interests many of our African American and Latino students who have developed an interest in issues of social justice and contemporary race relations. The program's theme is "Innovation out of Hardship." The course focuses on the social, cultural, and political context of 400 years of Black settlement and development in Liverpool and underscores the historical implications of the continued legacy of the city's former role as a major slave port. In addition to learning about the history of the slave trade, students become familiar with the contemporary cultural and social history of Liverpool. Participants take walking tours of the historical buildings and study the architectural imagery of the city. Additionally, students visit low-income neighborhoods in Liverpool and witness the effects of gentrification. Students are also exposed to other unique experiential components where they meet the members of the urban Liverpool community and listen to lectures given by speakers who are active with contemporary community issues. In a very real sense the students become immersed in the past and the present of Liverpool, using the entire city as a learning laboratory. One key highlight of the Liverpool Study Abroad Program is that students are able to see England through various lenses.

Many of our students have never had the opportunity to explore their ancestries. The Liverpool Study Abroad Program is a powerful global experience that allows students to see the relationship between the past and the present, and provides a better understanding of the historical connections between Africa, the Americas, and England. The program facilitates the exploration of the students' roots while emphasizing the development of global citizenship. These types of study abroad experiences can play an important role in identity development for many SSS participants.

Comments made by a number of respondents to our survey give us a window into some of the complex and wonderful insights they came away with:

- I realized that I have a thirst for knowledge when it comes to African-American history and going to England, taking the courses, learning first hand of Liverpool's history helped me realize that. As of now I am an African-American history minor.
- As an African American this trip was enlightening and helped me understand much more about the slave trade from a different standpoint.
- The identity change shocked me. In England, I was American, but in America, I am something else.
- Words can't explain how study abroad influenced the way I think. I know that what goes on here in the United States today is going on some place else.
- It was interesting to see how Hispanics were viewed in England. I was told by several people when I was there that I would be considered "Black." It was difficult for me to take a step back and look at the "categories" that societies place people in.
- For me it was very interesting to find Latinos in Liverpool and Scotland. The thought of meeting Latinos out there had not crossed my mind...for some reason I never pictured Latinos fleeing persecution and going to England. I realized that there is more to this world than the U.S.

Our students go to England intending to learn about "other people" and the past; they come home with new, more complex, and sophisticated understandings about themselves and about the world. Such understandings are just the beginning of their lifelong engagement with what it means to be a citizen in a culturally pluralistic nation and a globally interconnected world.

SSS Staff as Faculty Advisers

Our SSS Liverpool Study Abroad Program is designed specifically for our SSS students. A member of the SSS staff leads a cohort of SSS students in this program. In Liverpool these students participate in the Black Roots course with other students from the University of Liverpool and other American institutions. The faculty adviser plays a leading role in communicating with and supporting students during the predeparture phases of the program. This supportive network creates a bond and trust between the group and the faculty adviser long before they depart for England. Once in England, the faculty adviser coordinates activities, assists students when they feel homesick, provides academic support, and ensures program implementation. This description does not do justice to the relationship that the faculty advisers have with the students, one past participant's comments partly describes the bond that is developed:

> Our SSS adviser was great. She was always there for any questions we had. Always made sure everyone was all right and cared for us in a very special way. While she treated us like adults she also watched out for all of us like a mom would.

We take pride in the close relationships we foster within our program in general and these bonds are only strengthened during the 3 weeks that our students travel with each other and with staff. We have found that the role of faculty adviser is critical in our efforts to increase the numbers of students interested in study abroad programs. Students (and their families) feel more comfortable with their decisions to participate because an adult and peers that they know and trust are taking part in such an experience. As one survey respondent stated: "He helped us out in so many ways and really looked out for us. He was like our father, adviser, and our friend on the trip." Each year, a different member of our SSS staff accompanies the group to Liverpool. A majority of our staff members have now participated as faculty advisers in a study abroad program. This factor has been an important element to the success of our program and our advising practices. These students and our staff person return from their experience as advocates for study abroad, which, as we mentioned earlier, is very important in our efforts to recruit participants and to create a culture that values and promotes learning about the world around us. For many of our staff members, participating in this experience solidifies their beliefs in the power of our program. It might be that faculty and other university professionals also need to have such direct experiences with study abroad programs for first-generation students if we are to build a culture of *global citizenship for all* within the larger university community.

A RESEARCH AGENDA

In this description of our program we have detailed how the design of our study abroad program and the customized advising and orientation practices that we have developed take into consideration the unique needs and interests of many low-income and first generation college students. Based on our experiences and successes we propose a research agenda that seeks to identify study abroad policies and practices that are responsive and aligned to the unique needs of low-income and first generation college students to increase their participation.

There is little research on the influence of study abroad experiences on first generation college students' growth and learning. Pascarella et al. (2004) explain that research on first generation college students has typically fallen into three categories: (1) comparisons of these students to other student populations; (2) examination of transitions from high school to college; and (3) investigations of retention rates and future career attainment. The research on admissions and retention has been vital to efforts to increase the admission and retention of traditionally underrepresented students in colleges and universities; however, Pascarella et al. (2004) note that "surprisingly little is known about their college experiences or their cognitive and psychosocial development during college" (p. 250). We posit that research in the field must move beyond a focus on admission and retention toward a deeper understanding of this population of students' college experiences, in particular those related to study abroad. We need to understand how to provide access to the full range of vital, high-impact educational experiences that make up the curriculum of a 21st century college education, including study abroad programs. This research must move from increasing the numbers of students who participate in study abroad to the examination of the academic, cognitive, and social growth that result from participation. Such an agenda would expand on our attempts to identify policies and practices that meet the needs and interests of first-generation college students. Researchers must explore how their international experiences have impacted students not only when they return to campus, but beyond graduation and into their careers. These studies would require intense follow-up and longitudinal research.

Research must also examine the ways in which existing study abroad practices could be modified to attract and provide full access to first-generation students. In the field there is a tendency to point to students' limited financial means as the most common reason given for the low participation rates of this subgroup of students, a tendency that we feel oversimplifies and distracts us from considering other barriers to equal access to study abroad. Funding issues clearly pose a significant barrier for many of our students and while these issues must be addressed at the institutional level, solely focusing on financial barriers will not increase participation. It is our contention that many institutional practices make assumptions that do not consider the needs of first-generation college students. The "typical" study abroad applicant, one whose parents are college educated, enters into an advising session with an existing belief in the importance of study abroad and a predisposition that he or she will participate in such a program. We contend that many of these traditional institutional policies and practices related to study abroad make assumptions about what students should know before they undertake these experiences; assumptions that disregard some students' successful negotiation of the system and participation in such programs. Institutions of higher education expect students to have a degree of social or cultural "capital" before they enter college regarding the importance of and ability to partake in international experiences. Study abroad policies that are dedicated to providing equal access to study abroad experiences for all students must include the development of this very cultural capital through students' participation in such programs (Pascarella et al., 2004). Thus, the challenge for universities is to create initiatives to increase participation long before a student decides to study abroad. Increasing first-generation college students' participation in study abroad must begin as soon as students come to campus. This modification requires a systemic effort to create a culture that practically values and financially supports all students' participation in international experiences, while adapting the goals and content of the program offerings for a range of students' interests, needs, prior skills, and capabilities.

While the low participation rates of first-generation college students and students from historically underrepresented groups are increasingly discussed by policy makers and institutions, there has been limited research that seeks to examine study abroad practices that might increase the numbers among this population. We have put forward a challenge that alternative and innovative approaches to study abroad programs are necessary to increase the diversity of students participating in such programs. Obst et al. (2007) question why there has been so little focus on the low participation rates of first generation college students and minority students in study abroad, asking "[c]ould the answer lie on the premise that generally institutions of higher education stay away from customizing programs to the needs of all students...." (p. 5).

In this chapter we examined institutional practices and policies as they relate to addressing the needs of low-income, first-generation students; we have presented examples of "best practices" within a successful study abroad model. Our goal is to offer our experiences as a means for others to analyze policies and practices impacting the participation of first-generation students in study abroad. The SSS program has been planning and implementing study abroad initiatives specifically designed for first-generation students since 2001. So far, 100 SSS students have studied in England, South Africa, Cuba, and several European countries. Past participants have been introduced to a new way of thinking so they can begin to understand their role in becoming global citizens. In the process many productive partnerships have been developed, including the successful collaboration between the Center for Academic Programs and the Office of Study Abroad on campus. This relationship has allowed the Center to receive positive and constructive feedback that will assist us in identifying program areas for further development. For example, given the success of the Liverpool program, the Center is poised to evaluate various components of this initiative. In future assessments we propose to examine whether or not we are doing enough to infuse a global perspective into the curriculum. It is imperative to examine the concepts of intervention and autonomy as they relate to issues of empowerment. Although some of the survey responses offer glimpses of feelings of empowerment on the part of the students, we believe that more effort needs to be incorporated into the program to address these important issues.

We believe the Center has done a remarkable job of providing access to study abroad opportunities to first-generation students participating in the SSS program at the University of Connecticut. The SSS Study Abroad Program focuses on a specific population and offers an alternative to the traditional approach to study abroad. We created a model that may support others' efforts to increase access to these opportunities on their campuses for low-income, first-generation college students. The success of the University of Connecticut SSS Study Abroad model is a result of effective collaborations among critical units on campus that promote equal access and global citizenship for all students. Perhaps other institutions can benefit from our experience and implement initiatives that can successfully facilitate study abroad opportunities for first generation college students. In today's world of high competitiveness, we need every individual to develop a global understanding that will allow them to compete in a global economy.

NOTES

1. The Council for Opportunity in Education is a nonprofit organization, established in 1981, dedicated to furthering the expansion of educational opportunities throughout the United States. Through its numerous membership services, the Council works in conjunction with colleges, universities, and agencies that host TRIO Programs to specifically help low-income students enter college and graduate.
2. TRIO is Educational Opportunity for Low-Income and Disabled Americans. Federal TRIO Programs (Talent Search, Upward Bound, Upward Bound Math Science, Veteran's Upward Bound, Student Support Services, Educational Opportunity Centers, and the Ronald E. McNair Post-Baccalaureate Achievement Program) help students to overcome class, social, academic, and cultural barriers to higher education. They are funded under Title IV of the Higher Education Act of 1965. For more information on the TRIO programs, http://www.trioprograms.org.

REFERENCES

Abraham Lincoln Study Abroad Fellowship Program, Commission on the. (2005, November). *Global competence and national needs: One million Americans studying abroad.* Washington, DC. Retrieved June 19, 2008, from http://www.nafsa.org/_/Document/_/lincoln_commission_report.pdf

Friedman, T. L. (2005). *The world is flat: A brief history of the twenty-first century.* New York: Farrar, Straus & Giroux.

National Survey of Student Engagement. (2007). *Experiences that matter: Enhancing student learning and success.* Center for Postsecondary Research: Indiana University. Retrieved on June 18, 2008, from http://nsse.iub.edu/NSSE_2007_Annual_Report/index.cfm

Norfles, N. (2003, January 23–25). *Toward equal and equitable access: Obstacles and opportunities in international education.* Paper presented at the Global Challenges and U.S. Higher Education Research Conference. Duke University, Durham, NC. Retrieved June 18, 2008, from http://www.jhfc.duke.edu/ducis/globalchallenges/pdf/norfles_paper.pdf

Obst, D., Bhandari, R., & Witherell, S. (2007, May). *Meeting America's global education challenge: Current trends in U.S. study abroad and the impact of strategic diversity initiatives issues* (IIE Study Abroad White Paper Series, Issue Number 1). New York: Institute of International Education. Retrieved June 18, 2008, from http://www.iienetwork.org/file_depot/0-10000000/0-10000/1710/folder/62450/IIE+Study+Abroad+White+Paper+I.pdf

Pascarella, E. T., Pierson, C. T., Wolniak, G. C., & Terenzini, P. T. (2004). First generation college students. *Journal of Higher Education, 75*(3), 249–284.

Texas Tech University. (2008). *Scholarly review of literature on first generation college (FGC) students.* Retrieved June 10, 2008, from http://ram.tosm.ttu.edu/advising/pegasus/fgclitreview.php

Tym, C., McMillion, R., Barone, S., & Webster, J. (2004, November). *First generation college students: A literature review.* Texas Guaranteed Student Loan Corporation, Research and Analytical Services. Retrieved June 18, 2008, from http://www.tgslc.org/pdf/first_generation.pdf

Chapter 30

It's Not about You

The UConn Social Entrepreneur Corps Global Commonwealth Study Abroad Model

Ross Lewin
University of Connecticut

Greg Van Kirk
Social Entrepreneur Corps

UConn Social Entrepreneur Corps has given me invaluable experience and knowledge about sustainable development work that I will apply to different ventures in the future. We not only learned about successful development models, we saw them in practice and supported the people whose lives they were improving. The experience taught me the necessity and importance of the sharing of knowledge that is essential for successful development work. On both sides of development work we can teach and learn from those we are helping as they learn and teach us valuable lessons as well. (Richard Bogert, UConn Social Entrepreneur Corps, 2008, personal interview)

INTRODUCTION

Study abroad is moving from the margins to the center of the undergraduate curriculum. This move can be tracked in virtually every aspect of the field. Physically, universities are relocating study abroad offices from dingy buildings on the edge of campus to fresh spaces in the heart of university traffic. Instead of granting transfer credit for courses taken abroad, faculty are increasingly awarding students graded credit, the same as for students enrolled on the home campus. If once the almost exclusive bailiwick of foreign language departments, study abroad has become part of the curriculum of schools and departments across the university. Universities now articulate study abroad as part of their mission and academic plans. Even financially, university foundations are prioritizing raising money for study abroad to ensure widespread access to what is quickly becoming regarded as a sine qua non of a college education.

Yet as study abroad moves into the center of the undergraduate curriculum, the center of the curriculum is itself shifting. Specifically, it is shifting from faculty-centered teaching and student passivity to faculty-guided learning and student engagement. Study abroad has endeavored to stay abreast with these changes. While direct enrollment and "island" programming still predominates, there is a growing number of study abroad opportunities that integrate hands-on learning experiences. Internships with international companies have become an increasingly popular form of study abroad, yet the area of most dramatic growth has been in student internships in the host culture, particularly in community service governmental organizations, very often in countries outside of Europe and Oceania. The acquisition of high European culture is decreasingly the highest learning outcome of study abroad, replaced by the more explicitly civic goal of global citizenship.

Although study abroad has always valued experience beyond the classroom more than mainstream higher education, its latest trend of engaging students in community service internships follows recent trends on the home campus. While we generally regard study abroad's incorporation of these developments positively, demonstrative of its integration into undergraduate education, we caution in this chapter from simply copying them lock, stock, and barrel. There is a simple reason for this: transplanting ideas created for the home campus may not be feasible, effective, or ethical in study abroad. In particular, simply grafting student-centered learning and civic engagement models onto study abroad may be undemocratic, even imperialistic. In this chapter we offer an alternative view of global citizenship study abroad that asks for yet another shift, this time not a retreat from student-centered learning to faculty-centered teaching, but rather a progression from student-centered learning to community-centered development. We suggest, in fact, that designing programs that place the community first, rather than the student, is paradoxically the most effective way to realize the development of students intellectually, morally, and civically. In this chapter, we will thus review recent trends in higher education, how study abroad has been influenced by them, and why these trends may be particularly problematic in a global citizenship-oriented international environment. We then propose a new model of study abroad that works for the global commonweal and show how well it has succeeded through one example, the UConn Social Entrepreneur Corps in Guatemala, a program formed in partnership between the University of Connecticut and the Social Entrepreneur Corps.

THE STUDENT ENGAGEMENT MOVEMENT

Although student engagement can be traced back, as Schneider (2005) points out, to the student activism of the 1960s, the emergence of ethnic, gender, and urban studies programs, and the diversity and multiculturalism movements, it is currently driven by three priorities in higher education: assessment, experiential education, and civic education.

Until the 1980s assessment in higher education was largely academic. Scholars promoted assessment models to improve college teaching, but faculty rarely if ever implemented them. Beginning in the 1980s, however, university business schools woke up to the alarm of assessment sounded by prospective employers' complaints that university graduates did not come to them with the requisite skills. Eager to advertise high postgraduate job placement rates, business schools started analyzing their own curricula to ensure alignment with the needs of employers. Providing students with practical skills rose to the top of their priority list, leading many of them to place greater emphasis on engaging students in problem solving inside and practical internship experience outside the classroom.

In the mid-1980s the federal government, under then Secretary of Education William Bennett, began demanding accountability across universities to guarantee that U.S. college graduates had marketable skills, a mandate that has continued to this day, as witnessed in the 2006 U.S. Department of Higher Education report, commissioned by then Secretary of Education Margaret Spellings. As increases in tuition started outpacing inflation, taxpaying parents have had to foot a much larger portion of their children's college education, which has led them to demand that their children graduate with employable skills. Finally, as the percentage of public university budgets supported by the federal government has fallen precipitously, institutional fundraising has stepped up, with private donors underwriting a much greater portion of university life. To gain and maintain their support, private donors ask for "deliverables." Most of these stakeholders demand more engagement incorporated into the higher educational enterprise.

If outside pressure for assessment has driven student engagement, so too have the constituencies within the academy. Administrators and faculty alike understand that engaged students are better students. Emerging scholarship on teaching and learning holds that students attain higher levels of learning when the classroom is student-centered, requiring faculty to guide students through active pedagogies, such as collaborative learning, project-based learning, and experiential education, all of which require students to work on and then generalize from real life situations. The National Survey of Student Engagement (NSSE) has played perhaps the most dramatic role in focusing colleges and universities on greater student engagement. The president of NSSE, George Kuh (Kuh, Kinzie, Schuh, & Whitt, 2005) has demonstrated through data that, as one of Kuh et al.'s chapters is titled, "Student Engagement" is the "key to student success" (p. 7). Kuh goes beyond activities in the classroom to include areas that have been traditionally regarded as extracurricular, cocurricular, or value-added programs, including student government, campus associational life, learning communities and study abroad.

Civic education has been the third driver of student engagement. Civic engagement's history is long, dating back to the founding of U.S. higher education. Thomas Jefferson envisioned American higher education as dedicated to cultivating democratic citizenship and serving the public good, which by implication distinguished it from its English and German counterparts, which focused on the training of the aristocracy and the exclusive development of knowledge, respectively. In the 1980s two reports recycled this Jeffersonian vision. Frank Newman (1985) of the Carnegie Foundation for the Advancement of Teaching bemoaned the abandonment of the American tradition in favor of technical training and quantifiable outcomes, such as test scores. In its stead Newman called for a return to civic education:

> The most critical demand is to restore to higher education its original purpose of preparing graduates for a life of involved and committed citizenship.... It is essential that the purpose of liberal arts education be transformed so that it provides not only a broad base of knowledge and the requisite intellectual skills, but that it develops an entrepreneurial spirit and a sense of civic responsibility. (pp. xiv–xv)

And in 1987 then president of the Carnegie Foundation Ernest Boyer echoed Newman in his classic *College: The Undergraduate Experience in America.* Arguing for a change from "competence to commitment," Boyer concluded: "In the end, the quality of the undergraduate experience is to be measured by the willingness of graduates to be socially and civically engaged" (pp. 278–279).

Newman and Boyer link the cultivation of civic responsibility with more community service programming. Newman, for example, argues that "For a democracy to function, the role of volunteerism is essential" (p. 36). He asserts that, in addition to educating students about government and American history, "The college experience should also develop within a student a sense of country and community service" (p. 39). Boyer, for his part, "recommend[s] that every student complete a service project—involving volunteer work in the community or at the college—as an integral part of his or her undergraduate experience" (p. 218). At the core of both Newman's and

Boyer's arguments is higher education's responsibility to develop graduates who remain committed to engaging in civil society throughout their lives.

Evidently, the likes of Newman and Boyer were heard and realized in the service-learning movement. Since the 1990s service learning has distinguished itself from community service primarily through its focus not merely on outreach but also on learning and process, manifested by "structured reflection" writing exercises, which allow the students to abstract and generalize from their experience, and "reciprocity," which encourages communities to be the teachers of students rather than just the recipients of aid. In the last decade, service learning has increased dramatically in popularity, with institutions across the United States offering successful opportunities to undergraduates. Service is no longer regarded as merely extracurricular. It has now been more or less integrated into the undergraduate curriculum.

THE IMPACT OF HIGHER EDUCATION TRENDS ON STUDY ABROAD

As study abroad has moved to the center of undergraduate education, it has taken consistent steps toward integrating assessment, hands-on pedagogies, and civic engagement into its curriculum. Prior to this decade, the assessment of study abroad programming was scant, relegated to student evaluations and a few scholarly articles here and there. Recently, however, this has changed, with study abroad proactively policing itself. In 2005 the Forum on Education, established just a few years earlier, published its *Standards of Good Practice for Education Abroad*. Comprised of well over 200 questions, the *Standards* examine each aspect of the study abroad operation, from ethics, finances, safety, and security to the quality of the core curriculum. In 2007 the Forum followed the *Standards* with a single volume, *A Guide to Outcomes Assessment in Education Abroad* (Bolen, 2007a). Editor Bolen (2007b) explains its aim this way:

> Commitment to improving our work, political pressures, and growth as a field all contributes to the perception that outcomes assessment should be part of our education abroad agenda. Whether we've concluded outcomes assessment is important because of our need to foster productive program improvements, to convince doubters of the validity of our enterprise, or to convince state or federal officials to fund our work, we have become convinced for this type of research. (p. 1)

It is not, however, merely the desire to gain outside support from state and federal governments that has driven assessment in study abroad. Study abroad programs can cost more than twice what an in-state public university student pays for tuition and room and board, adding significantly to financial pressure on already overburdened parents who hear regularly from universities and their children that in this era of globalization a study abroad experience is an essential component of an undergraduate education. As funders of study abroad, parents thus need to be convinced that they are spending their money wisely. Given the cost, the demand, and the push, study abroad has also become the latest agenda item of university foundations. As university fundraisers visit their alumni and make their pitches, they are inevitably met by prospects who want to know what study abroad actually achieves. We submit that these pressures have quietly moved institutions to integrate more pragmatic elements into their study abroad programming.

Bolen's reference to the study abroad "doubters" also refers to those inside the university. As

Joan Gore points out in this volume (see chapter 17), study abroad has always met with skepticism from within the university, particularly from faculty, who have long viewed it as nothing more than an extension of the European grand tour or Swiss finishing school. This negative perception persists to this day. Despite the increased participation in study abroad, the skeptics' numbers continue to grow on account of the alleged homogenization of the world caused by global commercialism, which has led to more island programming that many faculty view as "neither significantly international nor truly educative" (Engle & Engle, 2002, p. 25). Given that credit is awarded exclusively by faculty, assessment has to be integrated into programming to sway them.

Yet, as Bolen indicates, the call within study abroad for greater assessment also aims to improve the quality of existing programs. What constitutes program quality has, however, changed. Up until recently, one might have assessed primarily for whether students mastered a foreign language or effectively immersed themselves in the host culture. While these remain goals, study abroad has now more or less adopted the higher education discourse more generally. Trudi Banta (2001) and Linda Suskie (2004) in their own works have established widely recognized assessment categories, including knowledge, skills, and attitudes, which they have deemed as the core competencies of a higher education. Study abroad has begun to mimic these categories. In 2003 the American Council on Education released a report on internationalization in which it specifically discusses "global" knowledge, "global" skills and "global" attitudes, and these categories have also found their way into study abroad assessment literature (Sutton, Miller, & Rubin, 2007). There are other assessment instruments out there, ones that test global awareness, intercultural sensitivity, and cross-cultural adaptivity, for example. These instruments share in common the desire to place the student at the center of the curriculum.

In addition to assessment, the student engagement movement has realized itself in study abroad through a new focus on hands-on experiences. It is no longer enough merely to have had the experience of studying and living in a different culture. Too many critics have complained that the study abroad curriculum is weak and inadequately integrated into the home curriculum. But rather than forcing faculty teaching home courses to get students to talk about their international experiences, study abroad progams are increasingly incorporating various types of hands-on pedagogies, including project-based work, field research, internships, and service learning. And in each case, there is a concerted effort to integrate more structured reflection exercises, which have been at the core of these pedagogies so that students can now actually compare and contrast cultures and become conscious of what they think and assume.

Study abroad has been, finally, influenced by the civic engagement movement, most visible in the recent focus on global citizenship. Despite the problematic advertising that Talya Zemach-Bersin discusses in this volume (see chapter 18), the global citizenship study abroad movement takes its inspiration from well-respected scholars. One of these is political scientist Benjamin Barber (1995), who in his best-selling *McWorld vs. Jihad* calls for the development of a global civil society:

> [D]emocracy demands new post-nation state institutions and new attitudes more attentive to direct responsibility people bear for their liberties. To be sure, global government, above all democratic global government, remains a distant dream; but the kinds of global citizenship necessary to its cultivation are less remote. Citizenship is first of all nurtured in democratic civil society. A global citizenship demands a domain parallel to McWorld's in which communities of cooperation do consciously and for the public good what markets currently do inadvertently on behalf of aggregated private interests. (p. 277)

547

Martha Nussbaum has also inspired study abroad professionals. In *Cultivating Humanity: A Classical Defense of Reform in Liberal Education* (1997), Nussbaum brings the discussion of global citizenship into higher education reform. Like Newman and Boyer, she also believes that college must go beyond the training of technocrats and include civic education. Nussbaum does not, however, merely believe that we need to create better U.S. citizens: "Many of our pressing problems require for their intelligent, cooperative solution a dialogue that brings together people from many different national and cultural and religious backgrounds" (p. 8). She calls for "world citizenship," which she divides into three parts: "the capacity of critical examination of oneself and one's traditions" (p. 9), "an ability to see themselves not simply as citizens of some local region or group but also, and above all, as human beings bound to all other human beings by ties of recognition and concern" (p. 10), and "the ability to think what it might be like to be in the shoes of a person different from oneself, " what she calls "narrative imagination" (pp. 10–11). Nussbaum's tripartite definition has become part of the discourse of study abroad, which is aggressively focusing its learning outcomes on conscious reflection of self and intercultural sensitivity.

CHALLENGES IN GLOBAL CITIZENSHIP PROGRAM DESIGN AND ASSESSMENT

Study abroad has recently embraced global citizenship into its programming. We not only witness this phenomenon in the large number of mission statements promoting this goal and the advertising for study abroad, as others in this volume have pointed out, but also in the several examples of global citizenship study abroad programming. There are, of course, the clear cases that have existed for some time, such as programs offered by the School for International Training (SIT), the University of Minnesota, Augsburg College, Brethren College, and The International Partnership for Service Learning. In addition, study abroad providers that have traditionally concentrated on intercultural development and academic integration into another culture's university system, such as IES Abroad, the Institute for Study Abroad (IFSA-Butler), and the Council on International Education Exchange (CIEE), now invite students to participate in internships and community service in virtually all of their programs. Many colleges and universities are also adding their own service-learning programs to their own menu of proprietary study abroad programs. At the University of Connecticut (UConn), for example, we can point to new service-learning programs in the Dominican Republic, South Africa, Mexico, and Guatemala, the latter of which we will discuss later in this chapter.

This surge of interest in community service organization (CSO) internships in study abroad marks a radical shift in the types of partnerships forged by university study abroad offices. Historically, study abroad offices have linked with foreign universities and third-party study abroad providers, both of which either share or adapt to their universities' missions. In creating programs focused on service learning, however, university study abroad offices find themselves increasingly partnering with CSOs that are guided by very different missions from their universities. Herein lie some challenges.

In contrast to colleges and universities, CSOs do not make student development—intellectually, personally, academically, morally, or civically—their core mission. They do not primarily serve students, but rather members of the community in which they work. In forming these marriages, universities and CSOs thus face the enormous challenge of satisfying the needs of both of their principle beneficiaries. This hurdle is no stranger to the larger field of service learning. The literature on service learning shows that university practitioners have repeatedly run up against the misgivings of community CSO leaders who have either felt that their university partners were simply transferring knowledge to the CSO's beneficiaries, or that the communities themselves became a means for the development of the student. Service-learning scholars and practitioners, recognizing the differential in power between the universities and the CSOs, have responded sensitively to this problem by articulating "reciprocity" as a necessary value. By reciprocity, they generally mean making sure that each partner receives an equal amount of benefit. The problem is, as many within the service-learning community have contended, that the universities almost always constitute the stronger partner in this relationship by dint of their generally superior financial situation and size. Following the principle of "reciprocity" may, therefore, sound better than it actually plays out in practice, which may be an even greater problem when partnering with CSOs in poorer countries in the world, which often confront even greater financial barriers than those in the United States.

The second problem encountered by a partnership between universities and CSOs is the degree to which each prioritizes the relationship. CSOs are typically small, financially strapped organizations. Integrating students into their projects has a huge impact on their day-to-day activities. Training, employing, and meeting the students' needs indeed consume a great portion of their energy. In contrast, universities, generally speaking, regard these internships as not much more than a marginal activity of their larger operations, especially with regard to undergraduate student programs. To be sure, land-grant institutions have been mandated to make community outreach a part of their mission. Yet this outreach has itself usually been shunted off to continuing or cooperative education offices and a small number of researchers. The pioneers of service-learning programs, who introduced student outreach into the curriculum, describe their own work as marginalized, seen more as a side show than part of the central mission of the university (Stanton, Giles, & Cruz, 1999). While individuals within universities thus seem to value the work of CSOs, the universities themselves do not usually respond in kind. As a result, CSOs do not feel appreciated, which can result ultimately in resentment, thereby jeopardizing the partnership. In study abroad programming that incorporates service learning, this problem can be magnified on account of distance, the fact that the university does not reside in the same town or even country as the CSO.

This university-centric relationship can also spill into the academic curriculum, especially when it comes to study abroad programming. Again, the published commentary on service learning reflects this problem. Service learning has usually been regarded as experiential and not academic. As such, it has been looked at askance by many faculty members who do not view it as academically worthy. To this extent, service learning butts up against the same faculty resistance as study abroad. When one then incorporates community service into a study abroad program, the amount of skepticism can be compounded. To address this problem, service-learning entities on campus work with faculty by often asking them to recognize a graded "journal course," which, they are assured, will not involve merely casual entries that recount one's daily work but will be intentionally designed reflection exercises that require, among other things, that they integrate their experiences into a wider context. Faculty may tolerate this solution when the service-learning component counts for just one course in a full-time semester's students academic load and a university faculty member guides the entire project. When, however, service learning constitutes the center of a program and that program takes place in an educational context very different from that on the home campus, faculty tolerance may decrease. In this scenario, faculty often respond by imposing their pedagogies onto a cultural and educational environment that precludes the successful implementation of the curriculum.

The final problem in developing these partnerships between universities and CSOs in poorer countries is the power differential between the two sets of beneficiaries, students and communities. Zemach-Bersin (2008) points to this problem, contending that students on her SIT program entered their Nepali homestays with a sense of entitlement. We have noted an entitlement problem on the UConn Cape Town program, which involves 3-day per week internships in CSOs across the city. We usually mean by the term *entitlement* that Americans benefit from White privilege or the privilege that comes from membership in a wealthy country. The entitlement problem generates, however, just as much from the fact that study abroad has become a consumer product. Students and their parents buy this experience at a high price. As consumers, then, students enter into this relationship as if it were contractual. They pay for goods and services, such as experiences and credits, and they want them delivered according to their expectations and as advertised. If unprepared for a study abroad experience working with CSOs in poor communities, and if they are not disabused of their fantasies, they will extend the assumptions of this contractual relationship into their relationships with members of the host communities. That is, students may treat the poor people with whom they are working as commodities for their consumption. They also want their credits' worth, which principally means that their first priority becomes their own academic development. The greatest risk of this contractual relationship is that it renders all aspects of international service learning about the development of the subject. Developing the student subject on the home campus makes perfect sense. Yet when we change the context to an international one marked by poverty, and when the program is focused mainly on helping communities in need, developing the student subject as a primary goal transforms itself into an act of colonialism, which, of course, contradicts the very goals of the program. The community members then end up having to satisfy those desires to keep the money coming from the students, which itself supports the CSOs that serve them.

The other problem with students is their abiding lack of knowledge and skills. American students often compensate for these deficiencies by calling on their national identity, marked particularly by the sense of exceptionalism drilled into them all of their lives. Even if critical of their government, U.S. students view themselves as somehow able to save the world. At the same time, they often invoke that uniquely American sense of pragmatism, articulated frequently as their "common sense" and "can-do" spirit. To be sure, these traits can and should be harnessed. But we must guard against students' delusions of grandeur. International service-learning programs, which often require students to carry out quotidian tasks and confront their own ignorance and ineptitude, can certainly humble students, leading to a greater sense of modesty. This work can, however, also frustrate students who have been told by their parents, their universities and their culture writ large that they stand at the center of the world. Given that CSOs do not usually have the financial or human capital to train students who are on site for the brief duration of a typical study abroad program, frustrated students often withdraw, left waiting to take orders that do not come, merely observing other people's contributions, even often getting in the way of other people's work.

This story is not new. In 1968 Ivan Illich articulated his displeasure with students going to poor countries to perform service. In a speech to students about to head off to Latin America, Illich scolded them for even going there, asserting that they had nothing to offer, and warning them that they could only do harm. A university faculty member who led a service-learning study abroad program in the Caribbean echoed Illich, maintaining that the impact of the nutrition and HIV-AIDS education her students were involved in was minimal. It would have been far better had they just sent the money for food and medicine. Yet she defended the enterprise on the grounds that the students came away much more sensitive and globally aware of issues of poverty and race than they were when they arrived. This faculty member went on to suggest that the only thing the students really provided to the communities was the money for the experience. In essence, the students catered to a tourist industry. Unfortunately, many students return from such experiences deluding themselves that they had made an impact.

In the end, the ultimate casualty of universities and CSOs entering into partnerships is their sustainability. Over time, conflicting missions can lead to tension and disinterest among all stakeholders. The CSOs feel dependent upon the univerities for cash, but they don't really know what to do with the students. The students leave either deluded into believing they made more of a contribution than they did, or disappointed that they made none. And the faculty feel resentful because they are called on to make adjustments to the agenda of the CSOs when they are already overtaxed with duties on their home campuses and do not recognize the academic value of what the students are engaged in.

NEW THINKING IN HIGHER EDUCATION AND STUDY ABROAD

Thus far we have argued that conflicting missions threaten the sustainability of the new partnerships in study abroad. Although these problems may appear insurmountable, there are several voices in U.S. higher education who provide us with new directions on how to get beyond them to create effective and sustainable global citizenship study abroad programs.

The first is The Association of American Colleges and Universities (AAC&U), which in its report *Greater Expectations: A New Vision for Learning as a Nation Goes to College* (2002) articulated a new vision of a "newly pragmatic liberal education [that] will prepare students for a dynamic economy and build civic capacity at home and abroad (p. xii). Three years later, one of the report's principle authors, AAC&U president Carol Geary Schneider (2005), reaffirmed this model, once again linking civic engagement to the resolution of social problems on a global stage:

> The "new academy" is centrally concerned not just with knowledge but also with educating students who are both prepared and inspired to address society's difficulty questions. This ethos places strong value on what it calls "engaged" learning—learning that emphasizes what students can do with their knowledge and that involves students, individually and collectively, in analyzing and working to solve significant problems in the larger world. (p. 127)

Key in both the AAC&U's report and Schneider's essay is a shift from a model of civic engagement that emphasizes charity and sensitivity to others to one which focuses much more explicitly on providing students with practical skills necessary to address real global problems.

AAC&U Vice President Caryn McTighe Musil also moves us in the right direction when regarding civic engagement. Like others, McTighe Musil (2003) admonishes universities for making civic engagement an after-hours event of the academic curriculum. Calling explicitly for its integration into every aspect of university life, she proposes a hierarchy of forms of citizenship, comprised of six levels: exclusionary, oblivious, naïve, charitable, reciprocal, and generative. McTighe Musil argues for moving beyond the charitable and reciprocal forms, as articulated in university outreach and service learning programs, to generative citizenship that actively develops the public good:

> This cumulative phase of generative citizenship has a more all encompassing scope with an eye to the future public good. The community is understood not as something separate and

apart but as one and the same, an interdependent resource filled with possibilities. Students move from civic engagement as a value to civic prosperity as a goal. They seek the well-being of the whole, an integrated social network in which all flourish. (p. 7)

By redefining the goals of civic education as prosperity, study abroad can now argue that the highest goal of its global citizenship programming should be to help promote the global commonweal.

McTighe Musil's citizenship ladder can be traced back to Harry Boyte and Nancy Kari (2000), who have long been involved in undergraduate civic education projects. Boyte and Kari level a serious criticism against the kinds of citizenship education defined by service learning. Like McTighe Musil, they recognize various forms of modern democratic citizenship. Rather than six levels, however, they identify three—civic, communitarian, and commonwealth—and show what role higher education plays in developing each. According to Boyte and Kari, civic citizenship, related to rights-bearing, representative government, is practiced primarily in the ballot box. Higher education contributes to the development of civic citizenship by cultivating students' expert knowledge and critical reasoning skills. Communitarian citizenship is defined by participation in civil society, the voluntary sector that lies outside work and government. For Boyte and Kari, higher education fosters communitarian citizenship, concerned with the development of the students' character, through moral education and service learning. Boyte and Kari save their greatest criticism for this form of citizenship:

> [U]nless ideals are connected to real work, they all too easily become sentimental or a clamor of competing moral claims. Thus, for instance, seeing community service as about teaching caring and concern feeds the thin associations of citizenship in "a thousand points of light," and the imagery of the heart, symbol of the volunteer. (p. 40)

Boyte and Kari regard commonwealth as the highest form of modern democratic citizenship. Commonwealth citizenship is quite similar to McTighe Musil's generative citizenship to the extent that it prioritizes developing students' creativity and experience necessary to make tangible improvements to the public good. For Boyte and Kari, higher education can achieve this goal by providing students with multiple opportunities to work on and analyze public works projects. Commonwealth citizenship creates "public problem solvers and co-producers of public goods" (p. 40).

Judith Ramalay, former president of the University of Vermont, is another voice useful to developing global citizenship study abroad. In her essay "The Perspective of a Comprehensive University," Ramalay (2000) argues for transforming the university into an agent of public good. Ramalay seems to draw on The Kellogg Commission for the Future of State and Land-Grant Institutions (2000), which reported a growing criticism by the public that these institutions were not serving the people of the state, but were dedicated primarily to creating knowledge for its own sake. The Kellogg Commission calls for a renewed commitment from universities, and for the first time changed the discourse from "outreach and service" to "engagement," calling for a "fully engaged university" dedicated not merely to transferring knowledge as a one-way street or engaging in charitable activities, but to working with communities in solving problems of the region and state. Ramalay expands on the Kellogg report by defining more precisely what constitutes an engaged university:

> A university must also be able to create conditions that support entrepreneurial activity that will enhance the economic base and promote opportunities for the citizens of the region it

serves and the state, if statewide issues are in its mission. This will be both our challenge and our opportunity as an engaged university for the twenty-first century. (p. 227)

By challenging the university to be entrepreneurial, she argues not merely for strategies to increase revenue but also for unleashing a creative spirit to improve the livelihood of citizens. We part from Ramalay only to the extent that we believe that public universities are no longer obliged merely to serve the citizens of their state and region but also to their counterparts around the world, given that both sides are so interconnected. Now is the time to consider developing programs in which the university, as well as faculty and the students are engaged in improving the public good around the world through an entrepreneurial spirit.

The noted scholar of teaching and learning L. Dee Fink (2003) helps us determine how to build effective study abroad programs, despite the fact that he never explicitly addresses the subject. Fink mirrors much of the work of past researchers interested in assessment, using the same essential triangle of goals, activities, and indicators of success, but he adds one more dimension that overdetermines each point on the triangle: "The Situation." The Situation, according to Fink, refers to the a priori conditions that inform our decisions. The Situation for study abroad programs that take place in the field and work with CSOs in relatively poor countries is the infrastructure, the fact that we have the same type of classroom facilities, faculty credentials, and faculty and student support services that home campuses do. Educational delivery is thus ipso facto delivered in a very different way, informing how we set goals, evaluate programs, and, perhaps most importantly, determine learning activities to achieve those goals.

DESIGNING AND ASSESSING STUDY ABROAD FOR THE GLOBAL COMMONWEAL

So far we have described recent trends affecting study abroad, what challenges they pose, and what proposals have been made in the last decade to help guide us to create more successful global citizenship study abroad programs. We now turn to describing our own program model, before analyzing how well this model has worked on UConn Social Entrepreneur Corps in Guatemala.

As mentioned above, one of the main struggles in developing global citizenship study abroad is to maintain a vital partnership between universities and CSOs. In order to solve this challenge, the first order of business is for the two partners to decide collectively what they share in common. Here we propose making "global citizenship" our starting point. We can assume that the guiding principle for most CSOs, and particularly for those with which universities will partner, is to serve the public good in the communities with which they work. Global citizenship, as defined by Boyte and Kari, lies at the center of their mission. At the same time, U.S. institutions of higher education of all types, including community colleges, private liberal arts colleges, and public universities, can refer to their own historical missions of serving the public good and creating citizens. Over and above that, given the radical transformation of the world as a result of globalization, universities can now articulate themselves as interested in the global commonweal, and not just the regional, state, or national. If we thus all begin with our desire to improve the global public good, the marriage between institutions of higher education and CSOs places itself on the right track.

The corollary of identifying a common mission is to prioritize our goals. Rather than dedicating ourselves first and foremost to students, we argue for aiming our goals at the development of the community using students. Given that study abroad is now entering into territory that lies outside the traditional parameters of teaching and learning and moves more into that sphere of university life that has been governed by outreach, we recommend that study abroad program designers and their CSO partners replace as its primary assessment tool the standard student assessment model that focuses on knowledge, skills, and attitudes with a modified version of the logic model framework (LMF). In contrast to student models, LMF is geared toward measuring community impact and raising money for CSOs. As such, they are more interested in outcomes based, either quantitative or qualitative, or what we might wish to call "impacts." The LMF matrix takes into account Dee Fink's emphasis on "The Situation." It also takes into account Schneider's and McTighe Musil's interest in producing students who can address global problems. What is the problem that we are trying to resolve? How do we go about resolving it? What resources do we need? What are our challenges?

One might consider thinking of this new model as a football team. On this team, there is a quarterback who decides the game plan as well as the particular plays. In this scenario, the quarterback is the CSO. The quarterback then assembles his players, each of whom is assigned a different role to help advance the entire team toward its short- and long-term goals. Creating a football team would seem to run in the face of democratic principles, which have traditionally guided service learning. After assessing the needs of the communities through direct conversations and data analysis, the CSO decides on its goal. It also then employs various players, based on their existing and potential knowledge, skills, and attitudes. Students, then, as well as the university itself, become players on this community development team.

In this same model, we also propose a very different model of learning. Traditionally, student knowledge, skills, and attitudes have been the goals, with learning activities designed to meet them. As we have mentioned, it has been the faculty guiding the active learning, with students playing an active role. While we still believe in proactive student learning, we argue for shifting emphases. In our estimation, student knowledge, skills, and attitudes are, for example, as much inputs as outputs. In order for the team to reach its community objectives and goals, it requires that students come to the game with certain skills sets. This requires planning, of course. It also requires on-the-spot training and practice. That is, we not only need to prepare students academically and morally before they go study abroad; we must also engage them in on-the-job training in order for them to make the greatest contribution. Acquisition of knowledge and skills, as well as new habits of mind, will take place. The more students are asked to do, the more knowledge they will need to acquire. The more they practice, the better their skills will become. The same holds true for attitudes. The goals of education will be achieved, but the strategy for realizing them is not making the program about them but about those communities in need.

We suggest that more study abroad partnerships focus on community development rather than community relief work. Although we value relief work, and by no means advocate for students and universities doing less of it, we contend that a concentration on development work will create solutions that are long-term and provide students and communities with skills that can be applied to other challenges they encounter. They will also avoid the illusion so often found in relief work of having solved a problem when, in fact, that problem can return immediately after the relief workers depart. As you will read in what follows, we are particularly interested in the social entrepreneurship model, as it dovetails so nicely with recent trends in higher education and its emphases on creativity and entrepreneurialism. We note that the AAC&U invited Bill Drayton, the founder of Ashoka, a foundation dedicated to advancing social entrepreneurship, to write a piece for *Peer Review* (Drayton, 2005). We now turn to telling our story of the partnership between the UConn and the Social Entrepreneur Corps.

CASE STUDY: UCONN SOCIAL ENTREPRENEUR CORPS IN GUATEMALA

UConn Social Entrepreneur Corps in Guatemala is a strategic partnership between UConn and Social Entrepreneur Corps. Its mission is to make tangible improvements in the lives of rural community residents in Guatemala by providing them with essential products and services at a low cost while at the same time enhancing the knowledge, skills, and attitudes of UConn undergraduates. We believe that the success of UConn Social Entrepreneur Corps in Guatemala is attributable to the question that framed our program design: How can we engage students in a way that facilitates the greatest community impact? On this program students focus on developing the community primarily and themselves secondarily. We contend that putting the community first has paradoxically led to the greatest benefit for students in all of the traditional student assessment categories, including knowledge, skills, and attitudes. In what follows we describe the basics of the social entrepreneurship approach, the community needs that generated a partnership between UConn and Social Entrepreneur Corps, the design model to meet those needs, the implementation of the pilot program, as well as the lessons learned and recommendations for improving the program in the future.

Social Entrepreneurship as an Approach

In order to analyze the problems addressed and the solutions implemented in UConn Social Entrepreneur Corps in Guatemala, we must first explain how the social entrepreneurship approach addresses the needs of poor communities.

Although social entrepreneurs have been engaged for centuries, from Johannes Gutenberg to Benjamin Franklin to Clara Barton to Florence Nightingale, only since the early 21st century has the term really entered the development lexicon. Although there is no universally accepted definition of social entrepreneurship, there is broad agreement that it describes an approach rather than any specific development model. According to the Schwab Foundation for Social Entrepreneurship, "[Social Entrepreneurs] pursue poverty alleviation goals with entrepreneurial zeal, business methods and the courage to innovate and overcome traditional practices." Indeed, they are concerned more with the "how" than the "what."

"Giving fish" usually refers to relief work, a form of assistance often required to provide emergency food, shelter, healthcare, and clothing resources after natural and human disasters. Relief work concerns itself primarily with immediate needs and to the logistics necessary to meet them as efficiently as possible. "Teaching to fish" refers to development work. Although development assistance may coincide with relief work, it more often than not directly follows or takes place independent of it. Development assistance supports individuals and communities as they mobilize themselves to create continuously higher standards of living over the short, medium and long term. Development assistance by and large supports education, healthcare needs, and income generation needs. If relief work provides critical assistance for people in dire need, development works creates opportunities for them to help themselves.

Yet as Bill Drayton (n.d.) states, "Social entrepreneurs are not content just to give a fish or teach how to fish. They will not rest until they have revolutionized the fishing industry." Social entrepreneurs attempt to create locally sustainable and globally replicable models that both "create" fish and fishermen where there were none before. David Bornstein (n.d.), author of *How to Change the World: Social Entrepreneurs and the Power of New Idea* writes: "Social entrepreneurs identify resources where people only see problems. They view the villagers as the solution, not the passive beneficiary. They begin with the assumption of competence and unleash resources in the communities they're serving." In effect, social entrepreneurs themselves are commonwealth citizens who not only help to produce public goods but help those who help to continue producing the public good. Social entrepreneurship is about long-term impact and sustainability. It is about achieving impacts in perpetuity.

Social entrepreneurship is ideally suited for study abroad. Through social entrepreneurship, students can gain practical knowledge, skills, and attitudes that will empower them to make a difference while studying abroad, as well as after they return. Social entrepreneurship study abroad also avoids the potential for paternalistic instincts that Ivan Illich worried so much about. Social entrepreneurship demands an approach whereby an ecosystem of sorts is created, and all stakeholders both add and derive value. It is this latter approach that is at the heart of the UConn Social Entrepreneur Corps in Guatemala model.

The Origins of the Social Entrepreneur Corps

The seeds of the UConn Social Entrepreneur Corps in Guatemala can be traced back to the founding of the nongovernmental organization Community Enterprise Solutions (CE Solutions) in May 2004. Greg Van Kirk and George Glickley generated the idea for CE Solutions after they each served 2 years in the Peace Corps. During his stint in Guatemala, Van Kirk recognized that tourists were regularly visiting the Guatemalan towns he was working in without spending any money. Identifying a problem, he received special dispensation from the Peace Corps to invest some of his own funds to start several businesses with local Guatemalan residents, including a restaurant, an Internet center, a hiking and trekking service, and an artisan store. Once these businesses successfully got off the ground, complete control over them was assumed exclusively by the local partners. The continued success of each of these businesses led Glickley to join forces with Van Kirk to develop an administration and funding mechanism to create other businesses that would provide basic products and services to Guatemalans. To create, fund, and support these businesses, Van Kirk and Glickley designed their microconsignment model, which forms the basis of UConn Social Entrepreneur Corps in Guatemala.

Their microconsignment model first emerged when Van Kirk donated money to a wood-burning stove project, which supplied a handful of stoves to an equal number of families in a local village. Like most Guatemalans, these families had always cooked campfire-style on their dirt floors. Cooking this way had long been recognized as extremely energy inefficient and harmful to the health of family members, particularly women and children who were spending a lot of time at home. Relief agencies had determined that the construction of inexpensive, locally manufactured, concrete stoves could immediately and dramatically reduce energy costs and improve the health and safety of family members. Van Kirk realized, however, that merely donating stoves severely limited the capacity for distribution. Once the relief money was expended, nobody else could get a stove. For Van Kirk, many more people could obtain these stoves if their distribution was built on a sustainable economy. Stoves would be locally manufactured, materials provided to local entrepreneurs on consignment and sold to poor families on an interest-free basis. The stoves would pay for themselves. The money saved in energy costs allowed families to repay these stoves within 6 months. The microconsignment model would not only employ manufacturers and sellers, but provide an essential, high-quality product at an affordable cost to poor, rural families.

Microconsignment is a microfinance model much like the microcredit model developed by

Nobel laureate Muhammad Yunus. Microcredit focuses on providing money to individuals to start new or expand existing businesses that sell products with a known supplier. Microcredit is neutral regarding what the businesses buy and sell; the targeted beneficiaries of this model are the entrepreneurs themselves. In contrast Van Kirk and Glickley's microconsignment model creates a way by which villagers get access to basic products and services through businesses created in partnership between the CSO and the locals. The success of the microconsignment model is predicated on continuous feedback. In contrast to micro-credit, the microconsignment social entrepreneurship model has two beneficiaries: the consumers who benefit from the products and, as a consequence, the entrepreneurs who earn money selling the products (plus the local manufacturers if applicable).

The microconsignment model can even help employ the consumers. For example, one of the businesses Van Kirk and Glickley developed using the model revolved around reading glasses. It is estimated that over 90% of people over 40 years old will need near-vision reading glasses to see up close. In rural Guatemala, there is no access to these glasses. Women weavers and teachers who depend upon their near vision lose their productivity at the very peak of their profession. In the microconsignment model, entrepreneurs are provided with marketing materials, training in giving eye exams, and the glasses themselves. They then travel to villages in areas where eye doctors rarely visit to give exams and sell these inexpensive glasses. By purchasing these glasses, weavers, most of whom are women and teachers, are able to extend their working lives for years.

In addition to starting a stove and reading glass business using the microconsignment model, Van Kirk and Glickley established water purification, energy efficient light bulb, and vegetable seed enterprises. Their success led to typical challenges associated with business expansion: the need for additional human and financial capital. During the first phase of this development, Van Kirk and Glickley established CE Solutions to generate the financial capital to support microconsignment expansion. They did not, however, want success to be dependent on the goodwill of others. In any case, this would eventually create the relief work problem: once the donors left, their businesses would fail. They solved this problem by establishing Social Entrepreneur Corps in 2005 as a sister organization to offer opportunities for students and recent graduates to volunteer in Guatemala supporting the microconsignment model's continuous innovations and growth. They had learned through working with recently graduated volunteers that fairly inexperienced individuals from diverse backgrounds could make a measurable impact in a short period of time. In addition, these volunteers had conveyed to them that they had gotten more out of their experience working within the model than they had in other more traditional study abroad experiences in which they had participated. Creating a mechanism for students to pay for a service to volunteer in Guatemala thus offered an elegant solution to the financial and human resource constraints that Van Kirk and Glickley had been confronting. Training and supporting students in many regards as apprentices who in turn funded the microconsignment work, was a much more efficient and effective use of time than dividing their time between fundraising and field implementation.

The first iteration of Social Entrepreneur Corps ran in the summers of 2006 and 2007 with student volunteers going to Guatemala for one of three 4-week stints. While the program worked well, Van Kirk and Glickley confronted challenges almost immediately in processing students and engaging them efficiently. Most students learned about Social Entrepreneur Corps through the Internet, and the CSO never knew until the last minute how many students it would actually be training and deploying. Vetting the written applications, as well as interviewing students and preparing them for arrival stretched its organizational capacity. It proved inefficient to offer three

4-week summer programs on the assumption that short-term programs would be most attractive to students in terms of time and money. Working with three separate groups, each of which needed an individual training program, meant that operating costs remained relatively high in proportion to community impact. Finally, since Social Entrepreneur Corps could not award academic credit, student motivation and expectations varied widely. Indeed, many students viewed this primarily through the exclusive lens of how the experience satisfied their own interests and desires.

The UConn Social Entrepreneur Corps Solution

The challenges confronting Social Entrepreneur Corps occurred at the same time that UConn was growing its study abroad program. UConn Study Abroad was not merely seeking to increase student participation, but to develop a set of programs that focused on providing students with international experiences that would prepare them to address social problems in their global contexts. In short, it was focused on developing global citizens. Social Entrepreneur Corp's need for financial and human capital to expand community businesses, along with UConn's desire to provide students with hands-on global citizenship experiences, led through a serendipitous meeting to the creation of UConn Social Entrepreneur Corps in Guatemala.

UConn and Social Entrepreneur Corps's first discussion centered on how to meet both community needs and university needs. They specifically asked:

1. How could students be engaged so that they would develop academically, personally, professionally, and civically while making a significant community impact?
2. How could the university and the CSO work together so that the larger and wealthier university's aim to serve students did not override the ability of the CSO to serve its clients?
3. How could students be best prepared so that they have the proper persepective and a base of knowledge and skills that would make them valuable to the CSO?
4. How could strengths be taken advantage of given the diverse resources, knowledge, skills, and experiences that each party provides to the equation?

As the critical first step, UConn and Social Entrepreneur Corps agreed to the guiding principle that their first priority was to effect sustainable commmunity impact. With this principle driving the parternship, they designated Social Entrepreneur Corps the quarterback of their development team. Social Entrepreneur Corps had established a leadership role on the ground, already successfully integrated students into its social entreprenership approach and, most imporantly, represented communities in need that the members of the partnership hoped to serve.

UConn and Social Entrepreneur Corps also agreed that if community impact were their goal, they would have to move away from traditional student assessment models to the logic model framework (LMF). Conversations between universities and CSOs often start with each asking the question: What are students going to do? Using the LMF as a guide, the partners asked: What are we trying to achieve for communities? Once we determined that answer, we then asked what can and should they do in order to achieve this goal, what do students need to know to realize this goal, and how would we know whether we achieved that goal. We decided that the combination of preparing them to be effective, engaging them in useful and feasible work, and measuring their impact on the entire process would result in high levels of learning. In this model, the students, just like staff members and other stakeholders, were subservient to the "quarterback." Students, that is, in the LMF were one of the inputs, and their output would be facilitated by employing them in activities to achieve community goals. Inputs and activities were divided, assigned, and designed so that all parties could bring to the table what they do best within the parameters of the larger goal of having the greatest community impact. Thus by deciding to use the LMF as the strategic framework for the guiding principle, UConn and Social Entrepreneur Corps sought to ensure that all resources would be expended to actually produce benefits for people.

Programmatically, the partners made several important decisions. First, they decided that to make this a study abroad program they would convey academic credit. Awarding credit allowed UConn to integrate it into the academic and study abroad curricula, and it gave the Social Entrepreneur Corps greater confidence in the motivation of the students. The UConn School of Business, the Honors Program, and the Department of Modern and Classical Languages took charge of the academic program by working directly with Social Entrepreneur Corps to shape the academic program. With this expanded team, UConn professors helped shape the assessment in a way that was consonant with the overall goals of the program.

All of the stakeholders agreed on an 8-week long program, twice the length of the Social Entrpreneur Corps volunteer program. Students would now have the opportunity to earn nine credits, including three credits for an internship, three credits for Spanish, and three credits for a course on social entrepreneurship. Doubling the duration of this program also enabled Social Entrepreneur Corps to reduce the time and money invested in training students, thereby increasing community impact.

In addition, the partners decided for just the first year to send the associate dean of the School of Business, the main university conveyor of course credit, to Guatemala for the first 3 weeks to participate as a student, including taking the intensive Spanish course, studying local Maya culture, and learning theories of social entrepreneurship as a development approach. By sending a faculty administrator, UConn and Social Entrepreneur Corps would theoretically gain a better understanding of how to improve integration between the needs of the CSO, community, and university.

Finally, UConn agreed to send a minimum of 10 students on the program for the first year, with the goal of ultimately sending a maximum of 20 each year. Sending a minimum of 10 students communicated the seriousness of UConn's investment. The University stakeholders assumed responsibility for the marketing and recruitment efforts, thus significantly reducing the funds that the CSO had hitherto allocated for those purposes, and enabling it to redirect precious resources to community needs. UConn also enrolled the students in health insurance. The lion's share of the application vetting process was conducted by the university, but both the CSO and representatives of UConn conducted oral inteviews of each applicant. Consensus was required between the two parties before the students were accepted.

The Program

Before arriving in Guatemala, students received syllabi, itineraries, as well as specific information related to safety, culture, and the specific projects on which they would be working. The CSO divided students divided into groups of eight based on language capabilities, competencies, and interests, and it integrated UConn students with other participants from Columbia, Notre Dame, and Duke. The UConn corps was the only group enrolled for academic credit.

Overview

In Guatemala, the program itself was divided into five phases: foundation building, initial field work, reflection and analysis, advanced field work, and summation. During the first foundation building phase, which took place at Social Entreprenueurs Corps headquarters in Antigua, students improved their knowledge, skills, and attitudes for greatest effectiveness in their field. They studied Spanish intensively, learned about Mayan culture, lived with local families, participated in dynamic discussions about best practices in development and relief work, visited development organizations, and organized into "virtual" CSOs; that is, small groups, each of which was tasked to different projects. In the second phase, the initial field work, students spent more than 2 weeks in a number of field sites across Guatemala working within the microconsignment model. During this phase, each student group also identified and analyzed the work of other CSOs in Guatemala. Students then returned to their initial training location where they refocused on Spanish language acquisition and analyzed their work so far in order to work more effectively during the second field work segment, the fourth phase of the program. The program ended by convening all the student groups back in Antigua where they handed in their deliverables, presented their work, and provided recommendations for the future.

The Projects

The 2008 UConn Social Entrepreneur Corps program focused on two overall goals: supporting the current and new microconsignment initiatives and assessing and funding work already underway by CE Solutions and other CSOs working in Guatemala. The program focused on five specific projects, Village Campaigns, ParaLaComunidad, Empresario Rural, Micro-Franchising, and CSO funding.

Village campaigns are the means by which the local entrepreneurs, working within the microconsignment model, create awareness, as well as market and sell their products and services. ParaLaComunidad is a Web site that provides local CSOs and community members with information about services offered in their regions. Gathering information for this Web site was a means to introduce CE Solutions to organizations, with the hope that they would develop into new microconsignment franchises. Empresario Rural is a Web site and newspaper that provides information on how to start and run small businesses to people who have never been thus engaged. Micro-Franchising is a channel to generate awareness, as well as market and sell essential products and services, with a local community organization acting as the entrepreneur. XSO Funding is an exclusively student oriented program designed to learn how to identify and analyze the work of CSOs based on student-driven criteria. Within this project, each virtual CSO group of students was provided with $400 and tasked with identifying, analyzing, and funding CSOs working in the field. This was in many regards their capstone project that brought all of their lessons learned into focus and forced them to make the difficult decisions that every actual CSO is confronted with everyday.

The Program's Logic Model Framework

Assuming that students reap the greatest benefit by working on projects that place the community first, the field work in which the students participated started with determining community outcomes. Only after specifying these outcomes, did the Social Entrepreneur Corps decide on student goals, indicators of success, indicator measurement techniques, and the student activities. This "cascade" of decisions starting with community goals and ending with student activities was key to the success of the model. The students engaged in six categories of activities; needs analysis, feasibility analysis, project launch, support, expansion, and evaluation. On certain projects there was a linear progression of these activities, in others there was not.

Needs analysis refers to student investigations and recommendations about how to address community and organizational challenges. Feasibility analysis is conducted when the needs have been ascertained and a solution is ready for design. Project launch refers to the initial implementation of the project. Support is provided to assist entrepreneurs and organizations as they launch a new project and/or execute an ongoing project. Students work on expansion to replicate geographically a successful project. Evaluation is a continuous process during every phase, from needs analysis to expansion.

Students engaged in all of these activities during the program, the importance of each being based upon the respective project priorities. Table 30.1 is the modified LMF used as the basis for, and outlines the student engagement.

The Impacts

As a result of effectively executing the modified LMF, the development team realized 100% of its student goals, which, in turn, made a profound impact on the organizations, communities, individuals, and entrepreneurs served (see Table 30.2).

CONCLUSION

Overall, the UConn Social Enterpreneur Corps in Guatemala proved successful. Students actually and tangibly made a contribution to improving the lives of poor, rural residents in Guatemala. In the process, they attained high levels of learning. They learned to identify and analyze problems as part of their work in determining how to expand new businesses, recognize new opportunities, and overcome the challenges given the conditions on the ground. To make these determinations, they had to gain knowledge about development work, theories of social entrepreneurship, local Guatemalan culture, and Spanish. They had to learn cultural differences in order to be effective on the ground. The learning was not done merely during the training period, but actually through the experience of working with local Guatemalan individuals and organizations to start up and expand existing businesses. Through these field experiences they deepened their understanding of development work, Spanish, and local culture. Importantly, they also learned team work in a cross-cultural setting.

When students returned from Guatemala, they had to prepare final projects and present them at a student-led symposium in the following fall semester. In preparing and executing this symposium, students learned that the value of this symposium went beyond getting additional credits. Indeed, the presentation was also designed to excite the university to intensify its partnership with Social Entrepreneur Corps and to raise more money to enable every student access to this experience. Ultimately, this presentation would benefit the communities in Guatemala.

In fact, the impact of their symposium was significant. Over 75 members of the community attended the student-led symposium, including members of the president's, provost's, and foundation's offices. A benefactor of the university who had supported the program through scholarships doubled the size of his gift. The UConn Foundation is now actively seeking support from other donors to support similar projects. The president's and provost's office has asked UConn Study Abroad to determine strategies for expanding this type of program. In their experience in Guatemala as global citizens, they also taught the university to become one as well.

Table 30.1 Logic Model Framework for UConn Social Entrepreneur Corps in Guatemala 2008

Project	Overall Desired Outcomes – Community	Organizational Short-Term Goals to Achieve Desired Outcomes	Student Activities based on Organizational Goals	Goal Indicators of Success	Indicator Measurement Technique
Village Campaigns	Access to essential products and services will have been created through individual entrepreneurial solutions	Entrepreneurs will be effectively supported during their village campaigns	Needs Analysis Feasibility Analysis Support Evaluation	Sales of products and services during village campaigns	Number of products and services sold during village campaigns
ParaLa Comunidad	Organizations and villagers will have gained access to critical information about local service providers	This new initiative will have been effectively launched	Needs Analysis Feasibility Analysis Pilot Project Support Expansion Evaluation	A sufficient database is created to launch the website	Number of organizational profiles collected
Empresario Rural	Rural and semi-urban small businesses will have gained access to critical business start-up, management, and growth information	This new initiative will have been effectively launched	Needs Analysis Feasibility Analysis Pilot Project Support Expansion Evaluation	Content is evaluated/ created and channels for distribution are created	Amount of content collected and number of papers handed out/permanent channels created
Micro-Franchising	Access to essential products and services will have been created through organizational entrepreneurial solutions	This new initiative will have been effectively launched	Needs Analysis Feasibility Analysis Pilot Project Support Expansion Evaluation	Micro-Franchises are created	Number of Micro-Franchises created
CSO Funding	Select organizations will have gained access to additional resources to help them achieve their respective missions	Appropriate funding opportunities will have been vetted and funding will have been provided	Needs Analysis Feasibility Analysis Expansion Evaluation	Organizations contributing to rural Guatemalan development are funded	Number, quality, and type of organizations funded

Table 30.2 *Community Impact by Students*

Student Projects	Impacts by Students on Community

Village Campaigns	▪ Supported women entrepreneurs during 26 product/service campaigns in 25 separate villages that previously lacked access
	
	▪ Supported 24 individual entrepreneurs
	
	▪ Supported these entrepreneurs in the sale of the following to low-income villagers:
	
	   ☐ 266 pairs of near vision glasses
	   ☐ 91 pairs of UV protection clear glasses
	   ☐ 32 pairs of UV protections sunglasses
	   ☐ 136 glasses cords
	   ☐ 288 glasses cases
	   ☐ 251 bottles of eye drops
	   ☐ 209 energy efficient light bulbs
	   ☐ Seven water filters
	   ☐ 162 vegetable seeds

ParaLaComunidad	▪ Collected approximately 40 distinct ParaLaComunidad profiles from organizations in four different regions ▪ Assisted NGO successfully launch the website www.paralacomunidad.com.
Empresario Rural	▪ Collected approximately 35 content interviews ▪ Distributed ca. 1,720 newspapers to over 105 individuals and small businesses ▪ Distributed ca. 2,300 newspapers to organizations setting up 15 displays and 26 distinct ongoing distribution points
Micro-Franchising	▪ Initiated and established from start to finish the foundation for 11 separate Micro-Franchises ▪ Trained eight Micro-Franchises that were selling products and services upon student departure
CSO Funding	Received approval and grants for the following: ▪ The publication of an advertising guide for women entrepreneurs ▪ The purchase of raw materials/training costs for a new wood burning stove initiative with a select Micro Franchise ▪ Books and materials for a newly formed rural library ▪ A current library outreach program ▪ Advertising and marketing outreach to help a bakery increase scale ▪ Material and human resource support for a community health organization ▪ The establishment of a program to teach weaving and earn extra income at an artisan cooperative

REFERENCES

Association of American Colleges and Universities. (2002). *Greater expectations: A new vision for learning as a nation goes to college.* Washington, DC: Author.

Banta, T. W. (2001). Assessing competence in higher education. In C. A. Palomba & T. W. Banta (Eds.), *Assessing student competence in accredited disciplines: Pioneering approaches to assessment in higher education* (pp. 1–12). Sterling, VA: Stylus.

Barber, B. (1995). *Jihad vs. McWorld: Terrorism's challenge to democracy.* New York: Random House.

Bolen, M. C. (Ed.). (2007a). *A guide to outcomes assessment in education abroad.* Carlisle, PA: Forum on Education Abroad.

Bolen, M. C. (2007b). Introduction. In M. C. Bolen (Ed.), *A guide to outcomes assessment in education abroad* (pp. 1–6). Carlisle, PA: Forum on Education Abroad.

Bornstein, D. (n.d.). Retrieved November 7, 2008, from http://www.pbs.org/opb/thenewheroes/whatis/

Boyer, E. L. (1987). *College: The undergraduate experience in America.* New York: Harper & Row.

Boyte, H. C., & Kari, N. N. (2000). Renewing the democratic spirit in American colleges and universities: Higher education as public work. In T. Ehrlich (Ed.), *Civic responsibility and higher education* (pp. 37–59). Westport, CT: The American Council on Education/Oryx Press.

Drayton, B. (2005, Spring). Everyone a changemaker. *Peer Review,* 8–11.

Drayton, B. (n.d.). Retrieved November 7, 2008, from http://www.ashoka.org/quotes/4047

Engle, J., & Engle, L. (2002). Neither international nor educative: Study abroad in the time of globalization. In W. Grünzweig & N. Rinehart (Eds.), *Rockin' in red square: Critical approaches to international education in the age of cyberculture* (pp. 5–22). Münster: Lit Verlag.

Fink, L. D. (2003). *Creating significant learning experiences: An integrated approach to designing college courses.* San Francisco: Jossey-Bass.

Forum on Education Abroad. (2005). *Standards of good practice for education abroad.* Retrieved October 15, 2008, from http://www.forumea.org

Kellogg Commission on the Future of State and Land-Grant Universities. (2000). *Renewing the covenant: Learning, discovery, and engagement in a new age and different world.* Washington, DC: National Association of State Universities and Land-Grant Colleges.

Kuh, G., Kinzie, J., Schuh, J. H., & Whitt, E. J. (2005). *Student success in college: Creating conditions that matter.* San Francisco: Jossey-Bass.

Illich, I. (1968, April 20). To hell with good intentions. Retrieved February 1, 2009, from http://en.wikipedia.org/wiki/Ivan_illich: http://swaraj.org/illich_hell.htm

McTighe Musil, C. M. (2003, Spring). Educating for citizenship. *Peer Review,* 4–8.

Newman, F. (1985). *Higher education and the American resurgence.* Princeton, NJ: Princeton University Press.

Nussbaum, M. C. (1997). *Cultivating humanity: A classical defense of reform in liberal education.* Cambridge, MA: Harvard University Press.

Ramalay, J. A. (2000). The perspective of a comprehensive university. In T. Ehrlich (Ed.), *Civic responsibility and higher education* (pp. 227–248). Westport, CT: The American Council on Education/Oryx Press.

Schneider, C. G. (2005). Liberal education and the civic engagement gap. In A. J. Kezar, T. C. Chambers, & J. C. Burkhardt (Eds.), *Higher education for the public good: Emerging voices from a national movement* (pp. 127–145). San Francisco: Jossey-Bass.

Schwab Foundation for Social Entrepreneurship. (n.d.). What is a social entrepreneur? Retrieved February 2, 2009, from http://www.schwabfound.org/sf/SocialEntrepreneurs/Whatisasocialentrepreneur/index.htm

Siaya, L., & Hayward, F. M. (2003). *Mapping internationalization on U. S. campuses: Final report 2003.* Washington, DC: American Council on Education.

Stanton, T. K., Giles, J. D., & Cruz, N. I. (1999). *Service-learning: A movement's pioneers reflect on its origins, practice, and future.* San Francisco: Jossey-Bass.

Suskie, L. A. (2004). *Assessing student learning: A common sense guide.* Bolton, MA: Anker.

Sutton, R. C., Miller, A. N., & Rubin, D. I. (2007). Research design in assessing learning outcomes of education abroad programs. In M. C. Bolen (Ed.), *A guide to outcomes assessment in education abroad* (pp. 23–59). Carlisle, PA: Forum on Education Abroad.

U.S. Department of Higher Education. (2006). *A test of leadership: Charting the future of U.S. higher education.* Washington, DC: Author.

Zemach-Bersin, T. (2008, March 7). American students abroad can't be "global citizens." *The Chronicle of Higher Education,* A55.

Contributors

Denise Saint Arnault is Associate Professor in the College of Nursing at Michigan State University, where she publishes on the Navajo and Michigan Native populations. Her research uses survey, clinical, and ethnographic methods to investigate the relationship between culture and mental health for Asian women abroad and immigrants to the U.S.

Jonathan A. Becker is Dean of International Studies and Associate Professor of Political Studies at Bard College, as well as Bard's Dean for Smolny College in St. Petersburg. He is the author of *Soviet and Russian Press Coverage of the United States: Press, Politics and Identity in Transition* (Palgrave, 1999, 2003) and earned his B.A. from McGill and his D.Phil. from St. Antony's College, Oxford.

Farrah Bernardino is Director of Study Abroad Programs at Georgia State University. She has presented widely on minority outreach in international education and holds a B.A. in Spanish from Emory and an M.A. in Spanish Literature from the University of Virginia.

Bryan Billings is Program Manager of the Bard-Smolny Study Abroad Program in St. Petersburg. He finished Columbia University in Russian Studies and has lived and worked in Russia and the former Soviet Union for several years.

Sergey Bogdanov is Head of the Division of Russian Language and Dean of the Department of Philology and Arts of St. Petersburg State University. He is Chair of the Scientific and Methodological Council for Russian Language and Culture of Speech of the Ministry of Education and Science of Russian Federation, and serves on the Russian government's Commission for Russian Language, the Board of Trustees of the *Russkiy Mir* Foundation, and the Board of Overseers of Smolny College.

Larry Braskamp is Professor Emeritus at Loyola University Chicago, Alumni Distinguished Professor at Central College, Senior Fellow at Association of American Colleges and Universities, and Senior Scientist at The Gallup Organization. He received his M.A. and Ph.D. in Educational Psychology from the University of Iowa. He co-authored most recently *Putting Students First: How Colleges Develop Students Purposefully* and the *Global Perspective Inventory*.

Robert G. Bringle is Chancellor's Professor of Psychology and Philanthropic Studies, and Director of the Indiana University–Purdue University Indianapolis's Center for Service and Learning. His scholarly journal articles, chapters, and books on service learning have earned him the Ehrlich Faculty Award for Service Learning and recognition at the International Service-Learning

Research Conference. The University of the Free State, South Africa awarded him an honorary doctorate for his scholarship on civic engagement and service learning.

Joseph L. Brockington is Associate Provost for International Programs and Professor of German at Kalamazoo College. He holds B.A., M.A., and Ph.D. degrees from Michigan State University. He has served on executive committees for NAFSA, the Association of International Education Administrators (AIEA), and the Forum on Education Abroad. He has published widely on study abroad and modern German literature, including co-editing the 3rd edition of *NAFSA's Guide to Education Abroad for Advisers and Administrators*.

William Brustein is Associate Provost for International Affairs, Professor of Sociology, Political Science, and History, and Alumni Professor of International Studies at the University of Illinois at Urbana-Champaign. He is past-president of the AIEA and serves on executive committees for the Association for Studies in International Education and the Commission on International Programs of the National Association of State Universities and Land-Grant Colleges (NASULGC). He chairs the Academic Affairs Committee of NASULGC's Commission on International Programs and helped draft *A Call to Leadership: the Presidential Role in Internationalizing the University*.

S. Megan Che is Assistant Professor of Mathematics Education in the Clemson University Eugene T. Moore School of Education, where she publishes on equity in mathematics classrooms, postcolonial mathematics education, and gender in math education. She contributes to a study abroad program to Azerbaijan that enables pre-service teachers to learn about cultural and social influences on teaching and learning.

Lisa Chieffo is Associate Director of the Center for International Studies at the University of Delaware, where she oversees 80 study abroad programs with an annual enrollment of over 1,500. She has led multiple research projects involving students abroad and has presented results at NAFSA conferences and published in *Frontiers* and in NAFSA and IIE journals. She received her Ed.D. in Educational Leadership from the University of Delaware.

Patti H. Clayton is Director of the Center for Excellence in Curricular Engagement at North Carolina State University, which builds capacity for and generates scholarship on community engaged teaching and learning. One of its core initiatives is "International Service-Learning," a cross-campus collaboration to support the integration of community engagement and international education. She is Senior Scholar with the Center for Service and Learning at Indiana University-Purdue University Indianapolis.

Connie Currier is Assistant Professor and Coordinator for International Programming in the College of Nursing at Michigan State University, where she teaches public health, international health, and health policy, as well as coordinates international initiatives, including study abroad programs in the U.K., Mexico, and Ghana. She has lived and worked in Africa as a Population Fellow (Zimbabwe), Peace Corps Volunteer (Ghana), and public health consultant.

Kenneth Cushner, Professor of Education at Kent State University, is author or editor of several publications in intercultural education and training, including: *Human Diversity in Education: An Integrative Approach, 6th ed.* (McGraw-Hill, 2009); and *Intercultural Student Teaching: A Bridge to Global Competence* (Rowman Littlefield, 2007). He is past Director of the Consortium for Overseas Student Teaching (COST) and President and Founding Fellow of the International Academy for Intercultural Research.

Ian Davies is Professor of Education in the Department of Educational Studies at the University of York, U.K. He is the editor of the international journal *Citizenship Teaching and Learning* and has written and edited numerous books and articles on citizenship education. He is a co-editor of the 4 volume reader *Citizenship Education* (Sage, 2007) and the *International Handbook on Democracy and Citizenship Education* (Sage, 2008).

Christina Davis is a Foreign Service Officer for the U.S. Agency for International Development and former International Program Manager at Bard College. She received her B.A. from Smith College and her M.A. in Economics from Western Illinois University.

Darla K. Deardorff is Executive Director of the Association of International Education Administrators (AIEA) at Duke University. She received her M.A. and Ph.D. from North Carolina State University and teaches graduate courses in international education and intercultural communication. She has published widely on international education, intercultural competence and assessment. She is editor of the forthcoming *Handbook of Intercultural Competence* (Sage, 2009).

Hans de Wit is International Higher Education Consultant and Editor of the *Journal of Studies in International Education* He has been Vice President for International Affairs of the University of Amsterdam, New Century Scholar of the Fulbright Program Higher Education in the 21st Century, and president of the European Association for International Education (EAIE). He has published widely on international education including the Organization for Economic Cooperation and Development and the World Bank, and has received awards from the University of Amsterdam, AIEA, CIEE, NAFSA and EAIE.

Mary Dwyer is President/CEO of IES Abroad. She was previously a faculty member at the College of Medicine and the Executive Associate Vice Chancellor for Research at University of Illinois at Chicago. She has consulted for numerous U.S. and international foundations, ministries of health/education, and the World Health Organization. She serves as Board Chair for The Forum on Education Abroad. She holds a B.A. from Mundelein College and a M.Ed. and Ph.D. in Public Policy Analysis from the University of Illinois.

Kike Ehigiator is Assistant Director, Program Development and Management in the Office of International Affairs at Georgia State University. She received undergraduate degrees from Obafemi Awolowd University in Nigeria and Mt. Saint Vincent University in Canada. She holds a M.A. in International Development Studies from St. Mary's University in Canada.

Robert A. Frost is Assistant Professor of Higher Education Leadership at Oregon State University (OSU), where he heads the Community College Emerging Leaders Institute. He serves as the Director of Education for Community Colleges for International Development and chairs NAFSA's taskforce on Education Abroad & Career Development.

Joan Gillespie is Associate Vice President for Academic Affairs and Assessment and Program Dean at IES Abroad. She has published and presented papers on programming and assessment in education abroad and the link between international education and global careers. She received her M.A. and Ph.D. in English Literature from Northwestern, and her B.A. from Vassar.

Susan H. Gillespie is Director of the Institute for International Liberal Education and Vice President of Bard College. She graduated from Radcliffe College and attended graduate school in Freiburg, Germany. She has published noted translations of philosophy, musicology, fiction, and poetry.

Allan Goodman is President and CEO of the Institute of International Education. Previously, he served as Executive Dean of the School of Foreign Service at Georgetown and authored several books on international affairs published by Harvard, Princeton and Yale, as well as *Diversity* *in Governance* by the American Council on Education. He helped create the first U.S. academic exchange program with the Moscow Diplomatic Academy for the Association of Professional Schools of International Affairs and was recently awarded the title "Chevalier" of the French Legion of Honour.

Joan Elias Gore is Director of Adult Education Travel Programs and Continuing and Professional Studies at University of Virginia, where she also served on the faculty. She earned her B.A. from the University of Toledo, M.A. from the University of Virginia, and Ph.D. in Communication and Culture/Educational Policy at the Institute of Education in London. She is the author of *Dominant Beliefs and Alternative Voices: Discourse, Belief, and Gender in American Study Abroad* (Routledge, 2005).

Lesa Griffiths is Professor of Animal Science and Associate Provost for International Programs at the University of Delaware. She received the U.S.D.A. National Award for Teaching Excellence, the University of Delaware Excellence-in-Teaching Award, the College of Agriculture and Natural Resources Outstanding Teaching Award, and the Mortar Board National Honor Society Faculty Award. She has accompanied almost 150 students on study abroad programs focused on international agriculture.

Fazela Haniff is Director of the Wits International Office, University of the Witwatersrand. A graduate of Ryerson Polytechnic University in Toronto, she worked for several years in the human rights community in Canada and South Africa, working with the Urban Alliance on Race Relations. She is past president of the International Education Association of South Africa.

Rebecca Hovey is the World Learning Engaged Global Scholar and an affiliated faculty member of the SIT Graduate Institute. Previously, she served as Dean of SIT Study Abroad, managing field-based programs in over 40 countries. She received her Ph.D. in City and Regional Planning from Cornell and has published extensively on international education, global citizenship, and critical pedagogy.

Kevin Hovland is Director of Global Learning and Curricular Change at the Association of American Colleges and Universities (AAC&U), where he directs curriculum and faculty development projects for the Shared Futures and the Educated Citizen and Public Health initiatives. He is the author of *Shared Futures: Global Learning and Liberal Education* (AAC&U, 2006) and executive editor of Diversity & Democracy: Civic Learning for Shared Futures. He completed his B.A. from Columbia and graduate work at Georgetown.

Amy Jamison is a doctoral candidate in the Education Policy program at Michigan State University, where she is writing on international higher education policy, the role of education in international development, and the history of higher education in Africa. She received a Fulbright-Hays Doctoral Dissertation Research Abroad Award to work in Tanzania. Jamison holds M.A. degrees from U.C.L.A. in African Studies and History and a B.A. from Hobart and William Smith Colleges.

Steven G. Jones is Associate Provost for Civic Engagement and Academic Mission at the University of Scranton. He worked in the Office of Service Learning, Center for Service and Learning, at Indiana University–Purdue University Indianapolis, where he coordinated faculty development and support activities regarding service learning, as well as the Service Learning Assistant Scholarship program.

Ayesha Kajee is Program Director of the International Human Rights Exchange (IHRE) at the University of the Witwatersrand and former head of the Program on Democracy and Political Parties at the South African Institute of International Affairs. Her research interests include human rights, transitional justice, education, gender, and politics, and she has worked extensively on African peer review, gender and remittances, and the African Union. She has taught in South Africa, the U.S., and the U.K.

Thomas Keenan teaches human rights, media, and literature at Bard College. He directs the Human Rights Program at Bard and is Academic Director of the International Human Rights Exchange in Johannesburg. He has written *Fables of Responsibility* (Stanford University Press, 1997) and edited *New Media, Old Media* (with Wendy Hui Kyong Chun, Routledge, 2005).

Charles Kolb is President of the Committee for Economic Development (CED) in Washington, D.C. CED is an independent, nonpartisan organization of over 200 business and education leaders dedicated to economic and social policy research and the implementation of its recommendations by the public and private sectors. He received his undergraduate degree at Princeton and his M.A. at Balliol College, Oxford University in Philosophy, Politics, and Economics. He holds a law degree from the University of Virginia.

Nikolay Koposov is Professor of History and Dean of Smolny College of Liberal Arts and Sciences of St. Petersburg State University. An historian by training, he is the author of *The Highest Bureaucracy in the Seventeenth-Century France* (Leningrad University Press, 1990), *How Historians Think* (Moscow: The New Literary Review Press, 2001), and *Down with the Cats' Massacre! Critique of the Social Sciences* (Moscow: The New Literary Review Press, 2005).

Tawana Kupe is Associate Professor of Media Studies and Executive Dean of the Faculty of Humanities at the University of Witwatersrand in Johannesburg. He holds a B.A. and an M.A. from the University of Zimbabwe and a D.Phil. in Media Studies from the University of Oslo. His teaching and research interests include critical political economy of the media and communication, and the democratic interactive potentialities of the Internet and online media.

Ross Lewin is Director of Study Abroad at the University of Connecticut. He earned his B.A. from the University of California, Santa Cruz and M.A. and Ph.D. in German Studies from Stanford.

James Lucas is Assistant to the Dean and Associate Provost of Undergraduate Education in the Office of the Provost at Michigan State University, where he works on campus internationalization, global education, and teaching and learning abroad. He has led four different study abroad programs and co-coordinates MSU's Freshman Seminar Abroad initiative with the Office of Study Abroad. He is completing a dissertation in higher education on male students' decision to study abroad.

Agida Manizade is Assistant Professor of Mathematics Education in the Clemson University Eugene T. Moore School of Education. Her research interests include geometry education, the pedagogy of mathematics, and educational technology. A native of Azerbaijan, she leads a study abroad program there for pre-service teachers.

Maria D. Martinez, Ph.D., is Director of the Center for Academic Programs at the University of Connecticut and consults on diversity issues related to first-generation, low-income, and underrepresented populations. She has developed study abroad opportunities at the University of Liverpool and at the University of Fort Hare, South Africa. She publishes on educational opportunities for low-income, first-generation, and Latino students.

Helen A. Marx, Ph.D., is Adjunct Professor in the Department of Curriculum and Instruction at the Neag School of Education, University of Connecticut. Her research focuses on intercultural sensitivity development within international experiences, particularly as they relate to teacher education programs.

Caryn McTighe Musil is Senior Vice President at the Association of American Colleges and Universities (AAC&U) and the author of *Assessing Global Learning: Matching Good Intentions with Good Practices* (AAC&U, 2006). She currently directs AAC&U's initiative Core Commitments: Educating Students for Personal and Social Responsibility, which engages students with core questions of ethical responsibility and citizenship. She received her B.A. from Duke University and her M.A. and Ph.D. in English from Northwestern University.

Valery Monakhov is Associate Professor of History and Director of Smolny College of St. Petersburg State University. He earned his M.A. from Leningrad State University and Ph.D. in American History from Herzen State Pedagogical University, where he also served as Dean of History and Vice Rector for International Relations. He is active in educational development and policy affairs at the national level and has played a leading role in developing liberal education in Russia.

Riall W. Nolan is Associate Provost and Dean of International Programs at Purdue University. A social anthropologist (Ph.D., University of Sussex), Nolan managed international programs at the University of Pittsburgh, Golden Gate University, and the University of Cincinnati before joining Purdue. Under his leadership Purdue won NAFSA's prestigious Simon Award for international education. Nolan presents frequently on international education practice and strategy.

Peter Pang is Associate Professor of Mathematics and Director of the University Scholars Programme (USP) at the National University of Singapore. He has served as President of the Singapore Mathematical Society and is currently a member of the Developing Country Strategy Group of the International Mathematical Union. He received the Public Administration Medal (Bronze) by the President of Singapore in 2006.

Earl Picard holds an M.A. and Ph.D. in Political Science from Clark Atlanta University. He is Senior Research Associate and Director of Program Management and Development in the Georgia State University Office of International Affairs. He received a Fulbright Fellowship to study abroad in Ghana and to teach in Lesotho.

Graham Pike is Dean of International Education at Vancouver Island University. He has consulted on global education for UNICEF in Africa, the Middle East, and Eastern Europe. He is the author of ten books on global education, environmental education, and human rights education. He is a Visiting Professor at the Center for the Study of Global Change, Indiana University and winner of the Canadian Bureau for International Education's *Innovation in International Education Award*.

William M. Plater is Director of International Community Development at Indiana University-Purdue University Indianapolis and Chancellor's Professor of Public Affairs, Philanthropic Studies, English, and Informatics. He served as the chief academic officer at IUPUI for nineteen years.

Rosalind Latiner Raby, Ph.D. in Comparative Education from U.C.L.A., is Senior Lecturer at California State University, Northridge in the Educational Leadership and Policy Studies Department. She is Director of California Colleges for International Education, a consortium whose membership includes eighty-four California community colleges and the Community College Representative for NAFSA Region XII and NAFSA Education Abroad Knowledge Community.

Preetha Ram is Assistant Dean for Undergraduate Education at Emory University. She received her Ph.D. in biophysical chemistry from Yale and Emory College's Excellence in Teaching Award for the Natural Sciences. She initiated Emory's first summer science study abroad program in

Siena and founded the Science Experience Abroad program in collaboration with the Center for International Programs Abroad, which received the Institute of International Education's Andrew Heiskell Award.

Bidya Ranjeet, Ph.D., is Director of Student Support Services (SSS) at the University of Connecticut, where she has helped create study abroad opportunities for low-income students. An advocate for South Asian women's interests, she publishes on domestic violence issues confronting women of South Asian heritage.

Howard Rollins is Professor of Psychology at Georgia Institute of Technology. Previously, he served as Associate Vice Provost for International Programs, where he facilitated study abroad opportunities for Georgia Tech students and fostered initiatives to further internationalize Georgia Tech, including the International Plan, which received the Institute for International Education's Andrew Heiskell Award. He is a past member of the Executive Committee of the Association of International Education Administrators.

Hans Schattle is Associate Professor of Political Science and International Relations at Yonsei University in Seoul, South Korea. He is the author of *The Practices of Global Citizenship* (Rowman & Littlefield, 2008), as well as recent articles in *Journal of Political Ideologies* and *Citizenship Studies*. He earned his D. Phil. at Oxford.

Adrian Shubert is York University's first Associate Vice-President International and a Canadian leader in internationalization. He is a faculty member and past department chair of York's History department. A specialist on 19th and 20th century Spain, he received a Guggenheim Fellowship and was named Commander of the Order of Civil Merit by King Juan Carlos.

James M. Skelly is Visiting Professor of Peace Studies at Magee College, University of Ulster in Derry, Northern Ireland; Senior Fellow at the Baker Institute for Peace & Conflict Studies at Juniata College; and Coordinator for Peace & Justice Programming for BCA Study Abroad. He was Associate Director of the University of California's Institute on Global Conflict & Cooperation; NYU's Center for War, Peace, and the News Media; and Academic Coordinator of the European University Center for Peace Studies in Austria. He holds a B.A. from the University of Minnesota, and an M.A. and Ph.D. from the University of California, San Diego.

Ellen Skilton-Sylvester is Associate Professor of Education and Director of Global Connections for the undergraduate curriculum at Arcadia University. An educational anthropologist and applied linguist, her research has focused on global citizenship, biliteracy, immigrant education policy, service learning, and teacher research as a form of professional development. She holds a Ph.D. in Educational Linguistics from the University of Pennsylvania.

Mindy Spearman is Assistant Professor of Elementary Social Studies Education in the Clemson University Eugene T. Moore School of Education. Her research interests include American educational history; teaching about sustainability and environmental issues; historical research methods; and school, museum, and university partnerships. She leads a study abroad program to Azerbaijan, which connects American education students with local educational professionals.

Bernhard T. Streitwieser (Ph.D., Columbia University) is Senior Research Associate at Northwestern University's Searle Center for Teaching Excellence. Previously, he served as the Associate Director of Northwestern's Study Abroad Office. He was a German Chancellor Fellow at the Max Planck Institute for Human Development and Education and a Research Analyst at the American Institutes for Research. He has published in international education, German education, and research methodology.

571

Daniel Teodorescu is Director of the Office of Institutional Research at Emory University and Adjunct Assistant Professor of Higher Education at The Pennsylvania State University. He completed his Ph.D. in Educational Administration and Policy Studies at SUNY Albany.

Dana Tottenham is Associate Director of the Center for International Programs Abroad at Emory University. She earned a B.A. from Emory and an M.A. in Anthropology from Georgia State University. She has taught introductory anthropology and first-year experience courses at Georgia State and is an active member of the Forum on Education Abroad and NAFSA.

Roopa Desai Trilokekar is Assistant Professor at the Faculty of Education, York University, Canada. Her scholarly interests include Canadian higher education policy; federalism and higher education; internationalization of higher education; student experiential learning through international study and work opportunities; diversity and education. She has recently completed a major study of the Government of Canada's role in internationalization and is currently editing Canada's *Universities Go Global* with Adrian Shubert and Glen Jones (University of Toronto).

Greg Van Kirk, an Ashoka Fellow, is Cofounder of Community Enterprise Solutions and Social Entrepreneur Corps, which design and implement innovative responses to long-standing rural development challenges. He began working in this field as a Peace Corps volunteer in Guatemala and has since served as an economic development consultant for development organizations in Latin America, Africa, and the Balkans.

Philip Wainwright is Associate Dean for International and Summer Programs at Emory University. Previously, he held a lectureship at Stanford, where he also served as an advisor for its study abroad programs. He earned a B.A. from Emory and a Ph.D. in Modern British History from Stanford.

Dieter Wanner is Associate Provost for Global Strategies and International Affairs at Ohio State University, where he is responsible for overseeing study abroad, international student and scholar services, and endowed and funded research centers. As a faculty member, he specializes in historical Romance linguistics and its interface with linguistic theory.

Adam Weinberg is Executive Vice President and Provost of World Learning, SIT. He previously served as Vice President and Dean of the College of Colgate University, where he designed Colgate's Residential Education program, which has attracted national attention for its innovative approach to civic education. He has worked with numerous organizations that connect universities and communities, including the Partnership for Community Development, the COVE, Democracy Matters and the Upstate Institute.

Margaret D. Wiedenhoeft is Associate Director of the Center for International Programs at Kalamazoo College. She received her B.A. in International Studies from Emory University and is currently pursuing her doctorate at Western Michigan University.

Talya Zemach-Bersin is a 2007 graduate of Wesleyan University and currently a graduate student in the Ph.D. program in American Studies at Yale University. Since studying abroad on an SIT program, she has published important articles, including "American Students Abroad Can't Be 'Global Citizens,'" and "Global Citizenship & Study Abroad: It's All About U.S."

Index

Page numbers in italic refer to Figures or Tables.

583

585 ■